DATE DUE			
OCT 2000			
		AUG 16 2012	

A HISTORY OF EAST CENTRAL EUROPE

Volume III

EDITORS

PETER F. SUGAR
University of Washington

DONALD W. TREADGOLD
University of Washington

A HISTORY OF EAST CENTRAL EUROPE

VOLUMES IN THE SERIES

* Forthcoming.

East Central Europe in the Middle Ages, 1000–1500

JEAN W. SEDLAR

UNIVERSITY OF WASHINGTON PRESS
Seattle and London

This book was published with the assistance of a grant
from the National Endowment for the Humanities.

Library of Congress Cataloging-in-Publication Data
Sedlar, Jean W.
    East Central Europe in the Middle Ages, 1000–1500 / Jean W.
    Sedlar.
        p.   cm. — (History of East Central Europe ; v. 3)
    Includes bibliographical references and index.
    ISBN 0–295–97290–4 (cloth : alk. paper).
        1. Europe, Eastern—History.   2. Central Europe—History.
I. Title.   II. Series.
DJK4.S93   vol. 3
[DJK46]
947—dc20   93–17820
                                                                       CIP

CONTENTS

FOREWORD

The systematic study of the history of East Central Europe outside the region itself began only in the last generation or two. For the most part historians in the region have preferred to write about the past of only their own countries. Hitherto no comprehensive history of the area as a whole has appeared in any language.

This series was conceived as a means of providing the scholar who does not specialize in East Central European history and the student who is considering such specialization with an introduction to the subject and a survey of knowledge deriving from previous publications. In some cases it has been necessary to carry out new research simply to be able to survey certain topics and periods. Common objectives and the procedures appropriate to attain them have been discussed by the authors of the individual volumes and by the coeditors. It is hoped that a certain commensurability will be the result, so that the ten volumes will constitute a unit and not merely an assemblage of writings. However, matters of interpretation and point of view have remained entirely the responsibility of the individual authors.

No volume deals with a single country. The aim has been to identify geographical or political units that were significant during the period in question, rather than to interpret the past in accordance with latter-day sentiments or aspirations.

The limits of "East Central Europe," for the purposes of this series, are the eastern linguistic frontier of German-and Italian-speaking peoples on the west, and the political borders of Russia/the former USSR on the east. Those limits are not precise, even within the period covered by any given volume of the series. The appropriateness of including the Finns, Estonians, Latvians, Lithuanians, Belorussians, and Ukrainians was considered, and it was decided not to attempt to cover them systematically, though they appear repeatedly in these books. Treated in depth are the Poles, Czechs, Slovaks, Hungarians, Romanians, Yugoslav peoples, Albanians, Bulgarians, and Greeks.

There has been an effort to apportion attention equitably among regions and periods. Three volumes deal with the area north of the Danube-Sava line, three with the area south of it, and three with both areas. Three treat premodern history, six modern times. Volume I consists of an historical atlas. Each volume is supplied with a bibliographical essay of its own, but we all have attempted to keep the scholarly apparatus at a minimum in order to make the text of the volumes more readable and accessible to the broader audience sought.

The coeditors wish to express their thanks to the Ford Foundation for the financial support it gave this venture, and to the Henry M. Jackson School of International Studies (formerly Far Eastern and Russian Institute) and its five successive directors, George E. Taylor, George M. Beckmann, Herbert J. Ellison, Kenneth Pyle, and Nicholas Lardy, under whose encouragement the project has moved close to being realized.

The whole undertaking has been longer in the making than originally planned. Two of the original list of projected authors died before they could finish their volumes and have been replaced. Volumes of the series are being published as the manuscripts are received. We hope that the usefulness of the series justifies the long agony of its conception and birth, that it will increase knowledge of and interest in the rich past and the many-sided present of East Central Europe among those everywhere who read English, and that it will serve to stimulate further study and research on the numerous aspects of this area's history that still await scholarly investigators.

Peter F. Sugar
Donald W. Treadgold

PREFACE

Centuries of Brilliance and Obscurity

The almost total neglect of medieval East Central Europe in histories of Western civilization hardly needs emphasis. While omission inevitably suggests that the period and the area hold nothing much of interest, quite the opposite is true. For the nations of this region, the medieval age is an important point of reference and a source of national pride: clearly more so than much of their history that came afterward, at least until the national renaissances of the 19th century. Diverse as these peoples were, they all experienced periods of brilliant achievement in the Middle Ages, which even to most historians are virtually unknown. The civilization of medieval East Central Europe, while undoubtedly influenced by the examples of ancient Rome, Byzantium, and Western Europe, was by no means merely derivative and second-rate. It does not deserve the historical obscurity to which it has been relegated.

In a word, the era from 1000 to 1500 was in many respects the Golden Age for the nationalities of East Central Europe. At one time or another during these five centuries, Bulgaria, Serbia, Hungary, Poland, and Bohemia all were major states playing a leading role on the European stage. The Romanian principalities of Walachia and Moldavia were less powerful, but still independent; and each had its moment of glory resisting Ottoman encroachments. In addition, the cultural achievements of the period were multifarious and of a high order. Medieval history is not dead in East Central Europe, despite its neglect in the West. Any visitor to the area at present will be struck by the efforts that governments have made to preserve their medieval heritage through the work of museums and the excavation and restoration of old churches, palaces, and works of art. Streets and public institutions in the late 20th century still bear the names of medieval monarchs.

Where exactly is East Central Europe? In the English language, this terminology (equivalent to the German *Mittelosteuropa* or *Ostmitteleuropa*) is rather imprecise. In the present book, it refers broadly to those countries occupying the geographical space between the Germanic and East Slavic lands (i.e., Germany and Austria on the one hand; Russia, Belarus, and Ukraine on the other). However, the region is sometimes included vaguely in "Eastern" Europe, suggesting that it is either an appendage of Russia (a reflection of recent political circumstances) or part of a vast, underdeveloped area beginning on Germany's eastern frontier. In fact, Poles, Czechs, and Hungarians firmly regard themselves as belonging to "Western," not "Eastern," civilization; and Romanians often affirm the same, despite their Eastern Orthodox heritage. On the other hand, foreigners are impressed above all by the enormous diversity of peoples and languages within this small space. The natives themselves, with some justice, tend to regard their own nationality as unique; and political nationalism (an expression of this feeling) is unquestionably a powerful force.

Is it intellectually justifiable to treat East Central Europe as a whole? The diversity of these countries cannot be doubted: certainly they lack any uniform character or culture. The multiplicity of ethnic groups and languages in the region is in itself an important reason for scholars' neglect of it. However, the area itself is not large: the total land surface of Poland, Hungary, the Czech and Slovak lands, ex-Yugoslavia, Romania, Bulgaria, and Albania together is not quite double that of Texas. Their geographical proximity is suggestive: countries lying so close together must surely have *some* features in common. In any event, their very diversity, as well as the fragmentary nature of most extant information about them, makes an effort at synthesis desirable.

In fact, the experiences of these lands in modern times have been remarkably similar. Not just for decades (the forty-four years of Soviet domination), but for centuries, all have been victims of their Great Power neighbors. Bulgaria fell to the Ottomans in 1396; Serbia in 1459; portions of Albania in 1477–78; Hungary at Mohács in 1526. Bohemia lost its independence to the Habsburgs at White Mountain in 1620. Poland was carved up by Prussia, Russia, and Austria at the Partitions of 1772, 1793, and 1795. From that time until World War I, these countries belonged to multinational empires—Ottoman, Russian, or German—although a small Serbian and later a Bulgarian state gained autonomy and finally independence in the course of the 19th century. The peace treaties following World War I brought these countries a precarious and short-lived liberty. Then after World War II the Soviet government enforced a single political system and an artificial sameness upon them all. Despite the revolutions of 1989, the traces of forty-four years of Soviet hegemony will not easily be eradicated.

The neglect of East Central Europe in Western historical scholarship may be attributed in part to the natural preference of most Westerners for what they consider to be their own cultural antecedents. Medievalists in the Western world concern themselves almost exclusively with Western Europe. (It is noteworthy that textbooks of Western civilization devote far more attention to ancient Egypt and Mesopotamia than to East Central Europe at any period.) Medieval history in general suffers from the predilection for "relevance," which usually means a modern orientation: the assumption that recent events (the more recent, the better) have more meaning for the people alive today than do those of a more distant age. Western specialists on East Central Europe—who are themselves not numerous—direct most of their attention to the 19th and 20th centuries, the period of national revival. On the other hand, historians native to East Central Europe usually study just their own nationality. Even their immediate neighbors hardly arouse much interest, except as they relate to the historian's own country. Hardly anyone calls attention to the "common European home."

The very diversity and complexity of East Central Europe makes an overview of the region difficult to achieve. Obvious problems include the multiplicity of languages in which the historical literature appears and the dispersal of this material in publications not widely available. Much of the material resists easy categorization. Scholarly monographs may exist on a certain subject for one country but not for another, or for one century but not for others. An attempt can be made to draw comparisons and contrasts; yet many gaps exist which historical scholarship has not yet filled. On the other hand, an organizational scheme and some cautious generalization are required to avoid burdening the reader with a mass of disconnected data. The present survey is thematic rather than chronological. Although it is aimed at the interested general reader, the complex nature of the subject makes unavoidable the introduction of numerous names and terms which are likely to be unfamiliar. At the same time, unnecessary references and excessive detail have been avoided wherever possible.

A very high proportion of the material in this book comes from monographs—often on rather specific small subjects—written by historians who are themselves natives of East Central Europe. In the years since World War II the nations of this region have devoted considerable resources to the study of their respective national pasts and published extensive collections of monographs by their own historians in German, French, or English translations. The results have gone far to remedy many previous lacunae in medieval scholarship. Furthermore, German and Austrian scholars have continued their traditional interest in the lands located just beyond their own eastern and southern frontiers. Without the efforts of these colleagues my own work would be significantly poorer. In accordance with the format of the History of East Central Europe series, a bibliographical essay replaces the usual scholarly footnotes.

A word is necessary on the knotty problem of geographical terminology, for which no satisfactory solution exists. Many localities in East Central Europe bear several names, depending on the period and the language in question. The use of modern terms when discussing ancient history is an obvious anachronism. On the other hand, the choice of names current at any particular period can be interpreted as a political statement. The language of place names can be highly controversial. When a place has changed overlords several times, confusion is compounded by referring to it by multiple names. What does one do, for example, about a town with a largely German-speaking population which was subject to Hungary for most of its history but now lies in Romania? Or about Balkan towns whose names during the Ottoman period only a Turk would recognize? The solution chosen in this book has been to use current place names for ease of location on modern maps, except when commonly accepted English equivalents are available. (For example, "Prague" and "Bucharest" are favored over "Praha" and "Bucureşti.") The anachronisms resulting from this method are sometimes jarring, but the alternative solutions (multiple names for a single place, or politically charged linguistic choices) seem worse. In some cases an alternate name is given in parentheses (but not necessarily *all* alternate names, in the interest of avoiding stylistic awkwardness). A concordance of place names appears at the end of the book.

Foreign words in general are anglicized. This permits terms used in more than one language area to keep the same form throughout and also avoids numerous phonetic difficulties for English speakers. First names of persons are similarly anglicized (except where no satisfactory English equivalent exists, as with the Hungarian "Béla"). Last names retain the original spelling unless they are well known in English (thus John "Hus," not "Husinec"). For greater clarity, similar institutions in various countries are given an identical name: thus "Diet" refers to the assemblies of lords and prelates which the various sources call "Parliament," "Estates," "Sejm" (in Polish), "Sobor" (in Serbo-Croatian), and so forth. In accordance with common (if inexact) English usage, the terms "Bulgar" and "Bulgarian," "Croat" and "Croatian," "Serb" and "Serbian," "Magyar" and "Hungarian" are (with some exceptions) used interchangeably. The Slavic-speaking inhabitants of Bohemia-Moravia are referred to as "Czechs," the speakers of Romanian as either "Vlachs" or "Romanians."

Since of all people a historian must be acutely aware of debts to one's predecessors, I owe greatest thanks to the scholars of many nationalities whose previous work on the history of East Central Europe has been indispensable in shaping a book of this scope. As for personal debts, I wish to thank particularly the Russian and East European Center of the University of Illinois at Urbana-Champaign and its founding director, Ralph T. Fisher, Jr., for facilitating my research over a period of many years. I am grateful as well to the Institute for East and Southeast European History in Vienna, to two NEH Institutes on Ottoman history directed by Norman Itzkowitz at Princeton University, to the University of Pittsburgh for granting me two sabbatical leaves and modest research support, and to my colleague Bernard J. Poole for invaluable help with the computer.

JWS
February 1993

NOTE ON PRONUNCIATION

An extensive discussion of pronunciation would take us much too far afield, but the following general considerations may be helpful to the reader unfamiliar with East Central European languages.

Stress: As a rule, Czech and Hungarian place the stress (accent) on the first syllable of each word; Polish accents the penultimate syllable, with few exceptions. In other languages (just as in English), the stress varies.

ą & ę (Polish): nasal sounds, sometimes transcribed into English as *on* and *en*
    respectively
c (Polish, Czech, Hungarian): like English *ts*, as in *cuts* (or Romanian ţ, below)
ć: no exact English equivalent, but sounds much like č to English speakers
č: like English *ch* in *church, cheap*
ch (Czech, Polish): aspirated *h*, as in the German *ach*; *not* like English *ch*
cs (Hungarian): like č above
cz (Polish): like č above
gy (Hungarian): like *di* in *adieu* (e.g., *Magyar*)
j: resembles the English *y* in *yes* in most languages of our region, but in Romanian
    it resembles the *g* in *rouge*. Since English speakers are often tempted to
    pronounce this letter like the *j* in *just*, in this book it is generally transcribed
    phonetically as *y* (e.g., *Nemanya*; in the original Serbian: *Nemanja*)
ł (Polish): like English *w* in *wall, west*
ń (Polish): like English *n* in *lenient*
r: rolled with tip of tongue
s: usually as in English, but in Hungarian sounds like *sh* in *show*
ś: no precise English equivalent, but sounds much like š to English speakers
š: like the English *sh* in *show, shift*
sz (Polish): like š above
sz (Hungarian): like English *s* in *sit*
ţ (Romanian): like English *ts* in *puts, cuts*
ž or ż: like English *g* in *regime* or *s* in *pleasure*

* Capital Cities

1. East Central Europe and neighboring lands, 1994.

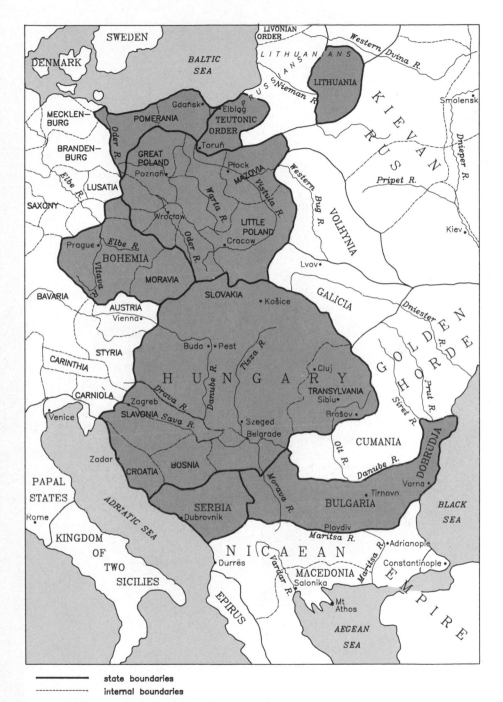

SWEDEN

DENMARK

BALTIC SEA

LIVONIAN ORDER

LITHUANIANS

LITHUANIA

Western Dvina R.

KIEVAN

Smolensk•

MECKLEN-BURG

BRANDEN-BURG

POMERANIA

Gdańsk•

Elbląg•

TEUTONIC ORDER

Nieman R.

RUS

Oder R.

•Toruń

GREAT POLAND

Płock•

MAZOVIA

Western Bug R.

Pripet R.

Dnieper R.

Elbe R.

LUSATIA

Poznań•

Warta R.

Vistula R.

VOLHYNIA

SAXONY

Wrocław•

LITTLE POLAND

Kiev•

Prague•

Elbe R.

BOHEMIA

Oder R.

Cracow•

Vltava R.

MORAVIA

Lvov•

GALICIA

Dniester R.

BAVARIA

SLOVAKIA

•Košice

GOLDEN HORDE

AUSTRIA

Vienna•

STYRIA

Buda• •Pest

Tisza R.

•Cluj

CARINTHIA

H U N G A R Y

TRANSYLVANIA

Sibiu•

Prut R.

Siret R.

CARNIOLA

Drava R.

Danube R.

Brašov•

•Venice

Zagreb•

SLAVONIA

Sava R.

Szeged•

Belgrade

CUMANIA

Olt R.

Danube R.

DOBRUDJA

Zadar•

CROATIA

BOSNIA

Varna•

PAPAL STATES

Rome•

ADRIATIC SEA

SERBIA

Dubrovnik•

Morava R.

Tirnovo•

BULGARIA

BLACK SEA

KINGDOM OF TWO SICILIES

Plovdiv•

Maritsa R.

N I C A E A N

•Adrianople

Durrës•

Vardar R.

MACEDONIA

Salonika•

Maritsa R.

Constantinople•

E M P I R E

EPIRUS

•Mt Athos

AEGEAN SEA

——————— state boundaries

---------------- internal boundaries

2. States of East Central Europe, ca. 1250. Adapted from Paul R. Magocsi, *Historical Atlas of East Central Europe* (1993), p. 17.

———————	state boundaries
- - - - - - -	internal boundaries
================	boundary of Holy Roman Empire

3. States of East Central Europe, ca. 1480. Adapted from Paul R. Magocsi,
Historical Atlas of East Central Europe (1993), p. 32.

East Central Europe
in the Middle Ages,
1000–1500

CHAPTER 1

Early Migrations

*T*wo thousand years ago in the days of the Roman Empire, the ethnic map of East Central Europe bore hardly any resemblance to its present configuration. On both sides of the lower Danube lived Thracian and Illyrian tribes, whose languages have left few traces in the speech of the region's present inhabitants except Albanian (which itself differs markedly from all other European tongues). North of the middle Danube and the Carpathian mountains, various Celtic and Germanic tribes lived in the lands which became Czechoslovakia and Poland. The modern nationalities map of East Central Europe is the product of massive migrations occurring early in the Middle Ages.

The earliest of the wandering tribes to establish a permanent and continuous presence in East Central Europe in historical times were Slavs (i.e., speakers of the Old Slavic tongue). Their gradual infiltration had certainly begun on a small scale by the 4th and 5th centuries, becoming a massive wave in the 6th and 7th. It is unlikely that any appreciable number of Slavs had inhabited East Central Europe previously; and earlier attempts to identify as such a prehistoric people living in Lusatia in eastern Germany have been largely discredited. The location of the Slavs' original homeland—the region where they first became a distinct ethnic group—remains a matter of some dispute. The bulk of the evidence seems to point to the region bounded approximately by the Vistula and Bug rivers to the northwest, the upper Dniester and western Dnieper rivers to the east, and the Carpathian Mountains to the south—that is, present-day Belarus (Belorussia, White Russia) and southeastern Poland.

In the earliest known period of history the overwhelming majority of Slavs who ultimately occupied most of East Central Europe resided somewhere else. They were an offshoot of the vast Indo-European people, who during the Neolithic period became separated from the larger linguistic group. About 2000 B.C. they formed part of a single Balto-Slavic mass. But by 1400–1200 B.C. the common speech of the Balto-Slavs had become differentiated into two distinct language groups: Baltic (the ancestor of modern Latvian and Lithuanian) and Old Slavic (also called Old Slavonic). Owing to subsequent migrations, the ancient Slavic tongue diverged still further into the various modern Slavic languages. Today the most widely spoken of these belong to the Eastern Slavic subgroup: Russian (or Great Russian), Ukrainian, and Belarussian (White Russian). East Central Europe is home to both the Western and Southern Slavic language subgroups, the former comprising Polish, Czech, and Slovak, together with some linguistic remnants like Sorbish; the latter including Serbo-Croatian, Bulgarian, Slovenian, and Macedonian.

In pre-Christian times the Balkan Peninsula was occupied by Illyrian and Thracian tribes speaking an ancient Indo-European tongue, only fragments of which survive today in a few scattered inscriptions. By the close of the first century B.C. most of this region had become part of the Roman Empire; and the Romans founded settlements there which became centers for diffusion of the Latin language and Roman culture. Thousands of Roman soldiers with their families came to settle as garrison troops in the new Roman towns, where they were joined by officials, merchants, and artisans. The majority spoke Latin and lived according to Roman customs. Thus the Thracians and Illyrians gradually lost their separate identities and became Romanized. Similarly the Roman conquest of Dacia (roughly the territory of present-day Romania) brought within the Roman sphere the tribes of that region, who were probably a northern branch of the Thracians. This occupation likewise had a Latinizing effect, except that its duration was comparatively short. Dacia remained subject to Rome for less than two centuries (A.D. 107–273)—far shorter than the period of Roman (and later Byzantine*) government south of the Danube.

The migration of the Slavs into East Central Europe was at first sporadic and small in scale. As with many other ancient tribal wanderings, its causes are obscure. As early as the first century A.D., isolated groups of Slavs began to move southward and westward from their homes in southeastern Poland and Belarus. Greek and Roman writers sometimes refer to the Slavs as "Venedi" or "Veneti," a name apparently of Celtic origin, which is preserved to this day in numerous place names having the root "vind" or "wend." Other Slavic groups moved west of the Oder River in the 2nd and 3rd centuries A.D., displacing the Germanic-speaking tribes of that region. The vast migration of peoples which was thus set in motion contributed to the fall of the Western Roman Empire by increasing the frequency and scope of Germanic attacks upon it. At the same time, Slavic groups also filtered into central Hungary, Dacia, and the Balkan Peninsula. In the 1st through 4th centuries A.D. some Slavs were certainly present in Pannonia (the former Roman province now comprising eastern Austria, western Hungary, and northern Croatia). Possibly others had moved as far south as Bulgaria and Greece by the 3rd century, although this is uncertain. In any

---

* The term "Byzantine" or "Byzantium" is used in this book to designate the government and territory of the Eastern Roman Empire from the 6th century onward.

event, some Slavic settlements undoubtedly existed south of the Danube several centuries prior to the much more extensive migrations of the 6th century A.D.

By the 4th century the migration of the Slavs from their trans-Carpathian homeland was well under way, although surviving historical sources take little notice of it. Evidently the Slavs did not leave their ancient territory in a single, sudden wave. Proof of this is the fact that the region north of the Carpathians remained full of Slavs in the 5th, 6th, and 7th centuries, just as it is today. The intermittent Slavic migrations differed sharply from the incursions of horsemen from the Eurasian steppe, whose advances were much more spectacular and destructive. The steppe dwellers lived by stock raising, which was the optimum means of survival on that flat, dry, treeless plain. The need to protect their flocks turned them into fierce mounted warriors, who frequently shifted from defense to offense and conducted plundering raids against their neighbors. Some of the steppe horsemen apparently constituted a permanent military caste of mounted cavalry forming the entourage of a chief. Under a talented leader these warriors sometimes parlayed their military prowess into major conquests. By contrast, the early Slavs were chiefly agriculturalists, on the whole far less belligerent than the steppe peoples. They moved gradually outward from their original nucleus, establishing fixed settlements wherever they went and constituting an easy prey for the mobile horsemen for whom warfare was a way of life.

The 6th century marked the high point of Slavic immigration south of the Carpathians and the virtual disappearance of the old Thracian and Illyrian tribes, already much reduced in size. Slavic settlements in Central Europe now increased greatly in number, while the new Slavic immigration extended much farther to the south than formerly. This movement of peoples was no longer a gradual, small-scale infiltration of peaceful agriculturalists whom the Byzantines could easily choose to ignore. The enormous wave of Slavic settlement soon led to conflict with the government at Constantinople, which maintained at least nominal control over the Balkan Peninsula south of the Danube. The earliest armed clash between Slavic and Byzantine troops apparently occurred in the year 517. In the following decades the Slavs conducted numerous raids across the lower Danube. Their frequent and wide-ranging attacks were often aided by the simultaneous aggression of mounted steppe warriors, particularly the Avars who occupied the central European plain between the last third of the 6th century and the end of the 8th. Multiple Slavic assaults on imperial territory south of the Danube and Sava rivers took place in the 6th century, which the Byzantine army was frequently unable to repel. Albania may also have been partially occupied by Slavs during this period, although the evidence on this point is inconclusive. Certainly Macedonia in the 6th and 7th centuries was filled with Slavs. Sources of the time refer to Macedonia as "the Slavic country" and describe it as very rich, doubtless partly because of plunder accumulated by the inhabitants on raids into Byzantine territory.

The Slavs who settled during the 6th century on the territory that later became Yugoslavia—probably in flight from the Avars—apparently were ruled in the 7th century by a warrior class of Iranian origin. Even prior to the great Slavic migrations, some degree of symbiosis apparently had occurred between the Slavs and the Iranian-speaking Sarmatians living north of the Black Sea. The terms "Serb" and "Croat" both appear to be of Iranian origin, while Iranian influences are evident in many other words which entered the Old Slavic language at an early date. Predictably, the discussion of Serb and Croat origins has been complicated by the reluctance of nationalist scholars to believe that foreigners might have provided the earliest ruling class for their nation. However, the domination of alien horse warriors over sedentary agriculturalists is hardly a unique phenomenon, as the case of the Bulgars well attests. While the name "Bulgar" today denotes a Slavic people, in the 7th and 8th centuries it referred to Turkic-speaking horsemen from the steppes of southern Ukraine, some of whom came to rule the Slavs of southeastern Europe.

As the area of Slavic settlement expanded southward into the Balkan Peninsula, the Latin-speaking population of the Adriatic littoral was partially displaced. Down to the close of the 6th century this coastal area remained secure against barbarian incursions. Although the interior of the peninsula was overrun, the main thrust of the Avar and Slavic attacks was directed toward Greece, where Constantinople and Salonika offered prizes far more dazzling than Balkan forest land. Dalmatia remained a secondary objective, protected by the mountain chain running parallel to the Adriatic coast. In the anarchy following the death of the Byzantine Emperor Maurice in 602, the Slavs had free run of the northern Balkans, at least until the Byzantines defeated the Avar-Slav assault on Constantinople in 626. Many of the Dalmatian towns were inadequately defended and easily occupied. The most important of them, Salona (Split), the site of Emperor Diocletian's famous 3rd-century palace, fell to Slavic invaders in 614. Part of the Latin-speaking population of the Adriatic coast now moved to the offshore islands, which remained in Byzantine hands long after the Slavic occupation of the interior. Other refugees settled on rocky islets separated from the coast by only a narrow channel, thereby founding the towns of Trogir, Dubrovnik, and Zadar. Still others retreated into the few well-fortified coastal settlements, some of which retained their Roman character as late as the mid-10th century.

Slavic occupation of the territory now known as Bulgaria was already extensive when the Turkic-speaking Bulgar horse warriors appeared on its borders in the late 7th century. Their settlement in this region was an indirect consequence of that Byzantine diplomacy which forever sought to play off one group of barbarians against another. Early in the 7th century the government at Constantinople gave its support to a Bulgar chieftain named Kubrat in his revolt against the Avars who then dominated the area north of the Black Sea. During the resultant upheavals, the Avars were driven westward, and Kubrat asserted hegemony over all the Bulgar tribes in Ukraine. One of his sons led a migration to the

Danube-Tisza plain, perhaps to join the Bulgar clans which had moved there earlier in the wake of the Avars. Another son established his chief residence on one of the islands of the Danube delta and about 650–70 began to rule over Dobrudja—that rectangle of land formed by the Danube's abrupt northward turn before it enters the Black Sea. In repelling an attack by the Byzantine emperor, who disliked the presence of barbarians so close to his northern frontier, the Bulgars chased the imperial troops southward. In contrast to their behavior on previous raids, this time they did not retreat north of the Danube, but stayed on to settle in Moesia, the Byzantine province south of the Danube and north of the Balkan Mountains.* Since the Slavs already present there were loosely organized and militarily too weak to resist, the much less numerous Bulgars established themselves as a ruling class over the sedentary Slavic agricultural population.

By the middle of the 7th century the great Slavic migrations had virtually ceased. All subsequent changes in Slavic settlement patterns in Europe proved comparatively minor, the principal one being the loss to the Germans of the territory west of the Oder River. Slavs now occupied most of present-day Poland, excluding only East Prussia with its population of Balts. Slavs formed the most numerous group in the area now comprising the Czech Republic, Slovakia, and Hungary, and dominated the territory south of the Sava-Danube line as far as the Adriatic Sea. Bulgaria had become largely Slavic in population; likewise Greece was home to extensive Slavic settlements. Significant groups of Latin speakers continued to reside in East Central Europe only along the Adriatic coast, the offshore islands, and sections of the Balkan interior. By the mid-7th century the Byzantine Empire had lost effective control of all but the fringes of the Balkan Peninsula.

Slavic settlement thus greatly reduced the territory available to the partially Romanized Illyrians and Thracians, who formerly had occupied a wide area in the Balkans. Apparently most of this indigenous population became absorbed into the Slavic flood, leaving only a remnant in the mountainous and largely inaccessible terrain of Albania. Place names in Albania bear witness to a Slavic presence there early in the medieval era, while place names in the Albanian language are missing altogether from that period. The earliest extant documentary reference to ethnic Albanians (or "Arbaneses") dates from the 11th century. These facts strongly suggest that the ancestors of today's Albanians cannot have occupied their present country continuously since the days of ancient Rome, since in that case at least a few ancient sources must have mentioned them. Unlike Dacia, about which the sources are similarly silent for nearly a thousand years, Albania lay well within the Roman and Byzantine sphere. Presumably the Albanians of

---

* This is a specific mountain range extending east and west across central Bulgaria, known in antiquity as the Haemus and in the Bulgarian language as Stara Planina. Its name unfortunately invites confusion with the term "Balkan" used to designate the entire peninsula.

the 11th century and afterward were descendants of the ancient Illyrians, pushed into the mountains by the invading Slavs and forced to adopt a pastoral life-style. The continuity between some ancient Illyrian sites and those later occupied by Albanians strongly suggests that this was the case.

The people known to medieval Europe as Vlachs—forebears of the present-day Romanians—were similarly forced to abandon their earlier homes in the Balkan lowlands. Ancestors of the Vlachs were the Latin-speaking (Roman or Romanized Thracian or Illyrian) inhabitants of the Roman Empire in south-eastern Europe, where Latin continued to be spoken as late as the 5th and 6th centuries despite the disappearance of effective Roman government in much of this region. In response to the pressure of the Slavic invasions in the 6th and 7th centuries, many of these Latin speakers evidently abandoned their farms and retreated into the hills with their livestock. Throughout the Middle Ages, Vlachs could be found in hilly or mountainous regions throughout the entire Balkan Peninsula, almost always living as stock raisers and herders. Indeed, in medieval usage the word "Vlach" became virtually synonymous with "shepherd," so that in many cases the historian cannot tell whether the term refers to an ethnic or an occupational category. Doubtless Slavic speakers were sometimes included under this rubric, although most Vlachs spoke a dialect derived from Latin. Without doubt the medieval Vlachs were a highly mobile people, who as pastoralists regarded migration as the natural response to unfavorable local conditions. In the southern Balkans most of them eventually became assimilated by the local Slavic or Greek population.

The political instability of the lower Danube plain—geographically an extension of the Ukrainian steppe—makes it unlikely that any group established itself there permanently during the thousand years after the Roman retreat from Dacia. Lacking any organized state structure, this territory (the future Walachia and Moldavia) came to be virtually ignored in historical documents. Its fertile grasslands lay wide open to invasion, while each new contingent of invaders from the steppe sought precisely the same grazing areas for its flocks. The rich but fatally exposed Danubian lowlands were subject to periodic incursions by successive waves of seminomadic peoples who occupied the country until they were pushed out or destroyed in turn by a new influx of invaders. Dacia after the Roman retreat was overrun successively by Goths (272–375), Huns (375–453), Gepids (453–566), and Avars (566–799); then by Slavs, Magyars, Pechenegs, Cumans, and Tatars (Mongols). Nowhere in East Central Europe were the conditions for permanent settlement less favorable. However, as the situation became more stable in the 14th century, many Vlachs migrated eastward from Transylvania to escape Hungarian rule; and the Romanian principalities of Moldavia and Walachia took form.

Transylvania itself was much less exposed to danger from the steppe, protected by the barrier of the Carpathian Mountains as well as by its own border defenses. How many or how few Vlachs may have resided there in the 11th century—the period when the Hungarian kings began to establish effective control over that eastern province—cannot be ascertained from any extant documentary evidence. The writers of medieval documents hardly considered such a question worth addressing. What is reasonably clear is that as far back as the records allow us to see, Transylvania has been a region of very mixed ethnic character. Hungarian and Romanian historians have each attempted to prove that their respective ancestors were the first to settle there. Romanians regard themselves as descendants of the (Thracian) tribes of pre-Roman Dacia intermingled with Roman settlers who allegedly have resided continuously in Transylvania ever since Roman times. Hungarians contend that a Vlach population entered Transylvania from the Balkan Peninsula only in the 12th century or thereabouts—an argument supported by the origin of some Transylvanian place names in the form of Old Slavic spoken at the time of the great Slavic migrations and by various Balkan influences on the modern Romanian language. However, the unspoken assumption behind this scholars' quarrel—namely, that prior occupation by a particular ethnic group justifies political rule by that same group even centuries afterward (i.e., at the present time)—is a modern notion, not a medieval one. The oldest extant documents from Transylvania, dating from the 12th and 13th centuries, make passing reference to both Hungarians and Vlachs. The actual number of persons belonging to each nationality is at best guesswork. A plausible estimate is that Vlachs constituted about two-thirds of Transylvania's population in 1241 on the eve of the Mongol invasion.

To complete the modern ethnic map of East Central Europe, the confederation of tribes known to Europeans as Magyars or Hungarians invaded the Danube-Tisza plain in 895–96, driving a permanent wedge between the Western and Southern Slavs. The new arrivals were a multi-ethnic and multi-lingual group in which the Megyeri tribe (i.e., the Finno-Ugric speaking component) formed a distinct minority, although they (and their language) subsequently came to dominate the whole. Like the Huns, Avars, and Bulgars before them, the Megyeri had arrived from the steppes of Ukraine. Evidently in the 820s or 830s they had abandoned their lands west of the Urals and moved to the region of the lower Dnieper and Don rivers. In 888–89 an attack of Pecheneg tribes pushed them out of this territory and forced them to flee westward.* The Megyeri then settled in a region they called Etelköz, or "river district," perhaps located somewhere between the Pruth and Dniester rivers (i.e., Bessarabia), or

* Certainly not all of the Finno-Ugric speakers joined the migration from southern Russia into Central Europe. Early in the 13th century, reports reached the kingdom of Hungary that speakers of the Magyar tongue could be found along the Volga River in faraway Russia. Three Dominican monks set out to find them. The only one who survived this journey, Friar Julian, succeeded in 1236 in locating his lost countrymen and reported back to Hungary that he had had no difficulty in communicating with them in his native tongue. A statue of Friar Julian with an appropriately patriotic inscription stands today on the Castle Hill in Budapest.

even farther south near the multiple mouths of the Danube. In any event, they did not remain there for long. According to tradition, the refugees in Etelköz drew up a Covenant of Blood with the federation of Onogurs then living on the lower Danube, by which they sealed a permanent union of their tribes. The Megyeri accepted the Onogur duke Almus as their supreme ruler and his son Árpád as military chief of their tribe.

The Danubians Onogurs, from whom the name "Hungarian" is derived, were descendants of those Onogurs who had lived in Pannonia during the previous century as partners in the Avar (or Avar-Onogur) federation. Ethnically they were related to the Turkic-speaking Bulgars, whom they also resembled in life-style. Driven out of Pannonia between 796 and 803 by Charlemagne and his Franks, they had since settled near the lower Danube; but with their advance into Central Europe in 895-96 they laid claim to their former domicile. Since according to nomad custom the newest member of a confederation always occupied the most exposed position during any military action, the Megyeri tribe under its Onogur chief Árpád led the way across the Carpathians. Traditional Hungarian historiography describes this event as a "taking of the land," or conquest, although various medieval documents refer to it as a "second coming." This latter term was accurate with respect to the Onogurs, which may explain why Western chroniclers who had long been aware of their presence along the lower Danube took no notice of this particular migration. However, for the Finno-Ugric Megyeri it was a first appearance in Central Europe. Within the confederation they soon became the dominant group, because their leader Árpád inherited his father's position as head of the entire tribal alliance and succeeded in founding a dynasty. Unaware of the multi-ethnic nature of this confederation, other Europeans referred to all of its members indiscriminately as "Magyars" or "Hungarians."

For the new immigrants the moment was propitious. The young Bulgar state, then engaged in bitter struggles with the Byzantines, could hardly exercise effective control over distant outposts in Central Europe. In Germany the East Franks, ruled by Charlemagne's weak heirs, had fallen into anarchy. According to all accounts, the Magyars' "taking of the land" encountered no serious resistance. The Danube-Tisza plain was then sparsely populated, its sandy wastes and marshes subject to frequent droughts and floods which made agriculture virtually impossible by the methods then prevailing. Only pastoral peoples like the Avars or now the Magyars, who required broad grasslands to feed their extensive herds, cared to live there permanently. Central Hungary in the late 9th century contained only some scattered Slavic and Avar remnants. Contemporary sources described it as "the Avar wasteland." The Magyars thus occupied the grassy plains and left the oak and beech forests of the Carpathian basin to the Slavs. However, they were not content to settle peacefully in their new homeland. Their horse warriors carried out wide-ranging raids into Western and Southern Europe, sowing terror wherever they went and taking numerous captives and plunder. In the more settled region west of the Danube, which was then ruled by Slavic dukes, many Slavs now abandoned their homes and moved southward into the area later known as Slavonia, between the Drava and Sava rivers.

The occupation of Hungary was the last wholesale migration of peoples into East Central Europe prior to the Ottoman conquests of the 14th century. Subsequent ethnic changes were smaller in scale and more gradual. The boundaries of Slavdom in northern Europe slowly retreated eastward, apparently because the settlement of Germans in the Elbe region became more intensive and the Slavs were outnumbered. Except for the Slavic-speaking Sorbs, who today inhabit linguistic enclaves in an overwhelmingly German environment, the Elbe Slavs became absorbed into the surrounding German population. Farther to the south, Turkic-speaking horsemen from the Ukrainian steppes continued to press westward into Central Europe, harassing eastern Transylvania and Poland, while retarding for centuries the formation of viable political units in Walachia and Moldavia. Toward the end of the 10th century Pecheneg tribes from the steppe settled in Moldavia and Walachia, conducting intermittent raids into Bulgaria. During the second half of the 11th century another steppe people, the Iazygs (or Uzes), replaced them as the principal danger to Transylvania's eastern frontier. Some of the Pechenegs fled into Hungary, where the Hungarian king employed them to guard his border districts. The Byzantine army conclusively eliminated the Pecheneg threat in two decisive battles in 1091 and 1122.

Toward the end of the 11th century, the Iazygs on the lower Danube were supplanted by Cumans, another steppe people who had established a loose overlordship over all of southern Ukraine. Groups of Cumans first moved into Moldavia as allies of the Pechenegs. In 1087 they crossed the lower Danube and occupied the plain on both sides of the river (i.e., Walachia and northern Bulgaria). Practicing no agriculture, they collected grain as tribute from the populations they subjected. In the 1190s they helped establish the Second Bulgarian Empire, participating in the armed struggles between Bulgarians and Byzantines. The onslaught of the Mongols into Europe—defeating a coalition of Cumans and Rus on the Kalka River in 1223—caused additional Cumans from Ukraine to flee westward. The Cuman hegemony in southeastern Europe lasted for about a century and a half. Finally in 1241, the Mongol invasion of Central Europe put an end to this "Cumania" in the Balkans.

Other significant ethnic changes took place in East Central Europe through government-ordered population transfers. The entire region in the Middle Ages contained large tracts of unoccupied land, where immigrant peasants formed welcome additions to the taxpaying population. If the newcomers possessed artisan skills or expertise in trade, so much the better. During the 10th century, the Byzantine government removed a number of Paulician heretics from the frontier regions of Anatolia and established them near Plovdiv in Bulgaria; these were primarily ethnic Armenians. In about 988, Emperor Basil II transferred other Armenians to Macedonia to serve as a bulwark against the Bulgars, with whom he was at war. In the 12th and 13th centuries large numbers of peasants and townsmen from Western Europe, primarily Germans but including an admixture of other nationalities, migrated into Bohemia, Hungary, and Poland. In the 14th and 15th centuries the expansion of the Ottoman Empire brought a considerable influx of Turks into the Balkan Peninsula, sometimes by forcible deportation from Anatolia. The new conquerors organized their European frontier regions into border marches and stationed Turkish soldiers in the garrisons. They also imported ordinary Turkish villagers or nomads as colonists, establishing them in particularly strategic spots. This was an obvious security measure—introducing a Muslim population among the local Christians—but useful also in order to repopulate districts devastated by war.

The largest Turkish immigration into the Balkans occurred during the initial period of Ottoman rule—the second half of the 14th century. In the eastern Balkans the area of Turkish settlement soon formed a solid belt extending from the Straits northward to beyond the Danube, where it made contact with the Tatars. In this way southern Bulgaria and Thrace became largely Islamized and Turkish speaking. After the decisive Ottoman victory at Černomen on the Maritsa River in 1371, Turks came to live in the principal towns of Macedonia (e.g., in Skopje and Bitolj), although rarely as yet in the villages. After Albania, Serbia, and Bosnia became subject to Ottoman control, some Turkish settlement occurred there also. However, in the 15th century most of the new Turkish immigrants into the Balkans were soldiers manning the garrisons, not peasants. The Christian inhabitants of the Ottoman Empire in Europe did not ordinarily adopt the Turkish language and life-style, nor did the Ottoman government encourage them to do so. For the most part, the Slavs, Hungarians, and Vlachs of the Balkan Peninsula preserved their ethnic character through nearly 500 years of Ottoman rule.

Another sort of migration was that of the Jews, who typically lived in the larger urban settlements, although some also resided in small country towns which maintained intimate links with the countryside. Jewish traders were active in many areas of East Central Europe at a very early date, although large-scale migrations of Jews into the region began only in 1096 in the wake of the First Crusade. From that time onward a steady flow of Jews moved eastward, especially into Poland, where their expertise in trade and finance was often very welcome and a number of princes offered them protection. The outbreaks of anti-Semitic violence which accompanied the Black Death (bubonic plague) in Western Europe in 1348–49 set off a second large wave of Jewish eastward emigration. Jews came to constitute an important segment of the urban class in East Central Europe, where town life was much less developed than in the West.

In sum, the great migrations into East Central Europe had ceased by the end of the 9th century. The Magyar invasion permanently divided the Western from the

Southern Slavs; and soon the Magyars themselves abandoned the life-style of the steppes for a more settled existence. The Old Slavic language began increasingly to diverge into its subsequent West, South, and East Slavic variants. Already by the 10th century the ethnic frontiers of East Central Europe had formed a pattern that would still be recognizable after a thousand years.

CHAPTER 2

State Formation

Modern notions of what constitutes a state or empire apply in only a limited way to the political formations of the early Middle Ages. "State" may be taken to mean an independent government with a territory, while an "empire" is a state uniting many peoples and territories under one ruler or ruling group. However, the salient characteristics of a modern state (fixed boundaries, a capital city, professional officials, an established legal system, and a standing army) are mostly absent in early medieval political units. The seminomadic peoples who dominated large parts of East Central Europe prior to the Slavic invasions possessed permanent military forces—consisting essentially of the entire able-bodied male population—but neither a fixed capital nor a bureaucracy or written law; and the boundaries of their territories were often only approximate. The early Slavic rulers each maintained a private entourage of fighting men and sought with varying success to appoint subordinates ("counts") to command military garrisons throughout their lands. In regions where enemies threatened to intrude, they made attempts to mark off the frontiers of the political unit with barriers of fallen trees or other obstacles. Nonetheless, the ruler had no permanent residence; government was conducted by orders issued on an ad hoc basis through his immediate servants; and law was based on custom. Historians cannot tell whether the earliest states were organized around a military aristocracy, aided by the preeminence of individual leaders, or whether the process of creating a state involved first the formation of tribes which later became consolidated into larger units. In either case the prestige of a ruling family and the personal authority of a leader over his armed entourage was the power which held a rudimentary "state" together. "Conquest" generally meant not direct control over a territory, but forcing a defeated group to pay tribute to the conqueror and provide soldiers for his wars.

The history of state formation in East Central Europe begins with the Roman Empire. Between the first century B.C. and the 5th A.D., the Romans extended their hegemony over all the lands bordering the Mediterranean Sea. In East

Central Europe the imperial frontier lay along the broad Danube, encompassing what is now western Hungary, most of Serbia, and all of Slovenia, Croatia, Bosnia-Hercegovina, Montenegro, Slavic Macedonia, Bulgaria, Albania, and Greece. During much of the 2nd and 3rd centuries, the empire extended north of the river to include the lands of present-day Romania. Although the western portion of the Roman Empire collapsed under barbarian pressure in the 5th century, the Byzantine (or Greek) half lasted until 1453, when the Ottoman Turks finally captured Constantinople, its magnificent capital. Byzantium owed its survival to an effective governmental organization, far superior to any which existed elsewhere in Europe at that time. Long after the demise of the Western Roman Empire, the ideal of a universal state, which the united empire had embodied, remained alive in a surprisingly pervasive tradition, a memory which ultimately became enshrined in the medieval Holy Roman (actually German) Empire. Furthermore, Byzantium provided a political and cultural model for the nascent Balkan states. However, Germany east of the Rhine and Hungary east of the Danube, together with all of the present-day Czech Republic, Slovakia, and Poland, never belonged to either half of the Roman Empire—a fact having profound consequences for their later evolution.

The serious process of state building in East Central Europe began earliest in those regions most influenced by the Byzantine or Roman example. The old imperial structures provided institutional models of a far more complex kind than the simple tribalism of the invading Bulgars, Slavs, or Magyars. Thus the Bulgars profited from geographical proximity to the Byzantine Empire, while the Croats absorbed Italian influences through the cities of the Adriatic littoral. Not surprisingly, a Bulgar and a Croat state came into existence considerably earlier than a Bohemian or a Polish one. Moreover, propinquity to the Greek and Roman cultural world was an important factor in the diffusion of Christianity. The process of early state formation placed the power of a central government firmly behind the new religion, while the institutional Church in turn gave ideological support to Christian governments.

The Byzantine government lost control of the interior of the Balkan Peninsula during the 7th century as a consequence of the Slavic migrations, internal political crises, and the Arab military threat to the southern frontier. Officially most of Dalmatia seems still to have acknowledged Byzantine sovereignty, since in 678 the emperor recognized the Croats' right to reside in the lands they already possessed. This presumably indicates that Constantinople had no choice in the matter. During this period several small Croatian political units came into existence. The earliest one was known as White Croatia, perhaps in memory of the former Croat homeland of that name north of the Carpathian Mountains. Its center lay on the Istrian Peninsula just east of Italy. By the end of the 8th century three distinct Croatian principalities had taken form: White Croatia and Red Croatia along the Adriatic coast, and Pannonian Croatia in the interior, separated from the other two by mountain ranges. The Croats remained at least nominal vassals of the Eastern emperor until Charlemagne, king of the Franks, conquered them early in the 9th century. Thereupon they exchanged Byzantine for Frankish suzerainty.

The earliest medieval state in the Balkan Peninsula took form soon after the year 681, when Bulgar horse warriors from the Ukrainian steppes invaded Byzantine territory, defeated a large Byzantine army, and established their hegemony over the Slavic and Latin-speaking peoples living between the Danube and the Balkan (Stara Planina) Mountains. Since no records survive of any resistance to this invasion, the Slavs perhaps welcomed the Bulgars as liberators from Byzantine taxation. For the government at Constantinople this attack occurred at a particularly unfortunate moment, when their response was hampered by a simultaneous threat from the Arabs in the south. Defeated by the Bulgars, the Byzantines for the first time were obliged officially to surrender some of their territory in the Balkan Peninsula. Their armies returned for a second Bulgarian campaign in 689, again unsuccessful. After this, Constantinople essentially gave up and left the Bulgars in peace. The newly established Bulgar state included not only the territory between the Balkan Mountains and the Danube, but also most of Walachia to the north of that river and Bessarabia as far as the Dniester. However, its center of gravity lay south of the Danube around Pliska, the capital. By the Bulgar-Byzantine treaty of 716, Bulgaria's southern boundary with Byzantium was established approximately along a line running from the northern shore of the Gulf of Burgas southwest to the Maritsa River.

The Byzantines remained unreconciled to the forfeiture of their Balkan lands. While forced by circumstances to recognize the Bulgars' conquests, they sought intermittently to restore their old boundary on the Danube. Even so, the Bulgars under Khan Krum (r. 802–14) gained major new territories in the northwest Balkans. Krum defeated the remnants of the Avars and united the Pannonian Bulgars with their fellows in the Balkan Peninsula. South of the Balkan Mountains a line of Byzantine fortresses prevented further advances into Thrace. Nonetheless, Bulgaria now extended from the northern Carpathian Mountains eastward to the Pruth River (or perhaps even the Dniester) and the Black Sea, and in the west touched the Frankish Empire on the Tisza River in Hungary. Khan Krum's successors gained additional lands in Macedonia, while Khan Boris (r. 852–89) arrogated to himself the exalted title of "tsar" (i.e., "emperor"). The late 9th and early 10th centuries were the Golden Age of this First Bulgarian Empire. During the brilliant reign of Tsar Symeon (r. 893–927), Bulgaria not only dominated the Balkan Peninsula but also became the center of an impressive Byzantine-oriented civilization.

Meanwhile, by the end of the 8th century the Frankish Empire had become the dominant power in Central Europe. After conquering the Avars of Pannonia and Dalmatia, Charlemagne organized this area into the march (i.e., borderland) of Friuli, ruled by a Frankish count. Paradoxically, in freeing the Slavs from Avar domination he ultimately made possible the development of independent Slavic principalities between the Danube and the Adriatic Sea. Pannonia and Dalmatia soon escaped Frankish control. The East Frankish realm and its successor, the German (or Holy Roman) Empire, never developed a strong central monarchy and imperial bureaucracy which might have kept the Slavs in subjection. Its chief offices were held by feudal lords who were far more interested in maintaining their own autonomous rule than in keeping the larger polity intact.

White and Red Croatia united to form a single state in the 9th century. However, the founder of the Croat national dynasty, Trpimir (r. ca. 845–64), reigned only along the Adriatic littoral, not in what later became inland Croatia, and clearly retained some political dependence on the Franks. Subsequently King Tomislav (r. 910–ca. 928), the most powerful monarch of independent Croatia, acquired the hinterland as far north as the Drava River and put an end to Frankish overlordship there. Politically Croatia declined notably after his death. The easternmost section (Red Croatia) broke away and the Serbs seized part of Bosnia, while the coastal town of Dubrovnik (Ragusa) became an independent city-state. Very little is known about the fate of Croatia during the 10th and 11th centuries. Clearly it never became a major power, except perhaps briefly under Tomislav. As an independent state it existed for only about two centuries prior to joining the Hungarian kingdom in the late 11th century.

Immediately to the north and west of Croatia lived the Slovenes, a comparatively small Slavic-speaking people who, like the Croats, came under Frankish domination in the 9th century. Cut off from contact with the Slavic tribes farther north by the Magyar occupation of Pannonia in the late 9th century, the Slovene population lived intermingled with Germans in the German-ruled territories now located in southern Austria and the (formerly Yugoslav) republic of Slovenia. In these regions, just as in Pomerania or Brandenburg, immigration pushed the boundaries of German settlement eastward, with many Slavic speakers becoming Germanized in the process. German domination of the Slovene-inhabited lands extended throughout the entire Middle Ages (and afterwards until the 20th century). As a consequence, the Slovenes developed a language and ethnic identity distinct from that of their Croatian neighbors, who became subject to Hungary late in the 11th century. The medieval Slovene-speaking population lived chiefly in the German-ruled duchies of Carniola, Carinthia, and Styria, which in turn belonged to the German (Holy Roman) Empire. No separate Slovene-speaking provinces then existed; and only in the year 1990 did an independent Slovenian state come into existence (roughly equivalent to the medieval duchy of Carniola).

The history of Serbia in the 9th and 10th centuries, like that of Croatia at the same period, is largely a blank page. Serbian tribes are known to have occupied the Balkan interior west of the Morava River and south as far as the Adriatic Sea. Presumably the Bulgars' expansion into this region prodded the Serbs into achieving a greater degree of unity than previously. Likewise the Byzantines were concerned to strengthen the Serbs as a counterweight to Bulgaria. The Serbian tribes of this period were grouped into several small principalities bordering the Adriatic coast: Duklja (Montenegro), Zahumlje (Hercegovina), and Trebinje situated between them. Byzantium claimed sovereignty over all three. (The geographical center of Serbia in the region between Belgrade and Skopje dates from the 12th century.) The powerful Bulgar Tsar Symeon (d. 927) incorporated the Serbian principalities into his empire and appointed their princes, but this arrangement apparently ceased at his death. Historical sources are silent concerning the fate of Serbia in the second half of the 10th century.

The Magyars who established themselves in Central Europe in the late 9th century were then just a coalition of tribes led by a military aristocracy. The real founder of the Hungarian state was King Stephen I, who accepted Christianity, married a Bavarian princess, assumed the royal title in the year 1000, and organized his government and church on Bavarian models. Eventually the kingdom of Hungary expanded into the entire Carpathian basin. From about the year 1025 it included Slovakia, the hilly country just south of the Carpathian Mountains, which was populated largely by Slavs.* Transylvania was incorporated only gradually during the course of the 11th century, until by the final third of the 12th century a separate Transylvanian province had been organized under the Hungarian crown. Meanwhile Hungary had received an enormous accretion of territory to the south by acquiring the kingdom of Croatia.

This union with Croatia occurred not through conquest but as a consequence of dynastic politics. The death of the Croatian King Zvonimir without heirs in 1089 was followed by a period of murderous feuds among the nobility and a situation of virtual anarchy. In response, a delegation from the town of Split invited Zvonimir's brother-in-law, King Ladislas of Hungary, to take over all of Croatia. Ladislas and his successor, King Koloman, met little opposition when they brought their army into Croatia between 1091 and 1097 and established Hungarian garrisons in the royal towns and fortresses. The northernmost region of Croatia, or Slavonia, became part of Hungary proper; but the remainder retained its separate identity. The Croats always insisted that their ancestors had chosen the king of Hungary as their ruler by free election, and in consequence felt entitled to insist on a special legal status within the Hungarian state. Hungary also acquired a claim to Bosnia, which the local nobility accepted in 1124 only after considerable resistance. The Bosnians cherished their independence, so that for long periods Hungarian authority there was purely nominal.

Bulgaria ceased to play a major role in Balkan politics after the death of Tsar Symeon in 927, although Tsar Peter, his son and successor, managed to maintain the integrity of the state for another forty years. Nonetheless, signs of weakness were already apparent during Peter's final decade. In 963 a provincial notable

---

* During the medieval era Slovakia was divided into counties on the usual Hungarian pattern and never formed a separate administrative unit. The term *Slovensko* (Slovakia) as a geographical designation begins to appear on documents in the mid-15th century.

(or "count") named Šišman rebelled and carved out an independent principality for himself from Bulgaria's western provinces (present-day Macedonia*
and Albania). Thus Bulgaria was already de facto split into two parts when
the Bulgar government precipitated the final catastrophe by refusing payment
of its customary tribute to Byzantium. To punish them the Byzantines invited
Prince Sviatoslav of Kiev to raid Bulgar territory. Sviatoslav complied; but when
he and his army showed no signs of intending to withdraw, the Byzantine Emperor
John Tzimiskes intervened to expel them. In the process he overran all of eastern
Bulgaria, which in 971 again became part of the Byzantine Empire.

The death of Tzimiskes in 976 permitted a temporary revival of the Bulgar
state, this time with its center of gravity in Macedonia. The four sons of Šišman,
collectively known as Comitopuli, or "Count's sons," ruled western Bulgaria as
an independent state. One of them, Samuel, killed or outlasted all his brothers
and proceeded to create a powerful army. With his centers of power at Ohrid
and Prespa in western Macedonia, Samuel had the advantage of relative distance
from Constantinople, while the Byzantines were occupied elsewhere. In 993 he
assumed the title of tsar. Samuel held a number of important fortresses and even
reconquered eastern Bulgaria, thus regaining much of the territory formerly held
by Symeon and Peter. By 996 he ruled not only all of the original Bulgar state but
also Thessaly, Epirus, and parts of Albania, while forcing the Serbian princes to
become his vassals. Nonetheless Bulgaria's resurgence was brief. The Byzantine
emperor at that time, Basil II (r. 976–1025), was a soldier no less capable than
Samuel himself, and he disposed of greatly superior resources. Beginning in
about 996, Basil began a series of meticulously organized campaigns into Bulgar
territory, placing Samuel increasingly on the defensive. By 1018 the restored
Bulgar state had ceased to exist, and the northern boundary of the Byzantine
Empire again ran along the Danube. There it remained for the following 170
years, while Byzantium underwent a military and political revival.

Meanwhile another Slavic state had come into existence within the semicircle
of the mountains that afterwards would mark the western frontier of the duchy
(later kingdom) of Bohemia. There the multiple sovereignties which existed
in the 9th and 10th centuries gradually became consolidated into two larger
units—Bohemia (in the narrower sense) in the northwest and Moravia in the
southeast.† In 1031 the two parts became permanently linked under a single ruler,
with Moravia recognizing the supremacy of Prague, the Bohemian capital. The
duchy of Bohemia was always subject to strong German influences, particularly

---

* Except where otherwise specified, this book employs the geographical term "Macedonia" in its older (and less precise) sense to encompass both Slavic Macedonia (the
former Yugoslav republic, together with a slice of the present-day western Bulgaria) and
Greek Macedonia.

† The term "Bohemia" sometimes denotes the entire kingdom, but at other times merely
its northwestern section. Wherever the narrower Bohemia (excluding Moravia) is meant,
this book will identify it specifically as a province or portion of the larger state.

from Bavaria. For several centuries the Bohemian duke was a vassal of the German emperor, holding Moravia as a border-march organized as a separate administrative area. The duke was required to pay tribute to the German emperor, attend his court on certain specified occasions, and participate in his campaigns. In the 13th century, Bohemia expanded northeastward to include Silesia, a region of numerous minor principalities then ruled by offshoots of the Polish Piast dynasty. On the other hand, Slovakia remained subject to Hungary, although the Czechs and Slovaks were kindred peoples sharing a common tongue.

The northernmost Slavs of East Central Europe were also the last to organize themselves politically. The earliest Polish state took form in the region known as Great Poland, or Wielkopolska (present-day western Poland). The treaty which its duke, Mieszko I, concluded in 963 with one of his German neighbors contains the earliest known reference to Poland in extant historical documents. Either Mieszko or his son Boleslav annexed the Cracow region (known as Małopolska, or Little Poland) and Silesia. Nonetheless the territory of the Polish state was still very much in flux in the 11th and 12th centuries. Old tribal divisions reasserted themselves periodically, especially in sparsely populated Mazovia (around Warsaw), which throughout the Middle Ages remained at least partly independent. A prolonged period of internal disintegration began in 1138. The semi-independent Polish principalities into which Poland now became divided lost even their common name—Polonia—which for the next two centuries referred to Great Poland alone. The region of Pomerania, along the Baltic Sea between the Oder and the Vistula, became a bone of contention between the German emperor and the Poles. Chiefly Slavic in population, it had long maintained a tenuous connection to Poland, but the emperor was able to assert feudal supremacy there. Although the de facto ruler of Pomerania in the 12th century was the Polish duke, he was formally a vassal of the emperor holding this duchy as a fief of the empire.

In the 13th century an entirely new type of state arose along the Baltic Sea east of the Vistula River, organized by the Teutonic Order of Knights. The Knights were a monastic military brotherhood founded in Palestine during the Crusades. After the crusading movement declined, the Order sought a new field of activity to justify its continued existence. In 1226 the Polish Duke Conrad of Mazovia, unable to protect his principality from the destructive raids of pagan Prussian tribes, invited the Knights to settle along his northwestern frontier.* Evidently he assumed that a Christian neighbor would be less dangerous than a pagan one. Although the Knights demanded extensive guarantees, Conrad agreed in 1230, after considerable hesitation, to recognize their suzerainty over whatever territory they might succeed in conquering from the Prussians. For

---

* These Prussians (who spoke a Baltic, not a Germanic, language) should not be confused with the German-speaking Prussians of later centuries who lived in this region (later known as East Prussia) as subjects of Brandenburg-Prussia and subsequently imperial Germany.

Poland it was a fatal mistake: exchanging a disruptive but primitive enemy for a far more powerful one possessing a superb military organization and powerful international connections. The Mazovian duke could scarcely have foreseen the consequences. The Knights' military skill, superior discipline, proficiency in diplomacy, and ability to attract recruits from all over Christendom soon made them a formidable rival, often an enemy, to the Poles on their common frontier.

The Teutonic Knights brought the first German settlers to Prussia in 1230. They began to build strongholds along the Vistula and the Baltic coast, most notably Toruń (Thorn), named after a fortress in Palestine. Their territory, separated only by semi-independent Pomerania from the German Empire, eventually extended eastward from the Vistula to the River Nieman. This new body politic, dominated by Germans, stood virtually alone in Europe in being governed not by a hereditary dynasty but by the elected head of a monastic organization. Nonetheless, in its expansionist impulses it scarcely differed from other contemporary states. In 1237 the Teutonic Knights fused with a similar but much smaller military order, the Livonian Knights (or Knights of the Sword), which had established a small principality at the mouth of the Western Dvina River in what is now Latvia. Although the two realms were not contiguous (between them lay Samogitia, a strip of land roughly equivalent to modern Lithuania), these two knightly monastic orders had in common their German character and crusading mentality. Together they formed a powerful bloc.

Meanwhile in the southern sector of East Central Europe, Serbia had evolved from a set of minor principalities under loose Byzantine suzerainty into an important power factor in the Balkans. In the 11th century the most important Serbian political units were Duklja (Dioclea), located on the southern Adriatic coast with a rugged mountainous hinterland (today's Montenegro); and Raška, farther east in the Balkan interior. After Duklja disintegrated early in the 12th century, Raška remained to become the nucleus of the future Serbia. The rulers of Raška in the 11th and 12th centuries fought intermittently with the Byzantines and made various unsuccessful attempts to acquire portions of Byzantine Macedonia. However, the death of Emperor Manuel Comnenus in 1180, followed by civil strife in the empire, created a power vacuum which allowed the Serbs to expand southward. By 1190 the Serbian state extended from the lower Morava and Drina rivers in the north to the coast of southern Dalmatia and Montenegro in the southwest and the Šar mountain range in the south (the present Serbian-Macedonian border). In that year the Byzantines were forced to recognize Serbia's conquests, although they continued to hold a strip of land along the Morava River which controlled the overland route to Belgrade. Even more favorable for Serbian ambitions was the capture of Constantinople in 1204 by the knights of the Fourth Crusade. Until 1261 West Europeans ruled the old Greek capital with its environs, now known as the Latin Empire of Constantinople, while the Byzantine emperors were confined to a small territory around the city of Nicaea in Asia Minor. Byzantine authority had now disappeared for all practical purposes from the Balkan Peninsula.

Concurrently with the rise of Serbia, a revolt in Bulgaria led to the founding of the Second Bulgarian Empire in 1185. The Bulgars had never forgotten their former dominance in the Balkans, despite their status as Byzantine subjects ever since the collapse of Tsar Samuel's empire in 1018. The example of the Serbs' success doubtless encouraged the Bulgars to bid for independence. Byzantium's current troubles, which included an attack by the Normans of Sicily on their possessions in Albania and Macedonia, created a favorable opportunity. In 1185 two Bulgar notables, the brothers John (Ivan) and Peter Asen, organized an uprising and raided the Empire's territories. Occupied in fighting the Normans, the Byzantine government could not respond effectively. By treaty in 1188 the government at Constantinople recognized the Asens' sovereignty over all of eastern Bulgaria between the Danube and the Balkan range—Bulgaria's original territory. The brothers went on to capture the great commercial center of Varna on the Black Sea.

The capture of Constantinople in 1204 provided a powerful stimulus to the Bulgarian revival. The Byzantine Empire was now split up into three mutually antagonistic states: the weak Latin Empire at Constantinople; a truncated Byzantine successor state with its capital at Nicaea; and the Greek-ruled state of Epirus in northwestern Greece. All three laid claim to the entire former Byzantine territory. In the Balkans the Bulgars competed with all three for dominance. Through a key military victory over the Latins at Adrianople in 1205 and another over the despot of Epirus at Klokotnica in 1230, Bulgaria became the most powerful state in the Balkans. With its capital at Tirnovo, this Second Bulgarian Empire reached its zenith under Emperor John (Ivan) Asen II (r. 1218–41), who briefly held most of the territories which had once belonged to Tsar Symeon. Nonetheless, internal troubles soon caused this newly ascendant Bulgar state to split apart. In 1246 the Nicaean emperor John Vatatzes reconquered large portions of southern Bulgaria, while the ruler of Epirus gained western Macedonia. In 1257 the region around the Danubian port of Vidin in western Bulgaria separated from Tirnovo and became independent. The reconquest of Constantinople by the Nicaeans in 1261 allowed the Byzantine government to take renewed interest in the Balkans and expand the frontier northward. Then in the 1280s and 1290s the Bulgar tsars were forced to become vassals of the Tatars of the Golden Horde, whose capital lay on the lower Volga River in Russia.

In 1322 eastern and western Bulgaria became united once more under a single ruler, only to be divided again in about 1360. This arrangement prevented Vidin and Tirnovo from coordinating a defense against their common enemy, the Ottoman Turks. However, the partition had little ultimate impact on the course of events. Time was running out for Bulgaria. Situated in the direct line of Ottoman expansion into Europe, with no prospect of significant military aid from its neighbors, it could hardly hope to withstand a major attack. After the Turks won a major victory at Černomen on the Maritsa River in 1371, the Bulgarian tsar as well as the princes of southern and eastern Serbia were obliged to become

Ottoman vassals. Tirnovo fell to the Turks in 1393, with Vidin following suit in 1396 after the battle of Nicopolis. These events inaugurated nearly 500 years of Ottoman rule over Bulgaria.

For Serbia the Ottoman advance proved equally disastrous. Beginning in the 1260s the Serbs had profited from a favorable external situation. The restored Byzantine Empire was scarcely able to control even the territory in the vicinity of its own capital, while Bulgaria had become a less formidable competitor than before. In the late 13th century the Serbs began moving the boundaries of their principality southward. Under its most powerful medieval tsar, Stephen Dušan (r. 1331–55), Serbia briefly became the most powerful state in the Balkans, ruling the former Byzantine or Bulgarian possessions in Macedonia, Albania, Epirus, and Thessaly. However, this expansion did not rest on a solid power base. The Serbian Empire quickly disintegrated after Dušan's death in 1355. Even during his lifetime, provincial nobles had enjoyed great power in their localities. After the battle of Černomen in 1371, Serbia was reduced to half of its former territory, with a center much farther north than before in the Morava valley. Local lords became increasingly autonomous; and the king (no longer called "tsar") held less power than some of his own nobles. After the battle of Kosovo in 1389 the remainder of Serbia became a Turkish vassal state, although its complete incorporation into the Ottoman Empire occurred only seventy years later.

Serbia's immediate neighbor to the west, the small and mountainous principality of Bosnia, enjoyed considerable de facto independence in the 13th and 14th centuries despite nominal subjection to Hungary. Its difficult terrain permitted the local lords frequently to ignore all central authority. Remoteness from the power centers of both Hungary and Serbia enabled the Bosnians to maneuver between their two powerful neighbors, usually managing to avoid subordination to either. However, several unusually capable rulers allowed Bosnia briefly to play the role of a great power in the 14th century. After about 1290 the country enjoyed virtual independence from Hungary and gained significant territory in Dalmatia at Serbia's expense. The Bosnian King Tvrtko I (r. 1353–91) acquired portions of western Serbia and most of the Adriatic coast south of the Neretva River. During the latter part of his reign, Tvrtko briefly ruled the strongest state in the Balkan Peninsula. However, local separatism remained strong in Bosnia, and after his death the country soon lost its preeminence. The Turks annexed portions of eastern Bosnia in the 1440s and 1450s, and went on to attack Hercegovina until its last fortress fell in 1481.

The 14th century also witnessed the emergence of two independent Vlach (i.e., Romanian) states between the Carpathian Mountains and the Black Sea— Walachia and Moldavia. Situated on the westernmost extension of the great Eurasian plain, their territory lay on the natural route taken by predatory steppe nomads from Ukraine on their raids into Central and Southern Europe. Over the centuries Goths, Huns, Avars, Pechenegs, and Cumans had all passed this way. The last to do so were the Tatars—offshoots of the Mongol Golden Horde which dominated large parts of Russia and Ukraine from about 1242 until 1480. Tatar hegemony over Moldavia and Walachia lasted until the mid-14th century, necessarily delaying the formation of stable state structures there. A series of joint Polish-Hungarian army campaigns between 1340 and 1355 finally relieved Tatar pressure on the Carpathian frontier. This military offensive pushed the Tatars out of the Balkans and back onto the Ukrainian steppes, making possible the formation of the Romanian principalities.

Walachia (meaning "Vlachland") was the first of the two to become an independent state, although the precise circumstances are obscure. A number of semi-autonomous Romanian political formations had existed even earlier in Walachia and Moldavia, subject to first to Tatar and later to Hungarian suzerainty. One Romanian tradition records that Walachia was founded by à Vlach conqueror riding down from the Carpathians in the 1290s. However, strong evidence suggests that this account of a "descent on horseback" is merely a legend subsequently invented to parallel the circumstances by which Moldavia was founded. More credible is the report that some Walachian lords in the Olt and Argeş river valleys chose as leader one of their number, a certain Basarab, who was probably of Cuman origin. Owing to internal strife in both Hungary and the Tatar realm, the timing was favorable. Basarab won several victories against the Tatars, united all of Walachia under his rule, and thus became the founder of a princely dynasty (ca. 1317). Victory over the Hungarians in 1330 enabled him to throw off vassalage to the Hungarian king. By the end of the century Walachia had expanded westward to the Carpathians and eastward to the Danube, reaching its easternmost limits with the annexation of Dobrudja in 1389.

The Moldavian state began as a Hungarian border district recently liberated from the Tatar yoke. There the Hungarian-installed governor aroused dissatisfaction among the local lords, culminating in 1359 in a successful revolt against Hungarian suzerainty. A royal Hungarian diploma of 1365 took note of the accomplished fact that Moldavia had detached itself from the Hungarian crown. Although still comprising only a minuscule area between the Pruth and Siret rivers, this small principality eventually became the nucleus of a larger state extending southeastward to include the Black Sea coast between the Danube and the Dniester rivers. About 1386 it annexed Tatar-dominated lands farther east, so that a document of 1392 could describe the Moldavian ruler as "prince as far as the edge of the sea." However, Walachia and Moldavia were rarely secure in their independence. Surrounded by more powerful neighbors, they perpetually had to struggle against Hungarian, Polish, and later Ottoman domination.

Poland was restored as a united country early in the 14th century after 175 years of division. Despite this long period of fragmentation, some awareness of the former unity of the state had persisted, helped by the fact that all of the semi-independent Polish principalities continued to be ruled by members of the original Piast dynasty (one of whom even bore the title of king). The process of reunification was well under way by about 1315, when a prince of that dynasty,

Vladislav IV (called Łokietek, or "thumb-sized," because of his small stature), brought together the provinces of Great Poland, Little Poland, and two smaller territories under his sole rule. His capable son Casimir III, known as "the Great," took advantage of the decline of the Tatar Golden Horde to annex additional lands in the southeast. Aware of his own limited resources, King Casimir chose not to attempt recovery of the formerly Polish lands in Silesia, which would have required war with Bohemia, their current overlord. In the north most of Mazovia remained independent, although Casimir managed to win a few of its many small principalities. Mazovia was incorporated into Poland piecemeal as the various Piast lines died out, the last one in 1526.

Significant as these gains were for Poland, they did not compare in magnitude with the union with Lithuania. Early in the 14th century Lithuania (Samogitia) was no more than a minor state along the Baltic Sea. Then under its Grand Duke Gedymin and his son Olgerd it expanded to include much of what is now Belarus and large parts of Ukraine. In this way the rulers of Lithuania came to exercise a loose sovereignty over the vast but sparsely populated territories on Poland's eastern frontier. Most of this area was occupied by Eastern Slavs, speaking some variety of the language now known as Old Russian; only Samogitia was ethnically Lithuanian. The Polish-Lithuanian union came about through a dynastic marriage in 1386 between the Lithuanian Grand Duke Jagiełło and Princess Jadwiga, heiress to the Polish throne. The consequence was an enormous joint state. Through client princes it was able for a while even to exercise a shadowy authority over the Tatars, since its territories in the south bordered on the realm of the Golden Horde. Thus Poland-Lithuania could be described (in the fond phrase of Polish historians) as extending "from sea to sea" (from the Baltic to the Black Sea), although in much of this area the Lithuanians ruled only indirectly. This dual state achieved substantial gains at the expense of the Teutonic Knights, most notably the transfer of West Prussia (eastern Pomerania) to Poland in 1466 after the Thirteen Years' War. By the original terms of union, Poland and Lithuania were linked only by allegiance to a single king, although gradually the ties were strengthened. Poland-Lithuania in the 15th–17th century was territorially the largest state in Europe after Muscovy, and unquestionably a major European power.

Even longer-lasting was the link established in the 15th century between Bohemia and Hungary. These two realms first became joined under King Sigismund (d. 1437), his son-in-law Albert (d. 1439), and the latter's son Ladislas (d. 1457), a child monarch who ruled only briefly. Following a short-lived experiment with "national" (i.e., nonroyal) kings—George Poděbrady in Bohemia (r. 1457–71) and Matthias Hunyadi in Hungary (r. 1458–90)—an assembly of notables in each kingdom chose as their next ruler Prince Vladislav, son of King Casimir IV of Poland. When Vladislav's son and successor, King Louis II, was killed in 1526 at the battle of Mohács fighting the Turks, the Habsburg monarchs—rulers of the lands immediately beyond Hungary's western frontier—inherited both thrones in accordance with previous dynastic arrangements. Thus Bohemia and Hungary together became part of the Habsburg Empire, where they remained until 1918.

Albania, today the smallest state in East Central Europe aside from the newly independent Yugoslav successor states of Slovenia and Macedonia, was never a sovereign country in the medieval era. From ancient times its location along the straits at the entrance to the Adriatic Sea had made it a prime zone of interference for both the Byzantines and various rulers of southern Italy. During much of the Middle Ages it was subject at least nominally to Byzantium. Even then it lacked separate administrative status, comprising only the eastern portion of the military district of Dyrrhachion (Durrës). In spite of its exceptionally rugged terrain, Albania possessed enormous strategic importance, since the most convenient overland transit route (and line of attack) from the Adriatic coast to Constantinople ran through its mountain valleys. Military considerations meant that the Byzantines took great care to fortify and garrison the Albanian mountain passes, thus effectively preventing the growth of native sovereignties. The towns of the Albanian littoral depended also on Byzantine sea power to keep open the commercial routes essential to their prosperity.

The decline of Byzantium made Albania a tempting prey for all its neighbors. In the 13th and 14th centuries, portions of the country changed overlords with great frequency, becoming subject at various times to the hegemony of Byzantium, Venice, Epirus, Bulgaria, Serbia, and Naples. Wealthy Albanian landed proprietors established multiple small principalities, while often serving as vassals of one of the occupying powers. Both Venice and the Ottomans watched carefully to see that none of these units grew strong enough to dominate the others. The closest approximation to Albanian unity during the Middle Ages was the League of Lezhë, organized in 1443 by the famous war-leader Skanderbeg to resist the Turks. Even this was merely a loose association of territorial lords who felt free to go their own way if they so chose. The League functioned only in the military domain, never as a government, although it did provide the first rudiments of Albanian unity.

The Ottoman Empire—the most powerful political unit ever created in medieval East Central Europe—originated as a small Turkish principality in Asia Minor (modern Turkey), where its initial conquests took place. After gaining a foothold in the Balkan Peninsula in the 1350s, the Ottomans moved gradually into Central Europe. The basis for their success was the military superiority of a centralized and well-organized state faced with disunited and mutually hostile smaller ones, whose Christian rulers were often not averse to calling in the Muslim Turks for aid in local dynastic quarrels. Ottoman power spread steadily and inexorably in the second half of the 14th and throughout the 15th century. In 1393 Bulgaria became a Turkish vassal state. In 1459 the Turks destroyed the last remnants of Serbian autonomy, and in 1463 annexed Bosnia. Fear of Turkish attack impelled most of the towns of central and southern Dalmatia to accept Venetian rule in 1412–20. Only Dubrovnik remained independent by paying a heavy tribute to the Ottoman sultan. Following the Turkish victory over the Hungarians at Mohács in 1526, Hungary lost its former position as a major Central European state. Thereafter, its northern and western sections were ruled by the Habsburg emperors and, the central plain (after 1541) by the Turks directly, while Transylvania became semi-autonomous under native princes.

Thus the Ottoman Empire in Europe in the 16th century extended from the Bosphorus to the middle Danube, encompassing central Hungary, part of Croatia, and all of Bosnia, Serbia, Bulgaria, and Greece. Somewhat more favorable was the situation of the Ottoman vassal states, Transylvania, Walachia, Moldavia, and Montenegro, which were ruled by native princes. Permitted to manage their own internal affairs, they were totally subservient to the Turks in foreign relations and liable to heavy tribute payments. The Habsburg-ruled portion of Hungary was technically a Turkish vassal state too, though this had little practical effect. All five were situated on the periphery of the Ottoman Empire, functioning as buffer zones between the regions under the sultan's direct authority and those that remained wholly beyond his control.

Ultimately the Ottoman Empire survived to become the most durable political structure ever established in southeastern Europe since the days of the ancient Roman and Byzantine empires. In a very real sense it was a Byzantine successor state, governing most of the former Byzantine territories in Europe, North Africa, and Asia Minor. The Ottomans ruled in Hungary and Croatia until 1699, in Bosnia until 1878. Serbia, the Romanian principalities, and Bulgaria became independent only in the 19th century. In the southernmost part of the Balkan Peninsula, Macedonia and northern Greece remained part of the Ottoman Empire until the First Balkan War in 1912 forced the Turks back upon the environs of Istanbul. In all of East Central Europe in the 16th century, only Poland-Lithuania retained its independence under native princes. Bohemia, western Hungary, and western Croatia became part of the Habsburg Empire, while the remainder of the area became subject to either direct Ottoman domination or vassalage.

CHAPTER 3

Monarchies

The principle of monarchy—the idea of government based on the hereditary rights of a particular dynasty—received virtually universal acceptance in the Middle Ages. East Central Europe was no different. In every country a designated family possessed rights of rulership which often dated back to very early times. Although the leading men of the tribe or nation might formally "elect" the monarch, their choice almost invariably fell upon a member of the recognized ruling house if such a person was available.

The manner in which a dynasty originally became "royal" was usually shrouded in legends of ancient vintage imbued with supernatural elements. The Bulgars traced their ruling family back to a period well prior to their initial settlement in the Balkan Peninsula, when their ancestors still resided on the steppes of Ukraine. According to the ancient "List of Bulgar Princes," the founder of the Bulgar royal dynasty was a certain Avitokhol (a name which may simply mean "ancestor"). The suggestion that Avitokhol was really Attila the Hun may justly be considered doubtful; but it is certainly conceivable that the same steppe dynasty which produced Attila may also have provided rulers for the Bulgars. Attila's son Ernach, who lived in Bessarabia, could be the same Irnik who stands second on the "List of Bulgar Princes." Mythical elements reminiscent of the life spans of Old Testament patriarchs are obvious in the alleged reign lengths of the ancient Bulgar khans. Avitokhol supposedly ruled for nearly 300 years, his son Irnik for an additional 145. Thereafter the Bulgar princes are said to have enjoyed more modest reigns. Byzantine historical sources confirm that the more recent names on the list represent real men.

An ancient Bohemian legend describes a mythical Golden Age during which the eponymous hero Čech and his companions arrived in their future country. When the people demanded a prince to rule them, Čech's granddaughter Libuša sent out an embassy with a white horse, announcing that she would take as her husband the man in front of whom the horse should stop. The horse led the envoys to a place called Stadice, where a certain Přemysl was plowing with his oxen.

Allegedly in this manner a peasant became the founder of Bohemia's Přemyslid dynasty. Likewise the origins of the Polish Piast dynasty are enveloped in legend, as in the story of divine envoys predicting the accession to the throne of Samovit, an early ruler; or Duke Mieszko I's miraculous recovery from blindness. Similarly the Árpád dynasty in Hungary claimed supernatural origin through a female ancestor fertilized by a celestial bird. Such legends enhanced the legitimacy of the ruling family by granting its members a more-than-human status.

In some cases the alleged beginnings of a dynasty were strikingly humble. The association of a sovereign with plowing the earth is a frequent motif in ancient legends, not only among the Slavs. The fairy tale of a wise peasant who becomes king by winning the hand of a princess appears in numerous variants throughout Europe. At a later period so lowly an origin would have been considered demeaning, but in early medieval times the notion of "plow" and "plowman" still possessed an element of magical significance, no doubt associated with the miracle of the earth's fertility. Přemysl's bark shoes were preserved in the royal castle in Prague as a souvenir of his alleged former occupation. The founder of the first Polish dynasty, Piast, was supposedly a peasant also. Whether or not this is true, he appears to have been a real person, ruling in Great Poland in the middle of the 9th century. The Serbian Nemanya dynasty claimed descent from a village priest, who was possibly a peasant as well. Similarly the Slovenes stressed their ruler's connection with the peasantry. Each duke of (Slovene) Carinthia in his enthronement ceremony was required to dress in peasant garments and submit to a ritual in which a free peasant asked him questions. Only afterward did the duke take the oath as sovereign and swear to be a just judge of the people.

Once a dynasty was firmly established, the single most important component of any monarch's legitimacy was the mere fact of descent from the founder. The ruling family of independent Croatia traced its lineage to a 9th-century prince called Trpimir, probably a near-contemporary of the Bohemian Přemysl. The first Hungarian royal dynasty was descended from Árpád, the tribal leader elected in the late 9th century. The crown of Poland became hereditary in the Piast family. All medieval Walachian princes derived their ancestry from Basarab, the 14th-century founder of the state. When these native dynasties failed to produce legitimate heirs, a new ruler was chosen, chiefly according to the closeness of his relationship to the previous ruling house, usually through the female line. Private-law elements also entered into the succession process, since the head of the family was entitled to select his successor, just as on any private estate; and his wishes carried great weight. Thus on rare occasions the eldest son might be passed over, although trouble was likely to occur as a result.

The right of succession to the throne was embodied in the dynasty as a whole, not just in its eldest male. In the first few centuries of state formation, the belief was common that "justice" demanded the division of the realm among all of a sovereign's sons. Thus the personal rights of members of the dynasty superseded the more abstract notion of state unity. This was the patrimonial principle of monarchy, according to which all of a ruler's sons possessed approximately equal rights, although the eldest male usually received some advantages over the others. Daughters were almost never permitted to rule in their own right, but they could transmit hereditary rights to their sons or husbands. Instances are numerous in which a country was divided among two or more of a ruler's sons. In independent Croatia, brothers or brothers' sons sometimes succeeded their father on the throne. The Polish Piasts observed no particular order of succession, since each son of the ruling duke was considered entitled to a territorial appanage; this notion served to promote the disintegration of the country in the 12th century. The Serbian Grand Župan (later King) Stephen the First-Crowned had an elder brother who ruled part of his realm and was nominally his subject. The Bohemian Přemyslid dynasty benefited from the fact that for several generations only one of the ruler's sons outlived his father; but the right of younger princes to appanages in the border region of Moravia subsequently caused many quarrels. In practice this patrimonial system functioned poorly, since the most able or energetic of the princes generally managed to drive out the other heirs and rule alone.

Attempting to regularize the succession process, Duke Boleslav III "Wry-mouth" of Poland in his final testament in 1138 prescribed a more elaborate arrangement, dividing his realm into four provinces, one for each of his sons. The eldest was to become grand prince and rule Little Poland from Cracow, the national capital, taking charge of foreign affairs and war for the entire country. This system was designed to provide for all of the sons without disrupting overall state unity; but in practice it caused endless difficulties. Theoretically the grand prince was supreme ruler, but in fact he held virtually no authority over the remaining appanages, which became further subdivided. The disruptive effect of this arrangement soon rendered the central authority merely nominal. For nearly two centuries Poland existed as a collection of semi-independent principalities, each ruled by a different branch of the Piast dynasty.

Hungarian rulers also divided their realm in a few cases, although this never led to a long-term disintegration of the state. King Koloman I in the 12th century gave one-third of Hungary to his rebellious younger brother Álmus, and Béla IV in the 13th century did the same for his insubordinate son Stephen. By medieval standards Hungary was a very large state, so that at times Croatia and Transylvania became virtually independent of the central government. Even then the principle of the king's supremacy was always maintained—however little it might be observed in practice. The early Bulgars considered all of the khan's sons equally entitled to rule; but apparently they never intentionally divided the realm. The Serbs occasionally followed the Byzantine example of appointing co-sovereigns, whereby a successor to the throne was officially crowned during his predecessor's lifetime. This practice helped prevent a throne conflict after the sovereign's death but also led to cases of double kingship, where two brothers, or a father and son, reigned simultaneously over the same territory. Thus King Stephen Dečanski and his son Stephen Dušan were crowned together in 1322, with Dušan receiving the title "Young King." Later when Dušan took the title of "tsar" (i.e., "emperor") he designated his young son Uroš as "king." In 1360, Tsar John Alexander of Bulgaria divided his realm in two, apparently to avoid disinheriting his younger son. In a less happy instance, the Serbian King Vukašin gave his eldest son Marko the rank of "Young King" not long before his own death at the battle of Černomen in 1371—leaving Marko with an imposing title hardly appropriate to the weak and vulnerable principality that he inherited.

The military character of kingship in the early Middle Ages sometimes favored the claims of a monarch's brother to the succession in preference to his son. Brother-right was more likely than son-right to produce a leader capable of wielding the royal power, particularly of leading the nation in war. Given the brief average life span in the Middle Ages, it often happened that a monarch died before his eldest son reached manhood. A country with a child king was likely to be torn apart by power struggles among members of the high nobility—a situation which produced weakness in the face of external enemies. The nobles themselves recognized the danger. For example, King Géza II of Hungary (d. 1162) wanted his fourteen-year-old son to succeed him; but the nobility, "according to the old Hungarian law" (as the notary phrased it), installed Géza's brother instead. In Bulgaria, Tsar Kaloyan (r. 1197–1207), an able military leader, followed his brother on the throne because the brother's son was young and the Bulgars' newly restored independence was seriously threatened by the Byzantines. Physical disability could also be disqualifying. An unmendable broken leg allegedly forced King Stephen Dragutin of Serbia to divide his realm with his brother Milutin (Uroš II) in 1282, so that until 1316 Serbia had two kings, called by contemporaries "King Stephen" and "King Uroš" respectively. This arrangement ultimately led to civil war. Brother-right was most likely to prevail in the early period of state existence, when kingship was most closely associated with military leadership. As the sovereign's functions in law, administration, and foreign policy increased in importance, strict primogeniture also became more common.

Predictably, conflict between the two principles of brother-right and son-right often led to internal strife. Usually it ended only after one of the contenders succeeded in dominating—often mutilating or murdering—his rivals. Since brother-right was still widely accepted in the early Middle Ages, civil war was the likely consequence when the son of a deceased ruler attempted to assert his lost rights vis-à-vis his uncles and cousins. For his part, the royal uncle generally wished to advance his own son at the expense of his nephew. Armed conflict was virtually certain unless death claimed one of the parties first. In order to prevent future dissension, even the most powerful rulers often attempted to satisfy their nearest male relatives by assigning them lands and titles, while maintaining at least in theory the supremacy of the crown. King Charles I of Bohemia (r. 1346–78) allowed his younger brother John Henry to become margrave of Moravia, thus inaugurating a separate though subordinate Moravian branch of the Luxemburg dynasty. In the Ottoman Empire no definite law or custom regulated succession to the throne. Any of a sultan's sons were eligible to inherit his power; and because Muslim law allowed a man to take four legal wives in addition to concubines, an Ottoman sultan ordinarily had many sons. This situation produced numerous power struggles, which often led to the murder of one or more of the contenders. Ultimately Sultan Mohammed II (r. 1451–81) raised fratricide to a legal principle by issuing a formal decree that whichever of his sons or grandsons subsequently gained the throne should have all his brothers killed "to ensure the peace of the world." Presumably he had in mind the protracted civil war (1402–13) among three sons of Sultan Bayezid I, still within living memory, which might easily have caused the Ottoman Empire to collapse if external circumstances had been less favorable.

The two Romanian principalities were in a class by themselves, since primogeniture was not always observed and any member of the ruling family was in principle entitled to take the throne. Princes succeeded one another on the two thrones with devastating frequency. Walachia suffered no fewer than forty-eight rulers in the 182 years between 1418 and 1600, for an average reign lasting no more than four years. Atrocious examples of fratricidal warfare occurred over the succession question, prompted by the princes' own insecurity and the perpetual readiness of foreign governments to intervene. Many throne contenders sought military aid from abroad. The brothers and sons of a Romanian voivode usually did not dare to reside in their native country, where their lives were perpetually at risk. Either they wandered about in foreign lands or accepted asylum from a neighboring ruler, who hoped to use them at some future date as pretenders. Princes who gained the thrones of Walachia or Moldavia were usually emigrants, both before attaining power and after being deposed. Unlike royalty elsewhere in Europe, the relatives of a reigning voivode received no appanages at home: ordinarily they held no estates whatsoever in their native principality. In view of this cruel and unregulated system of succession, the reigning sovereign could not permit his relatives to retain a base of power at home. Fugitives and pretenders were a constant threat.

Walachia and Moldavia were likewise unique in Europe in ignoring a principle which everywhere else was virtually ironclad—namely that the heir to the throne must be born of a legitimate Christian marriage. In practice the council of boyars in each principality felt free to select any member of the dynasty, legitimate or not, to be their sovereign. Several illegitimate descendants of Mircea the Old (d. 1418) reigned for a time in Walachia. The highly unstable political situation in both Romanian principalities made the usual distinctions in status difficult to uphold. Elsewhere in East Central Europe the stigma of illegitimacy virtually excluded a man from consideration. King Matthias of Hungary (r. 1458–90), who lacked legitimate offspring, attempted to secure the throne for his illegitimate son John; but once the father was safely dead the son's candidacy was quickly brushed aside. The authority of Andrew III of Hungary (r. 1290–1301), last scion of the Árpád dynasty, was seriously undermined by persistent though unconfirmed rumors of his paternal grandmother's adultery. Andrew's doubtful legitimacy made him unusually dependent on the good will of the nobility and high clergy. In consequence, he became the first Hungarian monarch who clearly owed his throne to election by a national assembly.

Only religious considerations justified in the popular mind a departure from the established order of succession. Thus the first Christian king of Hungary, Stephen I, disqualified his nearest male relative from the throne because he was a heathen, selecting instead his sister's son, the Venetian Peter Orseolo. Although a powerful group of lords contested this decision—the old nature religion was by no means extinct—ultimately the Christian party prevailed. The majority of Hungary's leading men had no wish to return to paganism; and a heathen monarch was clearly unsuitable for a Christian country. In Croatia a party among the lords seems to have recognized as king a powerful district chief named Slavac in 1074–75 because he supported the Slavic-language Church, which the papacy sought to abolish. In Bohemia the spread of Hussite beliefs led the Czechs to deny the throne to Sigismund of Hungary, whose hereditary title was undisputed, on the grounds that he was a rigid and intolerant Catholic. Hussite doctrine held that a sinful monarch could not demand obedience from his subjects. Radicals and conservatives alike agreed in demanding that any future Bohemian sovereign must uphold the Hussite Four Articles of Prague, which Sigismund declined to do. Bohemia for seventeen years was a kingdom without a king.

A dynasty was considered extinct upon the death of the last legitimate male heir to a throne. This happened in Croatia with the demise of the last Trpimirović in 1091; in Hungary with the Árpáds in 1301 and the Angevins (Anjou) in 1382; in Bohemia with the Přemyslids in 1306 and the Luxemburgs in 1437; in Poland with the main line of the Piasts in 1370. An interregnum then ensued, during which the nobility and high clergy of the country attempted to select a successor. In such cases the sons or grandsons of the late sovereign's sisters or the husbands of his daughters might all be candidates, presenting the nobility with a genuine choice. A candidate related only by marriage to a previous ruler naturally could not assert that the blood of the native dynasty flowed in his veins, but at least his own heritage had to be royal.

Even a very tenuous family connection would suffice if no candidate had a stronger claim. Thus in the 1090s the sole surviving relative of the late Croatian King Zvonimir was his widow Helen, sister of King Ladislas I of Hungary.* Helen

* English-language sources sometimes translate as "Ladislas" the Hungarian proper names "László" and "Ulászló," the Polish name "Władysław," and the Czech names "Vladislav" and "Ladislav," a practice causing much confusion. Hungary had five kings named "László" and two others called "Ulászló." The latter two belonged to the Polish Jagiellonian dynasty and were called "Władysław" in their native tongue, which becomes

had no blood right to the Croatian throne, although for a while she sought it—perhaps according to the Byzantine custom whereby a widowed empress represented dynastic legitimacy. However, the total extinction of the native dynasty, even in its collateral branches, permitted the Hungarian king to annex Croatia. In Bohemia John of Luxemburg (r. 1310–46) founded a new dynasty by marrying the sister of the last Přemyslid king, Wenceslas III. In Hungary, King Charles Robert (r. 1310–42) derived his rights from his grandmother, a sister of the Árpád King Ladislas IV, while the claim of his unsuccessful Bohemian rival was based upon betrothal to the daughter of the last Árpád, Andrew III. Prior to his death Casimir III of Poland (r. 1333–70) arranged for the succession of his sister's son, Louis of Hungary, who then ruled both realms. When Louis in turn died without male heirs in 1382, the husbands of his daughters Maria and Jadwiga gained the thrones of Hungary and Poland respectively. In this way inheritance through the female line gave rise to a new dynasty.

Since kingship in early times was so closely linked to personal leadership in war, women were automatically excluded from supreme power. This was true even when the queen rather than the king held hereditary rights to the royal office. Nowhere in East Central Europe was there any precedent for direct female succession to a throne. The women of a royal house were valuable chiefly as pawns in dynastic marriages; their inability to rule alone was everywhere taken for granted. But even if unable to transmit hereditary rights to a kingdom, they were useful in sealing political alliances, since family ties (even though sometimes ignored) represented the most secure guarantee of loyalty. Medieval opinion did consider it acceptable, if not exactly desirable, for a woman to rule as regent for her son if he was a minor, or for her husband during his absence from the country. Elizabeth, the wife of King John of Bohemia, directed the government while he was attending to his possessions elsewhere in Europe or fighting in foreign wars, which he did from sheer love of combat. When Louis of Hungary inherited the throne of Poland, his Polish mother Elizabeth served as his regent there.

King Louis deviated somewhat from the principle that only males might rule in their own names when he arranged to have his daughters formally recognized as his heirs. Maria and Jadwiga were accordingly elected "king" in Hungary and Poland respectively, although it was tacitly understood that their husbands would actually rule. Maria's husband Sigismund often issued official documents

"Vladislav" in the Czech language. Translating both "László" and "Ulászló" as "Ladislas" presents the anomaly of the Hungarian King Ladislas V (László V, r. 1453–57) preceding Ladislas II (Úlászló II, r. 1490-1516), as Langer's *Encyclopedia of World History* has it. For convenience in the present book only "László" is rendered as "Ladislas," while "Władysław" (in Hungarian: "Úlászló") becomes "Vladislav."

Bohemia also had a Duke Vladislav I (r. 1111–25) and Vladislav II (r. 1140–73). The enumeration began again when the dukes of Bohemia were recognized as kings. Two Bohemian dukes also bore the similar name of "Vratislav."

in both their names during her lifetime; but in matters of political importance he nonetheless insisted on his rights as sole sovereign. These two queens undoubtedly wielded far more influence than the typical royal consort. Jadwiga, not quite eleven years old when she assumed the Polish throne in 1384, developed considerable political acumen and became a person of real influence in the state. Esteemed for her numerous works of charity among the poor, she also provided for the foundation of Poland's first university with her gift of the crown jewels. Significantly, both Sigismund and Jagiełło continued to rule after the deaths of their wives, from whom their rights were derived, although neither royal pair had any living children through whom to transmit the dynastic heritage.

Informal influence by women was very different from direct rule, and depended entirely upon the personalities involved. An exceptional case was that of Empress Mara, daughter of Despot George Branković of Serbia and wife of the Ottoman Sultan Murad II. Mara at times played a direct role in foreign policy—an influence she owed both to her own undoubted abilities and to her equivocal position as the Christian consort of an Islamic ruler, which led both Christians and Muslims to have confidence in her. In 1444 she was instrumental in arranging the truce of Szeged between her father and her husband, which gave the Serbian despotate a further lease on life. As a widow she was apparently the only woman able to influence her stepson, the powerful Sultan Mohammed the Conqueror, who (so the documents tell us) "loved and respected" her. After the capture of Constantinople in 1453, hers was the chief voice in selecting patriarchs for the Greek Orthodox Church; and she also interceded with Mohammed on behalf of the monasteries on Mount Athos. He granted her a small territory to rule around the town of Serrai in Macedonia, where she maintained her own court surrounded by Serbian lords and monks. There she continued to intervene in Balkan affairs, signing contracts and letters with her father's seal. In the 1470s she served as mediator between the Venetians and Ottomans in the negotiations to end their sixteen-years' war (1463–79). Empress Mara's position was in every respect extraordinary. Most often the queen of a country possessed influence, if at all, either through having the king's ear or through the common practice of arranging the appointment of various relatives and hangers-on to high office. The wife of Andrew II of Hungary, Queen Gertrude, did this to such excess that eventually she was murdered by some of her numerous ill-wishers.

In early medieval times a royal marriage might even serve to promote Christianity. The wedding of a Christian princess with a pagan prince who agreed to be baptized was particularly rich in consequences, since it carried the promise of Christianizing his entire nation. Mieszko I of Poland in 967, Stephen I of Hungary in 1000, and Jagiełło of Lithuania in 1385—all recent converts to Christianity—combined marriage to Christian princesses with the promise of converting their realms. Even prior to the conversion of Lithuania, various Piast rulers of Mazovia (then an appanage only loosely connected to the Polish crown) had concluded at least four Lithuanian marriages, usually with the partner's express promise to become Christian. Such unions were considered justified only for urgent political reasons; and a newly baptized person was regarded with some suspicion. The betrothal of the future Casimir the Great with Aldona, daughter of the pagan Grand Duke Gedymin of Lithuania, aroused considerable opposition in Poland, although it was part of a valuable alliance against Poland's chief enemy, the Teutonic Knights. On the other hand, the newly baptized Grand Duke Jagiełło of Lithuania had little difficulty in being recognized as king of Poland, inasmuch as his marriage with Queen Jadwiga brought Poland an enormous accretion of territory. (This match was arranged, in fact, by a group of powerful Cracow lords.)

A more unusual case was that of Tsar John (Ivan) Alexander of Bulgaria (r. 1331–71), who divorced his first wife in order to marry a Jewess named Sarah, known as Theodora after her Christian baptism. Contemporaries praised the new queen for her intelligence, but her Jewish origin was not forgotten. This union, which was clearly a love match, had nothing to recommend it politically. Quite the contrary was true, since a different marriage might have brought Bulgaria a dynastic alliance. Years later John Alexander divided his realm into two parts in order to avoid disinheriting his son by Theodora, thereby weakening both sectors at a time when unity was indispensable for resisting the Turks. After the Ottoman Empire became a powerful Balkan presence, Christian princesses were sometimes married to Muslims, occasionally with the provision that the woman might retain her Christian faith. The Bulgar Tsar John Šišman III (d. 1393) gave his sister Thamar as wife to Sultan Murad I. Olivera, daughter of the Serbian Prince Lazar who died fighting the Turks at Kosovo in 1389, was married to Sultan Bayezid I. In 1433, the same year that he gave his daughter Mara to Sultan Murad II, the Serbian Despot George Branković betrothed her sister Katarina to one of the great lords of southern Hungary. Branković, an astute and flexible politician without strong loyalties, owed his survival as despot to a delicate balancing act between his two powerful neighbors. As Mara's dowry he was obliged to give Murad part of Serbia. However, Christian monarchs arranged Muslim marriages for their daughters only for compelling political reasons. The Church clearly disapproved of such unions, especially since Muslims were allowed to have four legal wives.

The importance of a monarch's hereditary title rested upon the belief that traditional dynasties possessed some inherent quality of charisma— vague and undefined though this might be. Thus throughout the Middle Ages in Western Christendom, the "king's touch" was thought to possess miraculous healing powers. However, rule by divine right was not a uniquely Christian notion. The pagan Bulgars also had believed that their khan held his position through God's favor, but was entitled to retain it for only as long as he ruled successfully. Disasters or illness were a sign that his power had waned or that God had withdrawn his grace. In that case he had to be killed, and his whole clan might be exterminated. Precisely this occurred in 756 following a major Bulgar military defeat, after which the khan's entire family was wiped out. Because monarchy was divinely sanctioned, hereditary rights to a throne in both Western and Eastern Europe were always considered superior to titles merely derived from election by an assembly of high nobility and clergy. In Western Christendom the seal of divine grace for a newly enthroned monarch was the ceremony of anointing with holy oil (for which good Biblical precedent existed). Even where election was regarded as an indispensable ritual in the transfer of royal power, it was not sufficient to grant legitimacy. Moreover, from the ruler's point of view the electoral procedure created an undesirable dependence on the electors, who were after all mere subjects. As a consequence, monarchs generally stressed their family ties to the native dynasty and professed to regard election as a mere supplement. Candidates for a vacant throne likewise emphasized their dynastic credentials, since ordinarily the assembly chose the man with the closest family relationship to the former ruler by blood or marriage. In some cases the monarch designated an heir in his own lifetime and asked the electors merely to confirm his choice. Usually they complied, although often at the price of concessions which significantly limited the royal power. Nonetheless, a candidate's position as the chosen heir of a previous monarch strengthened his link with dynastic tradition—always a crucial point in the Middle Ages.

The election of a monarch was a compromise practice, combining elements of public law with dynastic assumptions. In theory, it permitted "the people" (meaning in reality the high nobility and clergy) to make a free choice. In practice, the electors did not reach outside the charmed circle of the established dynasty, whose members were acknowledged to possess a "natural right" to the throne. Throughout medieval East Central Europe it was customary for an important segment of the upper class to participate in electing their sovereign. When a legitimate heir in the descending male line was present, the election became essentially symbolic, serving only to confirm the position of the "born heir" and to ratify his hereditary rights. In some cases of this type the formality of an election might simply be omitted. On the other hand, election became unavoidable whenever the previous dynasty died out in the male line. If two or more competing candidates possessed approximately equal dynastic rank, the outcome might be genuinely in doubt. For example, after the death in 1382 of King Louis (who concurrently had been king of Hungary), the Polish nobility declared its willingness to accept whichever of his daughters would agree to live in Poland. They selected Jadwiga, the younger of the two, in preference to her elder sister Maria, who had already been elected "king" in Hungary. Similarly in Poland in 1492 all the sons of King Casimir IV were considered eligible to succeed him. The eldest, Vladislav, was passed over because he already held the thrones of Bohemia and Hungary; the Poles wanted a monarch of their own. Instead they chose Casimir's second son, John Albert (r. 1492–1501). A by-product of the sovereign's election was to demonstrate a country's political independence. This was especially significant in the case of Bohemia, which belonged to the German (Holy Roman) Empire but did not wish to be absorbed by it. The Golden Bull of Emperor Frederick II in 1212 recognized the right of the Bohemians to elect their own monarch without first seeking approval from the emperor, who retained only the right of conferring symbols of office upon whomever the Bohemians chose. A subsequent Golden Bull issued by Emperor Charles IV in 1356 confirmed that the Bohemian kingdom was indivisible, and her king one of the seven electors of the empire.

Not infrequently in disputed elections the nobility split its vote, with each faction favoring a different candidate. The issue might then be settled by violence, with a subsequent election legitimizing the outcome. This happened in Hungary in 1162, when Ladislas II was elected by "all the nobles" after he had defeated his cousin in battle. A similar situation occurred in Hungary after the demise of the last Árpád ruler in 1301. The assembled nobility first elected Wenceslas II of Bohemia; but when Charles Robert of Naples invaded Hungary with a large army, they reconvened and transferred their allegiance to Charles. The two contenders actually possessed similar dynastic claims through the female line. Conversely, when Béla III of Hungary returned home from Byzantium after his brother's death in 1172, he had to fight for nearly a year before obtaining the crown. His status as legitimate heir of the Árpád dynasty was never in doubt, but some Hungarians feared he would be a tool of the Byzantines. The Bohemian prince Sigismund needed an army to gain the throne of Hungary, despite the fact of his betrothal to Louis the Great's daughter Maria. Only successful military action against a hostile noble faction permitted him to claim her as wife in 1385 and secure election in 1387 as king.

Superior hereditary rights could not in themselves compensate for a candidate's lack of military power. Monarchs were expected to have at their disposal sufficient armed force to repress internal discord and defend their borders. A medieval sovereign was above all a military leader who needed his own personal army. Probably for this reason, when Casimir the Great died in 1370 the Polish nobility passed over the collateral lines of the Piast dynasty and elected his sister's son, Louis of Hungary, since the native Piast princes controlled only small territories in Silesia or Mazovia. On similar grounds the Moravian line of the Luxemburg house was never considered for the throne of Bohemia, despite successive dynastic crises in the 15th century. The Hungarians in 1440 refused to elect Ladislas "Posthumous," infant son of their late King Albert, since they did not desire a long regency. On the other hand, if the nobles of a country perceived no immediate external threat to the kingdom, they might chiefly be concerned to preserve their independence from the royal power. In those circumstances, qualities of character and ability were not desired in a candidate, as happened in the Hungarian royal election of 1490. Reacting against the centralizing policies of the late King Matthias, the assembled nobility deliberately chose the amiable but ineffective Polish prince Vladislav, king of Bohemia (known as Vladislav "All

Right" because he invariably replied "all right" to any proposal). The weak
government which resulted from this choice rendered impossible any effective
Hungarian resistance to the Turks.

An additional function of a royal election was to demonstrate the sovereign's
ties with his people. In practice this was an occasion for the presentation of
demands by the leading secular and ecclesiastical lords. Peasants and even wealthy
townsmen, so it was assumed, would follow the lead of their social superiors. At
most, a newly elected monarch might show himself to the waiting crowd outside
the electoral assembly and receive their shouts of acclamation. A negative aspect
of election was that it sometimes rendered a country vulnerable to foreign
influences. Foreign agents might stir up mutual enmities among the lords or
succeed in bribing them. The Romanian principalities were particularly susceptible to such external pressures, situated as they were on the borders of two much
more powerful states, Hungary and the Ottoman Empire. Foreign intervention
often determined which member of a Romanian dynasty the boyars would elect
and how long he remained in power. In Hungary the first case of overt external
influence on a royal election occurred in 1490 with the choice of Vladislav "All
Right." In subsequent centuries Vladislav's native Poland would itself experience
many such elections.

A new sovereign was frequently required to give formal assurances that he
would respect the existing rights of the nobility and Church. He swore a solemn
oath—usually at the coronation ceremony—to respect the rights and privileges
of the "land." When a candidate's hereditary claim to the throne was weak, the
lords demanded additional privileges. Thus the nobility of Hungary in 1290 was
able to extract far-reaching concessions from Andrew III because his heredity
was disputed. Previously the Hungarian coronation oath had contained only
the king's promise to maintain the country's territorial integrity. Henceforth it
included an additional oath to uphold the "constitution," which meant all the
existing rights and privileges of the upper class. In this way a royal coronation
in Hungary assumed the form of a legal contract between king and "people."
As part of the agreement by which the Hungarian nobility finally recognized
Queen Maria's husband Sigismund as king in 1387, he had to promise to uphold
the traditional freedoms of the lords and prelates, to take their advice, to appoint
only Hungarians to office, and not to persecute any of his former opponents.
This was the first time in Hungarian history that a candidate for the throne was
required to make formal promises as a condition of his election.

In analogous fashion the Polish nobility utilized a crisis in the line of succession
to augment its privileges. Polish custom did not permit females to rule; and the
numerous Piast princesses who married abroad did not carry with them any
claim to the throne of Poland. In order to get one of his daughters accepted as
heir to his Polish kingdom, King Louis summoned the Polish nobility to a Diet
at Košice (Kassa) in 1374. In exchange for their assent to his dynastic plans,
he granted them extensive privileges and a legal basis for future claims which

seriously limited the royal prerogative. In cases of this kind the nobility became very conscious of its power. So too the Cracow lords who in 1383–84 negotiated the Polish-Lithuanian union and the accession of the Lithuanian Grand Duke Jagiełło were acutely aware that other dynastic combinations were possible. Four decades later Jagiełło himself was obliged to grant additional privileges to the Polish nobility and clergy before they would recognize the rights of his two sons to the throne. These princes, as offspring of his fourth marriage to a woman of nonroyal parentage, had questionable rights to the succession. The election in 1434 of the elder, Vladislav VI, marked the beginning of the practice whereby each Polish sovereign formally confirmed all existing rights and privileges of the nobility and clergy prior to receiving their oath of allegiance. The willingness of monarchs to make such concessions was not solely due to dynastic difficulties. It went hand in hand with the social transformation of the 14th and 15th centuries which rendered the great nobles virtually independent on their landed estates and increasingly difficult to coerce. They could assert themselves against the royal power more effectively than their forebears had done, and were correspondingly less awed by the prestige of the crown.

In both Poland and Hungary the rising power and self-confidence of the nobility led it to claim a legal right of rebellion against the king. The agreement between Sigismund and the Hungarian nobility in 1387 contained the extraordinary provision that if he did not remain faithful to his promises, the nobles were entitled to resist him by force. Although this radical stipulation was omitted in later electoral pacts, the precedent had been set. In Poland the legal right of resistance dates from the accession of Jagiełło's son Vladislav VI in 1434. This young king had to agree that if he did not keep the promises made at his election, the nobility was entitled to withdraw its allegiance. In Hungary the nobility even managed to legalize the anarchy which set in after the death of King Matthias. In the Diet of 1514 they approved the law code known as the Tripartitum, which not only established the legal equality of all Hungarian nobles but also authorized them to use armed force against the king. A somewhat different type of resistance to a monarch occurred in 1419–36 in Bohemia, when the Hussite party refused to accept Sigismund, their hereditary sovereign, and employed military force to turn back the five "crusades" he led against them. Only after Sigismund finally agreed to permit a modified form of Hussite worship was he permitted to enter Prague. His son-in-law and successor, Albert, was required to make the same promise, as well as swear that he would exclude all foreigners from the government of Bohemia.

In the mid-15th century the elective principle triumphed briefly over royal legitimacy in both Bohemia and Hungary when their nobilities each elected a sovereign who was not only unrelated to the traditional royal family but lacked any royal blood whatsoever. This extraordinary occurrence was the fruit of two unique situations. In Bohemia the decisive factor was the Hussite movement for religious reform, which led even moderate Hussites to view a strictly Catholic monarch as a threat to their religious and political liberty. In 1457 the Diet rejected alternative candidates from the French and Habsburg dynasties and elected George Poděbrady, leader of the Hussite party and longtime regent, as king of Bohemia. A powerful magnate and proven statesman, George was unquestionably the man best able to defend the Hussite form of worship. Furthermore, during the many years when Bohemia had functioned with no monarch whatsoever (1419–36), the nobility together with the leading townsmen of Prague had become accustomed to making their own decisions. In Hungary in 1458 the Diet elected as king the fourteen-year-old Matthias, son of the famed commander John Hunyadi. Too young to have made any important enemies, Matthias had inherited the largest landholdings in Hungary, while his father's military reputation suggested that he too might succeed in holding off the Turks. Certainly neither George Poděbrady nor Matthias Hunyadi could have hoped to become king if a suitable royal candidate had existed. At the same time, the beginnings of a genuine national sentiment are clearly discernible in the election of each of these "national" sovereigns. Hussitism was a consciously Czech (and sometimes anti-German) phenomenon, so that Poděbrady's prominence as leader of the Hussite party endeared him to his countrymen. In Hungary many lesser nobles in particular were pleased to note that Matthias was the first real Hungarian to occupy the throne since the demise of the Árpád dynasty in 1301.

Despite the undoubted political ability of these two national kings, both of them discovered by bitter experience that lack of royal blood was a deficiency impossible to overcome in the eyes of the wider Europe. Family ties to a traditional dynasty still provided a monarch's most important source of legitimacy. Although George Poděbrady had been born into the highest nobility of Bohemia, Matthias Hunyadi's grandfather had been a Transylvanian Vlach of modest social origin whose rise into the minor Hungarian nobility occurred through marriage. Moreover, George as the "Hussite king" suffered the additional handicap of religious heterodoxy. The foreign policies of both sovereigns were guided in part by attempts to overcome these inferior hereditary credentials. Early in his reign Poděbrady sought to increase his European prestige by allying himself with the German emperor, a faithful Catholic, in exchange for receiving Bohemia as an imperial fief—an act which inevitably prejudiced his status at home. Matthias tried to enhance his reputation by assuming the role of defender of the Catholic Church. Responding to the pope's promise to bless any religiously orthodox prince willing and able to overthrow the "heretical" Hussite monarch, he invaded the Bohemian kingdom and conquered Moravia, which he then held until his death. In this way the struggles of these two national kings for legitimacy were largely played out against each other. Most serious of all was the fact that Matthias's efforts to win recognition by conquests in Central Europe were undertaken at the price of ignoring the Ottoman danger on his southeastern flank.

Neither of these two "national" monarchs succeeded in founding a royal dynasty. Although he had three sons, George Poděbrady ultimately recognized that his position was untenable in the long run and renounced any hopes of securing the succession for one of them. Upon his recommendation, the Bohemian Diet in 1471 elected the Polish prince Vladislav to the throne. Religious requirements were not forgotten, since Vladislav had to swear an oath to observe the Basel Compacts, a moderate statement of Hussite principles, albeit one which no pope had ever approved. However, since Bohemia finally had a sovereign who was both Catholic and royal, the Roman pontiff scarcely protested. In Hungary the lack of royal blood caused King Matthias to suffer humiliating rebuffs in his efforts to marry into the leading royal houses of Europe. His attempts to found a dynasty were frustrated both biologically and politically. Having produced no legitimate offspring, he sought to arrange for the succession of his illegitimate son John Corvinus. However, once Matthias was dead the Hungarian Diet scarcely considered John's candidacy. Instead it chose genuine royalty—that same Vladislav II who was already king of Bohemia and appreciated for his good-natured willingness to approve almost any proposal.

An additional method of transferring royal authority, partially supplanting both dynastic rights and election, was the inheritance treaty. This was a gamble on royal longevity, a formal agreement between sovereigns to provide for the contingency that one of them might die without legitimate heirs. If this occurred, the surviving royal house acquired a legal claim to the throne of its extinct partner. Negotiated by the monarchs concerned, such treaties were sometimes ratified afterwards by an assembly of the nobility. However, they were openly based on the premise that royal power was essentially a private matter. Sovereigns regarded their authority as disposable at will, like any other personal possession. Inheritance treaties not only ignored the wishes of the leading class of a country but also provided foreign rulers with a welcome pretext for military intervention.

Several pacts of this type were arranged in the 12th and 13th centuries between various appanage princes in divided Poland. Far more important, however, were the inheritance treaties concluded between the Hungarian dynasty and the Habsburgs. In 1463, King Matthias signed a precedent-setting agreement with the Habsburg Emperor Frederick III, whose hereditary lands lay along the Hungarian border in what is now eastern Austria. This document stipulated that if Matthias died without heirs, either Frederick or his successor would occupy the Hungarian throne. However, when precisely that situation did occur in 1490, the Hungarian Diet ignored the treaty and elected the Bohemian King Vladislav II instead. A Habsburg army invaded Hungary in retaliation, but the Hungarians persuaded it to withdraw in exchange for a new agreement promising that a Habsburg prince would inherit the two thrones of Hungary and Bohemia if Vladislav II should have no sons. Both these arrangements were one-sided, since they gave the Hungarian dynasty no corresponding rights to the Habsburg lands. It happened that Vladislav did produce a son and heir, the future Louis II, so that a third inheritance treaty was signed in 1515, this time somewhat more favorable to Hungary. The agreement was sealed by a double marriage. Louis and his sister were betrothed to a Habsburg prince and princess, with the stipulation that if either the Austrian or the Hungarian ruling house died out, the surviving dynasty would fall heir to all the lands held by the other. This fateful accord proved to be extraordinarily rich in consequences. Louis II was killed in 1526 at the battle of Mohács, an overwhelming defeat for the Hungarians which placed most of their kingdom in Ottoman hands. Since he had no heirs, the Habsburgs asserted their rights to Bohemia and occupied western Hungary and Slovakia. In this accidental fashion the basis was laid for the Habsburg monarchy as a future great European power, particularly after the Turks were expelled from the remainder of Hungary in the late 17th century.

For a monarch's position to be fully recognized a formal coronation was highly desirable, even if not absolutely prerequisite. This ceremony required the nobility of the realm publicly to acknowledge the sovereign's authority, while the presence of high church dignitaries signified that royal power was sanctified by God. Normally the ceremony took place as soon as possible after a ruler's accession to the throne. In some cases he was even crowned twice, the first time while his father was still alive. This preliminary ceremony was designed to ensure an orderly succession by emphasizing the future monarch's right to rule; and it guaranteed his position as legitimate heir. On the other hand, the nobility generally disliked this procedure, since it created an accomplished fact which reduced their capacity for maneuver in the event of a future struggle for power. Only rulers who bore the title of "king" or "emperor" were crowned; those with lesser titles like "duke" or "prince" were not, although they might participate in a rite of enthronement. From the standpoint of relations with foreign powers, a formal coronation announced the monarch's independence vis-à-vis other sovereigns. At home it denoted his superiority to junior members of the dynasty.

Coronation was the most important ceremony of a king's reign—a solemn celebration with a pronounced religious character. As performed in medieval times it can be traced back to the old Roman-Byzantine custom whereby the emperor was elected by the Senate and afterwards acclaimed by the waiting crowd. Following the Christianization of the empire, this rite took on a sacred as well as a secular character. The Byzantine emperor was regarded as holy from the moment of his coronation, so that portrait artists painted his head surrounded by a nimbus. Pictures and mosaics often depict Christ, the Virgin Mary, angels, or saints setting the crown upon his head. At the ceremony itself the emperor was first raised on a shield and then acclaimed by the waiting crowd. Afterward a solemn procession made its way to the coronation church in Constantinople, where the emperor took communion and received the actual crown. As the patriarch held the diadem over his head, the assembled people cried out, "Holy!

holy! holy!" and "Long live!" The rulers of Bulgaria's Second Empire were also crowned in this manner. Whether an identical procedure was followed under the First Empire is unknown.

The coronation of kings in the Catholic West was similar. The basic ceremony was borrowed from the Carolingians, who in turn had taken it from the ancient Romans. Elevation to the throne was the decisive symbolic act which exalted the ruler above all his subjects and endowed him with the insignia of office. In Bohemia these included a cap or miter and a lance as the symbol of Saint Wenceslas,* the country's patron saint. In Hungary all royal coronations took place at Székesfehérvár, the burial place of King Stephen I, patron saint of the country. After the assembly of nobles had elected a new king they acclaimed him jointly with the common people who had gathered nearby. The country's highest-ranking prelate, usually the archbishop of Esztergom, anointed him with holy oil and placed the crown and mantle of Saint Stephen on his head. The new king received a scepter—a highly ornamented rod symbolizing authority—and a sword denoting military power. After being raised to the throne he pronounced the coronation oath, promising to respect the people's traditional rights. Finally the assembly swore faithfulness to their new sovereign and lifted him on their shoulders. For more than a century after Croatia's union with Hungary in 1102, the Hungarian monarch underwent a second coronation as king of Croatia. This latter rite was meant to soothe Croatian sensibilities by demonstrating that the country had not forfeited its identity through union with Hungary. However, when King Béla IV came to the throne in 1235 he refused to be crowned in Croatia, and the custom afterward died out.

The participation of a high-ranking churchman in the coronation rite was intended to lend the new ruler an added aura of legitimacy. The Church taught that royal power was divine in origin and that the king or emperor held his position "by grace of God." Christians drew a sharp distinction between the position of their own divinely sanctioned monarchs and that of heathen kings, which supposedly rested upon purely earthly considerations like tradition, custom, or election. Ecclesiastical confirmation also gave the Church an opportunity to interfere in selecting the sovereign. A prelate might even refuse, for his own reasons, to crown the recognized heir to the throne. This happened several times in Hungary during the 11th and 12th centuries: in one case because the heir was a heathen; another time because he was allegedly a usurper; and in the case of Béla III (former heir to the Byzantine throne) because the archbishop of Esztergom thought he was too pro-Byzantine. However, since the pope needed Béla's support against the German emperor, he ordered the archbishop of Kalocsa, the second-ranking Hungarian prelate, to place the crown on Béla's head.

Coronation by the pope in person rather than his legate, or (in the lands of

* This is the "Good King Wenceslas" of the famous Christmas carol. His actual title was "duke"; no rulers of Bohemia were entitled "king" before the 11th century.

Eastern Orthodoxy) by the patriarch at Constantinople, was a distinction normally reserved for emperors as opposed to mere kings. The German emperors,
as political heirs of Charlemagne, considered themselves the true successors of
the old Roman emperors and representatives of Christ on earth. The ideology of
this essentially German state required them to exert constant efforts to control
the city of Rome itself. Believing that their title could be validated only through
a Roman coronation, they insisted on making the long and costly journey to Italy
to be crowned by the pope. The pontiffs, for their part, feared imperial control
and did not want an emperor's troops in close proximity to the the papal court.
Thus Charles IV, journeying to Rome for his coronation in 1354, conformed to
papal wishes by viewing the sights of the city incognito. He could not receive
his crown from the actual pope, who then resided at Avignon; but a cardinal
officiated at the ceremony and Charles left Rome the same day. These imperial
coronations did not outlast the medieval era. Frederick III in 1452 was the last
German emperor to be crowned in Rome.

The Byzantine emperors had a better claim than the rulers of Germany to be
regarded as true heirs of Rome, since their Roman predecessors had transferred
the imperial capital to Constantinople in the 4th century. Byzantine sovereigns
were crowned by the highest dignitary of the Eastern Orthodox Church, namely
the patriarch of Constantinople, who in canon law held equal rank with the
Roman pope. Aspirants to the imperial throne did the same. When Tsar Symeon
of Bulgaria arrived with his army outside the walls of Constantinople in 913, he
arranged for the betrothal of his daughter to the youthful Byzantine emperor and
had himself crowned by the patriarch. However, Symeon could neither capture
Constantinople nor remain indefinitely in its suburbs; so after the Bulgarian army
withdrew, the Byzantine government reneged on its promise of marrying their
princess to a "barbarian." Greek historians afterward minimized the significance
of Symeon's coronation, alleging that the patriarch had deceived the Bulgarian
by placing only a headdress, not the real crown, on his head. After the soldiers
of the Fourth Crusade forced the Byzantine government out of Constantinople
in 1204, Emperor Theodore I Lascaris sought coronation by the patriarch as
a means of legitimizing his rump state at Nicaea as the true empire. On the
other hand, Stephen Dušan as ruler of Serbia had himself crowned emperor
by the lesser-ranking patriarchs of both Bulgaria and Serbia, since the patriarch
of Constantinople would scarcely have deigned to bestow the imperial title upon a
mere Balkan monarch. Undaunted, Dušan staged a brilliant coronation ceremony
copied from the Byzantine model, complete with a magnificent imperial crown
and scepter, and granted high-sounding Greek titles to his principal associates.

The title "emperor" (in Slavic: "tsar") was far more pretentious than that of
"king." According to medieval notions, it should indicate the sovereign of vast
and multifarious territories, who might also have mere kings as his subordinates.
In the ancient Graeco-Roman world the imperial title had applied exclusively

to the supreme head of state, whose capital was first at Rome and later at Constantinople. It denoted a claim to universal dominion which was jealously guarded by the Byzantine emperors even after their territories had shrunk drastically. Symeon of Bulgaria was the first Balkan ruler to designate himself "tsar," thus not only enhancing his own dignity but also announcing his intention of succeeding to the throne of Constantinople. Despite repeated failures to achieve this aim, he began calling himself "emperor of the Bulgars and Greeks" in 925 to indicate that he had not renounced his pretensions. Likewise Stephen Dušan of Serbia in 1345 termed himself "tsar of the Greeks" after capturing the important Macedonian town of Serrai; this was translated as "tsar of the Romans" in his Greek-language documents (since the inhabitants of the Eastern Empire still considered themselves "Romans"). Dušan's use of this title clearly indicated an ambition to supplant the Byzantine emperor, not merely to create a parallel Serbo-Greek empire.

The once-exalted title of "emperor" eventually became devalued with excessive usage and lost much of its former aura. It was borne not only by the rulers of Germany and Byzantium but also by a variety of Balkan princes. All the rulers of independent Bulgaria after 1218 called themselves "tsar of the Bulgars"; all but one also took the title "tsar of the Greeks." The Bulgarian and Serbian monarchs likewise copied Byzantine imperial insignia. On solemn occasions the tsar wore a bright purple robe worked in gold and decorated with pearls and precious stones. Upon becoming rulers of Bulgaria after 1185 the brothers Peter and John Asen—newly risen from the status of mere rebels—had themselves crowned with golden diadems and wore red shoes just like the Byzantine emperors. Tsar John Asen II (r. 1218–41) issued decrees authenticated in the Byzantine manner with gold seals, which symbolized world domination. Tsar John Alexander (r. 1331–71) had his portrait painted in the imperial Byzantine style with an angel holding the crown above his head, or with King David blessing him and an angel offering him a sword, to indicate that his authority came from heaven.

The title of "king" underwent a similar proliferation. In the early medieval period the ruler of even an important country might hold the less exalted rank of "duke" (in Latin: *dux*). Only three of the eight rulers of Poland between 963 and 1146 were crowned "king"; the rest were merely entitled "duke." During the period of disintegration of the Polish state (ca. 1138–1310), none of the appanage princes called themselves "king," although after the kingdom was reunified the royal title was revived. The Bohemian monarchs (with two exceptions) were entitled "duke" until 1198. The rulers of Bulgaria bore the pagan title of "khan" until they adopted Christianity under Khan Boris, who then became "king." Where a monarch was called "king," his brothers and sons often bore the title of "duke." This was roughly equivalent to the Slavic "voivode," which means "leader of warriors." This latter title was the usual designation for the rulers of Moldavia and Walachia, reflecting the fact that their main function was military leadership in a region constantly suffering from the incursions of steppe horsemen. (For analogous reasons the Hungarian governors of the Transylvanian royal counties, who were not independent sovereigns, were also called "voivode.") The chief princes of Serbia until 1217 bore the modest title of "grand župan"—a župan being merely a district chief. However, the Byzantines showed their scorn for all so-called barbarian monarchs by addressing them with rather modest Greek titles like "archon," which could describe almost anyone in a position of authority. Since the Balkan lands had formerly been imperial territory, the emperor claimed its rulers as his subordinates.

With the passage of time many a monarch whose original title was less than royal managed to become "king." However, this rise in status was considered legitimate only if confirmed by some higher authority—namely a pope, patriarch, or emperor. In countries subject to the Roman Church many rulers sought approval from the pope for a royal title. Tradition records (without much supporting evidence) that Tomislav, the most powerful sovereign of independent Croatia, received his crown from a papal legate in the year 924. King Stephen I (Saint Stephen) of Hungary allegedly received a crown from Pope Sylvester II in the millennial year 1000. Some doubt attaches to this story, since the only extant contemporary report of the matter states that Stephen received his crown through the favor of the emperor, not the pope. Certainly at the turn of the 10th–11th century no one yet claimed that all secular authority in Christendom came from Rome, or that the pope possessed the right to bestow and to take away kingdoms.

Serious attempts at giving effect to this theory of papal supremacy occurred only in the era of the so-called imperial papacy (1073–1303). The first pope to assert that the Hungarian monarchs owed their position to papal grant was Urban II in 1096, who said nothing about any crown. Duke Boleslav I "the Brave" (r. 992–1025) of Poland assumed the title of "king" with papal agreement in 1024, although apparently not as a gift from the pope; at the time he had already reigned as duke for over thirty years. His successor Casimir I was forced by the German emperor to renounce the royal title and revert to ducal status. Boleslav II "the Bold" (r. 1058–79) received a papal crown in 1076 as a reward for his zeal in reorganizing the Polish Church after a heathen reaction. Paradoxically, this same Boleslav was subsequently reponsible for the execution of Bishop Stanislas, Poland's future patron saint. An even closer relationship between pope and king ensued when a monarch agreed to accept a feudal relationship to the pope, holding his country as a fief and becoming the pope's vassal.

Even in the Balkan lands normally falling within the sphere of Eastern Orthodoxy, monarchs occasionally asked the pope to legitimize their titles. The official split between the Eastern and Western Churches had occurred only in 1054, and even then was not regarded by either side as definitive. The pope might grant a ruler a crown as a means of attaching him to Rome. In all such cases conditions were laid down which were intended to promote the spread of Latin Christianity in that ruler's territory. Thus Pope Innocent III (r. 1198–1216) permitted his legate in 1204 to crown the Bulgar sovereign Kaloyan, who thereafter called himself "tsar." Kaloyan in return swore that the Bulgarian Church recognized Rome's supremacy. This concession did not affect the dogmas or practice of the Bulgarian Church, but strengthened the country's international prestige. The first Serbian ruler to be called "king" (named "Stephen" like all the monarchs of the Nemanya dynasty) secured this rank by playing off the pope against the patriarch of Constantinople. When the patriarch refused him a crown, Stephen turned to Rome and was crowned by the pope's legate in 1217. Subsequently he returned to Orthodoxy but still retained the royal title, passing into history as King Stephen the First-Crowned.

Balkan rulers most often turned to the Byzantine emperor for purely secular titles. The fact that the Eastern Empire had survived while the Western Empire disintegrated meant that at Constantinople the superiority of emperor to patriarch was never seriously challenged. Moreover, the Byzantine emperor himself possessed an almost sacerdotal status. In the Latin West, on the contrary, the question of who held the authority to grant royal titles—pope or (German) emperor—was never definitively settled. In theory the pope represented the highest spiritual power in Christendom, the emperor the highest secular power. Nonetheless, the distinction was not absolute. According to prevailing opinion the emperor was also a consecrated personage, whose position was sanctified by God through papal coronation. Eventually the long and bitter quarrels between empire and papacy tended to give the emperor a more purely secular status. The fact remains that in the Latin West both emperor and pope at times granted royal titles.

The German emperor dispensed monarchical titles in his capacity as alleged heir of the Romans. Until the mid-11th century—before the stakes were raised by papal competition—he normally granted his vassals at most the rank of "duke." The rulers of Croatia, Bohemia, Moravia, and Poland were permitted to assume this title and to call their territories duchies. However, several German emperors ultimately saw fit to give out the title of "king" in order not to leave this prerogative to the pope. In 1086, Emperor Henry IV rewarded the Bohemian Duke Vratislav II for his services by naming him "king" of both Bohemia and Poland, although Vratislav held no authority over Poland and the title was not transmissible to his descendants. This amounted to a protest against the current Polish monarch, who had accepted a royal title from the pope instead of from the emperor. Two more Bohemian rulers in the 12th century also received imperial permission to call themselves "king"—Vladislav II* in 1158 and Ottokar I in 1198. In Ottokar's case the title was confirmed by the Golden Bull issued by Emperor Frederick II in 1212; and henceforth all the rulers of Bohemia were called "king." John of Luxemburg, elected to the throne of Bohemia by the Diet

---

* As "king" he of course became Vladislav the First. His royal title was personal, not hereditary.

in 1310, received a royal crown from Emperor Henry VII, who (not incidentally) was his own father. However, all titles granted by an emperor were valid only during the recipient's lifetime and did not devolve upon his successors. No one regarded the title conferred by imperial authority as equivalent to one acquired "by grace of God." Bohemia could consider itself truly a kingdom, as opposed to a mere duchy, only after the pope at Rome confirmed Ottokar I's royal status.

The Byzantine emperor did not grant royal titles at all. His vassals or allies received only Byzantine court titles—"proconsul," "patrician," or "despot"— even if at home they called themselves "king." Thus Tomislav of Croatia became "proconsul" after the emperor granted him permission to administer the province of Dalmatia, although he had long since entitled himself "king of the Croats." The young Hungarian Duke Béla acquired the Byzantine rank of "despot" in 1163 when he was betrothed to the emperor's daughter and became the official heir to the throne of Constantinople. This title had once been considered the virtual equivalent of "emperor," but fell into disuse in the 10th century until Manuel thus revived it. Thereafter at Byzantium it was routinely bestowed upon the emperor's son and heir. In the 14th century the title "despot" appears much more frequently, both in the empire itself and among various minor Balkan rulers having some claim to independent authority. Following the breakup of the old Serbian kingdom after the battle of Kosovo in 1389, "despot" became the official designation for the ruler of the reduced kingdom of Serbia. With the passage of time the title became linked to the despot's actual territory, which accordingly was known as a "despotate"—a significant departure from Byzantine practice. Even the most prominent hero of the Serbian folk epics, King Marko, became merely "prince" in this popular literature. The poets perhaps realized that the more exalted title (which he actually held) was out of touch with reality. Marko effectively ruled only a small principality in Macedonia. The willingness of the Serbian monarchs after 1371 to renounce the more grandiose appelation of "tsar" was not repeated elsewhere: the weak Bulgarian and Byzantine sovereigns of the 15th century retained the title despite their own insignificance.

Certainly nothing prevented a monarch from arrogating to himself an impressive title even if other states declined to recognize it. Often enough such a rubric constituted a claim to territory outside the ruler's own domain or signified a challenge to someone else's pretensions. Early in the 12th century the doge of Venice styled himself "duke of Croatia and Dalmatia" even though Hungary actually held those territories. King Emeric I of Hungary (r. 1196–1204) began calling himself "king of Serbia" after he succeeded in placing a protégé on the Serbian throne. Subsequent Hungarian monarchs retained this title long after it had ceased to have the slightest political reality. After adding Croatia to their realm in 1102 they termed themselves "king of Hungary, Croatia, and Dalmatia" even during those periods when the Dalmatian towns and islands belonged to Byzantium or Venice. After 1138 they added the title "king of Bosnia," although during most of the 12th century Bosnia was semi-independent. Conversely, the

Bosnian King Tvrtko in 1377 began calling himself "king of Serbia" after he acquired a small fraction of that country. Until Bosnia fell to the Turks in 1463, all of its rulers entitled themselves "king of Serbia and Bosnia" rather than just "ban of Bosnia"; a "ban" was a mere governor under the Hungarian crown.

The Byzantine emperor continued to enjoy high prestige and to use the imperial title even when he controlled only a drastically reduced territory around his capital of Constantinople. As heir of the old Roman emperors, he laid claim to nothing less than absolute world dominion, acquired through unbroken continuity from his imperial predecessors. Moreover, his semidivine status as God's representative on earth included the duty of protecting the Orthodox Church. In his transactions with foreigners he recognized no equality between them and himself. His treaties were issued only as acts of imperial grace in the form of privileges, not as agreements between two independent sovereigns. The coronation of the Frankish King Charlemagne as emperor by Pope Leo III at Rome in the year 800 aroused considerable hostility at Constantinople, although the Byzantine government was powerless to do anything but fulminate against this presumption. However, since the rulers of Germany considered themselves to be Charlemagne's successors, they appropriated his imperial title together with its claim to universal rule. In essence they adopted the old Roman ideology which insisted that only one God, one church, and one emperor could exist in the world, all centered at Rome. To maintain a Roman connection they persisted in seeking to control Italy at least as far south as the city of Rome. For their part, the Byzantines pointed out that the capital of the Roman Empire had been moved to Constantinople (East Rome) in the 4th century. Irrespective of political realities, the Byzantine emperor never renounced either his title or his ideological claim to universal dominion.

In some cases the royal crown as physical object carried great significance as a symbol of the state, meaning that the loyalty of subjects belonged to the crown and only indirectly to the monarch. Hungary constitutes the extreme example of this phenomenon. The linking of the royal crown with Saint Stephen, Hungary's first Christian king, imbued it with such mystical power that it came to be considered indispensable for a legal coronation. Whether or not Pope Sylvester II had sent an actual golden diadem to King Stephen I for his coronation in the year 1000, the object which was believed to be the crown of Saint Stephen had become by the 12th century a revered symbol of Hungary's independence. However, the Hungarian royal crown which exists today, lying in state in a Budapest museum, cannot have belonged to Saint Stephen. Actually it consists of two fused parts: a lower "Greek" crown and a "Latin" upper crown. The "Greek" portion was apparently constructed from a Byzantine women's diadem dating from the reign of King Béla III (r. 1173–96), while the "Latin" portion originated in the first third of the 13th century. Nonetheless, the tradition of the holy crown persists. Such is its hold upon people's affections that historical proofs even now cannot shake the belief of many Hungarians that it is a treasure once belonging to Saint Stephen himself.

This royal crown was considered essential for validating the position of a king of Hungary. In any contest for succession to the throne the contending parties made great efforts to secure it, sometimes with comic-opera effects. The first theft of the crown apparently occurred in 1270 after the death of King Béla IV, when his daughter Anna fled with it to the court of Ottokar II of Bohemia in hopes of using it to secure her son's succession to the throne. Béla's successor Stephen V had a new crown hastily crafted for his coronation in 1271, presenting it as the genuine article. The risk that the substitution would be noticed was slight, since the most recent royal coronation had occurred in 1245 when Stephen himself was crowned in his father's lifetime as "young king." The original crown evidently never returned to Hungary, since the Bohemian king himself harbored designs on the Hungarian throne. Its eventual fate is uncertain, because after 1279 the Hungarians ceased trying to recover it. Obviously at that time the ancient crown was not considered indispensable for securing the king's legitimacy, since both Stephen V and his son Ladislas IV possessed indisputable hereditary rights to the throne.

A monarch whose status was doubtful could not so easily renounce this sacred symbol. In 1290—the date which marks the accession of King Andrew III to the throne—Hungarian documentary sources for the first time identify the royal crown as specifically the crown of Saint Stephen. Inasmuch as Andrew himself was of questionable legitimacy, coronation with the crown that Saint Stephen had worn was meant to strengthen his position. Not coincidentally, it was precisely at this time that coronation with the traditional crown came to be considered essential. The founder of the Hungarian Angevin dynasty, Charles Robert (r. 1310–42), whose rights to the throne were likewise challenged, acted accordingly. The sacred object was not immediately available to him, since after Andrew III's death it was kept first by two of his rivals for the throne and later by one of the Transylvanian magnates, who was persuaded to give it up only under a papal threat of excommunication. Twice crowned with a substitute diadem (in 1298 and 1309), Charles Robert persisted in his efforts to secure the genuine article, with which he underwent a third and final coronation in 1310.

Vastly more damaging to Hungarian interests was King Matthias's struggle for the Holy Crown. In 1439, King Albert's widow, Elizabeth, had fled with it to the court of the German Emperor Frederick III, hoping thereby to ensure the succession rights of her infant son, the future Ladislas V. When the Hungarian Diet in 1440 elected Vladislav of Poland instead, it sought to remove any need for the traditional crown by issuing a formal declaration that the will of the people (i.e., the assembly of nobles) sufficed to create a king, and that the new crown which had been made specially for Vladislav's coronation possessed the same "virtue and mystery" as the old one. This legal innovation satisfied no one. When Matthias Hunyadi was elected king in 1458, he declared that recovery of the Holy Crown was a matter of national importance. Lacking either family ties to the previous dynasty or royal blood of any type, he desperately needed this sacred object to fortify his position. Matthias entered into negotiations with Emperor Frederick III, who demanded first 40,000 and later 80,000 gold guldens as his price for relinquishing it. This extraordinary sum was raised through a special tax on the population; and the Holy Crown returned to Hungary in 1463.

Likewise considered essential to a monarch's status was the maintenance of a splendid court, both to overawe his own subjects and to impress foreign visitors. The earliest courts of the rulers of East Central Europe were undoubtedly very simple affairs, probably just a wooden fortress on a hill, strengthened with walls and towers and set within an enclosure containing large courtyards, stables, kitchens, and a church. The residence of the royal family and their entourage was often quite primitive. In the early medieval period the throne itself might be no more than a stone seat. Four such seats have actually been preserved in Hercegovina, from which the former princes of the region pronounced judgments and presided over popular assemblies. Such simplicity rarely lasted for long. As the income and pretensions of a monarch rose, so did the magnificence of his residence, the impressiveness of his court ceremonies, and the opulence of his courtiers' dress.

Without question the imperial court at Constantinople outdid all rivals in its addiction to elaborate and expensive ceremonial. The Byzantine *Ceremony Book*, a product of the 9th–10th centuries, takes up over 800 printed pages with its minute descriptions of court rituals. Byzantine officials bore impressive sounding titles and appeared in public on feast days wearing clothes woven of gold thread set off by jeweled necklaces, and carrying richly decorated staffs. The monarchs of medieval Bulgaria and Serbia often imitated this high-flown style. They gave their officials Greek or Latin titles, referred to themselves not as "I" or "We" but as "My Empire," and copied Byzantine styles of court dress, particularly purple robes (the imperial color). The Bulgar Tsar Symeon sat among his nobles wearing a jewel-studded garment, arm rings, a purple belt, a gilded sword, and a necklace of coins. His nobles likewise adorned themselves with golden neck chains, belts, and arm bands. The princes and nobles of Serbia dressed in ceremonial robes of Byzantine type: long green or yellow caftans decorated with gold and pearls. Both Serbia and Bulgaria in the 14th century made increasing use of Greek titles and ritual, although neither could begin to compete in magnificence with Byzantium. Greek ambassadors who visited the Serbian court in 1268 and again in 1327 described it as crude and impoverished, which doubtless it was by comparison with the splendor of Constantinople. On the other hand, rulers in the Latin West had merely the now-impoverished Rome instead of imperial Constantinople as an object of imitation. Nonetheless, they too sought to enhance the magnificence of their capitals. Charles I of Bohemia (Emperor Charles IV) went to great lengths to beautify Prague. The

Hungarian royal capital of Esztergom with its monumental cathedrals and expensively furnished palace caused wonder even among Western knights en route to the Crusades who were accustomed to opulence. Hungary's continuing links to Constantinople resulted in certain efforts to imitate Greek imperial styles. Early in his reign King Béla IV attempted to introduce Byzantine magnificence at court by making himself personally inaccessible, receiving requests only in writing, and adopting Byzantine rituals. These innovations made him highly unpopular and failed to outlast the Mongol invasion of 1241, after which he found it advisable to conciliate his nobility rather than trying to impress them.

A sovereign's attempts to enhance his prestige through conspicuous display were not altogether a matter of vanity. Few medieval rulers felt safe from threats to their position, even from members of their own immediate families. Not infrequently a monarch's younger brothers, cousins, or nephews, and most often his sons, felt entitled to rule at least part of his realm, and occasionally sought to assert their claims through armed revolt. Duke Wenceslas of Bohemia (d. 929 or 935) was murdered by followers of his brother Boleslav, only to be later recognized as patron saint of his country. In Hungary King Koloman I (r. 1095–1116) faced serious rebellions led by his warlike brother Álmus. In Serbia Stephen Nemanya (r. 1168–96) founded a royal dynasty by overthrowing the rightful heir to the throne; and Stephen Dušan (r. 1331–55) made himself king by deposing his father, who was afterward strangled in prison. Stephen V (r. 1270–72) of Hungary revolted against his father, Béla IV. The list is long. Rebellions against constituted authority usually involved the extended family, since the rebel frequently sought aid from his royal relatives abroad, such as a sister's husband or wife's brother. Prevailing opinion in the early medieval period held that decency obliged such relatives to offer asylum. However, in order to be taken seriously, a pretender to the throne was expected to justify his claims in terms of dynastic or customary rights.

The special aura surrounding all members of a reigning dynasty produced strong reluctance to assassinate a sovereign. Monarchs who fell into the hands of their enemies were frequently punished not by death but by blinding. Rulers who owed their legitimacy to hereditary right were hesitant to set the example of shedding royal blood. Blinding was considered a comparatively humane penalty, since it deprived the victim of his ability to lead troops without actually taking his life. Moreover, a blind prince might still be useful in providing sons for his dynasty. Precisely this inhibition against murdering a king saved the Hungarian royal family from extinction in the early 12th century. King Béla II (r. 1131–41) was imprisoned in youth and deprived of his sight as punishment for rebellion against his sovereign. Nevertheless, he survived to rule as "Béla the Blind" and became the ancestor of all subsequent monarchs of the Árpád house. King Stephen Milutin (r. 1281–1321) of Serbia had his son Stephen blinded for rebellion; the son (who apparently had not totally lost his vision) took the throne in 1321. Known as Stephen Dečanski for his founding of the important Dečani monastery, he lived to witness a revival of the father-son conflict when his own son Stephen Dušan dethroned him in 1331.

The preparation which an heir to the throne received for his future position varied greatly from case to case even within a single dynasty. In the Latin West the eldest prince of a family often was trained chiefly in the military arts, which did not require a knowledge of reading and writing. A younger brother might receive a more literary education in anticipation of a career in the Church. Illiterate kings were by no means uncommon, since literacy was regarded as a skill appropriate chiefly for clerics or subordinate officials, but unnecessary for princes. It might happen that a royal child was purposely kept illiterate, like Casimir IV of Poland (r. 1447–92), evidently because the nobles who controlled the royal court during his youth felt they could assert themselves more easily against an ignorant sovereign. Nonetheless, even at a comparatively early period some princes in the West did receive the rudiments of a literary education. In 11th-century Poland these included Duke Boleslav I (d. 1025), who apparently could read; his son Mieszko II (d. 1034), who was praised for his knowledge of Greek; and Casimir II (d. 1194), described as fond of learning, who invited scholars to his court to discuss scientific and religious questions. Stephen I of Hungary (d. 1038), the presumed author of a small book of instructions for his son, was said to be well acquainted with the Bible. Two 11th-century rulers of Croatia reportedly acquired a good education in Venice: Stephen I (r. 1030–58) and his son Peter Krešimir IV (1058–73). King Koloman I of Hungary (r. 1095–1116), called "the Book Lover," was originally educated to become a bishop. However, even as king he pursued his theological studies, and astonished his contemporaries by taking more interest in books and in scholarly company than in typical royal pastimes such as hunting. As Renaissance influences reached northern Europe, book learning for princes became more common. The powerful Charles I of Bohemia (r. 1346–78) was educated at the court of his uncle, the king of France, and became a noted patron of Latin culture. Matthias I of Hungary (r. 1458–90), known as "Corvinus" from the raven on his family's escutcheon, was an accomplished Latin orator and lavish patron of Renaissance humanism. Even Casimir IV of Poland, although illiterate, spoke several languages fluently and took care to provide able tutors for his sons. Despite his own inability to read and write, he presided over the beginnings of the Renaissance in Poland and produced highly educated sons, four of whom became kings.

A very different attitude toward education prevailed in the Byzantine Empire, where urban society regarded knowledge of the Greek classics as valuable in itself, and upper-class children were taught reading and writing as a matter of course. Princes from East Central Europe who spent their youth at Constantinople, often as hostages or exiles, sometimes became cultured men with a real appreciation of art and literature. One example was Symeon of Bulgaria, who acquired an excellent Greek education during his long stay as a hostage at the imperial court.

Symeon became a proficient scholar with a taste for philosophy, and as tsar (d. 927) turned his capital of Preslav into a center of Greek influence. Béla III of Hungary (d. 1196), who resided at Constantinople for many years as heir to the Byzantine throne, was schooled in the Greek and Latin classics as well as in the government of the empire. King Stephen the First-Crowned (d. 1227) of Serbia received a Greek education. So did Stephen Dušan (d. 1355), the most powerful of the medieval Serbian kings, who was educated as a youth in enforced exile at Constantinople. Similarly conversant with Greek was the last important ruler of medieval Serbia, Despot George Branković (d. 1456), a subtle politician with a particular interest in theological questions.

Many rulers of medieval East Central Europe were effective sovereigns who deserve mention on any list of notable European monarchs. Certainly the founders of states belong in this category. Stephen I of Hungary (r. 997–1038), for example, organized the seminomadic Magyars into a state on the European model; Mieszko I (r. 960–92) and Boleslav I, "the Brave" (r. 992–1025), did the same for Poland. Stephen Nemanya (r. 1168–96) laid the foundations for the efflorescence of medieval Serbia. In the early 13th century Vladislav IV Łokietek of Poland and Charles Robert of Hungary served as "re-founders" who organized effective governments after long periods of anarchy. While their reputations have been overshadowed by the brilliance of their sons, Casimir III and Louis I* (both known as "the Great"), each performed the difficult preliminary task of defeating powerful appanage princes and autonomous great lords. Their combination of force and diplomacy made possible the achievements of their successors. King Tomislav (r. 910–ca. 928) was doubtless the most powerful ruler of independent Croatia but difficult to categorize, since so little is known about him. Among the sovereigns memorable as lawgivers were Stephen Dušan of Serbia, Charles I of Bohemia, Casimir III of Poland, and Matthias I of Hungary. Other monarchs were notable for their patronage of culture. The Bulgarian Tsar Symeon I (r. 893–927) promoted Slavic as well as Greek literature. Charles I of Bohemia (r. 1346–78) was responsible for the architectural development of Prague and founded the first university in Central Europe. Matthias of Hungary (r. 1458–90) encouraged Renaissance humanism and collected a great library.

Various kings of medieval East Central Europe were noted also for their military achievements. Among them were were Symeon I of Bulgaria, who sought repeatedly to capture Constantinople; Boleslav I the Brave of Poland, an incessant campaigner; Ottokar II of Bohemia (r. 1253–78), who created but lost a large Central European empire; Stephen Dušan of Serbia (r. 1333–55), who detached large areas from Byzantium and ruled an ephemeral empire of Serbs

---

* Louis ruled both his native Hungary and (more briefly) Poland, but only Hungarian historians call him "the Great." To the Poles (whose interests he neglected) he is simply "Louis the Hungarian."

and Greeks; Louis I of Hungary (r. 1342–82), who demonstrated great personal bravery on numerous foreign campaigns, the loot from which pleased his nobility without permanently benefiting his state; and Matthias I of Hungary, who ended his reign as ruler of Moravia and a portion of Austria as well, but whose conquests fell away immediately after his death. In the struggle against the Ottoman Turks, Sigismund as king of Hungary (r. 1387–1437) was an ineffective military leader. Nonetheless, he presided over the construction of extensive border fortifications which protected his realm for half a century. King Matthias fought most of his campaigns in the north and west, but his powerful army may well have deterred the Turks from seriously attempting the conquest of Hungary during his reign. The two outstanding medieval Romanian voivodes, Mircea the Old of Walachia (r. 1386–1418) and Stephen the Great of Moldavia (r. 1457–1504), overcame overwhelming odds to conduct successful holding operations against the Turks. Another effective anti-Turkish warrior was Vlad the Impaler of Walachia (r. 1456–62), notorious as the model for the Dracula legend, although he was hardly unique in his cruelties. The Ottoman sultans of the 14th and 15th centuries were on the whole able military leaders. In acquiring Balkan territory the most successful were Murad I (r. 1361–89) and Mohammed II (r. 1451–81), the conqueror of Constantinople.

Some rulers became known for their roles in religion, and several became canonized as saints. Saint Wenceslas of Bohemia (r. 920–29) was revered as the protector of his country, and commemorated in a famous old church song. Saint Stephen of Hungary was his country's first Christian ruler and a symbol of Hungarian independence. Saint Ladislas of Hungary (r. 1077–95) was known for his wise rule and support of the Church. Stephen Nemanya of Serbia likewise became his country's patron saint. In an era when religious intolerance was the norm, a few monarchs still strove to maintain religious peace. George Poděbrady (r. 1457–71), the "Hussite king" of Bohemia, managed the almost impossible feat of avoiding serious strife between the two forms of Christian confession within his kingdom. Casimir III of Poland was famous for his benevolence toward Jews and his toleration of Eastern Orthodoxy. On the other hand, Sigismund of Hungary (who was also German emperor) conducted five campaigns into Bohemia in his attempt to defeat the Hussite revolt. Louis the Great of Hungary aroused hostility with his efforts to force Catholicism on his Orthodox subjects.

Monarchy was unquestionably the central secular institution in all of medieval East Central Europe. The sovereign's judgment was the single most significant factor in decision making, even though he was obliged to consult his chief nobles and advisers on serious matters. Much depended upon his will, his energy, and his political talents. Heredity was inevitably a lottery which left his native abilities to chance; and a monarch's education was often haphazard. On the other hand, the hereditary principle held undoubted advantages, especially where primogeniture was the rule. It reduced the likelihood of disputed successions, while providing a form of legitimacy easily comprehensible to an unlettered and unsophisticated public. In the conditions of medieval life, transmission of power by inheritance within a ruling dynasty contributed to the maintenance of peace and order. This was of prime importance in view of the widespread ignorance, technological backwardness, and lawlessness which characterized the medieval age.

CHAPTER 4

Nobles and Landholders

A distinction between "great men" and ordinary men appears in many societies almost as soon as they come to historical notice. In other cases, important differences in status arise only later; and to some extent this development can be traced. Certainly in most of East Central Europe the notion of "nobility" carried no very precise meaning until about the 13th century. The word referred loosely to the most prestigious social class, namely: (1) persons who were free rather than enserfed, (2) persons who held land, usually as owners with hereditary tenure although possibly as fief holders with conditional tenure, and (3) persons who sometimes were also entitled to participate in political life. While the nobility was originally a military and landholding class, eventually it became distinguished by so-called noble or high birth (i.e., by heredity). Even then, titles of nobility could still be conferred through royal act. Prior to the 13th century any landholder identified as "free" (not bound to the land like a serf) was often loosely considered "noble." Until the 13th century the nobility of East Central Europe was in no sense a closed caste. It lacked the two distinguishing characteristics of nobility in the later meaning of the term: a firm hereditary basis and a separate legal status involving special privileges.

In early tribal and clan society, the leading social class did not hold land in individual possession. Among the early Magyars, all settled territory was regarded as the property of the clans living on it, while uninhabited areas belonged to the supreme leader, or king. Families had the right of land use—usufruct, not ownership. Individual ownership could be established only with the consent of the entire clan; and if a family died out, only the clan or tribe could inherit the land. Social distinction among the Magyars in this early period rested not upon landholding, but on a person's membership in a particular clan or tribe (which might be more or less powerful) and on his status within that group. The clan system prevailed for several centuries in Hungary, although the alleged blood relationship of clan members was clearly more theoretical than real. In early Polish society, the military class was also organized by clans, each one headed by an elder who was its most important male. As a landed nobility began to emerge in 12th-century Poland, it continued to maintain its clan ties and exhibit the clan coat of arms. Often the clan managed its property in common. Land belonging to any member could not be sold, exchanged, or given away without the clan's approval. Particularly in the 13th century, many cases in the Polish courts involved disputes between a buyer of land and the blood relatives of a deceased owner who disputed the sale.

Class differences existed even in this early society, despite the fact that all land was considered community property, not as yet marked off by precise boundaries. The Bulgars and Magyars, who prior to their migration into East Central Europe lived on the steppes north of the Black Sea, provide examples of such distinctions. When the Turkic-speaking Bulgars first occupied their present homeland in the 7th century, their war leaders already formed a dominant social group. Gradually this class was augmented by the addition of Slavic chiefs. Similarly, the Magyars who occupied the plain of Hungary in the late 9th century were ruled by clan chiefs. Magyar cemeteries dating from the 10th century testify to social distinctions: men and women of the highest class were interred in individual tombs, while those of less exalted status shared a common grave. Likewise among the Slavic peoples, class differences existed at an early date. Burial remains from 9th-century Moravia, for example, reveal that certain graves were rich in accoutrements, while others were nearly bare of them.

The term "boyar" or "bolyar" in medieval Bulgaria, Walachia, and Moldavia denoted someone of the privileged upper class, a person in contact with the supreme state power. The boyars were originally just military men, but as society became more settled they gradually became landholders. Boyar status did not necessarily denote great wealth, since "little" boyars existed as well as "great" ones. A boyar could own just a fraction of a village or ten villages. Great boyars occupied the highest military and administrative offices in the state, whereas petty boyars held lesser positions. They met in an assembly of the land to discuss important matters. The sovereign, who was essentially just the first among equals, ruled together with a council of boyars. Eventually the term boyar came to denote the entire landed upper class of Bulgaria and the Romanian principalities. The peasants who did the actual work of farming paid the boyars in crops, services, and (after a money economy began to develop) sometimes in cash as well.

The word boyar is of Turkic origin, introduced into the Balkan Peninsula by the Bulgars in the 7th century. As the Turkic-speaking Bulgar conquerors became Slavicized, they joined with the Slavic clan chiefs to form a single upper class known as bolyars. The origin of the Vlach (Romanian) boyar class is more problematic. It may have evolved naturally from the heads of Vlach villages and communities; or the ruling princes of Walachia and Moldavia may have created it by granting privileges to certain favored persons. Conceivably this class was actually Slavic by origin (a notion rejected by modern Romanian historians), if the Slavs who migrated into the former Roman province of Dacia in the 6th century imposed their rule over an older Latin-speaking population. Certainly the contacts between Slavs and Vlachs were extensive at an early date, since Slavic place names as well as proper names are abundant in the Romanian language. The word boyar apparently entered Romanian during the 9th–10th centuries when a Bulgar ruling class dominated ancient Dacia. In all of Europe, the only people who call their nobles boyars are the Bulgarians, Romanians, Russians, Lithuanians, and (formerly) Serbs.

In Poland and Bohemia the ruling duke's personal following, called a "druzhina," developed into a landholding class in the 11th and 12th centuries. These men owed their prominence to military service and to the sovereign's favor, not to heredity. The druzhina was an instrument of rule for the duke, as well as a fighting force and bodyguard under his command. Ability to wield a weapon was the essential qualification for belonging. The numbers involved were not large, sometimes just a few hundred men, more rarely a few thousand. The druzhina naturally claimed part of the booty after any successful campaign. In peacetime the duke endowed its members with land grants in order to ensure their loyalty. Paradoxically, the acquisition of property was precisely what enabled members of the druzhina eventually to become a landed nobility, resistant to the sovereign's control.

Nobility was nowhere a uniform category, not even where all nobles in theory were equal. Divisions into upper and lower were clearly recognized, at first only in practice, later often in law as well. The higher nobles—also known as "magnates"—possessed larger landholdings than their fellows and monopolized most of the high offices of state. Titles originally attached to an office ultimately became hereditary. In Hungary, the designation "baron" was at first just a term of respect for holders of high office. Later it became permanently attached to specific families. A somewhat lesser title was "count," which originally meant the head of a royal county. Later it was given to certain magnates irrespective of official function. When King Matthias (r. 1458–90) allowed a number of prominent families to bear the hereditary title of count, he turned what had already become a socially recognized class into a legal one. Finally, in 1498–1500 the Hungarian Diet drew up a list of a few dozen magnates who were entitled to maintain private armies (and in return were required to use them to defend the country in time of war). This measure had the incidental effect of marking off a sharp division between magnates and ordinary nobility, although legally all nobles continued to possess equal rights. In the Romanian principalities similar distinctions in rank were maintained: only important nobles were called boyars; lesser ones were known as viteji ("knights") or curteni ("courtiers"). In Poland, by contrast, all nobles bore only the title of pan (i.e., "lord"), with no further distinctions such as count or baron. Attempts to organize the Polish nobility into three separate ranks did not succeed. "Magnate," as a term to designate the richest and most powerful members of this class, was not a word the nobles applied to themselves.

Great magnates were sometimes enormously wealthy and disposed of impressive military power, enabling them to negotiate with sovereigns on virtually equal terms. As an example: in a period when the armies of an entire state rarely exceeded 25,000 to 30,000 men, the two Engjëllore brothers in northern Albania were capable by themselves of mobilizing a 5,000-man army without detriment to the cultivation of their numerous lands. Military force on this level inevitably became translated into political power. The Engjëllore were entitled to appoint the archbishop of Drishti—the highest prelate in Albania. The brothers undertook projects of governmental scope. Pal Engjëllore wrote in 1461 to the doge of Venice, his formal suzerain at the time, offering the services of 8,000 workers to build a defensive canal around the city of Durrës. He proposed to pay them all himself, half from his personal lands and half from the lands of the archbishopric. This feudal family was neither the largest nor the most powerful in 15th-century Albania.

The lesser nobility, or gentry, held either small parcels of land or sometimes none at all (although in Hungary a noble who lost his land also lost his noble status). In contrast to the magnates, barons, or counts, gentry were likely to be personally engaged in the work of their estates. In many cases their life-style scarcely differed from that of peasants. In Walachia and Moldavia, the viteji or curteni were small landowners who fought on horseback. They were particularly numerous in Moldavia in the 15th century, owing to the long wars against the Turks. Curteni, who are first mentioned in Walachian documents in the last quarter of that century, were landed proprietors owning one or two villages. They constituted the nucleus of the army of the two principalities, fighting on horseback together with the boyars. Gradations of rank and status existed even within this petty nobility. In Bohemia, for example, the upper gentry were those who owned at least one whole village and came from long-established noble families. Lower gentry were those of more recent noble origin who owned less than one village. Many Bohemian nobles were able appreciably to improve their status in the 1420s and 1430s through buying up landed property secularized during the Hussite revolution.

Both Poland and Hungary in the later Middle Ages were known for their unusually high proportion of petty nobility. According to one hypothesis, this noble class consisted of descendants of the old magnate families, pauperized through generations of subdividing landed property. Doubtless this is a partial explanation, since in both countries a noble's land was inherited equally by all of his sons, or if there were no sons, by his more distant male relatives. However, subdivision cannot account for the large number of minor nobles. If that had been a major cause, the nobility should have been more or less evenly distributed throughout a country. Precisely the opposite was true. Petty nobles were far more numerous in Mazovia, a border area of Poland in the medieval period, than elsewhere in the kingdom. The Szeklers of Hungary, a Magyar-speaking people with a distinct identity who resided primarily in the Transylvanian border districts, uniformly ranked as minor nobility.

The essential reason was geographical. The nobility was a military class, while the eastern borderlands of Poland and Hungary faced the Eurasian steppe, from which bands of mounted raiders frequently descended to plunder and burn. More fighting men were necessary in these exposed frontier areas than in the interior. Since medieval governments could not afford to pay standing armies, their only option was to grant land in the borderlands to men capable of defending their own property. These frontier fighters received guarantees of personal freedom and tax exemptions. They worked their land themselves, without serfs; and when danger threatened, they constituted the local defense forces. Even after the majority of agriculturalists in Poland and Hungary had become serfs tied to the land, these border dwellers retained their personal freedom—the hallmark of noble status.

Although in the later Middle Ages only peasants fought on foot, in earlier times the upper class of society had included foot soldiers as well as horsemen. The early Slavs, who had come to East Central Europe from well-watered agricultural lands, fought as infantry. However, steppe dwellers were accustomed to dry grasslands that were well suited to horses but marginal for agriculture. Accordingly, the early Bulgar, Croat, and Magyar aristocracy all fought on horseback. Ultimately the need for defense against steppe raiders forced the Slavs to develop cavalry also. The knight—who by definition fought on horseback*—became the dominant type of fighting man. Knights often ranked as petty nobles, although not invariably so. Knighthood presupposed a certain degree of wealth as well as equestrian skill, since a horse and armor were expensive and fighting on horseback required long practice. Until the time when nobility became hereditary, a man might rise to knightly status by adding to his property bit by bit until he could afford the necessary horse and equipment. Prosperous peasants could join in expeditions abroad, hoping either to collect booty or achieve military distinction (with its appropriate reward). Poorer men participated only in defensive warfare, which produced relatively little plunder.

A monarch could transform the members of his military retinue into knights by granting them land from the vast store of uninhabited territory that was considered royal property. Most often this occurred as a reward for faithful military service, or for some specific act of bravery in battle. In the latter case, the land-granting document referred to the precise occasion on which the warrior had distinguished himself. Medieval sources speak of nobles as created by the sovereign, or as recipients of the sovereign's grace. We know that the rulers of both Bohemia and Poland presented land to members of their entourage as early as the 10th century. The practice had become common by the 12th

* As in the French word for knight, "chevalier," from "cheval" (horse).

century. In Hungary, where the descendants of the original Magyar settlers were classed as nobility, most noble families by the 14th century could no longer trace their ancestry back to the settlement period. Rather they had acquired their lands through military services to the monarch. Hungarian clan names of the late Middle Ages reveal a substantial contingent of newcomers.

King Andrew II of Hungary (r. 1204–35), who needed a large army for his ambitious foreign policy, deliberately added to the number of his knights by ennobling men of the lower classes and granting them minor properties. Warriors of this type were known as "servientes regis" (i.e., royal servants) in contrast to nobles of more ancient origin. At first a clear distinction was observed between "servientes" and "nobles," as for example in the famous Golden Bull issued by Andrew in 1222. At that time the term "nobiles" referred only to the great magnates who had exacted this concession from a weak king. However, by the end of the 13th century the servientes had gained most of the same privileges as magnates, so that in practice the distinction between the two groups disappeared. In 1351, when King Louis reconfirmed the Golden Bull, the term "noble" encompassed a far larger class of people than had been the case in 1222, and included the landholders of Transylvania, Croatia, Slavonia, and Dalmatia as well as Hungary proper. Furthermore, the king could confer the rank of nobility on anyone he chose. After the shock of the Mongol invasion in 1241, Hungarian kings frequently bestowed noble status upon entire communities of free peasants in return for military service. Especially King Béla IV (r. 1235–70) augmented the number of his nobles in this way, creating a large class of people whose poverty made them virtually indistinguishable from serfs in their day-to-day lives. Similarly, in Moldavia and Walachia, it was common as late as the 15th century for the ruler to ennoble peasants who had distinguished themselves in battle.

In independent Croatia, by contrast, a nobility created by the monarch seems never to have existed. Like the Bulgar and Magyar conquerors, the Croat horsemen who dominated the Slavic agriculturalists of their region apparently evolved into landholders. A de facto nobility developed from among the district chiefs known as "župans," who were in a favorable position to make their landholdings hereditary. At a later date, only people who supposedly were descended from the original twelve Croatian tribes counted as noble. Probably if the independent kingdom of Croatia had survived longer, a nobility based upon royal service would have arisen in due time. In fact, this evolution was precluded by the union with Hungary. By the Pacta Conventa of 1102, which established the terms of union, the Hungarian King Koloman confirmed the Croatian nobility in complete possession of all its hereditary lands. Since the Croats were determined to retain a separate identity, they did not permit the king of Hungary to introduce a nobility based on service into their midst. South of the Petrova Gora hills (southeast of Karlovac), the Hungarian kings could neither acquire land for themselves nor grant any to nobles of their own choosing. However, this restriction did not apply to Croatia north of these hills, the region later known as Slavonia, which was governed by its own ban. Here the king freely donated landed estates to immigrant Hungarian or German nobles. The Croats drew a sharp distinction between these newcomers and their own native nobility, taking care that "foreigners" did not acquire property south of the Petrova Gora divide.

In Transylvania, where the Hungarian crown established its authority only gradually during the 11th century, a Vlach landholding class of indigenous origin survived into the 13th century. As Hungarians penetrated in greater numbers into the western and central parts of the province, these Vlach landholders eventually became displaced by nobles who owed their status to royal grant. In many cases, the former Vlach proprietors and their descendants acted as administrators of Vlach villages. As such, they were known by the generic name "knez," a Slavic word again suggesting the Slavic origin of the Romanian upper class. However, in the eastern borderlands of Transylvania, where the Hungarian presence was minimal, the Vlach knezi retained their property in full ownership. This situation produced the anomaly that in western and central Transylvania the term knez usually referred to a Vlach village administrator, whereas in the borderlands it denoted a Vlach landholder. Similarly known as knezi were the men who cleared new lands in the Transylvanian frontier districts. These entrepreneurs founded new villages with the tacit or explicit consent of the royal government, which always looked with favor upon new settlement. They held their property by what was known as "knez law," meaning that it was hereditary, but subject to taxes and military service.

In 14th-century Hungary the Angevin kings—a French dynasty by origin—sought to bring Hungarian land tenure into closer conformity with West European feudal notions. According to feudal law, all rights to land were derived exclusively from the sovereign. This principle led the Angevins to legalize the de facto landholding of the Vlach knezi through royal acts of privilege, which officially granted them the rank of minor nobility. Decrees of this type almost always confirmed the ancestral possessions of the knezi, as opposed to conferring new ones. Indeed, a formal title to one's lands was considered in itself an act of ennoblement, even if this was not specifically expressed in the document. Like all Hungarian nobles, the knezi were required to serve in the army. King Louis I in 1366 even established a legal distinction between the knezi recognized by royal letters, whose testimony in court would be weighed like that of nobles, and others whose evidence would count for less, like that of village judges. In addition, many families of knezi had their nobility verified by charters of donation or by a public ceremony of taking possession. Since the rank of knez was attached to the land, not the person, loss of the land automatically meant the loss of nobility.

King Louis and his successor, King Sigismund, both issued draconian edicts to the effect that non-Catholics—meaning primarily the Vlachs, who were overwhelmingly Eastern Orthodox in religion—should be deprived of both their possessions and their noble rank. Quite possibly such decrees were intended chiefly to please the pope, the patron of the Angevin dynasty, since both monarchs knew perfectly well that the military power of the knezi would make them difficult to dislodge. The legal situation of the Vlachs changed for the worse after 1437, when the act of the Transylvanian Diet known as the Union of the Three Nations failed to include them among the three privileged categories of inhabitants in the province (Hungarians, Saxons, and Szeklers). Nonetheless, instances still occurred in which Vlachs were confirmed in their rights of nobility in recompense for "faithful and loyal services" rendered to the crown, particularly in the anti-Turkish wars. Conversely, religious discrimination persuaded a number of Vlach knezi to accept Catholicism, abandon the Romanian language in favor of Hungarian, and thus fuse with the Hungarian nobility. If they did this, the highest offices of state would not be closed to them, even though their Vlach origin would be remembered. The brilliant military and political career of John Hunyadi provides only the most striking example of a more general phenomenon. Hunyadi's Vlach father enhanced his original social status by marrying a woman of the gentry class, thus setting the stage for his son's further advancement. However, nobles of Vlach origin remained a rarity in 14th- and 15th-century Hungary outside of the Transylvanian borderlands, even though the Turkish danger permitted a certain increase in their number by offering opportunities for military distinction.

Settlers of German ("Saxon") origin in Transylvania also enjoyed noble or seminoble status. The Saxon *graeves* or counts, who were the headmen of villages, belonged to the lowest level of the Hungarian noble hierarchy. Evidently they owed this position to their own or their ancestors' services, either as warriors or as "locators" bringing settlers into underpopulated regions. A Saxon count, however, was not the proprietor of his village, and could not demand feudal services from his peasants. The king of Hungary merely authorized him to exercise the functions of policeman and judge under the general surveillance of royal officials. A Saxon count did hold certain material advantages, such as the right to maintain a mill in his village and receive a portion of the revenue from fines. Thanks to this economic power, most of these counts succeeded eventually in making their offices and property hereditary. They tended to become Magyarized, adopting the life-style of the Hungarian nobility as they did so.

Similarly the Szeklers of Transylvania never became serfs, but served as a mobile military force in the borderlands. From about the 14th century onward their status was that of petty nobles, which meant freedom from serfdom and exemption from taxes. While in theory all Szeklers were equal, significant property differences did arise among them; and some of their common lands eventually became privatized. Like the Saxon counts, their upper class sought to live in the style of the Hungarian nobility—an ambition precipitating a revolt of the less-privileged Szeklers in 1465. Nonetheless, the traditions of community property and juridical equality among the Szeklers made it difficult for even the wealthier ones to acquire extensive private estates analogous to those of the Magyar county nobility. In consequence, some Szeklers entered royal service in order to be eligible for the land grants with which the king rewarded his loyal associates. Men of this type sometimes played a role both in the Magyar noble counties and in the Szekler districts. King Matthias in 1473 assured the Szeklers of their right to army service, thus guaranteeing their status as free men rather than serfs.

Upward mobility became more difficult in East Central Europe in the 13th century. As state boundaries became more firmly fixed and plundering expeditions rarer, booty became less available as a source of wealth. To be sure, profits from a victorious campaign might still enable a man to buy a village; and landownership created a presumption of nobility. The mere fact of military service was an asset, since in the popular mind nobility was associated with the profession of arms. However, any would-be noble needed an income sufficient to procure a horse and weapons for himself. He had to learn the art of fighting on horseback—a skill few peasants had the opportunity to master. Fortunately for the ambitious, the survival of light cavalry traditions in Eastern Europe set the minimum level of required equipment considerably lower than in France or the German Empire.

The notion of nobility as derived from service to the monarch continued even after heredity was recognized as the determining factor. This transition is visible in Hungarian documents of the late 13th and early 14th centuries, which speak of nobles ambiguously as "servant and noble," or "noble servant," meaning in a broad sense a member of the king's retinue. Only in the second half of the 14th century did the concept arise of nobility as an ancient class with deep historical roots, originating independently of the king's will. In Walachia and Moldavia, which attained statehood only in the 14th century, the great nobles or boyars even in the 15th century were sometimes referred to as "servants" of the ruling prince. However, as the nobility sought increasing independence from royal control, its members began to propound the notion that high social position came from "noble birth" rather than royal service. This emphasis upon birth made noble status a permanent value, rather than a temporary one like property or political influence. After nobility came to be regarded as a matter of heredity rather than service, it also ceased to involve any obligations. Nobles thus attempted to have their rank recognized in a legal sense. From the 14th century onward, they sought to limit the occasions on which military service could legitimately be demanded of them. In particular, they refused to fight beyond the borders of their own country unless they were paid.

In Poland and Hungary in the 13th and 14th centuries, recruitment into the noble class occurred primarily among persons already close to the noble way of life. This sometimes came about through military service, but frequently also by managing an estate. To gain acceptance into the noble class, suitable manners and a knowledge of noble customs were essential. These were assets often possessed by people who had served in the households of powerful lords, but difficult to attain otherwise. The surest method of becoming noble was to acquire landed property, either through marriage, success in trade, or as a reward for faithful service at some lord's court. The new estate owner could then pretend to noble ancestry and attempt to impress his neighbors by a display of extravagance, hospitality, and refined manners. Persons of this type often constructed fantastic genealogies for themselves. In Great and Little Poland they typically claimed descent from the nobility of Mazovia—a region conveniently distant, but well known for its numerous class of impoverished gentry. Men of foreign origin often found it easier than natives to sustain the pretense of nobility, since their claims were difficult to disprove.

Of course wealth alone could never confer on a person the social status provided by hereditary nobility. For this reason, rich merchants were often not satisfied with possessing money, houses, and shops, but sought also to acquire nobility by purchasing rural estates. Noble rank was associated with landholding, whereas few nobles resided in towns. Indeed, municipal councils often prohibited nobles from living in towns, fearing that the nobles' military skills and connections at the royal court would enable them to infringe upon municipal privileges. An alternate route to ennoblement for a townsman was marriage to a noblewoman, usually one without a dowry. Whereas a bridegroom of noble rank automatically expected a dowry, a commoner might willingly dispense with one in view of the girl's high status. Accordingly, a noble but impecunious father often decided that the financial advantage of marrying his daughter to a rich merchant's son outweighed the stigma of the latter's inferior social position. If the merchant himself afterward claimed a fictitious nobility, the groom and his father had little choice but to support the pretense. Conversely, a man of the middle or lower nobility might improve his finances by marrying the well-dowered daughter of a wealthy merchant. Social relations were eased if the nonnoble relatives subsequently joined the nobility. A number of prominent Polish noble families bore titles derived from the villages purchased by merchant ancestors. The same was true of Bohemia, where many town patricians or servants of the king or Church entered the lower nobility.

Another possible route to ennoblement was adoption into a noble family. A recognized nobleman could admit a commoner to his coat of arms and thus accept him as a blood brother. These adoptions, which occurred with some frequency in Poland, generally took place within court circles and required money and influence in high places. Often they occurred as a by-product of marriage arrangements. Finally, great nobles often felt obliged to ennoble the professional warriors attached to their households, since custom decreed that magnates be surrounded by persons of comparable rank. Not only did prominent nobles close their eyes to the plebeian background of such people; they actually encouraged the commoners' ambitions and corroborated their pretense of noble ancestry. Furthermore, a magnate needed a large clientele of lesser nobles in order to influence his district assembly, in which only nobles could vote.

The status of noble families ancient in origin and well known in their districts was usually considered unchallengeable, not requiring documentary proof. On the other hand, nobles of more recent provenance, or persons merely aspiring to noble status, found formal proofs indispensable. For example, in Hungary by the 1330s royal grants were generally considered the sole source of noble property. Unless a person could produce a charter of donation, his claim to noble rank was considered doubtful. The royal chancellery issued charters of nobility in great numbers. If the original documents had been lost, duplicates were issued. However, since many noble families had acquired their land through purchase, exchange, or private gift, they lacked written deeds. In such cases they sought out aged witnesses to attest to their reputation as nobles in their districts, or instigated a court process to verify their lineage. Deprivation of noble status was not uncommon. Degradations occurred by which fictitious nobles were reduced to bourgeois or even peasant status. On occasion, genuine but impoverished noble families lost their noble rank.

Since nobility conferred in one country was also acknowledged abroad, a person might claim to hold noble rank in his place of origin. Then a court might be asked to decide who was noble and who was merely pretending. In Poland, for example, no specific institution existed to settle these questions. At first the local courts made such determinations; later the royal courts and the district assemblies did so. This procedure was undertaken only in response to a formal accusation that someone had usurped noble status. Cases of this type became rather common in Polish courts in the late 14th and the 15th century. Frequently the accused person initiated the proceedings himself, in order to remove any suspicion concerning his true origin. He organized a trial, paid an accuser, and purchased the necessary witnesses. Inasmuch as false testimony was often impossible to refute, the usual result of such trials was to confirm the person's noble status—in effect creating a new noble. To disprove a usurper's claim to noble ancestry was difficult in that age of few documents and faulty communications.

Eventually, of course, a reaction set in on the part of persons who wished to preserve the nobility as a closed caste. The frequency of false claims and forged documents of ennoblement had caused noble status to become devalued. Thus a Polish statute of 1505 prohibited marriages between nobles and townspeople and restricted noble status to persons with two noble parents. In Bohemia by the end of the 14th century, the rising prosperity of the towns threatened to overwhelm the old nobility with newly ennobled persons of middle-class origin. Consequently, the existing nobles sought to prevent the further penetration of commoners into their ranks. Whereas in former times noble status could often be acquired through the purchase of landed property, now heredity assumed decisive importance. Documents of the period frequently mention "noble birth" or the lack of it in connection with particular persons. While this expression was never precisely defined in law until the end of the 15th century, it referred in general to membership in a family of long-established noble status dating back at least several generations. In this way noble rank was separated from wealth, and the awareness of class distinctions became sharper. Nobles increasingly felt that their own inherent superiority (i.e., "noble blood") set them apart from common freemen and serfs and entitled them to special privileges.

As upper class status became more precisely defined, nobles increasingly were expected to observe certain norms of conduct. The code of chivalry demanded that a noble knight be more than just a brave and skillful fighter. He was expected also to fight fairly, behave politely in society, and refrain from violence against women of his own class. Noble rank thus acquired idealistic overtones by becoming equated with a standard of conduct higher than that of townspeople or peasantry. By following chivalric rules, petty nobles emphasized that they too were of noble birth. In this way the concept of "gentry" (lesser nobility) or "gentle" birth became associated with "gentlemanly" behavior. The assumed moral superiority of this class, added to its heredity, provided ideological justification for its social and legal privileges. Moreover, only certain occupations were considered worthy of a noble's superior status. To serve the sovereign, the Church, or a higher lord in some military or administrative capacity was regarded as commendable, but employment in commerce or any of the artisan trades was degrading and disqualifying. Since military service was viewed as particularly "honorable," many a minor noble earned his living as a mercenary soldier. In this way John Žižka, a petty Bohemian noble turned soldier of fortune, gained the experience enabling him to become the leading Czech commander in the Hussite wars.

Noble status also involved the use of a coat of arms, or heraldry. In Hungary and Poland heraldry was much influenced by models from France, Germany, and Bohemia. The Hungarian King Charles Robert (r. 1310–42), drawing upon the French and Italian traditions of his family, introduced banners, crests, and coats of arms for his nobility. The Hungarian lords eagerly embraced this new fashion, which they viewed as increasing their social prestige. Charles Robert also promoted a chivalric life-style at court, sponsoring knightly tournaments and founding an association of knights. In Poland as well, heraldic symbols became popular in the 14th and 15th centuries. Documents of the latter century mention more than two hundred Polish clans possessing coats of arms. It often happened that several families, or even several dozen, bore a single coat of arms, which sometimes (but not always) indicated that they had ancestors in common. Nobles of very modest pretensions, tilling their lands like any peasant, might use the same heraldic symbols as powerful lords. In itself the coat of arms was often quite plain—a small shield with pictures of animals or indications of geographical origin. In Poland the noble coats of arms were simple in design and rarely partitioned, in contrast to those of France, where heraldry was well developed.

During the Renaissance a new concept of nobility came into existence, which disregarded both property holding and noble birth. This was the notion that true nobility demanded individual ability, good manners, and literary culture. In the 15th century this idea attained little currency outside of Italy, where many ruling princes or their immediate ancestors had risen from modest beginnings. However, King Matthias of Hungary (r. 1458–90) sought to justify his rule on this principle and applied it in appointing officials for his centralized monarchy. Matthias himself was greatly disadvantaged by the fact of his insufficiently high birth, which prevented him from marrying into any of the major royal dynasties of Europe. Much of his policy was directed toward overcoming this obstacle. In consequence, he and his humanists eagerly promoted the Renaissance concept of noble honor as based on faithfulness, hard work, humaneness, and service. These ideals were plainly expressed in the lawbook that Matthias issued in 1486. All the same, the Hungarian Diet reverted to the older dynastic idea in 1490 when it elected a prince of the Polish Jagiellonian dynasty as his successor.

Nobles both great and small enjoyed legal prerogatives denied to commoners. They were entitled to participate in political life, especially in provincial assemblies, even if their economic position scarcely differed from that of rich peasants. In Bohemia during the Hussite period, this fact of belonging to the "political nation" added greatly to their influence. Polish laws of 1422, 1430, and 1433 forbade the king to arrest, punish, or confiscate the property of a noble without a court judgment based upon written law. Unless caught in the act of committing a crime, a noble could not be imprisoned prior to judgment. To be sure, nobles without land might find their rights restricted. For example, in Poland they were disqualified from holding offices of state, and—unlike the rest of their class—were answerable to the district courts rather than royal tribunals. However, disabilities of this type were provisional, since in principle poverty could not erase noble rank. If an impoverished noble managed somehow to purchase (or even rent) an estate, his full noble rights were restored. At times the meetings of the nobility (the Diet or Estates) exercised great influence upon the sovereign, determining his policies and effectively limiting his scope for action. If a royal dynasty died out, the nobility of the country gathered in an electoral assembly to choose the new monarch.

The lesser nobility naturally sought to insist that all nobles—from the wealthiest to the poorest—should be recognized as fully equal in law and entitled to enjoy identical rights and privileges. In both Hungary and Poland they succeeded in enshrining this principle in the law of the land. In 1222 the Hungarian gentry class forced King Andrew II to issue his Golden Bull, granting them the same legal status as the greatest lords in the land—a concession confirmed by King Louis I in 1351. The famous codification of Hungarian law known as the Tripartitum, completed in 1514, declared that all nobles possessed "the same liberty and the same nobility." Similarly in Poland, by the end of the 14th century all nobles were recognized as belonging to a single legal "estate." In Lithuania, joined to

Poland in 1385, a rough equality seems also to have existed within the boyar class, although certain distinctions were observed between ordinary boyars and princes of the ruling dynasty. However, the Lithuanian lawbook of 1468 provided that both groups had the same rights and obligations. Admittedly, legal equality could not alter the fact that enormous differences in wealth and social standing existed within the nobility. As in Hungary, so also in Poland-Lithuania, the vaunted equality of all members of the noble class existed more in theory than in reality. Particularly in Transylvania, the minor nobility suffered considerable harassment at the hands of the magnates. Some Hungarian gentry even joined the widespread peasant insurrections of 1437 and 1514, although as the peasants' demands became more radical the petty nobles tended to abandon these awkward allies and go over to the camp of the magnates.

The creation of dual states—Hungary-Croatia and Poland-Lithuania—naturally had a tendency to equalize the position of the nobility in both sectors. The Croatian nobles always ranked as equals of their Hungarian counterparts, both socially and legally, which was certainly one reason why they never seriously challenged Hungarian hegemony. In Poland the equalization process proceeded more gradually. The Horodło agreement of 1413 encouraged the Polish nobility to "adopt" Lithuanian noble families, thereby giving the latter legal equality; but this applied only to Catholics and not to those who remained Orthodox in religion. Social amalgamation of the two nobilities occurred very slowly. A decree of 1434 declared Catholic and Orthodox nobles to be juridically equal, although in reality this principle was probably not much observed before the end of the 15th century. A more genuine equality resulted from the fact that many Lithuanian nobles eventually adopted Catholicism and became Polonized in language and culture.

Feudal relationships in the West European sense of the term rarely existed in medieval East Central Europe. Most nobles were directly subordinate to their sovereign and owed no allegiance to any intermediate lord. Oaths of fealty or ceremonies of vassalage creating a special bond between one noble lord and another were virtually nonexistent. At the same time, landholding differed from the West European feudal model by the fact that most nobles held their land in full ownership. They owed military service to the monarch not as parties to a feudal contract but simply as members of the military class. A few exceptions to this general rule did occur. In Bohemia during the 10th–12th centuries, the counts and castellans who administered the various districts were ordinarily the vassals of the ruling duke. They held their districts (usually comprising a fortress or castle with agricultural land attached) as fiefs, but at the same time possessed land of their own nearby. Vassalage subsequently disappeared in Bohemia, so that by the end of the 12th century most noble estates had become hereditary property. In the 14th century the kings of the Luxemburg dynasty, influenced by French models, sought to introduce Western feudal principles into Bohemia. The attempt was not successful. The Bohemian nobility was accustomed to holding its estates in complete hereditary possession and resisted being transformed into vassals. Only in the regions newly added to the kingdom, such as Silesia, could the Bohemian monarchs establish fiefs to any extent.

The Hungarian kings in the 11th and 12th centuries were often powerful enough to give away land only as fiefs rather than as freeholds. In the 11th century they sometimes granted estates even to foreigners in exchange for services at court or in the army. However, the kings had no authority to dispose of the land belonging to the native clans, much of which was transformed into individually held allods as the clan ties became weaker. Since many of the same men who owned allods also held fiefs from the ruler, while conversely the fief-holding knights sometimes acquired clan lands, the older distinction between fiefs and allods came to be generally ignored by the end of the 13th century. All landed property in Hungary had become in effect hereditary, and its owners were considered noble. The only difference was that if direct heirs were lacking, collateral heirs could inherit the former clan property, whereas land that had originated as a fief reverted to the king. The landholders naturally disliked this restriction; and by the Golden Bull of 1222 they forced King Andrew II to permit free disposition of all property. As a further concession to the nobility, King Louis I in 1351 established the right of entail (i.e., making all land the possession "in perpetuity" of its noble clan). Since landed estates could no longer be sold, the law now excluded "new men" and tended to make the nobility a closed class, although it still permitted the estates of clans extinct in the male line to revert to the crown. The same decree extended complete hereditary rights to all noble property, whatever its origin. Women, however, could inherit property and leave it to their heirs only by the king's "special grace," though daughters were entitled to a portion of an estate to be paid in money, and widows sometimes administered property on behalf of underage sons.

Similarly in Poland, most noble land was owned unconditionally and free of feudal restrictions. With few exceptions, Polish nobles were not the sovereign's vassals. He, in turn, was not entitled to any of the typical privileges of feudal overlords, such as the payment of aids, reliefs, or rights of wardship over minor heirs. Nor did an estate escheat to the monarch when a landholder died without direct heirs. By the 13th century even collateral heirs were allowed to inherit property if the deceased owner had no direct descendants. When the heir was a minor, his relatives held custody both of his land and his person and arranged for whatever military service was due from the estate. Feudal customs were observed in Poland only in those relatively few cases where land was held as a fief. Then the vassal took an oath of fealty to his lord, and ceremonies of homage were performed. Such land could not be sold, exchanged or divided without permission of the overlord. In newly acquired territory, where the sovereign could more easily ignore vested interests, conditional landholding was more common than elsewhere.

In Poland, as in Hungary, pressures inevitably developed to equalize all forms of landholding in the state. Especially during the second half of the 15th century, many Polish fiefs became transformed into freehold estates, or allods. This could occur in a variety of ways. Sometimes by fraudulent statements a noble got a court to agree that the land in question was not a fief at all; or he paid a sum of money to his overlord in exchange for freedom from feudal burdens. A monarch might give his personal consent to a change in the status of a fief. However, whatever the mode of landholding, every noble in Poland was the sovereign's direct subject and swore loyalty to him personally. In contrast to Western Europe, where the fealty of vassal to lord often outweighed the obligation of loyalty to the sovereign, most Polish knights did not do homage to the men under whose banner they fought. The intermediate loyalties characteristic of West European feudalism were practically nonexistent.

One type of feudalism did exist in those parts of East Central Europe which were either directly controlled by Constantinople or strongly influenced by its example. When Bulgaria reverted to Byzantine rule in 1018, its territories were organized on the Byzantine model into military fiefs called pronoias. Although this reduced the legal rights of nobles over their landed property, the Byzantine government won the loyalty of many of the Bulgarian boyars by presenting them with titles and offices. Eventually the boyar class became amalgamated with the Greek feudal aristocracy; and in the course of the 12th century, most of its landholdings became hereditary property. In the 14th and 15th centuries the independent state of Serbia also adopted the Byzantine pronoia system. However, military fiefs never became universal in that country; and fief holders did not constitute the principal component of the Serbian army. Ordinary freemen, peasants, and herdsmen as well as the possessors of freeholds served as soldiers in Serbia. In Walachia and Moldavia, hereditary landownership and feudal fiefs existed side by side. The boyars' property, which in many cases antedated the founding of the state, was held in full ownership. In other instances the ruler granted fiefs to his followers as recompense for "right and faithful service."

Unlike every other state in medieval East Central Europe, the Ottoman Empire never developed a true nobility in the sense of a hereditary class with high social status and privileges recognized by law. Although landholding was the prerogative of the military elite, most Ottoman subjects in the 14th and 15th centuries held their land only on conditional tenure. Any Muslim who distinguished himself in battle might receive a certificate from his military superior entitling him to apply for a military fief, called a timar. If the fief holder continued to perform well, its size might be increased. Ottoman timars were assigned at first by the provincial governors, although after 1530 the central government at Istanbul assumed this function. Officials of the sultan exercised strict control over fief holders. The timars of men who had failed to carry out their assigned duties were confiscated.

In essence a timar was the right to collect a certain set of taxes, which might or might not have a territorial basis. Typically, although not always, it was a farm worked by peasants who paid the military landholder in agricultural products. Its value was calculated in monetary equivalents. The minimum timar in Ottoman Europe was supposed to be worth about 3,000 akçes, in Anatolia about 2,000 akçes. This represented the approximate cost of supporting one cavalryman. A small timar holder was required only to perform military service himself; those who held larger estates were supposed to supply proportionately more troops and equipment. The timar system originated only in the mid-14th century in the Ottoman Empire; and until the 15th century it played a secondary role in the state. Then under Sultan Murad II (r. 1421–51) Ottoman military feudalism reached its full development. A complete registration of these military fiefs, recording the name, annual income, and duties of each fief holder, was carried out for the first time in 1431. The Ottoman timars closely resembled the earlier Byzantine pronoias.

Compared to the typical landholding noble in Christian Europe, an Ottoman timar holder, or timariot, was not a particularly privileged person. The land he occupied was not his own. Continuance of a timar in the same family was possible only if a son took over his father's duties. (Such continuance was in fact common practice; if the son was a minor, a substitute could serve in his place.) However, the son's timar would be smaller than that of his father unless it already stood at minimum value. The state strictly regulated the income a timariot was permitted to receive from his holding, which severely limited his ability to exploit his peasants. Even the holder of a very large timar, called a zeamet (one supposedly worth 20,000 akçes or more), could scarcely expect to attain the virtually independent status of the great magnates of Poland or Hungary. Moreover, a timariot's welfare depended heavily on the success of the sultan's military campaigns, which entitled him to share in the plunder. The Ottoman landholder was not a noble, but merely a cog in a military machine, replaceable at will by the sultan. His immediate superior was not a feudal lord, but a government official in the chief town of his district.

Not all property in the Ottoman Empire was subject to the restrictions of the timar system. A small number of privileged persons were permitted to hold land outright. An estate of this type, called a "mülk," was granted in perpetuity and involved no obligations to the state. In contrast to a timar, which was merely the right to collect revenue, a mülk was a specific piece of land. Once acquired, however, it could be bought and sold. Among the persons entitled to hold a mülk were members of the Ottoman ruling dynasty; high officials in the army, the civil administration, or the sultan's court; descendants of the former aristocracy of the Anatolian emirates or the Christian states of the Balkans; prominent military leaders; and Islamic high clergy. Especially in the fertile lands of the Balkans, which had been ruined by warfare, mülks were granted with the specific purpose of encouraging the owners to repopulate them. However, the central government at Istanbul retained control even over mülks by periodically confirming the owners' rights. Moreover, the gift of a mülk by one sultan was not binding on his successors.

In practice, most mülks were eventually transformed into vakifs, or pious foundations. A vakif was an irreversible gift, the income of which was designated for religious or charitable purposes. The donation was registered in the courts and could not be confiscated or forcibly purchased by the state. Qualifying as vakifs were not only mosques and Islamic religious schools, but also contributions to public welfare such as hospitals, hostels, bridges, wayside inns, drinking fountains, water pipes, and dowries for orphan girls. The donor might be Muslim or non-Muslim as long as the gift did not promote a non-Islamic religion; thus gifts to Christian churches or monasteries were not eligible. The vakif system provided a roundabout way for the holders of mülks to make their property hereditary. The owner of a mülk could set it up as a vakif, appointing himself and his descendants as administrators and employees of the foundation. The family then enjoyed whatever income remained after the expenses of the charity had been met. In theory the administrator of a vakif should take no more than a tenth of its revenue for himself, although in reality he disposed of its entire income.

Vakifs had an advantage over timars and zeamets in that their ownership was stable. Islamic Sacred Law forbade anyone to alter the status of a pious gift. Moreover, the managers of the foundations were never absent on campaign. As a consequence, many vakifs became quite prosperous, producing agricultural surpluses for the market. Others were neglected, since the administrators who profited from them spent as little as possible on their maintenance. Many high officials who were legally the sultan's slaves took advantage of the vakif system, despite the fact that Koranic law forbade slaves to hold property. Each new sultan upon ascending the throne had to confirm all existing vakifs; and the Ottoman respect for religion usually ensured that he did so. However, the system lent itself to obvious abuses, created powerful vested interests in landholding, and reduced the central government's control over the state. Presumably for these reasons, Sultan Mohammed the Conqueror (of Constantinople) abolished all mülks and vakifs in 1465–68. This act aroused such a backlash that his successor, Bayezid II, a relatively weak ruler, restored them all and even granted new ones.

The system of conditional land tenure which predominated in the Byzantine and Ottoman empires was thus the exception in medieval East Central Europe. In Bohemia, Poland, or Hungary, land was ordinarily held in full ownership; and the same was generally true in Bulgaria, Serbia, Bosnia, and the Romanian principalities, despite some examples of pronoia tenure. This meant that most landholding was not specifically linked to military service, which constituted a separate obligation. Naturally, the connection between the two remained very close, since land was the primary source of wealth and every knight had to provide his own horse and armor. The nobility was by origin a military class, and continued to regard itself as such even after the noble cavalryman had become obsolete in actual practice. Mounted warfare was a primary feature distinguishing nobles from peasants, who participated in war either not at all or as ordinary foot soldiers or auxiliaries. (Impecunious nobles sometimes also served on foot if they could not afford a cavalryman's equipment.) The nobility as a class never disputed its theoretical obligation to assist in defending the country, even while asserting its right to "noble freedom" (i.e., independence from the central government's control). Service in the army, together with landholding, was the mark of noble status; and it carried great prestige.

Whether a monarch actually received the military service to which he was entitled was another matter. In Poland during the period of disunion (ca. 1138–1310), the appanage dukes could sometimes enlist their nobles' services only by granting them new privileges. After the monarchy had become more centralized, King Casimir the Great (r. 1333–70) imposed military service as an obligation upon all landholders. Polish statutes from the end of the 14th century onward recognized a formal link between military service and landholding, although this still fell far short of a feudal obligation. Holders of both fiefs and allods were supposed to provide fully equipped cavalrymen at their own expense, in numbers proportional to their incomes. The royal courts punished those who failed to do so by imposing fines or confiscation of estates. In Hungary, an unlimited military obligation applied at first to everyone who held land derived from a royal grant. However, since so many knights balked at serving in foreign campaigns, King Andrew II (r. 1205–35) increased the size of his army by granting large parts of the royal domain to warriors of nonnoble origin. These so-called servientes became in effect minor nobles; and King Louis's decree of 1351 recognized them as such. In Bosnia the nobles were even more independent than in Hungary. Not only did they enjoy full ownership of their properties but the monarch (whether the Hungarian or the Bosnian king) was unable even to confiscate the land of persons who refused military service.

As nobles became more autonomous on their estates, they became correspondingly less willing to follow their sovereign on campaigns abroad. This was especially true if the principal objective of a war was aggrandizement of the ruler's family. Whenever possible, the nobility insisted on distinguishing between service within their country, which they performed more or less willingly and at their own expense, and service abroad, for which they expected to be reimbursed. Although Croatia and Hungary shared a king, the Croatian nobles assumed the cost of their military service only as far as the Drava River (Croatia's northern boundary with Hungary). Beyond that point the Hungarian king paid the expenses. The Bohemian nobility in 1158 refused to participate in Duke Vladislav's Italian war until he promised to underwrite the entire cost of the expedition and make participation voluntary. In 1310 or 1311 King John of Bohemia formally conceded that the military obligation of his nobles was limited to the defense of the homeland. Similarly in Poland, the usual rule was that knights who owned property were entitled to be paid if they fought outside the realm, whereas fief holders had to serve in the army at their own expense wherever the king led them. Throughout the 15th century the Polish courts tried to enforce this rule. Nonetheless the incidence of noncompliance was high, as shown by the fact that the royal courts confiscated 2,400 knightly estates after the Polish nobility refused to follow King John Albert on his Walachian campaign in 1497. In Hungary initially all knights whose land was derived from royal grants were subject to unlimited military service—a requirement not imposed upon the holders of hereditary property. However, when the distinction between fiefs and freeholds disappeared in Hungary in the 13th century, the entire landholding class demanded payment from the king for fighting beyond the frontiers.

Wars instigated by powerful nobles, either against the central power or against each other, frequently led to anarchy in a country. Throughout the 13th century, jealousy between the nobles of Great and Little Poland frustrated all attempts to unite the Polish lands. In Bosnia noble anarchy became endemic after the death of King Tvrtko I in 1391—a situation which facilitated the conquest of Bosnia by Hungary. (At one point the Hungarian King Sigismund had 120 prominent Bosnian lords thrown from a cliff into the Bosna River, an ordeal which none survived.) Even the threat of imminent foreign invasion sometimes failed to moderate the nobles' self-destructive feuds and their fatal propensity to behave like independent sovereigns. During the Mongol advance into Hungary in 1241, the Croatian nobility refused to heed King Béla IV's urgent pleas for aid, arguing that their army could not leave the country without prior approval by the Croatian Diet. Likewise in Hungary itself, many nobles permitted their dislike for King Béla to blind them to the Mongol threat. In Bosnia and Croatia in the 15th century, not even the immediate prospect of Ottoman conquest could moderate the incessant feuds of a nobility which was perfectly willing to call in the Turks to settle its disputes. Similarly, when the death of King Matthias in 1490 freed the Hungarian nobility from his strong hand, this class was more concerned to assert its legal rights against the sovereign than to defend the country against the Turks.

The building of private castles—large and often imposing stone structures fortified for defense—was a major element in the growing power of the nobility in the 14th and 15th centuries. Until the age of gunpowder a castle provided a very effective form of protection against enemies, as well as a socially prestigious residence. Castle-building became a competitive activity, since when one noble built such a structure others felt compelled to do likewise. However, minor nobles were unable to afford such expense. A castle could not be constructed simply by using local peasant labor, but required skilled craftsmen, who had to be paid. The possession of castles gave great nobles the security they needed to intimidate their lesser fellows. As a result, many small or even medium landholders lost control of their property to some predatory neighbor who forced them to join his military retinue or become his tenants or serfs. This proliferation of castles accentuated the differences between the upper and middle nobility and led to the emergence of an oligarchy controlling enormous concentrations of land. It also weakened the power of the monarch vis-à-vis the great magnates. The Hungarian kings, for example, tried to prevent nobles from building castles without a royal license. Unlicensed castles sprang up all the same.

As the gap between upper and lower nobility widened, the magnates often made lesser nobles into their clients. In Hungary the petty nobility became linked to the oligarchs through the institution known as "familiaritas." Small landholders who were too impoverished to continue as independent proprietors often joined the so-called family of a powerful neighbor. The magnate and the familiaris drew up a service contract with definite time limits, specifying the duties of both parties. Either party could dissolve the relationship at will; and no feudal obligations were involved. The usual functions of a familiaris were military—policing the lord's estate and protecting his property and servants. He might also serve as the manager of an estate, collecting dues from the serfs and giving judgment in serfs' quarrels. In exchange he received maintenance and a salary, either in cash or in natural products. In contrast to West European vassals, a familiaris was sometimes not noble at all, although the legal distinction between noble and nonnoble was upheld even if they both performed the same functions. For example, commoners fought directly for their lord and fell under the lord's jurisdiction in criminal cases, whereas nobles fought with the county nobility and were entitled to be judged by a royal judge.

A Hungarian noble who became a familiaris retained both his original land-holdings and his noble status. If he held property when beginning his service, he usually presented it to his lord but retained the use of it; and if he left the lord's service he got his property back. Like all nobles, he paid no taxes or customs duties and retained his right to appeal to the royal court, except in questions connected with his service. Together with his lord he attended the gatherings of the county nobility, the sessions of the county court, and the meetings of the national Diet. He constituted part of the lord's loyal clientele, analogous to a small political party. If his lord held an important public office, he might carry out complex political duties. Often he acquired extensive estates through his services to the magnate and lived in the same lordly style. On the other hand, he remained bound by the services for which he had originally received property from the lord. Upon the latter's death the land the familiaris had been granted reverted to the lord's estate.

The growth in power of the landed nobility meant that frequently the more prominent members of this class dictated the sovereign's choice of his own officials. Indeed, the position of many nobles as royal officeholders in the counties, districts, or provinces became a major source of their power. Their offices usually became hereditary in practice, even though in theory they were not. As the nobility on its landed estates became increasingly independent of royal control, its monopoly of office also became more pronounced. In Hungary, for example, the royal counts, bans, and voivodes insisted that these positions be passed on to their descendants. Already in the 12th century, the king rarely granted offices in the counties or at the royal court to nonnobles; in the 14th century, nobles held all such positions. Through the institution of familiaritas and the assemblies of county nobility, the magnates ruled the counties as hereditary property, either personally or through their adherents. The Angevin prince Charles Robert, in his efforts to become king of Hungary, was obliged to renounce the freedom to choose his own chief officials in exchange for receiving the noble oligarchs' oath of loyalty. Then after consolidating his position he gradually deprived the magnates of their offices and installed less powerful nobles in their places, defeating several military rebellions in the process. A monarch who was less determined or a less commanding personality—for example, Sigismund (r. 1387–1437)—was often at the mercy of his own nobility.

In Bohemia as early as the 13th century the chief offices of state were occupied by secular or clerical lords whom the king could not easily control. In 1394–1405 the Bohemian upper nobility insisted upon its right to hold all important offices in the capital as well as in the provinces. Exceptions were allowed only for positions requiring some particular expertise. For example, in provincial administration the scrivener, whose job required literacy in Latin, could be a minor noble; but his inferior social status required that he sit separately from his colleagues. At the royal court a petty noble might hold only the office of mint master, which demanded financial ability. In Poland the chronicler Gallus Anonymous (d. 1118) already argued that only men of the upper nobility should hold important positions in government, which suggests that the practice was not yet fully established in his time. In 1505, however, the nobles in the Great Sejm forbade the king to create any new offices or officeholders without their approval and tenured the existing royal officials for life, which deprived the king of control over his own administration.

The nobility also acquired a virtual monopoly of high office in the Church. In the early medieval period in East Central Europe it could still happen that a man of very modest antecedents rose to become a bishop. At that time the Church had been rich only in land, not in disposable income. However, since ecclesiastical estates were not subject to division by heredity or alienation, the Church's holdings constantly grew through pious donations. As the population increased, this property became more valuable, enabling bishops and abbots to live in comparative luxury and enjoy considerable political influence. As a consequence, positions in the church hierarchy gradually came to be monopolized by the nobility. In Hungary as early as the mid-13th century almost all bishops and abbots were of noble origin. By the 15th century, nobles held virtually all higher ecclesiastical offices in Bohemia and Poland as well. In Poland the Diet legalized this monopoly in 1505 by a statute which specifically required that all upper church officials be noble, with a few exceptions for men with university degrees. Since family connections were clearly more important than qualifications for office, the higher a bishop's social position at the time of appointment, the younger he was likely to be. Pastoral services were provided by subordinates or not at all, while the titular officeholder merely collected the revenues of his see. Nonetheless, despite a few strikingly unqualified appointees, many prelates of this period were university trained. Some had acquired valuable experience serving the king as chancellery officials or diplomats.

Among the legal advantages possessed by many noble estates was "immunity," i.e., exemption from government control over their lands. The monarch's officials were forbidden to enter an estate enjoying this privilege. The royal courts exercised no jurisdiction there; and no taxes could be collected from anyone or on anything on the premises. The landowner became in effect a petty sovereign, exercising virtually total control over his peasants and other nonnoble residents on his property. If royal officials tried to assert authority on an immune estate, the noble proprietor was entitled to resist them by force—a right sometimes expressly stated in his charter of privileges. The Church, with its large landholdings, usually led the way in demanding and receiving immunities for its lands. Experience proved that concessions granted to churchmen could not long be denied to nobles. Weak monarchs gave away many formerly royal rights to private individuals; and even strong rulers could not always resist the importunities of powerful subjects. Whereas immunities originally were granted only to favored lords on an individual basis, subsequently they were bestowed on the entire noble class as a body.

Judicial immunity for noble estates applied at first only to relatively minor crimes (low justice). However, by the end of the 13th century in Poland the Church enjoyed total immunity for virtually all of its property, even in cases of crimes involving capital punishment (high justice). By the 14th century such immunity was a normal privilege of the Polish nobility as well. The Bohemian nobility during the 13th and 14th centuries acquired the right to judge all cases involving peasants. The few exceptions concerned villages subject to town law—a situation beneficial to the peasants in question, since town law offered greater protection than noble law. Otherwise the landholder was for all practical purposes an absolute lord over his dependents. The larger noble estates maintained two courts: a higher court for capital crimes, over which the lord himself presided; and a lower court for minor cases, which the estate manager, or bailiff, decided in conjunction with the villagers. The most common penalties were fines and corporal punishment.

In Hungary, where the monarchy was more powerful than its counterparts in neighboring lands, noble immunities were never complete. The charters of immunity received by certain lords in the late 12th and especially the 13th century allowed them to judge minor crimes commited by their dependents, but not crimes involving the death penalty, which was reserved for the judges of the royal curia. Even on their private estates the nobles were obliged to respect royal decrees as well as the "customs of the land." County officials could legally enter an immune estate; and if a lord's court committed injustices the lord himself could be tried before the king. In the 14th and 15th centuries a few nobles did receive royal permission to judge capital crimes; and some may have done so whether authorized or not. Nonetheless, on the whole, "high justice" in Hungary remained a royal prerogative.

Whenever possible, the nobility insisted upon paying no taxes to which it did not specifically consent in an assembly of the land. In Hungary the Golden Bull of 1222 specified that only the king's own peasants should pay taxes to him directly; all other peasants would pay their lords. King Louis as ruler of Poland in 1374 abolished all previous tax obligations of the Polish nobility, retaining only a small symbolic tax per unit of land held, which in reality was a burden on the peasants. (Previously some, but not all, of the Polish nobles had enjoyed this privilege.) Similarly in Lithuania, the charter of 1434 exempted the boyars from all payments to the grand duke and permitted them to tax their peasants themselves. Nonetheless, even formal guarantees of tax exemption were not always effective in practice. In Hungary during the reigns of the energetic monarchs of the Anjou dynasty (1310–82), the lesser nobles were often unable to realize the tax freedom to which in theory they were entitled. On the other hand, the private armies of the great magnates made such men too powerful to be easily coerced. The Angevin kings were strong enough to collect considerable revenue simply by virtue of their royal supremacy. However, King Sigismund (r. 1387–1437) exercised much less control over his nobility, who in 1405 managed to gain exemption from paying even the church tithe. Finally King Matthias (r. 1458–1490), by effectively exploiting his regalian rights, centralizing his government, and building up a powerful army, could intimidate the nobles of the Diet on many occasions into voting an extraordinary war tax.

Noble immunities existed in the Balkans as well; and there too they gradually became more extensive. When Bulgaria returned to Byzantine rule in the 11th century, the Bulgarian boyars possessed only incomplete authority over their tenants, while peasants paid taxes directly to the government. Then as the landholding nobility became more powerful, its members began to collect this tax themselves. Gradually the boyars acquired partial or complete freedom from governmental interference on their estates and assumed extensive rights of jurisdiction over their dependent peasants. While in theory the pronoia system remained in force, the government at Constantinople found it increasingly difficult to exercise authority over the boyar landholders. This situation continued to exist under the Second Bulgarian Empire (1187–1393), when the boyars became even more independent than their Byzantine counterparts. Landed property enjoyed complete freedom from taxation, while the dependent peasants, who no longer paid state taxes, had become serfs tied to the land. To some extent the Byzantine government had been able to limit the landholders' powers; but the rulers of the Second Bulgarian Empire did not dare to try. Byzantium lay just across the southern frontier, a still powerful opponent perpetually ready to support separatist tendencies. A system of noble immunities also existed north of the Danube in Walachia. Medieval Walachian documents provide a long list of officials forbidden to enter the domains of nobles with immunity rights.

The Ottoman conquest eliminated the power of the heredity nobility through-out the Balkan Peninsula and brought about its destruction as a distinct class. Many of the native Balkan nobles died fighting the Turks. Others fled northward or westward to Catholic-ruled territory or (if they stayed behind) were forced to become peasants. A few managed to retain their ancestral lands on condition of performing military service for the Turks. They held no real power vis-à-vis the centralized Ottoman regime; and if they remained Christian they became second-class citizens in a Muslim state. As a result, the native nobility disappeared in Bulgaria, Serbia, and large parts of Hungary, leaving solely a subject peasantry. Only in Bosnia and Albania did a portion of the native nobility retain its former status, making these countries unique in the Ottoman Empire in possessing a hereditary noble class. Here the Turks did not interfere on any large scale with the existing structure of landholding. Many Bosnian lords retained part of their ancestral property as timars or zeamets, which made for continuity of occupation and reinforced their influence as a class. These holdings were often supplemented by land confiscated from the peasantry. Very early in Ottoman Bosnia the practice was established of awarding timars and zeamets to local landowners only. More-over, Bosnians were usually permitted to transmit their estates to their heirs. One reason for this special treatment was that both Bosnia and Albania consisted largely of mountainous terrain difficult for a distant government to control. A more important factor was that both regions had become strategic frontier areas facing the Turks' two most formidable enemies in Europe—the Habsburg Empire and Venice. Finally, the population of both areas was known to be relatively indifferent to religion. This made their acceptance of Muslim rule easier and reduced the possibilities of interference from Catholic powers abroad. Eventually the majority of landholders in both Bosnia and Albania became Muslims. As such they were accepted into the Ottoman elite, which was religious rather than national in character.

Compared to its Christian predecessors, the Ottoman government clearly permitted its landed class much less autonomy on its estates. Far from enjoying administrative and judicial powers over their peasants and servants, Ottoman timar holders had to tolerate the interference of state officials. Often they were required to set aside half their revenue for the benefit of their military superiors. Despite their elite status as warriors and (usually) Muslims, the timariots could not totally dominate the people living on their lands, since in cases of conflict between a landholder and his dependents the local Muslim judge arbitrated the disputes. Sometimes, though not invariably, the owners of mülks or vakifs were allowed to collect the poll tax from their peasants in person. However, even these favored landholders could not easily assert themselves against the Ottoman government. Neither their status nor their property was protected by law; and the sultan could confiscate their land at any time, with or without reason. Surviving documents attest that this did in fact happen, particularly at the hands of Mohammed the Conqueror.

Nobility as an institution in medieval East Central Europe was ultimately the product of a rural agricultural society. Despite the steady growth of towns throughout our period, land remained without question the most significant source of wealth. At an earlier period, agriculture had been too primitive and too poorly organized to afford a landholder much profit. By the 13th century, it was universally recognized as a supremely desirable possession. Territory which had formerly been the property of an entire tribe or clan became divided into individually held estates, while monarchs sought to purchase military service and personal loyalty by giving away lands belonging to the crown. Thus endowed with the principal wealth of society, the nobility developed into an exclusive social class with far-reaching privileges. Until such time as central governments found ways to control a larger share of society's resources, landed nobilities would remain a powerful force in East Central Europe.

CHAPTER 5

Peasants, Herders, Serfs, and Slaves

*P*easants and animal herders comprised the great mass of the population everywhere in medieval Europe. Whether free people or serfs, they occupied the next-to-lowest rung of the social ladder, superior only to slaves. Little respected in their own time, they have received slight attention in historical records. Thus the surviving information about them is scanty; and generalizations must be made with care. Certainly it is safe to say that most medieval people lived out their lives largely within the boundaries of their own villages or districts, hardly aware of the wider world. Nearly all were illiterate. The agricultural tools and techniques they used were primitive, while their crops often yielded little more than bare subsistence—sometimes not even that. Nevertheless, peasants and herders constituted the foundation of medieval society, producing the food supplies upon which all classes of society depended.

The earliest form of agriculture in East Central Europe was the slash-and-burn variety, which provided good crop yields for a few years in the ashes of the burnt trees. Within about three years after the original conflagration the soil nutrients were largely exhausted, so that farmers were forced to move elsewhere to begin the process all over again. Among the Slavs the slash-and-burn method was largely abandoned in the 7th century in favor of plowing. This transition necessarily brought about social changes. Whereas slash-and-burn required a large group of people to control the fire, the adoption of plow agriculture made possible a smaller work unit consisting of extended families or even nuclear families. Thus the most common unit of peasant settlement became the village. Laid out on a defined space, it gradually replaced the vague territorial claims and frequent migrations of the clans.

The typical village was a small cluster of dwellings containing between a few dozen and a few hundred inhabitants. Quite often the grasslands, pastures, forests, and streams in the vicinity were regarded as belonging to all the local people together. In some places individual farmsteads existed also. The type of settlement which prevailed was largely a function of topography. In Serbia, where the hilly terrain made villages impractical in many areas, individual farms were quite common, consisting of houses set in the midst of fields, vineyards, and orchards. The farmers might be either minor nobles or peasants. In such regions only woodlands and pastures were held in common, not tilled fields. Likewise in the Carpathian Mountains of Transylvania or the Beskids of southern Poland, peasant houses were widely dispersed in the midst of family plots. In regions of gentle hills, villages tended to be strung out along winding roads. Settlements in the plains were more compact, crisscrossed by several streets with houses set closely together. In villages founded according to German law, a square layout according to a fixed plan was typical.

The type of productive activity prevailing in any area was also a function of geography. Whereas agriculture was the principal occupation of plains dwellers, stock raising and farming were found in roughly equal proportions in the hills. In the mountains and on the steppes, herding predominated. In Slovakia, for example, where the Carpathian Mountains block the arrival of moisture from the sea, droughts present a perpetual threat. The Slovaks compensate for the uncertainty of agriculture by supplementing their incomes with animal husbandry. The grass crop is sufficiently abundant that winter and summer pastures lie in close proximity and nomadism is unnecessary. By comparison, the much drier steppe north of the Black Sea has traditionally been a region of seminomadic grazing and very little agriculture.

A common residential pattern in the villages of medieval East Central Europe was an extended family of some kind. Nuclear families were not unknown, but the larger kinship group offered greater economic security in an uncertain environment, since its members could help one another. In Poland the so-called large family typically included three generations of men with their wives and children. The entire family worked the land together under the direction of the father or grandfather, and constituted the basic unit of social life. Similarly the Serbian zadruga, or commune, which certain 19th-century nationalists idealized as a specifically South Slav institution, was a kinship-based peasant organization scarcely different from the patriarchal family systems of other peasant societies. In Albania a system of joint cultivation and land use functioned in the 15th century as a means of defense against the Turks. Extended families survived in the Balkans even well after the Middle Ages. A family elder dominated the group, assigned tasks to its members, and managed the joint finances. Most often the unit consisted of a father and his married sons with their families, or in other cases brothers and their families, with either the father or one of the sons acting as head.

The nature of the crops grown in any locality naturally depended heavily on weather. Most common in Bohemia were rye, oats, wheat, barley, millet, and legumes, although some villages also produced wine, hops, flax, and hemp. Farther north in the colder climate of Poland, millet was the most popular grain, since it would grow even under relatively unfavorable conditions and could easily be processed into gruel, the dietary staple of the poorer classes. Other cereals were raised chiefly for sale in order to pay taxes. In Hungary millet tended increasingly to be replaced by more valuable cereals such as wheat or barley. Many fruits and vegetables were cultivated as well: apples, pears, peaches, cherries, grapes, and plums. On the Adriatic coast and in Macedonia the olive was the most valuable fruit. Cattle, horses, sheep, pigs, goats, and poultry were raised as an adjunct to agriculture. As markets developed, various agricultural and animal products were offered for sale in towns. In Hungary wine was an even more important product than grain. Landlords received so much wine as rent that the taverns they owned contributed significantly to their incomes. Similarly along the Adriatic, viticulture was widespread. In Walachia both lords and peasants maintained vineyards. In some cases the land belonged to one person and the vines to another, bringing considerable income to the owners. The Serbian red wine was preserved in caves in wooden barrels or in large jars, then transported on horseback in large casks or goatskin bags.

A significant rise in agricultural productivity during the Middle Ages can be attributed to technological improvements. Iron-tipped plows came into wide use between the 6th and 10th centuries—a decided advance over purely wooden implements. An improved plow with a vertical knife, horizontal plowshare, and moldboard spread to East Central Europe from the West. Its iron plowshare turned the furrow over instead of merely scratching the surface of the earth. This new plow, harnessed to a team of horses or oxen, could be used on terrain previously considered too difficult to cultivate; and it also permitted a more intensive use of the older farming areas. Another innovation was the horse collar, a deceptively simple device unknown to the Romans but enormously important in medieval agriculture. By removing pressure from the horse's windpipe it permitted the animal to pull heavier loads without choking, and made possible the hitching together of many animals to draw a plow. Since draught animals were now indispensable (eight or ten oxen to each plow), cattle breeding soon outstripped horse breeding. An incidental result of this change was to improve soil fertility through the increased use of manure. Finally, the three-field system of crop rotation, known in Western Europe since the 9th century, began to spread eastward in the 11th. Whereas the old two-field system had involved a simple alternation of planted and fallow fields each year, the new method required that only one-third of the arable land be left fallow. Another third of the available area was planted with winter crops of wheat or rye, and the remaining third with summer crops of oats, barley, and especially legumes, which restored nitrogen to the soil. Three-field rotation eventually came to prevail almost everywhere in East Central Europe, resulting in correspondingly higher crop yields. Nonetheless peasants did not always appreciate the advantages of this improved method, even as late as the 12th and 13th centuries. In the German-law villages newly founded in Poland at this time, the authorities had to impose the system by fiat.

Peasants were the principal craftsmen of the medieval period prior to the growth of towns and a money economy. Most craftwork was done either in villages by peasants producing articles for their own use or by artisans in the service of a monarch, bishop, or lord and directly dependent upon him. Their tools were few and simple. Village craftsmen remained peasants in their attitudes and life-styles, often combining their trades with agricultural labor. Only a small minority, like blacksmiths or silversmiths, received supplies from any distance; most got raw materials from their own village or one nearby. In early medieval times artisans rarely produced for an area larger than their lord's domain. Those who worked in the vicinity of administrative centers were somewhat better off than villagers, since they had the advantage of a more assured market and stood under the immediate protection of a lord. As urban life developed after the 12th century and the demand for artisan products expanded, more craftsmen set themselves up in towns.

In some parts of medieval East Central Europe animal herding was the primary means of livelihood. In Albania the inhabitants of the coastal districts evidently lost their connection with agriculture in the 6th and 7th centuries in the wake of the Slavic invasions. Adopting a pastoral life-style, they survived by tending sheep in the mountains, migrating twice annually between winter and summer pastures. These mountaineers regularly raided the plains settlements, supplementing their incomes with plunder. The Magyars had been herders on the Ukrainian steppes prior to invading Central Europe; and even in Hungary, stock raising was their principal means of support. They avoided the thick beech and pine forests which could not be used as pasture, leaving these to Slavic, German, or Vlach peasants. Travelers of the 12th century described Hungary as one vast grazing area, interrupted only occasionally by patches of cultivated land. The Magyars spent their winters in villages set alongside riverbanks, often in shelters hollowed out of the earth. In spring they sowed their seed, then moved on to the grasslands where they lived in tents. At harvest time they returned to their villages. Their winter habitats were usually near a fortress, while summer residences were located in the vicinity of pastures.

Similarly the early Serbs lived primarily from stock raising, an occupation well suited to their hilly country. (The region known as Serbia in the 12th century faced the Adriatic and included the rough terrain of Hercegovina and Montenegro.) The chronicler William of Tyre, passing through Serbia in 1168 on his way to the Holy Land, described the local people as warlike mountaineers, rich in milk, cheese, butter, meat, honey, and wax. The Serbs that he observed lived entirely from the products of their herds, although we now know that they also practiced a moderate agriculture in the valleys. Hog raising was a primary activity in medieval Serbia just as in modern times, thanks to an abundant supply of acorns for pigs to feed upon in the thick oak forests. Hunting was also important: bears, wolves, stags, boars, rabbits, martens, and foxes were abundant. Fishing was carried on everywhere in the lakes and streams. Beekeeping was widespread: not only peasants, but monks and even kings kept large apiaries. Honey was much in demand as a sweetener before sugar became available, while beeswax was used to make candles. Honey was also the basic ingredient of mead, the most popular fermented beverage of the period.

Stock raising continued to be widely practiced in East Central Europe long after agriculture had become the dominant economic activity. Many animal herders were Vlachs (ancestors of the modern Romanians), who spoke a language derived from Latin. Subsisting on the products of their flocks, they lived in the mountainous regions of southern Poland, Transylvania, and the Balkan Peninsula. Their sheep supplied them with meat, leather, fat, wool, skins, and particularly the milk from which they produced several different types of cheese. Donkeys or mules were their beasts of burden on the stony mountain footpaths; and they raised small horses for sale in the plains. Vlach herders maintained close contacts with the inhabitants of the Adriatic coastal districts, to whom they sold salted pork for the provisioning of ships. The towns of Kotor and Dubrovnik employed Vlachs to tend their horses, oxen, sheep, goats, pigs, and beehives, sharing with them half-and-half the gains and losses from this activity. Other Adriatic towns regarded the Vlachs as a nuisance and tried to prevent them from using municipal territory for grazing their flocks. For example, the Hungarian king ordered in 1379 that "all Vlachs residing in our city of Šibenik, and often causing damage there, must leave." Similarly the ban (governor) of Croatia found it necessary to exclude all Vlachs from territory belonging to the town of Trogir. Apparently these decrees had little effect. Perhaps the ban did not try to enforce them, but more probably the Vlachs simply ignored them.

The rents and services rendered by peasants to their landlords and to their sovereign varied greatly, not only from place to place but also according to whether the peasant was a freeman or serf. These obligations usually were defined by tradition rather than by law, and for that reason frequently went unrecorded. They can be classified either as labor services (corvée), deliveries of natural products, or money rents. Labor included not only work in the fields but also the building and repair of fortifications, castles, manor houses, roads, and bridges. Guard duty might be included, as well as hospitality for the monarch's officials and servants on their travels throughout the country. Deliveries of natural products could involve either sharecropping or a fixed amount in taxes. The obligations of free peasants were not always onerous. For example, the oldest known Polish lawbook, which was used in the district of Elbląg in Prussia and dates from the 13th century, lists the burdens of free peasants as follows: (1) providing horses for the ruler's messengers and transportation for his goods; (2) spending three days a year mowing the landlord's fields and three more in cutting his grain. A free peasant was entitled to leave his village at any time, provided that he first planted the crop and paid his yearly rent. If he had received a tax exemption at the time of settlement, he had to compensate his lord for the years of tax freedom. To be sure, these financial provisions often made departure difficult or impossible in practice. Sometimes a peasant was forbidden to leave his plot unless he found a substitute to take his place. Already in the 14th century King Casimir the Great's statutes for Great Poland specify only a few cases in which peasants could legally abandon their plots, while his statute for Little Poland permitted only one or two peasants per year to leave an estate.

With the spread of a money economy, rents in cash gradually replaced payments in labor services or natural products. In Bohemia money rents were collected in some regions as early as the 12th century and became common in the 13th and 14th, particularly in regions producing wine and fruit for sale at markets. The Teutonic Order in Prussia also allowed corvée to be transformed into rent payments. In Hungary by the end of the 15th century nearly all peasants paid at least some of their rent in cash. The sum due might be calculated either per unit of land or according to the value of the products (e.g., a gulden instead of a hog, five denars instead of a goat). Landlords sometimes extracted additional amounts without legal title, for example for the use of meadows or forests. Often the transition to money rent began when the lord assessed a tax in coin upon the peasant market towns that developed on his estates. These places were typically hamlets of five hundred to a thousand inhabitants which served as local centers of production and exchange. According to one calculation, by the end of the 15th century in Hungary approximately one-fifth of all peasants (roughly half a million people) lived in settlements of this type, which often enjoyed the same legal rights as towns.

Peasants sometimes welcomed the change to a money economy, though at other times they resisted it. Cash rents forced them to sell their produce on the market, irrespective of the current state of the economy. In times of high agricultural prices this could be very advantageous, while if prices were low virtually nothing might be left after the payment of taxes. In either case, money rent freed the peasant from his former humiliating subservience to the landlord or the landlord's agents, who either inspected his crop or directly supervised his work. Cash rent encouraged the peasant to produce a surplus, and (if he was a serf) sometimes even enabled him to purchase his freedom. On the other hand, the development of a money economy encouraged landlords to develop a taste for luxury goods which could only be purchased for cash in towns. This impelled them to raise rents, causing the peasants much misery.

Whether a free agricultural population—consisting neither of serfs bound to the land nor of slaves who were owned outright—existed in the early medieval period is a question not easily answered. Conditions varied widely from country to country, and even within a single region. Nevertheless, it is clear that when the great Slavic migrations came to an end in the 6th–7th centuries and the tribesmen settled down to agriculture, serfdom was unknown. Settled areas were held in common by the clans or tribes. In Bulgaria, for example, serfdom apparently took root only gradually. When the Bulgars entered the southeastern Balkans, they were seminomadic herders. They could and did tax the Slavic agriculturalists who had earlier taken possession of this territory; but until they themselves settled down to agriculture they could not reduce the subject population to serfdom. In the 8th and 9th centuries the majority of agriculturalists in Bulgaria remained free people. Similarly in Bohemia and Poland, when state structures began to develop in the 10th century most peasants seem to have been personally free. Until well into the 11th and 12th centuries they lived either on their own plots or on land belonging to the monarch which he allotted for their use.

Indeed, in the early medieval period peasant settlements were mere islands of cultivated land surrounded by vast expanses of forest and woodland. The eventual economic dependence of peasants upon landholders (a status which was not yet serfdom) arose in response to the prevailing conditions of semi-anarchy. In the Balkan Peninsula in the 5th–7th centuries the Slavic, Avar, and Bulgar invasions destroyed much of what remained of the old Roman government. Farther north in East Central Europe, the Slavs moved into areas where no effective state structure had ever existed—the present territory of Poland, the Czech Republic, Slovakia, and most of Hungary—or where organized government had long since ceased to function, as in the former Roman provinces of Pannonia and Dacia. The replacement of tribal society by centralized governments took time, while a lack of basic security compelled people to make their own arrangements for protection. Moreover, poverty forced the free warriors of the tribe to settle down to agriculture after they were no longer able to support themselves from the booty derived from raiding expeditions.

As society became more settled and governments more powerful, pressures increased to reduce the agricultural population to serfdom. Land was plentiful almost everywhere, but without labor it was useless. Landholders with military obligations needed to assure themselves of a steady income from peasant labor and dues in order to afford the equipment necessary for war. Governments wished to facilitate tax collection and guarantee that the landholders could afford to perform military service. Peasants were unorganized, isolated in the countryside, and essentially powerless to resist the restrictions imposed upon them. Thus a ruler and his principal warriors could use force or threats of force to compel peasants to work for them. Conversely, free peasants might voluntarily accept submission to powerful overlords in exchange for physical protection. Furthermore, untilled earth was regarded as the sovereign's property, which he was entitled to give away. Monarchs had little alternative but to grant lands to their chief followers in exchange for military and political support. In this way the state played a vital role in the creation of private property. On the other hand, landed proprietors came to exercise increasing influence over central governments. They demanded laws to assure themselves of a secure labor force, which meant legal authority over the peasants on their estates and restrictions on peasant mobility. In this way, serfdom was born.

Some early monarchs tried to prevent the settlement of peasants on private land, since this conflicted with the concept of the free warrior and also weakened the ruler's authority. In early 11th-century Hungary, King Stephen I decreed that "no count or knight may make a free person a serf," although contractual arrangements between landholders and freemen were permissible as long as the freemen's status was preserved. A law of King Ladislas I later in the century shows that he accepted arrangements between private landholders and freemen which did not turn the latter into serfs. A decree of his successor, King Koloman, refers unmistakably to "freemen who work on the land of others." On the other hand, in Poland in the early 13th century the categories of freeman and serving man were mutually exclusive, meaning that a freeman could not serve a private landholder. Only the sovereign was entitled to a freeman's services. Ruinous fines were imposed on private persons (meaning great nobles or magnates of the Church) who took free people "under obedience" because this infringed on the sovereign's rights.

Even after centralized states came into existence, the right of ordinary people to move in search of better conditions remained unquestioned. Abandoning one lord for another was a common occurrence, as individuals sought to improve their economic status or fled from war zones. In Hungary the freedom to migrate was an ancient right, supposedly dating back to the foundation of the state. Hungary in the 11th and 12th centuries was still largely a pastoral country, where members of the tribes remained free people subject only to their sovereign. The class of true peasants, as opposed to herders engaging in occasional agriculture, was for a long time relatively small. The spread of serfdom was hindered at first by the fact that so much of the land still belonged to communities of herdsmen. At the same time, the warriors assigned to the royal fortresses constituted a class of half-peasant freemen engaging in agriculture between campaigns. Legally free in the sense of being directly subject to the sovereign rather than to a private lord, they were forbidden to leave the property of the fortress because of their service obligations. Many such persons ultimately became full-time peasants. However, the distinction between free and unfree was not very clear in Hungary, so that in the course of time more and more of the fortress people secured the right to move. On the other hand, as agriculture gradually replaced herding, the property of the clans was broken up into private estates which were held mainly by nobles and churchmen. Gradually the free Magyar clansmen were transformed into serfs. At times prisoners of war augmented the serf population.

This deterioration in the status of agriculturalists might be termed the "first serfdom." It was a virtually inevitable accompaniment to the process of state formation and the creation of large private landholdings, since the estate owners needed peasant labor, and peasants possessed few options in the underdeveloped rural society of the Middle Ages. Gradually, the growth of towns and the effect of foreign immigration in the 13th and 14th centuries inaugurated an era of increased peasant freedom in Bohemia, Poland, and Hungary. On the other hand, immigration was notably smaller in scope and correspondingly lesser in impact in the Balkan Peninsula. Except along the coasts of the Adriatic and Black seas and in a few mining districts, towns were poor and far apart. The growth of large landed estates led to widespread serfdom, with peasants living under the jurisdiction of private landowners or monasteries. Finally, the Ottoman conquests in the Balkans in the mid-14th century and afterward created a form of state serfdom. The government at Istanbul set the regulations governing peasant life, while the Ottoman military class held the land as fiefs. In the northern sector of East Central Europe, the trend toward increased peasant freedom was reversed during the 15th century. Thus began what is termed "the second serfdom."

Serfdom was nowhere a uniform category. Medieval documents offer so bewildering a variety of terms for the various degrees of bondage that scholars are not always certain which words can reliably be translated as "serf." The distinguishing mark of serfdom was the condition of being bound to a particular piece of land and forbidden to leave. Persons with this status were commonly described as "recorded people" (adscriptici), indicating that their tie to the land was listed in official documents. Serfdom was hereditary, so that the children of serfs were serfs also. On the other hand, a serf usually could not be evicted from his land. This was a form of security which during periods of economic distress might easily be more valuable than the right to leave. Certainly serfs occupied a position superior to that of slaves, although the distinction was sometimes barely discernible in practice.

Even after being deprived of all rights to move, peasants were still considered direct subjects of the sovereign power, paying taxes on their own account and entitled to use the royal courts. Theoretically a person's free status was not affected when he became a tenant on an estate. In 13th-century Poland, for example, free peasants still enjoyed a limited access to the royal courts. This included the right to sue their own lords, although the remnants of peasant landownership had largely disappeared by this time. By the end of the century even freemen in Poland had become subject to their landlords' jurisdiction in practice. All the same, until nearly 1500 the sources continue to call such persons "liberi," or free people. The crown reserved the right to tax them, although they also owed rent and various dues to their immediate lords. Only as bondage became more firmly entrenched were peasants removed from all contact with a superior governmental authority, thereby becoming entirely subordinate to their lords. In Bohemia, on the other hand, liberi are almost never mentioned in official records. The terms for "peasant" indicate various degrees of servitude. At a comparatively early date, Bohemian peasants appear to have been tied to the land.

Typically the men performing military service were personally free, juridically subject to their sovereign rather than to any private lord. They regarded themselves as free warriors, full members of their clan or tribe, and were treated as such even if they supported themselves partly or wholly by agriculture. The

Szeklers of Transylvania were soldiers of this kind, living as a privileged minority in the Hungarian borderlands. They cultivated communal lands as free people, scarcely differing in life-style from any other tillers of the soil. Until the end of the 15th century they retained their original military organization, as granted by King Stephen I in the early 11th century. Since the Szeklers ranked as minor nobility, their lands could not become part of any lord's domain. Their villages differed from ordinary peasant settlements in being fully autonomous. All Szekler men participated in village self-government. Perpetually ready to fight at the king's command, they paid no taxes to the royal authorities. They even objected strenuously to the church tithe until finally King Sigismund exempted them from it. A similar category of border fighters existed in the eastern provinces of Poland, also living from the products of agricultural labor. The origins of these people as a class have never been satisfactorily explained. Like the Szeklers they ranked as petty nobility, leading some historians to regard them as the pauperized descendants of great magnate families. More probably they were originally free warriors who escaped tenant status and eventual serfdom by accepting a military obligation.

Communities of free Vlach peasants were numerous in Transylvania as late as the mid-13th century. Some of them persisted until the mid-14th century, and in peripheral regions even into the 15th. The king's officials did not disturb them, preferring instead to enlist the villagers' cooperation in the defense of the border. Likewise free were the Vlach shepherds of the hill country, many of whom turned to agriculture only in the 15th and 16th centuries after falling into the power of noble landholders. However, the efforts of the Transylvanian nobility to impose serfdom on the Vlachs were counteracted by the willingness of free Vlach peasants and herdsmen to move east of the Carpathians into Walachia and Moldavia. Many free Vlachs abandoned Transylvania for the newly established Romanian principalities, where state structures took form only in the 14th century. There too the landholding boyars could not do much to hinder peasant migration. The two principalities were small and weak, menaced by powerful neighbors and continually unsettled by the assaults of marauding steppe horsemen or Turkish irregulars. The power of the ruling voivodes suffered accordingly, leaving the landholders without effective aid from the state. Until the mid-16th century most peasants in Walachia and Moldavia still lived in free villages, especially in the Carpathian foothills but often in the plains as well.

Peasant self-government in a limited form existed in many areas of medieval East Central Europe at a fairly early date. In Croatia, where each extended family or clan usually had its own village, the heads of the clans represented their people in assemblies of the district. Generally the Croatian nobility did not interfere with the internal affairs of the clan, except occasionally to influence the choice of a new clan head. In Poland in the 11th and 12th centuries a single organization for knights, free peasants, and serfs existed in each district, or "opole," charged with delimiting estates, pursuing criminals, and collecting taxes. However, the powers of the opole declined after the 13th century, when an increasing number of villages came under German law. In Hungary and Bohemia, village headmen were elected to regulate day-to-day affairs, subject to general supervision by estate managers and governors of fortresses. These headmen allocated and collected the rent due to the king or landlord and handled minor judicial matters. Similarly, villages in Moldavia and Walachia were governed by councils of "old and good men" who gave judgment, apportioned whatever taxes the current voivode saw fit to impose, and selected the men assigned to join the army. However, in much of East Central Europe during the 13th century and after, an increasing number of landed estates received immunity from the monarch's jurisdiction. This made the peasants direct subjects of the landholder, who might or might not find it convenient to respect traditional peasant institutions. On the other hand, in the Balkans under Ottoman rule the landholders did not have such authority. The central government often permitted peasant communes to function with minimal interference, since they involved the villagers in mutual guarantees for paying taxes and catching lawbreakers. In mountainous Albania and Montenegro the communal system was particularly well entrenched, and the Turkish authorities chose not to disturb it.

Occasionally an enterprising peasant could win his freedom. One method was to prove himself a capable soldier. Although serfs ordinarily formed no part of medieval fighting units, those who accompanied their lords to war in a menial capacity sometimes found opportunities to join a battle. Lords normally were happy to find capable warriors for their private armies, and sometimes granted liberty to loyal followers who fought well. Indeed, a lord could emancipate his serfs for any reason, either by public declaration or in his last will. The Church emphatically approved of such acts. Without challenging the institution of serfdom as such, it taught that liberating one's serfs was a Christian virtue. Other serfs gained freedom by purchasing it themselves. The development of a market economy enabled some of them to earn the money to buy their liberty, either by compensating their lords for lost labor or by paying other people to take their places.

Nonetheless, the most common route to emancipation was flight. Often large groups of peasants, or even entire villages, abandoned their lords en masse in order to seek a better life elsewhere. The existence of large uncultivated areas in East Central Europe and the widespread lack of labor power made this undertaking relatively easy. Somewhere another lord would be only too willing to employ the fugitives, frequently offering attractive conditions of service. Peasant runaways occasionally found refuge in forests, where they formed powerful groups of outlaws. Many peasants who settled in the newly established "guest" villages of Poland, Bohemia, or Hungary in the 12th and 13th centuries were probably fugitive serfs from Germany or Flanders who had left their native places illegally. Others, no doubt, were serfs from closer to home. In Poland, for example, the flight of serfs greatly increased in the first half of the 13th century, precisely the time when immigration from abroad gained impetus. Presumably the agents who promoted this foreign migration asked no inconvenient questions; and the previous status of foreigners could scarcely be ascertained in any case. Even within a single kingdom or province, peasant flight was difficult to prevent. The incentives were too great; and landholders could usually be found whose need for extra hands outweighed any feeling of solidarity with the nobility as a class. In any event, governments in the Middle Ages were incapable of undertaking extensive internal police operations.

Naturally those nobles—usually the less powerful ones—who stood to lose labor through peasant flight tried hardest to prevent it. Legal procedures were available whereby a lord could regain his fugitive serf in a public judicial process. The laws which prohibited peasant migration and imposed punishments on offenders were often very severe, on both the runaway himself and anyone granting him refuge. For instance, a Serbian law of 1354 provided that anyone receiving a fugitive was subject to confiscation of all his property—a penalty equivalent to the one for high treason. Captured serfs were cruelly tortured by having their hair burned and noses split. The harshness of the prescribed punishments bore witness to the difficulty of preventing the offense. The mere existence of free towns encouraged peasant flight, since in large parts of Europe serfdom did not exist within town walls. Not surprisingly, the nobility tried whenever possible to limit town freedoms. In Poland, for example, the nobles used their control of the Great Sejm to pass laws forbidding the towns to receive peasants.

Despite all the hardships of their position, serfs were usually still better off than slaves, who comprised the very lowest class in medieval society. Slaves were property pure and simple, lacking even the security of land tenure normally vouchsafed to serfs. Having no guaranteed rights, they could be bought, sold, exchanged, or even killed by their owners without compunction. No doubt in practice the distinction between serfs and slaves was often scarcely noticeable, although serfs theoretically enjoyed a higher status in law. Both groups were at the complete mercy of their lords, upon whose personal characteristics their treatment depended. However, slavery was a fact of life in East Central Europe well before the advent of serfdom. It was commonplace under the Roman Empire, so that all the late Roman law codes provide for it. The Slavs at the time of the great 6th-and 7th-century migrations already held slaves; and often they enslaved part of the indigenous population in the regions they occupied. The conquered peoples frequently possessed slaves of their own. The Byzantine Empire, including its Balkan territories, retained a significant number of slaves down to the end of its existence.

People became slaves in a variety of ways. In early medieval times a major objective of armed raids was the capture of slaves, which meant that many were war captives. Slave status might result from inability to pay one's debts, or from crime: thus the death penalty could be commuted into a sentence of slavery. Freeborn persons sometimes sold themselves into slavery to extinguish their debts. Poverty-stricken parents might sell their children as slaves to nobles or to the Church. Medieval laws fully recognized the legality of slavery. For example, the laws of King Stephen I of Hungary in the early 11th century treated slaves as persons totally without rights. In Poland the offspring of slaves automatically became slaves as well. A Serbian law of the early 13th century permitted a man to sell his faithless wife into slavery if she had no property; obviously, the wife herself was considered property. In the 14th century the Serbian law code of Tsar Stephen Dušan as well as the laws of the Dalmatian towns simply assumed the existence of slavery.

Slaves certainly were present in every state of medieval East Central Europe, although their proportion in the total population is unknown. Polish rulers in the 11th century established entire villages of slaves to perform artisan work or other services. Similarly in Bohemia, entire villages consisted of slaves or near slaves with specialized abilities, for example vinetenders, blacksmiths, and beekeepers. The same was true of Hungary, where slaves with professional capabilities were often employed by the monarch and the military chiefs. Others worked as domestic servants. In Walachia and Moldavia many gypsies and Tatars became slaves. However, the incidence of slavery tended to decrease in late-medieval times. Many slaves managed to escape from their owners and settle elsewhere. Like fugitive serfs, some probably found work in the new towns and villages established during the eastward immigration movement. Landlords discovered that slaves were less productive than serfs, who were allowed to keep some of the fruits of their labor. The slave trade became subject to various legal restrictions. By the end of the 12th century, outright slavery had largely disappeared in Bohemia, Poland, and Hungary. Most slaves had merged into the class of serfs.

In the Ottoman Empire slavery bore a very different connotation than in Christian Europe. To be a slave (kul) of the sultan was neither a disgrace nor a mark of low social status. Quite the contrary: many members of the Ottoman government, including the highest administrators and sometimes even the grand vizier, might legally be slaves. The employment of slaves as high officials gave the sultan absolute power over these subordinates and served to guarantee their loyalty. The sultans themselves took slaves as wives or concubines; thus from the mid-15th century onward, many of the reigning sultans had been born to slave mothers. On the whole, however, slaves or freed slaves occupied the lowest rank in Ottoman society. Slave labor predominated on the estates owned by the sultan or high-ranking officials, rich private individuals, or religious foundations. Certain segments of the economy, such as the silk industry, were dependent on slave labor. Aside from their value as an unpaid work force, slaves were advantageous to their owners because human beings constituted an investment easily convertible into cash. Moreover, many of the legal restrictions protecting ordinary people did not apply to slaves.

Slaves traditionally came from the non-Muslim world as prisoners of war, as the gift of friendly rulers, or simply as merchandise purchased at a slave market. Natural increase operated as well, since the children of two slave parents were slaves likewise, although under Islamic law the children of a marriage between one free and one slave partner counted as free. On the other hand, Islamic law forbade the enslavement of anyone who was either Muslim by birth or the inhabitant of an Islamic state. All such persons were entitled to the sultan's protection. In practice the Ottoman government blatantly violated its own principles through its policy of child tribute, known as devşirme. This regular roundup of Christian boys from its Balkan territories increased in scope as Ottoman territorial expansion slowed down and the number of captives decreased. Beginning on a small scale, devşirme came to involve a total of between 15,000 and 20,000 children in the thirty years of Mohammed the Conqueror's reign (1451–81). These children were legally the sultan's slaves. After a period of training and conversion to Islam, most served as soldiers in the Janissary corps, although some also occupied administrative positions. Devşirme was never challenged on legal grounds in the Ottoman Empire, doubtless because the government considered it vital to the welfare of the state. Child tribute was superior to other methods of acquiring slaves because it provided a greater choice of human material. Presumably this explains why most of the slaves who attained high rank under the Ottoman sultan were of devşirme origin, although child tribute actually furnished only about one-third of all the slaves in the empire.

The continued existence of Ottoman slavery depended on a constant renewal of the supply, since bondage was frequently a temporary condition. Aside from flight, an Ottoman slave sometimes had opportunities to win his liberty by legal means. In many cases he worked under a limited-service contract, known in Islamic law as mukataba. Such agreements had the advantage of providing the master with good service for a fixed period of time, since lifelong slaves tended either to be unmotivated or to escape. The owner was forbidden to alter the contract to the slave's detriment, but might do so to the latter's advantage, for example by shortening the period of service. Under certain contracts of the mukataba type a slave was permitted to work independently and keep his earnings, which later he might use to buy his liberty. Manumission of slaves was a fairly common practice, since the Koran treated this as an act of piety. On many occasions the sultan freed some of his slaves in order to celebrate an important event like a military victory, circumcision of a son, or recovery from an illness. Sometimes he also freed the women of his harem, who thereby became eligible for marriage.

In the northern portion of medieval East Central Europe, conditions for the lower classes generally were improving in the 13th century. One important reason was certainly the rise of towns, which provided some rural people with an alternative to serfdom. This was particularly true of Bohemia, where towns were comparatively numerous and prosperous. It was also a factor in Poland and Hungary. Furthermore, the development of a money economy permitted the commutation of peasant dues from natural products into cash rent. The nobles' desire for urban luxury goods, available only for money, made them prefer this form of payment. As monarchs discovered that mercenary troops were more effective than the general levy of the nobility, they too preferred to receive taxes in money, since mercenaries had to be paid in cash. Through commutation of services and dues, many serfs became transformed into tenants who paid rent for the land they worked. Sometimes they could earn enough to buy their freedom.

The ambition of high-ranking persons to attract settlers to their private lands proved favorable to peasant freedom, since most regions of medieval East Central Europe were underpopulated. The disintegration of the Polish state in the 12th and 13th centuries had the incidental effect of promoting peasant liberation. The relatively weak Polish appanage princes felt constrained to give away large tracts of land, while the new landholders competed for the peasants' services. Hungary in the 13th century still contained enormous empty spaces. Even in the 14th century Western travelers were struck by the sparseness of population in that fruitful country. Monarchs, bishops, and nobles in Poland, Hungary, and Bohemia all promoted immigration from abroad, chiefly in an effort to increase their incomes and satisfy their growing taste for luxury and magnificence. Religious institutions needed labor power for the large landholdings they had accumulated over the years. New settlers meant higher returns from the land by rendering forests and swamps arable, permitting greater intensity of cultivation, and creating large fields which made improvements like the three-field system feasible. As a consequence, immigrants from abroad, known as hospites or "guests," were given special privileges as an inducement to migration.

A tremendous wave of agriculturalists from Western Europe—most often from Germany or Flanders—found new homes in Poland, Bohemia, or Hungary in the late 12th and the 13th centuries. Extant sources do not comment on their motives, but the wish for economic improvement was certainly paramount. Energetic peasants were willing to undertake the backbreaking task of clearing previously untilled woodlands and forests in return for tax concessions and recognition of their status as free people. Monarchs offered the immigrants tax exemption for a fixed number of years (usually three to five) and a guarantee that they were at liberty to move once they had fulfilled their obligations. Private landowners offered prospective settlers freedom from rent and dues. Although the lord himself retained ultimate ownership of the land, the immigrants received hereditary tenure together with a precise agreement delineating their rights. These were advantages they had not usually enjoyed in their native places. Some limitations on peasant freedom nonetheless continued in force. Although the scope of village self-administration was enlarged, the village head tended to be the agent of the territorial lord; and he exercised authority accordingly. In Bohemia the landholders retained legal juristiction over their peasant-colonists—a significant restriction on their freedom.

In Hungary, German immigration became very extensive after the mid-12th century, although some had occurred earlier in frontier areas. Compact enclaves of German settlement appeared on royal land in the Zips district of Slovakia and in eastern Transylvania around the towns of Sibiu and Braşov. Other German villages sprang up throughout Transylvania. The Teutonic Knights' brief occupation of the Braşov region (1211–25) stimulated an influx of Germans both there and across the border into Moldavia. Immigrants from Western Europe, whatever their country of origin, were known throughout Transylvania as "Saxons" and enjoyed special privileges. In judicial proceedings involving only "low justice" (i.e., cases not involving the death penalty) they were freed from the jurisdiction of royal judges. They could also select their own priests, although ordinarily in royal villages the king made all appointments to church positions. Saxons were permitted to hold markets free from state taxes and dues. Wherever they resided in compact communities they received rights of self-government.

The second great wave of Saxon immigration into Hungary occurred under the patronage of great private lords. Usually these later settlements did not form ethnic communities of sufficient size to make self-government feasible. In any case, a private estate owner could not offer his colonists the same advantages that settlers on the king's land enjoyed. He could not free them from royal taxes, though he might refrain from demanding excessive rents for himself. As patron of the churches on his lands, he could allow the settlers free choice of priests; but he could not exempt them from tithes owed to the bishop. Nonetheless, colonists on private land enjoyed more extensive rights than the indigenous peasantry. They received guarantees of personal freedom, royal protection, and exemption from military service.

Many German immigrants also took up residence in Bohemia, Poland, or Prussia in the 13th century. The earliest wave struck the regions in closest proximity to Germany itself, namely western Bohemia and Silesia (which at that time was populated largely by Slavs and ruled by Polish princes). In Prussia the Teutonic Knights actively promoted the immigration of German peasants as part of their policy of settling the wilderness. Colonization was an organized movement for the profit both of its sponsors—monarchs, bishops, or great nobles—and its agents, known as "locators." The earliest locators usually were townsmen of German origin who had purchased settlement rights from some monarch or lord. They received legal documents, known as location acts, authorizing the foundation of new villages or improvements in the legal status of old ones. If a village lay on royal property, the monarch himself executed the document for the locator's benefit, while reserving supreme legal authority to himself. If a private lord wished to found a village, he secured appropriate permission from his sovereign. The location document described the rights and obligations of everyone concerned.

The locator's first task was to find peasants willing to move to a new and unknown region. For this purpose his contacts in Germany often furnished a basis. Next he established the village and parceled out its land among the inhabitants. Usually he also became the first village head, or mayor. The locator's relation to the lord of the village was based on the hierarchical practices of West European feudalism. The lord retained ultimate ownership, while the locator became a vassal of sorts. Representing the lord in the village, he headed the village court, collected income and rents for the lord, and accompanied him to war. In return the locator received his own farmstead, plus a third of the income and judicial fines collected in the village, while reserving the other two-thirds for the lord. Usually he also enjoyed other privileges, such as permission to maintain a tavern or mill. His office was hereditary. The villagers received leases in perpetuity that obligated them to work the land and pay the required taxes. On royal land they received tax exemptions, or on private land rent concessions. These would be valid for a longer period in a village founded "from bare roots" than in an existing one.

The legal principles according to which this immigration took place went by the general name of "German law." In the 12th and 13th centuries several versions of this law were introduced into parts of Prussia, Poland, Bohemia, and Hungary. Technically German law was emphyteutic law, meaning that ultimate rights over the land in question remained with the owner, while the tenant's lease was permanent, fully heritable, and salable. German law fixed tax burdens "for always" by a firm and precise agreement which could not arbitrarily be changed at the lord's discretion. Peasants subject to this law were required only to pay royal taxes and make certain payments to their lords, supplemented at times by minor labor services. For their part, the landlords were assured of a definite yearly income from the tenants, based on the usual (and generally quite accurate) medieval assumption that prices would remain stable indefinitely. Tenants could abandon their land only under specified circumstances, thereby avoiding the threat that the lord might suddenly be left without labor. Moving required the prior agreement of the lord (in practice: the village head), who ascertained whether the peasant's obligations had been fulfilled. Finally, villages founded under German law were entitled to exercise self-government. Since many such villages were closely linked to towns which also possessed German law, their status probably represented an extension of the town's privileges. If a village was located on an estate exempt from royal jurisdiction, it too was exempt. This immunity provided the peasants with certain advantages. It meant that for minor crimes they had only to deal with the village head, not with minor officials of the royal courts, who were less accessible and prone to cause delays or legal obstructions.

The privileges granted to foreign immigrants inevitably put pressure on the monarchs and lords to accord equivalent rights to natives. Gradually some of the characteristics of German law were extended to villages originally having no connection with immigration. Inhabitants of older settlements sometimes purchased the right to live under German law. At times they might even be required to do so, since the lords profited financially from the sale of German-law rights. However, in most localities the older legal regime continued in force. At the end of the immigration wave in Poland, German law applied only to a minority of villages even in the regions most accessible to Western influences. In Silesia only about one-third of the villages ever received this law, while in Great Poland and the western section of the duchy of Cracow the proportion was about one-fourth. Elsewhere the incidence was much lower. Customary native law remained particularly strong in the outlying eastern regions of Poland, particularly in Mazovia.

In Bohemia and Hungary the grant of German law to existing villages brought important improvements in the peasantry's legal position. The process of equalizing the status of old and new settlers coincided with the last years of the immigration wave. By the end of the 14th century most Bohemian peasants held their land in hereditary tenure. In Hungary, too, the privileges accorded to "guests" (hospites) had the effect of creating a relatively independent peasantry. By the 14th century in Hungary a uniform class of peasant tenants had emerged, the so-called jobbágy. (This term had earlier been applied to the armed retainers or lesser officials of the royal fortresses.) Among the most important improvements granted to peasants by German law or its equivalent were the freedom to migrate, security of tenure, and rents which were fixed rather than arbitrary. Under this law a peasant could leave his lord once he had fulfilled his obligations in dues and services, since the relationship was one of free tenant to landlord, not personal dependence on a feudal superior. Moreover, the peasant had a hereditary right to retain his holding. He could not be evicted once he had paid his rent and performed the required services for the lord. His rent, calculated according to the amount of land leased, was paid partly in money and partly in produce. The few labor services demanded of him were comparatively minor in nature.

In Hungary the increased freedom of peasants in the 14th century proved detrimental to the less affluent landholders. The great lords could often attract peasants to their estates from the lands of the lower nobility by offering financial inducements. To eliminate this competition, which incidentally worked to the peasants' advantage, King Louis in 1351 decreed a uniform land rent for all Hungary, payable in addition to church tithe. It amounted to one-ninth (nona) of all peasant produce. The same law formally confirmed the peasants' freedom to migrate if they had paid all their debts—a right confirmed by subsequent decrees in 1391 and 1397. However, the king and the nobles did not have identical interests in this matter. The king viewed peasant migration rights as a welcome check on the power of the nobility, but the lords feared being left with many vacant holdings. The attempts of some lesser nobles to enhance their personal incomes by increasing the peasants' dues foundered precisely upon this fact of free movement. In the 15th century free peasants were very numerous in Hungary, while serfdom had virtually disappeared. In theory all peasants possessed migration rights, although in practice the lords sometimes resettled people arbitrarily. Many peasants either owned their own land or paid rent as free tenants, while the use of forests, meadows, and rivers was free to everyone. Whatever surplus remained after paying rent and taxes the peasants could dispose of as they wished. Similarly they could buy, sell, or bequeath their property. Many seem to have bought vineyards. Hungarian peasants of the 15th century were apparently quite well-off by comparison with their counterparts in Western Europe.

However, the virtual cessation of foreign immigration in the second half of the 14th century proved detrimental to peasant life in East Central Europe. Economic conditions made colonization no longer feasible. The settlers were required to pay normal money rents and taxes once their initial exemptions had expired. This they could afford to do only by bringing grain to the market. More grain was offered for sale than the towns of the time could absorb; and an agrarian crisis ensued. As a result, colonization ceased to be a source of profit for its sponsors and organizers. Moreover, local resistance developed to the cutting down of forests and woodlands, which served the medieval economy as a source of timber and pasture and as a hunting area for the nobility. Finally, the Black Death (bubonic plague) of 1347–50 sharply reduced the reservoir of potential immigrants by causing a drastic reduction in the population of Western Europe. The privileged position of foreigners no longer functioned to improve the status of local people.

In the northern sector of East Central Europe the peasants' condition gradually deteriorated in the last years of the 15th century. Reinforcing the effects of the end of large-scale immigration, the value of money fell drastically. This was a Europe-wide phenomenon, initially favorable to peasants whose rents were fixed. As a consequence of this inflation, the landowners now became poorer while their expenses increased. Meanwhile, they had become accustomed to a higher standard of living. Their only means of gaining additional profit from the land was by raising the peasants' rents. Since nobles were influential at the royal courts and in the national assemblies, they succeeded in doing so. Moreover, instead of cash payments, the peasants once again were forced to deliver a portion of their crop to a lord, since its real value was not affected by changes in the value of money. During the same period, mercenary soldiers increasingly were assuming the nobility's former military role, leaving many lords little choice but to stay at home and pay more attention to their estates. They sought to utilize formerly untilled ground, and even confiscated some of the land traditionally belonging to peasants.

More decisive still in the worsening of peasant life was the growth of large agricultural estates, both secular and ecclesiastical. The material resources of the great magnates gave them a power of intimidation which ultimately proved detrimental to the peasant's status. Much worse was the transformation of many noble estates into miniature, semi-independent kingdoms through the application of so-called immunities. On an estate enjoying immunity, the only effective law was the will of the lord and the decisions of his private court. No royal official could exercise authority over immune property or over the people who lived on it. No agent of the monarch was entitled to set foot on such an estate without the owner's express permission. At first the peasants did not always experience this situation as harmful to themselves. They were freed from taxes and services to the monarch and now had to deal only with a single overlord. However, these same lords could no longer be prevented from demanding increased rents and labor. Juridically the change was clearly deleterious, since it broke the peasants' link to the government of the country. Persons living on immune estates lost the right of appeal to the royal courts against a lord's injustices. Immunity rights tended to reduce everyone on an estate to a single class of dependent peasants, who ultimately became serfs. The peasants had no recourse except outright revolt—a desperate measure unlikely to improve their situation.

Another crucial element in the deterioration of peasant life in the 15th century was the development of an important foreign market for agricultural products. The growth of towns in Western Europe had created a large demand for food-stuffs which could be supplied only by imports. Especially those Polish nobles whose lands were located near water transport found it possible to dispose of large agricultural surpluses at a profit. The result for the peasants was a drastic limitation of their former rights. In the absence of technological inno-vation, an increase in production could be attained only by additional labor. Armed with immunity rights, the lords could essentially do as they pleased with their peasants. Through their control of the national assemblies—an increasingly important element in the political life of Bohemia, Hungary, Poland, and Royal Prussia in the 15th century—they could and did pass laws binding peasants to the soil. No other social class existed at that time which might have restrained them. The growth of towns, which in Western Europe offered discontented peasants the possibility of escape, had failed to keep pace farther east. With a few exceptions—Gdańsk, Cracow, Prague, or Buda—the urban centers of East Central Europe were relatively small and powerless. They could neither absorb an oppressed peasantry nor compete with the nobility in political power. Thus the last years of the 15th century witnessed the renewal of serfdom in East Central Europe—precisely at a time when serfdom was fast disappearing in the West.

Hungary offers a good illustration of this process. In the 15th century, Hungar-ian lords increased their links to the West European market by exporting cattle and wine. Since these products required peasant labor, the lords employed all possible means to block peasant migration. One method was to charge very high rent for land, since the law permitted a peasant to move only if he had paid all his debts. Hungarian documents of the 15th century leave no doubt that the nobility at this time began collecting higher rents and dues contrary to ancient custom.

Widespread violence against peasants occurred as well, including kidnapping. Similarly in Poland, many nobles augmented their incomes by supplying grain and cattle products to Western markets. The acquisition of West Prussia in the Thirteen Years' War (1454–66) opened the port of Gdańsk to a lucrative Polish export trade. Whereas corvée labor formerly had been set at only a few days per year, by the end of the 15th century Polish peasants worked a minimum of one day per week, and on some ecclesiastical manors two or three days a week. They lacked legal remedies because their ties to royal jurisdiction had been broken. Where German-law villages existed, the lords bought up the mayors' rights and appointed their own men to administer the villages.

Serfdom thus resulted from corvée, rather than corvée from serfdom. In Hungary and Poland the nobility used its political influence to secure laws reducing and eventually eliminating the peasants' freedom to migrate. Only in Royal Prussia was the situation somewhat better, illustrating once again the strong correlation between prosperous towns and a free peasantry. Towns were larger and wealthier in Prussia than elsewhere in the Polish kingdom, and their ties to the peasant economy were close. The existence of important urban markets and the demands of the export trade meant also that the price of wheat was higher in Prussia than elsewhere. As a result, hired labor became profitable and serfdom unnecessary. Conversely, where the export of wheat did not pay—namely, in the regions remote from the Baltic Sea (Little Poland, the upper Dnieper valley, or the border wilderness of Mazovia)—peasants continued to pay money rents and were not enserfed.

Peasant resistance to the abuses and extortions of the landlord class was not uncommon. Malingering was one frequent response to oppression; deliberate provocations were another. At times the peasants cut wood in the lord's forests, led their animals to feed on the lord's pasture, or hunted and fished in the forests and lakes reserved for the lord's use. If sufficiently aroused, they might even burn the lord's property or kill the lord himself. Usually such outbreaks were local in nature, escalating only rarely into serious disturbances. Predictably, the worsening conditions of peasant life produced more than the usual number of rebellions. In Transylvania many small-scale uprisings occurred during the first third of the 15th century. Agricultural implements were transformed into weapons; castles, manors, and monasteries were burned down. Finally, in the spring of 1437, masses of Transylvanian peasants rose up in an outburst of violent fury. The spark which set off this rebellion was an increase in the church tithe; but high taxes and the curtailment of peasant migration were additional grievances. Another ferocious peasant uprising broke out in Hungary in 1514, likewise fueled by economic hardship and resentment at the nobles' privileges. Both revolts were brutally suppressed, as peasants fought with farm tools against nobles with vastly superior arms and training. Afterward the nobles imposed still further legal restrictions on the peasantry.

In the southern sector of East Central Europe, the interlude of comparative peasant freedom which occurred in Poland, Bohemia, and Hungary in the 13th–15th centuries never happened at all. Bulgaria reverted to Byzantine control in 1018 after several centuries as an independent state. As elsewhere in the Byzantine Empire in the 11th century, the number of large landed estates rose substantially in Bulgaria, enabling powerful landholders to attach increasing numbers of people to the land as serfs. Landless tenant farmers who had previously been free to move now worked plots received from their lords and were not permitted to leave. On the other hand, peasants with land who had voluntarily commended this property to a lord in exchange for protection, or whose ancestors had done so, retained the right to rent out their plots and even to transfer them to other lords. Small independent farmers evidently were rare in Bulgaria, perhaps even nonexistent. For Serbia, our earliest solid information about peasant conditions dates from the 13th–14th centuries, at which time most peasants apparently were tied to the soil. Large landed estates certainly existed in Serbia; and the lords evidently worried about serf discontent, since the 14th-century law code of Tsar Stephen Dušan prohibited serfs from holding meetings. However, Serbian peasants had few alternatives to serfdom except along the Adriatic coast. There a flourishing urban life existed; and peasants were both personally free and owned hereditary property.

Owing to the relatively late formation of the two Romanian states, the transition to serfdom occurred later there than elsewhere in East Central Europe. Probably most peasants in Walachia and Moldavia were comparatively free when these principalities took shape in the 14th century. Nonetheless, peasants paid taxes to the ruler and the boyars in wheat, wine, sheep, hogs, honey, wax, and fish. They performed labor services as well. In the 15th century the ruling voivodes continually imposed heavier taxes on the population in response to the Turks' growing demands for tribute. However, peasants who had commended their property to a lord retained the right to bequeath it; and with the lord's permission they could change masters or even buy themselves free. Documents from the end of the 15th century mention a special tax paid as compensation for lost labor by peasants who left their lord's domain. Eventually the development of grain production for the market had the same detrimental effect on the peasantry of Moldavia and Walachia as it did in Poland or Hungary. The two Romanian principalities were rich agricultural regions, favorably located for the shipment of grain from ports on the Black Sea. Toward the end of the 15th century the boyars intensified their exploitation of the peasants, demanding increased amounts of forced labor and rent. They put new lands into production, reinforced their administrative and judicial rights over dependent persons living on their estates, and sought to suppress the right of peasant migration. The cases in which they failed to do this probably indicate that the ruling voivode at that time was powerful enough to oppose them. Peasant rents continually increased in the course of the 15th century in both Moldavia and Walachia, although corvée seems to have remained fairly constant.

The Ottoman conquest of the Balkans represented little more than a change of overlords for much of the agricultural population. Most peasants still lived on someone else's property: either Turkish military fiefs (timars), the land of religious foundations (vakifs), or the privately owned estates (mülks) of high Ottoman dignitaries. All free peasants of the conquered nationalities, whether Christians or Muslims, were classified as re'aya (singular: ra'iya), or "flock"; the sultan was their "shepherd." Unlike the serfs of Christian Europe, peasants in the Ottoman Empire were not subject to the legal jurisdiction of their landlords. Justice was the function of the local Islamic judge. Compared to the former Christian lords of the region, who had been quite free to act arbitrarily, the men who held Turkish military fiefs were much more strictly controlled by the central government. Ottoman laws sought to preserve the country's ability to support the military system, which meant that officials in the districts were supposed to prevent fief holders (timariots) from exploiting the peasants for personal benefit. In any case, the timariots were so frequently absent on campaign that they could not exercise continuous personal supervision over their tenants. On the other hand, decrees of the sultan which were aimed at protecting peasants on military fiefs did not apply to the workers on privately owned estates. Often these latter were slaves or former slaves, which in itself gave them less protection than ordinary re'aya possessed.

In villages located on timar land, the sites of the peasants' houses and attached gardens counted as private property. Trees, vines, and usually buildings were likewise privately owned, although the land on which they stood was not. Arable and pasture land was state property, although the peasants held the right of use, known as tasarruf (as opposed to ownership), in permanent and hereditary tenure. They could not be evicted unless they failed to cultivate the land. One purpose of these legal arrangements was to avoid the inheritance provisions of Islamic law, which prescribed the division of private property among a number of heirs and would have caused excessive fragmentation of land that was owned outright. Since the Sacred Law said nothing about the inheritance of usage rights, when a peasant died his land passed without difficulty to his sons jointly, or to a daughter if sons were lacking. If a peasant on a timar wished to leave his plot, he could either find a replacement who would assume his tax obligations or he could pay a fee to the timariot, who would then find another cultivator. This sum was to cover the loss to the fief holder in case another tenant could not be found immediately. If the abandoned farm was given at once to another tenant, the fee was not paid. In practice this right of migration usually did not mean much, since without the agreement of the timariot a peasant could not take advantage of it. Inasmuch as tax rates were set by the central government, peasants saw little purpose in moving from one estate to another. The urban economy was too undeveloped to absorb an extensive unskilled work force; and a peasant who abandoned his land to move to town was taking a serious risk. For all these reasons, peasant flight was not a serious problem in the Ottoman Empire. Given the centralization of the system, a runaway was unlikely to improve his condition. The earliest decree that categorically prohibited peasant movement dates from the reign of Bayezid II (r. 1481–1512).

Many provisions of Ottoman legislation differentiate between re'aya and "free" peasants. Re'aya belonged to the sultan and lived either on timars or vakifs, while free peasants worked their own land and owed obligations only to the state, not to private landholders. Most peasants in the empire were re'aya. An imperial order listed the taxes and services they owed; and no one was entitled to impose any others. A landholder could lose his land if he contravened the regulations. Even for vakifs, which as charitable foundations were otherwise exempt from state interference, the central government set norms for peasant exploitation. Re'aya were usually exempt from corvée, except for such minor services as carrying the landholder's produce to market, reaping his meadow, and providing hospitality upon request. Sultan Mohammed II (r. 1451–81) issued a decree stating that peasants could be forced to work for their lords no more than seven days per year, and only three days if they had other obligations to the state. This restriction hardly injured the Ottoman timar holders, who in any case were too often absent on campaign to take much advantage of labor services. They preferred payment in cash or in kind.

In contrast to the timariots, the owners of private estates, or mülks, had a free hand in exploiting their peasants. Since the Ottoman sultans often made gifts of mülk estates to important persons for the express purpose of repopulating war-torn districts, the owners benefited from the government's policy of exiling people from other regions of the empire where their presence was considered superfluous. Chiefly this meant the removal of Turkish peasants from Anatolia into the fertile but devastated lands of the southeastern Balkans. Despite this practice, however, the chief source of labor on mülk lands was slavery. Usually the owner of a mülk was either a military officer who himself had carried away dozens of slaves as plunder or a high official who could afford to buy slaves at the market. Since slaves were not protected as re'aya and paid no taxes to the state, the government had no interest in them and the landholder could exploit them at will. Unlike re'aya, slaves were compelled to cultivate part of the landowner's personal land and give him half the produce. Even if freed from slavery they did not become re'aya, but remained legally subject to their former master and still paid taxes to him.

Altogether the situation of the Balkan peasants under Ottoman rule was certainly no worse, and probably somewhat better, than under the preceding Christian regimes. Decrees of the sultan set limitations on the taxes and services that could be demanded of peasants. The landholders might at times abuse their authority, but by the 15th century the central government was strong enough to enforce a considerable degree of control. Security was much improved, since internally the Ottoman Empire was at peace. Wars among local Balkan lords had ceased to devastate the land and ruin the peasants' crops. However, individual peasants were certainly no freer than before—probably less so, since the Ottoman government supervised them more efficiently than its Christian predecessors had done. Christianity was a tolerated religion, but Christians were second-class citizens. Since the majority of Balkan peasants did not adopt Islam, a great gap was opened between the Turkish rulers and most of their Balkan subjects.

In East Central Europe as a whole, most peasants saw their legal rights, social status, and material comforts deteriorate in the course of the 15th century. Compared to the position of nobles, clergy, or townspeople, their status was unenviable. Although far more numerous than the other classes in society, they lived in a basically rural environment which offered them few options. Altogether the peasantry is the great neglected element in medieval history. The surviving records have much to say about kings, nobles, and churchmen; but medieval chroniclers evinced little interest in the lives of the great rural majority. While the social pyramid rested on a peasant base, peasants themselves were regarded as important only on the rare occasions when they impinged upon great events. Owing to this class bias, our information about them is sadly fragmentary and incomplete.

CHAPTER 6

Towns and Townspeople

*B*oth the Western and the Eastern European types of town were represented in medieval East Central Europe, with the boundary between them following approximately the demarcation line dividing the Latin from the Greek Church. A town of the Western kind was subject to a legal regime very different from the one prevailing in surrounding areas. Its inhabitants by definition were free people; and the principle that "town air makes free" was generally respected. The activities most characteristic of urban life—artisan production and trade—were recognized as requiring very different conditions from those suitable for agriculturalists, warriors, or clerics. From the 13th century onward, the larger towns of Bohemia, Hungary, and Poland on the whole followed the Western model, receiving royal charters that spelled out their rights. On the other hand, the Eastern, or Byzantine type of town never acquired a similarly privileged status. It was subject to direct control by officials of a central government, who intervened on a regular basis in commercial and artisan life. No legal boundary divided town from countryside, since both were equally subject to state authority. This situation was typical of the towns of the Balkan Peninsula, except on the Adriatic littoral.

In the Middle Ages hardly any urban settlements could boast a population much greater than that of a modern small town. A large city by medieval standards contained 10,000 to 50,000 people. In the year 1500 only six European cities held over 100,000 inhabitants. Three of these lay in Italy—Naples, Venice, and Milan—while two others were located on the periphery of the continent—Istanbul and Moscow. Paris was the sixth. The largest city in the German Empire was Cologne, with 30,000 to 40,000 inhabitants. Prague and Lübeck each held perhaps 25,000 to 30,000. Even these modest figures represented a doubling of their populations of a century and a half earlier. On the whole, East Central Europe was much less urbanized than Western Europe. Gdańsk was the largest city in the region, owing to the Baltic wheat trade. Its population reached perhaps 30,000 toward the end of the 15th century (compared with 15,000 in 1400). Buda and Pest, which together formed the largest urban concentration in Hungary, may have held

22,000 to 25,000 people. Cracow, the capital of Poland, probably counted 10,000 inhabitants in the mid-14th century and 15,000 by 1500. Each of the principal towns of Transylvania—Cluj, Sibiu, and Braşov—probably had between 4,500 and 5,500 people in about 1450. No urban area in either Western or Eastern Europe in the medieval period compared even remotely in population with the great cities of the ancient world. Constantinople at its height in the 4th century held about 400,000 people, but had greatly declined since that time. On the other hand, even a smallish medieval town of 2,000 to 3,000 inhabitants assumed much greater importance in the economy of its region than far larger agglomerations do at present. Settlements of this size were significant centers of commerce, culture, and administration.

Medieval Latin documents use different words for the several types of urban settlement, although the terminology is far from consistent. The distinction often observed in English between "city" and "town," referring chiefly to size of population, did not apply. The word *civitas* in Latin (translatable as either "city" *or* "town") meant a fortified place surrounded by walls. Another type of town was called *oppidum*, a word perhaps best rendered as "country town," which designated an intermediate type between town and village. An oppidum was an unfortified settlement, differing from a village in enjoying certain legal privileges which villages did not, such as a charter of incorporation and its own mayor and jurors, who were permitted to decide legal cases. It served as a market-place and a center for locally oriented artisan activity, while retaining a pronounced agrarian character. In some cases an oppidum might be larger than a civitas. However, both types of town clearly differed from villages, which were purely agricultural settlements inhabited by peasants.

Medieval towns arose in a variety of ways. Some evolved from the artisan colonies adjacent to the court of a king, bishop, or lord. Others began as markets along well-traveled (often ancient) commercial routes. Communities of miners constituted a third type. A town had a life-style quite unlike that of its surrounding region, even though many town dwellers still kept gardens or tended vineyards. Many of the earliest medieval towns began as administrative centers. Subsequently they might attract enough artisans and merchants to become economically viable on their own. However, unless a settlement was favorably situated along convenient trade arteries, this was unlikely to happen. In the legal sense, a town originated when its inhabitants agreed by sworn oath to form a corporation (in Latin: *universitas*), which gave them a recognized status and enabled them more easily to defend their rights. If a place developed into something larger than a mere hamlet, it eventually required some type of market law for the conduct of its affairs. At first this mostly meant customary rules, which grew up naturally according to need. Then as towns became larger and more numerous, the norms had to be formalized. Finally, if the town was not to be taxed out of existence, control or interference by the local nobility had to be prevented. Towns of the

Western type achieved this independence when they began to govern themselves. The ruler of the territory guaranteed their rights by charter.

In the southern sector of East Central Europe, some medieval towns had been continuously inhabited since Roman or even Greek times. To be sure, the invasions of Goths, Slavs, Avars, and Bulgars in the 5th to 7th centuries had destroyed many such places and caused the abandonment of others. Most of the Greek towns in the eastern Balkans succumbed to the invaders. Nonetheless, this massive barbarian influx failed to ruin all of the urban centers. Walled settlements were often able to defend themselves successfully. On the Adriatic and Black Sea coasts and along the Danube River—the old imperial frontier—many ancient towns continued in existence despite severe impoverishment. Among them were Durrës, Shkodër, and Lezhë in Albania; Zadar, Trogir, and Budva in Dalmatia. Here Roman settlement had been more extensive than elsewhere in East Central Europe, owing to the importance of sea commerce and the establishment of Roman garrisons along the Danube. In Roman times such towns often had paved streets laid out in a regular pattern, water conduits and baths, marketplaces, temples, public monuments, and theaters where animal combats, gladiatorial contests, and races took place. Around the square or forum in the center of town stood a municipal hall or curia, a temple, and a courthouse. Roman houses were typically built of stone or brick, and outfitted with a heating system conveying hot air through hollow tiles located under the floor and inside the walls. Medieval towns did not approach this Roman standard.

The need for protection from barbarian enemies mandated the establishment of settlements in places well situated for defense. Since both Slavs and steppe horsemen were inexperienced navigators, the sea formed an effective barrier against attack. Zadar (Zara) was the only town in Dalmatia to survive the Slavic invasions, enabling it to retain its character as a Roman municipality well into the Middle Ages. Its location on a peninsula extending into the Adriatic rendered it easily defensible. Zadar's landward side consisted of an isthmus only 500 meters long, protected by a wall and towers. After the 7th-century Slavic onslaught on Dalmatia, new settlements were founded on some of the small rocky islands protruding above the water line along the coast, separated only by narrow channels from the mainland. Thus when invading Slavs captured the Roman town of Epidaurus, its surviving inhabitants moved to an island some ten miles away. This was the origin of Dubrovnik (Ragusa), subsequently the wealthiest and most influential trading town in Dalmatia. Later the original island became linked to the mainland, forming a peninsula. Survivors from Salona, a major Roman center destroyed by the Slavs in 614, sought safety nearby in Emperor Diocletian's well-fortified palace, which became the nucleus of the new town of Split. Kotor (Cattaro) and Bar (Antivari), south of Dubrovnik on the Gulf of Kotor, were founded shortly after the Slavic invasions on narrow stretches of land wedged in between the mountains and the sea.

The Slavs in the 6th and 7th centuries had little use for towns, which they called "walled tombs." Many of the places they captured became uninhabited and simply went to ruin. Later some of the old walled enclosures were put to use as fortresses; and certain formerly Roman towns came back to life as the centers of bishoprics. A number of modern settlements, of course, have grown up on the same favorable sites as Roman ones formerly, even if urban life there was not continuous. One such example is Plovdiv (Philippopolis) in Bulgaria, regarded in Roman times as "the most brilliant metropolis in Thrace." Perched on hills overlooking the Maritsa River, it commands the Thracian plain along the famous "diagonal" route from Belgrade to Constantinople. If the interval between decline and revival of a place was not too long, new towns on the old Roman sites often bore names which were Slavic or Albanian variants of the former Latin or Greek ones. Thus Scupi in Macedonia became Skopje; Naissus in Serbia became Niš (Nish). Serdica in Bulgaria held out against the barbarians until it was just a tiny settlement around the Greek Church of Holy Wisdom (*Sophia*), from which it takes its modern name of Sofia. Even today much of the Roman plan of Sofia survives, so that streets in the center of town run parallel to and sometimes above the old Roman ones. Where decades or centuries intervened before a town revived, the name changed altogether. Thus Odessos became Varna, Viminacium became Braničevo, Singidunum was reborn as Belgrade.

As the Byzantine government lost control of most of its Balkan territories during the 6th and 7th centuries, towns in peripheral regions were often left to their own devices. They developed a high degree of municipal autonomy which obliged their rulers to assume a dual civilian and military role. "Byzantine" Dalmatia was largely a fiction after the early 7th century. Recognizing this fact, the emperor in 998 appointed the doge of Venice as his official representative for the territory. The change made little practical difference to the towns, which continued to administer themselves. While nominally under Byzantine suzerainty, they maintained only slight contact with Constantinople. During the 11th century, elected officials called priors functioned as the chief authorities in most Dalmatian towns. The prior of Zadar, himself a member of the local upper class, served concurrently as governor of Byzantine Dalmatia. Although this position gave him the double function of local dignitary and imperial official, he ruled the town jointly with a council of respected citizens. Both the prior's functions and his formal relationship to Constantinople appear to have been only vaguely defined. Zadar's connection to the other Adriatic towns was equally loose.

In medieval Bulgaria most towns were of relatively recent origin, not continuous with old Roman settlements. Pliska, the first capital of the Bulgar state, was at first just a large walled camp set in the middle of a plain. After the Byzantines destroyed it in a war early in the 9th century, Khan Omurtag rebuilt it with imposing fortifications, a palace of massive stone blocks, and sanctuaries for the Bulgars' pagan religious observances. Preslav, which became Bulgaria's capital in 893 when the country turned Christian, contained stone palaces and fortifications which were even more impressive. Proclaiming the grandeur of the powerful Tsar Symeon, this city was graced by towers lining the approaches to the sovereign's palace and large buildings on either side of the street. Churches and residences at Preslav were decorated with murals or mosaics and embellished with marble, copper, silver, and gold. No European city outside the Byzantine Empire could pride itself on comparable splendor at so early a date. In addition, a number of Bulgar towns flourished around the mouths of the Danube. The Rus "Chronicle of Nestor" reports for the years 969–72 that the Kievan Prince Sviatoslav captured eighty towns on the lower Danube—doubtless an exaggeration, but nonetheless indicative of important urban activity in that locality. Sviatoslav himself declared that he preferred the town of Pereiaslavec on the Danube to his own capital of Kiev in Ukraine.

Dobrudja, the rectangle formed by the great bend of the Danube as it nears the Black Sea, was the site of important trading towns throughout the Middle Ages. One was Silistra (ancient Durostorum), which flourished in the 10th to 12th centuries, and which the traveler Idrisi described as "a town with markets overflowing, splendid town squares, wonderful and perfect buildings." Farther north lay Kilia (now extinct) on the northern branch of the Danube delta and Cetatea Alba (Belgorod) along the Dniester estuary, both important Byzantine possessions in the 13th and 14th centuries. Tirnovo, the capital of Bulgaria in the 14th century, was described by the Serbian monk Gregory Camblak as "a very large city, handsome and surrounded by walls," with a population of 12,000 to 15,000 persons. It stood on a splendid site on two hills separated by the Jantra River. Town life also revived along the eastern Adriatic in the 11th century. Split, Trogir, Zadar, and Dubrovnik attained considerable importance as trading ports where products from overseas were exchanged for those of the Dalmatian hinterland. By contrast, no important urban life existed in the interior of Serbia and Croatia prior to the 12th century. Towns in medieval Serbia generally consisted of only a market and a collection of wooden huts situated in the vicinity of a fortress—itself a primitive affair—which might serve as a refuge in times of danger. A similar situation prevailed in Bosnia, where the largest population centers were likewise little more than the extensions of fortresses. When the Roman Church in the 13th century wished to establish a bishop's see in Bosnia, not a single town existed in which to locate a cathedral.

Archaeological excavations on the territory of the Western Slavs have revealed the existence of urban settlements dating from as early as the 8th century. Mikulčice in Moravia, containing a prominent ducal residence with a stone palace and imposing basilica, was set on a fortified hill surrounded by suburbs. Staré Město in Moravia was similar in layout, whereas Nitra in Slovakia consisted of as many as four fortified centers set close together, with open settlements nearby. Szczecin (Stettin) and Wolin at the mouth of the Oder prospered in the 10th and 11th centuries from the Baltic trade as well as from the production of pottery and articles of metal and amber. Prior to the introduction of Christianity, both towns were noted for their elaborate pagan temples. A fortress was erected at Gniezno in western Poland as early as the end of the 9th century; and another already stood on the site of Cracow in the 10th century. By the first half of the 11th century, the Polish duke possessed sixty or seventy fortified settlements, each with at least one suburb inhabited by artisans.

Very few places deserving the name of "town" existed in Poland, Bohemia, or Hungary before the 11th century. Local chiefs ruling from fortified strongholds dominated groups of villages, while the overlord, whom the Latin sources often call *dux* ("duke"), possessed no fixed domicile. Instead he moved constantly among his various residences, which were actually primitive wooden fortresses. Consolidation of small political units into a rudimentary state led to the establishment of permanent or semipermanent settlements for the monarchs and their growing entourages. These centers, or "capitals," were usually located at places favorably situated for both communication and defense. The fortresses themselves were typically located on hilltops, protected by ramparts of wood and earth as much as 10 to 20 meters wide and about 10 meters high. Eloquently testifying to the ever-present danger of attack, their construction was a major undertaking. Even the maintenance of existing fortifications involved considerable effort and expense.

At first the population of many early towns consisted chiefly of the military men and serving people surrounding either a lay lord or a bishop. If the lord was an important person, the settlement soon attracted artisans to its suburbs and peasant settlers to its vicinity. If favorably located, such places sometimes developed into genuine trade centers. Such was the case with Prague, the chief residence of the duke of Bohemia, which was already an important town in the 10th century. Similarly Olomouc (Olmütz) and Brno (Brünn), where the Moravian margraves held court, had developed some commercial activity by the 11th century. Prior to the 13th century, such trading centers remained exceptional. Even in Bohemia, more urbanized than either Poland or Hungary, a so-called town (*urbs* or *civitas*) was usually little more than the seat of a royal official or a spiritual or lay lord. Sometimes the manor house of a large agricultural estate served as the nucleus of a small settlement, with a church, a peasant village, and a market, inn, tavern, or tollhouse. The court of a prince or bishop naturally attracted settlers on a larger scale, since craftsmen were always in demand to provide for the requirements of court personnel. Around or beneath the ruler's residence, suburbs populated by cobblers, armorers, cooks, bakers, and various other tradesmen grew up. Eventually these artisan settlements took on a life of their own as suppliers of products to the hinterland. Then they became enclosed by walls of earth and timber and began to look like real towns.

An urban center could only develop where sufficient and secure food supplies were available, which in most cases presupposed the existence of farming communities nearby. Reciprocally, peasant settlements which functioned as markets and suppliers of artisan goods grew up on the outskirts of towns. A village of this type (in Latin: *suburbium*) bore an ambiguous character. Closely tied to the town economically, it might be subject to the jurisdiction of a municipal court but pay rent to a territorial lord. A suburban village presented an expressly rural aspect, containing peasant houses and meadows, an extensive land area, and large cultivated surfaces. Its layout contrasted sharply with the narrow housing lots inside the walled towns. Originally such villages were purely agrarian communities of peasants, although urban dwellers gradually encroached upon them, buying up land for gardens. For the most part, only the smaller towns had links of this type with villages. Larger trading centers frequently did not, probably because they were located on navigable rivers or along a seacoast where they could import food by ship.

The discovery of important mineral deposits led to the founding of towns near the mines, often in otherwise inhospitable locations. Typically the inhabitants were German immigrants possessing the necessary technical expertise for extracting the ores. Everywhere in East Central Europe these miners were known as "Saxons," apparently because the laws which governed their settlements had been adapted from a mining code developed at Goslar in the Harz Mountains of Saxony. Intensive silver mining began in both Bohemia and Hungary in the 12th century. In the Bohemian kingdom the principal centers were at Jihlava (Iglau) and Kutná Hora (Kuttenberg). Mining activity in Hungary was concentrated in the mountains of Slovakia. There Banská Štiavnica (Schemnitz) already flourished in the 12th century as a center of silver extraction, while Banská Bystrica (Neusohl) specialized in copper. Kremnica (Kremnitz), founded in 1328, became the most important of all the Slovak mining towns by virtue of producing larger quantities of gold than any other locality in Europe. Transylvania too was rich in minerals. King Béla IV in the 13th century authorized German miners to erect towns and markets "beside the Cumans" in the Carpathian Mountains of eastern Transylvania, with the stipulation that they would prospect for gold and silver. In Poland several towns grew up near salt mines, particularly at Wieliczka and Bochnia near Cracow. In Pomerania along the Baltic coast, Kołobrzeg (Kolberg) owed much of its prosperity to salt springs nearby.

Mining in the Balkan Peninsula occurred chiefly in Serbia and Bosnia, where it dated back to Roman times. After long neglect, some of the old Roman mines were reopened in the 13th century. Just as in Bohemia or Hungary, the Balkan mining towns were populated largely by Germans, popularly known as "Saxons." Whether the Germans arrived on their own initiative or at the invitation of monarchs is not clear. In any event, a great efflorescence of mining activity occurred in both Serbia and Bosnia in the second half of the 14th century, precisely the period when metal production in Central Europe was in decline. The Saxon miners in the Balkans enjoyed a privileged legal status. The Serbian Despot Stephen Lazarević (r. 1389–1427), for example, granted them representation in the administration and law courts of their communities; decreed fixed prices on bread, meat, and artisan services; and guaranteed sufficient supplies for their work. These favors were not extended to the native inhabitants of the towns. Serbia's wealth in metals—derived chiefly from Novo Brdo in the Kosovo region and Srebrenica in eastern Bosnia—contributed enormously to the power of the state. Profits from Srebrenica's rich silver deposits financed the imperial conquests of Tsar Stephen Dušan in the 14th century. Inevitably, this silver-producing town became a pawn in the power politics of the region, fought over by Bosnia, Serbia, and Hungary. When conquering Serbia and Macedonia in the 15th century, the Turks hastened to seize Srebrenica and Novo Brdo before proceeding to subdue the rest of the country.

Except for mining settlements, very few new towns appeared in the interior of the Balkans during the medieval era. However, in northern East Central Europe urban growth was extensive in the late 12th–15th centuries, particularly the 13th. The earliest of these new towns were usually sponsored by the monarchs. Then in the 14th and 15th centuries many more were founded by spiritual and secular lords whose estates enjoyed immunity from royal taxation and justice. The conquest of Prussia by the Teutonic Knights in the 13th century also promoted town formation. The Knights secured each newly subjugated area by building fortresses in strategic spots, with the consequence that settlements of artisans and traders arose outside the fortress walls. At least at first, the Knights and the townsmen often behaved as allies. Both were conscious of their strongly German and Christian identity amid a foreign, half-barbarous, and pagan population.

In contrast to the haphazard arrangement of most older towns in East Central Europe, many of the new settlements which arose in the 12th and 13th centuries were laid out according to a plan. This was particularly true of the ones inhabited by foreign colonists. A typical new town was built around a central plaza, either square or rectangular in shape, from which streets led outward like the spokes of a wheel. The most important public buildings, such as the principal church, town hall, cloth hall, and various guild houses, were located around this plaza. Streets were narrow, not only for easier defense, but so that the largest number of houses could occupy the smallest possible space. Members of a single profession, guild, or nationality tended to live in a single street, or at least in the same section of town. Frequently the streets were named after the inhabitants, like "French Street," "Cobblers' Street," or "Candlemakers' Street." At first the streets were merely dirt tracks, but later might be covered with boards. East Central Europe lagged considerably behind the West in this respect. Whereas paved streets already existed in Italy in the 12th century and in the larger towns of Western Europe by the 15th, pavement was a rarity in Central Europe until the end of the Middle Ages. Even major towns like Cracow, Poznań (Posen), or Wrocław (Breslau) contained dirt streets, which in wet weather turned into bogs and during droughts became hard crusts, creating clouds of dust. Swine and cattle wandered about or were driven through the town on their way to pasture. After a rainfall, merely to cross over from one side of a street to the other became hazardous. Blocks of wood were sometimes set out to facilitate pedestrian traffic in wet weather. The filth can well be imagined.

Houses in urban locations initially were built of wood, creating the notorious propensity of medieval towns to catch fire. At a later date the better dwellings were often of stone or brick. To save space, town houses frequently contained two or even three stories, with the second floors of adjacent buildings connected by elevated covered bridges. Well-to-do townspeople decorated their walls and floors with colored rugs, which might even be embellished with silver and gold thread. They ate at tables with tablecloths and sat on benches, three-legged stools, or chairs. Their dishes were made of wood, which was often painted in various colors, while drinking cups might be of glass, wood, or pewter. For lighting, the patricians used wax candles in chandeliers or lanterns; humbler people used torches or resinous wood. In both rich and poor households, precious objects were kept in wooden chests or in sacks decorated with embroidery. In the Muslim quarters of Balkan towns, houses were built of heavy stones. They faced inward toward a courtyard, which might also be surrounded by walls. The outsides of Muslim houses were usually simple and severe in style, the interiors typically rich and colorful.

Military considerations were paramount in the placement and layout of medieval towns. Owing to the superiority of high ground for defense, settlements were often situated on fairly inaccessible high plateaus or hills, sometimes beside the bend of a river. The advantage of the site was then enhanced by surrounding the town with walls which originally were constructed of wood or earth, and only later of stone. The concept of "town" was so closely associated with the idea of defense that in many languages the word for "town" is derived from "fortress," like the Serbian *grad*, Polish *gród*, Hungarian *város*. As early as the 7th or 8th century, the limestone bluffs above the Vistula River on the site of Cracow were surrounded by embankments built of wood, stone, and earth. By the late 14th century, Cracow was completely encircled by stone walls averaging ten meters in height and strengthened by a series of towers, fourteen of which have been identified. Pliska, Bulgaria's earliest capital, was a military camp enclosed by two concentric circles of defenses—the inner one a wooden palisade, the outer one made of earth. After a Byzantine army destroyed Pliska in 811, its walls were rebuilt in stone. In 11th-century Albania the walls of Durrës (Durazzo) were so wide that four horsemen could ride abreast on top, while towers eleven feet high enhanced its security still further. However, most towns in the Balkan interior were too impoverished to build solid fortifications, and at best could erect only wooden palisades. Travelers from Western Europe rarely failed to notice the absence of walls around Balkan towns.

Strong monarchs generally promoted town fortification as a means of national defense despite the danger of feudal separatism which this entailed. The Mongol invasion of Europe in 1241 had proved that only castles with powerful stone walls could resist the onslaught of the formidable steppe warriors. Hungary had borne the brunt of the Mongol attack, losing a large proportion of its inhabitants in the process. King Béla IV, whose policy until that time had been to diminish the nobles' power and privileges, afterward actively encouraged them to build fortifications. Castles and walled towns offered the only hope of resisting a future incursion from the steppe. Near the spot where the Mongols had crossed the Danube, citizens of Pest established a new town directly across the river on the high hills of Buda. This favorable natural location was soon strengthened further with walls, towers, and moats. In the 1260s a similar quest for security impelled the population of Zagreb in Croatia to move to a high hill nearby and fortify the site. Entrance into a town situated in this way was possible only through gates which were permanently guarded and closed at night.

Unless the defenders were either negligent or pitifully few in number, a well-fortified town on a hill was virtually impregnable until the age of gunpowder. In some cases its walls were strengthened by towers for additional protection. Often the inner town, or citadel, was located at a spot difficult of access, usually a high hill or cliff. Within this enclosed space stood the residence of the lord, the cathedral (if the town was a bishop's seat), and the homes of privileged citizens. The middle and lower classes lived in the outer town below, which frequently was surrounded by another wall. Private buildings often became part of this defense system. The market was located in front of the town gate, since security considerations prevented its being held within the town itself. The proximity of the wall gave the tradespeople some protection. An important gate might be defended by a second gate or bastion with a trench alongside. This was an Arab invention known as a barbican, introduced into Europe by soldiers returning from the Crusades in the Holy Land. However, after the Ottoman conquest the towns of the Balkan Peninsula frequently lost their fortifications. The size of the Ottoman Empire meant that places located far from the frontier did not fear foreign attack, and defense became irrelevant. As a consequence, the Turks razed some of the existing fortifications in the Balkans and allowed others to fall to ruin. In many cases they resettled people from relatively inaccessible sites onto the plains, in order to have them nearer the communication routes.

The towns often developed sufficient military power to make them a factor in local struggles. Armed citizens' organizations sometimes fought the troops of the local bishop or joined one of the factions vying for power at the national level. For example, the towns of Dobrudja, located along the mouths of the Danube or the Black Sea coast, constituted the first line of defense against marauders from the steppes. After Byzantine control was reestablished there in the late 10th century, citizens of these towns played an important role in protecting the empire. In the 1060s and 1070s Pechenegs, Iazygs, and Cumans from southern Ukraine launched attacks along the lower Danube. Finding that imperial officials supplied little help, the towns of Dobrudja formed a league and rebelled against Byzantine overlordship. This organization survived from 1072 to 1094, until the revived Byzantine government under Emperor Alexius I Comnenus reestablished imperial control over Dobrudja in a series of difficult campaigns. The defensive role of these towns declined in the 12th century, owing in part to the reduced threat from the steppe.

From a military standpoint the safest town in medieval East Central Europe was probably Dubrovnik, which was never conquered despite a series of attempts. Situated on a rocky peninsula projecting into the sea, and protected on the land side by mountains as well as by walls and moats, Dubrovnik could neither be taken by assault nor starved into surrender, since its navy could always provide supplies. Various Serbian rulers in the 12th to 14th centuries sought to acquire the town, but without success. At times Venice conducted naval warfare against it, until in 1444 Venice, Aragon, the pope, and the German emperor recognized its neutrality by international agreement. Soon thereafter, Ottoman contingents appeared along the Adriatic. Dubrovnik reinforced its defenses in preparation for the expected assault, but none occurred. The Turks made no effort to conquer this town, but demanded instead the payment of a sizable tribute, which undoubtedly profited them more. Dubrovnik remained immune from enemy attack during the next three and a half centuries, until the appearance of Napoleon's army in 1805.

From a monarch's vantage point, a town was first and foremost a source of tax revenue. Towns depended on trade; and as the royal lands inevitably decreased in size over time (owing to the political imperative of granting estates to faithful followers), rulers became increasingly dependent on the income derived from market tolls, customs duties, and coinage. In any case, long distance commerce and mining created riches far exceeding the revenue to be gained merely by taxing peasants or lords. Mining towns were much fought over, since their silver and gold could be used directly as money. Townsmen might also be useful to a monarch for their financial expertise—a field in which nobles were usually incompetent. Typically the kings employed town merchants or bankers to handle their financial affairs. Dubrovnik's independent status even allowed it to provide asylum for princes and nobles in political difficulty at home. The rulers of the town successfully resisted foreign pressure to have them extradited. Furthermore, Dubrovnik functioned as a safe repository of treasure for foreigners. The Serbian Despot George Branković, whose throne was seriously threatened by the Ottoman advance in the 15th century, deposited large sums at Dubrovnik for safekeeping. Many lesser Serbian nobles did likewise, protecting themselves against future contingencies which might oblige them to flee.

Finally, towns served as sources of prestige for a kingdom, particularly if they were noted for fine buildings and an active cultural life. King Ottokar II of Bohemia (r. 1253–78) enlarged his capital of Prague by laying out a new district, the so-called Small Side, along the Moldau (Vltava) River. Prague "New Town" was founded on the direct initiative of King Charles I (r. 1346–78), who pursued a policy distinctly favorable to the urban classes. He fostered economic development by enhancing security in the Prague streets, improving roads and bridges, and granting commercial privileges. This able and enlightened monarch, who as Charles IV was also German emperor, sought to make his capital the grandest city of the empire. At Prague he founded the first university in Central Europe and sponsored many projects to beautify its public spaces. Particularly noteworthy are Saint Vitus Cathedral on the castle hill overlooking the city and the exquisite Charles Bridge across the Moldau, both of which still stand.

Admittedly, the towns of East Central Europe—even those of the Western type—never attained the independent status typical of their counterparts in Western Europe. The latter were sometimes so powerful that sovereigns could use them as counterweights to the landed nobility. This did not occur in East Central Europe. Nonetheless, monarchs jealously guarded their right to erect new towns, most of which were established on royal land. Only unwillingly did they authorize the foundation of urban settlements on property belonging to the Church or the nobility. In Bohemia, for example, no one but the ruler could grant a town the rank of *civitas* and authorize it to hold a market or build an enclosing wall. Individual lords usually received such privileges only when the central authority was weak; and if possible the sovereign afterward withdrew his permission. Historical records furnish many examples of monarchs who attempted to take over private markets and towns, frequently with success. The reverse process also occurred. Sometimes a ruler attempted to raise money or purchase political support by selling one of his royal towns to a private lord.

The process of founding new towns, termed "location" (*locatio* in Latin), was carried out by authorized agents of the territorial rulers known as "locators." These were the men who persuaded foreign townsmen to migrate eastward and handled the practical arrangements. The method was similar to that which brought peasants to settle in new villages and open up virgin agricultural lands. The locators roamed far afield in Germany and Flanders, offering inducements to merchants and artisans to immigrate. Location might involve either the establishment of a new town or a change in the status of an old one. A key attraction was the promise of German law, which included rights of municipal self-government and judicial authority, together with a set number of years of tax freedom. If enough people with German-law privileges settled in an already established community, this law was extended to all residents within the town's boundaries, whether German or not. Thus natives and foreigners benefited alike. In some cases, however, location privileges specifically excluded the native element. For example, the Polish Duke Boleslav V in the 13th century expressly instructed his locators not to admit any more Poles into Cracow. His purpose was naturally not to promote Germanization but to avoid angering the lords of the neighborhood by drawing taxpaying tenants away from their native villages. Reportedly his instructions on this matter were not strictly observed, however.

If a town was established on entirely new ground, the locator conducted immigrants to the site and laid out a town square and streets. For himself he reserved a generous grant of land and the right to retain a portion of the municipal taxes. Usually he became the town's chief official, a combined mayor and judge with hereditary rights to his office. The overlord of the town was his direct superior. If several entrepreneurs had shared in establishing a town, it might have several such officials. However, only a minority of "locations" produced completely new settlements where none had existed before. Foundations on new ground generally required the clearing of virgin forests, which the Teutonic Knights undertook on a large scale in the wilderness of Prussia. More typically, "location" simply meant establishing a new community on the outskirts of an old one, giving rise to innumerable places named either "Old Town" or "New Town." The "New Town" might receive German law, while the adjacent older center remained subject to the customary law of the land. If a citadel, cathedral, or fort which was crucial to a town's well-being already existed, the establishment of a "New Town" might not be feasible. In such cases German law might be granted to only a portion of the older settlement. Finally, "location" might denote the act of removing a town from the direct administration of the territorial lord and placing it under a new jurisdiction, which typically meant German law.

Municipal autonomy was a powerful incentive to the development of new towns. Monarchs could not, of course, evoke the economic conditions necessary to make a settlement flourish. But they could provide a propitious atmosphere—personal freedom for the inhabitants, the right to transfer and inherit property freely, and a considerable degree of local self-government. Political autonomy was greatly preferable to domination by a territorial lord, who usually had little comprehension of the conditions required to make commerce flourish. The profit-oriented and unwarlike mentality of the urban commercial classes was far removed from the military spirit of the typical king or noble, who drew his income from tolls, taxes, and the agricultural labor of serfs but understood little or nothing of handicraft production or trade. Monarchs as well as lesser territorial lords despised merchants and artisans as social inferiors and regarded towns primarily as sources of revenue. Unless prevented, they tended to ruin the towns with taxation. On the other hand, certain conditions were indispensable for commerce to flourish, such as laws regulating the enforcement of contracts, collection of debts, protection of goods in transit, and the safe transfer of funds. Townsmen placed a high value on self-government precisely in order to avoid interference with their means of livelihood. To ensure that excessive taxation would not strangle trade, they preferred to pay a fixed sum in taxes to the monarch and then allocate the burden among themselves.

Grants of autonomy to the royal free towns did not emancipate them entirely from the monarch's authority. Not all municipal charters included rights of jurisdiction over capital crimes (high justice), which might have to be judged by royal officials, although usually the elected town magistrates could judge lesser crimes (low justice). Townsmen continued to bear a heavy tax burden. However, the earlier, unpredictable financial exactions now became fixed, permitting a greater rationalization of economic activity. The ruler no longer demanded "extraordinary" taxes. Ultimately, the restriction of German law just to new towns proved impossible to maintain; and this law had to be granted to many older places as well. Finally, the attractive force of the royal free towns often obliged landed magnates to grant analogous rights to the settlements on their own private estates. Occasionally a private town became quite prosperous, like Debrecen in Hungary, although most such places lagged far behind the royal foundations in economic vitality. Legally they were also less autonomous, since the overlord with his appointed officials held the lion's share of the authority, while the citizens lacked the right of appeal to the king. No matter how privileged such a town might be, its inhabitants were legally the lord's serfs.

The towns of Prussia received their charters of rights from the grand master of the Teutonic Order of Knights, who regulated their commerce as well as the admission of foreigners. Nevertheless, they prospered from the Baltic trade and became quite autonomous in practice. Representatives of the Prussian towns met together regularly at the port city of Gdańsk (Danzig) or the grand master's own capital at Malbork (Marienburg), despite the Order's disapproval. After 1370 such meetings were held nearly every year. Six of the most prosperous towns—including Gdańsk, Elbląg, Toruń, and Chełmno—joined the Hanseatic League, thereby establishing an ongoing link with the leading towns of northern Europe in an association for mutual protection and economic advancement. The Prussian towns at times conducted hostilities against foreign states with which the Teutonic Order was at peace, or acted as a neutral power in negotiations between the Order and Lithuania.

The grant of German law to a town did not necessarily mean that its population was ethnically German, but merely that it enjoyed approximately the same legal rights as the free towns in Germany itself. Slavic, Magyar, and Vlach settlements also received this law. However, the means by which town law was acquired were not everywhere identical. Municipal autonomy in Western Europe had developed gradually, whereas in East Central Europe it arrived later and in finished form. The towns of Poland, Bohemia, or Hungary did not win their rights in a struggle against territorial lords, but usually as free grants. They obtained German law because the monarchs found this a useful way to promote town development, whereas the customary law of the land took no account of the special features of urban life. Disputes over commercial issues were better left to town judges who understood them than to noble judges who did not. However, this reception of German law as the sovereign's gift certainly had its effect in producing the typically passive attitude of the townsmen in East Central Europe toward royal power. Except for Dubrovnik and Gdańsk, no municipalities in this region became independent republics comparable to some of the towns of Italy or Flanders or to Hamburg, Lübeck, and Bremen in Germany.

Mining towns, however, possessed special privileges even beyond the ordinary ones granted to towns. These included far-reaching rights of self-government, a separate legal regime, and independent municipal courts. In the Balkans, where the inhabitants of such towns were largely Catholic in a region overwhelmingly Orthodox, they were permitted to hold Catholic worship services. Fundamental to the existence of mining towns was the right to exploit local ore deposits, together with an exemption from most taxes and from military service. Occasionally the town received other favors, such as freedom from customs duties and permission to utilize the local woods, waters, and roads. These privileges were so profitable that in order to retain them, town governments sometimes forced their citizens to contribute to the maintenance of mines in which the ores had become exhausted. In general, the work of opening and operating the mines was undertaken by societies of entrepreneurs capable of supplying the indispensable technical expertise. Sovereigns found it necessary to grant extensive rights to these private investors in order to assure themselves of sufficient gold and silver for monetary purposes. The metal was directly transformed into coinage in the mining centers. (When silver or gold was discovered on privately owned land, the monarchs often simply confiscated the property.) The miner's trade was highly esteemed in medieval society, probably because of its connection with money. Miners considered themselves socially superior to the practitioners of other crafts.

Even in privileged towns not all inhabitants enjoyed equal status. The term "citizen" applied for the most part only to established merchants and artisans, while the majority of poor urban dwellers, such as ordinary laborers or servants, were simply "inhabitants." The citizens of a town usually bore extra obligations as well as rights. For instance, at Braşov (Kronstadt) in Transylvania any citizen who refused an elective office paid a penalty in cash. The right to be a witness in court was likewise limited to citizens, probably because this involved a financial guarantee. Citizenship was hereditary, and its acquisition by outsiders was a complex process. In Poland a person who desired this status had to pay a fee and present documents to the town council testifying to his legitimate birth, upright moral character, and permanent residence in the town. (However, the king could confer legitimacy if this was in question.) Unmarried persons either had to marry within a year or purchase a town house. Provisions of this type naturally favored wealthy aspirants and made citizenship difficult to obtain for new arrivals from the villages. Finally, the candidate had to be Catholic, which excluded persons of Orthodox or Jewish faith unless they changed their religion. In the 15th century the adherents of Hussitism—a pernicious heresy in the eyes of the Polish church—were required first to renounce their errors. These restrictions aside, citizenship was well worth having, because it conferred important rights. Only citizens could become artisans, belong to a guild, engage in trade, or hold office in the town government.

Nobles and clerics, regardless of their place of residence, were not considered citizens of a town unless they specifically accepted its jurisdiction and received municipal rights accordingly. Nobles sometimes took this step when they bought or inherited property in town, perhaps because (at least in Hungary) the law of the realm specified that nobles were obliged to use the town courts in disputes over such property. Otherwise they were subject only to the general law of the land, whereas clergy were answerable to the ecclesiastical courts. Members of both groups were exempt from municipal taxes, even if they held extensive urban properties. Occasionally the local authorities tried to prevent nobles from buying land in a town, but usually without much success, since residence near the court of a king, bishop, or high royal official could be very advantageous. For the nobility such a town provided valuable contacts and social opportunities, whereas merchants and artisans saw it as a possible place to sell their goods. In any case, whether the resident nobles held citizenship or not, their social standing gave them a strong influence on a town's culture and life-style.

In the towns of Bohemia, Poland, and Hungary the most prestigious citizens were usually merchants, particularly those engaged in long-distance trade. Affluent businessmen formed a patrician class; and the government of the town was ordinarily in their hands. Their numbers were constantly augmented by immigration from Western Europe, primarily from Germany. Patricians often disposed of considerable wealth, lived in fine houses, and patronized education and culture. In some cases they were forced to share their monopoly of local administration by admitting some of the lesser merchants or the more successful artisans to the town council. Artisans were nearly always less well-off than merchants, and in many towns bitter struggles over control of local government erupted between the two groups. To resolve this conflict, King Casimir III of Poland in 1368 issued a decree that half the Cracow town council must be composed of merchants and the other half of artisans. Economic conflicts were frequently aggravated by nationalist or religious tensions, since so many of the patricians were ethnic Germans. This was particularly true of Bohemia in the early 15th century, when middle-class Czech Hussites in Prague created their own organs of national leadership and displaced the heavily German patriciate. Thereby the Germans lost much of their former political influence, and many of them fled abroad.

The attitude of merchant patricians toward the landed nobility was a mixture compounded of fear, antagonism, and envy. Even the relatively secure royal towns feared the territorial lords who ruled the surrounding countryside, controlled significant military power, and aspired to appropriate the town's wealth for themselves. As members of a superior social class, nobles possessed status and privileges. An impecunious and illiterate nobleman outranked even the richest and most cultivated bourgeois gentleman. One consequence of this situation was that well-to-do townsmen did their best to imitate the tastes and manners of the nobility. They enjoyed giving themselves noble airs, for instance by joining social organizations modeled on the associations of knights. Marriages between poor nobles and the daughters of wealthy townsmen were not uncommon. Merchants frequently strove to enter the noble class by purchasing landed estates or marrying into noble families. Some succeeded and changed their life-styles accordingly, since business activity was considered degrading for members of the nobility.

In the Balkan towns, which were generally of the Byzantine type except on the Adriatic coast, merchants and artisans were significantly less independent than in the West. The monarch supervised and regulated all commercial activity, while large artisan shops were state property. In towns of this kind the patrician class consisted not of middle-class merchants, but of nobles, high churchmen, and important state officials. The central government appointed the chief officials— governor, judge, and notary—although in certain privileged towns the leading citizens were allowed to participate in deliberations of the law courts. Power at the local level rested almost wholly with the landed aristocracy, which restricted access to leadership to men of its own class. In Moldavia (just as in Muscovy) the sovereign himself was the richest merchant in the country, monopolizing the trade in wax, honey, expensive furs, gold, silver, and thoroughbred horses. He held priority in the purchase of any imported wares. The right to build mills belonged not to locator-entrepreneurs or mayors of towns, but to nobles or monasteries. In Bulgaria the town patriciate in the 13th and 14th centuries consisted largely of boyars, high military or civil officials, and prelates. Men of this class held economic power in both town and countryside, using their serfs in the stores and workshops which they owned in town as well as on rural estates. Even if the patriciate included a few nonnoble merchants, the main economic and political power belonged to noble lords. In Transylvania (eastern Hungary) some of the towns initially showed a mixture of Western and Byzantine traits. An example is Braşov, where some of the patricians were lesser nobles who continued to control outlying villages. However, even in Transylvania most towns had begun to resemble their Western counterparts by the final third of the 14th century. The upper class consisted of merchants and financiers, whereas the older noble families had either died out or withdrawn to the countryside. In their place came new German merchants, who rarely bought villages or married into noble houses.

Town handicraftsmen produced a variety of finished articles, either for sale in their own shops or for local merchants to sell abroad. Their activities were organized in much the same way as in Western Europe. Apprentices came to live and work with a master in their trade for a certain number of years, as specified in a written contract. The master provided them with room, board, and clothing; and at the end of the period of service he paid them an agreed sum of money. Examples of early apprenticeship contracts have survived from Dubrovnik, and are probably fairly typical of those in force elsewhere. An apprentice at Dubrovnik was usually between ages nine and thirteen when he began service with a master, and remained with him for three to four years. Both boys and girls could become apprentices, although boys did so far more often. Girls were most likely to be trained in spinning wool, a trade monopolized by women. The apprentice's hours of work were virtually unlimited; indeed, most

contracts specified that he or she would work "day and night." After completing
the appropriate training, a young craftsman (now a journeyman) might either
remain with the old master or join another, who would provide a loan and a
place to work in exchange for a promise to remain with him for one to three
years. Persons over age eighteen sometimes served under shorter apprenticeship
contracts. Conversely, they might arrange to work for a master for a fixed wage
while learning the trade.

As town artisans became more numerous and more market oriented, they
organized themselves into craft guilds. Examples stood ready to hand in the
Balkans, since guilds with elaborate rules had existed for centuries in the towns
of the Byzantine Empire. Similarly, the artisan guilds which appeared in Germany
in the 12th century provided a model for the organizations that arose somewhat
later among the heavily German artisan class of Poland, Bohemia, and Hungary.
Persons engaged in virtually every conceivable occupation belonged to guilds; and
town authorities generally respected the independence of these organizations.
The guilds laid down strict specifications for each type of product, with no
changes allowed. The price of each article was firmly fixed. Leaders of the
guild upheld its regulations, punished violators, and settled disputes among the
members. Guilds also functioned as religious brotherhoods, social organizations,
welfare societies, and as citizen militias to aid in the town's defense. On public
occasions the members marched in solemn procession through the streets. The
number of guilds in any locality naturally varied according to population. In
smaller towns all artisans might belong to a single guild, whereas in larger
places each craft specialty had its own organization. The oligarchic structure
of the guilds resembled that of many town governments. Only masters of a
trade who maintained independent workshops could participate in the ruling
assemblies of their guild, vote for guild elders, or join in decision making,
although everyone in that guild's line of work was obliged to belong to the
association.

The ethnic composition of towns was often very mixed. Despite the absence
of reliable statistics, it is clear that native speakers of German constituted a high
proportion of the urban dwellers in medieval Poland, Bohemia, and Hungary.
Many came originally from the eastern borderlands of Silesia or Brandenburg—
areas of mixed German-Slavic population which were geographically not too
distant. The "Saxon" miners whose presence is recorded in Bosnia and Serbia
from the mid-13th century onward typically had resided earlier in the mining
regions of Slovakia. Since urban development had occurred earlier in Germany
than farther east, enterprising German miners or merchants frequently regarded
the embryonic towns of Bohemia, Poland, or Hungary as rich fields of opportunity. The German element was particularly strong in Bohemia, but dominant
likewise in the towns of Pomerania, Silesia, and Carniola (Slovenia) and highly
prominent in those of Great Poland, Little Poland, and the mining regions of

Serbia and Bulgaria. Other ethnic groups were represented to a lesser extent—especially Flemings, Frenchmen, and Italians.

Native-born merchants in the towns of East Central Europe could not easily compete with the men of foreign origin, who were usually more experienced in the techniques of large-scale production and long-distance trade. Frequently the newcomers possessed considerable investment capital and international contacts. Mining in particular required extensive investment, for which foreign capital was essential. Firms of bankers and merchants in Germany maintained close ties with colleagues farther east. The Fuggers of Augsburg, for example, formed a close partnership with the Thurzó family in Hungary and kept permanent representatives in Buda. Under the so-called German law, settlers of foreign origin enjoyed privileges of self-government which were not always granted to natives of the country. Moreover, as members of the propertied class, foreigners tended to dominate the town governments. Municipal record books which list the names of citizens (i.e., persons with political rights) tell the tale. From the 13th until the mid-15th century, ethnic Germans owned most of the wealth and dominated the patrician class of Prague, Cracow, Buda, and Cluj. Among the urban lower classes the proportion of natives was certainly much higher, although even approximate figures would be mere guesswork. Medieval town books rarely recorded the names of the humbler artisans, common laborers, or servants who lacked rights of citizenship. Many such people were undoubtedly peasant immigrants from the surrounding villages.

Other foreigners besides Germans played major roles in certain municipalities of East Central Europe. A massive immigration of Frenchmen resulted from the king of France's journey through Hungary en route to the Second Crusade in the mid-12th century. This produced "Latin" quarters in the suburbs of what were then the two chief Hungarian towns—Esztergom (Gran) and Székesfehérvár (Stuhlweissenburg). Farther south the Dalmatian littoral was home to many Italians as well as Latin speakers—cultural heirs of the ancient Romans. In the towns of Macedonia or Bulgaria the predominant foreign element was Greek, especially south of the Balkan (Stara Planina) Mountains and along the Black Sea coast. Following the Ottoman conquests in the Balkan Peninsula, Turks from Anatolia settled in various towns of that region, giving them an Oriental appearance. Armenians were numerous in some places in Poland-Lithuania; and Jews were present in towns virtually everywhere in East Central Europe. Important Jewish communities existed in Bohemia, Poland, and Hungary as early as the 12th century, and were greatly augmented in the 13th and 14th centuries. In contrast to other immigrant groups, which included both townsmen and peasants, the Jews were almost exclusively town dwellers. Barred from associating with Christians in the regular municipal governments, they developed their own form of self-administration called the "kahal," composed of an elected council of elders headed by a rabbi. The kahal allocated and collected the taxes which municipal authorities demanded from the Jews; and it handled the community's internal affairs. Disputes with Christians were settled by a representative of the monarch.

In the towns the Jews were treated as a separate group; and a variety of special restrictions applied to them. Forbidden to hold landed estates, and usually excluded from the artisan guilds, they developed compensating skills in commerce. Some Jews became moneylenders, a field in which open Christian competition was lacking, since the medieval Church condemned "usury" as sinful. In the underdeveloped economies of East Central Europe, the Jews' financial expertise was very welcome, inducing many monarchs to encourage Jewish immigration. A number of kings and lords protected the Jews, borrowed money from them, or employed them as tax collectors. A distinct Jewish quarter grew up in many medieval towns, which often contained a "Jews' Street." As early as the 11th and 12th centuries in Prague, an autonomous Jewish community flourished near the royal castle of Vyšehrad, governed according to Jewish law and taxed directly by the ruling duke.

The tendency of Jews to inhabit a particular section of town, while common, was also voluntary in medieval East Central Europe. Segregation provided safety in numbers against the violence sometimes perpetrated on Jews by Christians. Whenever popular emotions were aroused, Jews proved vulnerable to mob attack. This was demonstrated in Bohemia, for example, by the outbreaks against Jews during the Crusades and during the Mongol invasion of Europe in 1241 (which came dangerously close to striking at Bohemia). However, nowhere in East Central Europe were Jews required to live in closed ghettos until nearly the end of the 15th century. In many towns the houses of Christians and Jews stood side by side. An early instance of compulsory resettlement of Jews occurred in Cracow in 1494, when the looting of the Jewish quarter after a fire led the municipal authorities to relocate its residents to a tract of open land on the outskirts of town. The new suburb was named "Kazimierz" in memory of King Casimir III (r. 1333–70), who had been a notable friend of the Jews. Walls were built around the new settlement to create a segregated enclosure. Subsequently many other communities in Poland forced their Jews to move to a certain street or designated district. These ghettos were often surrounded by walls to reduce as far as possible the contacts of Jews with Christians.

Muslim townsmen were fairly uncommon in East Central Europe prior to the Ottoman period, although in some places a few Islamic merchants were in evidence. In the 12th century in Hungary, Muslims were permitted to reside only in towns containing a bishop's residence—a measure doubtless intended to keep them under surveillance. Pest was largely a "Saracen" town until the 1230s, when pressure from the Church forced the Muslims to withdraw and Germans took their places. Soon after the Ottoman conquests a process of Islamization began in many parts of the Balkan Peninsula, at first mainly through the influx of Turkish soldiers and artisans supplying the army. Newly fortified Ottoman towns, like Elbasan in Albania, acquired a large population of Turkish soldiers and other immigrants from Anatolia. At Skopje in Macedonia, captured by the Ottomans in 1391–92, Muslims comprised about three-fifths of the population in 1450. A century later the proportion was over four-fifths. This increase was only partly due to immigration, since some of the Muslims were converts from Christianity. The commercial and military centers of the Balkans in particular tended to have Muslim inhabitants by the middle of the 15th century, with the percentage increasing down to the end of the 16th century.

An important distinguishing feature in the life of Western style towns was political autonomy, which meant self-government, a separate judiciary, and freedom from the interference of royal officials except in specified circumstances. Admittedly, this autonomy was everywhere a matter of degree. Even within a single region no uniform set of privileges applied to all towns. Each one made its own arrangements with the monarch and received a separate charter of privileges. However, in royal free towns the economically dominant merchant class was permitted to establish local governments and courts sympathetic to its interests, thus avoiding the state courts which generally favored the nobility. Town autonomy also encouraged an independent spirit on the part of the citizen class. In sharp contrast, self-government did not exist at all in the towns of the Byzantine Empire. While many Byzantine towns prospered economically, the ever-present imperial officials treated the business class as an adjunct to state policy.

The earliest examples of municipal autonomy in East Central Europe occurred in Dalmatia, where both geography and history favored urban development. The towns of the Adriatic coast grew wealthy from maritime trade, which financed not only their military defense but also the tribute which neighboring powers often demanded as the price of leaving them in peace. Affluence and autonomy went hand in hand. Politically the most independent as well as the richest of the Dalmatian towns was Dubrovnik, which conducted an extensive sea commerce and also maintained close connections with the Balkan hinterland. For a long time the nominal overlord of Dalmatia, Byzantium, was militarily too weak to exercise direct authority there. The towns' obligations to Constantinople—which indeed gave them very inadequate military protection—were probably limited to paying an annual tribute and providing occasional naval assistance. In domestic matters the Dalmatian towns were self-governing. Left essentially to their own devices, they developed into oligarchic commercial republics.

After the millennial year 1000, it was rare that any single government controlled all of the Dalmatian towns. Hungarian suzerainty over Zadar, Šibenik, Trogir, and Split—a consequence of the union with Croatia—survived with occasional interruptions from the 12th until the 15th century. This hegemony scarcely affected local liberties. Dalmatia was the farthest outpost of Hungary's power to the south; and the Hungarian king was well aware that the ruling oligarchies of the merchant towns would resent any infringement of their accustomed freedoms.

The letter of privilege which King Koloman granted to Trogir (Trau) in 1108 served as a model for the other Dalmatian towns in Hungarian possession. Koloman promised to limit his financial demands on Trogir to two-thirds of its customs revenue and to collect no other taxes. He would appoint a bishop for the town only in accordance with the wishes of clergy and people, although a royal count would reside there as his personal representative. Citizens of the town would be entitled to trade freely throughout the Hungarian kingdom and emigrate freely with all their goods. Juridically they would be answerable to the town court and to none other. If the king in person chose to visit Trogir, hospitality for him and his entourage would be voluntary. These privileges greatly surpassed any which the royal towns in Hungary itself enjoyed at that time.

Hungary's major competitor for control of Dalmatia was Venice. This formerly minor city-state set amid the lagoons of northeastern Italy had become a commercial and naval power of pan-European importance by the 13th century. The Dalmatian towns lay on her very doorstep, not only as trade rivals, but as strategic danger points if they fell into hostile hands. Whenever the Venetians controlled one of the Adriatic towns, they severely restricted local autonomy but did not altogether destroy it. They insisted on acting as middlemen for the buying and selling of goods in Dalmatia, prohibiting the towns from dealing directly with foreign merchants or even with each other. This mercantilist system, while never fully enforced, ensured that the Dalmatian towns could not undersell Venetian wares. In each town a count was appointed to look after Venice's interests; and the formidable Venetian fleet reinforced his authority. The count presided over an elected municipal council, managed the judiciary, and took charge of military affairs. Decisions of the town council required his approval. In 1358, after three wars with Venice, Hungary gained at least nominal ascendancy over the entire Dalmatian coast from Rijeka (Fiume) to Durrës. Then in the 1420s the Venetians returned, this time to exercise a more permanent hegemony over Dalmatia. Trade restrictions became tighter, while the commerce of the towns declined significantly. Dubrovnik alone escaped the Venetian stranglehold by remaining under nominal Hungarian suzerainty.

Despite the overlordship of Byzantium, Hungary, Venice, or Serbia, a fairly high level of political autonomy prevailed even in the smaller towns of Dalmatia. At Kotor, for example, which was Serbia's major port, popular assemblies dominated local government in the 13th century, while a more aristocratic regime prevailed in the 14th. Either way the town conducted its affairs without much reference to its formal sovereign. Dubrovnik's governing system was more complex. The principal ruling body was the Senate, whose 45 members always came from a single, restricted group of patrician families and held office for life. A so-called Minor Council of eleven nobles and judges enforced market regulations, preserved law and order, and served as a supreme court. The larger body known as the Major Council, with about 300 noble members, acted as a legislature and also elected the Senate and Minor Council. The Senate dealt with foreign states and proposed laws; but these could go into effect only after the Major Council and the archbishop had approved them.

Dubrovnik's position was exceptional, since foreign control was minimal and did not seriously prejudice either the town's prosperity or its ability to govern itself. During the century and a half (1205–1358) of Venetian hegemony, Dubrovnik was obliged to accept a resident Venetian count as well as certain limitations on its navigation, but nonetheless retained its municipal freedoms. Except for collecting customs duties on all imported goods, Venice did nothing to prevent Dubrovnik's trade with the hinterland. After the town returned to Hungarian rule in 1358, it enjoyed almost total independence, successfully resisting the attempt of King Louis to install his own representative there. Even the Ottoman Turks—the most powerful suzerains yet to appear in the Balkans—saw the advantage of respecting Dubrovnik's autonomy. The town's favorable defensive position would have rendered conquest difficult in any case, quite aside from its location distant from the center of Ottoman power. Thus the Turks merely collected tribute, while Dubrovnik retained its independence in exchange for substantial annual payments. In 1459 the sultan granted its citizens complete freedom to trade anywhere in the Ottoman Empire. Dubrovnik's tribute to Istanbul became stabilized after 1481 at 12,500 ducats annually. The maritime towns farther north escaped Ottoman control altogether. Owing to Venice's protectorate over most of the Adriatic littoral, the Turks failed to gain more than a tenuous foothold anywhere on the Dalmatian coast north of Albania.

The mining towns of Serbia and Bosnia, partners of Dubrovnik in the Balkan commerce, enjoyed autonomy of the kind usually found only in Western Europe. Most of the miners were in fact ethnic Germans (locally known as Saxons), whose specialized skills were in short supply. To induce potential settlers to immigrate, the overlords of the towns granted them extensive legal privileges—personal freedom as well as the right to elect their own town councillors and freely practice their (Catholic) religion. Eventually these rights had to be extended to all the inhabitants of the Saxon towns, irrespective of ethnic origin. The typical mining settlement in the Balkan interior consisted of a heterogeneous mixture of entrepreneurs and laborers. It was ruled by a council of twelve sworn citizens, or jurors, who exercised both administrative and judicial functions and shared power with a chief magistrate, or count. The spatial boundaries of the town were precisely marked off, clearly separating it from its rural and feudal environment. However, the Balkan mining towns never developed a patrician upper class capable of monopolizing public functions. They failed to attain the same independence as the towns of Dalmatia, which were able even to pursue their own foreign policies on occasion. A count representing the territorial power was always present, while customs officials (actually tax farmers) looked after the monarch's financial interests. The wealth of the community was divided among the sovereign, the mining enterpreneurs, and the merchants, who together controlled local political life. A few small nonmining towns also sprang up in Serbia and Bosnia in the late 14th and 15th centuries, usually in the vicinity of fortresses or important intersections. Their local governments seem to have followed the usual Saxon pattern; but none of these places acquired much importance. The interior of the Balkan Peninsula remained the least urbanized sector in all of medieval East Central Europe.

The towns of Bohemia originally were governed by representatives of the sovereign, whose supervision sometimes extended to quite petty affairs. Local self-government evolved only gradually in the course of the 13th and 14th centuries, with the oldest known grant of liberties to a Bohemian town dating from 1223. Certain towns eventually succeeded in restricting the role of the royal magistrate and placing a mayor and councilmen at the head of affairs. However, each case involved separate negotiations between the leading citizens and the sovereign; and each town received its own charter delineating its specific rights and privileges. Prague, for example, gained permission to construct a town hall—the symbol of autonomous government—only in 1299. When actually built in 1338, this edifice was the first of its type in the kingdom. Elected mayors became common in Bohemia during the 14th century; but not until the 15th century were most towns permitted to choose their own municipal councils. The four most privileged towns in Bohemia were the Old Town and New Town of Prague (adjacent, but separately governed); Kutná Hora (Kuttenberg), second only to the capital in importance because of its rich silver mines; and Cheb (Eger) in the far west, a possession of the German emperor. Mining towns were also comparatively privileged, although their special character demanded a somewhat different set of regulations. A relatively early grant of privileges to the Moravian town of Jihlava in the mid-13th century was later widely imitated for mining communities elsewhere. However, even the most favored towns in Bohemia were less independent than the free imperial towns of Germany.

The Hussite period introduced a major change in the political role of Prague, since the refusal of the Bohemians to accept Sigismund of Hungary as their sovereign created a power vacuum. From 1419 to 1436 the Prague municipal council assumed direction of national policy. The composition of this body also had changed as a result of a mass exodus of Germans from the capital in 1420. Many residents for the first time had become eligible to participate in town government by purchasing confiscated German property. On its own authority Prague now summoned the Bohemian Diet, sent ambassadors abroad, and imposed or deposed the governors of castles and mayors of towns. In collaboration with the two most radical Hussite centers, Tabor and Hradec Kralové (Königgrätz), it conducted the war against the forces of King Sigismund and took a leading part in the deliberations of the Diet. Although Prague's political influence declined after 1434, when a force of conservative Hussites (Utraquists) defeated the radicals at the battle of Lipany, townsmen continued to be influential in Bohemia through their curia in the Diet down to the end of the 15th century.

In Hungary municipal liberties date back to the mid-12th century, when the country's earliest capital, Székesfehérvár, received its charter of privileges. This document permitted the town's citizens to elect their own judges and hold a market free from customs duties. The Hungarian kings apparently recognized that such liberties encouraged the immigration of skilled craftsmen, which in turn promoted general prosperity. Hungarian royal charters usually gave towns the right to elect a judge, jurors, and a governing council. Within a privileged town the king or his representative served only as appeals judge from the decisions of town courts. Royal tax collectors were not permitted to enter the free towns, which collected their taxes themselves and merely turned over the required sums to the king's treasury. By the early 13th century various important Hungarian towns—Székesfehérvár, Esztergom, Bratislava, and Sibiu—had been freed from the authority of royal officials and given the right to self-government and trading privileges. The mining towns likewise were exempt from royal interference, except for the obligation to pay a small tax and deliver their ore to the king.

The model for town rights in Hungary was the privileged status typically granted to the foreigners known as hospites (i.e., "guests") to encourage them to settle in the kingdom. These "guests" were guaranteed the right to live according to their own customs, choose their own judges, and pay a tax in money calculated according to the amount of land they held. Such privileges permitted the foreign communities to develop independently in their own fashion. Usually the "guests" lived in towns or villages which had received similar freedoms. In the 13th century some Hungarian artisans (often former serfs) obtained a status similar to that granted to foreigners, although Hungarian law prohibited the immigration to towns of serfs who still owed legal obligations to their masters. In outlining hospite privileges, the charters make numerous references to the rights of townsmen according to German law, which obviously served as a point of reference. The specific features of hospite status in Hungary show the clear influence of German law as it was applied in Poland or Bohemia.

The unprecedented destruction caused by the Mongol invasion of Hungary in 1241 delivered a major setback to town development. After this storm had passed, King Béla IV attempted to revive town life. He issued more extensive urban privileges than any of his predecessors had done, granting the towns important rights of self-government and judicial independence. He also promoted the immigration of skilled artisans from Germany and Italy. These colonists received the typical municipal freedoms, including exemption from the authority of county officials and valuable trade concessions. Béla issued numerous documents transforming the hospite communities into legally recognized towns. He not only confirmed all of the towns' former rights, but also granted new ones. This policy continued into the 14th century and helped to attract a considerable influx of new settlers. By a decree of 1351, King Louis I encouraged the Hungarian towns to build fortifications, exempting the ones that did so from payment of the standard "ninth" (nona) tax. Nonetheless, only eight towns in Hungary—among them

Buda, Bratislava, Sopron, and Pest—were recognized as free royal towns possessing significant rights of self-government, although the Slovak mining towns
also received important privileges.

In every country, the free royal towns tended to be larger and more prosperous
than the others. They also constituted a small minority of the total. Secular
and ecclesiastical lords did grant some privileges to the settlements on their
estates, advisable if they wished to retain their inhabitants. Nonetheless, private
towns typically lagged far behind royal ones with respect to legal and economic
autonomy. Their situation also tended to deteriorate over time. As more and
more noble estates acquired legal immunity from royal jurisdiction, private towns
became increasingly subject to the direct authority of their lords. Judges chosen
by the community were allowed to handle only minor cases, while the lord
himself judged everything else. Although in theory an appeal from the lord's
justice to the monarch was possible, the superior social status of nobles vis-à-vis
townsmen must have made this procedure infrequent at best. King Sigismund of
Hungary actually pawned or sold many of his royal towns to the nobility, thereby
converting them into private towns and the free townspeople into serfs. For a few
years (1405–10) Sigismund experimented with a policy of granting privileges to
towns; but when the expected increase in revenue did not materialize he reverted
to his former habits. After the first decade of the 15th century very few Hungarian
towns saw their legal status improve.

Municipal self-government existed in Poland as early as the 13th century,
subject to the sovereign's overall authority. The free royal towns were semi-
independent ministates, supreme within their walls and subject to a very different legal regime from the one which prevailed in the rest of the country.
Royal officials could not tax them, nor the royal courts judge them. The towns
paid the monarch an agreed rent in exchange for the right to hold a tax-free
market. Court cases involving commercial transactions were handled by a market
judge with specialized knowledge of trade matters, who also made sure that the
sovereign received the rents and fees to which he was entitled. As in Hungary,
however, towns in Poland which were located on noble estates lacked autonomy.
A lord with immunity from royal jurisdiction held the supreme authority and
appointed officials of his choice to oversee the town's affairs. Even in royal towns
the monarch could revoke the privileges that he or his predecessors had granted,
which the nobility sometimes induced him to do.

In Polish royal towns the instrument of self-government was usually an elected
council. In principle it shared power with an assembly of citizens which was
supposed to approve all important taxes and laws; but this body was too large
for efficiency. The council exercised executive functions and also protected the
town's interests vis-à-vis the monarch. Although the king or his representative
always exerted great influence on the choice of council members, the fact that
the latter usually served for life gave them a certain independence. Town councils in Poland initially were subordinate to their chief magistrates or mayors.

Subsequently, conflicts between mayors and councils became so common that many towns, Cracow among them, simply purchased the mayor's office. In the case of lesser royal towns, the king himself might buy this office and assign an official called a starosta to represent him. The larger towns also hired a few permanent employees. The most important was the notary, who attended all sessions of the municipal council, recorded its decisions, collected the town's income, and managed its financial affairs. Small towns which could not afford a professional notary often employed a priest or teacher for this work. The notary had to be an educated man, well acquainted with the law as well as literate in German in order to handle German-law cases. He also needed fluency in Latin, the prevailing administrative language in Poland until the 16th century.

The towns of Prussia by the 15th century had become increasingly irritated by the Teutonic Knights' continual interference in their affairs. This monastic military organization was not only their political superior but also a competitor in trade. Fortified by a papal dispensation, the Knights carried on trade for their own profit. In many cases they claimed a preferential right to purchase imported goods. Finally Gdańsk, the largest and wealthiest of the towns, took the lead in organizing a league of Prussian towns and nobles which sought to replace the sovereignty of the Knights with that of the king of Poland. In the ensuing Thirteen Years' War (1454–66), the financial resources of the towns (i.e., their ability to hire and pay mercenary troops) proved a decisive factor in their victory. In West Prussia (henceforth Royal Prussia), which the Teutonic Order was obliged to cede to Poland, the towns received extensive rights of self-government. In Gdańsk, Toruń, and Elbląg—the three principal towns—the Polish king was represented only by a royal starosta, himself a townsman. He thus found it impossible to make the royal will prevail against local opposition. All three places acquired the privilege of coining their own money. Gdańsk became a semisovereign territory similar to the great Hanseatic towns in Germany. Toruń acquired similar rights through a succession of royal grants, although its territory was smaller. Moreover, Gdańsk took responsibility for guarding the security of the Baltic seacoast. It possessed its own army and warships, concluded contracts and commercial alliances with foreigners, and took part in the wars of the Hanseatic League.

The opposite situation prevailed in Byzantine-controlled towns, which never evolved into genuinely self-governing communities. Clearly these municipalities were incapable of providing examples of self-government to the Balkan peoples who at various times inherited or conquered them. In Bulgaria and Serbia—Byzantine successor-states in this respect, as in others—the monarch ruled the towns directly. The same was true of the Romanian principalities. No legal distinction existed between the population of town and countryside. The towns also played virtually no role in national politics. In contrast to the usual West European pattern, not all the inhabitants of such places were legally free, since some were dependent peasants belonging to churches or monasteries. No trace existed of any local self-government. Only the Orthodox Church possessed some autonomy.

In Albania, where Byzantine authority remained fairly effective until interrupted by the establishment of the Latin Empire (1204–61) and then after 1285 was partially restored, urban autonomy was never allowed to develop. The prime strategic importance of Albania ensured that it would not experience the benign neglect which Venice or Hungary accorded to the towns of Dalmatia. The Albanians themselves were apparently content with this situation. The town dwellers were chiefly Greek speakers, well aware that their commercial prosperity depended on links with the Byzantine lands. At no time did Albania ever attempt to detach itself from the empire; and no independent political units of any size ever took form there. The few elements of municipal self-government which arose in Byzantine Albania remained rudimentary. An assembly dominated by merchants existed in the south at Vlorë (Valona) and clearly possessed some legal status. At Durrës a popular assembly met occasionally, although apparently not at regular intervals. Its powers were poorly defined, and the Byzantine administration never recognized its legal validity. No elected officials functioned at Durrës. The Dalmatian style of town government, characterized by genuine local control through a popular assembly and elected executive, appeared nowhere in Albania. The Neapolitan or Venetian governors who succeeded the Byzantines took care to prevent any such development, while Albania itself continued to be a pawn in the power struggles of its greater neighbors. Long wars disrupted the commerce of the towns, broke many of their old ties to the Greek world, and encouraged predatory behavior on the part of native Albanian lords, whose outlook was predominantly tribal and feudal.

Economically the Byzantine-ruled towns of the Balkans were quite prosperous by comparison with those of medieval Bulgaria or Serbia. They possessed walls and towers for defense; and some also contained a citadel for the town garrison, where the governor and military commander resided. Most such towns were largely Greek in population even when the hinterland was Slavic. In contrast to medieval Germany or Italy, where a weak central authority permitted the urban merchant and artisan classes to govern themselves, in the Balkans a landed aristocracy played the leading role even in towns. After Bulgaria returned to Byzantine rule early in the 11th century, some of its towns became part of feudal estates, which the central government assigned to members of the nobility in exchange for military and administrative services. The town magistrates received lifetime (and later hereditary) tenure. This system continued in force even after 1185, when Byzantine hegemony had ended and a Bulgarian tsar ruled the country. Towns controlled by nobles sometimes became centers of local separatism. This happened in the 1240s, when Byzantine military forces captured a number of Bulgarian towns simply by bribing their overlords.

The transfer of the Balkan towns to Ottoman rule in the late 14th and the 15th centuries thus denoted no sharp break in the style of urban government. The

Ottoman sultan named an administrator for each town and a military commander for each fortress. Larger towns were divided into districts, each with its own public buildings (mosque, bath, market) and its own gates. The superintendent of the market and the commander of the local soldiery served as police. An Islamic judge, or kadi, settled disputes and supervised local government, although native (i.e., Christian) laws and customs which did not contradict Islamic law were respected. The kadi together with an official inspector policed the markets to ensure that no shopkeeper was giving short weight. The inspector also enforced market regulations and collected various dues. If necessary, the population was called out to aid in the town's defense. Local assemblies under the Ottoman regime were permitted to regulate certain matters pertaining to property rights, education, and religion, but held no judicial power.

Like its Byzantine predecessor, the Ottoman state interfered extensively in the economic life of the towns. Government decrees regulated the supply of raw materials, the volume of production, the prices of goods sold at the markets, and the legal rate of profit. In setting and enforcing these rules, local officials worked closely with the guilds. To guard against popular uprisings—always a danger, since most townsmen possessed weapons—inspectors made certain that adequate food supplies were always available. They acted also to prevent speculation in food products. The maximum profit on artisan goods was fixed at ten percent, with certain exceptions; and competition was strictly forbidden. All producers were supposed to have equal access to raw materials. Most trades in the Ottoman Empire were carried on by Muslims and non-Muslims alike, although certain ones were reserved to Muslims only. Christian artisans were not numerous in the Turkish-controlled towns of the Balkans in the 15th century. Many shops belonged to Islamic religious foundations; and artisan guilds affiliated with political and religious societies played an important role in town life.

The existence of town autonomy in certain parts of medieval East Central Europe cannot conceal the fact that even the freest towns had a limited impact on national policy. They projected little authority beyond their own boundaries, and normally did not even attempt to translate commercial prosperity into political influence. Town representatives were admitted to the Diets of Bohemia and Croatia in the 13th century, but with little practical effect, since the nobility was in overall control. Townsmen joined the Hungarian Diet only in the 1440s, where they did assert their right to participate as a separate estate. The two major exceptions to this general lack of influence—Prague during the Hussite wars and the Prussian towns in the Thirteen Years' War—showed that a potential for effective political action did exist if the towns possessed sufficient financial resources. However, leading townsmen were usually fully absorbed in commercial affairs and became politically involved only on a local level, if at all. In any event, they could never outvote the nobility in the national assemblies; and the nobles treated them with overweening arrogance. In the Byzantine sphere the weight of tradition added its contribution to this political impotence. The urban centers of the Greek world had not experienced self-government since ancient times. The towns of independent Bulgaria and Serbia had known none either, aside from those few on the Adriatic coast which at times acknowledged a loose Serbian overlordship. The Balkan towns were not represented in the assemblies of the land, which seem to have been gatherings of nobility and clergy alone. In any case, they had no wish to quarrel with the monarch, whom they often regarded as their protector.

In Poland the approval of the towns was sometimes required for important acts of state. The seven largest Polish towns joined the nobility in 1343 to guarantee King Casimir III's treaty with the Teutonic Knights. King Louis of Hungary subsequently solicited the towns' promise to recognize one of his daughters as heir to his Polish lands. In 1384 during the interregnum after his death, townsmen and nobles together formed the Confederation of Radom to preserve order until a new monarch could be elected. In 1430, representatives of the Polish towns agreed to support the succession of one of King Vladislav Jagiełło's sons, appending the great seal of Cracow to this document. In theory the Polish towns had the right to send delegates to the national Diet, or Great Sejm; but the nobility disliked their presence and the townsmen often failed to come. Those few town representatives who did appear were usually from only the largest places (Cracow, Vilnius, and Lvov), and even they were not permitted to vote. Polish townsmen on the whole perceived no danger in their abstention from national affairs and took little interest in the business of the commonwealth. Rather than join forces for common ends, each town separately sought privileges from the monarch.

In every country the towns and the nobility tended to be rivals. Nobles living on rural estates were irritated by the wealth of the towns, the asylum they sometimes provided to refugees, the high prices of their products, and the foreign ethnic origin of many of their leading citizens. Alliances among towns were rare, thus limiting their citizens' potential influence. Even in Bohemia and Hungary, where the towns eventually were recognized as an estate in the national assemblies, their actual political role was secondary. In Poland at the end of the 15th century the towns lost all right to participate in national affairs. The noble class in all three countries tried by various means to prevent the influx of rich townsmen into their ranks—a tendency which became especially pronounced in Poland. In 1496 the Great Sejm forbade townsmen to acquire property in land (which might facilitate their entrance into the nobility), limited the rights of townsmen to hold office in the Church, and mandated that nobles who adopted town occupations would lose their noble status. After this time the only town which retained a voice in the Great Sejm of Poland was Cracow, the capital, which participated only when its own affairs were under discussion.

By the end of the 15th century the great age of urban development had come to an end in East Central Europe. Town life in Bohemia had been adversely affected by the Hussite wars and the concomitant hostility of the Catholic Church. In Poland, where townsmen had often been more prosperous than nobles in the 14th and 15th centuries, the urban centers now grew more slowly than the agricultural sector and suffered under increasing legal restrictions. In Hungary the towns' economic power was attenuated by the rising taxes and forced loans imposed by King Matthias to finance his perpetual military campaigns. Many Hungarian towns showed an absolute loss of population from the middle of the 14th century until the end of the 15th. However, the Dalmatian towns continued to flourish in the 15th century in spite of Venetian economic regulations, and succeeded in maintaining their traditions of self-government. The towns of the Balkan interior had always been weak economically, aside from a few mining centers. Many of them undoubtedly continued to exist under Ottoman administration as centers of trade and crafts. Although possessing no political autonomy of any kind, they had never known any under their native rulers either. Ottoman officials alone held administrative and judicial authority, while councils of elders in the towns and villages were able to exercise only a limited jurisdiction over property disputes and religious affairs. The Ottoman official class maintained an essentially parasitic relationship to the Balkan towns, using them as sources of credit and lending operations. Strict state regulation prevented the development of an economically independent urban bourgeoisie, which might later have exercised genuine autonomy.

Thus by the close of the 15th century, even the free royal towns of medieval East Central Europe had failed to live up to their earlier promise. Their evolution was interrupted and their independence truncated by economic and political circumstances largely beyond their control. Even at their height the towns of this region had been generally smaller and less prosperous than those of France, Italy, Germany, or Flanders. Subsequently the gap would become wider. In the early modern era, impoverishment and political impotence would combine to seal off the towns of East Central Europe from serious participation in the great economic and cultural advances of the European continent.

CHAPTER 7

Religion and the Churches

The Slavs, Bulgars, and Magyars who settled in East Central Europe between the 5th and 9th centuries were for the most part not yet Christian. Rather they were polytheists who practiced some form of nature worship, based on the belief that the forces of nature were divine beings to whom they must sacrifice. The early Slavs, for example, had a cult of springs, rivers, and lakes and regarded the damp earth as the divine source of all life. They believed in the existence of evil beings like devils, witches, and vampires with uncanny powers as well as beneficent nymphs, river sprites, and fairies. The Slavs thought of the soul or spirit as an almost material essence, bound only loosely to a human and animal frame. It regularly left the body during sleep and wandered about, usually in the form of a bird. The boundary between life and death was flexible, since the departure of the soul during sleep allegedly caused the body to die, while its return brought the flesh again to life. Spirits of the dead were thought to remain in contact with living people and influence their fate for either good or evil. The ghosts of dead relatives were objects of ancestor worship. Of the various deities worshipped by the Slavs, the most powerful was a god of light, sun, and fire named Svarog, Swarożyc, or Świątowit. Despite a multiplicity of gods, no class of priests is known to have existed among any of the Slavic peoples. Chiefs of tribes and fathers of families led the religious activities of the clan. Temples seem to have been rare, although the island of Rügen in the Baltic Sea was known for its impressive shrine dedicated to the god Świątowit.

The pagan Bulgars and Magyars brought with them to Europe various beliefs typical of the Ukrainian steppe, their previous homeland. They held that nature was permeated by spirits or souls that could pass from person to person or from animals to people and back again. The soul which gave life to a human body lived on after death in the form of a spirit or shadow. Honor was paid to the spirits of dead ancestors in order to invoke their protection. Shamans played an important role in establishing contact with the supernatural. These wise men were believed to be powerful magicians capable of bringing rain, lightning, and thunder, preventing flood and fire, annihilating an enemy through witchcraft, and communicating with the world of the spirits. During their ceremonies the shamans created considerable tumult by drumming, jumping about, shouting, and singing. At times they sank into trances, during which they claimed to make contact with the spirit world. Empowered with this superior knowledge, they then offered advice to people. The paganism of the Bulgars and Magyars was closely linked to the old clan system. Many Bulgar clans claimed a divine origin. The ruler's family allegedly possessed some elements of supernatural power which inhered in the blood. This belief led to the custom of drinking animal blood, especially from the skull of a powerful man. Each Magyar clan maintained a fireplace around which stood the idols of clan and family, often forged of gold or silver. A sacred fire burned eternally there, which if extinguished was supposed to bring bad luck to the household. Like many other dwellers on the Ukrainian steppe, the Bulgars and Magyars identified one of their deities as the creator of heaven and earth. The Bulgars called their highest god "Tangra," a deity widely known among the Turkic peoples. The Magyars named the supreme author of the universe "Isten." No doubt this qualified monotheism facilitated their subsequent acceptance of Christianity.

The Byzantine Empire in the 6th and 7th centuries was unable to prevent the incursion of Bulgars and Slavs into its European territories. However, it could and did promote Christian missionary activity among these pagan peoples as a means of bringing them within Byzantium's sphere of influence. The Bulgars had already acquired a passing acquaintance with Christianity in their old homes on the steppe, where a few Bulgar princes had accepted baptism early in the 7th century. Subsequently the Bulgars became overlords of a partially Christianized Slavic population in the Balkan Peninsula. Nonetheless Christianity in the Balkans was too closely associated with Byzantine political ambitions to have much effect until the 9th century, when Constantinople was forced to recognize the existence of an independent Bulgar state. Emperor Basil I (r. 867–86) promoted the conversion of Serbia—then a small principality between the Drina and Morava rivers and the Adriatic Sea—probably using Latin missionaries from the Dalmatian towns under Byzantine control. At the same period the dominance of the Franks in the westernmost sector of East Central Europe created strong pressures in favor of Christianity. To some degree Bohemia, Slovenia, and the western parts of Hungary and Croatia apparently were Christianized even before the Franks arrived. However, their incorporation into the Frankish Empire enabled the Church of Rome to insist upon the total extermination of paganism, by force if necessary.

Most of East Central Europe in the 9th and 10th centuries lay beyond the effective reach of the Frankish or Byzantine empires and accepted Christianity at the instigation of native rulers. Individual conversions aside, the existence of state structures was an essential prerequisite for massive and rapid Christianization, since only an organized government could provide the necessary support for imposing the new religion upon an often recalcitrant population. A monarch was able to offer armed protection to Christian missionaries, establish churches and monasteries, and donate land for their maintenance. He could suppress heathen ceremonies, destroy pagan shrines, and put down resistance by force. For the populace as a whole, instruction in the essentials of Christian belief often lagged well behind the official conversion of a country. The early missionaries set a very modest standard for their new converts. This sometimes amounted to nothing more than participation in Christian ritual and the avoidance of overtly pagan practices, out of fear that excessive strictness might be counterproductive.

Several compelling reasons existed for the early medieval rulers of East Central Europe to accept Christianity. The new faith was recognizably the key to a more advanced civilization. Moreover, adherence to Christianity was politically essential for any ruling house that wished to be treated as an equal partner in the European state system. Dynastic marriage alliances—the principal cement of interstate relations—were possible only between fellow Christians, or upon the pagan partner's promise of timely baptism. Christian governments could justify military campaigns against heathen neighbors on the pretext of conducting a missionary war. The East Frankish rulers and their successors, the German emperors, often sought to impose their religion as an adjunct to political hegemony over their Slavic neighbors. In the conversion of the Croats, Czechs, and Poles this military pressure played a decisive role. By contrast, the Byzantines showed considerably more finesse in their treatment of the Balkan peoples. Byzantium was a status quo power concerned to preserve rather than expand its territory. It supported missionary activities abroad for the practical reason that Christian nations were less likely than pagan ones to be hostile. Its prompt military reaction in the 860s to the threat of papal domination in Bulgaria was exceptional, impelled by the competition between Catholicism and Eastern Orthodoxy and by Bulgaria's geographical propinquity to Constantinople. Ordinarily the Byzantine government did not seek territorial expansion at the pagans' expense. Christianity was merely one tool among many in a sophisticated foreign policy.

Among the pagans themselves, internal opposition to the acceptance of Christianity could be formidable. This was especially true of the Bulgars and Magyars, among whom the warrior ethos of the steppe remained alive long after they had settled in East Central Europe. A few prominent men among the Bulgars received Christian baptism in the 8th century, although on the whole the aristocracy of that period continued to follow the traditions of steppe culture. However, the conquests of Khan Krum (r. 803–14) in the northern Balkans added a considerable Christian population to the Bulgar state. Concurrently the social separation between the Bulgar ruling class and the Slavic agriculturalists was beginning to break down. Pressures from the Byzantine government certainly played a role in the decision of Khan Boris to accept Christianity in the year 863. Boris may also have calculated that it would be advantageous to unite his

Bulgar and Slavic subjects in a single church. Another factor was the undoubted attractiveness of Byzantine high civilization, with which many Bulgar nobles were already acquainted.

Similarly resistant to Christian baptism were the Hungarians, who in 895–96 established themselves west of the Danube in Pannonia. Like the Bulgars, they were steppe warriors whose life-style clearly contradicted any notion of Christian virtue. Conversion was out of the question as long as their devastating campaigns of plunder and destruction continued in Western Europe. However, in 955 the decisive defeat of a Magyar invading force at Lechfeld near Augsburg in Germany largely put an end to these predatory incursions. Acceptance of Christianity was essential if Hungary was to become a recognized European state. Thus in the 970s the Hungarian ruler, Duke Géza (r. 972–97), asked the German Emperor Otto I to send him Christian missionaries. Subsequently he and his son and heir, Stephen, were baptized. This act also proclaimed Géza's choice of Latin rather than Greek Christianity, despite the fact that Byzantine missions had functioned in eastern Transylvania for the previous quarter of a century. The adoption of the Latin rite may have owed something to German pressure, but probably more important was the fact that Hungary's political center of gravity lay west of the Danube near the border with Austria. Géza himself did very little to support missionary activity. His personal beliefs are unknown, but he continued to perform sacrifices to heathen deities as well as to the Christian God. The actual conversion of the Hungarians to Christianity dates only from the reign of his son Stephen I (r. 997–1038), who proved a loyal friend to the pope and granted the Church extraordinary privileges.

The Christian Church was the best-organized institution in all of medieval Europe. Modeled on the organization of the Roman Empire, it also appropriated much of the imperial terminology. All Christian lands were organized into provinces and dioceses, which normally coincided with political divisions. An archbishop or metropolitan bishop supervised the clergy within his church province, while subordinate bishops headed the dioceses or bishoprics and administered the parishes there. An archbishop was entitled to summon synods at which his bishops and the abbots of important monasteries in his province gathered to discuss church affairs. According to canon law, bishops were supposed to be elected by the clergy of their dioceses, and archbishops by the bishops. The five canonical patriarchs of Rome, Constantinople, Alexandria, Antioch, and Jerusalem—all theoretically equal in rank—stood at the summit of this hierarchy. Any important decisions of a bishop required confirmation by one of these five. Nonetheless, a bishop was essentially the master within his own house; and his cathedral was the principal church of the diocese.

The most influential of the five patriarchs in the medieval Church were the pope at Rome and the patriarch of Constantinople, since by the 8th century the other three operated in predominantly Muslim states. However, the powers of pope and patriarch were by no means equivalent. Owing to the fragmentation of the Roman Empire in the West, bishops in the Western Church exercised great authority in secular affairs. The disappearance of Roman imperial government meant that the papacy at Rome never developed a tradition of subservience to the state. Although controlled at times by the German emperor or the Roman mob, the pope was not permanently associated with any one political authority. By contrast, the Eastern Church was an integral part of the state organism. The patriarch of Constantinople and the emperor theoretically were equals, although in most respects the emperor was supreme. He exerted enormous power over ecclesiastical policy through his influence on the election of the patriarch and the bishops, who comprised the Holy Synod, the ruling body of the Church. Church councils met at the emperor's command, or at least under his protection; and he ratified all their more important decisions. Cooperation between emperor and patriarch was the norm, and conflicts rare. Seldom did the patriarch fail to bend to the emperor's will.

Until the final quarrel in the year 1054, the Western (Catholic) and Eastern (Orthodox) Churches regarded themselves as two halves of a single body. All the same, the pope and the patriarch competed for the allegiance of the Balkan peoples. The pope wanted them to adopt Christianity in its Latin form and acknowledge the ecclesiastical supremacy of Rome. The Greek patriarch and Byzantine emperor likewise sought to dominate the Balkan Slavs, but did not insist upon Greek as the sole liturgical language. Indeed, when a Slavic ruler named Rastislav in the year 863 invited the Byzantine emperor to send him a Christian bishop, the emperor was more than willing. He commissioned two eminent Greeks of Salonika, Constantine (better known by his monastic name of Cyril) and his brother Methodius, to develop a written language for the use of the Slavic peoples. These two apostles (who were later canonized as saints) were not the first to translate religious writings into Slavic, since some preliminary work had been done earlier by Bavarian missionaries. However, they were the first to invent a Slavic alphabet and undertake translations into Slavic on a major scale.

The importance which Constantinople attached to this project is indicated by the quality of the the two men chosen to carry it out. Constantine-Cyril was a renowned linguist, a priest, and a teacher of philosophy at the palace school in Constantinople. His brother Methodius was a high-ranking imperial administrator and diplomat. Presumably the two men had learned Slavic in their native Salonika in northern Greece, a region which contained many Slavs. Their initial task was to create an alphabet for the Slavic language, so that the major religious texts could be translated. For this purpose Cyril supposedly invented the alphabet now known as Glagolitic. (The so-called Cyrillic script named after him is actually of later vintage.) The two apostles next undertook the massive labor of translating ecclesiastical literature from Greek into Slavic, beginning with the text of the Byzantine liturgy or Mass. According to one ancient source, Methodius translated the complete Old and New Testaments into Slavic, perhaps with some assistance. At that time his versions could easily be understood by all Slavs, since the great migrations were then of relatively recent date and Slavic essentially was still one language. The separate Slavic tongues of modern times had not yet diverged to the point of mutual incomprehensibility.

The question of a Slavic liturgy, however, quickly became enmeshed in the struggle between pope and patriarch for control of the new Slavic churches. The liturgy—the prescribed ritual used in divine worship—contained sacred texts not to be taken lightly. For the churches within the boundaries of the empire the Byzantine government exerted strong pressure in favor of using Greek, which indeed it regarded as the only civilized tongue. However, as an element of foreign policy, it accepted vernacular liturgies in regions beyond the reach of Constantinople's political authority. Liturgical books already existed in Coptic, Ethiopian, Syriac, Georgian, Armenian, and Gothic. The Byzantines understood that nations newly converted to Christianity responded best to a faith professed in a language they could comprehend. On the other hand, the Church of Rome had long used nothing but Latin and was loath to break with this tradition.

In part the question of liturgical language was a struggle over political power, expressing the conflict between a pro-Frankish and a pro-Byzantine political orientation. The Frankish clergy supported Latin, the language of the Western Church, whereas the Eastern Church upheld the use of Slavic. Since in theory Christendom still constituted a single body, each side sought the approval of the pope for its position. However, papal attitudes on this issue showed great ambivalence, changing several times within just the two decades of the Cyril-Methodian mission. On the one hand, a Slavic liturgy would clearly be useful in attracting the Slavs to Christianity. On the other hand, the Latin language gave unity to the Western Church. Moreover, liturgies in vernacular tongues had become associated with heresy, because churches which had adopted the Arian interpretation of Christianity used them. (The Arian Bishop Ulfilas, for example, had produced a splendid rendition of the Bible into Gothic.) Fears were expressed that translations produced in distant mission fields, even by true Christians, might prove inaccurate and thus inadvertently promote heresy. Finally, the feeling persisted that a "barbaric" language like Slavic, so newly reduced to writing, was unworthy of the Christian sacred scriptures and the Christian Mass. Some theologians argued that only three languages in the world—Hebrew, Greek, and Latin—were capable of expressing the true word of God.

In Bulgaria the Christian worship services at first were conducted exclusively in Greek. Khan Boris (after a brief flirtation with Rome) accepted Christianity from Byzantine sources in 866, and Greek missionaries arrived in Bulgaria to spread the faith. Progress was slow. Clerics ignorant of Slavic occupied all the posts in the Bulgarian church hierarchy and delivered their sermons in Greek. In the beginning this situation was unavoidable, since time was needed to train native priests. Moreover, in the decade of the 860s Cyril and Methodius had merely begun the work of Slavic translation, whereas Greek was the official language of pagan

Bulgaria. Nonetheless Khan Boris welcomed the Slavic-speaking clergy who came his way, perceiving that they would be helpful both in spreading Christianity and in increasing the Bulgarian Church's independence from Constantinople. On the other hand, the Bulgar aristocracy, which was not yet fully Slavicized, favored the sophisticated Greek clerics from Constantinople. High-ranking Bulgars presumably looked down on Slavic as the language of a subordinate social class. Boris may also have considered it advisable to keep the Greek and the Slavic clergy separate. In any event, he retained the Greek priests at court and sent the Slavic ones to work in the provinces. In 886 he dispatched the Slavic-speaking priest Clement, a future saint, to organize a mission in Macedonia. This diocese, with its center at Ohrid, became a major center for missionary activity among the Slavs. It used the Slavic rite and Glagolitic alphabet.

By the end of the 9th century the victory of the Slavic Church in Bulgaria was assured. In 893 a great assembly of notables, summoned by Khan Boris to meet at Preslav, resolved to replace the Greek priests with Slavic ones and to adopt Slavic as Bulgaria's official language. This assembly also decreed the use of the Cyrillic alphabet, which thereafter became the dominant script both for Old Slavic and for its modern derivatives in all Eastern Orthodox lands. Cyrillic was simpler than Glagolitic and much closer in form to the Greek alphabet—an obvious advantage in Bulgaria, where Greek had long been the language of official documents and carried great cultural prestige. These acts of the Bulgar assembly angered the Byzantine government, which regarded the Greek-speaking Church as a bulwark of its political influence. It first expelled all Bulgarian merchants from Constantinople and then in 894 resorted to arms. The new Bulgar Tsar Symeon I defeated them, and peace was concluded in 896.

The assembly's decision in favor of Cyrillic created a linguistic cleavage between the two halves of the Bulgar state. In western Bulgaria (i.e., Macedonia) the Glagolitic alphabet brought by Clement and his disciples remained dominant at first. However, at the capital of Preslav in eastern Bulgaria the sacred texts were all transcribed into Cyrillic and edited to conform more precisely to the Slavic speech of that region. Glagolitic gradually ceased to be used there at all. Indeed, Bulgaria in the 10th century became the Slavic world's leading center for the dissemination of both religious and secular works in the Slavic tongue and Cyrillic script. From Bulgaria Christian influence spread westward into Serbia, where the Slavic liturgy aided greatly in its reception. Although the restoration of Byzantine rule over Bulgaria from 1018 to 1185 led to strong pressures to re-Hellenize the Church, the Bulgar patriarchate with its center at Ohrid continued in existence. In any event, by this time Bulgaria had already played its historic role in the formation of Slavic Christianity. "Old Bulgarian," more commonly known as Old Slavic or Old Church Slavic (or Slavonic), became the permanent ecclesiastical language in all the Slavic countries professing Eastern Orthodoxy, as well as in the Romanian principalities until the 18th century. However, as a sacred tongue it ultimately suffered the same fate as Latin. Originally a vernacular understandable throughout the Slavic world, it eventually became petrified in a form incomprehensible to the vast majority of worshippers.

Christianity in the Balkans remained rigidly Byzantine and traditional despite its Slavic dress. Its dogma had been established by church councils in the early Christian centuries and was no longer flexible. In any event, the ritual formalities and canonical rules of the faith appeared quite sufficient to its new converts. Their concerns lay with matters of practice (i.e., rituals, fasts, and dress) rather than doctrine. The same held true in those other parts of Europe which received their Christianity from Rome. Medieval churchmen on the whole failed to acquire much theological sophistication. A bare knowledge of reading and writing was considered enough, and frequently even this was not attained. The newly converted nations of East Central Europe remained largely unaware of Christianity's rich heritage of religious thought. For the Orthodox clergy especially, who were generally more tradition-oriented than their Catholic colleagues, the chief aim was to preserve the true faith in its original purity. Even missionary activity was relegated to the background. On the other hand, everywhere in medieval East Central Europe Christianity became strongly impregnated with popular beliefs.

In Croatia the question of the liturgical language was not definitively settled for centuries, largely because the country was so divided in its ethnic character. Whereas the hinterland was overwhelmingly rural and Slavic, the Dalmatian coastal towns were chiefly Latin in culture, maintaining numerous overseas contacts and proud of their Roman heritage. Along the coast the Latin liturgy prevailed, reinforced by the attraction which Latin culture continued to exert upon the ruling class. On the other hand, the majority of the native Croatian nobility and clergy favored the Slavic liturgy and Glagolitic script. Papal pronouncements on the subject had minimal effect. The pope in his letter to the synod of Split in 925 described the Slavic tongue as "barbaric," and warned the Dalmatian bishops that henceforth all church services must be conducted in Latin. This synod was dominated by pro-Latin delegates. When it forbade the further recruitment of priests who did not know Latin, it obviously envisaged the gradual suppression of the Slavic priesthood. Nevertheless it decreed that Slavic would continue to be acceptable where Latin-speaking priests were not available. In light of the Croatian nobility's continued attachment to their language, plus a well-founded fear that Tsar Symeon of Bulgaria might intervene to support the Slavic side, insistence on Latin evidently was felt to be unwise.

As a consequence, the Slavic and Latin liturgies continued to exist side by side in parts of Croatia. The language question was raised at another synod of Split in 1059–60, which this time totally outlawed the Slavic liturgy and forbade the ordination of priests ignorant of Latin. In this case church practice as well as language was at issue. The Slavic-speaking priests observed certain customs of the Greek East. Many had wives and families, which the Eastern Church permitted, but which the Western Church was currently seeking (not always with success) to suppress. The Slavic clergy, with their beards and long hair, resembled Orthodox priests in external appearance. Accordingly the synod forbade clerics to grow beards or wear their hair long, to get married, or if already married, to retain their wives. Two popes in succession confirmed these decisions. This dispute divided the Croats along the lines of social class as well as language. The majority, which consisted of (mostly provincial) Slavic clergy, lower nobility, and the Slavic-speaking general population, opposed the synod's decision. A smaller but more influential group, composed of higher clergy, upper nobility, and court personnel, favored the changes. The latter naturally prevailed.

Great dissatisfaction ensued when the synod's decrees were proclaimed to the clergy and people of Croatia. The fact remained that most of the Slavic priests were married men who ministered to the peasantry and wished to retain their families. Most were likewise ignorant of Latin—"raw and uneducated," according to the highly partial pro-Latin chronicler Thomas of Split. For the first time some persecution of Slavic priests occurred in Croatia. In obedience to the synod's decrees, royal officials closed the doors of all Slavic churches and prevented the saying of Mass in Slavic. Even this did not mean the end of the Slavic Mass in Croatia, which continued to be said more or less secretly in remote parts of the country, especially on the island of Krk. Nearly two centuries after the decrees of 1060, a Roman pontiff finally acknowledged that the Slavic liturgy could not be abolished by fiat. In 1248 and 1252 Pope Innocent IV authorized its use in those bishoprics where it already existed and where the clergy did not know Latin. Thereby the Church of Croatia became unique in the Christian world in using the Western form of the liturgy in a Slavic tongue, differing in some respects from the Eastern liturgy, which had been translated from Greek rather than Latin.   In Bohemia the Slavic rite never became dominant, although it maintained a precarious existence in the country in the 10th and 11th centuries. Disputes apparently arose quite early over the question of the liturgical language, since in 973 the pope approved the foundation of a bishopric at Prague with the specific provision that it *not* use Slavic. Subsequently the Bohemian Duke Břetislav I (r. 1034–55) introduced a Slavic liturgy into the monastery at Sázava. However, this move was clearly not to the liking of either the Latin clergy or the papacy. In 1057 the next Bohemian Duke, Spytihnev I, expelled the Slavic monks from Sázava in hopes of receiving papal authorization for a royal crown for himself and the elevation of the Prague diocese to the rank of archbishopric. (He failed on both counts, though the German emperor did grant him the title of "king" for his lifetime.) Subsequently Duke Vratislav II (r. 1061–92) reintroduced the Slavic liturgy at Sázava. During his reign this monastery became the center of Bohemian religious and intellectual life.

The Holy See as well as the Church in Germany (where Latin had always been used exclusively) remained hostile to Slavic. Ultimately the pressures from these two sources proved irresistible. Bohemia was a vassal of the German Empire, while the bishops of both Prague and Olomouc (in Moravia) were canonically subject to the archbishop of Mainz. Duke Vratislav asked the permission of Pope Gregory VII to preserve the Slavic liturgy, arguing that the incomprehensible Latin of the Mass was a hindrance to piety and led to errors and misunderstandings. The pope, who was concerned above all to preserve church unity, denied this request in no uncertain terms. Vratislav's successor Břetislav II, acknowledging the Latin clergy's continued hostility to Slavic, forced the Slavic monks out of Sázava in 1096. This act brought to an end the attempts to found a Slavic-language Church in Bohemia. Traces of the Slavic rite nonetheless survived in the Czech religious vocabulary, testifying to its former links with the Slavic and Glagolitic tradition of Croatia. But virtually all the Glagolitic manuscripts produced in Bohemia were destroyed, aside from a few that were preserved in Russia.

In some parts of Poland a Slavic liturgy may have been used as late as the 1030s. The chronicler Gallus Anonymous (ca. 1115) mentions two Christian rites coexisting in Poland before 1022. Several old Polish churches are dedicated to Procopius, the Slavic abbot of the Sázava monastery, who was canonized in 1204. The pope's insistence in 1038 that the Piast prince Casimir "the Restorer" impose the Latin rite on the Church strongly suggests that this was not the only option. Despite this evidence that a Slavic Mass existed in Poland at one time, no Polish texts of that liturgy have survived, presumably because at a later date worship in any language other than Latin came to symbolize an antipapal attitude. With the single exception of Croatia, where the Slavic liturgy and Glagolitic alphabet maintained a tenuous existence, the dividing line between the Latin and Slavic liturgical languages ultimately corresponded almost exactly to the boundary between the Western and the Eastern Church (i.e., between Catholicism and Orthodoxy).

Pagan monarchs who decided to accept Christianity naturally sought to do so in a way which would not unduly compromise their political independence. The Bulgars, who occupied territory wrested from the Byzantine Empire, were particularly sensitive to the threat that conversion to Christianity would involve Byzantine interference in their affairs. Thus Khan Boris in 863–64 asked the East Franks rather than the Byzantines to send Christian missionaries to Bulgaria. His request greatly angered the Byzantines, who regarded as intolerable the extension of Frankish and papal influence so close to their own capital. Upon hearing of Boris's request, the government at Constantinople immediately declared war and forced the Bulgars to renounce the Frankish connection. Bulgaria now accepted Christianity in its Eastern form. Nonetheless Boris was dissatisfied with the degree of control which Constantinople sought to exert over the new Bulgarian Church. When he could not persuade the Greek patriarch to grant Bulgaria its own archbishopric, he offered his allegiance to the pope at Rome. Then the pope likewise proved reluctant to authorize an autonomous Bulgarian Church, leading Boris to reopen negotiations with the patriarch. This time he received more favorable terms, although somewhat less than full ecclesiastical independence, since the archbishop of Bulgaria would still have to be consecrated at Constantinople. In 870 Bulgaria returned to the Eastern Church. In retaliation the pope excommunicated all the Greek bishops and clergy serving in Bulgaria—a merely symbolic gesture, since Rome did not control the situation.

The Polish Duke Mieszko I (r. 960–92), feeling the pressure of German expansionism on his western frontier, chose to receive Christianity from Bohemia. His marriage in 964 to the Christian princess Dobrava of Bohemia doubtless included the stipulation that he would accept her religion. The princess brought Christian missionaries to Poland in her entourage; and Mieszko himself was baptized in 966. In deciding for a Bohemian orientation the Polish duke no doubt sought to undercut the position of the archbishopric of Magdeburg, which had been founded in 962 by the German Emperor Otto I as a headquarters for missionary work among the Slavs to the east and (not incidentally) for the spread of German influence. After Mieszko's conversion, the popes on the whole supported Poland in its quarrels with the German Empire, refusing to let the Magdeburg diocese interfere. In 990 or 991 Mieszko sent an embassy to Rome which donated the whole of Poland (perhaps as a fief in the feudal sense) to the Holy See. The exact meaning of this act remains uncertain, since the document in which the gift is recorded, known by its first two words "Dagome iudex," is ambiguously worded. However, a special relationship of some sort was clearly established between Poland and the papacy at that time. This link with Rome—prestigious but nonthreatening—offered Poland a degree of security against any pretensions by the Magdeburg archbishops or the German emperors to intervene in Polish affairs.

Whether Poland's relationship to the Holy See should be described as vassalage (i.e., feudal dependence) remains a disputed question. The Poles paid an extraordinary tax to the pope—the so-called Peter's pence—which was assessed upon very few other European nations. (The papacy repeatedly demanded this payment from Bohemia, but without success.) Peter's pence in Poland may have begun as a quid pro quo for the papal agreement of 1038 which released Casimir I from his monastic vows, enabling him to ascend the throne. At first the Polish ruler paid this tax out of his own resources. Later it became a head tax charged to the whole population; and beginning in the 13th century, papal agents came to Poland to collect it. However, payment was somewhat irregular, so that at times the pope had to insist upon arrears. Peter's pence was collected in Poland until the 16th century, when influences stemming from the Protestant Reformation caused it to be abolished. Apart from this tax issue, the pontiffs frequently intervened in Poland's internal affairs, particularly in matters concerning the division of territories and inheritance rights. During the period of political fragmentation in Poland in the 13th century, a number of minor Polish princes voluntarily accepted papal protection. Polish state documents as well as papal bulls at this time occasionally note that "Poland is directly subject to the Roman Church."

Despite the official acceptance of Christianity by every major state in East Central Europe by the year 1000, heathenism in the region remained far from dead. The independent Slavic tribes living along the Baltic coast between the Elbe and the Vistula rivers continued to worship pagan gods. In part this was a reaction against the ruthless methods of German missionaries in their midst, for whom conversion to Christianity was frequently a thinly disguised shield for the land hunger of the East German nobility. The Baltic peoples of East Prussia and Lithuania remained largely pagan until the 13th century, when the Teutonic and the Livonian Knights arrived to conquer and convert them. Similarly heathen were the Cuman tribes which settled in the 13th century in eastern Hungary (Transylvania) and in Walachia and Moldavia, then known as Cumania. Even when the ruler of a country willingly accepted Christianity, the process of converting his realm usually involved force or the threat of force. Pagan shrines were destroyed; persons loyal to the old beliefs were persecuted. Inevitably, the pressure for immediate and large-scale conversions meant that newly baptized persons received only the most superficial initiation into Christian doctrine. The pagan aristocracy consisted of military men with little inclination to observe rules imposed by priests or to admire Christian ideals of otherworldliness and piety. Rude warriors remained attached to their old heathen rites and regarded Christian codes of behavior as irksome. Biding their time until the central power showed signs of weakness, this warrior class then organized revolts which sought to extirpate Christianity and restore paganism. Particularly serious uprisings of this type broke out in Bulgaria, Poland, and Hungary.

Bulgaria experienced a heathen reaction after Boris, its first Christian king, abdicated in 889 and retired to a monastery. His son and successor, Vladimir, acquiesced in the wish of a group of influential nobles to reintroduce pagan ceremonies. Furious at this reversal of his policy, Boris in 893 came out of seclusion, defeated Vladimir in battle, blinded him, and took steps to organize the Bulgarian Church more adequately for the future. Prior to resuming the monk's cowl he established his second son Symeon on the throne. The Bulgar capital was transferred from Pliska, with its old heathen associations, to a new location at Preslav near Boris's own monastery. In Poland the earliest known heathen revolt broke out in 1022, more than half a century after Duke Mieszko I had accepted Christianity, although earlier disturbances may have gone unrecorded. Certainly the dynastic struggle which erupted in Poland in 1034 demonstrated that paganism was far from dead in the country, and that hostility to the Christian Church simmered beneath the surface. For half a dozen years Poland was engulfed by a heathen uprising in which nearly the entire church organization of the country was wiped out. So many bishops and priests were killed that some bishop's sees were left vacant for years afterward. The Polish Church had to be reestablished from virtually nothing. In Hungary King Stephen I's efforts to Christianize his subjects had included ruthless measures against paganism. However, in 1046 after his death a series of ferocious anti-Christian rebellions broke out along the Tisza River. The old heathen tribal leaders hated the foreign prelates and officials whose influence had displaced theirs. Instigated by one of these dispossessed chiefs, the rebels murdered every Christian they could find, especially foreign priests, and ransacked and burned many churches. A second pagan-inspired rebellion flared up in 1060. It too failed. Hungary's leading men, whether genuinely Christian or not, recognized the impossibility of remaining pagan in a Europe dominated by Christian states.

The Prussian tribes who lived to the north of Poland along the Baltic Sea were among the last people in Europe to be converted. They also proved particularly recalcitrant. A heathen uprising in 1224 wiped out a mission founded earlier in Prussia by a group of Cistercian monks. In 1226, Duke Conrad of Mazovia invited the Teutonic Order of Knights to establish settlement in Prussia to help subdue the country. A crusade against the heathens was preached throughout Europe, and the pope declared that anyone who joined it would have his sins forgiven. The first Teutonic Knights arrived in Prussia in 1230 and took energetic measures to expand their control over the country. The warriors themselves did not seek to save souls; their task was to make the territory safe for Christian missionaries and converts. Whether they actually forced the native Prussians to accept baptism at sword's point is a disputed question. Certainly the Teutonic Order viewed conversion of the heathen as the justification for its activities in Prussia, which otherwise would have appeared as quite ordinary wars of conquest. However, the Knights treated even baptized Prussians as inferiors and often turned them into serfs. The result in 1260 was a very widespread and well-coordinated uprising. The Prussians captured many of the Order's fortresses in the interior of the country, though not those along the Baltic or the Vistula, and sacrificed their Christian captives to pagan gods. Not until 1273 did the Christian overlords of Prussia succeed in completely suppressing this revolt.

The Teutonic Order of Knights was a monastic organization including warriors of both knightly and nonknightly rank, together with clerics and lay brothers and sisters who performed service functions. All lived in the fortresses belonging to the Order and took the usual monastic vows of chastity, obedience, and poverty. Prospective members had to show that they were not the property of any lord, while married men were required to leave their wives, and men claiming knightly status had to offer proof of sufficiently high birth. Warriors of nonknightly rank did not fight in full armor and were allowed fewer horses than the knights. Aside from the parish priests who were coopted into the organization, clerical members were expected to educate the others in spiritual matters, copy useful books, and occupy the various offices necessary to the Order's functioning. Lay brothers served in the fields or workshops. The lay sisters (who were not counted as full members) were pious menial workers from the lower classes since women of a higher status were not desired in the Order. The lay sisters wore gray cloaks, worked in the hospitals, prepared food, and looked after the brothers' clothing.

They lived in houses next to the brothers' cloisters and received spiritual direction from them.

Discipline was stern in the Teutonic Order. Everyone spent at least five hours a day in prayer and spiritual exercises at the prescribed canonical hours. Each member was allowed only two sets of clothing—rough robelike garments in a "clerical" color (i.e., black, white, brown, or gray) with a black cross, which was the Order's distinctive emblem. (Lay brothers and sisters wore only a half-cross.) Men of knightly or clerical rank were distinguishable by their white cloaks. The warrior monks, who in combat wore complete armor over their monastic dress, had to practice regularly with their weapons. Meals were simple, with many days devoted to strict fasts. Knightly entertainments (such as tournaments or hunting) and conversations outside of the monastic residence were forbidden. Members were also not allowed to live in towns, ride out alone, read or write letters, or associate with persons in secular life. Any contact with the heathen (other than war against them) counted as a grievous offense equivalent to desertion and resulted in expulsion from the Order. The number of actual knights in the organization was never large: probably never more than a thousand at most. Their ranks were supplemented periodically by professional soldiers from all over Europe, especially from the German Empire. The Teutonic Order's military campaigns in Prussia and Livonia kept the crusading ideal alive in western Christendom long after the principal Crusades to the Holy Land had come to an end. To have fought against the enemies of Christ in Prussia was a source of pride, even though many of the participants were minor nobles in need of employment, inspired chiefly by the hope of glory, plunder, and ransoms.

Uprisings of the heathen against their conquerors were ultimately defeated everywhere in Europe. However, the beliefs which had inspired them did not disappear so easily. A substantial residue of paganism persisted in East Central Europe for many centuries even after Christianity had become the officially recognized faith. The average Christian remained convinced that the world of nature was pervaded by spirits of all kinds. Fairies and nymphs, devils and witches were at least as real to medieval people as the Christian saints. Marriage remained a secular, not a religious rite. Ancient customs concerning death and burial continued to be observed; and the return of dead spirits was greatly feared. As a concession to popular superstition, even the Church's calendar contained many feast days of pagan origin which were only superficially Christian.

The transformation of nominal Christianity into a true faith of the people was the work of generations of priests and missionaries. At first many of these were foreign monks. In the Orthodox lands of East Central Europe the largest number were Greeks; in the Catholic lands, Germans. In many cases the language barrier was a serious obstacle. Bulgaria was relatively fortunate in this respect, since its traditional cultural ties with Byzantium meant that some educated Bulgars knew Greek already. A knowledge of German was widespread in Bohemia, which was part of the German Empire and maintained strong links with the great monastery of Saint Emmeram at Regensburg, the chief point of departure for missionaries to the Czech lands. Nonetheless, for a long time the shortage of Czech priests caused difficulties. Most offices in the Bohemian ecclesiastical hierarchy were occupied by Germans, who frequently did not learn Czech. Germans dominated to a lesser extent in the Polish Church, where Bohemians likewise played a key role, aided by the marked similarity between the Czech and Polish languages. For Hungary the German diocese of Salzburg provided many missionaries. However, communication was a serious problem for them, since the Magyar tongue resembled no other except Finnish in either Eastern or Western Europe. The fact that most foreign missionaries did not speak Hungarian, while the first native Hungarian priests generally came from the lower classes, made it difficult for the proud Magyar warriors to accept the new faith. Ultimately, however, the training of native priests was an indispensable prerequisite to any large-scale conversion of the population.

A central element in both Eastern and Western medieval Christianity was monasticism. Monastic life exemplified the supreme Christian ideals of the age: devotion to God's service in chastity, poverty, and obedience to one's ecclesiastical superiors. Until the 12th century in the Catholic lands of East Central Europe most monasteries followed the rule of Saint Benedict, which stressed work as well as prayer and did not encourage unbridled asceticism. Benedictine monasteries were often founded in remote forests far from any centers of population, which forced the monks to clear the land for farming and turned them into colonizers. Their presence inevitably attracted peasant settlers, so that in time the monastic foundations became less isolated. By comparison, Orthodox monks concentrated their efforts more upon meditation, prayer, and fasting. Their asceticism was carried to greater lengths; and tendencies toward mysticism were prominent among them.

The organization of monastic life also differed considerably from East to West. Catholic monks belonged to federations known as orders, whose activities crossed many diocesan boundaries. Each order had a constitution and founded houses for its monks in accordance with specific priorities. New orders were established only with the approval of the pope, who also exercised general supervision over their activities. By contrast, monastic orders did not exist in the Orthodox world. Ordinarily the local bishop supervised the monasteries in his diocese, although some houses were subject to a metropolitan bishop or even to the patriarch of Constantinople. A few, like the famous houses on Mount Athos in Greece, stood under the direct orders of the Byzantine emperor. While in general all Orthodox cloisters followed the rules originally prescribed by Saint Basil in the 4th century, each one was a separate foundation with its own rules. Some contact among them was maintained by the fact that Orthodox monks often made a practice of wandering from one monastery to another, as a kind of spiritual pilgrimage. However, the lack of institutional support caused many of the Eastern foundations to fall into disrepair and cease to exist within a relatively short time.

A further point of contrast with Western Christianity was the fact that in the Eastern Church monks monopolized all positions in the ecclesiastical hierarchy. Bishops, archbishops, and patriarchs invariably were monks. The archbishop of an Orthodox country was usually by origin a nobleman who had won his spiritual credentials by assuming the monk's cowl, living for a while in one of the monasteries on Mount Athos, and making the pilgrimage to Jerusalem. Orthodox monks, unlike their Western counterparts, were also at liberty to reenter secular life or engage in a variety of worldly activities if they so desired. Frequently they migrated from one monastery to another. This wandering favored the spread of theological influences and promoted a sense of belonging to the world of Orthodoxy as a whole.

Monasteries also served a variety of nonreligious functions. The earliest schools of medieval Europe were established in abbeys; and most authors of medieval histories, annals, and chronicles were monks. Private persons often deposited important documents in the monasteries for safety, such as records concerning the purchase and sale of property, division of estates, manumission of slaves, and wills. The authority and prestige of the major monastic institutions provided the best possible guarantee that the documents would be preserved. In Hungary the great abbey of Pannonhalma served for centuries as the literary center of the country and produced many documents for the royal chancellery. In towns the monks often managed hospitals, schools, orphanages, and old age homes. Moving freely among the population, they exhorted believers to greater piety, gave advice, and strongly influenced public opinion. Balkan rulers donated funds to cloisters in Greece or Asia Minor in order to obtain financial support abroad during their periods of exile. Owing to the rarity of towns in the medieval Balkans, monasteries also served as bishops' residences.

The Orthodox monasteries in Europe generally adapted their rules from one of the famous Greek cloisters of the Near East. The monks lived a communal life, practicing silence, humility, frequent fasting, and sleeplessness. They prayed frequently, sang hymns, and performed numerous prostrations. On festive occasions their worship services sometimes continued without interruption through an entire night. Monks ordinarily ate only fish and vegetables, no meat, and little wine. Their cloisters typically were located in isolated spots with large surrounding properties, on which they planted vineyards and orchards. By virtue of their example and their reputation for holiness, the monks exerted great influence over the population of their region. Those who sought an even more strenuous regimen became hermits in the mountains or forests, sometimes living in caves, sometimes out in the open with only trees or brush for shelter, where they were subject to all the vagaries of the weather.

The monks themselves ran the gamut from the illiterate and superstitious to the most highly educated men of their time. In either case they were greatly revered by the Orthodox population, which viewed them as holy men especially close to God. Lay Christians from all ranks of society undertook pilgrimages to famous monasteries, while poor folk sought alms in front of their gates. A common way for a layman to demonstrate piety was to make gifts to a cloister. Monarchs and nobles presented the monastic orders with uninhabited forested lands, hoping not only that the monks would clear the area for settlement but also that an invading enemy would hesitate to desecrate property dedicated to religion. Some monasteries were rather small affairs with no more than ten to twenty resident monks. When the original founder died, his heirs sometimes repossessed the land and the monastery itself disappeared. Other establishments, particularly the royal foundations, became holders of enormous properties which permitted their inhabitants to live in a comfortable and often very secular life-style.

Many Orthodox monarchs made generous gifts of land and treasure to more than one monastery, including some on Mount Athos (in Byzantine Thrace) and others in Palestine. All Serbian rulers beginning with Stephen Nemanya I (r. 1168–96) built at least one monastery church, considering this as essential for their souls' salvation. Powerful Balkan lords competed in zeal to found monasteries and endow them with rich gifts. Noblewomen embroidered rich sacerdotal vestments in gold thread for the monks. The abbots collected dues and received labor services from the peasants on their domains just like any secular lord. Eventually the monasteries won "immunities" from royal taxes and feudal services, thereby creating a precedent for other religious institutions and ultimately for secular landholders as well. It was not unusual for young noblemen and occasionally noblewomen as well to embrace the monastic life. Following Byzantine custom, Orthodox rulers sometimes took monastic vows when they felt death approaching. Owing to the equation of celibacy with purity, monks in the Orthodox world were regarded as morally superior to priests, who could marry and have families and engaged in agriculture and stock raising to supplement their incomes. The parish clergy received plots of land in hereditary tenure or the use of tax-free land, but for the most part lived on the same economic level as the peasantry.

Certain Orthodox cloisters became noteworthy as cultural institutions, specializing in the work of copying and translating church books. The foundations at Preslav and Ohrid in Bulgaria or Neamţ in Moldavia were particularly famous for this. However, the preeminent center of Orthodox literary and artistic life was Mount Athos, the home of an entire complex of monasteries. Located in Thrace on a peninsula jutting into the Aegean Sea, it benefited from easy communication by both sea and land to Salonika and Constantinople. Athos was an autonomous monastic republic, founded in the second half of the 10th century upon a wave of enthusiasm for the ascetic life. Its cloisters gained great prestige, both because of the monks' holy life and because of the literary activities conducted there. Rich patronage came from many foreign sovereigns, including the rulers of Bulgaria, Serbia, and Walachia, who sought in return to receive the monks' blessings. The monasteries of Athos attracted men of many nationalities, although the Greek element was dominant. While the cloisters excluded no one on ethnic grounds alone, several of the houses on Athos acquired a specific national character. The Zograf monastery was chiefly Bulgarian, while Hilandar was Serbian.

The growing wealth of the monasteries inevitably led to laxity in standards, whereby the monks' vow of poverty was largely ignored. In the Latin West in the 12th century a wave of church reform led to the founding of two new monastic orders—the Cistercians and Praemonstratensians—both of which soon became firmly established in Hungary, Bohemia, and Poland. The Cistercians were particularly noted for their energy and expertise in clearing and coloniz-ing land. Forbidden to spend money on themselves or in ornamenting their churches, they invested their surpluses in land and ultimately became wealthy. One example of a successful Cistercian enterprise was the Goldenkron monastery in Bohemia, which owned nearly a thousand square miles of land with seventy villages. Moreover, the Cistercians established important ties with high society by serving as confessors to kings and tutors for royal children, among them the offspring of the Hungarian King Béla III. The Praemonstratensians made missionary activity their primary concern, going out into the world as beggar monks or itinerant apostles to teach and proclaim the faith. Both Cistercian and Praemonstratensian monks remained in close contact with their French mother houses. Their abbots and priors were required to appear every third year at the general assemblies of their order in Cîteaux and Prémontré respectively, while the daughter houses received visits every third year from their superiors in France. In this way important cultural ties were forged between France on the one hand and Bohemia, Hungary, and Poland on the other.

The attachment of simple people to Christianity in the Middle Ages was enhanced enormously by the cult of saints. Less remote and awe-inspiring than God, Jesus, or even Mary, the saints could be approached for help in times of trouble. Both the Eastern and the Western Church encouraged reverence for saints, who were persons noted for exceptional holiness, miraculous works, or outstanding contributions to the Church. Their statues or pictures were promi-nently displayed in churches, and an official procedure was developed for can-onization. Many of the most popular medieval literary works were lives of saints, whose pious deeds and ultimate martyrdom were presented to the populace as worthy of admiration and emulation. Members of royal families were often made saints by the Church, so that their cults became associated with the dynasty's attempts to create loyalty to the state. A saint from one's own royal house or kingdom became a point of pride. Monarchs often intervened in Rome to have their candidates canonized.

Bohemia became the first land of Western Christendom to produce a native saint—the young Duke Wenceslas (d. 929), who captured the Czech imagination at an early date. He became the subject of numerous legends praising his charity to the poor, his protection of widows and orphans, his endowment of churches, and his humane concept of justice. Despite many later competitors, Wenceslas (Václav) remained the most beloved of all the Czech medieval saints. Other Bohemians were canonized in the 12th century: Ludmila, the grandmother of Wenceslas; Procopius, the abbot of the Sázava monastery; Vitus, for whom the great Prague cathedral is named; and Sigismund, the patron of the Přemyslid dynasty. Hungary in the 11th century also produced several royal saints: Stephen, its first Christian king; his pious son Emeric, who died before he could reign; and King Ladislas I, a devout sovereign as well as a chivalrous soldier. From the 13th century came two royal Hungarian female saints: Elizabeth, the daughter of King Andrew II; and Margaret, the daughter of Béla IV. The Slovenes acquired a patron saint in Virgil, the learned 8th-century Irish monk and missionary who founded the first churches in Slovene territory. The Bohemian saint John Nepomuk, who died in 1393, attracted little attention until in the 18th century he became the object of a Jesuit-sponsored cult designed to counteract the popularity of the Hussite martyrs. Nepomuk's claim to martyrdom was that as vicar-general of Prague he had helped thwart the wish of King Wenceslas IV to erect a new bishopric for one of his cronies. The king had him arrested, tied up, and thrown into the Moldau River, where he drowned.

In Poland the first recognized saint was Adalbert (Vojtěch), a high Czech noble and bishop of Prague who moved to Poland after the duke of Bohemia had massacred his family. Famous for his asceticism and intense religiosity, Adalbert invited martyrdom by becoming a missionary to the fierce heathen Prussians, who killed him in 997. Ultimately both Czechs and Poles claimed him as a national saint. The Polish Duke Boleslav I ransomed his corpse and had it buried with great ceremony at Gniezno, recognizing that possession of a holy martyr's body was a national asset. Adalbert was canonized as early as 999, and his shrine at Gniezno attracted many pilgrims. Then in 1039 the Bohemians stole his body during their invasion of Poland, diminishing the importance of his cult for the Poles. The new patron saint of Poland was Archbishop Stanislas of Cracow, who was murdered in 1079 while saying Mass in the cathedral. According to legend, the Polish Duke Boleslav II killed this future saint with his own hand after accusing him of plotting against the throne. The truth or falsity of the charge is now impossible to judge, but outrage at the deed sufficed to drive Boleslav into exile. Stanislas ultimately became the most revered of all the Polish saints.

The Eastern Orthodox Church produced its own saints. Among them were Cyril and Methodius, the 9th-century apostles to the Slavs, as well as Methodius's disciples Clement and Naum, noted for their work in spreading Christianity in Macedonia (i.e., western Bulgaria). The most famous Bulgarian saint was John (Ivan) of Rila, who founded the important Rila monastery in the 10th century. In his "Spiritual Testament" John formulated a rigorous set of rules for cloisters which combined personal asceticism with manual labor and community life. Ultimately he abandoned his own foundation in order to undergo the still more rigorous trial of total solitude. Saint John of Rila belongs in the rich tradition of holy hermits which occupies so prominent a place in Eastern Orthodoxy. Much less typical was the Serbian Saint Sava, who combined a lifelong devotion to monasticism with great political skill in advancing the cause of his royal house. The son of Grand Župan Stephen Nemanya, Sava (his monastic name) fled as a youth of seventeen to the holy mountain of Athos, where he entered a cloister. Together with his father, who late in life joined him as a monk there, he established the Hilandar monastery for Serbian monks. This foundation soon became the preeminent center of Serbian Orthodox piety and learning.

Without question Sava was a towering figure in medieval Serbian ecclesiastical and cultural life. As the influential abbot of the Studenica monastery, founded by his father, he introduced the monastic rule already in effect at Hilandar and established many additional monastic retreats. Together with his brother, King Stephen the First-Crowned, he founded the great monastery of Žiča which became Serbia's leading shrine. In 1219 he undertook the mission to the Byzantine emperor and patriarch at Nicaea by which the Serbian Orthodox Church gained autocephalous status (i.e., full administrative and judicial sovereignty) together with the right of all future Serbian archbishops to be elected by their own suffragans. The patriarch then consecrated Sava himself as the first archbishop of Serbia. Returning home in 1220, Sava proceeded to reorganize the Serbian Church, probably with eleven bishoprics (including three on territory formerly subordinate to the archbishopric of Ohrid). In 1229 he journeyed to Jerusalem, where he established hospices for Serbian monks and pilgrims and visited the famous monastery of Saint Sabas. The rule of that monastery had become widely adopted in the Orthodox monasteries of the East by this time; and upon his return home in 1230 Sava introduced a modified form of it into Serbia, known as the Jerusalem Rule. Ultimately both Sava and his father Stephen Nemanya (now known by his monastic name of Symeon) became recognized as saints in Serbia. However, only Sava ranked as such abroad, since the patriarchate of Constantinople disliked granting this distinction to laymen.

The differences between the Eastern and Western branches of Christianity grew more pronounced with time. Centuries of separate existence had led to important variations in practice, particularly during the 7th to 10th centuries when the Muslims' near-monopoly of Mediterranean shipping cut off most East-West contacts. The Greek and Latin liturgies diverged from each other in both form and content, the Greek one being more complex. The Western Church insisted on a single ritual chanted only in Latin, while the Eastern Church tolerated many languages. Greek priests wore beards; Latin ones shaved. The Greeks performed baptisms by immersion, the Latins by sprinkling with water. Orthodox Christians prayed standing; Catholics knelt. For communion the Orthodox used leavened bread; Catholics used unleavened bread.

Theological formulations differed as well. The Roman Church imposed strict definitions of dogma, while Orthodoxy kept many doctrines purposely imprecise, leaving fundamental issues unresolved. Orthodox theologians believed that certain elements of the faith were better left mysterious, inasmuch as no human being could know the mind of God. Toward philosophy and logic, the crowning achievements of the Greek intellect, they evinced considerable skepticism. Perhaps because they knew it too well, they regarded the philosopher's search for exact formulas as dangerous to the faith and conducive to hair-splitting. Orthodoxy never developed fixed views on transubstantiation, purgatory, or divorce—key issues destined to shatter the unity of the Roman Church during the Protestant Reformation. On the other hand, Orthodox thinkers preserved great respect for tradition as such. Aware that the ecumenical councils of the early Church (4th–7th centuries) had pronounced upon many difficult points of doctrine, they generally felt that the practices of centuries should not be altered.

Particularly divisive was the Western Church's insertion of the word *filioque* into the Nicene Creed, the fundamental statement of Christian faith as proclaimed by the Council of Nicaea in the year 325. The Eastern Church taught that the Holy Spirit originated with God the Father alone and passed from the Father "through the Son." The Western Church countered that the Spirit proceeded from the Father "*and* the Son" (in Latin: *filioque*), a formulation which treated Jesus as co-eternal with the Father. Quite aside from the fact that *filioque* was an innovation of Western origin and abhorrent to traditionalists for that reason, conflict over this single word in the Creed involved two quite different concepts of the person of Christ. Compromise was impossible, since the primacy of the Father over the Son was the point in question. The Orthodox Church refused to accept *filioque*, while the Roman Church insisted upon it. Another disputed point concerned the position of the Roman pope, who claimed authority over the entire Christian Church. The Greek-speaking East regarded the pope as merely one of the five ecumenical patriarchs, albeit the first among equals. The Greeks insisted that direct authority over the Eastern Church belonged only to the patriarch of Constantinople.

Still another basic difference concerned clerical celibacy. During its first thousand years of existence the Church had permitted ordinary parish priests to have wives (as long as they married before ordination), although monks always took vows of chastity. In the Western Church the rule of celibacy existed for priests as well. Nonetheless, prior to the 11th century the popes had never seriously attempted to enforce this rule, knowing full well that the task would be stupendous. Parish clergy were unavoidably exposed to sexual temptations in the course of their duties, whereas priests who were already married resisted giving up their wives. Finally the reforming pontiffs of the 11th and 12th centuries resolved to make the necessary effort to compel observance of the rule. Predictably, the task proved enormously difficult.

In Bohemia the effort to enforce priestly celibacy began in the 1140s with the mission of a papal legate, who ordered all married priests to renounce their wives and deprived those who refused of their sacerdotal offices. Nonetheless, it was only in the 13th century in Bohemia that clerical celibacy was enforced with some consistency. The Church in Poland issued injunctions on the subject of celibacy for the first time in 1197. Soon afterward the energetic Polish Archbishop Henry Kietlicz began to enforce the rule by conducting frequent visitations in his diocese and suspending offenders from their priestly functions. However, his successors showed less zeal in this cause, which made only modest progress in Poland during the Middle Ages. In Hungary, where a strong monarchy was powerful enough to impose its will on the Church, the kings proved reluctant to force this issue. One complication was that the Orthodox Church, with its legitimately married priests, retained many outposts in eastern Transylvania in the 11th and 12th centuries—a situation bound to make celibacy for Catholic priests difficult to uphold. Nonetheless, under pressure from the papacy a series of Hungarian church synods gradually tightened the rules. Not surprisingly, the question of priestly celibacy became one of the most stubborn obstacles to a reunion of the Eastern and Western Church. The Roman hierarchy had fought too hard against its own clergy on this point to permit any concessions.

The year 1054 is the usual date given for the final and definitive schism between the Eastern and Western Church, although for a long time afterward much of Christendom behaved as though nothing had happened. Pope and patriarch had already quarreled more than once over their respective spheres of administrative jurisdiction in the Balkans. For centuries these two ecclesiastical potentates had competed for the allegiance of Balkan Christians. Then in the 1030s adventurers from Normandy—adherents of the Latin Church—began to occupy Byzantine-held territories in southern Italy. The pope now claimed ecclesiastical jurisdiction over this region, which the Greek patriarch refused to concede. Papal legates were sent to Constantinople to resolve the dispute, but agreement proved impossible to achieve. The legates then excommunicated the patriarch; and subsequently a council of the Eastern Church condemned everyone who supported the pope. The impasse was total. Nevertheless no one at the time expected the estrangement to be permanent. Efforts at reuniting the two churches occurred intermittently down to the eve of Constantinople's fall to the Turks in 1453.

The enmity between Greeks and Latins increased rather than diminished over time. The behavior of the Western Crusaders who passed through the Byzantine Empire on their way to Palestine created an enormous backlash. By the refined standards of Byzantine civilization the Latins were crude and uncivilized rustics, arrogant and overbearing. Too many of them plundered and murdered, burned towns, destroyed churches, stole sacred objects, and treated Orthodox Christians with contempt as "schismatics." The Byzantines were shocked that Latin bishops and priests carried weapons and participated in battles, murdering with the same hand which held the sacred host. For their part the Westerners felt aggrieved that the Byzantines did not better appreciate the high purpose of their odyssey to the Holy Land, for which the pope had promised great spiritual rewards. The crowning indignity occurred in 1204, when knights of the Fourth Crusade captured Constantinople and attempted to impose Latin Christianity upon the population. After the restoration of Greek rule in 1261, the Byzantine clergy and public remained unremittingly hostile when—desperate for Western aid to save the tottering empire—the emperor and patriarch on several occasions agreed to a union of churches.

The theory of a universal Church in a universal state required that an emperor must have a patriarch or pope by his side. Both the Byzantine and the German empires claimed to be universal states. Thus the Greek emperor had his patriarch, and the German emperor sought to control Rome. However, lesser rulers with imperial pretensions likewise wanted their highest ecclesiastical official to be a patriarch. Symeon I of Bulgaria, who aspired to the throne of Constantinople, unilaterally raised the archbishop of Bulgaria to this dignity in 917 or 919. After the Byzantine reconquest of Bulgaria in 1018, this patriarchate, centered at Ohrid in Macedonia, was reduced to the rank of archbishopric. In 1235, John Asen II, who called himself "tsar" (i.e., "emperor"), wanted a Bulgarian prelate again to hold patriarchal rank. Since the Byzantine government at Nicaea needed John's alliance against the Latin Empire, it agreed to recognize this title, and a second Bulgarian patriarchate was established at the Bulgarian capital of Tirnovo. Subsequently, Stephen Dušan of Serbia, who also termed himself "emperor," naturally wanted a patriarch too. In 1346 he held a church council at Skopje which raised the archbishop of Serbia to that rank, with his seat at Peć. However, in canon law unilateral elevation by a mere Balkan monarch meant nothing. No one ever regarded a patriarch of Bulgaria or Serbia as equal in status to the patriarch of any of the ancient Eastern sees.

Rulers of every rank wished to preside over a Church independent of foreign powers, which meant that the country's leading prelate must rank at least as an archbishop. Some monarchs successfully negotiated this independence at the same time that their realms officially became Christian (e.g., Boris of Bulgaria and Stephen I of Hungary). Others acquired an archbishopric only later, like Stephen the First-Crowned of Serbia, who in 1220 gained the Greek patriarch's approval for an autonomous Serbian Church. In Poland the missionary bishopric of Poznań dated from the time of Emperor Otto I (r. 936–73), but the archbishopric of Gniezno was founded already in the year 1000, with a territory comprising nearly the entire Polish state. When King Casimir the Great conquered new territories in Galicia in the 14th century, he arranged with the Greek patriarch to establish a separate archbishopric for Galicia's Orthodox population. The object was to detach Poland's new subjects from the jurisdiction of the metropolitan of "Kiev and All Russia," whose headquarters were in Moscow. By contrast, Bohemia until the 14th century was included in the territory of the German imperial Church; and the German emperors were entitled to invest the bishop of Prague with his insignia of office. After many efforts by the Bohemian monarchs to win an independent archbishopric for Prague,

Charles, the heir to the throne (later King Charles I), finally achieved this in 1344.

Since the Roman pope and Greek patriarch both desired genuine authority over their churches, they resisted as far as possible the demands of secular monarchs for church autonomy. But while the Greek patriarchs could not exercise secular authority, the popes became a major force in European politics. Their independence of lay rulers, at least in theory, gave them not only spiritual freedom but also great flexibility in political maneuver. In the period of the so-called imperial papacy (1073–1303), the Roman pontiffs claimed entire countries as papal fiefs. Proclaiming that spiritual power was superior to secular power, they claimed the right to install or depose kings, and declared that total submission to the Holy See was indispensable for salvation. Even in the 14th and 15th centuries they could seriously undermine the position of any secular ruler who refused them obedience.

This situation often led contenders for a throne to try to strengthen their position through papal support. One such case involved King Zvonimir of Croatia, who attempted to fortify a weak claim to the throne by declaring himself the pope's vassal. Zvonimir swore an "unbreakable feudal oath . . . to always be true to my lord, Pope Gregory [VII], and his legally elected successors" and "to fulfill everything which the pope or his legate have obliged me to do, or will require in the future, without hesitation." He lived up to these commitments also, participating in several foreign campaigns to fight the pope's enemies. Precisely this excess of loyalty led to his undoing. In 1089 when a pope again requested military aid, Zvonimir summoned an assembly of the land to the field of Knin and appealed to his nobles to join the new war. Some of the Croatian nobility evidently felt that this was carrying subservience too far. Shouting that they had no wish to fight for the pope, they provoked an armed melée in which the king was killed.

A pope intervened in Hungary on several occasions to place one of his protegés on the throne. The Angevin rulers of Naples, related through the female line to the Árpád dynasty, were semipermanent papal allies who served as counterweights to the attempts of the German Emperors to control northern Italy. When the last Árpád king of Hungary in the direct male line died in 1290, the pope declared Hungary a papal fief and by virtue of his alleged feudal supremacy granted the country to King Charles II of Naples. Disregarding this move, the Hungarians elected Andrew the Venetian, a descendant of King Béla IV through the female line, who accordingly took the throne. When Andrew in turn died in 1301 without heirs, the pope encouraged a younger member of the Angevin house, Charles Robert of Naples, to press his claims. The Neapolitan prince captured Buda that same year, while the pope excommunicated its citizens for supporting the rival candidate. Finally after years of civil war, a majority of the Hungarian lords in 1308 accepted Charles Robert as king and permitted the papal legate to confirm his election. After this the pontiffs ceased to claim Hungary as a papal fief, but continued to promote the cause of the Angevin dynasty. In 1403, Pope Boniface IX sought to depose King Sigismund of Hungary, with whom he had quarreled, by supporting (in vain) a pretender to the throne of Hungary.

When Christianity was established initially in Bohemia, Poland, and Hungary, the rulers automatically assumed the right to appoint bishops or archbishops to dioceses located on their territories. The official Church at first registered no objection to this practice. In Hungary the first Christian king, Stephen I, organized the ecclesiastical hierarchy himself, dividing the country into ten dioceses and appointing the bishops. Similarly the rulers of Poland assumed the right to collect taxes and demand feudal services from the lands of any vacant bishopric until a new bishop could be installed. On the whole, church and state still acted as allies rather than competitors. From the mid-10th to mid-11th centuries the German emperor not only made all appointments to bishoprics in his lands, but even selected the Roman pope. This practice came to an end in the 1070s, owing to the investiture controversy between emperor Henry IV and Pope Gregory VII over the question of who was entitled to grant a bishop the symbols of office. According to canon law, long since fallen into disuse, no layman should ever appoint a bishop or perform the investiture ceremony. A bishop was supposed to be elected by the canons (clergy) of his cathedral.

The popes described their efforts to assert the power of appointment as a matter of the Church's spiritual well-being, thus playing upon the fears which medieval people commonly held concerning their own salvation. Opposition to a pontiff's wishes allegedly prejudiced the soul's chances of entering Heaven. The pope could also make use of weapons which were by no means negligible in the Middle Ages. Papal excommunication excluded a person from all contact with good Christians. The papal interdict or ban closed all churches in the affected area and rendered unavailable the most essential church services, including baptism and extreme unction. Popes of the 11th–13th centuries demonstrated more than once their willingness to employ such methods. Until spiritual penalties of this type became devalued through excessive use, they threatened to arouse popular anger against the guilty monarch and disturb the peace of the realm. Fear of papal punishment impelled most secular rulers to observe at least the outward forms of canonical election to bishoprics.

In practice the most important churches of a country were usually controlled directly by the monarch. Smaller churches on private estates were regarded as the property of the landowner, who collected the income from "his" church and appointed its priests. However, by the 12th century some bishops had begun to challenge the lay ownership and domination of these "proprietary" or private churches. Councils held in 1123 and in 1139 at the Church of the Lateran in Rome went on record as forbidding laypersons to be the proprietors of churches or make priestly appointments. These Lateran councils decreed that only a bishop could invest a priest with his office, although secular lords might propose candidates. Political realities dictated otherwise. In many cases a lord or his ancestors had founded a particular church and regarded the appointment of its priest as his right. Kings possessed their own churches, exercising the same rights of patronage. The church hierarchy now began to promote the compromise notion that a landowner was "patron" rather than "proprietor" of the churches on his property. A patron in theory would consider the spiritual welfare of his church as paramount and treat as secondary his temporal interests (e.g., his share of the tithe and the fees that the priest collected for his services). This new concept made little difference in practice. A monarch now simply presented his candidates for church office to the bishop of the appropriate diocese, who usually confirmed the choices more or less automatically. The nobles on their private estates continued to install or remove clergy as they pleased.

Nonetheless, the system of church appointment gradually was modified. In Bohemia in the early 13th century the cathedral chapters of both Prague and Olomouc obtained the right to elect their own bishops, although the king retained his old prerogative of presenting a candidate. Only in the 14th century did the Bohemian Church actively supervise the installation of priests. Even then the practice was for the archbishop to honor a noble's choice of appointee for any church located on his property, while the noble recognized the archbishop's right to confirm him. The reformers had more success in Poland in the 13th century, owing to the fragmented state of the country at that period. Archbishop Kietlicz (appointed 1199) insisted on free election of bishops by the cathedral chapters, abolition of lay investiture, tax freedom for church estates, and various other changes which would have made the Church virtually independent of the state. When the Cracow duke (titular suzerain over all Poland) resisted these measures, the pope excommunicated him and the duke was driven from the realm. His successor took the lesson to heart, placed Poland under papal protection, and permitted the free election of bishops. In 1207 for the first time in Polish history, the canons of Cracow cathedral chose their own bishop—the learned chronicler Vincent Kadłubek. Thereafter, free election remained standard practice in Poland for as long as the country remained divided. Following the reunification and strengthening of the monarchy in the 14th century, however, the king in effect usually made these appointments. The cathedral chapters still held an election; but the king's candidate generally won, and the pope then confirmed him.

In Hungary, which was a more powerful kingdom than either Bohemia or Poland in the 12th and 13th centuries, the reformers had less success in the matter of church appointments. Although the king agreed to observe the formalities of canonical election, he retained considerable real control over the process. At a synod in 1106, King Koloman renounced his former right to grant church positions outright, but continued to exert great influence in designating the candidates, merely doing so less openly than before. Hungary's status as a major power in Central Europe impelled the pope to treat him with caution. For most appointments the king reached prior agreement with the canons or monks concerned, who then proceeded to elect the royal candidate. Conversely, the pope usually requested the king's approval before confirming an election. If the king and cathedral chapter could not agree on a candidate, the pope was supposed to decide, and usually he accepted the monarch's choice. Nonetheless, in many cases a bishop designate was allowed to possess his see and collect its revenues even before the pope confirmed him. The provisions of canonical election were sometimes ignored entirely. Persons with high political connections, particularly the king's relatives, sometimes received high church offices even when youth, lack of education, or scandalous morals made them wholly unsuitable. The right of individual lords to control their private churches was repeatedly confirmed by the Hungarian Diet and formally recognized by the papal curia.

The popes attempted to bring some important church appointments under their personal control through the doctrine of papal "reservation." As supreme heads of the Church, they claimed the right to name candidates to ecclesiastical benefices irrespective of the wishes of either the cathedral canons or the king of the country. Local clergy, however, greatly resented the pope's appointments, which diminished their own chances for preferment in the Church. They railed against "foreign clerics," who were often members of the papal curia being rewarded for loyal service. Pressures for local appointment intensified with the rise of a university-educated class in the 14th century, since many graduates sought careers in their national churches. By this time the substantial and growing revenues of ecclesiastical benefices had made them increasingly attractive to the upper classes, especially when no corresponding duties were required. A benefice might provide a student with the leisure for scholarship, but might equally well finance a noble's high living. Other benefices were supposed to involve duties, but the holders usually neglected to perform them. For example, at an earlier period the canons of the cathedrals had lived in the chapter houses and actively assisted their bishops in celebrating Mass and administering the dioceses. However, by the middle of the 14th century most canons held benefices which enabled them to live privately and hire substitutes to conduct church services. Some maintained elementary and secondary schools and served as notaries public. Others merely collected the revenue to which their benefices entitled them.

Eventually the efforts of the popes to claim rights of church appointment collided head-on with the growing national self-awareness of the secular states. The papacy began increasingly to be viewed as a foreign institution. More important, the Church in the course of centuries had acquired such enormous economic and political power that no monarch could afford indifference to the identity of his bishops and abbots. In 1403 a serious clash over papal reservations erupted between Pope Boniface IX and King Sigismund of Hungary, who had resisted the pope's claim to make appointments in the Hungarian Church. In retaliation Boniface took the drastic step of encouraging a pretender, Ladislas of Naples, to overthrow the king. Despite a pronounced coolness toward Sigismund, the majority of Hungarian nobles refused to support the papal action. In 1404 they retaliated in the Diet by approving a statute which expressly forbade the pope to appoint clergy in Hungary. National sentiment had been aroused. In 1445 the Diet formally ordered the newly elected regent, John Hunyadi, to defend the interests of Hungary vis-à-vis the Roman curia. Since the papacy refused to yield on the question of church appointments, clashes recurred from time to time. In practice, when the Hungarian rulers needed the pope's political support, they sometimes still acceded to his demands—for example, by formally requesting him to nominate their designated candidate.

King Matthias (r. 1458–90) carried state authority over the Hungarian Church to still greater lengths. He did not even bother to ask the pope to make appointments, but only to confirm them. In handing over an ecclesiastical benefice he did not wait for the pope's approval. Matthias knew that he could count on the support of his nobility for an antipapal policy, and he made it plain that without royal permission no papal candidate would be allowed to take office in Hungary. Bluntly he told the pope (probably with some exaggeration): "The Hungarians would rather give up Catholicism and accept heresy than to permit the Holy See to make appointments to benefices in Hungary without the king's consent." During Matthias's reign, not a single bishop took office in Hungary without royal permission. In one particularly notorious case, he forced the pope to name a seven-year-old Italian relative of the queen as archbishop of Esztergom, threatening that in the event of refusal he would permit the child to assume the office anyway. Bishops could challenge such abuses only indirectly, often by insisting that appointees must either have (or subsequently acquire) a suitable level of education.

The Church in Catholic Europe financed its activities largely through the tithe—an obligatory payment of one-tenth of every sort of income. This tax was assessed on grain and other agricultural products, on the increase in the herds, and even on the proceeds from tariffs, tolls, and coinage. In theory everyone paid it—nobles, townsmen, peasants, and the king himself, although eventually many nobles secured exemptions for their personal estates. A relatively small part of the total—in Hungary no more than one-fourth at best—was assigned to the lower clergy for the care of souls, with the rest going to the bishops and cathedral chapters. In many cases the right to collect tithe was assigned to lessees, or tax farmers. This meant that the Church itself did not bear the costs of collection, while laypersons drew a profit from it. In theory this system also enabled the Church to receive the proceeds in money rather than in natural products, though frequently this was not achieved. Like any other tax, the tithe was often resented. The great Transylvanian peasant revolt of 1437–38 was caused in part by abuses in collecting it, reinforced by ecclesiastical sanctions against people who failed to pay. Particularly galling to Eastern Orthodox believers was the fact that they were obliged to pay tithe to the Catholic Church, although strictly speaking only Catholics were supposed to be liable for it.

When historical sources quote exact figures for ecclesiastical property, the amounts are impressive. Cases could be multiplied many times over. For example, in 1136 the archbishopric of Gniezno in Poland owned 149 villages, and by 1500 its property had increased to 303 villages and 13 towns. The Bohemian Church in the mid-13th century owned approximately 1,000 villages and 600 manorial estates. Monastic estates in Bohemia and Moravia, belonging to just 34 such institutions, comprised approximately one-third of all the land in the kingdom. Since this wealth greatly exceeded the amount necessary to maintain the monks and the parish clergy, the Church endowed many benefices which required the holder to perform no corresponding services. At the end of the 14th century in Prague, 700 "minor orders" were conferred each year, entitling the recipient to an income free of all obligation. In light of such figures, the bitter hostility of many radical Hussites in the 15th century toward monks and monasteries is hardly surprising. Ordinary working people, even if sincerely pious, hated the monks as parasites.

The Church in the Orthodox lands was also very rich, holding enormous properties which the monarch could not tax. Particularly wealthy were certain establishments in Macedonia. The monastery of Saint George near Skopje owned 27 villages at the beginning of the 14th century. The famous Rila monastery in 1378 held over 20. The monasteries on Mount Athos were especially well endowed, particularly Hilandar, which in the 13th and 14th centuries possessed more than 100 villages, chiefly in Serbia and Macedonia. At the end of the 14th century Hilandar was apparently the richest landowner in the Balkan Peninsula. In Walachia in the 14th–16th centuries, monastic property occupied about one-fifth of the territory. In many cases, monasteries abroad held title to such estates, thus providing a means of economic support for the Walachian princes in their frequent periods of exile as well as a foothold back home.

By contrast, the parish clergy everywhere were poor, due in large part to the excessive proportion of the Church's income taken by the hierarchy. A few reforming popes tried to ameliorate this situation. Thus the Third Lateran Council in 1170 forbade bishops, abbots, or other prelates to impose new taxes, raise old ones, or demand additional payments for themselves. In even clearer fashion the Fourth Lateran Council in 1215 blamed patrons and bishops for the fact that priests received so small a part of the Church's revenue. While the middle clergy—deacons and archdeacons—had various means of increasing their incomes, it was clear that the living standard of the lower clergy was unacceptably low. In Poland even as late as the 15th century many parishes remained without priests for years at a time, usually because of the low salaries offered. Priests in rich areas sometimes simply appropriated the income of the parishes and hired poorly paid vicars to perform the pastoral duties. Very few educated clerics wished to serve a congregation, preferring instead the more lucrative positions as ecclesiastical officials, for example, as canons of a cathedral.

Not infrequently secular monarchs were able to share in the Church's revenue, if only because their cooperation was required for its collection. In Hungary in the 14th century, King Charles Robert permitted papal officials to collect the tithe only on condition that they turn over one-third of the yield to him. This system proved very profitable for the royal treasury, since all the expenses of tax-gathering were borne by the Church. Whereas previously the king had placed obstacles in the path of papal tax collectors, now he sought to ensure that the sums they took in should be as large as possible. Charles Robert also acquired income from the Church by demanding payment from bishops newly installed in their dioceses, by retaining the income of vacant benefices for himself, and by requiring New Year's gifts from bishops and archbishops. If he dared, a monarch could exercise direct control over church revenue. In 14th-century Poland, King Casimir III insisted that all landed property unable to show a valid title should revert to the crown. Sigismund of Hungary confiscated the possessions and income of the prelates who supported the pope in the plot against him in 1403. King Wenceslas IV of Bohemia fully expected to share the profits from a sale of indulgences proclaimed by the pope in 1412. Outraged when the Hussite reformers criticized him for this, he ceased to treat them with his formerly benign tolerance.

In Catholic and Orthodox Europe alike, church property ordinarily was exempt from royal jurisdiction and taxes. Anyone with clerical status was excused from providing the monarch, the noble lords, or the towns with labor services or taxes in natural products or cash. For example, in Bulgaria in the 13th and 14th centuries the monasteries enjoyed full and irrevocable domination over their possessions. The tsar's officials had no access to monastic lands, carried out no functions there, and were forbidden to interfere in any way with activities on the property. They could not collect taxes or punish the dependents of a cloister (monks, overseers, serfs) even for acts committed elsewhere. The same system prevailed in Serbia, where the monasteries received services, natural products, or money from their dependents, but the monarch could not touch them. Monastery officials judged the peasants, punished them, and retained whatever fines were collected. Similarly in Catholic Bohemia, the king in 1222 exempted everyone living on ecclesiastical estates from the authority of state officials. A strong monarch like Casimir III in Poland could sometimes compel payment of a plow tax or household tax from church estates; and he demanded that the holders of church property either provide military service or give up their lands. However, when the central government was weak, the Church demanded additional privileges. In 1381 the Polish clergy claimed the right to pay no taxes at all on their lands. Finally they agreed to remit a small sum, defined as a voluntary gift rather than a tax.

The level of antagonism between Catholic and Orthodox believers was certainly greater in the 13th and 14th centuries than previously. Precisely in East Central Europe, where the two forms of Christian worship were often juxtaposed, hostility and intolerance were on the rise. Catholics commonly regarded the Orthodox as "schismatics" or "heretics" who ought to be converted to true

Christianity, whatever the method. Orthodox believers had equally little love for Catholics. However, the Catholic states were stronger than their Orthodox rivals, which gave their rulers greater opportunities to practice intolerance. In predominantly Catholic Hungary the adherents of Orthodoxy—meaning primarily the Vlachs of Transylvania—became subject to increased Catholic pressures in the second half of the 13th century. Some Vlachs responded by moving eastward across the Carpathians to settle in "Cumania"—the future Walachia and Moldavia.

King Louis of Hungary (r. 1342–82) showed a bigotry in religious matters well beyond the usual intolerance of the period. Political motives doubtless played a role in this—a strongly pro-Catholic policy would strengthen his ties to the pope—though such excesses were hardly necessary just to retain papal support. Louis's uncle, King Casimir III of Poland, showed far more benevolence toward his newly acquired Orthodox subjects in Ukraine without thereby forteiting papal favor. By contrast, Louis proclaimed that Hungary was a Catholic kingdom and began persecuting the Orthodox Church, despite the large number of his subjects who were Orthodox in religion. In 1366 he ordered the expulsion of all Orthodox priests from his realm (an order that must often have been circumvented). Louis was a strong exponent of forcible conversion, which he probably believed would strengthen his political hold on his kingdom by making it uniform in religion. After conquering the principality of Vidin in western Bulgaria in 1365, he installed Hungarian lords and Franciscan monks there who attempted to impose Catholicism on the primarily Orthodox population. Missionaries were permitted to baptize nearly a third of the inhabitants of Vidin according to the Catholic rite. However, military reverses soon rendered these conversions null and void, since in 1369 an army of Bulgars, Serbs, and Vlachs drove the Hungarians out. Louis also forced a majority of the Orthodox in Transylvania to be rebaptized as Catholics, which could only be done by force or threats of force and created considerable ill-will. He issued decrees that only Catholics could be recognized as nobles in the Hungarian kingdom, thus relegating the largely Orthodox Vlach population to the status of a permanent underclass. (Conversion to Catholicism removed this disability.) No organized Orthodox church hierarchy was permitted to function on Hungarian territory. As late as 1571, when Transylvania had become an autonomous vassal principality under Ottoman suzerainty, Orthodoxy was not among the four legal religions (Catholic, Lutheran, Calvinist, Unitarian) recognized by the provincial Diet. The faith of the numerous Vlach population was treated as nonexistent.

Enmities between Catholic and Orthodox believers intensified in Poland also. By the middle of the 12th century, the relative tolerance formerly prevailing between them had begun to wane. The envenomed atmosphere produced by the Crusades played its part in these developments; and the papacy sharpened the conflict by stressing the differences rather than the affinities between the two forms of Christianity. Hostility to Orthodoxy was very pronounced among the Polish clergy by the beginning of the 14th century. Inevitably, the laity absorbed these prejudices. Conflicts became even more acute when King Casimir III annexed the principality of Halicz (Galicia), which included the important trading city of Lvov. This eastern territory was largely Orthodox in religion, but also contained Armenians of the Gregorian rite. Casimir actively promoted the advance of Catholicism in Halicz, even persuading the pope to renounce part of his usual tithe to help finance the wars against Orthodox "schismatics." Nonetheless the Polish king refused to authorize forcible conversions, fearing that such a policy would undermine his authority. Henceforth in Halicz a Catholic, an Orthodox, and an Armenian hierarchy functioned side by side.

In 1385 the union of Poland with Lithuania brought an immense Orthodox population into permanent association with the Polish state. The Lithuanian Grand Duke Jagiełło, who had abandoned paganism for Catholicism in order to become king of Poland, continued Casimir III's policy of religious toleration. However, the Orthodox Church did not receive equality of status. Its bishops were nominated by the Polish king, who was naturally a Catholic. By the terms of the Union of Horodło in 1413, which strengthened the legal bonds between Poland and Lithuania, only Catholic nobles received full political rights. This policy encouraged conversions to Catholicism on the part of certain Lithuanian noble families, but contributed to a sense of grievance among those who remained Orthodox. Furthermore, the hierarchy of the Catholic Church disapproved of religious toleration. Papal bulls in 1509 and 1515 proclaimed (largely ineffective) crusades against the Orthodox population of Poland-Lithuania.

Another area of Catholic-Orthodox tension existed along the eastern shore of the Adriatic, where adherents of the two forms of Christianity lived in close proximity. Most of Dalmatia and parts of northern Albania were Catholic, with links to the Latin culture of Italy. Intermittent Byzantine hegemony had brought in a Greek population as well, especially at Zadar and Split. During the intervals of Hungarian control, most of the Greek churches were given to Catholics. The final cessation of Byzantine rule in Dalmatia, nominal as it often had been, proved detrimental to the adherents of Orthodoxy. A synod of Latin bishops meeting at Split in 1185 declared that the Orthodox were heretics and therefore anathema. Dalmatia in the 13th and 14th centuries was controlled exclusively by Catholic powers—either Hungary or Venice—which inevitably caused the situation of the Orthodox to deteriorate. In 1314 the last Orthodox church in Dalmatia was confiscated, forcing its priests to conduct services in private houses. Actually this religious intimidation was not to the taste of the Venetian governments which controlled the Adriatic littoral after 1409. Interested primarily in commercial affairs, they had no wish to alienate their Orthodox subjects. However, the popes exerted strong pressure on the Venetian authorities to help win over the "schismatics." Unable to avoid giving some support to the Catholic Church's proselytizing efforts, Venice acquiesced in requiring the Orthodox population of Dalmatia to recognize the authority of the Latin bishops.

The population of Albania was already split between Orthodoxy and Catholicism when the advent of Islam in the late 14th century added a third element to the religious mixture. The southern sector of this small country was dominated by Orthodoxy, the northern by Catholicism, with an area of encounter in the center around Durrës and Krujë. The active commercial life and cosmopolitan atmosphere at Durrës were conducive to a fairly high level of religious toleration. However, the popes considered Albania a "mission" country because of its partially Orthodox population. Missionary friars began arriving there in the 1230s. Proselytizing efforts, added to military conquest by the pope's Angevin allies from south Italy, caused Catholicism to make advances in the northern part of the country, although Orthodoxy continued dominant in the south. Mountainous terrain rendered much of Albania difficult of access and its clergy relatively independent. Thus Catholicism did not overtly appear as the pope's instrument, which always repelled the Orthodox. Ultimately the dividing line between the two churches in Albania stabilized approximately along the Shkumbi River in the center of the country.

Serbia likewise contained both Catholic and Orthodox believers. The interior was overwhelmingly Orthodox, the Adriatic coastal towns largely Catholic. The ruling Nemanya dynasty was Orthodox; but its founder, Stephen Nemanya, gave rich gifts to both Catholic and Orthodox churches. The pope clearly had hopes of winning the entire country for Catholicism when he granted a royal crown to Nemanya's son (Stephen the First-Crowned) in 1217. Although that monarch returned soon afterward to Orthodoxy, he permitted a Catholic hierarchy to operate parallel to the Orthodox one in Serbia. On the other hand, Tsar Stephen Dušan's law code in the 14th century already showed considerable anti-Catholic prejudice, prescribing severe punishments for anyone attempting to convert Orthodox believers to what it described as the "Latin heresy." Dušan's code also prohibited marriages between Orthodox and Catholics, referring to the latter as "half-believers."

Nothing could better illustrate the deep-seated hostility between the Eastern and Western churches than the persistent miscarriage of efforts to unite them. The fifty-seven-year tenure of the Latins at Constantinople had failed utterly to impose Catholicism on the recalcitrant Orthodox hierarchy and population. Nonetheless, after the Greek dynasty of Nicaea returned to Constantinople in 1261, the Popes openly sought to restore the Latin Empire by force. If successful, this would have resulted in papal supremacy over the Orthodox Church. The Pope's ally, Charles of Anjou, had acquired his kingdom of Naples with papal aid in 1268, and now was eager to invade Byzantine territory. To forestall him, the Greek Emperor Michael VIII (r. 1259–82) promised to unite the two churches himself. At the ecclesiastical council held in 1274 at Lyons in France—conveniently distant from Byzantine territory—the Greek delegation accepted church union on papal terms, including papal supremacy, *filioque*, and the use of unleavened bread in the Mass. From the pope's perspective, a union sponsored by the Greek emperor was more likely to succeed than one dictated by a Catholic prince. For his part, Michael VIII certainly realized that the Union of Lyons was unacceptable to his Orthodox subjects. He sought to conceal its exact provisions, assuring the population of Constantinople that the agreement denoted no real changes. His purpose was to gain time, and in this he succeeded. It was 1281 before the pope became totally convinced of the Greek emperor's insincerity and pronounced him a schismatic who ought to be deposed. Charles of Anjou now laid plans to attack Constantinople in 1282, but the massive Italian uprising known as the "Sicilian Vespers" forestalled him. Michael VIII's tactics had achieved their objective, but his subjects were not grateful. Instead they reviled him for his alleged "heresy" in acceding to church union at all. His son Andronicus II immediately repudiated the Union of Lyons upon succeeding to the throne in 1282.

The same military weakness which in 1274 had led Michael VIII to approve church union brought about a similar effort in the 15th century. Once again beset by the threat of imminent conquest, this time by the Ottoman Turks, the beleaguered government at Constantinople sought to gain Western military support through concessions in religion. At a church council held at Ferrara and Florence in 1438–39 the Greek delegation accepted Rome's position on all disputed points, including papal supremacy and retention of *filioque* in the Nicene Creed. The Orthodox would be permitted a few deviations in practice: namely, the Greek language and liturgy and leavened rather than unleavened bread in the communion service. These few concessions scarcely veiled what amounted to total surrender on the part of the Eastern Church. At the same time, the issue of church union threw a clear light on the limits of the Byzantine emperor's supremacy. When vital points of theology were at stake, especially involving concessions to the hated Latins, he could not carry his subjects with him. To them, as to the medieval mind in general, acceptance of true doctrine was absolutely essential to salvation. Ultimately many Orthodox believers attributed the fall of Constantinople in 1453 to God's anger at the unfaithful emperor.

Heresy was, of course, entirely a matter of definition, signifying a departure from the authorized dogmas of an established religion. The Eastern Church held that true doctrine had been determined once and for all by the ancient ecumenical councils, and further emendations were neither necessary nor desirable. The Western Church accepted the pope's authority to issue binding decrees on matters of dogma. Both Catholics and Orthodox believed in the ideal of a united Church and held that only one doctrine (its own) could possibly be true, although deviations might be allowed in the precise form of worship. Differences threatened the unity of the Church, and must be suppressed. Characteristically, the principal groups which the medieval Church accused of heresy regarded themselves as reformers, not heretics. They quarreled with the institutional Church, but did not intend to found new religions. Bogomils, Bosnians, and

Hussites all considered themselves to be better Christians than the clerics who persecuted them.

The origins of Bogomilism are obscure, since both the Orthodox and Catholic churches afterward took care to obliterate all traces of it. This dualist creed flourished in Bulgaria from the 10th through the 14th century, although at present its teachings are known almost exclusively from the works of its enemies. The Bogomils believed that both God and Satan have existed from all eternity. God is the author of the heavenly, invisible world; Satan has created the visible and material one—the universe. The human soul is an angel fallen from heaven and now imprisoned in a material body; but after the Last Judgment it will return to its original home. The body of Christ while he lived on earth was an illusion, since everything physical is the work of Satan. His death on the cross was also unreal. Jesus taught people how to liberate their souls; this is the meaning of redemption. Sacraments which employ material elements like water for baptism or bread and wine in the Eucharist are Satanic. Salvation occurs through fasting and prayer. The Bogomils therefore rejected the Christian sacraments, images, the cross, and the Mass on the ground that they belonged to the material world, not the spiritual. The most esteemed members of the Bogomil sect were its monks, known as the Perfect, who renounced all earthly goods and led a strictly ascetic life. They rejected violence, marriage, and meat eating and spent much time praying. All the Perfect, male or female, were allowed to preach. The Bogomils had no ecclesiastical hierarchy, although a bishop headed their community. In Bulgaria the sect split into two branches, known respectively as Bulgarian and Dragovitsian. The latter professed a strict and consistent dualism, while the more moderate Bulgarian branch regarded Satan not as a being which had existed from the beginning of time, but rather as a fallen angel.

Bogomilism is often considered an offshoot of Manichaeism, a dualist religion of Persian origin which became widely popular in the late Roman Empire. Another possibility is that it originated within Bulgaria itself, either in protest against the Greek-dominated Church or as a Christian offshoot which placed particular emphasis on the role of the Devil. Since the Bogomils considered themselves Christians and did not separate from the Church, but merely declared their own doctrines to be more correct than those of official Christianity, this is a distinct possibility. Certainly Bogomilism expressed strong dissatisfaction with the institutional Church. The typical Orthodox priest was scarcely superior to laymen in either education or morals. By contrast, the itinerant Bogomil monks (the Perfect) were serious ascetics who attracted support by setting an example of disciplined behavior. They practiced strict celibacy and engaged in frequent prayers and fasts. Apparently their teaching included elements of protest against social injustice. The 10th-century Bulgarian priest Kozma, who wrote a polemical tract against Bogomilism, reported: "They revile the wealthy, hate the Tsar, ridicule the elders, condemn the boyars, regard as vile in the sight of God those who serve the Tsar, and forbid every serf to work for his lord." Kozma condemned the Bogomils as hypocrites who merely pretended to be virtuous. Nonetheless, the social aspect of this heresy seems to have been merely a subordinate feature in what was essentially a religious movement. Since Bogomils regarded the world as Satan's creation, they obviously could not accept the idea that God condoned the existing social order.

In the late 12th century the Bogomil sect spread from Bulgaria into Serbia, where Grand Župan Stephen Nemanya employed the Byzantine laws against Manichaeism to punish its leaders. Some Bogomils were burned to death; others had their houses and property confiscated and were driven into exile. The last of them, mostly nobles, were either baptized by Archbishop Sava or expelled from the country early in the 13th century. Serbian sources after this time cease to mention the Bogomils. In Bulgaria, where Bogomilism had reached its height in the 13th century, Tsar Boril actively persecuted its adherents. In 1211 he summoned a church synod at Tirnovo which proclaimed the Bogomil doctrine to be anathema. His reasons for taking this step are not clear, since Bogomilism was a powerful sect in Bulgaria and his predecessors had left it alone.

A subsequent threat to the established Church in Bulgaria was the popular type of mysticism known as Hesychasm. Originating in the monasteries of Mount Athos in the 14th century, it afterward spread widely throughout the Orthodox world. Hesychasm encouraged contemplative silence as a means of attaining personal inner tranquility and knowledge of God. Its adherents devoted themselves to solitary meditations, causing them to see a supernatural light which filled them with ecstasy. A synod of the Bulgarian Church in about 1355 pronounced a curse on both Bogomils and Hesychasts and banned their elders and priests. Nonetheless Hesychasm not only survived but inspired an important Bulgarian literary movement in the late 14th century. Since the Hesychasts regarded language as not just a vehicle for expression but as a component in itself of divine truth, they were eager to correct the existing translations of Old Slavic texts on the ground that textual errors could lead to heresy.

Significant departures from accepted Christian practice also occurred in Bosnia in the 13th century. These have usually been identified as Bogomil and attributed to influences emanating from Bulgaria. However, the evidence for this view is far from conclusive. A separate Bosnian Church certainly existed at this period, differing in various respects from both Catholicism and Orthodoxy. A small dualist movement may even have been present in some areas. Nonetheless, no real proof exists that the Church in Bosnia ever accepted Bogomilism. The country was a mountainous and isolated European backwater, where nonstandard religious practices could easily have developed simply through ignorance. Already in the 1220s Bosnia had somehow acquired a reputation for "heresy," although what this actually meant in practice is far from clear. With papal encouragement a Hungarian army invaded the country in the 1230s in order to wipe out this alleged deviation. The impression gained by later historians that the Bosnian Church was

Bogomil or dualist is chiefly derived from 15th-century Italian sources, poorly informed about local conditions.

Moreover, Catholicism to the Bosnians had come to be irrevocably associated with Hungarian aggression. Presumably for this reason, the independent-minded nobles of central Bosnia severed their connections with the Hungarian Catholic hierarchy in the mid-13th century, and organized their own autonomous Church around an existing order of monks. Its theology probably consisted of poorly understood Catholic beliefs combined with various local peculiarities which appeared heretical to outsiders. Other Europeans referred to the monks of the Bosnian Church, and sometimes even to its lay members, as Patarenes. Most Bosnian nobles probably adhered to this home-grown religious organization in the 14th century, since in most of the country none other existed. At the same time, there is no reason to believe that the Bosnian Church played any political role or that the nobility made any particular efforts to defend it. During the same period, Catholicism retained its hold on portions of northern Bosnia, while the Orthodox Church remained dominant in Hercegovina.

The Bosnian Church throughout its existence remained essentially a monastic order. Its monks were known as krstjani (i.e., "Christians"), a name suggesting that only they could be true Christians. Since the monks lived in cloisters and did not preach, their influence over the general population was minimal. Nearly all the rulers of independent Bosnia after the middle of the 14th century were Catholics, although the nobility included adherents of all three Christian faiths—Bosnian, Catholic, and Orthodox. Evidently no social barrier prevented contacts among members of these three confessions. However, on the eve of the Ottoman conquest the king sought military aid from the pope, who made it a condition that action must first be taken against the Bosnian Church. Thus in 1459 for the first time a Bosnian monarch began persecuting some members of this native institution, offering its clergy the choice between conversion to Catholicism or exile. Most chose conversion. Despite this capitulation the pope failed to provide any practical assistance for Bosnia, which fell to the Turks in 1463. The Bosnian Church disappeared soon afterward, and many Bosnians subsequently adopted Islam.

The Franciscan and Dominican brotherhoods were a new phenomenon in the religious history of Europe in the 13th century. Founded early in the century in Italy and southern France, they gained considerable influence in East Central Europe shortly afterward. Their task was to preach the Catholic faith and combat heresy. Unlike monks in the traditional orders, who sought isolation from society in order to avoid worldly temptations, the Franciscan and Dominican friars moved freely among the population. In principle they were mendicants (i.e., beggars), supporting themselves only upon whatever alms the population saw fit to give them. Recognizing that part of the heretics' appeal lay in their criticism of abuses within the Church, they were strong supporters of church reform, and sought to encourage a deeper Christian spirituality through inspirational preaching. Because the upper church hierarchy was so enmeshed in politics and luxurious living, the Franciscan and Dominican orders organized themselves on a new principle. Bypassing the authority of local bishops, they swore allegiance instead to the head of their own organization, who reported directly to the pope at Rome. The friars concentrated their proselytizing efforts on the towns, which supplied many of their members and most of their financial support. They also organized a limited number of convents for women. Since the urban population in Bohemia, Poland, and Hungary was so strongly German in the 13th century, many friars in those countries were ethnic Germans even though native born.

Houses of the mendicant friars multiplied with astounding rapidity in East Central Europe. They attracted members of high society like the future Saint Margaret, daughter of Hungary's King Béla IV, who became a Dominican nun. A new monastic organization of Hungarian origin was that of the Eremites of Saint Paul, or Paulicians, founded in 1262. This order was not mendicant, since the brothers did not preach; but in contrast to the more traditional Benedictine monks, they did maintain certain relations with the towns. Pious folk visited their houses on pilgrimage. The new order developed rapidly under the patronage of royalty or great magnates, who often were buried in their churches. The Paulicians built most of their cloisters in wooded mountains, especially in the northern region of Hungary, and generally avoided towns, although they maintained one house a few miles from Buda. In 1382 they founded the monastery of Częstochowa in Poland, home of the famous Black Madonna altarpiece, which remains to this day a focus of fervent Catholic religiosity.

The Dominicans in particular recognized the need to raise the educational and moral level of the parish clergy. They established an extensive school system to train preachers and confessors, opening their schools to Catholic clergy of any order. It was clear that the practice of oral confession, known for centuries in monastic communities but now spreading into the parishes, required educational preparation on the part of the confessor. The training of a Dominican brother was much superior to that of an ordinary parish priest, which was one important reason for the friars' appeal. Since the Dominicans were known for their religious learning, the Church also called upon them to preside over the tribunals of the Inquisition, which by their very nature demanded theologians capable of distinguishing between orthodoxy and heresy. The Inquisition came to East Central Europe relatively late—two-thirds of a century or more after its original founding in 1233 by the pope. In Bohemia it was introduced in 1297 and functioned very actively after 1315. In Poland it arrived in 1318 and operated at least until the mid- 16th century.

Unlike most other religious institutions, the houses of the Dominicans and Franciscans on principle were not dependent on permanent endowments. The friars were well aware that if they lost the people's good will they would also lose their donations and fees. As an exception to this rule, they did permit endowments in eastern Poland, where the population was largely Orthodox and local support was unreliable. However, in Catholic lands the Dominican and Franciscan houses acquired such an appeal that nearly all princely courts wished to have one in their vicinity. The larger establishments contained scores of friars, while smaller ones had a minimum of twelve or sometimes even fewer. In many respects the mendicant brothers duplicated the work of the parish priests, preaching and listening to confessions. People sought them out for material, spiritual, or medical aid, often preferring them to their own parish priests. Not surprisingly, the priests often resented these competitors, whose activities caused them a loss of revenue. At the turn of the 13th–14th centuries the pope required all mendicant orders to give one-fourth of their revenue to the parishes in which they operated. Even this sum proved inadequate to offset the losses to a parish when friars moved into its neighborhood.

The same enthusiasm which promoted the spread of the mendicant orders also encouraged military crusades against Europe's remaining pagans. In the 13th century many such people still lived on the grasslands along the lower Danube, a region loosely subject to Hungarian domination but open to the repeated incursions of steppe raiders. Also predominantly pagan were the vast territories of Lithuania beyond Poland's eastern frontiers. The eradication of heathenism was a slow process, while conversion to Christianity frequently took place by means of conquest, violence, and intimidation. Although such methods inevitably evoked resistance, the superior military power of the crusaders also suggested to its victims that the Christian god was more powerful than their own traditional deities. Prussia's subjugation by the Teutonic Knights led to the conversion or extermination of the native (i.e., Baltic-speaking) Prussians. The Cumans of Hungary gradually accepted Catholicism, while in Cumania itself—the usual designation for Walachia and Moldavia in the 13th century— the pagan Cumans eventually were driven back onto the steppes or absorbed into Orthodoxy. The territories subject to Lithuania officially became Christian after the union with Poland in 1385, and the pagan element slowly disappeared there. By the end of the Middle Ages the open worship of heathen deities had largely ceased in East Central Europe, although many ancient beliefs persisted. At the same time, the pagans themselves often recognized that Christianity was the vehicle of a higher civilization, richer and more complex than their ancient polytheism and better able than simple nature worship to explain the human condition.

Such considerations scarcely affected the Muslim and Jewish minorities of medieval Europe. Heirs themselves to a rich religious tradition, both groups proved highly resistant to Christianization. Long before the advent of the Otto- man Turks an extensive Islamic population already resided in the borderlands of East Central Europe. The majority were Turkic or Turkic-related, including the Khazars, Pechenegs, Cumans, and Iazygs. Muslims lived among the Danubian

Bulgars in the 9th century, which explains the reference to "Saracen" books in Pope Nicholas I's letter to the Bulgar Khan Boris. Those Muslims known as Maghrebians, who were probably Pechenegs, fought as light cavalry for Hungary in the 11th and 12th centuries and were noted for their bravery. The Khazars (Chorasmians) served both as auxiliary troops and as traders and coinmakers. On the whole the Muslims lived in compact village communities. Most of the men were soldiers, but some engaged in commerce as well. Their numbers began to decline early in the 13th century, as efforts to convert them to Christianity became more intense.

The arrival of Cuman tribesman in eastern Transylvania and Moldavia in the 13th and 14th centuries greatly augmented the Islamic population of those regions. (Many Cumans remained pagans; a few had accepted Christianity.) The Hungarians responded with various prejudicial decrees against these so-called Saracens and Ishmaelites. King Andrew II (r. 1205–35) prohibited Muslims from becoming state officials (e.g., tax collectors or coiners of money) and required them to wear a distinct dress. King Charles Robert in 1341 ordered all his non-Christian subjects to be baptized or leave the country. The Hungarian law code known as the Tripartitum, approved by the Diet in 1514, contains a variety of discriminatory provisions against Muslims. It directed them to build churches for Christians and violate the commands of their religion by eating pork, while forbidding their daughters to marry fellow Muslims and encouraging Christians to spy on them. However, the Ottoman conquest of Hungary in 1526 prevented wide application of these measures.

Similarly unwilling to accept Christianity were the Jews. Numerically and economically they were far more prominent than the Muslims, forming a significant portion of the town class in many parts of East Central Europe. The Jews cultivated a religious tradition much older than Christianity; and rarely did they accept Christian baptism except under the threat of violence. Their earliest large-scale migration into East Central Europe occurred in the aftermath of persecutions suffered in the Rhineland in 1096 as a side effect of the First Crusade. Until that time they had generally been left in peace. However, Christian preachers now found that stirring up religious fanaticism was an effective means of encouraging their listeners to take the crusader's vow. Hostility to Jews on theological grounds was an old story. Christian doctrine taught that the Jews were guilty of Christ killing, for which crime they should be degraded forever. The Fourth Lateran Council at Rome in 1215 decreed that Jews must wear identifying badges, so that Christians would not unwittingly be contaminated by their presence. The Council of Basel in 1434 ordered the Jews to live in ghettos separate from the Christian population. Canon law forbade Jews baptized against their will to return to Judaism, or Jewish parents to reclaim any of their children who had been baptized by force. Jews who became Christian, whether willingly or otherwise, automatically forfeited all their worldly goods, since in theory all

Jewish property belonged to the king. Jewish converts to Christianity usually lived in miserable poverty and often had to beg for a living.

Religious calumnies against the Jews were widely believed, even in the face of contrary evidence and explicit denials by several popes. A common theme of anti-Semitic propaganda was the claim that Jews murdered innocent children (never adults, since innocence was essential) in order to use their blood in worship services. In 1247, Pope Innocent IV strictly forbade Christians to accuse Jews of this crime, but the suspicion that they practiced it refused to die. Nonetheless, the Roman popes' record of toleration for Jews was far better than that of the lesser clergy, not to mention the common people. Rome generally disapproved of forced baptism and anti-Semitic violence, which contradicted the belief in Christianity's inherent superiority. Successive pontiffs declared that ritual murder was contrary to Jewish principles and rejected allegations that Jews poisoned the wells of Europe or made a practice of desecrating the holy wafer used in the Eucharist. On the other hand, friars and parish clergy tended to share the popular superstitions and often disseminated such beliefs.

The first massacres of Jews during the Crusades to the Holy Land occurred as a result of clerical preaching, and three of the most murderous bands of Crusaders were led by priests. Many subsequent accusations against Jews, especially concerning ritual murder or desecration of the host, originated with local priests and monks or were spread by them. Any monarch who granted privileges to Jews laid himself open to accusations of enmity toward Christ. Dominican and Franciscan friars promoted the burning of Jewish books and perpetuated the inflammatory notion that "the Jews" had killed Jesus (despite the New Testament's clear evidence that the Roman governor Pontius Pilate was the official responsible for ordering his death). When Dominican friars came to the synagogues to preach and compelled Jews to listen, they were sometimes accompanied by unruly mobs of Christians. Finally, Jews faced the mortal threat of the Inquisition if they attempted to renounce Christianity after being forcibly baptized. Since the court of the Inquisition was empowered to deal with matters of blasphemy, witchcraft, and usury, it sometimes succeeded in bringing Jews to trial.

Usually it was the Church that attempted to restrict the Jews' rights, whereas the monarchs and nobles who profited from their services sought to protect them. A Polish church synod meeting at Wrocław in 1266 under papal sponsorship issued extensive regulations concerning the Jews, requiring them to reside in separate sections of towns or villages set apart from the Christian sector by a hedge, wall, or ditch. To avoid offense to Christian sensibilities, Jews were told to lock themselves in their houses whenever a Christian religious procession passed through the streets. No town could possess more than one synagogue. Jews had to wear a peculiarly shaped hat or be punished if they did not. The council repeated the ancient canonical enactments forbidding Jews to keep Christian servants or exercise any public functions. A Hungarian church synod held at Buda in 1279 required Jews to wear a ring of red cloth sewn onto the front of their garments in order to make their identity obvious to the general public. In Bohemia in 1399 the Church caused the execution of eighty Jews by claiming in court that a certain Jewish prayer contained blasphemies against Jesus.

If rigorously applied, the anti-Semitic decrees would have transformed the Jews into a totally separate social caste. In reality, edicts of this type were frequently not enforced. The Jews were needed for their expertise in commerce and moneylending, so that often the monarchs protected them. King Casimir III of Poland (r. 1333–70) was particularly noted for his friendliness toward the Jews. He ordered royal officials to prevent the Catholic clergy from molesting them, and announced that unfounded accusations against Jews would be punished with death. Casimir specifically forbade the standard anti-Semitic allegations, for example, that the Jews used Christian blood in their Passover ceremonies or desecrated the host. Then in the 15th century the situation of the Polish Jews deteriorated. Casimir's tolerant attitude had aroused resistance, especially among the clergy. Jagiełło, the pagan-born king of Poland (r. 1386–1434), felt obliged to demonstrate his Catholic loyalties by taking a hard line against the Jews. The first serious persecutions of Jews in Poland occurred during his reign.

One of the worst actions took place in 1399 in Poznań, where Jews were accused of stabbing three holy wafers allegedly stolen from the local Dominican church. Rumors spread that the host had spurted blood, thereby confirming the dogma of Christ's real presence in the Eucharist. As punishment for allegedly instigating this crime, the Jewish elders of Poznań were condemned, tortured, tied to pillars, and roasted alive over a slow fire. For more than three centuries afterward the Jewish community of Poznań was required to pay an annual fine to the Dominican church from which the wafers supposedly had been stolen. In Cracow in 1407 a major riot broke out after a priest announced from the pulpit that Jews had killed a Christian boy and thrown stones at a priest. Worshippers rushed into the streets to take vengeance upon "Christ's enemies" by looting and burning Jewish houses. Afterward the children of the slain Jews were all forcibly baptized. King Casimir IV (r. 1447–92) was denounced for protecting the Jews. When the Polish army lost a major battle to the Teutonic Knights in 1454, the clergy blamed the king's toleration of Jews and heretics for the disaster. Since Casimir needed the Church's assistance in conducting this war, he revoked all the previously granted Jewish privileges. Catholic hostility to the Hussites of Bohemia also recoiled upon the Jews, who were accused of supplying these supposed heretics with money and arms. Dominican friars denounced both Jews and Hussites, while crusades against the Hussites began with massacres of Jews.

The antecedents of Hussitism date back to the so-called *devotio moderna* of the mid-14th century, a movement for religious inwardness which included the moral obligation to imitate Christ in practical life. In Bohemia the new religiosity was stimulated by a series of extraordinary preachers. The first was the Augustinian friar Konrad Waldhauser, whose reputation led King Charles I to invite him to

Prague in 1358. Waldhauser's sermons in Latin and German as well as his own strictly ascetic life made a strong impression. His immediate successor was John Milíč of Kroměříž, a Czech from Moravia, who resigned his position as a canon of the Prague cathedral in order to become a penitential preacher. Delivering his sermons in both Czech and German, Milíč was enthusiastically received by members of both nationalities. Like Waldhauser, he practiced a severe asceticism: wearing only a simple unwashed tunic, beating himself with rods, fasting, and praying for hours daily. He denounced ecclesiastical abuses, particularly simony, luxury, clerical concubinage, lay appointment of bishops. and mendicant friars who sold indulgences and accumulated riches. Boldly he referred to the German emperor as Antichrist. Among his works of charity, Milíč founded a school for preachers as well as a community for reformed prostitutes. To avoid the suspicion of heresy he took care to declare his loyalty to the pope, whom he called upon to support reform in the Church. Accused of heresy nonetheless, he was defended by the Prague canons, who prevented his coming to trial.

The Czech reformers concentrated their activities on the Bethlehem Chapel, a new church in Prague founded by a group of prominent citizens specifically to promote popular preaching in the Czech tongue. Completed in 1394, it provided space for 3,000 persons. Priests at the chapel propounded an inspirational brand of religion largely devoid of dogma or ritual. Exhorting people to repent of their sins and transform their lives through imitation of Christ, the Czech preachers emphasized spiritual awakening and moral reform, not theology. Since the congregation at the Bethlehem Chapel knew little or no Latin, worship services emphasized sermons and religious music in the Czech tongue. Among the most active leaders of this new movement were Thomas Štítný, the author of various inspirational writings and translations, and Matthew of Janov, whose treatises exalted primitive Christianity and criticized the Roman Church for worldliness, hypocrisy, and lack of charity. The Prague townspeople gave the reformers wide support, while King Wenceslas IV and the ecclesiastical hierarchy at first tolerated this religious ferment, probably because the Czech preachers had powerful backing.

Unfortunately for the reformers, they were immediately suspected of heresy by association with the name of John Wyclif (d. 1384), the radical English theologian who in many respects was a forerunner of Protestantism. In the 1390s a number of masters and scholars at the university in Prague had come under his influence. Wyclif defined the Church as the totality of Christians predestined for salvation—a radical concept which denied special status to the clergy. He argued that clerics possessed spiritual authority not by reason of holding office but only if they led virtuous lives which bore witness to their state of grace. In his opinion, individuals ought to stand in a direct relationship to God, which meant abolishing oral confession to priests and reducing the status of the sacraments. Wyclif's English translation of the Bible was the first complete version in the vernacular making the Scriptures accessible to a public ignorant of Latin. His insistence that the Church should not own property and that honest work ought to be valued above begging (contrary to the friars' viewpoint) spoke to the strong prevailing hostility against the clergy and the mendicant orders. Ultimately his advocacy of communion for the laity "in both kinds" (i.e., in both bread and wine) would become the most compelling theme of the Hussite movement.

John Hus himself was originally just one among several prominent religious reformers in early 15th-century Prague. Circumstances transformed him into a martyr and symbol of the movement which later bore his name. Born in southern Bohemia in 1369, he took a master's degree at the university in Prague in 1396 and in 1400 was ordained a priest. In 1402 he became chief preacher at the Bethlehem Chapel, where his sermons in the Czech language gave the reform movement a distinctly popular cast. He also won adherents in high places, among them Queen Sophia, who made him her confessor and often went to hear him preach. Hus was not an original theologian, but rather a gifted speaker and popularizer. His powerful sermons against clerical vice and his call to return to the purity of the early Church convinced many simple people to support the intellectual leaders of the reform. Hus's teachings did not openly contravene the Church's doctrines, but his strictures unquestionably undermined its authority. Pope Gregory XII cited him for judgment in Rome and in 1411 excommunicated him for not appearing.

The popular mood in Prague became more tense in 1412, when an emissary of the pope arrived to promote the sale of indulgences. Believers were told that the purchase of an indulgence would free them from doing penance for their sins; and the king as well as the Church expected to profit from the sales. This traffic in indulgences had the same radicalizing effect on Hus as on Martin Luther a century later, when it provided the spark that ignited the Protestant Reformation. Hus was mortally offended at the indulgence trade and the crude claims made by salesmen on the Church's behalf. According to Catholic doctrine, an indulgence should be granted only after a sinner had sincerely repented of his sins. However, the hawkers of indulgences promised exactly the same spiritual rewards in exchange for money. At this point Hus's preaching went beyond mere advocacy of spiritual renewal and challenged the Church on a matter of economic significance. He not only inveighed against indulgence selling, but went on to question the pope's right to demand obedience from Christians. Thereupon the pope laid an interdict on Prague, forbidding all religious services in the city as long as Hus remained there. To counteract this edict, Hus went into voluntary exile in south Bohemia, where various noble families protected him. He continued to preach, often under the open sky; and people traveled long distances to hear him. At this time he composed two influential Latin treatises: "On Simony," a vigorous attack on the purchase of spiritual goods; and "On the Church," which developed Wyclif's concept of predestination. His writings in Czech also circulated very widely. Their literary quality made them popular and contributed to Hus's growing stature as the foremost representative of church reform.

The issues raised by the reformers led to public disturbances in the streets of Prague and caused serious tensions in the university, where the reform tendency had many adherents. King Wenceslas IV at first vacillated between support for the conservatives and for the reformers, until the Hussites offended him by opposing the sale of indulgences, in which he had a personal financial stake. Uncertain how to handle the growing controversy, he finally appealed for judgment to the church council then in session at Constance, which promised Hus a fair and impartial hearing. Hus himself hoped that by defending himself before the assembled prelates he could clear himself of the charges of heresy. Bearing a safe-conduct from Emperor Sigismund, he arrived at Constance late in 1414. Three weeks later the cardinals there had him imprisoned; and the emperor refused to honor his own safe-conduct. In vain the nobility of Bohemia sent four joint letters of protest to Constance.

The agenda of the Council of Constance probably doomed Hus's case in advance. This Council had assembled primarily to settle the scandal of the Great Schism (1378–1418), which had given the Western Church two competing popes. Many leading prelates now supported the brand of reform known as conciliarism, which sought to replace papal absolutism by a system of representative government in the Church. They could not afford to prejudice their case by any suspicion that they tolerated heresy. Furthermore, the bishops and cardinals themselves were prime beneficiaries of precisely that corrupt system which the Czech reformers criticized. Representatives of the Council first sought to make Hus publicly repudiate certain doctrines of Wyclif, which he claimed he had never held. Instead he offered to renounce any of his statements which could be proven from Scripture to be false. This appeal to Biblical authority challenged the Church's key claim to authority—namely, that it alone could be the judge of divine truth. Hus was never granted the fair hearing that he had been promised. In June 1415 he was brought before the Council and accused of heresy. Although never convicted, he also refused to recant, and accordingly was burned at the stake. In Bohemia the news of his martyrdom aroused a flood of outrage and set off a wave of disturbances. Undeterred, the Council one year later condemned to death Hus's friend and fellow reformer Jerome of Prague.

The deaths of Hus and Jerome at Constance turned them into martyrs and radicalized the Czech reform party. When one year later the archbishop of Prague placed the Bohemian capital under interdict, this act became a call to rebellion. Priests obedient to the Church refrained from administering the sacraments, but others of the Hussite party took their places. In this fashion a large segment of the Bohemian Church passed into Hussite hands. A further innovation was the introduction of the Mass in Czech. Encouraged by Jacob of Stříbro, Hus's successor as chief preacher at the Bethlehem Chapel, Czech translations of the Latin liturgy had appeared as early as 1415. Thereby the reform movement clearly emphasized its Czech character and separated itself from the German element in Bohemia. Hussitism became identified with Czech nationality, whereas ethnic Germans living in Bohemia remained loyal on the whole to the traditional Church. Nonetheless nationality was never the dominant issue in the reform movement. In principle, if not always in practice, the Hussites attempted to distinguish between people who supported the reform and those who did not. Their emphasis on preaching in Czech was directed not against German but against the monopoly of Latin.

Ultimately the question of communion in both kinds for lay believers became the principal issue dividing the Hussites from their opponents. According to Catholic theology, the bread and wine used by a priest in the Mass, or Eucharist, are transformed by a miracle into the actual body and blood of Christ. This is called the real presence. By consuming these elements the believer feels himself united with the Savior himself. However, in the Western Church in the 15th century only priests were permitted to drink the wine, while ordinary worshippers were restricted to bread only. Curiously, in view of the centrality of this issue in the Hussite controversy, the Roman Church itself for centuries had routinely given the wine to lay communicants during Mass. It modified this practice only in the course of the 12th century, apparently in order to simplify the service. Since Catholic theology defined each of the elements singly as equivalent to the two together, no serious objection seems to have been raised at the time. However, the Bohemian reformers aspired to share in the miracle of the Eucharist. Denial of the wine signified for them the refusal of equal spiritual rights to the laity. The cup or chalice became the unifying symbol of the entire Hussite movement.

The Church's position on the Eucharist exemplified the reformers' general criticism of priests as lazy and indifferent, eager only to get through the service as quickly as possible. Denial of the cup looked like totally unjust favoritism to clerics, contradicting the practice of Jesus himself at the Last Supper. Communion in both forms (in the Latin phrase: *sub specie utraque*) became the minimum demand of even the most conservative Hussite reformers, who accordingly became known as Utraquists. By the end of 1415, the year of John Hus's death, most congregations in Prague had begun to dispense communion to the laity with both bread and wine. The practice soon spread to other towns in Bohemia, until finally the rural population took it up. This issue became so explosive that in many places priests who refused to give lay believers the cup, or chalice, were driven from their churches. Hus himself stood diametrically opposed to the Council of Constance on this issue. In one of his last letters from prison he had approved of communion for the laity in both kinds, whereas the Council in June 1415 had solemnly condemned the practice. In 1417, the university in Prague declared itself in favor of the chalice, but did not go as far as the radical Hussites, who argued that communion in both kinds was absolutely essential for salvation.

The religious ferment of these years in Bohemia gave rise not merely to moderate demands for reform but also to radical tendencies which excluded any possibility of reconciliation with the Roman Church. South Bohemia had been in a state of excitement ever since Hus's exile there. The sermons of the reform preachers and the revelation of God's Word in the Czech vernacular had enthralled masses of simple people. Worshippers undertook pilgrimages to the mountains, where Mass was said under the open sky and the laity received communion in both bread and wine. Similarly in Prague New Town, one of the capital's three boroughs, radical religious ideas took root among the Czech craftsmen and laborers. Fiercely puritan in outlook, the Prague radicals particularly resented the wealth and opulence of the churches and monasteries, whose artistic treasures they sometimes destroyed in riots. At the same time King Wenceslas IV was under strong pressure from the Council of Constance and its newly elected pope (Martin V) to reconcile Bohemia to the Church. In summer 1419 the king forbade Hussite services in all but four Prague churches and appointed anti-Hussite councillors for Prague New Town. This edict led to the famous "defenestration," in which an excited mob threw the newly appointed councillors to their deaths from the windows of the Town Hall. Two weeks later Wenceslas died of a stroke.

Early in the year 1420 a sizable group of Hussites from south Bohemia organized a communal settlement on top of Hradiště Mountain, calling it by the Biblical name of Tabor. Mass was recited in Czech and communion given in both kinds; but innovations of a much more radical kind were introduced as well. The Taborites treated their priests not as bearers of divine grace like the Catholic clergy, but as ministers and servants of the community. Their priests wore laymen's clothes and could marry if they wished. Divine service consisted of reading and explaining the Scriptures in Czech, singing Czech hymns, praying, and receiving communion. The Taborites abolished oral confession on the ground that only God could grant absolution from sins. They denied the existence of purgatory and rejected all sacraments except baptism and communion. Detesting the worship of saints, they viewed paintings and statues of saints as forms of idolatry. A similar, but less radical Hussite brotherhood known as the Orebites established its own communal settlement on a hill in eastern Bohemia named after the Biblical Mount Horeb. Together the Taborites and Orebites became the principal military arm of the Hussite revolution.

The moderate Utraquists had no wish to break definitively with the pope. Instead they sought an accommodation which would permit moral reform in the Church together with communion for the laity with bread and wine. On the whole they were of a higher social class than the radicals of Prague or Tabor and saw nothing wrong with luxurious churches or elaborate divine services. Sensitive to threats to property, they objected to the destruction of works of art and architecture by puritan lower-class radicals. However, despite considerable tension between the moderate and radical Hussites, both groups saw the need for a united front. In May 1420 after much discussion, representatives of the two tendencies agreed upon a common platform. Known as the Four Articles of Prague, it demanded: (1) freedom of preaching, which meant sermons based on the Scriptures and delivered in the vernacular; (2) communion for the laity in both kinds, allowing all believers to experience mystic union with Christ; (3) clerical poverty (i.e., a Church without property), to eliminate the abuses that inevitably accompanied wealth; and (4) both prohibition and punishment of specific sins. A long list of such sins was appended, including such well-established practices as simony, the sale of indulgences, Mass said for money, and hypocritical begging.

This religious revolution was accompanied by a political crisis. Since the death of the childless Wenceslas IV in 1419, the Bohemian throne had belonged by right of inheritance to his younger half-brother Sigismund, the same who had betrayed John Hus at Constance. The Hussite party would accept him as king only if he promised to respect freedom of worship in Bohemia. Sigismund refused. As German emperor and king of Hungary, he could hardly afford to make this concession, which would have alienated his other subjects as well as the Church. Instead he proclaimed a crusade against Bohemia, supported by a papal bull stigmatizing the Hussites as heretics. Between 1420 and 1432 Sigismund led five separate campaigns into Bohemia, each one an ignominious failure. After this both sides were ready for peace, and a Hussite delegation met with representatives of the Council of Basel to discuss possible conditions for a settlement.

Meanwhile within Bohemia the Hussites were at odds among themselves. The Utraquists had come to regard the radicals as the main obstacle to the attainment of peace by some reasonable compromise; and tensions rose. In May 1434 a moderate and a radical Hussite army clashed near the village of Lipany in north Bohemia, where the Utraquists won a victory that largely eliminated the radicals as a military factor. This result cleared the way for the compromise known as the Basel Compacts, drawn up and accepted in final form in 1436 by the assemblies of Bohemia and Moravia and by King Sigismund. Based on the earlier Four Articles of Prague, the Compacts recognized both Catholicism and Utraquism as legal faiths in Bohemia. The Council of Basel formally declared that communion in both kinds was not heretical. Finally in 1436, seventeen years after inheriting the crown of Bohemia, Sigismund entered Prague as king.

Sadly, the Basel Compacts did not bring permanent religious peace to Bohemia. As the work only of a church council, not a pope, they were weakened by the decline of the conciliar movement after the ending of the Great Schism. Successive popes interpreted the Compacts in so narrow a fashion as to render them virtually meaningless; and no pope was ever willing to ratify them. Nonetheless, Utraquism remained the dominant form of Christianity in Bohemia for nearly two centuries, until the victory of international Catholicism over the Bohemians at White Mountain in 1620. Similar in doctrine to Catholicism, it remained faithful to the chalice for the laity and to the reforming principles of Hus, who was venerated as a martyr. The Taborite organization continued in existence, although much reduced in numbers, while the Orebites disappeared entirely. Meanwhile the Utraquist Church developed into an independent religious body with its own archbishop, John Rokycana, elected by the Bohemian Diet in 1435. Organizationally it was hampered by its insistence that only a bishop properly confirmed by Rome could perform the sacred act of ordaining priests. In consequence the Utraquist Church suffered from a shortage of clergy, although some priests managed to get ordained in Poland, Hungary, or Italy. No satisfactory solution was ever found for this problem, since no pope would confirm Rokycana as archbishop.

The terms of the Basel Compacts as well as the memory of the Hussite wars convinced both Utraquists and Catholics in Bohemia of the need to tolerate one another. George Poděbrady, the Hussite leader who was elected king (r. 1457–71), always insisted that he was ruler of "both kinds of people." Nonetheless the dominant Utraquist party denied toleration to the still more radical sect known as the Unity of Brethren (later as Bohemian or Moravian Brethren), who established their own organization in about 1459. In many respects the Brethren were spiritual heirs of the Taborites, except that they refused to use military force in defense of their convictions. They accepted the pacifist and ethical ideas of Peter Chelčický (1390–1460), the greatest religious philosopher produced by the Czech nation. Originally the Brethren were a society of rural Christians who lived piously and sought to imitate Christ's example by engaging in simple manual labor. To avoid persecution they moved to Moravia, which became the center of the brotherhood.

George Poděbrady, the "Hussite king," was a very able statesman who maintained religious peace in Bohemia against formidable odds. The Basel Compacts had established a precarious balance between Utraquists and Catholics in that strife-ridden country. While Utraquists were in the majority, Catholics were too strong a minority to be overridden and could always count on support from abroad. As long as both parties were prepared to observe the Compacts, religious peace was maintained and George could claim to be as orthodox in religion as any sovereign in Christendom. However, the peace proved to be temporary. The Catholic Church remained unreconciled to the secularization of most of its Bohemian property, which in 1400 had amounted to at least a third of the kingdom. The pope and the Catholic hierarchy insisted on a severely limited interpretation of the Basel Compacts. In 1462 Pope Pius II (better known as the humanist Aeneas Sylvius) formally abrogated any obligation of the Church to abide by them. Later Pope Paul II encouraged King Matthias of Hungary to conduct a crusade against Bohemia to eliminate Hussitism by force. This pressure made it impossible for George Poděbrady to found his own royal dynasty. Nonetheless the Czechs insisted that the king they elected after his death, the Polish Catholic Vladislav II, must accept the Basel Compacts as a condition of taking the throne. By this time it was abundantly clear that any attempt to impose a single form of worship on Bohemia could only lead to strife. In 1485 the Diet passed the statutes of Kutná Hora, which permitted freedom of choice between Utraquism and Catholicism in Bohemia. Religious toleration thus became the law of the land; and in 1512 these statutes were reconfirmed and declared valid forever. In fact they survived only until 1620, but long enough to bequeath their tradition to the Protestant Reformation.

Hussite influences spread from Bohemia abroad, especially to Poland, where the similiarity between the Polish and Czech languages rendered communication easy. In Poland the Hussites found numerous supporters among the nobility and townspeople, partly as an expression of opposition to the Catholic clergy. However, conditions were more favorable for the spread of Hussitism in Bohemia than in Poland, where the towns played a smaller political role and were less independent of the monarchy. Cracow's university remained a bulwark of Roman Catholicism, while the king and the church hierarchy in Poland actively persecuted Hussites. King Jagiełło, still living down the stigma of having been born a pagan, also hoped for papal support in his ongoing conflict with the Teutonic Knights in Prussia. In 1424 he issued an edict empowering the church courts to persecute "heretics" (i.e., Hussites) and deliver them to the secular arm. Numerous acts of Polish cathedral chapters in the 15th century record punishments imposed on accused Hussites.

Hussite ideas found an echo also in the Hungarian kingdom, particularly in Croatia and Transylvania, where intermittent Turkish raids had created an unstable situation. Some clerics who had studied at Prague began preaching Hussite doctrines. In 1432 a Hussite-led revolt broke out in Hungary, first in the areas adjacent to Bohemia, then in Transylvania. The pope sent a special Inquisitor to Hungary who took forcible measures aimed at subjecting both the Hussites and Orthodox Christians of the kingdom to the Church of Rome. In response, many Hungarian Hussites moved across the border into Moldavia, where they sponsored the earliest translation of the Bible into their native vernacular. Some of the persecuted Polish Hussites also went to Moldavia, where the ruling voivode, Alexander the Good, rejected demands to extradite them. Certain major similarities between Hussitism and Eastern Orthodoxy, the dominant faith of the Romanians, perhaps made Alexander sympathetic to their cause. Like the Hussites, the Orthodox practiced communion in both kinds, denied the supremacy of the pope, and (here resembling Taborites but not Utraquists) permitted the marriage of priests. In the 15th century Moldavia was the only state in Europe outside of Bohemia itself where Hussites were free from persecution.

Meanwhile Orthodoxy was under siege in those parts of the Balkans overrun by the Turks. In this first phase of their European conquests, the Ottoman sultans had yet to evolve a consistent religious policy, which therefore varied from place to place. In theory, Christianity was a tolerated religion in all Muslim states. Islamic religious law defined Jews, Christians, and Zoroastrians as "People of the Book," superior to mere pagans because they possessed sacred Scriptures revealed by God. Nonetheless, a number of Christian bishoprics in Ottoman Thrace and Macedonia had to be abandoned in the 14th century. Some prelates were imprisoned, while others fled, and still others were prevented from carrying out their duties. Some Christian church property was confiscated. The Church became impoverished, and many Christian communities were left without priests.

As long as the Byzantine Empire still stood, the Turks viewed Eastern Orthodoxy as politically suspect, because inextricably linked with the enemy. The situation of the Balkan Christians improved noticeably after the conquest of Constantinople in 1453, which transformed the Greek patriarch into an Ottoman subject. Political considerations no longer stood in the way of granting Christians the toleration prescribed by the Koran for "People of the Book."

Ottoman authorities only rarely exerted pressure on a conquered population to accept Islam. Although Christians and Jews were naturally considered inferior to Muslims, they were entitled to protection from the Islamic state and free practice of their religion. Indeed, the special head tax paid by non-Muslims, the jizya, constituted an important part of Ottoman state revenue. Not surprisingly, non-Muslims found many salient reasons for conversion to the religion of the conquerors. Undoubtedly fear played a role during the conquest period; and once a person had accepted Islam, reversion to Christianity or to Judaism was punishable by death. Muslims enjoyed a lighter tax burden than unbelievers, as well as a favored legal position. Christian testimony was not accepted as evidence in Islamic courts. At times Christians suffered from petty persecution and discrimination at the hands of Ottoman officials. Sumptuary regulations governed the clothes they could wear, the animals they could ride, and the weapons they were permitted to carry. Positive inducements operated also, such as the prestige of belonging to the dominant religious body of the empire. By comparison Christianity was the religion of an underclass.

During the initial period of Ottoman hegemony in the Balkans, only isolated individuals took the step of conversion to Islam. Subsequently entire villages and districts did so. A significant intermixture of Christian and Muslim beliefs occurred on a popular level, owing to the many survivals of pagan nature worship and the lack of theological sophistication among simple people. Islamic folk religion easily incorporated Christian practices like baptism and the cult of saints. Muslim pilgrims visited Christian shrines where saints or holy relics were believed to work miracles. Conversely, Christians were attracted to Muslim sanctuaries by pious legends claiming that the Islamic holy men honored there were identical to particular Christian saints or had secretly been converted to Christianity. Integration of this type undoubtedly made it easier for Christians to accept Islam at a time when conversion had become advantageous for other reasons as well.

In Bosnia and Hercegovina, which formed part of the Ottoman Empire after 1463, a particularly large segment of the population eventually accepted Islam. The Bosnians were by no means rigidly attached to one religious orthodoxy. They had long since become accustomed to the comfortable coexistence of three versions of Christianity—Catholicism, Orthodoxy, and the indigenous Bosnian Church. Many Bosnians undoubtedly preferred the Turks to the Catholic Hungarians, who had conducted wars of conquest against them in the guise of religious crusades. Contrary to a widely held assumption, Bosnian nobles were not required to accept Islam in order to retain their estates. Nor did any massive Turkish colonization occur in the country. Apparently Bosnia's conversion to Islam was largely voluntary, beginning in the towns and spreading slowly into the rural areas. The population lacked strong attachment to either Catholicism or Orthodoxy, so that conversion to Islam was not difficult for them. Under somewhat analogous circumstances, Islamization made great inroads in Albania also. Just as in Bosnia, the mountainous hinterland was relatively impenetrable to the influences of international Christianity. Some Albanian lords changed their religion several times as political circumstances dictated. Moreover, as a military state, the Ottoman Empire offered many outlets for the warlike qualities of the Albanian clansmen. Men who wished to rise in the sultan's service naturally accepted Islam; and a majority of the Albanian people eventually did likewise. About a third of the population remained faithful to Orthodoxy, while Catholics became a small minority.

In Bulgaria, conquered by the Ottomans in 1396, Christian worship was subject at first to certain restrictions. To avoid giving offense to Muslim sensibilities, Christian churches in Sofia were required to be small and narrow, half-buried in the earth, and surrounded by high walls. Normalization of economic and social life eventually brought about greater tolerance for Christians and their institutions in Bulgaria. However, for nearly a century after the Turkish conquest very little Islamization occurred. In Macedonia (western Bulgaria) the process gained momentum only after about 1480. Ottoman records show that in strategically located towns like Skopje or Bitolj, Muslims had become a majority by the end of the 15th century. For the most part, this change was attributable not to conversions but to an influx of Turkish colonists employed by the Ottoman military establishment. Similarly in eastern Bulgaria, relatively few Christians converted to Islam. The principal exceptions were the so-called Pomaks who lived in the Rhodope Mountains. Islamization in Bulgaria was chiefly due to the planned settlement of Turkish peasants from Anatolia.

An important contributor to the spread of Islam in the Balkans was the Sufi movement. The Sufis were ascetics and mystics, similar in many respects to Christian monks. Famous Sufi Muslim teachers attracted groups of disciples who eventually organized themselves into brotherhoods or orders and maintained their own meetinghouses or monasteries. Each Sufi order advocated a unique tarikat or "path" (i.e., a spiritual discipline through which the believer sought direct contact with God). The orthodox ulema—the recognized scholars and experts in Islamic Sacred Law—tolerated the Sufis as long as they did not openly reject Islamic doctrine and ritual. However, Sufi beliefs and practices were frequently quite heterodox. The Sufi adepts obeyed no central religious authority, since neither popes nor church councils existed in the Muslim world. Islamic doctrine had taken form gradually over the centuries through the consensus (ijma) of learned men. This absence of centralized control doubtless facilitated to the Sufis' departures from mainstream Islam.

Sufi beliefs consisted largely of mystical doctrines intermixed with popular superstitions, some of which can be traced to Syrian, Persian, or Indian sources. Since the Sufis were dedicated to poverty, they were popularly known as dervishes, or "poor men." Each Sufi brotherhood cultivated its own methods and ceremonies, which in many cases orthodox Muslims regarded as highly objectionable. The famous "dancing" dervishes, for example, performed a ritual which entailed revolving on the right foot until dizziness gave way to ecstasy. This "dancing" was accompanied by music and the recitation of poetry. Other dervishes recited set formulas or even consumed drugs in order to produce a similarly ecstatic effect. In addition to such proceedings, the Sufis engaged in prayer and fasting. Some Sufi brotherhoods emphasized mystical contemplation, conducting their affairs in secret and avoiding all external symbols. Others mingled with the public and were easily recognizable by the members' headdress. Many Sufi houses also served as centers for charitable activities.

The dervish orders flourished mainly in towns, where they established close connections with the Muslim artisan guilds. Financial support came from religious foundations (vakifs) endowed by the Ottoman sultans or other prominent men. The dervishes also enjoyed great popularity with the general public, which regarded them as intermediaries between this world and the next. Simple folk were impressed by their rule of poverty and their mystical rites and customs, which often reflected vestiges of ancient cults. A few Sufis were believed to possess supernatural powers which gave them the reputation of saints. Pious Muslims visited the tombs of such holy men in order to invoke their intercession with the divine power—a practice upon which orthodox Islam frowned. The essentially pantheistic nature of Sufi beliefs prevented them from drawing sharp distinctions between one religion and another, so that even devout Christians often looked upon them with favor. The Sufis' approach to life contrasted sharply with the legalism and rationalism of the orthodox Muslim ulema. Nonetheless the activities of the dervishes gave Sufism an extraordinary hold on all classes of Muslims, who scarcely noticed the discrepancy between Sufi beliefs and the prescriptions of Islamic Sacred Law.

The most famous of the dervish orders were the Bektashis, whose organization apparently dates from the early 15th century. Actually the type of belief they represented had long been popular among the Turkish tribesmen of Anatolia. The Bektashis professed an eclectic mixture of popular religious ideas, including relics of Asiatic shamanism and old Turkish folklore. Shamanist influence is particularly evident in the ritual of the whirling dervishes. The Bektashis looked tolerantly upon all religions and attached little importance to externals. They did not demand conformity to the standard Islamic observances, such as prayer five times daily and fasting during the month of Ramadan. Unlike most other Muslims in the Ottoman Empire, who professed stricter forms of Islam, they permitted wine drinking and allowed their women to go unveiled in public and mix with men in society. To many Balkan Christians this form of Islam cannot have appeared uncongenial. During the 15th century the Bektashis obtained a firm foothold in the Janissary corps, many of whose members were products of the Balkan child tribute or former war prisoners whose conversion to Islam had been either superficial or involuntary. In fact the Bektashis accepted certain quasi-Christian doctrines, such as belief in the efficacy of confession and a Trinity consisting of Allah, Mohammed, and Mohammed's son-in-law Ali. To Muslims of this type, all religions were equally valid.

The Ottoman sultans, whose notions of sovereignty drew no distinction between the sacred and the secular, naturally tended to favor the legalism of the ulema over the mysticism of the Sufis. Muslims believed that legislation, administration, and justice should rest upon a religious foundation; and the theologically minded ulema supplied the necessary legal underpinning. As experts in Islamic law, the ulema served the Ottoman state as judges, basing their decisions on the precepts of the Koran and the Traditions of Mohammed. Theocratic assumptions also made it logical for the Ottoman sultans to distinguish among their subject peoples on the basis of confessional allegiance. Thus each religious group in the empire became a separate legal entity; and the sultan allowed the head of each one to exercise wide jurisdiction over its members. This was the basis of the so-called millet system, which in its essentials had a long history. The ancient empires of the Romans, the Sassanians of Persia, and the Caliphs of Baghdad, among others, had all permitted some of their subject communities to retain their own laws under a traditional leader answerable to the head of state.

Until the conquest of Constantinople in 1453, the Ottoman sultans had controlled their Orthodox subjects through local bishops. However, once the Greek patriarch himself became an Ottoman subject, he was eligible to assume important political functions in the theocratic Ottoman system of government. Sultan Mohammed II (the Conqueror) appointed the Christian scholar Gennadios as the first ecumenical patriarch, giving him authority over all other Orthodox Christian prelates in the empire. The independence of the two surviving Balkan patriarchates, Tirnovo and Peć, was suppressed, while the Serbian archbishopric at Ohrid was abolished altogether. The ecumenical patriarch received a high ceremonial rank, presided over his own court of law, and even maintained a prison. For most purposes, including the payment of taxes, his legal jurisdiction extended over all Orthodox Christians in the empire. (His position in the Ottoman system naturally did not alter the canon law, which regarded all five patriarchs as equal.) At the same time Mohammed II appointed a chief rabbi, whose powers over all Jews in the empire resembled those of the patriarch over Christians. Finally the Armenians, who adhered to the (Monophysite) Gregorian Church, were recognized in 1461 as forming their own millet. Because the head of the Armenian Church, the Catholicos, did not reside on Ottoman territory, the sultan chose the Armenian bishop of Bursa as head of this millet. Since no new millets were established after this time, any non-Muslims who later became subject to the empire but were neither Orthodox Christians nor Jews were included in the Armenian one.

By means of these arrangements the Ottoman sultans permitted the leaders of the various faiths to exercise wide authority over their flocks. Each religious community constituted a kind of state within the state, subject to the sultan's overall jurisdiction. For the religious leaders themselves, this situation held many advantages. The Greek patriarch, for example, often became personally wealthy. He received special privileges, such as the right to wear the insignia of office, bear arms, ride a horse, and have an escort of Turkish soldiers, which helped in collecting taxes. Ironically, this leader of Orthodox Christians exercised more real authority in Ottoman times than his predecessors had enjoyed under the Byzantine Empire, since it was through him that the sultan dealt with Christian affairs. On suitable occasions the patriarch and/or the bishops received letters of privilege from the sultan called berats, enumerating their privileges and obligations. The patriarch's court became the chief judicial authority for Christians in the Ottoman Empire. It employed Byzantine legal codes and sometimes even adjudicated the quarrels of Christians with Muslims.

Nonetheless, the position of the patriarch was fundamentally insecure. Berats were valid only until the death of the sultan who issued them; his successor had to reconfirm them. All prelates were wholly dependent on the sultan's favor. Most of the Orthodox patriarchs who held office in Ottoman times were insignificant figures who had attained their positions through bribery or intrigue. Usually they were permitted to serve only brief terms of office. The Orthodox Church in the Balkans, deprived of patronage from a native dynasty and nobility, was no longer the cultural force it had been previously. On the other hand, Ottoman religious policy at least made possible the Church's survival as an institution. While some church buildings were destroyed or converted into mosques, the majority were left untouched and allowed to function. Ottoman authorities did not prevent the repair of old churches and occasionally even permitted the construction of new ones. Not surprisingly, most Christian churches built in the Ottoman period were modest structures reflecting the limited economic means of the Christian middle class and the reduced size of the monastic communities.

The Catholic Church under the Ottoman regime fared far worse. The Turks' principal military opponents in Europe were Catholics, while the popes strongly supported anti-Turkish crusades. The sultan's government viewed Catholicism as a particular threat in Bosnia, owing to that country's location on the borders of Catholic Hungary with the German Empire looming beyond. This strategic situation produced the paradox of a Muslim government attempting to coerce into Orthodoxy any Catholics who resisted conversion to Islam. In the Balkans the Catholic clergy felt personally unsafe as well as unwelcome, exposed to outbreaks of religious fanaticism on the part of both Muslims and Orthodox Christians. Catholic bishops whose dioceses lay in Ottoman territory rarely occupied their sees, disguising themselves as simple Franciscan friars if they traveled there at all. As a result, the bishops neglected their flocks, while the Church in the Ottoman Empire suffered a chronic shortage of priests. Balkan Catholics often acquired the habit of attending Orthodox services and in the end usually accepted Orthodoxy altogether.

For the Christian peoples of the Balkans the Church was the only culture bearer that mattered in Ottoman times. No secular literature or art existed for them, aside from orally transmitted folktales and the architectural remains of an earlier period. Even religious art and literature were scarcely cultivated. Contrary to the Balkan nationalist mythology of a later age, which treated the Ottoman period primarily as an oppressive "yoke," the Turks did not normally destroy Christian manuscripts or the monasteries which preserved them. All the same, these institutions became greatly impoverished. Their former patrons, the Christian monarchs and upper nobility, had either been destroyed, exiled, or absorbed into Islam. The educational system declined correspondingly. Mount Athos represented a partial exception, perhaps because it submitted to the sultan in 1383 prior to being directly threatened by his troops and thus escaped the usual fate of conquered territories. The Athos monasteries prospered by selling their agricultural products and managed to preserve their reputation as bastions of pure Orthodoxy. Their Greek character diminished somewhat when the Holy Mountain began to attract more Slavic monks. However, the overall cultural level definitely declined. The Byzantine upper class which formerly had supplied the Athos monasteries with highly educated recruits and financial patronage no longer existed. Alternate sources of support were unavailable.

The favorable legal position of Christianity in the Ottoman Empire was useful propaganda for the Turks in their ongoing military campaigns in Europe. Moreover, the dissension between Eastern and Western Christianity ensured that favorable treatment of the Orthodox Church would not strengthen the Catholic West. Outright religious persecution was rare and temporary in the Ottoman Empire. On the other hand, discrimination on religious grounds was an essential part of the system. Like Christianity, Islam considered itself the only true faith. Ottoman law imposed various restrictions on the Christian churches—for example, that their steeples could never rise higher than the domes of the mosques. New churches could seldom be built, only old ones repaired. Church bells were prohibited. Christians were required to worship quietly, without display, and always show due deference to Muslims. Despite such handicaps, the position of non-Muslims in the Ottoman Empire was decidedly better than that of non-Christians or alleged heretics under Christian rule. Ottoman subjects were not obliged to reside in ghettos, and found no secular occupations legally closed to them. Violence against non-Muslims was uncommon. They were not forced to choose between exile and martyrdom.

Thus in the course of the 15th century the religious picture in East Central Europe changed dramatically. Whereas Catholicism retained its monopoly in

Poland and Hungary, Bohemia experienced the massive Hussite revolution which turned the Czechs into forerunners of the Protestant Reformation and furnished an early and rare example of religious toleration. The religion of Islam, supported by the government of the Ottoman Empire, became a major force in southeastern Europe. A significant Muslim Turkish population settled in the Balkan Peninsula, where the Orthodox Church was now subject to an Islamic state. Orthodoxy per se was not persecuted in the Balkans, but its institutions lost their intellectual eminence. The 16th century would see these religious upheavals continue on a larger scale. The Protestant Reformation was destined to evoke few echoes in Ottoman-ruled territory, but elsewhere in East Central Europe its effects would be profound. Bohemia, Poland, and Hungary would acquire important Protestant minorities in the new century as religious conflict entered a new phase.

CHAPTER 8

The Art and Practice of War

Warfare is an activity as old as the human race itself. In this respect the inhabitants of medieval East Central Europe formed no exception whatsoever, as archaeological remains as well as surviving documents amply attest. Whether the soldier or the saint was more highly esteemed in medieval society is a moot point; but certainly in secular life the warrior had no competitor for the admiration of his peers. Physical courage and skill with weapons conferred prestige far above the humble labor of the agriculturalist, the dexterity of the artisan, or the cleverness of the merchant. The warrior exulted in the excitement of the armed clash and the opportunity to prove his prowess; for war was the supreme test of manhood. At the same time, medieval warfare presented certain intensely practical problems which were not easily solved. The feeding of an army on campaign created almost insuperable difficulties. Relatively few supplies could be carried on the march; and no district was capable of providing sufficient food and fodder for thousands of men and horses for any length of time. In virtually every war zone a bitter struggle erupted between the local peasantry seeking to conceal its animals and foodstuffs and soldiers trying to seize them by force or threat of force. Thus the size of an army which could live off the land in this way was necessarily limited; and famine was a common accompaniment of war.

In the 6th and 7th centuries A.D., when the Slavic peoples undertook their great migrations, Byzantium was the dominant military power of southeastern Europe. Heir to the remaining lands of the old Roman Empire, this East Roman Empire with its Greek ruling class was not ordinarily an aggressive state. From the late 6th century onward it aspired chiefly to preserve the territorial status quo, which nonetheless denoted hegemony over an enormous land mass in both Europe and Asia. The army reforms of Emperor Maurice (r. 582–602), which for the most part remained in effect, involved a strictly defensive strategy, centered upon a small professional force and massive fortifications situated along the frontiers of the empire. Although in the course of centuries the Byzantines would suffer shattering defeats and staggering territorial losses, they succeeded in preserving the core of the empire and a high civilization for nearly a thousand years after the fall of Rome in the West. Superior numbers alone cannot explain this phenomenon, since the Greeks were often greatly outnumbered by the forces of their enemies. Technological superiority does not account for it either, because Greeks and barbarians often fought with similar weapons. The key lay in organization, discipline, strategy, and planning.

By the time of the Slavic invasions in the 6th century, the Byzantine army had become primarily a cavalry force. This marked a nearly complete departure from the practice of the ancient Romans, who had relied primarily on the shock tactics made possible by the stern discipline and drill of their heavy infantry. However, the government at Constantinople was obliged to deal with a succession of hostile horsemen—Huns, Avars, Pechenegs, Magyars, Cumans—who roamed the flat grasslands of Central Asia, Ukraine, and southeastern Europe. Semi-nomadic in life-style, most such groups entered the empire as raiders in search of plunder rather than as invaders seeking to capture territory. Sheer necessity demanded that the Byzantines adapt to the nature of these enemies. They gave up the effort to keep their frontiers inviolate and created instead a defense in depth. This new strategy was based on a highly mobile field force, capable of reaching the invasion point quickly and concentrating troops for battle if necessary. Since infantry was normally too slow for this purpose, cavalry became the primary component of the army. When enemy raiders invaded imperial territory, the Byzantine cavalry tracked and harassed them, impeded their advance, picked off stragglers, and kept the nearest military headquarters informed of their location. Meanwhile the local garrison remained sheltered behind the walls of a fortress. The commander of the fortress then chose a favorable moment to ride out with his cavalry, seeking either to ambush the raiders, trap them in a pass already occupied by the infantry, or force them against a frontier obstacle. These tactics deprived the intruders of their most important requisite: a safe return home with their plunder.

Along the Byzantine frontiers infantry continued to be useful in the defense of fortresses, as garrison troops, or for small expeditions in the mountains. Raiders from the steppes were unable to break a steady line of heavily armed foot soldiers carrying shields, spears, and swords. The bows of the Byzantine light infantry could shoot farther than the smaller bows of the steppe warriors, whose horses usually wore no protective armor. Facing the Byzantine infantry, their riders were likely to have their mounts shot out from under them before they could come within range to attack. Byzantine light infantry was also useful whenever enemy raiders had to leave their horses behind to cross the imperial frontier, which in the Balkans meant the Danube River. Steppe horsemen when dismounted were fairly helpless, having never learned to fight on foot. Finally, the Byzantine light infantry was useful in blocking the raiders' line of retreat; and it could move faster than wagons loaded with booty. On the other hand, no type of infantry could catch up with steppe warriors on their swift horses, who relied for victory upon speed rather than steadfastness or heavy armor. Cavalry was indispensable for a viable defense against them.

The Byzantine officer corps, drawn largely from the Greek aristocracy, demonstrated a high average level of ability as well as professional pride. At the same time it possessed relatively few of the attributes of chivalry as understood in Western Europe. The typical Western knight loved war for its own sake. Battle meant the clash of heavy cavalry in a frontal charge, while only men of inferior social standing fought on foot. The French or English medieval knight admired courage and daring regardless of the objective, and believed firmly in the offensive as the most effective form of combat. Greek warriors scorned such an attitude. The standard Byzantine manual of military tactics, compiled by Emperor Leo the Wise (r. 886–912), expressed nothing but contempt for the Western code of chivalry, which produced needless loss of life. To the rational Greek mind the best proof of generalship was a campaign successfully concluded without a major battle. This was the least costly form of warfare in both men and treasure. The Byzantines never forgot that their empire had numerous enemies and many long frontiers to defend. They considered legitimate any trickery which promised success, such as false surrenders or spurious negotiations used as cover for an ambush. Many times the skillful Greek diplomats achieved with bribes a result which could only have been attained at greater cost through warfare. Byzantine scholars studied in great detail the military capacity and habits of potential enemies and devised appropriate counterstrategies to match. They took it for granted that the barbarians would usually possess numerical superiority, but could be outwitted through ruse, stratagem, and superior organization.

Once the transition to cavalry had occurred, the Byzantines' superior military organization gave them a distinct advantage over their enemies. By the 8th century, successive emperors had transferred many provinces from civilian to military rule, with a general as the head of provincial government. These militarized political units, called themes, each supported a permanent army corps. The themes were linked by good roads which connected places of strategic importance and permitted the quick movement of troops. A Byzantine army traveled with an extensive wagon train, including eight to ten days' worth of supplies for situations in which the army outran its baggage. At each overnight stopping place, field engineers organized the digging of entrenchments, which they surrounded by ropes and a thick chain of pickets farther from the camp so that a surprise enemy attack became virtually impossible. Such systematic planning made the Byzantine defenses relatively independent of the talent of individual generals or the quality of the soldiers. Nothing less could have preserved this remarkable empire in existence for a thousand years after the fall of Rome in the West.

The pivots of the empire's defensive strategy were its numerous fortresses. Permanent garrisons based upon these strongholds guarded every Byzantine frontier, supplementing the mobile field army which the emperor could use at his discretion. The fortresses functioned as protected supply depots with agricultural settlements nearby to furnish provisions. An enemy force might invade Byzantine territory with relative ease, but without benefit of an adequate supply system it could survive only by foraging. At that point it became easy prey for the imperial troops, who were stationed near their supplies and could concentrate superior force in any threatened district. However, a Byzantine general did not often see combat. When danger threatened he typically retired with his army to the safety of a fortress. Hostile troops might surround the walls of this stronghold but could seldom capture it, since lack of supplies eventually forced the raising of the siege. Areas of particular strategic importance possessed especially heavy fortifications. One such region was Dobrudja, the rectangular territory lying between the last great bend of the Danube and the Black Sea. Another was Albania, situated at the western end of the chief route from the Adriatic through the mountains to Salonika and Constantinople. Albania's imposing fortifications were carefully maintained, since if these defenses fell, Salonika lay wide open to a land invasion from the west.

The imperial capital of Constantinople was the best-fortified city in Christendom, with magnificent stone walls which repeatedly proved impregnable against attack. Located on a triangle-shaped peninsula, the city was protected on its land side by a moat over 60 feet wide and at least 22 feet deep which could be filled with water piped from the hills. Behind the moat stood an outer wall about 27 feet high, with square and semicircular towers projecting from its face to provide for flanking fire. Inside this wall was a covered passageway to shield the transfer of troops, and behind it a battlemented inner wall 15 feet thick and 30 feet high to furnish cover for archers. Prior to the age of gunpowder, no hostile force was ever able to breach these powerful landward defenses. In the 7th and 8th centuries Avar, Persian, and Saracen forces all blockaded Constantinople and attempted to starve it out, but to no avail. The Ottoman Turks likewise fell short on several occasions, succeeding in 1453 by only the narrowest of margins even with the aid of cannon against a pitifully small defending force. On the other hand, the sea side of Constantinople was protected by only a single wall. Normally the Byzantines employed their superior navy to repel attacks from that direction; but the weak emperors who ruled after the death of Manuel Comnenus in 1180 neglected the fleet. This enabled the men of the Fourth Crusade in 1204 to capture the city by moving close to the sea wall on Venetian ships. The Byzantines' recapture of Constantinople in 1261 happened almost by accident. A Greek general reconnoitering in the suburbs discovered that its Venetian defenders were absent, forced an entry into the city through a narrow secret passage, and opened a gate from the inside to admit his troops. In both cases a somewhat more capable defense might easily have prevented capture.

This weakness at sea was exceptional, since throughout much of its history Byzantium maintained the finest war fleet in the Mediterranean, protecting the coastal cities as well as the sea-lanes. Each naval district of the empire underwrote the cost of the ships assigned to it. The fleet drew much of its manpower from the sailors of the merchant marine, since Byzantium was a major commercial power. Thus when Venetian competition had caused the Byzantine share of the Mediterranean trade to decline in the 10th century and afterward, one result was a serious diminution in the quality and quantity of the empire's naval personnel. The Byzantine navy also possessed a unique incendiary weapon in the so-called Greek fire, a viscous substance which burned brightly even when it fell upon stone or iron. Invented at about the time of the Arab siege of Constantinople in 673, it created havoc in the enemy's ranks. Greek fire proved catastrophic to successive Arab navies attacking Constantinople, and similarly decisive in destroying the Rus fleets in 941 and 1043. For defense on land it could be squirted from tubes mounted on city walls. Water only made it burn more brightly, so that sand or vinegar was required to extinguish it. The composition of Greek fire was secret, and remains imperfectly known even today.

For centuries the Byzantine fleet enjoyed a virtually unchallenged superiority over all opponents. Its ships patrolled the Danube whenever that river formed part of the empire's northern boundary (i.e., when the Bulgars did not control it). Greek ships easily outclassed the primitive boats of the Slavs who attempted to capture Salonika in 626. Naval dominance was similarly decisive in repelling the far more dangerous attacks of the Arabs, particularly in 673 and 717. Although the fleet declined in the 9th century when the emperors of the Isaurian dynasty economized on armaments, this eclipse was temporary. In the 10th century the Byzantine navy prevented Bulgar river vessels from entering the Black Sea; and it proved indispensable in the wars with Venice and the Normans of south Italy. In the 11th and 12th centuries the troops needed to counteract Pecheneg and Cuman raids were transported by ship in the Black Sea. Constantinople, with its magnificent location on the Bosphorus, enjoyed an exceptionally favorable strategic position for purposes of naval defense. Any rival fleet approaching from the Mediterranean Sea had first to negotiate the narrow strait of the Dardanelles, while the city itself was surrounded by water on three sides.

Protection of the empire's land frontiers proved more difficult. The Danube boundary presented no insuperable barrier to raiders from the opposite shore. Although a strong line of fortifications protected the southern bank of the river, frequently too few troops were available for its defense. The Slavs who entered Byzantine territory in the 5th and 6th centuries did so largely by means of infiltration and plundering rather than outright conquest. Primarily agriculturalists, they generally lived in village settlements widely separated from one another along riverbanks. When they fought, it was as foot soldiers, sometimes (but not invariably) protected by heavy shields. Byzantine sources describe the Slavs as brave warriors, but poorly armed. Their usual weapons were wooden bows and poison-tipped arrows, supplemented by hammers, axes, and clubs for hand-to-hand fighting. When attacked they fled into the forests and swamps, attempting to entice the opponent to follow in order to shoot at him from the cover of the trees and underbrush. From their earlier homeland on the well-watered plains of Belarus, the Slavs brought considerable expertise in river navigation, which enabled them to conduct attacks from boats. Although good swimmers who fought well in streams and swamps, they could not easily compete in cavalry warfare. The mobility of their troops was limited not only by lack of practice in horsemanship but, more important, by the need to remain close to their fields, without which they would starve.

Despite the damage they wreaked on the towns of the Balkan Peninsula, the Slavs did not threaten the actual survival of the Byzantine Empire. At times the imperial government even used Slavic troops as part of its defenses against other invaders. The Slavs were formidable to the Greeks only when they kept to the mountains, where their archers and javelin-throwers could harass an invader from inaccessible positions or make sudden assaults on the flanks or rear of invading columns. On a plundering expedition in the plains they could easily be ridden down by Byzantine cavalry, since they lacked discipline and wore no defensive equipment except for large round shields. At first unable to attack fortified towns at all, the Slavs soon learned to use ladders to scale town walls. However, they lacked the siege machinery necessary to capture strongly fortified places, as witness their inability to take Constantinople in 626 or Salonika in 675–81, despite repeated attempts and the assistance of Avar steppe cavalry.

For defense the Slavs built forts protected by earthworks and wooden walls, usually in marshland or wooded country where the population could take refuge in times of danger. Their earliest fortified settlements were protected only with palisades (i.e., sharpened wooden stakes). Eventually these crude defensive arrangements began to be superseded in favor of a stronger type of fort surrounded by solid embankments of earth. For example, at Poznań in Poland in the 10th and 11th centuries the embankments stood over 60 feet wide and 30 feet high, strengthened by a nine-foot outer ledge of stone-filled wooden boxes covered with clay as protection against fire. The main body of the fortress was built of wood. Fortifications of stone were rare everywhere in Europe until about 1100 except where old Roman citadels remained in use, as in Serbia or Bulgaria. Stone castles were both too expensive and too difficult to construct for the craftsmen of that period. Instead the Slavs surrounded rocky heights with ditches and fallen trees or built artificial mounds which they enclosed by ditches and palisades. In early Croatia, for example, the fortress and royal residence of Knin was built on the edge of a rocky precipice above the river which wound around its base, dominating the main roads leading from the interior of the country down to the coast.

The Croatian military class, like that of the Bulgars in the 8th and 9th centuries, may have been of non-Slavic steppe origin, perhaps Iranian. Certainly the early Croats conducted their wars in a style unknown among the Slavs. The elite of the army fought as highly mobile light cavalry armed with bows, arrows, and lances, employing swift movements and surprise attacks. Foot soldiers were evidently of a lower class, supplying the forces for garrison duty. Independent Croatia became a significant military power under King Tomislav (r. ca. 910–28), who allegedly could put into the field 100,000 infantry and 60,000 cavalry. His fleet included 80 galleys carrying 80 men apiece and 100 cutters holding 10 to 20 men each, aside from the galley slaves who rowed them. His navy could transport 5,000 soldiers at one time. These figures, supplied by the Byzantine historian and Emperor Constantine Porphyrogenetos, would make the Croat navy only slightly inferior in numbers to its Venetian or Byzantine counterparts at the same period, although the Byzantines possessed larger ships. On the other hand, the Croats at this date apparently did not possess siege engines such as stone throwers or wall breakers. When faced with stone fortifications, they could only withdraw. Croatia's prominence in Tomislav's day was exceptional in the history of that country. Within the next generation its military position declined considerably.

The successful establishment of a Bulgar state in the Balkans in the 7th and 8th centuries was possible chiefly because at that time the Byzantines were fully occupied with the Arab military threat to their far more valuable territories in Asia Minor. Even after settling down in southeastern Europe, the Turkic-speaking Bulgars continued to fight in the typical fast-moving style of the steppes. They wore helmets and armor (doubtless both of leather) and fought with spears, swords, bows and arrows, and axes. Deserters from Byzantium taught them to construct war machines and siege equipment. In the 9th century the Bulgars proceeded to build themselves a system of triple earthworks for protection in depth against the horsemen of the steppe. In front of this defensive line they created a no-man's land—a wide but sparsely populated swath of territory where the unavailability of food and booty would obstruct any hostile invasion. Along the Black Sea coast they threw up embankments and dug ditches to prevent hostile landings on the beaches. The Bulgars' most formidable defenses, however, protected them against the Byzantine Empire to the south. Here on the Bulgar-Greek frontier they constructed the barrier the Greeks called the "Great Fence" or "Great Ditch" of Thrace, namely a high rampart and a trench, which merchants were permitted to cross only with letters of safe-conduct. The Bulgars' system of fortifications was not static. As their frontier advanced they built new earthworks and reinforced the older ones with stone walls.

Although the Byzantine government in the 9th and 10th centuries was forced to recognize the existence of independent Bulgaria, it never ceased to regard the Danube as the empire's rightful boundary. With a strong military emperor at Constantinople, Bulgaria became vulnerable. In 971 the regent (later emperor) John Tzimiskes restored the old Byzantine frontier on the Danube with his victory against an opposing force of Bulgars, Rus, Pechenegs, and Magyars. Emperor Basil II (r. 976–1025) followed up this success by reconquering western Bulgaria (i.e., Macedonia). Dedicated to religion as well as war, Basil wore a monk's robe under his armor, but was nonetheless capable of monstrous cruelty. In a series of campaigns beginning in about 998, he invaded Bulgaria nearly every year, each time penetrating farther into Bulgar territory. Basil was a superb organizer, who showed the meticulous attention to detail characteristic of Byzantine practice at its best. Establishing his base camp at Plovdiv, he moved methodically forward with his well-equipped and well-disciplined troops, garrisoning strongpoints along the route. His advance was accompanied by systematic destruction and pillage aimed at eliminating all sources of resistance. The Bulgar Tsar Samuel (r. 976–1014) was a capable military chief, but the odds against him became progressively less favorable. Repeatedly he fell upon the Byzantines with ambushes and sudden attacks, but was obliged to remain continually on the defensive. In a decisive battle in 1014, Emperor Basil surprised the Bulgar army near Salonika and won an overwhelming victory, taking 14,000 prisoners. He then ordered the blinding of ninety-nine out of every one hundred Bulgar captives, leaving each hundredth man with a single eye in order to lead his companions home. This atrocity marked the virtual end of the restored Bulgar state. Soon after viewing the miserable remnant of his army, Samuel died. In 1018 Bulgaria collapsed altogether, while Basil added to his imperial titles that of "Bulgar-Slayer."

In the 9th century a new contingent of horse warriors, known to Europeans as Magyars or Hungarians, proceeded to terrorize Europe. Bands of these horsemen appeared in Germany as early as the year 862, but began to settle permanently in what is now central and western Hungary only in 896, where they met with little opposition. Thus encamped in the heart of Europe, they conducted devastating raids many hundreds of miles from their home base. Arriving unannounced before some unfortified town, the Magyars typically sacked and burned it before the startled inhabitants could organize a defense. If faced with armed resistance they could quickly alter their objective or retreat, which gave them great flexibility. Owing to their superior mobility, they rarely engaged in open clashes. The object of their campaigns was not territory but plunder. They placed a high value on precious metals, which they used for display; and on captives, whom they sold as slaves. In Christian lands the churches suffered in particular from their depredations, since the sacred gold and silver vessels used in the Mass were both valuable and easy to carry away. The Magyar leaders were always purchasable—quite willing to leave entire regions alone or to conclude peace in exchange for gold and silver. On the other hand, they seem to have been impelled by some sense of mission. When the captured chiefs Bulcsú and Lél were asked why they tormented Christians, they replied, "We are the revenge of God, chosen by Him as a whip over you."

The Magyar warriors were feared for their speed, maneuverability, and ability to surprise. They conducted scouting operations and posted watch with great care. In battle they advanced not in one solid mass but in small bands which attacked the enemy from all sides, letting fly a stream of arrows. On the other hand, they generally bypassed fortresses in order not to waste time on sieges.

When faced with organized resistance, the Magyars usually chose to avoid open combat, seeking out protective terrain instead from which to discharge a volley of arrows and stones upon their enemies. After the initial barrage they formed a dense battlefront and advanced at a gallop, striking the opposing soldiers from horseback with their spears or short, crooked sabers. Although individually they were excellent shots, their favorite tactic was to overwhelm the enemy with a shower of missiles. Only when this had broken up the enemy formations did they attempt to attack individual knights. Often the Magyars appeared unexpectedly in the rear of the enemy to overwhelm him with arrows and cut off his retreat. Separate units showed enormous discipline in working together and were capable of great speed and mobility. These characteristics rendered the Magyar warriors vastly superior in combat to the often more numerous, but also more individualistic, knights of Western Europe. However, the Byzantine Emperor Leo the Wise (r. 886–912) in his standard work on military tactics pointed out that lightly armed mounted troops could be ridden down by heavy cavalry. He advised his horsemen to close with them at once rather than endure a hail of arrows discharged from a distance.

The Magyars were splendid riders who had developed the art of cavalry warfare to a high degree of perfection. Their equestrian expertise was the result of spending most of their time in the saddle: guarding their herds, hunting, sometimes even eating and sleeping. Wooden palisades, earthen walls, ditches, and even medium-size streams scarcely hindered their advance, since their horses could jump over ditches and walls, climb hills, and swim across rivers. The use of stirrups—an invention of unknown origin which reached Western Europe only in the 8th century—enabled their riders to stop, start, or turn very suddenly, either separately or in formation. The skilled Magyar horsemen, standing erect in their stirrups, could release arrows in all directions while their horses were in motion. Foot soldiers were at an enormous disadvantage against these mounted men shooting down at them. Magyar warriors were dangerous not for their numbers, which were often quite modest, but for the swift movements and surprise tactics which counteracted their numerical disadvantage. In order to maximize speed and avoid overloading their horses, they wore very light armor: just mail shirts, hard leather helmets, and hair braided so as to protect the sides of the neck. Each soldier was supplied with three or four horses, which he rode by turns in order not to tire any of them. His weapons were the bow and arrow, a slightly bent saber, short spear, and hatchet. Packhorses rather than baggage wagons carried supplies, enabling this cavalry to cover 25 to 30 miles in a day and follow narrow roads or mountain paths inaccessible to other armies. Using little-traveled routes, the Magyars were able to surprise their enemies with sudden attacks from unanticipated directions.

The Magyars were also masters of deception. After an unsuccessful attack they often withdrew suddenly, pretending defeat. Not infrequently the opposing heavily armed cavalry fell into this trap, pursued them, and got drawn into swamps or forests where they were devastated by arrows and stones from hidden Magyar detachments. By pretending to flee in the midst of battle the Magyars encouraged the enemy army to break ranks in pursuit. Then they turned swiftly, showered their disorganized opponents with arrows, and slaughtered them in hand-to-hand fighting. In defending their own territory the Magyars typically practiced a scorched-earth policy, systematically destroying all food supplies to prevent the enemy from living off the land. They removed the inhabitants of the threatened district, burned whatever foodstuffs could not be transported or hidden, and drove away all cattle in the path of the enemy. The object was to entice the invader into the interior, where he could gradually be exhausted through skirmishes and lack of supplies. Avoiding open battle whenever possible, Magyar archers harassed the enemy until he was forced to withdraw. For example, such tactics brought about the defeat of the German Emperor when he invaded Hungary in 1030 and 1050.

Western Europe was utterly unprepared, and at first paralyzed, by the Magyar onslaught. The chief recourse of its inhabitants was prayer, constantly reiterated in the Christian churches, begging God to save his people from this Asiatic scourge. However, initial helplessness gave way eventually to efforts by the victims to modify their own military style. The Germans observed that the Magyar attackers were incapable of besieging walled towns or standing firm in hand-to-hand combat, and could be overpowered most easily during a retreat, when they were tired and loaded down with booty. Emperor Henry I (r. 919–36) set his people to work building defensible enclosures where the population could take refuge. Many of these new fortifications consisted merely of a ditch and a bank of earth with a wooden palisade; but they reduced the yield from raids and forced the Magyars to commit larger forces to battle. Henry also spent years teaching the Germans to fight on horseback until he had created a force of well-disciplined heavy cavalry which fought as a unit. Eventually these measures proved their value. In 933, Henry overwhelmed a large force of Magyars in a decisive battle at Merseburg on the Saale River, where for the first time German cavalry could follow the enemy horsemen at equal speed.

As the first important victory over steppe cavalry in central Europe, Merseburg proved to be a turning point. Indeed, by this time the more heavily armed Germans had achieved military superiority over the Magyars, who wore only light defensive armor and rode horses relatively small in size. The number of destructive raids diminished. Then in 955 a large Magyar force returned to Germany to try its luck once more. Emperor Otto I (r. 936–73), leading a coalition of German princes, met it along the Lech River near Augsburg. In the ensuing battle the Magyars employed their usual tactics of feigned retreat, showering the enemy with arrows, but this time the German line held firm instead of breaking ranks as expected. Then Otto ordered a charge of his heavy cavalry which drove the enemy back against the river. Prevented by this obstacle from fleeing, the Magyar light cavalry was helpless against the more heavily armed

Germans. Many were killed, and even more drowned while trying to cross the stream. Emperor Otto's victory at Lechfeld largely ended the Magyar threat to Western Europe.

As the Magyars gradually gave up raiding for agriculture, they began to construct border defenses along their frontiers. First they erected barricades in the north and east, facing those same steppe lands from which they themselves had earlier descended upon Central Europe. After the defeat at Lechfeld in 955 they built similar barriers against the states of the West. This defensive system, known as the gyepü line, consisted of piles of stone and earth, rows of fallen trees, ditches, artificial hedges, and earthen entrenchments. It utilized any natural obstacles provided by the terrain, such as hills, rocks, and swamps. Beyond this line the Magyars maintained a border wasteland, an area of scorched earth which required two days' march to cross. Entrance into Hungary was permitted only at designated points. The Hungarian kings also erected fortified strongholds along the mountain passes leading across the frontier. In the 11th and 12th centuries these were invariably constructed of wood and earth rather than stone, sometimes as adaptations of Roman walls or Bronze Age mounds. However, such fortresses were much too few and far between to provide an adequate frontier defense. Turkic-speaking steppe peoples like the Pechenegs, Iazygs, and Cumans were frequently able to penetrate into Transylvania through the passes of the eastern Carpathian Mountains. Usually the Hungarian troops repulsed these invasions in open pitched battles without the aid of fortifications.

Successive monarchs strengthened the gyepü barrier by establishing new settlements near the frontier and granting the inhabitants various privileges in exchange for military service. For example, King Géza II (r. 1141–61) sent an embassy into the steppes to attract "suppressed and poor Muslims and Turks, who shoot well with arrows" to settle at strategic spots along the Carpathian Mountain passes into Transylvania. He offered them the status of freemen in exchange for military service, and invited land-hungry peasants from the Rhineland to immigrate on similar terms. Most of the Hungarian border settlements were located beside the great army roads, from which sentinels could watch for enemies and announce their approach. When King Andrew II permitted the Teutonic Knights to settle in the Braşov region of Transylvania in 1211, he thereby plugged the last gap in the gyepü line.

Other states of East Central Europe likewise constructed frontier defenses consisting of earth, fallen trees, or even more formidable barriers if the political situation seemed to require it. In the 12th century the Byzantines erected barricades along their border with Serbia for protection against the rising Serbian state. The Poles set up similar barriers against both Lithuania and the Tatars of the Golden Horde. Polish frontier fortresses were built of earth and wickerwork until at least the 14th century, when some were replaced by stone castles. Bohemia was geographically more fortunate—actually a natural fortress in itself. The mountains and thick forests which formed a complete semicircle along its northern, western, and southern border rendered penetration by an enemy extremely difficult. Bohemia's border·defenses, consisting of felled trees and brushwood, therefore were concentrated along the few roads leading through this frontier wilderness.

These obstacles were not always adequate to their purpose, however. The Magyars' gyepü line, which eventually surrounded the entire country, offered adequate protection against European invaders and sometimes even against steppe horsemen like the Pechenegs and Cumans. But it proved utterly ineffective against the Mongols, who simply tore the barriers down when they descended upon Europe in the 13th century. The only obstacles which proved capable of stopping the Mongols were castles surrounded by stone walls, plus the Danube River until it froze over. After the Mongol retreat, stone began increasingly to replace wood for castle-building in both Poland and Hungary. Nobles and prelates as well as monarchs erected enormous fortresses with crenelated stone walls, towers, bastions, and moats filled with water. Less affluent lords built smaller versions of the same. Thus the fortified castle came to dominate warfare, since a hundred good soldiers could hold a strong fortress against thousands of attackers.

As society became more settled in East Central Europe, armed forces usually became organized territorially rather than merely on the basis of loyalty to the ruler. In independent Croatia the military establishment was based upon the župans, or districts, each of which raised its own military contingent by a partial or general levy. In time of danger the troops from many župans joined together under the command of the king or (after the union with Hungary) the ban. In the 10th century the king of Croatia required his landed nobility to supply a certain number of cavalrymen, archers, and foot soldiers from their own resources. Since most of the cavalry wore armor, which only the wealthy could afford, poorer nobles served as infantry. Important nobles were also responsible for building frontier fortresses, taxing the peasants of the district for this purpose. However, the traditional župa military organization disappeared in the 12th century. Its replacement was a system in which each nobleman on his estate possessed a private army corresponding in size to his personal wealth and ambition.

In Hungary proper every free man in principle owed unconditional military service to the monarch, which meant that he had to serve at the king's command whenever summoned. This obligation was not derived from the contractual ties of vassal to lord, as in the developed feudalism of Western Europe. Originally it was part of the automatic loyalty which an armed retinue owed to its chief. However, by the 12th century the descendants of the original Magyar invaders had become landowners who were no longer eager for combat. Experience also showed that the king could not rely on them for campaigns outside the country. The nobility's unwillingness to fight abroad was legalized in the famous Hungarian Golden Bull, extracted by rebellious lords from King Andrew II in 1222. This document abolished any legal obligation to serve in foreign campaigns and limited a noble's required service within Hungary itself to a mere fifteen days. After that time had elapsed he was free to go home regardless of the military situation. Needless to say, these concessions drastically restricted the usefulness of the nobility to the king, who was left with little alternative but to take into his service many common freemen and foreign mercenaries.

In Poland likewise a gradual transition took place from the system based on the ruler's armed retinue to one based on landholding. In the first period of the Polish state the sovereign maintained a private retinue called a druzhina, part of which he kept near his person while the rest garrisoned his fortresses. This war band was the force which held the state together. The early Polish dukes conducted pillaging expeditions abroad which furnished these men with slaves, animals, and treasure. Combined with land grants from the ruler, the proceeds from successful raids enabled the warriors of the druzhina gradually to transform themselves into a powerful landed nobility. The call-up of this landholding class became the basis of Poland's armed strength. By the 13th century every man who held land according to what was called "knightly" or "military" law was required to serve in the army if physically able to do so. Unless excused, he was expected to arm himself at his own expense and report for each military call-up accompanied by a suite of armed warriors from his estate. The number of the latter depended on the extent of his lands and his rank. Landholders unable to fight in person, like clerics or knights' widows, had to send substitutes or buy exemption by paying a sum of money to the royal treasury.

Cavalrymen in heavy armor comprised the principal military forces in both Western and East Central Europe from the mid-11th to the mid-14th century. As the threat from the light cavalry of the steppe slowly receded, mobility became less crucial. Armor became heavier and more cumbersome, both in order to protect the wearers and to provide greater shock effect during a frontal assault. This also made it more expensive. Since Western Europe was on the whole richer than East Central Europe, the weight and extent of the knights' armor tended to decrease as one traveled eastward. However, even there the need to provide horses and armor for warfare contributed to a growing division of social classes. War became an activity necessarily restricted to noble landowners and their retainers, who evolved into a class of professional cavalry. They alone fought on horseback, since ordinary folk could not afford either war horses or armor. Peasants accompanied their social superiors on foot as servants or laborers to care for the spare horses, locate supplies, carry messages, build and repair fortresses, fell trees to block the enemy's road, or perform the hard work of laying siege to fortified places, which nobles scorned to do.

The Church accentuated this social division by prohibiting weapons which threatened to undermine the dominance of heavy cavalry. One such weapon was the crossbow, essentially a miniature ballista, which came into use in the

11th century. It consisted of a wooden handle with a groove along the top which held an iron bolt. The bow crossed it at right angles, and the bowstring was pulled back by a lever or winch attached to the handle and worked by hand or foot. The larger ones required several men to operate. Unlike the older bow, which fired only wooden shafts, the crossbow discharged metal bolts with sufficient force to penetrate chain mail. While the older bow required long practice to aim accurately and powerful muscles to pull it repeatedly, the crossbow demanded less skill and strength. Its range was greater also. It could more readily be used by men of the lower social class, who had neither the leisure to practice archery nor the opportunity to develop their skills in knightly tournaments. A series of papal anathemas in the 11th and 12th centuries forbade the use of the crossbow except against pagans and infidels. Predictably, these strictures were largely ineffective. More to the point was the fact that some of the knights themselves despised missile weapons as unchivalrous because they struck an enemy at random and reduced the importance of accurate aim. Moreover, missiles could be fired faster from the older bows than from crossbows.

Infantry was sometimes present on the battlefields of medieval Europe even during the years when cavalry was most dominant. However, it rarely contributed to the outcome; and the chroniclers usually ignore it. Indeed, foot soldiers were often the principal losers in a defeat, since the victors ruthlessly cut them to pieces while the knights either rode away in safety or, if captured, were held for ransom. Cavalry warfare alone carried military prestige. In Syria during the First Crusade (1096–99), when many horses died for lack of forage, the Crusaders won several important victories when some of them were forced to fight on foot. However, even this practical experience of the value of infantry failed to alter what had already become a fixed prejudice in favor of mounted warfare. Back home in Europe most battles continued to be fought with cavalry alone. By the 12th century even the Hungarians had adopted the heavy armor of the Western knighthood and abandoned the light-cavalry tactics which formerly had made them the scourge of Europe. Only in the borderlands facing the steppe did their close kinsmen and allies, the seminomadic Szeklers of Transylvania, continue to fight in the old way. Speed and mobility remained essential in encounters with steppe raiders. After the Mongol invasion in the 13th century the royal army of Hungary relied heavily on light-cavalry units of Cumans and Szeklers, which were effective in pursuing an enemy but virtually useless for siege operations. The Szeklers also served at times as light cavalry in the advance guards or rear guards of the main Hungarian forces. In the 13th and 14th centuries the Bulgar monarchs employed Cuman and Tatar steppe horsemen in the same fashion.

For several centuries after the Magyars' defeat at Lechfeld in 955, mounted steppe warriors ceased to plague Europe in any major way. This proved to be merely a reprieve. The Mongols who struck at Poland and Hungary in 1241 were the most dangerous light cavalry which had yet afflicted the European continent. Bred on the bleak treeless plains of Mongolia, they had learned the arts of horsemanship and archery, surprise, ambush, and missile attack as valuable survival skills. Hunting, herding, and theft were their chief occupations; and all their possessions could be carried on the backs of animals. Like other steppe dwellers, the Mongols were capable of complete self-sufficiency, living entirely from animal products. However, they often conducted a lively trade with neighboring sedentary peoples like the Chinese, selling their horses in exchange for linen, grain, arms, silk, and precious stones. Alternatively, they exploited their military superiority to impose tribute payments upon subject populations. The struggle for existence in the harsh climate of Inner Asia gave the people and animals of the steppe an extraordinary toughness and endurance. The horses could survive without fodder, just on twigs and tree bark, and knew how to dig out grass from under a covering of snow. The Mongols' most severe problem was finding sufficient grass and water for their numerous mounts, since the availability of pasture determined the size and range of their armies.

The Mongol armies which invaded Europe in the 13th century actually comprised men from many Inner Asian tribes, united for the first time in the late 12th century by the Mongol chieftain Jenghiz Khan ("Very Mighty King"). The Europeans knew these intruders as "Tatars" (actually the name of one of their component tribes)—a word which suggested appropriately that they had come from "Tartarus" (i.e., Hell). Jenghiz created the formidable military machine with which he and his descendants overran vast territories in Central Asia, China, and Persia. In 1221 the Mongol general Subutai led an exploratory campaign westward over hitherto unprecedented distances across Central Asia and into Georgia and the Crimea. Everywhere victorious, his army in 1223 smashed a disorganized coalition force of Rus and Cuman princes on the Kalka River north of the Sea of Azov. Having ridden over 5,500 miles in two years and won more than a dozen major battles against superior numbers, Subutai returned home loaded with plunder. Then for the next fourteen years the Mongols concentrated their attention upon subduing China.

The assault into Europe was resumed in 1237 under Jenghiz's grandson Batu, who had inherited the Mongols' westernmost territories bordering on Russia. Actual direction of the campaign lay with Subutai, his chief of staff. Unique among the Mongol war leaders, Subutai was not a member of Jenghiz's dynasty, but had reached this position of eminence through sheer military genius. For three years the Mongol armies ranged over Russia and Ukraine, capturing and destroying the principal towns and slaughtering the population. Then in the autumn of 1240, Batu sent an embassy to the Hungarian King Béla IV, demanding that he render homage to the Great Khan of the Mongols. To the proud Béla, Christian ruler of one of the major kingdoms of Europe, subjection to a pagan nomad chief was unthinkable. Nonetheless he could not persuade his nobles to take the Mongol threat seriously. Béla himself was so unpopular that many of the Hungarian lords were indifferent to his plight or even glad of it. Some actually laughed at him, refusing to believe that mere steppe warriors would dare to attack the powerful king of Hungary. While the Hungarians quarreled, the Mongols crossed the frozen Dnieper River in December 1240, capturing and burning the ancient Rus capital of Kiev. Thereafter they moved westward against only token resistance. A mere three weeks after taking Kiev they pitched their camp on the border of Poland, where Subutai outlined his strategy for the coming campaign.

The Mongol plan of invasion was totally unprecedented in its scope, calling for a coordinated advance along a 600-mile front between the Black and Baltic seas. At his disposal Subutai probably had no more than 100,000 men. His key objective was Hungary, which at that time was not only the richest and strongest state of East Central Europe but also a country of flat grasslands providing ample pasture for horses. Since Subutai was aware that once he crossed the Carpathian Mountains into Transylvania he would have a Polish army on his flank and rear, his strategy was to send three armed columns westward simultaneously. A northern contingent under the Mongol princes Baidar and Kadan would sweep through Poland—a land then in a state of anarchy with no central power capable of organizing serious resistance. This maneuver would crush all threats to the security of the main invasion. In the center the principal Mongol army under Batu would conduct a two-pronged attack into Hungary, remaining in close contact with the northern troops through signals and messengers. Once Batu had located the chief Hungarian force, his central and southern armies would unite. Their task was to lure the Hungarians into the field until the northern flank was secure and the force under Baidar and Kadan could join them.

In February 1241 a Mongol advance guard began the attack on Poland by burning and sacking the towns of Lublin and Sandomierz. The Poles were caught totally by surprise. However, since the object of the invasion was to draw off the northern European armies from Hungary, Baidar and Kadan had to wait for them to be mobilized. The Mongol troops in Poland probably numbered no more than 20,000 men, but the two princes nonetheless divided them in order to spread alarm as widely as possible. They knew that the Mongol light cavalry could always outrun any European force seeking to oppose them. Kadan led one detachment northward into Lithuania, went on to invade East Prussia, and then hastened to rejoin the rest of the northern army in Silesia. Meanwhile Baidar advanced on Cracow. When Polish troops emerged from behind the town walls, the Mongols staged a feigned retreat. The Poles pursued them, only to be annihilated in an ambush eleven miles from the city. Early in April, Baidar moved into Silesia and began to besiege Wrocław. Meanwhile, near the town of Legnica (Liegnitz) Duke Henry of Silesia was hastily assembling a motley array of Polish light cavalry, supplemented by some Moravian and German infantry. When Baidar learned that King Wenceslas I of Bohemia was marching to join the Poles, he raised the siege of Wrocław and hurried northward to forestall him.

On April 9, 1241, the Silesian duke led his forces out to meet the Mongol army. Less well informed than his opponents, he was unaware that Wenceslas was only a day's march away. Even without Bohemian aid, the Poles and their allies possessed superiority in numbers. Nevertheless, the Mongols prevailed by their usual stratagem of pretending to give way in the center, then falling upon the flanks of their opponents from ambush. Hearing of the Poles' defeat, the Bohemian king fell back to collect reinforcements from Thuringia and Saxony. It hardly mattered that Baidar and Kadan had too few men to face him in the field, since their real assignment was to keep the Bohemian army away from Hungary. Accordingly they drew Wenceslas after them into Moravia, where they spent fourteen days devastating much of the province. Meanwhile Wenceslas stood with his army in Bohemia, apparently feeling too weak to attempt an attack. The cherished belief of some Czech patriots that their king saved Western Europe from the Asiatic scourge thus lacks historical foundation, since Wenceslas neither met the Mongols in battle nor impeded their grand strategy.

While Baidar and Kadan were laying Poland waste, the central Mongol army under Batu advanced through Moldavia into northern Transylvania, capturing the chief towns in its path. The southern wing under Kuyuk and Subutai ravaged Moldavia and Walachia prior to entering Transylvania from the south. By mid-March of 1241 all of Hungary east of the Danube was in the grip of the Mongol pincer. In response to this advance, King Béla IV summoned all the Hungarian lords and their retainers to gather at Buda in mid-February. They assembled on schedule, joined by a cavalry force of Cuman refugees whom Béla had allowed to settle in Hungary several years earlier. However, the Hungarian lords minimized the Mongol danger. With extraordinary short-sightedness they agreed to fight only if the king first granted them new legal privileges, which he refused. They also demanded the expulsion from Hungary of the Cumans, whom many Hungarians suspected of being a Mongol fifth column. However, Béla refused to dismiss a valuable ally experienced in the art of steppe warfare. The stalemate between the king and his army continued into the middle of March, even as messengers arrived with news that the Mongols were attacking the Carpathian passes on Hungary's eastern border. The situation deteriorated still further when disgruntled Hungarian nobles assaulted the Cuman chief Kötöny, who commited suicide rather than letting himself be slaughtered. Furious at this act of treachery, the Cuman army immediately broke camp and rode away toward the Balkans, devastating the countryside and sacking several towns as they went. Thus on the eve of their decisive encounter with the Mongols the Hungarians had lost their most capable military allies.

At the end of March 1241 the Mongol army reached the left bank of the Danube just outside of Pest. Then suddenly it turned and rode away toward the east. The Hungarian lords interpreted this withdrawal as due to fear at the sight of their own superior forces. On the verge of abandoning the field and returning home, they now scented victory and did not wish to be left out. In actuality the Mongols were now poised for a decisive battle. On April 7, King Béla ordered his army to pursue them. Three days later the Mongols crossed the single stone bridge over the Sajó River near the place where it joins the Tisza and proceeded some distance beyond. Arriving at the Sajó that same evening but finding no trace of the enemy, the Hungarians pitched camp on the western side of the river. Secretly that same night the Mongols threw a wooden bridge across the Sajó farther north, enabling their forces to recross the river upstream and place themselves on the flanks of the sleeping opponent. Caught unawares, the Hungarians were surrounded early the next morning and trapped between the Mongols and the river. Resistance collapsed entirely as the encircled army dissolved in chaos. King Béla and a few of his knights succeeded in breaking out of the enemy ring, but the main Hungarian force never managed to assemble in battle order. Many of the knights attempted to flee through a gap in the encirclement, where the waiting Mongol light cavalry cut them down.

Following their victory on the Sajó the Mongols fanned out across eastern Hungary, terrorizing the inhabitants. With the onset of winter they resumed their westward advance. Crossing the frozen Danube on Christmas day of 1241, they attacked various towns west of the river and advanced toward Austria. Meanwhile Kadan led a Mongol detachment into Croatia in pursuit of King Béla. The defeated Hungarian monarch managed to elude them, although he was treacherously imprisoned en route by Duke Frederick of Austria, who forced him to purchase his freedom with the crown jewels and three counties in western Hungary. In February 1242, Béla reached the Adriatic, taking refuge first on the unprotected island of Rab, then farther south in the island fortress of Trogir near Split, from which a ship could take him to Italy if necessary. Continuing in pursuit of the fugitive king, Kadan's forces did not fare well in Dalmatia. An army of Croats drove them off a battlefield near Rijeka, inflicting severe casualties. As the Mongols moved down the coast, supplies ran short; and the mountainous terrain provided no grass for the horses. Bypassing Split, which was too well fortified to be taken by storm, Kadan and his army rode into northern Albania.

Then suddenly and without warning—inexplicably to the Europeans—the invaders retreated. In March 1242, while the Mongols were plundering south-western Hungary, messengers arrived from the Mongol capital of Karakorum to report that Great Khan Ogadei had died. The princes of the dynasty would have to elect a new khan, who might subsequently wish to reallocate the lands and armies of the empire. While the situation was thus in flux, Batu could not afford to be far away in Europe. He may even have welcomed the excuse to establish himself in an independent position in Russia and Ukraine. In any event, the Mongol forces now recrossed the Danube and abandoned Hungary, while Batu's army withdrew through Transylvania and Moldavia. Kadan returned via Bulgaria, receiving the submission of the new king of that country prior to joining Batu near the Danube mouths. While the rest of the leadership continued onward to Mongolia, Batu halted at Sarai, his base camp on the Volga some 60 miles north of the Caspian Sea. Here he established a capital of his own and began to organize a government. The conquered Rus princes pledged allegiance to him and his successors, henceforth sending their tribute to Sarai, not Karakorum. The wealth of Sarai quickly became legendary, causing the Mongols of the Volga to be known henceforth as the Golden Horde.

Unquestionably the Mongols were far more effective militarily than any of the steppe horsemen who had previously plagued Europe. This was a consequence of their occupation of north China, the home of an ancient and refined civilization whose people had studied war as a science for many centuries. The result was "the grafting of a wise and subtle Chinese head onto a Mongol body." Always brave and hardy warriors, the Mongols enhanced their military effectiveness through the strategy and techniques learned from this conquered people. Applying intelligence to the art of war, they prepared their campaigns with great care. Their spies and secret agents brought back detailed information about the territories they proposed to invade. Mongol generals received reports on the political situation in the target countries as well as the terrain and the strength of opposing armies. Prior to conquering China, the Mongols had known nothing of artillery or siegecraft, but they learned quickly. They adopted various Chinese noisemaking and flame-throwing devices as well as the Chinese light and heavy catapult, which they used either for hurling rocks at enemy fortifications or for throwing incendiary devices.

The Mongols owed their military superiority to a combination of skill and discipline, superior generalship, utilization of all possible manpower, and the ability to take advantage of an opponent's weaknesses. They specialized in sudden attacks, encirclements, and isolation of the enemy army. Above all they favored ambushes and feigned retreats. Although the rank and file of their army included conscripts of many nationalities speaking a variety of tongues, Mongol leaders maintained excellent communication on the battlefield by using multicolored signaling flags, or at night flaming torches. Swift couriers enabled them to coordinate the movements of armies hundreds of miles apart. The effectiveness of these methods was evident in their invasion of Europe, for which the coordination was flawless. Comparison of the key dates speaks for itself. On April 9, 1241, Baidar and Kadan smashed the Polish and Silesian armies at Legnica. On April 10, Kuyuk destroyed the army of Transylvania at Sibiu, 500 miles away. On April 11, Batu and Subutai annihilated the main Hungarian army on the Sajó River.

Mongol warfare was essentially a more sophisticated version of the military style long prevalent on the Eurasian steppes. Indeed, the Mongols fought very much as the Hungarians themselves had done in the 9th and 10th centuries, but which their Europeanized descendants had since forgotten. Wholly at home in the saddle, where they spent most of their waking hours, the Mongols rode horseback with consummate skill. All able-bodied adult males below the age of sixty fought in the army. By means of long practice and drill they learned to execute well-planned, quick, and precise movements calculated to confuse their opponents and excite panic. Their flying invasion columns could cover fifty miles in a day. Riding in close formation, they often overpowered their enemies by shock tactics. However, the bow and arrow were the weapons that ordinarily brought them victory. The Mongols disliked a melée at close quarters, preferring to aim from a distance. Their archers could shoot accurately in every direction, even backwards in retreat, although they often preferred to release a volley of arrows, each half a yard long. The peoples they defeated usually had the impression of being overwhelmed by enormous hordes. In fact this was an illusion created by speed and mobility, since the Mongols were usually inferior in numbers to their enemies. To compensate for this disadvantage, discipline was fierce. In each unit of ten men, if even one fled the scene of battle, all the others were executed. A unique feature of Mongol practice was the habit of beginning hostilities early in winter, when other armies typically rested and could be caught unprepared. The horses at that season were strong from a summer out to pasture; foliage no longer concealed the presence of enemies; and deep rivers could be crossed on ice.

The equipment the Mongols carried with them was adapted to their style of rapid movement and the need to transport all supplies on horseback. Unlike armies operating in agricultural regions, they could not expect to live off the land, although their horses could pasture on the grasslands. To keep the horses from tiring, each warrior possessed several mounts and rode each one in turn. On campaign the Mongols carried their supplies in airtight inflatable bags made of skins, which could be used as life jackets for crossing rivers. Food consisted of yogurt, millet, horse meat, horses' blood, fermented mare's milk, and occasional game. The cavalry carried light bows made of horn for rapid fire on horseback and heavy bows for sieges, while frontline troops were equipped also with hooked lances for dragging an enemy out of the saddle. In addition, each man had a wicker shield covered with heavy leather. Men in the front ranks wore iron helmets and leather armor sewn with overlapping metal plates, while those in the rear were more lightly equipped. To reduce the toll from wounds, each warrior wore next to his skin a long, loose undershirt made of raw silk. An arrow which pierced armor usually failed to cut the silk, but instead carried the cloth with it into the wound. Then the silk could be twisted around the arrow and gently withdrawn from the body, doing minimal damage to the surrounding tissues.

An inseparable part of Mongol military practice was the commission of atrocities, to an extent rarely equaled before or since. Not for nothing did Europeans consider these Asiatics as the scourge of humanity. The Mongols used terror as a political weapon and committed frightful massacres in a thoroughly methodical and cold-blooded fashion. The hard life on the steppe had made them sullen and callous, capable both of suffering without complaint and killing without mercy. They observed the rule laid down by Jenghiz Khan that any resistance to their armies meant death. The populations of villages harboring troops, or of castles or towns which surrendered after a siege, were butchered without mercy. Neither men, women, nor children were spared. At best a few of the younger captives might avoid death by being sold into slavery. Sometimes an opposing unit which laid down its weapons and surrendered was incorporated into the Mongol army, where it was placed in the vanguard to absorb the brunt of the next assault. Some of the Mongols' conquests were achieved through treachery. Their agents rode ahead of the main forces, promising mercy to those who submitted peacefully. This enabled them to occupy many fortresses or towns without a battle, although the helpless people who surrendered were often slaughtered anyway. In other cases the Mongols apparently kept their word. Certainly some regions of Central Asia prospered under Mongol rule, while others were permanently transformed into wastelands.

In Hungary the Mongols employed treachery. After the victories of 1241 they announced that anyone willing to submit to their rule could safely return home. Many villagers now emerged from hiding to undertake the year's planting and provide food for the invaders. Then after the harvest was completed the Mongols massacred or enslaved these same peasants in order not to leave potential enemies in the rear during further campaigns into Western Europe. Such trickery they regarded as a legitimate military tactic. Unquestionably the Mongols were callous victors who seem to have taken pleasure in the sheer misery of the vanquished. Nonetheless, their famed cruelty was cool and systematic, not a wild and uncontrolled barbarism. In order to control immense territories with limited forces, they thought it necessary either to frighten the conquered populations into submission or to kill them. They regarded terror and deception as no different in principle from any other weapon of war, effective in striking fear into enemy hearts and inducing surrender. At times their savagery appeared purely gratuitous, serving no conceivable military purpose—perhaps because it was so habitual. For example, on the retreat from Europe, Batu released all his prisoners and announced that they were free to return home. The captives had scarcely set out when his troops overtook and massacred them.

Some of the Mongols' success in Europe is attributable to the weakness and division of their opponents. The quarreling princes of Rus were unable to form a united front, while Poland in the 13th century had dissolved into anarchy. Neither country possessed a central government capable of organizing an effective defense. Conceivably a European army under competent leadership might have defeated the Mongols or at least caused them serious losses; but they never encountered any such force. King Wenceslas I of Bohemia (r. 1230–53) was a strong monarch who by early 1242 had collected a massive army; but the Mongols retreated without attacking him. The Polish light cavalry was not equipped to meet the Mongols on anything like equal terms. Clad merely in leather jerkins, armed with lances, but lacking missile weapons of any kind, it could not respond to the Mongols' hail of arrows. A Polish infantry was nonexistent. The Hungarian resistance was undermined by the nobility's dislike of proud King Béla IV, and by Béla's own inadequate generalship. Neighboring Christian states provided no assistance. The German Emperor Frederick II and Pope Gregory IX were actively hostile to one another. Early in 1241 while the king of Hungary was pleading for help to meet the Mongol threat, the pope was preparing a crusade against the emperor, whom he had excommunicated for alleged heresy. Emperor Frederick in turn considered it more important to fight the pope's Lombard allies in Italy than to resist the Mongols. Another Frederick, the duke of Austria, not only failed to aid the Hungarians but even sought to profit from their debacle. With such mutual antagonism at work, no united front against the invader was possible.

On the other hand, the Mongols themselves were not immune from internal discord. The timing of the great khan's death was fortuitous; but dissensions among the Mongol princes undoubtedly hastened their retreat from Europe. The likely successor to Ogadei as great khan was Kuyuk, who was Batu's enemy. Ogadei had permitted Batu to command armies drawn from the entire Mongol Empire; but if Kuyuk became great khan, this indulgence certainly would cease. Thus it made sense for Batu to consolidate his hold on the north Caspian steppe. Moreover, his spies by this time had doubtless conveyed the intelligence that Western Europe was unsuitable terrain for a pastoral way of life. When the Mongols first occupied Hungary, they behaved in a manner suggesting that they meant to occupy it permanently. They even went to the extent of minting their own coins. However, the fact was inescapable that Mongol military power demanded vast numbers of horses: three or four for each mounted warrior. This in turn required access to extensive grazing lands, since a pastoral, subsistence economy did not produce crops for fodder. Even the grasslands of Hungary, the European country most suited to their life-style, were insufficient to support Mongol military dominance for any length of time. A much larger area was needed for that purpose, like Ukraine or Mongolia.

Quite aside from this logistical problem, the topography of Western Europe did not permit the advantageous use of Mongol military power. The landscape was marked by mountains, swamps, thick forests, and miserable roads. In contrast to Poland or Hungary, stone castles were already common in Western Europe by the 13th century; and the quantities of grass needed to feed large numbers of horses were lacking. Under such conditions the Mongol cavalry could not have functioned effectively. In dense woodlands, horsemen must keep to narrow trails that provide easy targets for concealed sharpshooters. In marshlands, the horses' feet sink into the soggy ground. In the mountains, small local forces can easily block an army's path. Speed and rapid turning movements—the advantage possessed by light cavalry—are impossible in such country. In Western Europe the Mongols would have been out of their element, and undoubtedly they knew it. Certainly it was not fear of their opponents' military power which prevented them from returning to Europe after the retreat of 1242. Their next major westward expedition, in 1256, was directed toward Persia and Syria, not Europe.

With fear and trepidation the Europeans for decades awaited a new Mongol onslaught. The danger was self-evident, inasmuch as the Golden Horde on the Volga continued to threaten Europe's eastern borderlands, but no large-scale attack upon Central Europe ever recurred. In 1259 a detachment of Mongols (now usually known as Tatars) crossed into Poland, sacked the towns of Sandomierz and Lublin, burned Cracow, and perpetrated widespread massacres. For the Poles this incursion proved vastly more destructive than its predecessor in 1241, which had been essentially a flanking operation to protect the invasion of Hungary. However, after three months the Mongols returned unopposed to Russia, while the territories west of Poland remained unaffected. The last Tatar invasion of East Central Europe occurred in 1285, led by Nogai, the khan of a breakaway faction of the Golden Horde. Nogai's armies entered Transylvania to aid the ill-starred Hungarian king, Ladislas "the Cuman," against his own nobility. The next year they again attacked Sandomierz and Cracow in Poland but on this occasion the Poles were not tempted to engage them in the field. The garrisons of the two towns successfully defended their walls and did not venture outside. The Tatars captured and sacked some smaller places and proceeded to devastate the Polish countryside. However, by this time their soldiers were no longer the fierce steppe warriors of former days. Failing to find easy plunder in Poland, they retreated in 1287 to Volhynia. Bulgaria suffered from their raids for several decades more; but the Tatars never returned in force to East Central Europe.

The Mongol interlude throws considerable light on the nature of warfare in 13th-century Europe. Because no major threats from the steppe had arisen since the 10th-century Magyar incursions, European knights were totally unprepared for an attack of the Mongol type. Europe's military class had chosen to sacrifice mobility on horseback in favor of better armored protection. The mail shirts of the early medieval period, consisting of thick cloth tunics covered with little metal scales, strips, or iron rings, had given way in the 13th century to chain mail and plate armor. Arrows fired from a crossbow, the typical knightly weapon of the 11th-14th centuries, could not pierce heavy steel plate. A knight outfitted in full armor was virtually immune to serious injury unless he was knocked off his horse. However, this armor obliged the horse to carry a weight of between 300 and 400 pounds and drastically reduced the rider's mobility. A man thrown from his mount was unable to get up without assistance. Heavy armor also caused the European knights to prefer huge chargers, which moved more slowly than the smaller and quicker horses of the steppe. Finally, armor dictated the limits of tactics. Heavy cavalry could not move swiftly, since both men and horses were too quickly exhausted. Surprise, stealth, and ambush became nearly impossible. Indeed, Western knights came to consider such expedients unfair and unchivalrous. Not surprisingly, they easily fell victim to the Mongols' superior speed, mobility, and tactics.

In military intelligence and the execution of maneuvers the Mongols were vastly superior to their European opponents. Mongol armies were highly trained to carry out complicated movements on command. Their leaders did not fight in person, but stayed in the rear to control the course of the battle. By contrast, medieval European generals usually fought in the ranks, which demonstrated their courage but gave them little control over events once an encounter had begun. Battle tended to be a melée of simultaneous individual combats in which personal bravery and daring were the most valued qualities. European warfare at the time of the Mongol invasion was essentially a clash of heavily armored warriors meeting head-on. The skills which the knights had acquired through long practice in tournaments, jousts, and hunting were purely individual. Moreover, medieval European armies were unaccustomed to fighting together. Often they assembled just for a single campaign. No time was available for training as a unit, owing to the limited period during which the nobles were required to serve and a lack of sufficient funds to pay mercenaries. In any event, medieval knights were unwilling to submit to discipline. An inadequate command structure complicated this situation. European armies were usually composed of separate contingents whose chiefs acknowledged no overall authority. Leadership was determined by social rank, not by military expertise. A monarch might be in nominal command of an army, but he could not dictate strategy to the great lords of his kingdom. Any magnate at the head of a personal military retinue felt perfectly free to act as he pleased. At most he might accept orders from his immediate overlord, the king, but certainly not from another lord of social status comparable to his own. Many a battle was lost when one or more of the independent lords decided to abandon the field.

Furthermore, medieval European commanders possessed only minimal geographical knowledge. Scouting was virtually unknown and surprises were rare. Battles often took place by prior arrangement between the contending parties. Officers had no maps, so that even opposing forces spoiling for a fight might have difficulty in finding one another. An example of this occurred in 1260, when the respective armies of Bohemia and Hungary stood poised for battle, only to discover that the river Morava lay between them. The Bohemian king politely offered to let his opponents cross the river unhindered, or failing this, proposed that the Hungarians grant him the same courtesy. Such procedure conformed perfectly to the code of chivalry, whatever its defects from a military standpoint. The Hungarian king—the same Béla IV who had earlier escaped the Mongols by a hairbreadth—selected the first option and the clash took place. An ineffective commander, Béla lost the battle despite having his choice of terrain. Another example of inadequate prior scouting occurred in 1422, when the Poles invaded the territory of the Teutonic Knights but failed to find the Knights' army. In this instance no battle occurred at all. The Mongols did not permit such fiascos. They attached great importance to intelligence operations, and their leaders demonstrated thorough knowledge of the territory on which they fought. In their European campaign of 1241, with no better means of communication than messengers on horseback, they successfully coordinated the operations of three armies along a 600-mile front.

Amid the Mongols' long string of victories, it is noteworthy that they usually could not capture fortresses or walled towns except by treachery. This was not due to any lack of siege equipment or ability in siegecraft. Unlike most steppe warriors on campaign, they brought along engineers to operate battering rams and catapults. Their packhorses even carried dismantled siege engines capable of hurling huge stones for distances of more than 400 yards. In Hungary the Mongols captured the fortified town of Esztergom after bombarding it with heavy missiles, filling up its moat unhindered, and overwhelming the garrison with their superior numbers. The town lay in a flat plain where this method could be effective; but they still failed to take Esztergom's royal citadel, which stood on a hill. On the whole they preferred to avoid sieges, which slowed up their advance and deprived them of the mobility which was one of their chief advantages. Often they chose simply to avoid fortified places; and the sieges they did attempt usually failed. Certainly in the invasion of 1241 the Mongols showed themselves more interested in plunder than in territory. Fortified settlements were hardly worth the effort required to capture them. Swift cavalry raids provided a richer harvest of loot than long and expensive stationary warfare, which immobilized and demoralized the army and carried no guarantee of victory. The speed and fighting skill of the Mongol horse archers would largely have been wasted on sieges.

Moreover, siege operations were largely unnecessary in Poland and Hungary. Both countries were nearly devoid of stone fortifications, and their flat terrain provided few natural obstacles. Polish nobles in the 13th century did not live in stone castles capable of being defended, but in wooden manor houses. Where town fortifications existed at all, they usually consisted merely of a ditch, a mound, and a wooden stockade which could easily succumb to fire. The situation in Hungary was only slightly better. The country had not experienced a serious invasion for centuries, and in 1241 it possessed very few stone fortresses. The old county strongholds were built of either earth or a combination of stone and earth protected by wooden stockades. Stone-and-mortar construction was rare except for royal residences like the citadels at Esztergom, the capital, or Székesfehérvár, the coronation city. These two, plus the fortified abbey of Pannonhalma, successfully resisted the Mongol onslaught of 1241. In Moravia the Mongols failed to capture the fortified towns of Olomouc and Brno. They could not break the defenses of the Kalnik fortress in northern Croatia, where King Béla IV of Hungary took temporary refuge; and they failed to capture a single fortified town in Dalmatia.

All this was noted at the time, impelling the Bohemians and Hungarians to revamp their defense systems after the Mongols retreated. In Bohemia the king and the nobles built many new stone castles even after the fear of the Tatars had subsided. In Hungary twice as many such strongholds went up between 1242 and 1270 as in the country's entire previous history. King Béla IV personally was responsible for more than half of this new construction, while great nobles and high officers of the crown undertook most of the remainder. Whereas previously Béla had tried to strengthen royal authority against both lay and clerical landholders, now he positively encouraged his great nobles to build stone castles, despite the fact that these fortified structures increased their ability to resist royal control. He even handed over suitable sites to men having the means to fortify them. Earthworks were no longer considered adequate for defense purposes. All the new castles were built of stone linked by mortar. Most were located on steep hills or rocky crags accessible only from one narrow side, whereas the older edifices had generally been set just on small hills. Sites that were protected by a river or marshes were favored as well, although water was not a major obstacle to an attacker because it could freeze in winter or be drained off by a ditch.

Most of the new castles built in 13th-century Hungary consisted of a circular wall or ramparts enclosing an open space, with a tower in the middle as the second line of defense. The majority were quite small, with an enclosed area of perhaps 30 by 50 yards, so that relatively few men were needed to prevent capture. Some castles were placed at strategically important locations which controlled major trade routes, while others were designed primarily as places of refuge and situated far off the beaten track. However, these castles did not form part of a consolidated defense system. Nobles built them wherever they chose on their own estates. The new structures were not intended to shelter the population at large but rather to protect the landholders, their families, their military retainers, their gold and silver treasures, and the very crucial title deeds to their properties. The space was much too limited to receive the people of the surrounding villages. A castle on a steep rock might send out smoke signals to warn the neighborhood of an enemy's approach; but peasants were expected to fend for themselves.

Town governments also constructed many new fortifications in the 13th and 14th centuries. Since an invader could rarely afford to bypass a major center of trade and communications, these defenses contributed to the security of an entire district. Urban fortifications at first consisted merely of wooden palisades surrounded by trenches, although stone walls with towers and gates were sometimes added later. To enter the town through a gate might require crossing a ditch via a bridge which could be lifted up only by special machinery. The bridge when raised transformed itself into a barricade with sharp iron pegs on the outside. In some cases the more important town gates were defended by a second gate called a barbican, which was a bastion extending beyond the wall. Gates were closed at night and opened only by special permission. However, medieval urban fortifications were always expensive, usually rudimentary, and often inadequate. Too few soldiers and weapons might be available to repel an attack, or too few provisions stored up to withstand a siege. The walls might begin to crumble if no funds were available for repairs. Certain towns which were badly in need of protection were never fortified at all, no doubt because of the cost.

By the 14th century many towns of East Central Europe possessed fortifications of some kind. Larger places usually exhibited the most impressive defenses. If the location of an old settlement made adequate fortification impractical, a new one might be founded close by at a more favorable spot. The later Croatian capital of Zagreb originated in this way. Border towns near the steppe in Poland and Transylvania were more likely to be fortified than settlements in the interior. Churches were often surrounded by strong walls which allowed them to serve as refuges for the population in time of danger. Such fortress churches were particularly common in the Saxon districts of Transylvania as protection against roving bands of steppe marauders or Turkish irregulars. The Saxons developed a distinct style of church architecture in which the church walls formed part of a defensive barrier, complete with peepholes and firing slits. Even some peasant villages in Transylvania provided themselves with fortifications built out of massive stone blocks. These were usually situated on cliffs, particularly in the exposed southern borderlands. Strongholds of this type were common also in Walachia and Moldavia in the 14th and 15th centuries.

The capture of well-built castles was a difficult proposition, and until the age of gunpowder the advantage lay clearly with the defense. Since the weaker party usually preferred to retreat behind fortifications rather than fight, medieval campaigns involved few actual battles. Siege machines like bores or battering rams were incapable of beating down stone walls 15 to 20 feet thick. Escalades were virtually impossible unless the defense was extremely lax. Mining was out of the question if the fortress was built on solid rock or surrounded by a lake, a marsh, or a moat. Therefore the defense of a castle or fortified town was generally a static affair. The defenders attempted to hold the outer walls or, failing that, the tower within. If the garrison was large enough, it might attempt to break out and provoke a pitched battle in front of the walls in order to prevent a blockade. However, this procedure was risky and would not be attempted if a relief force was expected. The only certain method for taking a fortress was by starving it out; but here the contest lay between the patience of the besieging army and the provisions available within the walls. Medieval armies were unwilling to remain in service for a long campaign, while the exhaustion of locally available food and fodder restricted the length of stay in any one place. On the other hand, a castle with ample supplies might hold out for months if its defenders could avoid becoming demoralized. In a region rich in castles and walled towns, military expeditions often proved utterly futile. Campaigns tended to become plundering raids which robbed the peasants but avoided the strongholds. Alternatively, an invader might concentrate on reducing a single fortified place in hopes of gaining the plunder within.

The warrior elites of Bohemia, Poland, and Hungary all tended to imitate West European styles of warfare, but with a time lag. The Magyars, who had fought as light cavalry in the 9th and 10th centuries, changed to the Western style of heavy armor within a century or so. Obliged to fight the Germans on occasion, they had little choice but to meet them on terms as equal as possible. Light cavalry was entirely at the mercy of heavy cavalry when confined within a narrow space or forced up against a natural obstacle like a river, unless it was equipped with bows and arrows, which horsemen weighed down with metal armor were incapable of wielding. While light cavalry was well suited for hit-and-run warfare and could easily outrun heavy cavalry on the wide open spaces of the steppes, it was useless for frontal assaults or shock tactics. Thus if they could afford it, the knights of East Central Europe generally adopted the Western preference for heavy armor. Their military equipment became quite similar to the Western type, merely more rudimentary and lower in quality. If as a rule they were less heavily armored than their Western counterparts, this was rather the consequence of poverty than of choice.

Light cavalry adapted to local conditions remained the standard for warfare on the eastern borderlands of Poland and Hungary down to the end of the Middle Ages. Here the usual opponents were lightly armed steppe raiders or Turkish irregulars. In Poland even as late as the 14th century, poor nobles still fought as lightly armed cavalry or even as foot soldiers. However, a mobile light cavalry force wielding bows and arrows could sometimes overcome the relatively inflexible heavy cavalry of the West. For example, at the key battle of Marchfeld in 1278, the Hungarian light cavalry contributed significantly to the victory of its ally, the German Emperor Rudolf I. At issue was the claim of the Bohemian King Ottokar II to various fiefs in Austria. Both sides used cavalry only; and the number of combatants was unusually large. The Hungarians employed a mixed force of horse archers from the borderlands in conjunction with heavily armored knights of the Western type. This was a combination long favored by the Byzantines; and Marchfeld again demonstrated its effectiveness. The Hungarian light cavalry outflanked and largely surrounded the heavily armed Bohemian horsemen, while King Ottokar was killed.

During the 14th century the armies of Western Europe increasingly began to adopt infantry tactics. Swiss pikemen in dense columns and well-organized English longbowmen demonstrated that highly disciplined foot soldiers, trained not to break ranks, could prevail over the individualistic heavy feudal cavalry. The increasing use of firearms in warfare aided in this development. Firearms began to be employed in Western Europe in the second quarter of the 14th century, and by the end of the century could be found in most of the towns of the Adriatic coast and in Hungary. By 1378 cannon were being manufactured in Dubrovnik; the first recorded use of this weapon in Dalmatia occurred that year in the defense of Kotor against a Venetian attack. Early in the 15th century the Serbian despot Stephen Lazarević possessed cannon similar to those employed in Western Europe. By the late 15th and early 16th century, infantry equipped partly with firearms and partly with pikes had become the decisive military arm in the West. However, the military class of East Central Europe was slow to follow suit.

When the Poles fought the Teutonic Knights in the battle of Tannenberg in 1410, both sides used cavalry in a manner hardly different from that of two centuries before. The Poles won by hard fighting, not by superior tactics or armament. The best army of 15th-century Hungary—the mercenary force of King Matthias which was known as the Black Army—still depended chiefly on light cavalry. Matthias's infantry was superior to the Hungarian foot soldiers of former times, but certainly less effective than the contemporary Swiss pikemen. The dissolution of this force after the king's death in 1490 left Hungary with an infantry of very poor quality, armed for the most part just with bows and arrows at a time when this weapon had largely become obsolete elsewhere in Europe. Only some of the militia from the northern provinces and the soldiers supplied by the towns carried firearms. The expense of heavy armor still dictated that the bulk of the Hungarian army would consist of light cavalry. However, more than half of the troops supplied by the great magnates were supposed to consist of heavy cavalry, except in the southern borderlands. There the light cavalry was still crucial to defense against Turkish marauders. In the late 15th century many of these Hungarian border fighters were Serbian refugees from the Turks who had overrun their homeland.

The series of Crusades to the Holy Land which began in 1096 included relatively few participants from East Central Europe, except from Bohemia, which was part of the German Empire. Hungary and the Balkan lands were peripherally involved, however, because Crusaders who took the land route to Asia necessarily passed through these regions. Some Crusaders favored the old Roman road known as the "Diagonal" across Hungary via Belgrade, Sofia, Plovdiv, and Edirne to Constantinople. Others followed the Dalmatian coast to Durrës in Albania and from there took the Via Egnatia across Macedonia to Salonika and the Straits. Like all medieval armies, the Crusaders lived off the land, frequently plundering without paying for what they took. Many behaved like the proverbial plague of locusts—looting, destroying, and raping as they went. Disorderly and undisciplined, they often became embroiled in bloody conflicts with the local inhabitants. Christian monarchs along their route could not easily refuse cooperation with an enterprise blessed by the pope and infused with great religious significance. However, as news of the Crusaders' depredations spread, even pious rulers turned against them.

The first armies of Crusaders which set out for Palestine were not the ones assembled under papal sponsorship and led by great nobles. Rather they formed a People's Crusade, independent bands of mostly poor folk roused to enthusiasm by popular preachers. Many believed that Jerusalem must be recovered for the faith prior to Christ's second coming. Several such groups were inspired by the preaching of a barefoot itinerant French monk known to history only as Peter the Hermit. An advance detachment of Peter's followers led by the French knight Walter the Penniless reached Hungary's western frontier in May 1096 and received permission to cross the kingdom. King Koloman was watchful but not initially hostile. He supplied the Crusaders with provisions, enabling them to travel without incident as far as his southern border on the Sava River opposite Belgrade. There when some of the men tried to rob a bazaar they were captured, stripped naked, and sent across the river into Byzantine territory. The Greek commander at Belgrade was unprepared for the Crusaders' arrival. Since he had no surplus food for them, they began to pillage. Eventually they reached Niš, the military headquarters of that Byzantine province, where the governor supplied them with provisions and an escort to Constantinople.

Meanwhile another body of poor Crusaders, led this time by Peter the Hermit in person, arrived on Hungary's western border. King Koloman again was friendly, but warned that pillaging would be punished. He permitted the crusading army to cross his territory only on condition that it pay for what it needed and take nothing by force. Serious conflict was avoided until the Crusaders approached the Danube frontier, where they heard rumors of their predecessors' troubles. A dispute over a pair of shoes led to a riot in which allegedly four thousand local people were killed. Next the army forced its way across the river, captured and pillaged Belgrade, and set the town on fire. Farther into Byzantine territory at Niš, some of the men got into quarrels in the marketplace and burned a few mills, while others attacked the town's fortifications. Byzantine troops then routed and scattered them, causing the loss of about one quarter of the crusading force. When Peter and his remaining men reached Constantinople, Emperor Alexius I allowed them to camp in the suburbs, where they committed numerous thefts, broke into houses, and even stole the lead from church roofs. The emperor treated them with forbearance, but was clearly eager to be rid of them. Both groups of Crusaders had barely moved into Asia Minor when the joint army of about 20,000 men was wiped out near Nicaea in its first clash with the Turks.

Other contingents of this People's Crusade, leaving Germany to join Peter in the East, gave an even worse account of themselves. In April 1096 a preacher named Volkmar set out from the Rhineland with about 10,000 followers, while a second preacher, Gottschalk, led a somewhat larger group. A still more numerous band accompanied Count Emich of Leisingen, a petty noble and experienced soldier already known for his lawless behavior. Ultimately none of these forces got much beyond the Hungarian border. Volkmar's followers entered northern Hungary from Bohemia after conducting a bloodbath of Jews at Prague. They behaved in so rowdy a fashion at Nitra in Slovakia that a Hungarian army intercepted their march, killing many and scattering the remainder. Gottschalk's warriors had scarcely crossed the Hungarian frontier from Bavaria before they began robbing the peasants of their grain, wine, and livestock. King Koloman surrounded them with troops, forced them to relinquish their weapons and stolen goods, and then sent his army to annihilate them. Gottschalk's entire following perished in this slaughter. When Emich's still larger and better-armed force reached the Hungarian border a few weeks later, fresh from slaughtering Jews in the Rhine valley, Koloman flatly refused to let them across. Nonetheless, they succeeded in forcing their way into Hungary after six weeks of skirmishing. While they were besieging the fortress of Moson its garrison came out and routed them. Few of Emich's followers reached home alive.

The more respectable armies of the First Crusade passed through Hungary without trouble. The first was headed by two French barons, Duke Godfrey of Lower Lorraine and his brother Baldwin, who arrived on the Hungarian border in the late autumn of 1096. Mindful of his experiences with previous Crusaders, King Koloman suspected their intentions. However, Duke Godfrey made a favorable impression; and ultimately he and Koloman agreed on the conditions under which the Crusaders could cross Hungary. The leaders promised to control their troops, while Koloman agreed to supply them with ample provisions at fair prices. Duke Baldwin and his family remained behind as hostages for the troops' good behavior. These Crusaders marched peacefully across Hungary, with Koloman and his army shadowing them all the way. As soon as Godfrey and his followers had safely crossed the Sava into Byzantine territory, Koloman released the hostages and parted from Baldwin with a kiss of friendship. Ultimately this French army reached Palestine and went on to participate in the capture of Jerusalem.

Another group of Crusaders led by Count Raymond of Toulouse left France in October 1096, traveling through northern Italy and down the coast of Dalmatia. On that barren Adriatic shore the men suffered severely from the attacks of wild local tribes, who regarded these foreigners with undisguised hostility and harassed them with forays from ambush. The Crusaders retaliated by mutilating any guerrillas whom they captured. The natives of the coastal districts refused either to sell their produce or to serve as guides, but instead abandoned their villages and fled into the interior. The last effective Croatian king had died in 1089, and Dalmatia at that period was subject to no effective central authority. Fortunately, Count Raymond's army carried ample provisions in its baggage and lost no one through starvation, though by the time it reached Albania the men were suffering from hunger. From Durrës the Crusaders followed the Via Egnatia to Constantinople, accompanied by Byzantine soldiers. Ultimately they, too, joined in the capture of Jerusalem.

The Second Crusade to the Holy Land in 1147 also took the overland route through Hungary. Led by the German emperor and king of France respectively, the two main armies traveled separately in order to avoid quarrels. First the German Emperor Conrad III* arrived on the Hungarian frontier with about 20,000 men, including his vassal, the duke of Bohemia, with many Bohemian nobles. This time the ruler of Hungary was no longer the forceful Koloman, but seventeen-year-old Géza II. The young king was unable to restrain Conrad's troops from committing robbery and arson. In order to avoid open hostilities he

---

* Strictly speaking, Conrad III was only king of Germany, since he was never crowned in Rome.

resorted to the unpleasant expedient of bribing them with food and money. On Bulgarian territory the Crusaders began to pillage, refused to pay for what they took, and slaughtered anyone who protested. They instigated a riot at Plovdiv, where they burned the town's suburbs but found the walls too strong to attack. The Byzantine Emperor Manuel I sent troops to accompany their march; but this only provoked further clashes. Conrad's forces burned down a monastery and killed all the monks, while Byzantine soldiers killed stragglers from the German army. Quite different from this disorderly conduct was the behavior of the French Crusaders, led by the pious and chivalrous young king of France, Louis VII. Arriving on the Hungarian border about a month after the Germans, Louis concluded a friendship alliance with King Géza; and his army moved through Hungary without incident. However, this Second Crusade ended in ignominious failure. A Seljuk army annihilated nine-tenths of the German force; and after a futile attack on Damascus, both monarchs left for home.

The Third Crusade in 1189–92 again touched Hungary and the Balkans. This time only the German contingent chose the land route, while the French and English traveled by sea on Venetian ships. The Germans experienced few problems in Hungary, where King Béla III received Emperor Frederick Barbarossa with royal splendor. But the situation in the Balkans had changed drastically since the death of the Byzantine Emperor Manuel I in 1180. Imperial garrisons still held the fortresses along the main road to Constantinople, but Serbian and Bulgarian brigands freely attacked the Crusaders as they marched. Emperor Frederick suspected the Byzantines of inciting these marauders, although in fact the Byzantine Emperor Isaac II was simply too weak to control his own provinces. In the region between Belgrade and Sofia the Germans found everything in ruins, a consequence of frequent hostilities in recent decades between Hungarians and Byzantines. The Third Crusade ended in disaster like its predecessor. On the march across Asia Minor, Emperor Frederick drowned accidentally in a stream, possibly due to the weight of his armor; and the German army disintegrated.

The principal Crusades to the Holy Land were already finished before any Hungarian monarch became actively involved. King Béla III had taken the Crusader's vow, but died in 1196 before he could set out. The one Hungarian king who did reach Palestine—Andrew II, as part of the Fifth Crusade—profited not at all from his transparently self-serving efforts. Andrew, who was related through his wife to the Latin emperor of Constantinople, hoped to promote his candidacy for that throne by impressing the pope with a show of piety. To finance his Crusade he resorted to the dubious expedient of alienating large tracts of royal land. When a rival contender won the Latin throne, Andrew lost much of his zeal for crusading, but remained bound by his vow, which he dared not renounce. This Crusade was badly organized from the beginning. Lack of provisions caused many would-be participants to turn back. In the late summer of 1217, Andrew took his army to Split on the Adriatic coast, where he discovered that only two ships capable of making the voyage to Palestine were available. Leaving most of his army behind, he departed with only a small force. After arriving in the Holy Land he undertook no serious military action. His half-hearted attempts to capture a few Turkish fortresses proved futile; and despite threats from the papal legate, he departed after a few months. To compound this farce, he was captured in Bulgaria on the return journey and held for ransom. As the price of his release he was forced to renounce two Hungarian border fortresses.

The successive failures of so many crusades naturally diminished the Europeans' enthusiasm for further military adventures in Palestine. However, wars for the faith could still be fought against pagans and heretics within Europe itself. The most famous campaign of this type was mounted in 1208–13 against the Albigensians of southern France, whose dualistic theology was anathema to the Christian Church. The less well-known crusade against Bosnia in 1234–38 was similar in motive. The Bosnians evidently were suspected of Bogomilism, a faith related to the Albigensian heresy in that both were distant offshoots of Persian Manichaeism. In 1234, Pope Gregory IX promised spiritual rewards to anyone who would join a proposed war against the alleged Bosnian "heretics"; and he authorized the Hungarian Duke Koloman to lead this crusade. Bosnia was a borderland which the Hungarians had dominated in the past; and presumably they wanted an acceptable excuse to invade it now. Hungarian troops occupied northern Bosnia, although the central region successfully resisted. Seven years later the Mongol onslaught forced the Hungarians to withdraw, allowing Bosnia to revert to its formerly independent status.

The crusading ideal was kept alive in the 13th and 14th centuries by an organization of German warrior monks, the Teutonic Order of Knights. Founded in Palestine during the Third Crusade to care for sick or wounded German soldiers and pilgrims, in 1198 it received papal approval to become a military order as well. As such it participated in no major actions in the Holy Land, and soon transferred its main operations to Europe. The Order first accepted an offer from the Hungarian King Andrew II to settle in the Braşov region of southeastern Transylvania, a strategic location dominating major passes through the Carpathians. Expecting the Knights to help fight the heathen Cumans beyond the mountains, Andrew in 1211 granted them extensive lands and privileges. However, the Order's energetic proceedings and independent dealings with the papacy suggested an ambition to carve out an autonomous principality on the model of the Crusader states of Syria and Palestine. Andrew began to fear that these activities would undermine his own claims to the land. In 1225 he accused the Knights of encroaching on his royal prerogatives and expelled them from Transylvania by force.

The Order found a new opportunity for crusading along the Baltic coast, where the Prussian tribes remained heathen, and where Lithuania was destined to stand for another century and a half as the last major pagan outpost in Europe. In 1226 the Polish Duke Conrad of Mazovia invited the Knights to help him defend his northern frontier against the destructive incursions of the wild Prussian tribes. The Knights were willing, but determined to avoid another experience like the recent debacle in Transylvania, and insisted on making their position legally secure. The grand master of the Order, the clever diplomat Hermann von Salza, prolonged negotiations until in 1230 the Mazovian duke finally conceded most of the disputed points. The Order received extensive lands along the Vistula, with permission to retain any territory captured in future from the Prussians, plus a series of powers appropriate only to a sovereign state, such as the right to establish coinage, tariffs, and a salt tax. In theory the grand master stood in a vassal relationship to the duke of Mazovia. However, he soon achieved a fully independent position, first by persuading the German emperor to treat him as equal to "a prince of the empire" and afterward by becoming a direct vassal of the pope in Rome.

The first contingent of Teutonic Knights arrived in Prussia in 1230. From their starting point around Chełmno (Kulm) they built a series of fortresses along the northern Vistula which became stepping-stones for further territorial acquisitions. The Order conducted numerous military campaigns against the pagan Prussians and occasionally against Christian Poland as well. Within a short time it had acquired extensive landholdings. Skillfully it utilized its international contacts, powers of organization, and diplomatic expertise to expand its territory. The Order's campaigns into Prussia were carried out crusader fashion with the assistance of visiting warriors from all over Europe, particularly from the German Empire. Foreign knights regularly rode into Prussia for the campaigning season to find adventure and booty, returning home each winter. The Order required the pagans whom it defeated in battle to accept baptism and receive Christian missionaries on their territory. This aspect of its activities provided moral justification not only for its devastating campaigns against the heathen Prussians, but also for the state structure which it erected in the conquered lands. Membership in the Order became much sought after by the sons of minor German knightly families. Within a short time the Teutonic Knights had become a dominating force in the politics of northeastern Europe, a competitor and often an enemy of Poland. In 1260 they suppressed the last great pagan rebellion in Prussia and achieved supremacy over the last of the independent tribes there.

Religious conviction combined with intolerance of other faiths veiled the self-serving motives behind many medieval wars, transforming them into holy enterprises blessed by the pope. Military expeditions for the ostensible purpose of spreading Catholicism continued for centuries along the eastern frontiers of European Christendom. The Teutonic Knights' almost yearly forays against the still-pagan Lithuanians in the 13th and 14th centuries counted as crusades. King Casimir of Poland and his nephew King Louis of Hungary fought on their eastern borders against pagans and "schismatics" (i.e., Eastern Orthodox) in the mid-14th century. As the Muslim Turks pressed farther into the Balkans, a succession of popes sought to have them turned back. The two major anti-Ottoman campaigns of the medieval period, defeated respectively at Nicopolis in 1396 and at Varna in 1444, were officially termed crusades, as was Hunyadi's successful defense of Belgrade in 1456. The wars between Hussites and Catholics were regarded by both sides as battles for the faith.

Religiously inspired wars began in Bohemia in the 15th century when Sigismund, king of Hungary and German emperor, inherited the Bohemian throne. Resolutely opposed to the Hussite religious reforms, he refused to guarantee freedom of worship in Bohemia. The Hussites' refusal in turn to renounce their beliefs made hostilities inevitable, although Sigismund's enormous military resources made their attitude appear suicidal at first. At this point a hitherto obscure mercenary captain stepped forward to lead the Bohemian resistance. John Žižka was a minor noble in his sixties, whose modest origins would have prevented his rise to prominence in ordinary times. An adherent of the radical wing of the Hussites, he was also an experienced soldier who had lost one eye in combat. He now revealed himself to be a military leader of genius. Through sheer ability and force of character he became a leader of the Czech nation and one of the foremost military innovators of all time. In view of the unremitting hostility of most of Catholic Europe, it is difficult to believe that the Hussite movement could long have survived without him.

The resources with which Žižka began this struggle looked hopelessly inadequate at first. His original army consisted chiefly of peasants armed with agricultural implements plus townsmen carrying pikes, lances, or sometimes crossbows. The old soldier adapted his methods to his material. Under his direction the Hussites established a military stronghold and training camp on the steep hill of Tabor, some fifty miles southeast of Prague. Žižka ordered it fortified with double and triple walls, towers, and a moat, thus rendering it virtually impregnable. There he subjected his green troops to the discipline of military exercises on a training ground—an innovation quite alien to medieval habits. To enhance morale and accustom his troops to combat he led them in small-scale attacks on neighboring Catholic monasteries. This enabled his men to capture weapons and provided a considerable loot of gold and jewels for the Hussite war chest. The soldiers of Tabor were full of zeal for a holy cause. Anticipating Oliver Cromwell's Army of the Saints in England two centuries later, they combined stern military drill with regular prayers and hymn singing. Moral discipline was rigorous. Žižka strictly prohibited and punished drinking, brawling, and womanizing. He taught his soldiers to consider themselves tools in God's hands and instruments for the execution of God's law. This religious enthusiasm was an indispensable part of the Hussites' armory, and contributed in a very substantial way to their military successes. With never more than 25,000 troops they achieved their victories despite small numbers.

In 1420, Pope Martin V (the same whose election had recently brought the Great Schism to an end) proclaimed a crusade against the Hussites and entrusted Emperor Sigismund with carrying it out. Sigismund scarcely needed this authorization, which fully corresponded to his own inclinations. Ultimately he led five separate military campaigns against Bohemia, aided in each case by enormous superiority in numbers. All five were not only disastrous but humiliating. The emperor was an ineffective general and many of his troops were mercenaries, while the Czechs benefited from superb leadership and morale. For the first campaign, in June 1420, Sigismund led an army of Germans to the outskirts of Prague. There Žižka's tactical moves prevented him from taking either the city or its surrounding hills, which the Czechs had covered with entrenchments. In August 1421, Sigismund undertook a second and still larger crusade, for which the pope had promised indulgences and absolution from sins to all volunteers. The crusaders' failure to capture the small Bohemian town of Žatec, which held firm after six separate assaults, combined with Žižka's already formidable military reputation to undermine the attackers' morale. At the mere news that a Hussite army was approaching, the Germans hastily broke camp and fled.

Later that same year Sigismund invaded Bohemia from Hungary with an army commanded by his capable Italian general, Filippo ("Pipo") Scolari. Through a clever maneuver Pipo took Kutná Hora, the second-largest town of Bohemia, placing Žižka's forces at a considerable disadvantage between the town and the Hungarian army. Seemingly trapped, Žižka executed a surprise tactical move which drove the Hungarians from their positions and broke the encirclement. In a series of follow-up actions he forced the emperor out of Bohemia by the end of 1422. Amazingly, these feats were the work of a blind man, for in June 1421, Žižka had lost his one good eye to an arrow wound. He now directed the fighting by relying on subordinates for precise descriptions of the terrain and the location of the enemy forces. The loss of his sight evidently did nothing to shake Žižka's self-confidence or his ability to command. Indeed, he won his greatest victories *after* becoming blind, rather than before. By the time of his death late in 1424, his associates had thoroughly learned his methods. His second-in-command, the ex-priest Procopius, assumed leadership of the army; and the series of victories continued. The Hussites now began to take on an aura of invincibility, as their successes suggested that perhaps they were really God's chosen people. The fear that this might be true seriously demoralized their enemies.

The Hussite wars continued almost without interruption for fourteen years, 1420–34. Sigismund's fourth crusade into Bohemia in 1427 proved an utter fiasco. The Hussites' military reputation had shaken the confidence of his troops so thoroughly that they fled merely upon hearing that the Czechs were approaching. During that same year, the Hussites carried their campaigns into Germany and Austria for the first time. Once again their reputation had preceded them, so that their mere approach usually caused the Germans to turn and run. When skirmishes actually took place the Czechs invariably prevailed. A war of religious propaganda accompanied these foreign expeditions, as the Hussites disseminated thousands of hand-copied pamphlets. Launching a fifth crusade in 1431, Sigismund tried for one last time to impose his will on Bohemia by military force. This final invasion merely confirmed the verdict of its predecessors. Near the town of Domažlice an enormous German army fled in disorder without even encountering the Czechs. In the end, Hussite troops met their only important defeat at the hands of other Hussites. At the battle of Lipany in 1434 the conservative Utraquists overcame the radicals from Tabor, with both sides employing the methods they had learned from Žižka. The Utraquists' victory enabled them to dominate Bohemian political life for the remainder of the century.

The distinguishing feature of Hussite military tactics was the use of the wagon fort. This idea in itself was no novelty, since the steppe dwellers for centuries had fought behind their wagons. Žižka presumably had observed the practice during his earlier service on the Polish-Lithuanian frontier, although farther west in Europe it was still unknown. His use of the wagon fortress began as a defensive measure. The few resources at his disposal obliged him to employ any means at hand, which meant farm wagons and implements. Žižka trained his peasant troops to move forward in a formation which allowed the wagons on short notice to form a closed circle, linked by chains. The horses were unhitched and kept within the enclosure. To repulse an attack, the men stood on the wagons swinging flails and poles with long, sharp hooks that were capable of unhorsing a knight. Typically, when the attackers had exhausted themselves beating against the wagons, Žižka's men on foot and on horseback sallied out through the gaps between the wagons to complete the victory. This was an effective device against an opponent overwhelmingly superior in cavalry, especially if the enemy was armed only with bows and arrows rather than artillery, which could have blown the wagons to bits. The Hussites themselves possessed only limited numbers of cavalry, since most Bohemian noblemen who might have fought on horseback were either hostile or at least uncommitted to the cause.

The key to Žižka's system was to choose a position which the opponent was obliged to capture in order to attain some objective. He then set up his wagon forts in a way that compelled the enemy to attack at a disadvantage. Armored knights on horseback, who at first refused to take such improvised defenses seriously, were astonished to find the humble wagons surprisingly resistant to attack. To be sure, this method presupposed that the enemy would take the offensive, which at first during the Hussite wars was usually the case. Later the Czechs' reputation became so formidable that hostile troops simply refused to assault the wagon forts, as happened during the German invasions of Bohemia in 1427 and 1431. The Hussite wagons could also roll forward as moving fortresses, permitting slow and deliberate aim by men shooting from inside through loopholes. In their later campaigns the Czechs overran German territory with stunning speed, following the principle that mobility was better protection than body armor. They also departed from the normal conventions of medieval warfare by pursuing a beaten enemy after a battle in order to render their victory more complete.

Žižka was also an innovator in his use of firepower. After his first successes, when some of the Czech towns had rallied to his side, he obtained access to facilities for arms manufacture which supplied him with small handguns and primitive artillery pieces. He was the first European commander to maneuver on the field with cannon of medium caliber, which he mounted on carts in the spaces between wagons. These field pieces could propel stone balls weighing up to a hundred pounds into massed units of hostile cavalry. At first the effect was more psychological than material, since the noise of exploding gunpowder frightened the enemy soldiers and horses more than the stone balls harmed them. This artillery enabled the Hussites not only to block or discourage the approach of enemy forces, but also to dislodge them from a position or force them back. At the key battle of Kutná Hora, for example, Czech field artillery drove the Hungarians from their positions. Žižka also introduced the use of small firearms for large bodies of infantry, eventually equipping a third of his infantry with handguns. These were highly useful in fighting the German feudal cavalry, since armor by now had become so heavy that at ordinary battlefield range it resisted arrows and bolts fired from crossbows.

Artillery was a comparatively new phenomenon in Žižka's time, since warfare was still in the process of being revolutionized by gunpowder. When ignited, this chemical mixture imparted a much stronger impetus than tension or torsion to the propulsion of missiles. As an explosive it was far more destructive than a merely incendiary compound like Greek fire. On the battlefield it rendered the armored knight utterly obsolete, since not even the heaviest armor offered sufficient protection against it. Cannons fired by gunpowder greatly reduced the significance of fortresses, because a threatened army was no longer able simply to retreat to the safety of the nearest walled stronghold. Stone walls and ramparts lost much of their previous effectiveness when artillery became capable of reducing them to rubble. A fortress still retained some value, since an invader had to capture it if he did not wish to leave its defenders in his rear when he moved forward. The protection offered by stone walls, though no longer as effective as formerly, was much better than none at all. On the other hand, the old rules governing fortress construction had to be revised. Ditches surrounding the walls of castles and cities were widened and strengthened with masonry. Low, broad bastions jutting out into a ditch were built to permit flanking fire by the defenders. Instead of a high cliff, the preferred location for a settlement was now a wet plain with ground too soft to support the weight of artillery.

Admittedly, cannons produced only a limited effect when they were first employed on the battlefield in the latter half of the 14th century. Their rate of fire was poor and their range mediocre. Their weight made transport difficult; and an advancing army was often able to spike them once the first salvo had been fired. Improvised fortifications such as ditches, banks of earth, and palisades had to be thrown up in the field to prevent this from happening. Cannons were of little use in defending walled towns, since medieval walls were not strong enough to serve as emplacements; the shock from the explosion would do more damage to the walls than to the enemy. Only in the mid-15th century did the larger cannons begin to employ lead shot; at first they fired only stone balls. Handguns were in effect miniature cannons. The earliest model, which fired lead bullets, consisted of an iron tube clamped to a staff. The powder was ignited by a match applied to a touchhole. The butt of the staff rested on the ground to absorb the recoil, forcing the gunner to aim high and inaccurately. Precise aiming was impossible anyhow since two hands were needed to fire the gun. Early in the 15th century the first true handgun appeared with a shorter stock to permit firing from shoulder to breast. The Hussites in the 1420s were the first to use such handguns on a large scale.

Any account of the Hussites' military success must take full account of the genius of Žižka. This experienced old soldier understood how to make the best possible use of meager resources and inspire his men. He insisted on regular and methodical drill, strict discipline, and a clear division of function among his troops—practices virtually unknown in medieval European warfare. Žižka unerringly analyzed the terrain in order to select the most advantageous locations for setting up his wagon forts. He was capable of quick decision, swift moves, and tactical surprises. After his death in 1424, his successor, Procopius, employed the same methods. The generalship of these two leaders was compounded by the religious enthusiasm and daring of their men, who often attained an objective through boldness alone. On the other hand, the Hussites never faced a really competent enemy. Ultimately Žižka's system proved to be an anomaly in the history of warfare. Improvised to meet specific circumstances—namely, the need for inexperienced troops to hold their own against far larger professional forces—it could not readily be applied under different conditions. One weakness of Žižka's strategy was that it depended heavily on an opponent's willingness to attack or his readiness to flee. The cumbersome horse-drawn wagons were incapable of pursuing an enemy who retreated in good order. Moreover, when artillery came to play a major role on the battlefield, wagons provided a poor defense.

In the course of the Hussite wars, religious fanaticism sometimes caused both sides to behave savagely. Catholic authorities in Bohemia were responsible for burnings, drownings, and mass slaughters of Hussites. In turn, Hussite crowds in Prague stormed Catholic cloisters and churches, setting fire to the buildings and expelling or killing the clergy. The capture of hostile towns by either side was sometimes accompanied by scenes of horror and misery. Since resentment against idle clergy living in luxury gave an important impetus to the Hussite revolt, Catholic monks were particularly at risk if they fell into Hussite hands. Žižka permitted Catholic priests and monks to be burned to death, although he made a point of sparing the lives of women and children. On the other hand, Hussite troops seem not to have engaged in sexual excesses, which their religious principles forbade. In this respect they differed sharply from the foreign armies who opposed them, especially Sigismund's Hungarian mercenaries. The latter often began their depredations even before reaching Bohemian territory. Religious fanaticism on both sides was reinforced by ethnic antagonism between Germans and Czechs, who often lived side by side in Bohemia itself, as well as by a kind of nationalist hostility between natives of Bohemia and the foreign troops in Sigismund's employ. Distinctions tended to be ignored in the heat of conflict, so that German soldiers were inclined to regard all Czechs as Hussites, while Czechs sometimes treated all Germans as Catholics. Neither assumption was always true. However, it explains why Sigismund's troops at times killed anyone they encountered who could not speak German, while Hussites on occasion burned Germans to death in barrels.

Žižka's military innovations did find imitators among the peasants of Transylvania. In 1437 a major uprising occurred in that province, beginning with peasant protests against a recent increase in church tithes and labor services. The disturbances soon assumed massive proportions. Four to five thousand peasants gathered on Bobîlna hill north of Cluj (Kolozsvár), where they built a fortified camp resembling the Hussite stronghold at Tabor. Some lower-class townsmen and a few petty nobles joined them. The site was excellent, since the heavy surrounding forests would prevent a cavalry charge, while the summit itself provided a large open area. The peasant rebels showed considerable military skill, indicating that many of them must have had previous army experience. On Bobîlna hill they achieved a notable victory over an attacking army of nobles, but were too cautious to pursue and destroy the retreating enemy. Ultimately the uprising spread over a wide area of Transylvania, with the rebels capturing several important towns. However, no religious ideology inspired this movement; and the peasants lacked a leader of outstanding ability. Devoid of any overall strategy, they dissipated their strength in local and uncoordinated actions. Meanwhile the nobles organized their own military forces. The outcome of the rebellion demonstrated once again that peasant soldiers were no match for better armed and organized professional troops. The final battle occurred at Cluj, which had opened its gates to the peasants. An army of nobles besieged the town, forced the rebels to surrender, and killed the peasant leaders. Bloody reprisals followed.

Another of Žižka's imitators was the Hungarian general John Hunyadi, who like him faced the problem of resisting superior forces—in this case the Ottoman Turks. Hunyadi had learned the soldier's trade in the wars against the Hussites in Bohemia, and later served as a mercenary captain in Italy. On becoming commander of the army of southern Hungary in 1440, he introduced the Hussite style of warfare. Like Žižka, he set up his camps as wagon fortresses and used horse-drawn wagons to transport his infantry. Indeed, the core of his army consisted of Bohemian mercenaries, supplemented on occasion by peasant troops, sometimes in great number. Although the Hungarian nobility regarded his methods with contempt, Hunyadi soon demonstrated their effectiveness. With a primarily peasant army he achieved a major victory over the Turks in March of 1442 near Alba Julia in Transylvania, and a still more impressive triumph a few months later in Walachia, using Hussite tactics. As a reward for outstanding services, he received extensive estates from the Hungarian king, enabling him to finance his wars in part by hiring mercenaries with the revenues from his own lands.

Hunyadi lacked the option of calling upon a general levy of the entire nobility, which already had become a rarity in his time. In Hungary after the mid-13th century the king no longer demanded that men with military obligations serve in person, but merely that members of the nobility supply a prescribed number of fully equipped knights. Thus the armies of Hungary and Croatia came to be composed in large part of private war bands called "banderia," each fighting under its own banner. The king and the ban of Croatia each maintained such a unit; powerful lay magnates and prelates of the Church did likewise. Even minor noblemen often kept some private troops, as did each Croatian župan and some of the towns. Most of these forces were called up in the general levy, although loyalty to their lord usually outweighed loyalty to the king. Frequently the banderia were used to settle personal disputes between nobles, or between nobles and the king. In the 14th century these private armies formed the chief component of the Hungarian military forces. The members were called familiares (i.e., "family") and swore fealty to their lord, but were paid as mercenaries. The tie of dependence lasted for only a limited time and did not affect a man's noble status or property. These banderia troops were supplemented by companies of independent lesser nobility headed by the royal count of their home county, or (if appropriate) by the Transylvanian voivode, the ban of Slavonia or Croatia, or for the Cumans the palatine.

In Transylvania, more diverse in population than the rest of Hungary, service obligations varied for each legal category. The Szeklers historically had combined personal freedom with the obligation to serve in the army; and they retained this status throughout the 15th century. Many had become peasants, too poor to equip themselves as light cavalry, but continued to serve as infantry. Unlike peasants elsewhere in the kingdom, they could not legally be enserfed. The Szekler foot soldiers were poorly armed, but useful in skirmishes against similarly equipped Turkish irregulars. Among the Vlachs of Transylvania only the local chiefs, or knezi, served in the army; ordinary Vlachs did not. The Transylvanian Saxons were personally exempt from military service, but were obligated to provide a fixed number of soldiers. They hired mercenaries to defend their towns, and also sent fighters to the royal army under the command of local magistrates. Special regulations applied to soldiers guarding the frontier, who were allowed (like nobles) to hold hereditary property.

The fact that the lower nobility in 14th-century Hungary had ceased to form the backbone of the army was a function of their life-style. Aside from those few who became familiares of the king, a baron, or a prelate, most petty nobles now lived in country villages. They had lost their former warlike spirit, and often differed but slightly from peasants in their way of life. Their principal distinguishing mark was the right to serve in war at the king's call and under his direct command, which was regarded as a privilege belonging to nobility alone. The military effectiveness of this minor nobility was limited. Not only were they too impoverished to arm themselves adequately; they also lacked organization and leadership. Furthermore, they were inclined to suspect that the county count, who was supposed to lead them, might actually wish to restrict their autonomy. Often they appeared at the general levy on foot or on poor horses useless for combat, clad not in armor but in peasant dress, armed with sticks instead of swords. At the same time, the growing Turkish danger meant that Hungary needed a larger and better army.

The defeat of a major Christian coalition by the Turks at Nicopolis in Bulgaria in 1396 made clear the obsolescence of the general levy of the nobility and emphasized the need for a different type of army. Thus the Hungarian Diet which met at Timişoara the following year created a new military system, decreeing that all landowners must provide one archer for each twenty peasant households on an estate. Many of these troops would obviously come from the nobles' own banderia, but presumably some of the new recruits would be peasants. To minimize expense, the new soldiers would be outfitted only as light, not heavy cavalry. The units raised in this fashion were known as the militia portalis (a porta, or "gate," being a taxable unit). At the same session the Diet confirmed the principle that the nobles personally were not required to fight outside Hungary. King Sigismund promised not to call upon the nobility for military service at all unless the banderia of the lords together with his own private forces proved unable to prevent a hostile army from invading the country. After this time he only once summoned the general levy of the nobility for one of his numerous wars, that of 1432 against Bohemia. The wealthier nobles were unwilling to fight, and the lesser ones were generally too poverty-stricken to function effectively as soldiers. The militia portalis, albeit a slight improvement over the general levy of the nobility, was still too cumbersome and disorganized to resist a major Ottoman attack. However, by introducing certain peasants to the use of arms, this new militia had the unintended effect of preparing the ground for the great peasant revolt of 1437–38.

Later in the 15th century King Matthias created another type of military unit—a powerful mercenary army financed by increased taxation. Subsequently known as the Black Army, this was a permanent force owing allegiance only to the king. At its greatest strength it consisted of 20,000 horsemen and 8,000 infantrymen. Light cavalry formed its largest and most effective component, although it also included a fair number of infantry and some artillery. Its successes were largely due to a centralized command, good coordination between the various elements, and a high level of discipline. This army was the key instrument of Matthias's ambitious foreign policy, although to some extent he still made use of the older units: banderia, noble levy, and militia portalis. However, the Hungarian lords greatly resented Matthias's centralized government and accompanying taxation. Wishing to recover some of their former importance, they deliberately neglected to pay the king's army after his death. When the troops responded by plundering, a force of nobles annihilated them—a fateful loss to the military power of the kingdom.

The Polish nobles also resisted army service, while continuing to insist on their distinct identity as a military class. At every opportunity they sought to increase the king's obligations toward themselves, while decreasing their own toward him. Throughout the 14th century they generally insisted that the king was required to compensate them for war service beyond the frontiers of the state, pay their ransoms if they were captured, and make good their material losses from combat, especially in horses. These stipulations were written into law at the Diet of Košice (Kassa) in 1374. However, the nobles' responsibility for military service if the country was invaded remained unchanged. Statutes of 1458 and 1459 further defined their obligations according to the size of their lands and incomes. In contrast to West European feudal practice, this service was due only to the king and to no other lord. The penalty for failure to appear when summoned, accompanied by the requisite number of armed horsemen, was either a monetary fine or confiscation of property. The rulers of Poland in the 15th century did not hesitate to impose these punishments.

By this time the Polish nobles had ceased to be an effective fighting force. Just as they discussed matters of state in the Sejm (Diet), so also in the army they tended more to deliberate than to follow orders. Besides, the more they became personally involved in estate management, the less they were inclined to go to war. Especially if their dependent peasants performed labor services instead of paying taxes in cash, constant supervision was essential. Military service became a burden which nobles were happy to avoid by hiring mercenaries, particularly since the taxes for paying the mercenaries fell upon peasants and townsmen. The Thirteen Years' War between Poland and the Teutonic Knights (1454–66) was fought largely by hired troops. The king named a leader for them called a hetman, at first on a temporary basis, although in the 1520s this office became permanent. Mercenary soldiers had become necessary not only because of the nobility's military ineffectiveness, but also because the great landed estates of Poland in the 15th century generally enjoyed "immunities" from royal taxation and royal justice. The king had lost much of his power to insist on army service from his nobility. More and more rarely did he summon them to war. Nevertheless the nobles took care to maintain the fiction that a military obligation still existed, since this was the ostensible justification for their privileged status in society. They also did not want the king to strengthen his position by establishing a permanent professional army.

Quite different was the military system of the Ottoman Turks, who ultimately placed all their troops under centralized governmental control. This was a gradual achievement, culminating only under Sultan Suleiman the Magnificent in the 16th century. The initial Turkish attacks upon Europe were conducted by more or less autonomous groups of raiders operating along the Byzantine frontier. Many of them were members of nomadic Turkic tribes driven westward by the Mongols into central Anatolia, which was ruled at that time by the Seljuk Turks. Taking advantage of the tribes' warlike proclivities, the Seljuk sultans set them the task of defending exposed border regions. At first the sultans were able to keep these tribal warriors more or less in check—for example, by detaining their leaders at court as hostages—in order to preserve good relations with Byzantium. Then in 1243 at Kösedagh a Mongol army dealt the Seljuks a disastrous defeat, causing the Seljuk empire in Anatolia to disintegrate into semi-independent principalities. During the following century, the Turkish border fighters were subject to only minimal outside authority. Owing allegiance just to a local chief, they conducted frequent plundering expeditions against neighboring lands, initially seeking booty rather than territory. Their opportunities for profit increased considerably after 1261, when the Byzantine government returned from Nicaea to Constantinople and transferred many of its troops to Europe. The Turkish frontier fighters soon discovered that the Byzantine defenses in Asia Minor had become significantly weaker than before. Indeed, the Greek emperors of the 14th century often hired Turkish mercenaries to help them in their dynastic struggles or in Balkan wars.

The founder of the Ottoman state, Osman or Othman (r. 1290–1326), was originally no more than a minor Turkish tribal chief commanding a few hundred mounted warriors and ruling a small area along the Sea of Marmora just beyond the eastern edge of the Byzantine Empire. Success made him bolder and attracted many new recruits to his banners, including men from the other Muslim states of Asia Minor. The fortuitous location of his lands gave the raiders easy access to Europe. Like the earlier Christian Crusaders to the Holy Land, these Islamic fighters were driven by material as well as religious impulses. The lure of plunder, adventure, and the hope of acquiring rich new lands obviously played a major role; but religion was also an important source of inspiration. The Koran had imposed upon Muslims the obligation of jihad, or holy war against unbelievers, until such time as the whole world accepted Islam. Quite aside from whatever worldly ambitions these soldiers may have cherished, they viewed themselves as ghazis, warriors for the faith. This did not prevent them from attacking other Muslim states, but it did make them prefer Christian enemies. A ghazi's courage was fortified by the conviction that if he died in battle, his entrance into paradise was assured. He also possessed a heavy dose of fatalism, believing that Allah alone determined the moment of a man's death, which no human act could alter. Ottoman warriors saw themselves as part of a community of believers dedicated to the struggle against infidels.

During the reign of Osman's successor Orkhan (r. 1326–61), under whom a rudimentary governmental structure took form, better-organized armies began to replace the semi-independent frontier raiders. In the early 1350s Turkish troops achieved their first permanent conquest in Europe by crossing the Dardanelles and overrunning the Gallipoli peninsula. The Byzantines attempted in vain to dislodge them. Strategically this location was precious, since it afforded the Ottoman armies an unimpeded passage into the Balkan Peninsula. From that time onward, Turkish irregulars conducted plundering expeditions into Europe each year, both on horseback and on foot. The leaders of these war bands usually acknowledged the suzerainty of the Ottoman sultan, although their operations were largely beyond his control. At first their raids did not result in territorial losses to the Christian states. However, the damage they wrought and the burden they imposed on the defenders clearly diminished the ability of the Balkan peoples to resist the later, more sustained onslaughts of the regular Ottoman army.

The bulk of the Ottoman forces always consisted of cavalry, which at first meant chiefly the lightly armed mounted warriors typical of the steppe. Light cavalry were useful for overwhelming enemy troops with arrows as well as for harassing and dispersing them; but for shock tactics heavy armor was indispensable. Orkhan created the first companies of heavily mailed horsemen known as sipahis, armed with lance and scimitar for hand-to-hand combat. Originally serving just as the sultan's bodyguard, by the mid-15th century they had become a major component of the Ottoman army. Most sipahis were Turks who had been brought up in the tradition of arms. The Ottoman sultans also employed two types of irregular auxiliary troops. The azabs were a kind of militia, lightly armed foot soldiers who manned the provincial garrisons and were available if necessary to build earthworks or serve as oarsmen. The akindjis were light cavalrymen, volunteer irregulars who received no pay but lived from the spoil of their raids. Generally they were sent out two days in advance of the regular Ottoman army to plunder and exhaust the opponent. By encouraging enemy soldiers to give chase, the akindjis could often bring about a clash with the regular troops. While not particularly efficient for ordinary combat, they sometimes proved useful as scouts. Their principal function was pillage, for which purpose they fanned out across an entire district ahead of the army on the march. Eventually they were either superseded or absorbed into regular military units. In addition, the Ottoman army at first also included a number of free peasants. Organized along tribal lines and known as müsellem, they later became transformed into regular auxiliary forces.

A key element in the Ottoman military machine were the Janissaries (*Yeni-cheri*, or "new troops"), an infantry force paid directly from the sultan's treasury. Their function was to stiffen the resistance of the light cavalry, who were useless for defense and prone to panic when attacked. Initially the Janissaries fought with bows and arrows, although early in the 16th century they turned to firearms. At first they were largely prisoners of war who had become the sultan's slaves, since Muslim law granted the sultan one-fifth of all war booty. Janissary troops appeared in the Ottoman ranks as early as the battle of Nicopolis in 1396, although still in a secondary role. During the 15th century they slowly became a more central component of the army. As the corps expanded, so that war prisoners ceased to be available in sufficient numbers, the sultans resorted to the system known as devşirme, or child tribute. This human tax, attested for the first time in 1438, apparently was introduced in gradual fashion in the course of the 15th century. Christian peasant boys from the Balkan provinces of the empire were forcibly recruited, converted to Islam, and given a thorough military training. Those who qualified were enrolled as Janissaries. Required to live in barracks, they were forbidden to marry or to engage in commerce or industry until retirement. In certain respects they resembled a fraternal organization, wearing a distinctive headdress and maintaining close ties with the Bektashi order of dervishes. Owing to their superior military education, the Janissaries developed into the planning staff of the Ottoman army and proved receptive to technical innovation. For example, it was they who procured the heavy artillery that played a key role in the Turks' capture of Constantinople in 1453. Despite their slave status, they eventually wielded immense political power as the only regular armed force at Istanbul.

In the European part of the Ottoman Empire in the 14th century the sultans established a system of military landholding, which by the mid-15th century had become the principal support of their cavalry. The government gave out large tracts of land as fiefs called timars in exchange for army service. The sipahis resided on their fiefs when not on campaign and supported themselves from taxes on peasant crops and livestock. Part of this produce they converted into cash in order to provide themselves with the necessary horses and military equipment. A timar holder who failed to fulfill his military obligations lost his rights to the land. Conversely, free Muslims from the border units who distinguished themselves in battle were entitled to apply for timars, while men who already held timars might be awarded larger ones. If a timar yielded an income above 3,000 akçes (the legal minimum supposedly needed to support one cavalryman), the landholder was required not only to serve in the army personally but also to provide one fully armed horseman for each additional 3,000 akçes of his revenue. Timar-holding sipahis constituted the bulk of the Ottoman armed forces in the 15th century. As the empire expanded, larger areas became subject to this landholding system, although it was not imposed upon autonomous tribute-paying vassal states like Walachia and Moldavia.

Conquered lands in the Balkans supplied the Ottoman sultans with many of their soldiers, including Bulgars, Serbs, Albanians, Macedonians, and Greeks. Often such men continued to serve under the command of their native princes. By joining the Ottoman army they received tax exemptions and permission to live on state-owned land. Except in chronically insecure territories like Albania or Serbia, many timar holders down to the end of the 15th century were allowed to remain Christians, although Muslims certainly outnumbered them. Christian populations also performed auxiliary military services, again in exchange for privileges. Some took care of the horses and located appropriate spots for pasturage and camps. Others guarded the mountain passes, maintained bridges, piloted ships, acted as messengers, built fortresses and barracks, or cleared and leveled the roads prior to any important military offensive. Vlachs living in the Balkans served as frontier guards and raiders. However, unlike the Romans, the Ottomans did not maintain military roads in good repair. Their chief concern was not speed but the safety of the traffic. They provided for this by granting special status to the population living along the most vulnerable stretches of roadway.

In terms of military effectiveness the Ottoman system was far superior to West European feudalism. The timar-holding cavalry were a professional force, not a semi-independent and fractious nobility. They served at the command of the sultan or his designated subordinates and owed loyalty to him directly, not to any intermediate lords. Whereas the European feudal armies of the 14th and 15th centuries often insisted on serving for no more than forty days a year and refused to fight abroad unless they were paid, Ottoman troops went wherever their commanders led them and stayed for the length of the campaign. To be sure, European mercenary armies were likewise unaffected by time limits or geographical restrictions; but typically they were recruited from the dregs of society, whereas the Turkish professional soldiers were considered an elite. Strict discipline and centralized leadership gave the Turks a decided advantage on the battlefield over the individualistic and undisciplined European knights. Enveloping tactics, turning movements, feints, and ambushes became a decisive element in Ottoman victories, whereas the heavily armed European knights generally limited themselves to head-on assaults and were incapable of maneuvers. The Ottoman army also enjoyed ample financial support, which enabled it to employ foreign experts and techniques regardless of the expense.

Superior organization also gave the Ottoman army a decided advantage. Its commanders knew how to move large masses of troops in segments to keep the various units from interfering with one another's movements. An efficient logistical system allowed them to put into the field much larger armies than any European state of that time could muster. Local resources naturally were utilized whenever possible, especially forage; but the existing level of economic development and low population density in most areas placed a severe upper limit on the number of men and animals that could live off the land. Thus the Turkish authorities collected and stored staple items, primarily grain, in advance. Bread was baked on location and carried into the field by carts or beasts of burden. The Ottoman army went on campaign with two or three months of food reserves, enabling it to fight at much greater distances from home base than any comparable European force of the late medieval period could manage. Ordinarily the troops set out from Istanbul in early spring and returned in late autumn, which left the summer for fighting. Too little food, forage, and lodging would be available to support a large force in the field in winter; and the timar-holding cavalry could not afford to leave their land and peasants unsupervised for too long a time. Since the average speed of march was about ten miles per day, Hungary lay at the outer limit of Ottoman military operations in Europe. At that distance a decisive battle had to be fought within a thirty-day period, or the entire campaign would be for nothing. Owing to these constraints, the Ottomans needed fifteen years to consolidate their control over Hungary even after destroying the bulk of the Hungarian armed forces at Mohács in 1526.

Until a relatively late date the Ottoman sultans possessed no navy, since the horsemen from Western Asia who had founded the empire were unfamiliar with seafaring. Moreover, Turkish town dwellers did not ordinarily engage in overseas commerce, so that no merchant fleet existed to be mobilized for defense. For their first incursions into Europe the Ottomans hired Genoese transports to ferry their troops across the Straits from Asia. Then, as the empire expanded, their ambitions did likewise. To defeat the Venetians, who controlled many strategic points along the Aegean coast, a navy was indispensable. Accordingly the sultans began to construct their own war fleet, consisting of galleys built on the Italian model and manned by crews of Italians, Greeks, and Catalans. These vessels were normally propelled by rowers, but also carried a few sails for use when no conflict was in the offing. Since the naval technique of the time consisted of ramming and boarding enemy vessels, ships in battle had to be maneuvered with oars. Only later did the development of naval gunnery cause galleys to be abandoned in favor of sailing ships.

The Ottoman advance into Europe was marked by occasional major battles, frequent minor ones, and more or less constant border raids by bands of irregulars. In 1371 a major disaster for the Christians occurred on the Maritsa River near Černomen in Thrace. Aroused by the attempt of two Serbian princes to attack the new Ottoman capital of Edirne (Adrianople), a Turkish army surprised the Serbs in their camp under cover of night and won a smashing victory. Černomen was the most important Ottoman military success in Europe prior to the capture of Constantinople in 1453. However, it never attained the literary renown of the Serbian defeat at Kosovo Polje ("Blackbirds' Field"), which became a major theme in Serbian epic poetry. On the plain of Kosovo in 1389 the Ottoman army led by Sultan Murad I clashed with an allied force of Serbs, Albanians, and Bosnians under the command of the Serbian Prince Lazar. Both armies were largely annihilated and the two leaders killed, although after the battle was over the Turks held the field. In the narrower military sense this contest was probably inconclusive. Nonetheless, it destroyed the Balkan states' powers of resistance; and it became enshrined in Serbian folklore as the supreme national tragedy. Nearly the entire Serbian fighting force (between 12,000 and 20,000 men) had been present at Kosovo, while the Ottomans (with 27,000 to 30,000 on the battlefield) retained numerous reserves in Anatolia. After Kosovo the Serbian princes were unable to offer further resistance. Many were forced to become Turkish vassals and fight for the sultan thereafter.

The battle of Kosovo left Hungary as the Ottomans' major antagonist in Europe. However, King Sigismund was less concerned to confront the Turks than to appropriate the territories of his smaller Balkan neighbors. His invasion of western Bulgaria in 1392 led directly to the Ottoman counteroffensive of 1393, which resulted in the capture of Tirnovo and the destruction of eastern Bulgaria as an independent state. In the aftermath the Turks killed many Bulgarian nobles and deported others to Anatolia. They tore down not only fortress walls and other military strongholds but also palaces, churches, and monasteries. Having annexed all of eastern Bulgaria, they were now favorably positioned on the lower Danube to move into Walachia and Transylvania. In 1395 the Walachian voivode Mircea the Old fought them at Rovine on the Argeş River in what was apparently an indecisive battle, since both sides claimed victory. Mircea dealt the Turks several sharp defeats and temporarily deflected their advance away from his lands.

The so-called Nicopolis Crusade of 1396 marked the last serious effort of Catholic and Orthodox Christians to cooperate in a war against the Turks. This enterprise was publicized in Europe as a great Christian offensive against the Muslim enemy, although in fact by that date the crusading ideal had retained very little inspirational power. The Hungarian King Sigismund headed the expedition, aided by contingents from France, Germany, Italy, and Poland. Accompanied by a river fleet, the combined army moved southeastward along the Danube, to be joined downriver by Serbs and Walachians. From the beginning the campaign was plagued by divided leadership and the undisciplined arrogance of many of the knights. En route the Crusaders committed innumerable acts of robbery, rape, and violence. Although Vidin, the capital of western Bulgaria, surrendered without resistance, Nicopolis (Nikopol) was nearly impregnable, towering above the Danube on a high plateau and surrounded by double walls with towers. The Crusaders began to besiege the town, although they were short of siege machines and lacked cannons, which at that date were too clumsy to be dragged from one end of Europe to the other. Arrogantly assuming that the Turks were too alarmed by their presence to fight, the Crusaders spent fifteen days carousing outside the walls of Nicopolis. Meanwhile Sultan Bayezid I interrupted his siege of Constantinople and hurried to meet the Christian threat in the Balkans.

On hearing that Bayezid was coming, the Crusaders hastily prepared for battle. However, dissension in their ranks led to fatally uncoordinated operations. The Hungarians, who had ample experience with Turkish tactics, proposed that the French heavy cavalry hold back as a reserve to guard against a flanking attack by the Turkish light cavalry. The French were offended at this suggestion, which they interpreted as a ploy by King Sigismund to win all the military glory for himself. Medieval notions of chivalry and honor caused them to regard warfare as a fair fight on even terms. Since their battle experience consisted largely of frontal charges by heavy cavalry, they had little or no experience of enveloping tactics, which were more suitable for light cavalry than for knights in full armor. Insisting on the "honor" of beginning the conflict, the French cavalry at Nicopolis initially broke through the Turkish front lines, but soon was surrounded and cut down. Meanwhile Sigismund and the rest of the army fought a separate engagement, equally catastrophic. Voivode Mircea of Walachia left the field early, having no wish needlessly to antagonize the Turks. Sigismund's beaten troops retreated in complete disorder to the Danube, where many of them drowned in flight.

Following their victory at Nicopolis the Ottomans established a new border province in western Bulgaria, with its center at Vidin on the Danube. From this vantage point their raiding parties penetrated ever more deeply into southeastern Europe. Then in 1402 the Ottoman advance into Europe was interrupted by a major setback suffered in Asia. Sultan Bayezid I (r. 1389–1402), known as the Thunderbolt for his lightning campaigns, had overrun many of the Muslim-ruled principalities of Anatolia with an army of Janissaries and the troops of his Christian vassals. These conquests brought the boundaries of the Ottoman Empire in the East to the Taurus Mountains and Euphrates River. However, pious Muslims were shocked at this wholesale offensive against fellow believers. It so happened that during the same period the ferocious Mongol conqueror Timur had been conquering vast territories in Central Asia, and in 1402 appeared in Anatolia, thus threatening the Ottoman eastern provinces. This emergency impelled Bayezid to strengthen his forces with cavalrymen from the Muslim principalities he had so recently defeated. During the course of a fierce battle fought near Ankara, these troops deserted en masse, while Bayezid was totally vanquished, captured, and died in captivity the following year. Civil war broke out among his sons, so that for years the Ottoman Empire was on the verge of disintegration.

For the duration of this civil war (1402–13) the Ottomans were unable to conduct a full-scale invasion of Europe, although Turkish raids into Transylvania, Walachia, and Serbia continued. Finally the Transylvanian peasant revolt of 1437 inspired Sultan Murad II to undertake his most ambitious military effort into the Balkans up to that time. In a major campaign in 1439 his forces captured the important fortress of Smederevo in Serbia after a bombardment of three months' duration. His advance guard moved onward in the direction of Buda, but heavy rains apparently caused its retreat. In the same year the Turks burned and looted in the Braşov area and for eight days besieged the Saxon town of Sibiu. Although the town's successful defense against the sultan's entire European army forestalled a permanent Ottoman presence in Transylvania, the Turks made an important advance at Serbia's expense that year by capturing virtually the entire Serbian despotate. No help was forthcoming from Hungary, where the nobility was too occupied with the problem of succession to the throne to raise an army. The road to Bosnia lay open. Ottoman troops returned to the Balkans in April 1440 to lay siege to Belgrade, where the Hungarian army repulsed them. Although Turkish raiders continued to plunder in northern Serbia, the great Danubian fortress held out.

Chiefly responsible for the defense of Transylvania at this period was John Hunyadi, whose appointment as voivode in 1441 gave him ample opportunity to demonstrate his military and organizational talents. In 1442 he responded to an Ottoman surprise attack near Alba Iulia by raising an army from the surrounding countryside and defeating the Turks in a major battle. His tactics were to place his best troops in the center of the line, sending the light cavalry to attack from the flanks, and then exploit the enemy's confusion. Following this victory he crossed the Carpathians into Walachia with an army of about 15,000 Szeklers and mercenaries and inflicted a crushing defeat on a Turkish force several times larger than his own. This was his first use of Hussite wagon forts with mounted guns, and also the first time that a sizable Ottoman army had suffered a major defeat in Europe. Hunyadi followed up this success in the autumn of 1443 with an ambitious foray into the Balkans, his so-called Long Campaign. Presumably he had calculated that the Turks' European army, following its usual practice, had already dispersed for the winter; and he also knew that the sultan was then in Asia Minor. Bypassing the fortresses garrisoned by Turkish troops, he penetrated far into Ottoman-held territory. His army moved southward to the Balkan Mountains before lack of provisions forced its return to Belgrade.

These successes persuaded the sultan to propose a ten years' armistice. Initially the Hungarians appeared to accept his terms; but not long afterward they resumed the war. Hunyadi's spectacular Long Campaign had raised the hopes of Christians that now the Turks might be expelled from Europe altogether. This impression was deceptive. Although the Hungarians had won every battle they fought and taken thousands of prisoners, all the major fortresses of Serbia except Belgrade still lay in Ottoman hands. Hunyadi had defeated only garrison troops, not the main Turkish army. Nonetheless, in autumn of 1444 the decision was taken to continue the campaign, under circumstances much less favorable than before. The expedition was hastily and carelessly planned, with the Christian forces notably smaller and less disciplined than in the previous year. However, the Venetians had promised to block the Straits with their ships to prevent the sultan from transferring his army from Asia into Europe. Led by Hunyadi and Vladislav, the young king of Hungary and Poland, the Christian army marched through Bulgaria to the town of Varna on the Black Sea. At Varna, Hunyadi received word that Sultan Murad II had already crossed over to Europe with his entire army. (Genoese aid to the Turks was suspected, although never proven.) In due course the sultan arrived at Varna with his army of between 60,000 and 100,000 men, as against only 19,000 to 20,000 for the Christians. Well aware of the odds they faced, Hunyadi and Vladislav nonetheless felt that honor forbade them to turn back without fighting. In the first stages of the battle the Hungarians held their own. Then panic broke out when Vladislav was killed and the Turks held his severed head high on a lance for everyone to see. The battle of Varna became a rout comparable to the disaster at Nicopolis nearly half a century earlier. Among those Hungarians who survived the slaughter, many subsequently died of disease or were murdered by local peasants, whom they had plundered not long before. Hunyadi was one of the few to make good his escape. For several years after this catastrophe, he limited his military operations to the defense of Hungary's frontiers.

The Ottoman and Hungarian military forces of the 15th century were actually well matched in quality and composition, although numerically the Turks were far superior. Hungary disposed of a formidable levy of light cavalry consisting of both bowmen and lancemen, as well as a heavy cavalry which had adopted Western arms and armor. Unlike the Serbs and Bulgarians, who put masses of tribal infantry into the field, the Hungarians had no native infantry at all and rarely hired mercenary foot soldiers. However, they sometimes allied themselves with countries possessing such forces, which permitted them to use a combination of cavalry and infantry tactics. The possibilities open to a mixed force of this kind were well illustrated at the second battle of Kosovo in 1448. Hunyadi, who was now the richest landowner in Hungary, had raised an army of 24,000 men from his private resources, including German and Bohemian infantrymen armed with handguns to supplement his Hungarian cavalry. Sultan Murad II met him at Kosovo, on the historic battleground where in 1389 the Turkish victory had sealed the doom of the Serbian Empire. This time the sultan brought onto the field a force of at least 60,000 men, including Janissaries with muskets and a contingent of artillery. Both sides placed infantry at the center of their line and cavalry on the wings, with the German and Bohemian infantry thus facing the Janissaries. In a two-day battle the Ottomans gradually gained the upper hand, but at the cost of heavy casualties on both sides. This second battle of Kosovo demonstrated conclusively that Hungary by itself was incapable of defeating the Turks in the open field. Although the Christian side lost, the high casualties in both armies did prove that infantry forces which held firm were capable of sustaining a long resistance to Ottoman arms. Contributing to Hunyadi's defeat was the fact that the Serbian despot George Branković remained neutral, fearing the loss of his principality (newly restored by the truce earlier that year) if he offended the Turks. Finally, the Albanians who were marching to Hunyadi's aid arrived too late.

The leader of the Albanians was the intrepid warrior Skanderbeg, who had surfaced a few years previously to take up his countrymen's struggle against the Turks. Born the son of a minor Albanian lord who had accepted Ottoman suzerainty, Skanderbeg as a young man was sent as a hostage to the sultan's court, where he adopted Islam and received a good military education. After serving the sultan faithfully in campaigns in both Europe and Asia, he became a high-ranking military commander; thus his Turkish title of "beg." The personal impulse for his revolt may have arisen when the Turks appropriated his family's hereditary lands in Albania. In any event, after the Ottoman defeat at Niš in

1443 (during Hunyadi's Long Campaign), he deserted the sultan's army together with about 300 followers. Arriving at Krujë in Albania, he publicly embraced Christianity and ordered the impalement of anyone (including captured Ottoman officials) who refused to follow his example. Then he reoccupied his family's former lands. The same year an assembly of Albanian lords met in the town of Lezhë, where it organized a league to fight the Turks and elected Skanderbeg as commander in chief.

From that time until his death in 1468, Skanderbeg was the Ottomans' most determined opponent. He harassed their troops intermittently with guerrilla tactics and occasionally won a major battle. In 1450 he held the fortress of Krujë against an army led by the sultan himself, thereby bringing his remote and mountainous land to the notice of a broader European public. However, Albania was a small and poor country ruled by semi-independent tribal lords. Skanderbeg himself was constantly harried by rivals at home, and his army was never large. His efforts to win assistance from Christian powers abroad proved largely fruitless. On the other hand, the rugged terrain of Albania offered numerous possibilities for defense. Skanderbeg's strength lay in defensive warfare in the inhospitable territory which he and his warriors knew intimately. For twenty-five years he successfully withstood the Turks from his mountain strongholds, at a period when virtually no one else in Europe seemed either able or willing to organize serious resistance.

Long after the Ottomans had created a major empire in the Balkans, the great metropolis of Constantinople still held out against them. Situated on the narrow straits between Europe and Asia and surrounded by sea on three sides, it enjoyed an unrivaled location. In earlier times the Greek fleet had always protected the city and supplied it by sea, although in the mid-15th century the government had become too impoverished to maintain a navy. The once-powerful Byzantine Empire by this time had been reduced to a small district surrounding the capital, although until now Constantinople's massive fortifications had rendered the city virtually impregnable. Even in the new age of gunpowder its walls constituted a serious obstacle to any would-be conqueror. Significantly, the young Sultan Mohammed II, who took the throne in 1451, was the first Ottoman ruler to show a serious interest in artillery. In his service was a brilliant Hungarian armaments maker who had recently produced improved models of cannon. This man had earlier offered his services to the Byzantine Emperor Constantine XI, but Constantine could neither afford the salary the technician demanded nor supply the required raw materials.

The final Ottoman assault on Constantinople in 1453 differed from all previous attempts in its use of cannon and by the fact that for the first time an attacker held command of the sea. Sultan Mohammed II had collected a large fleet, while the regular Turkish army numbered perhaps 80,000 men. (All contemporary estimates are unreliable.) By contrast, the entire Christian force at Constantinople

consisted of no more than 5,000 Greeks and 2,000 foreign mercenaries—a pitifully inadequate number despite the advantage naturally accruing to defenders
ensconced behind fortifications. No Western government paid serious attention
to the Byzantine emperor's desperate appeals for help. The prevailing assumption was that Constantinople, which had withstood so many attacks in the past,
would do so again. The Venetians and Genoese were ambivalent about offering
aid, since they traded very profitably with the Turks and had no wish to offend
them. The pope would not commit himself to act without some assurance that
the union of the Catholic and Orthodox churches, agreed upon at the Council
of Florence in 1439, had been put into effect. (However, the papacy's meager
assistance to the loyal Catholic Skanderbeg held little promise that such help,
even if given, would have sufficed to save the city.)

In 1453 the main Ottoman attack on Constantinople was expected along its
walls on the landward side. However, the dearth of Christian troops meant that
no defense in depth was possible. Only the outer fortifications and not the inner
ones could be manned with soldiers. The Genoese captain Giovanni Giustiniani,
a soldier reputedly skilled at defending walled cities, was appointed to the overall
command. The few cannons that the Byzantines possessed were of limited use,
since when fired they damaged the city walls. In any case, very little gunpowder
was available. On the other hand, the Turkish cannons were unwieldy, and so
difficult to keep on their platforms that the larger ones could be fired only seven
times a day. All the same, they did enormous damage. Men and women came
out from the city every night with boards and sacks of earth to plug the gaps
torn in the walls by each day's bombardment. Constantinople's position was far
from hopeless. In attacking a single gate the Turks' numerical superiority was
worthless, since it could not be brought to bear in a narrow space. On the whole
the Christian defenders had heavier armor than the Turks, enabling them to risk
their persons more boldly, while Giustiniani showed great energy and courage
as war leader.

Sultan Mohammed proposed to wear out the defenders by continuous bombardment until their provisions ran short. Nonetheless, after a siege of fifty-four
days, his final victory was almost accidental. A small group of Turks managed to
enter the city through a gate which had carelessly been left open. To eliminate
this exposed force would not ordinarily have been difficult, except that at this
very moment Giustiniani, the Christian commander, was being carried wounded
down to the harbor. Perceiving this, most of his soldiers concluded that the battle
was lost and sought to escape to the waiting ships. This left the Greek emperor
Constantine to fight on alone with his troops. Observing the sudden panic of the
defenders, the Turks charged again; and in the ensuing confusion the open gate
could not be closed. As additional Turks poured into the city the defense quickly
collapsed and the looting commenced. Islamic law prescribed that any city taken
by force must be delivered over to three days of pillage and the population
reduced to slavery. However, since Sultan Mohammed (thereafter known as

"the Conqueror") intended to make Constantinople his capital, he halted the destruction after the first day. In any case, by the evening of the victory very little booty remained to be taken. The Byzantine Empire, which had survived drastic territorial losses and numerous assaults on its splendid capital in the thousand years since the fall of Rome in the West, now passed out of existence.

For another half-century Christian Europe's resistance to the Turks held at the Danube line. In 1454 the sultan mounted a major campaign against Serbia and began to besiege its principal towns. Here an army led by John Hunyadi surprised and defeated him, burned Vidin, and laid waste the region of Niš. Hunyadi's final success came at the defense of Belgrade during the Turkish siege of 1456. This key fortress, ceded to Hungary by the Serbian despot in 1427, was favored by its splendid location on a cliff at the junction of the Danube and Sava rivers. The citadel was protected by five forts, three on the hill and two below on the Danube, with good towers, considerable artillery, and a harbor enclosed by a chain. Apprehension that the Turks might capture this strategic location inspired one final Christian crusade against the infidel. The Franciscan friar John Capistrano undertook a preaching tour in southern Hungary, enjoining his listeners to join Hunyadi's army. The peasants of that region, so often exposed to the attacks of Turkish irregulars, understood the danger and responded in considerable numbers. In the meantime the Turks had set up a naval block-ade around Belgrade, but Hunyadi broke through it. Although Turkish can-non did serious damage to the walls of the fortress, the principal Ottoman attack was pushed back with tremendous losses when Hunyadi ordered flam-mable material to be thrown onto the heads of the attackers in the trenches surrounding the citadel. Finally the Turks gave up, burned their war machines, and retreated by night, leaving most of their cannons behind. An epidemic of plague had broken out in the Ottoman camp which now claimed many Chris-tians victims as well, including Hunyadi himself within a month of his great victory.

Although Belgrade was thus spared a Turkish occupation, the same was not true of Serbia, which hitherto had maintained a precarious existence as an Otto-man vassal state. Despot George Branković had built himself a massive strong-hold at Smederevo on the Danube, finished in 1430 in record time. Overlooking the broad river some twenty-five miles east of Belgrade, it was a powerful fortress laid out in the shape of a triangle with twenty-four towers. At an earlier period it would have proved almost impregnable. However, thick walls and high towers no longer provided adequate defense against the new weapon of gunpowder. Smederevo's existence as an effective citadel was brief, since the Serbs were too weak to defend it against Turkish cannons. Initially captured by the sultan in 1439, it was restored to the Serbian Despotate in the peace negotiations following Hunyadi's Long Campaign of 1443. Its ultimate surrender to the Turks in 1459 brought the last remnant of Serbia's independence to an end. The defenders of the fortress offered no resistance, since Ottoman control of the surrounding countryside had rendered its long-term position hopeless.

For the next sixty-five years Belgrade remained the farthest outpost of Hungarian power in the Balkans, the key to the southern system of border defenses. Construction of this fortified line had began in the 1420s under the direction of King Sigismund's capable Italian mercenary captain, Pipo Scolari. The core of the system lay along the stretch of frontier most exposed to the attacks of Turkish garrison troops in the vassal states of Bulgaria and Serbia. The Hungarian king granted estates in this region to many South Slav lords whom the Turks had expelled from their former lands. Together with Serb peasants who had fled Ottoman rule, they played an important part in organizing its defense. Although warfare continued intermittently along the frontier, the position of Belgrade inhibited any direct Turkish approach into Transylvania from the south. For many years the Ottomans deflected their military pressure westward and eastward in a two-pronged movement toward the Adriatic and the north coast of the Black Sea. In a quick campaign in 1463 they overran Bosnia, where political disorder and long-standing resentment at Hungarian aggression had caused many of the inhabitants to prefer Turkish to Christian rule. From Bosnia outward they conducted major plundering expeditions into Dalmatia, Croatia, and Austria. Hercegovina, Bosnia's neighbor to the southeast, was the object of numerous Turkish attacks from 1465 until 1481, when it became part of the Ottoman Empire. The Hungarians now established additional fortifications on the Croatian border.

Dubrovnik, the richest and best-fortified town in Dalmatia, responded to the Ottoman danger by deepening its moats and tearing down all the buildings and trees near its gates. Surprisingly, these precautions proved to be unnecessary. The Turks evidently had no wish to undertake a long siege of this well-defended merchant town, which could be supplied indefinitely by sea. Croatia suffered from numerous Turkish raids during the 15th century, but the objective was plunder and captives rather than territory. On the opposite flank of the Ottoman advance, Transylvania also defended itself successfully. Sheltered by the two Romanian principalities and by the Carpathian Mountains, this Hungarian province had no regular system of defensive works on its eastern borders except for the royal fortresses guarding the passes through the mountains and a few well-fortified Saxon towns like Braşov and Sibiu. In 1479 the Turks mounted a major campaign against Transylvania through Walachia and the Carpathian passes. Near Alba Iulia a Hungarian force overtook the retreating Ottoman army laden with booty, and defeated it in a particularly bloody battle.

By the mid-15th century lack of naval power no longer hindered the Turks' military operations, although previously this had been their principal weakness. The first Ottoman warships were built in the reign of Sultan Murad II (r. 1421–51). His successor Mohammed the Conqueror (r. 1451–81) enlisted the help of Genoese sailors and navigators from Galata, the "foreign" suburb of Istanbul, who aided him in building war galleys. The Ottoman navy played an important part in the invasion of Serbia in the 1450s. For the siege of Belgrade in 1456, Sultan Mohammed forced the local Christian population to construct a hundred boats outfitted with guns on the Morava tributary of the Danube. However, even he considered a fleet primarily as a form of transport, not as an independent striking force. No naval battles of any significance were fought during his reign, although toward its close he possessed approximately 500 large vessels, including many war galleys. To capture the Black Sea ports of Kilia and Cetatea Alba from the Moldavians in 1484, his successor Bayezid II employed about a hundred ships to transport his troops, together with siege machines, munitions, and other provisions. No enemy ships hindered their passage; and with the capture of these two ports, the Black Sea became an Ottoman lake.

In the Adriatic Sea the Ottoman navy was held in check by Venice, which saw to it that the sea routes remained open for its maritime traffic. The Venetians' dependence on overseas trade made them ambitious to control as much as possible of the eastern Adriatic coast. In the 15th century they succeeded in dominating many of the offshore islands together with some Dalmatian towns. By contrast, the Ottomans never gained control of more than a few isolated places in Dalmatia, despite their occupation of the hinterland. They held fragments of the coast—the town of Skradin near Šibenik, the mouth of the Neretva River, and the area around the Bay of Kotor—but Venetian fortresses, artillery emplacements, and ships prevented their access to the open sea.

The two Romanian principalities of Walachia and Moldavia stood fully exposed to Turkish incursions in the second half of the 15th century. Their populations were obliged to be almost constantly at war, while the armed forces which their leaders could muster were scarcely equal to the magnitude of this struggle. In 1461–62 the Turks carried out a major invasion of Walachia. Calling upon every able-bodied male in the country to join his army, Voivode Vlad III collected between 22,000 and 30,000 men. The Turks opposed him with about 60,000 effectives and 20,000 auxiliaries. Unable to risk an open battle with this disparity in numbers, Vlad conducted strategic retreats, a scorched earth policy, and guerrilla attacks. In this fashion he was able to mount repeated strikes against Turkish garrisons on both banks of the Danube. Vlad's most famous exploit occurred early in the winter of 1462, when he crossed the Danube with a large army and carried out a surprise night attack on the sultan's own camp. The result was a bloody massacre, which removed the Ottoman threat to the Walachian capital of Tîrgovişte and forced the Turks to retreat.

Vlad III was doubtless an intrepid fighter against the Turks, and as such was remembered in Romanian folklore. His reputation abroad was very different, owing to his unique contribution to the horrors of warfare. As his cognomen "the Impaler" testifies, he made a practice of killing his opponents by having sharp stakes driven through their vital organs. While he was hardly the inventor of this form of torture, he did make a point of exhibiting the results in full public view in order better to intimidate his enemies. In one such demonstration, probably in 1459, he had the impaled corpses of about 500 of his murdered boyar opponents displayed outside his palace and beyond the walls of his capital. In 1462, shortly after his successful night attack on the Ottoman camp, the Turks allegedly discovered more than 20,000 impaled and rotting carcasses in a gorge just outside of Tîrgovişte. Numerous horror stories were told of Vlad's extravagant savagery, for example that he cut up the bodies of captured Turks with his own hands; or that while confined to a Hungarian jail he could not resist trapping and dismembering the rats in his cell. Whatever the truth of such tales, his reputation served to make him the prototype for the legendary vampire Dracula in European folklore.

The outstanding Romanian champion in the anti-Ottoman wars was Stephen the Great, voivode of Moldavia (r. 1457–1504). Stephen's repeated successes in resisting the Turks proved that lightly armed infantry, if well led, could be surprisingly effective even against Ottoman heavy cavalry. His troops used horses only for transport to and from the battlefield to enhance their mobility, while in actual combat they fought on foot. The Turks were his most dangerous opponent, although he also fought the Hungarians, Poles, and Tatars, resisting as long as possible the repeated attempts of his more powerful neighbors to reduce him to vassalage. When he refused to pay the Ottoman tribute in 1474, this was in effect a declaration of war, and the sultan responded by invading Moldavia. With much inferior forces Stephen surprised the enemy in January 1475 near the town of Vaslui and won a major victory. However, the Ottoman army returned in 1476, reinforced by an attack on Moldavia from the north by the Tatars of the Crimea. While unable to avoid defeat himself, Stephen nonetheless prevented the Tatars from effecting a junction with the Turks; and the sultan failed to capture a single Moldavian fortress.

The Turks' dominant position around the Black Sea created heavy pressure on the two fortified coastal towns that remained in Moldavian hands: Kilia on one of the Danube's northern mouths, and Cetatea Alba on the right bank of the Dniester. Both places depended for their prosperity on maritime trade; and by 1475 they were the only Black Sea ports that had not yet submitted to Ottoman domination. Commerce was their lifeline; and their merchants needed Turkish permission to trade along the Black Sea littoral. Thus the hostilities between Stephen the Great and the Ottomans greatly complicated the towns' situation. In 1484 a large Turkish army and fleet returned to Moldavia, again in conjunction with the Crimean Tatars. Both Kilia and Cetatea at that time possessed ample munitions and provisions; and neither was weak in defenses. Cetatea's stone walls, for example, were over fifteen feet thick and strengthened with towers, while its moat was 35 or 40 feet wide, over 7 feet deep, and filled with water from the Danube. Nonetheless in 1484 both towns opened their gates to the Turks after a short siege. Evidently the local merchants had decided that their future prosperity depended on joining the Ottoman Empire.

For Moldavia, however, this loss had the disastrous effect of cutting its links with the sea.

Despite this defeat, Stephen the Great's overall record of success was remarkable, given the odds against him. Aside from his exceptionally long reign and his own military and political skill, he could credit the fact that Moldavia, like its Walachian neighbor, called to arms a very large proportion of its total population. This so-called great army, summoned only in times of extreme danger, included men of every social class. Walachia's armed forces in the 15th century contained 30,000 to 40,000 men in wartime—a very large number for a country with only about half a million people. Stephen the Great's army was even larger—50,000 to 60,000 men out of Moldavia's total population of perhaps a quarter million. Stephen required every man capable of bearing arms to serve in the army when called upon; and peasants knew that they were defending their own lands. Only this mass mobilization can explain how a small state like Moldavia could hold off the mighty Ottoman war machine as well as it did. Neither of the two Romanian principalities could afford to exempt any significant number of its inhabitants from military service or from the taxation which financed the hiring of mercenaries. Also important was the fact that Walachia and Moldavia in the 15th century contained few serfs, but many free landholding peasants. Since only a small part of the army consisted of boyars with personal armed followings, the ruler exercised considerable direct authority over his troops.

Meanwhile the military position of Hungary continued to deteriorate. King Matthias had paid slight attention to his southern frontier; but at least during his reign the southern border defenses were adequately maintained. However, the Hungarian nobility resented his authoritarian rule; and in 1498–1500 after his death the Diet voted to divide the war tax (which it had reluctantly retained) between the nobility and the king. This new measure listed the names of a few dozen magnates who were required to appear with a contingent of armed men in the king's camp, and decreed that the garrison troops on the southern frontier would be financed from the king's share of the war tax. In effect this legalized the right of the magnates to maintain private armies. It also partly reconstituted the old banderia system, which the Diet of Timişoara had abandoned in 1397; and it complicated the process of calling up the armed forces. However, Hungary's tax base continued to shrink, largely because of the continual Turkish depredations in the borderlands. Even when the country was officially at peace, irregular warfare continued along the long southern frontier. By 1510 most of the Hungarian border fortresses stood in the midst of virtually uninhabited territory and had to be supplied with food and ammunition by regular military expeditions. When the Ottoman Sultan Suleiman I appeared in 1521 with a large army just outside of Belgrade, the fortress surrendered after a siege of two months. Before the Hungarian army could be mustered, this crucial position had already fallen.

The loss of Belgrade removed the last major obstacle to a Turkish thrust at the heart of Hungary. On August 29, 1526, Suleiman's troops faced a Hungarian force which was staggeringly inferior in numbers, comprising no more than 50,000 to 60,000 men against about 150,000 for the Ottomans. The two armies clashed near Mohács, not far from where the Drava River meets the Danube. After a promising initial charge by the Hungarian cavalry and infantry, the Ottomans annihilated the small Hungarian army in a single afternoon; and the king drowned in flight. This battle marked the end of Hungary as an independent state. The Turks marched northward along the Danube to Buda and Pest, which they first plundered and then burned. They also moved south into Croatia and Slavonia, capturing most of the fortresses still in Hungarian hands. These successes marked their last permanent territorial acquisitions in Europe, although in 1529 and 1683 they went on to besiege Vienna. Ottoman hegemony in Europe now extended over most of the territories once held by Byzantium at the height of its power. Thus nearly a thousand years after Justinian's attempt to restore the Roman Empire, Constantinople (now Istanbul) had become the capital of another great imperial state, extending outward to encompass vast territories in both Europe and Asia.

CHAPTER 9

Governments

---

*T*he most basic role of a central government in the Middle Ages was simply to hold the state together, protecting the territory and preventing regional or local authorities from becoming too autonomous. An effective monarch needed his own military force as well as the means to persuade or coerce others to fight for him. Centralization demanded permanent officials to oversee the collection of taxes, hear court cases, and enforce a uniform law throughout the land. The ancient Roman Empire had possessed all of these characteristics, and its Byzantine successor continued to do so until its demise in 1453. Not surprisingly, the newly formed states of East Central Europe all imitated to some extent the structure of the old Roman or Byzantine officialdom. Roman models were transmitted indirectly to Bohemia, Hungary, and Poland by the example of the medieval German (later called Holy Roman) Empire, which itself drew heavily upon classical Roman traditions. Even more obviously, the Byzantine government throughout the medieval era interacted with (and sometimes ruled) the lands of the Balkan Peninsula.

The development of political centralization was a gradual process. Prior to the formation of organized states in East Central Europe, the heads of clans (small units allegedly based on blood ties) and tribes (larger organizations of multiple clans) exercised a rudimentary governmental authority. Power was highly decentralized, although weaker tribes often acknowledged the hegemony of stronger ones. In the 6th and 7th centuries the Slavic chiefs who migrated with their peoples into East Central Europe possessed no far-reaching powers. Leadership of a tribe (for none of these chiefs can quite be called kings) typically rested with a single family; yet the tribal head was essentially only the first among equals, holding limited powers. An assembly of the most eminent men of the tribe made all important decisions. When the Bulgars and Magyars entered Central Europe, they were similarly organized into tribal units linked by the authority of a chief or khan. Unlike the Slavs, they were pastoral peoples practicing agriculture in only a limited way. However, they were better organized for war than the Slavs, which meant that their leaders occupied a more exalted position.

Among the Slavs as well as the Bulgars or Magyars, the head of a tribe was a military chief, the leader of warriors bound to him by personal ties of kinship and loyalty. His position was often enhanced by real or fictitious descent from an illustrious ancestor and by the notion that he ruled through the favor of God. However, it was his status as war leader which gave him authority over his fellows. Success in battle, which satisfied his military retinue by letting them enrich themselves with plunder, naturally increased his prestige. Gradually these chiefs of war bands evolved into the heads of territorial units. Relationships which originally were personal in nature developed into an authority based on supremacy over a territory, although personal loyalty remained a significant factor in the chief's dominance. Even after the association of tribes had become a better organized political unit, the strength of the union depended to a dangerous degree on the sovereign's personal qualities. Under a weak monarch, especially a succession of weak ones, a rudimentary state could disintegrate altogether, either to be conquered by outsiders or simply to dissolve into its component parts. The abstraction which in modern times is called a "state"—namely, a territory and people under a continuous government—was a concept foreign to the Middle Ages. The medieval mind was accustomed to thinking in the more human and concrete framework of loyalty to the person of a monarch.

Why monarchs were obeyed, and how a particular family or dynasty came to be regarded as sole possessor of the right to rule, are matters lost in the obscurity of unwritten prehistory. Monarchical authority was everywhere considered "natural," no doubt on the analogy of the father's dominance over the family. The monarch himself was believed to possess a special charisma in the form of extraordinary (sometimes more than human) personal qualities and a force of attraction derived from his membership in the recognized ruling house. This dynastic idea was an important component of power throughout all of medieval East Central Europe. However, in no country did a monarch's title and pedigree suffice to make people obey him. Military force was essential, so that many rulers in the early medieval age surrounded themselves with a group of experienced fighting men. In Poland this was the druzhina (i.e., "companions"); in Hungary it was a contingent of practiced horsemen fighting in the style of the steppes, who accompanied the leader on plundering expeditions and fought with him against his enemies. Bonds of personal loyalty were strong between the monarch and his warrior retinue; but fighting men still needed to be fed and equipped; and they expected rewards for their services. Naturally these royal war bands sought to profit from the booty taken on campaigns and from the tribute paid by neighboring princes as the price of being left in peace.

When the Bulgar steppe dwellers moved into the southeastern Balkans about 680, their military class subjugated the agricultural Slavic peoples already living there. For several generations afterward the Bulgar and Slavic clans lived essentially separate lives, each following its traditional customs. This autonomy of the parts was a pattern typical of the seminomadic confederations of the steppe. The Bulgar khan held supreme civil, military, and judicial power, but internally the various tribes managed their own affairs. The khan's autocracy was limited by ancestral custom and his need to conciliate the various clan chiefs. Then in about the middle of the 9th century the Bulgar leadership introduced a greater degree of centralization by organizing its territory into nine counties and three larger "lands." In the center lay the so-called Inner Region, a core area lying between the Danube and the Balkan (Stara Planina) Mountains, which continued to exist as a distinct geographical unit until eastern Bulgaria fell to the Byzantines in 976.

The steppe dwellers known to Europe as Magyars or Hungarians invaded Central Europe in 895–96 as a confederation of tribes. In the manner of other peoples of similar background like the Khazars and Avars, they were ruled by a triumvirate of chiefs who exercised supreme authority. These chiefs also commanded the strongest military retinues, with which they forced the component tribes and clans of the alliance to pay tribute and provide fighting men upon demand. At first each tribe held all its territory in common. Then gradually the heads of the tribes and clans became local aristocrats who disregarded the former land boundaries in the attempt to expand their power. The chiefs also established centers for specific productive purposes (e.g., fishing, hunting, artisan work); and the people who lived in such settlements tended to lose their tribal consciousness. The ruthless centralization policy carried out by Duke Géza (r. 972–97) made him the effective founder of the Hungarian Árpád monarchy. By fighting the tribal leaders who opposed him, Géza succeeded in appropriating much of their territory and installing his own appointees in the defeated tribes' strongholds. His son, King Stephen I, continued this policy. Stephen converted the tribal and clan lands into districts which later became the basic units of Hungarian administration—the counties—each headed by an official called an ispán (i.e., "count"). By the end of his reign he had brought two-thirds of Hungary's population under his direct authority.

A comparatively high degree of centralization for so early a period prevailed in both Poland and Hungary during the first two centuries of their existence as states, despite the limitations of abysmally poor communications and the almost total lack of a state bureaucracy. The monarch's retinue had a personal interest in promoting his authority, since the military campaigns which he led resulted in the capture of booty and slaves to be sold for profit. Moreover, both Hungary and Poland were in the process of expansion—likewise a profitable situation, since additional potential tribute payers became subject to the sovereign's authority. Such circumstances ceased to exist when a more effective armed resistance by neighboring peoples terminated the era of easy expansion and plunder. At the economic level prevailing in the early Middle Ages, a monarch was unable to support an armed following from his own resources alone. Once the possibilities for plunder had diminished, his treasure quickly became exhausted. The warriors began to settle down on the land and went to war less often.

With plunder eliminated as a major form of income, and commerce a distinctly minor affair in the early medieval period, a ruler's principal source of wealth was land. All land which was not specifically the property of either the Church, the tribes, the clans, or particular individuals belonged in theory to the sovereign. Since East Central Europe was very sparsely populated in the 10th-12th centuries, this meant an enormous expanse of territory. The monarchs granted tracts of land to their military followers, who could then equip themselves for warfare out of their own resources. In this way the members of the retinue became private landholders, residing not in the ruler's immediate vicinity but on scattered estates throughout the countryside. Distance from the royal court inevitably made them less dependent on the sovereign and less inclined to obey him. Nonetheless, he had no other means of providing himself with a military force. Most parts of medieval East Central Europe never experienced a feudal system of the type prevailing in France or England, where land was often granted as fiefs (i.e., in exchange for a vassal's promise to perform military service whenever summoned). This meant that landholding was not ordinarily linked to a military obligation in any formal or legal way, since in principle, if not always in practice, all able-bodied men owed this service to their sovereign. In most cases a landholder did not perform a ceremony of vassalage to a superior lord or swear a formal oath of loyalty. Nonetheless the prospect of a gift of land as a reward for faithful war service was the principal method by which a monarch attracted the loyalty of subordinates. The extent of a ruler's personal authority depended largely upon the extent of his estates.

Early medieval Croatia provides one example of a country in which the rulers were unable to establish a strong territorial base. Even its most powerful monarch, Tomislav (r. 910–ca. 928), possessed only the ancestral estates of his house together with certain lands acquired through forfeiture. Not surprisingly, monarchy in Croatia never became a powerful institution. The two Romanian principalities of Walachia and Moldavia, which attained statehood only in the 14th century, provide an even more striking (and better attested) case of the weakness of monarchs devoid of extensive personal landholdings. Since the Romanian rulers were land poor, they lacked the single most important means of attracting support from the nobility. Documents from Walachia record that only four of its numerous (and usually short-lived) medieval sovereigns held land or possessed villages, either before or after taking the throne—an astoundingly small number, even assuming that some relevant evidence is missing. Frequent changes on the throne and the constant appearance of pretenders with foreign support weakened the principalities politically, while wars of succession crippled them militarily. To a considerable extent, medieval Walachia and Moldavia were pawns of their more powerful neighbors.

Precisely the opposite situation prevailed in Hungary. The invading Magyars had the good fortune to settle in a sparsely populated area in which large uninhabited zones separated the areas of tribal settlement. Early in the 11th century, King Stephen I took possession of these essentially empty regions in the name of the crown. By thus creating a giant royal demesne without infringing on the possessions of the tribes and clans, he established the basis for the economic power of the monarchy. Similarly in early medieval Bohemia, the sovereign owned extensive tracts of uncultivated ground which provided the foundation for state power. In Poland likewise the monarch was entitled to treat all conquered territory as his own. Everywhere in East Central Europe in the early period of state formation, royal lands supplied the indispensable basis for centralized government. Their gradual privatization in the 13th century, by weak or spendthrift rulers seeking political support or money, greatly enhanced the position of the great landed magnates and led to a crisis in royal authority. In the 14th century the rise to power of new dynasties in Bohemia and Hungary partly reversed this situation. The Luxemburg kings possessed important properties elsewhere in Europe which added to their authority in Bohemia, while in Hungary the first Angevin monarch, Charles Robert, confiscated enormous landed wealth from his enemies in the process of fighting his way to the throne.

Inasmuch as political power was closely linked to the influence of religion, support from the established Church was indispensable to a ruler. The Church needed the state to protect its various activities, just as the state needed the Church to provide divine justification for the monarch's exalted position. Moreover, since few persons in medieval Europe except clerics could read and write, churchmen were essential collaborators in the business of government. Whenever written documents were required, men of clerical status composed them and wrote them out. The sovereign was expected to enrich the Church with his gifts; and if he was also noted for personal piety, this enhanced his reputation and authority in the country. High-ranking churchmen participated in state affairs on the same basis as powerful aristocrats, and indeed were themselves often members of noble families. Clerics served as royal diplomats and as officials in the state chancellery. Frequently they interfered with decisive effect in politics. The pope competed with secular monarchs for the right to appoint high ecclesiastical dignitaries. Nor did he hesitate to intervene in the internal affairs of a country where he felt that the interests of the Church were at stake, for example by supporting the Teutonic Knights in Prussia or the claims of the Angevin dynasty of Naples to rule Hungary.

Once a state had been formed and the clans and tribes had forfeited their autonomy (although usually not their identity), the supreme ruler in principle enjoyed enormous authority. In theory his power was unlimited, despite the fact that some of his leading men might in fact exert enormous influence. The sovereign had the sole right to appoint or remove officials, grant land to anyone he chose, exercise final judicial authority, and make war and peace. In Bohemia, for instance, the position of the ruling duke was legally unlimited prior to the 13th century. His right to demand military service from all the able-bodied men of the nation was unquestioned; and the country's most powerful men had not yet become semi-independent landed proprietors. The Bohemian duke was the source of law as well as its executor. He exacted various labor services and taxes from his subjects, both in money and in kind. He could establish new taxes by decree, in addition to tolls, customs, and market fees. He alone possessed the privilege of coining money. Although a vassal of the German emperor until the mid-14th century, the duke of Bohemia (who began to be called "king" only in the late 12th century) was fully independent in internal matters. This patriarchal absolutism was possible in the 11th and 12th centuries because as yet the Bohemian landed nobility was too weak to restrain the sovereign's power. Still in the future lay the formation of a national assembly or diet through which the noble class could set limits to monarchical authority.

The king of Hungary in the 11th and 12th centuries was perhaps the most autocratic sovereign in Europe. Although necessarily limited in power by the primitive technology and undeveloped organizational forms of the period, he stood far above his countrymen in the extent of his authority. He ruled through officials called "counts" whom he appointed to wield administrative and judicial authority in the counties. All able-bodied men in Hungary were required to serve in the royal army, whether they were landholders or not. No fief law prescribed that land was held on condition of military service. The material basis of the king's power was his personal wealth—the fact that until the 13th century his landed estates were far larger than anyone else's in Hungary. All territory lying in the interstices between counties or along the frontier, much of it sparsely populated or uninhabited, ranked as royal property. The German chronicler Otto of Freising, writing in about the year 1150, marveled that the Hungarian king could judge his nobles without benefit of a jury; that he monopolized the right of coinage; and that even a low-born royal official could imprison a powerful lord. Compared to the decentralized German Empire, where regional authorities generally governed without reference to the emperor, all this was quite remarkable.

Despite their recognized supremacy, few medieval monarchs could consider themselves immune from revolts instigated by their own leading men. In most cases the rebel nobles sought merely redress of grievances, but occasionally they aimed at replacing the occupant of the throne. Serious uprisings occurred in both Hungary and Poland in the 11th century, stimulated in part by antagonism toward the growing power of the state and the imposition of Christianity. The Poles, for example, expelled one monarch in 1035 and another in 1078. In Hungary a pagan uprising followed the death of King Stephen I; and throughout the 11th century, opponents of the Hungarian royal house allied themselves with the pagan Cuman and Iazyg tribes residing beyond Hungary's eastern frontier. After Bulgaria was reincorporated into the Byzantine Empire in 1018, the Bulgars twice mounted a serious challenge to Byzantine authority. The first such rebellion broke out in 1040, led by a scion of the old Bulgar dynasty, Peter Delyan. The second occurred in 1072–73, when a group of Bulgar nobles sought to place a Serbian prince on the throne. Eventually in 1185–86 the brothers Peter and John (Ivan) Asen led a successful revolt against Byzantine hegemony, resulting in the reestablishment of independent Bulgaria. Somewhat different in motive was the Bulgar rebellion of the 1270s led by the swineherd Ivailo. Inspired by mystic visions, Ivailo claimed that God had destined him to save Bulgaria from the Tatar hordes which were then devastating the country. After several victories over these intruders he defeated the forces of the legitimate, but ineffective tsar; and for a time most of Bulgaria submitted to his authority. Ivailo married the widowed queen, was briefly recognized as tsar himself, and defeated two Byzantine armies sent to Bulgaria in support of a pretender. Ultimately he was assassinated at the instigation of his old enemy, the Tatar khan.

The Croats apparently never revolted against Hungarian overlordship, presumably because their nobility was content with its semi-autonomous status under the terms of Croatia's union with Hungary. On the other hand, the Bosnians more than once resisted with violence the claims of Hungary to suzerainty over their country. Bosnian nobles rebelled in 1366 against their own King Tvrtko, who had returned from exile and reestablished himself in power with Hungarian aid. The Hungarian King Matthias faced at least two major internal rebellions. One occurred in 1467 in Transylvania, prompted by the excessive taxation required to finance his wars; it was separatist in motive. In 1471 he defeated a more serious conspiracy led by his closest advisers, who were disturbed by his growing power, his counselors drawn from the lesser nobility or town class, and his neglect of the Turkish danger. Matthias stifled both revolts by a combination of diplomacy and force. In rare cases the nobility of a country kidnapped the sovereign in order to realize some objective. In 1386, for example, Croatian lords who supported a rival candidate for the throne captured Queen Maria and killed her mother. Rebellious Bohemian lords in 1394 imprisoned King Wenceslas IV for over two months, during which time they also took over the royal chancellery. Ten years later they staged a repeat performance. A group of Hungarian oligarchs imprisoned King Sigismund of Hungary in 1401 until he agreed to a marriage alliance with one of their number. Occasionally the right to rebel even acquired a legal basis. The Hungarian Golden Bull, granted by King Andrew II in 1222, expressly conceded the right of nobles to resist the monarch if he broke the promises contained in that document. This dangerous provision was somewhat modified in a revision of the Bull issued in 1231; but the precedent remained. In Poland beginning in 1434 each king upon accession to the throne was required to confirm the rights of all his subjects in a sworn document which specifically authorized the nobility to renounce obedience to him if he violated his promises.

The Ottoman Empire, firmly entrenched in the Balkans by the 15th century, was tightly enough organized to be virtually immune to rebellion. Prior to the year 1500 only the Albanians ever rose up against it, led by the famous Skanderbeg. Even they could merely harass the Ottoman forces, not expel them from the country, despite the advantage of Albania's exceptionally inhospitable terrain. Usually when the Turks conquered a territory they either eliminated or coopted the native nobility, thus depriving the population of its natural leaders. They effectively controlled even outlying regions of their empire, having at their command the resources of an enormous land mass in both Europe and Asia. Although civil war (1402–13) among the three sons of Sultan Bayezid I presented the Ottoman subject peoples with an obvious occasion for revolt, none seized the opportunity to do so. Nor did the Turks' immediate enemies—Hungary, Serbia, and Byzantium—encourage such action. On the contrary, Serbs and Hungarians joined one of the contestants, the future Sultan Mohammed I, for the final battle against his brother.

Many rulers of medieval East Central Europe lacked a permanent capital city, but instead traveled incessantly among their various domains. For example, the king of independent Croatia shuffled constantly between one and another of his various fortresses. The rulers of Serbia in the 13th and 14th centuries owned about twenty royal residences, enabling them to reside in the mountains in summer and in the warmer valleys in winter. In the early days of the Ottoman Empire the capital was wherever the sultan pitched his tent. The sultan usually remained with his army in the field, traveling with an enormous retinue that included officials, archives, and the state treasury. After the conquest of Adrianople (Edirne) in Thrace, probably in 1369, the Turks transferred their center of operations to Europe. The magnificent Byzantine capital of Constantinople on the Bosphorus resisted their attacks until 1453, when it became the Ottoman capital of Istanbul. Even the Holy Roman (i.e., German) Empire, despite its grandiloquent title, never acquired a fixed capital in all its centuries of existence. The emperor remained constantly on the move, residing in various castles belonging either to him or to the Church.

In some instances a capital city was established early in a country's history but later was moved elsewhere, usually to conform to a change in the state's center of gravity. The first two Polish capitals stood in the western province of Great Poland, first at Poznań and then at Gniezno. The latter town remained the seat of the Polish archbishopric, but early in the 12th century the government moved south to Cracow, where it remained for five centuries. At that period the present Polish capital of Warsaw was a minor outpost in the remote and sparsely settled northern province of Mazovia. The Teutonic Knights, who maintained several hundred monastic houses throughout Europe, kept their capital at Venice until 1309, when the grand master moved to Malbork in Prussia to be closer to the Order's main theater of operations. In Hungary both the royal court and the residence of the primate were originally at Esztergom, near where the Danube makes its 90-degree turn southward. However, the coronation city of the kings was Székesfehérvár, located in the center of the ruling dynasty's private domains on the pilgrimage route to Jerusalem. In 1323, King Charles Robert established his capital at Visegrád, a few miles north of Buda on a steep cliff overlooking the Danube. Buda (across the Danube from Pest) was often used for ceremonial purposes during the 14th century, though its full establishment as a capital was delayed until Sigismund built a palace there in the early 15th century. Visegrád was not abandoned entirely, but in time was allowed to decay.

In Bulgaria, Preslav replaced Pliska as capital in 893, both in order to escape Pliska's pagan associations and because the country had expanded southward. The Second Bulgarian Empire had its capital at Tirnovo, where the hereditary lands of the ruling Asen dynasty were situated. When the state split into two parts, Vidin on the Danube became the capital of the western part. Walachia knew four different capitals prior to 1500, each one farther south than its predecessor. The first two, Cîmpulung and Curtea-de-Argeş, were located for security reasons in the western mountains. In 1385 the capital was moved to Tîrgovişte, 45 miles northwest of Bucharest, a town too exposed to Turkish raids to be of much consequence at the time. Bucharest functioned after the mid-15th century as the winter capital (Ottoman campaigns normally ended in October). It became sole capital in the 17th century after the Turks destroyed Tîrgovişte. The Serbian state developed in the 12th century around the town of Raška in what is now southern Serbia, but Turkish pressure eventually rendered this location untenable. After the Serbs' defeat at the battle of Kosovo in 1389, Belgrade served briefly as capital of the much reduced despotate, thus completing Serbia's transformation from an Adriatic into a Danubian state. Uniquely for East Central Europe, Bohemia never had any capital other than Prague.

Even after a permanent capital had been established, the sovereign frequently went on tour. Because no real administrative apparatus existed in the early medieval period, the royal court could easily be moved. The government was located wherever the ruler happened to be. In that age of primitive communications, such royal peregrinations were the best possible means of keeping in touch with the leading men of the realm. The personal ties created in this fashion played an important role in holding the state together. Royal processions also permitted ordinary people to view their monarch in the flesh, magnificently attired and accompanied by a splendid retinue. Displays of this type promoted loyalty by exposing the public to the reality of the sovereign's presence. In any event, the year-round maintenance of a royal court, which included hundreds of people and horses, would have constituted an undue burden on any district. It was easier to move the court to the supplies than the supplies to the court.

In some parts of East Central Europe the monarch's crown came to be regarded as the symbol and embodiment of the realm. This attachment to a semisacred material object marked a transition stage between the purely personal loyalties common to tribal societies and the more abstract concept of a political unit independent of the sovereign's person. The leading men of the country (the nobility) were described as "members of the crown," natural representatives of the nation as a whole. In its symbolic aspect, the "crown of the Bohemian realm," like the "crown of Saint Stephen" in Hungary, assumed the status of a legal personality superior to both the king and the assembly of the nobility. Similarly, the expression "crown of the Polish kingdom" signified the entire Polish realm as distinct from the monarch himself. The crown symbolized the country as an independent entity, relegating to second place the older patrimonial notion of the state as property of the royal house. For Poles the phrase "crown of the kingdom" eventually came to mean all the territory they regarded as historically theirs, including lands which did not then belong to the Polish state. However, the importance of a particular royal crown as physical object was carried to greatest lengths in Hungary. Beginning in 1290 with the accession of Andrew III, whose claim to the throne was doubtful, possession of the crown was closely linked to the status of the monarch as legitimate ruler. The "Holy Crown of Saint Stephen" was believed to incorporate the whole power of the state and constitute the source of its law. Coronation with this diadem was essential in giving a Hungarian sovereign the legal right to rule. The Hungarian law code of 1514, known as the Tripartitum, recognized no distinction between the crown as embodiment of the realm and as material object. In Serbia the crown of King Stephen "the First-Crowned" held a similar position. Accordingly, Sigismund of Hungary was prevented from staging a formal coronation for himself as king of Serbia and Bosnia because the Serbian crown was not in his custody.

Byzantine government in the Balkan Peninsula was quite different from the rudimentary political structures farther north. Byzantium was a highly developed, centralized state run by officials who were usually well-educated laymen rather than churchmen. However, Byzantine administration became increasingly militarized after the 7th century. Whereas under the older Roman system a clear line had been drawn between military and civilian functions, now the highest unit of provincial government became the theme, or military district, with a strategos, or general, as governor. Lesser territorial units were dominated by the military establishment even if they did not officially rank as themes, although most were converted to theme status by the end of the 9th century. This system came to dominate the Byzantine-held provinces of southeastern Europe. Nonetheless, the towns of the Dalmatian theme remained largely autonomous, merely paying a small tribute in gold to the strategos as a symbolic recognition of Byzantine overlordship. Durrës in Albania, the center of another theme, was the principal Byzantine port on the Adriatic and the base for a considerable Greek fleet. Along the Black Sea coast the Paristrion theme, established in 971, included northeastern Bulgaria and Dobrudja as far as the mouths of the Danube. Extending at times even north of the river, Paristrion served as a bulwark against the nomads of the steppes. Bulgaria after the Byzantine reconquest of 1018 was likewise divided into themes and districts in which native Bulgars were allowed to play only minor roles. Greek garrisons were established in key towns, and the Byzantine tax system was introduced.

Another highly centralized state was Prussia,* founded in 1230 by the Teutonic Order of Knights. Primarily a charitable organization elsewhere in Europe, the Order in Prussia was above all military in character, viewing its task as the extirpation of paganism and winning the lands on the southern shore of the Baltic Sea for Christianity. In 1234 the pope granted the Order complete rule over Prussia, where it eventually acquired direct ownership over two-thirds of the land area, either by conquest or by purchase. The houses of the Teutonic Order in Prussia—numbering about a hundred by the year 1400—were fortified centers of defense and administration, in which a strict monastic regime prevailed. The brothers of the Order held all public offices in the state, receiving only a modest maintenance allowance for their services. The power of the elected grand master approached that of an absolute monarch, although he ruled in conjunction with a council of commanders. He possessed the exclusive right to make war, conduct foreign policy, collect taxes, and exercise high justice. In many respects the Knights' regime in Prussia resembled the government of Sicily, where early in the 13th century Emperor Frederick II had introduced the most modern and efficient administrative system of his time. Since the Teutonic Order included clerics as well as military men, its members on average easily surpassed the contemporary European standard for education and competence. Prussia was divided into districts with a well-organized financial system that supplied the state with a regular income and enforced a single monetary standard. Although the Order lost West Prussia (Pomerania) to Poland in the Thirteen Years' War (1454–66), it continued to rule the remainder of the country until Prussia was transformed into a secular state in 1525 in response to the Protestant Reformation.

The Ottoman Empire was likewise a highly centralized state, although it origi-nated in the late 13th century as something quite different—a rude frontier princi-pality on the eastern edge of the Byzantine Empire, ruled by tribal warriors. Mili-tary success led to enormous territorial expansion, until eventually the Ottomans governed a vast multinational empire which incorporated most of the former Byzantine lands. However, the degree to which the Ottoman administrative system was indebted to Byzantine precedent is a matter of dispute, inevitably colored by the nationalistic impulses of modern Greeks and Turks. Without doubt many non-Turks held government posts in this empire. Christian officials of the former Byzantine and Balkan states often found posts in its governing apparatus, both on the local and the imperial level. Greeks handled finance and Jews commerce, while Italians, Greeks, and Catalans manned the fleet and Germans the artillery. Nonetheless, Muslims (sometimes quite recent converts) constituted the ruling class.

---

* "Prussia" as ruled by the Teutonic Knights included territory west of the Vistula (known as West Prussia or later as Pomerania) and east of the Vistula (East Prussia).

Like its Byzantine predecessor, the Ottoman state was a bureaucratic theocracy. The sultan was the unquestioned source of all authority, leader of the Holy War against the unbelievers. Only he could grant any privilege or impose any tax. In each district of the empire he appointed two officials with independent spheres of authority—the bey as the local executive and the kadi (Muslim judge) for legal matters. Legally the bey could not inflict any punishment without first obtaining an order from the kadi, who in turn was not allowed to execute his own judicial sentences, although as government servants certainly neither one was entirely immune to official pressures. Soldiers subject directly to the sultan's orders were quartered in the principal cities of the empire, which prevented local officials from exercising power arbitrarily. The sultan also disposed of an extensive intelligence service, a fact well known to the population, which resulted in a widespread fear of spies. This was no vain precaution, inasmuch as Venice alone is known to have sponsored at least a dozen attempts on the life of Sultan Mohammed II.

A key factor in this governmental centralization was the specific Ottoman form of slavery. The Turks did not invent this system, which had existed much earlier in the Abbasid Caliphate in Syria (750–1258) and in the Islamic sultanates of Egypt and Iran. However, the older Islamic states had used slaves chiefly for military service, while leaving official posts in the hands of men who were Muslims by birth. The Ottomans followed this example until the mid-15th century, when they began to utilize slaves for administrative purposes also. The principle of the slave system was the same in either case, since its purpose was control. The sultan could exercise maximum authority over slaves, who possessed neither influential relatives nor any private wealth. A slave could normally be trusted to obey orders, since if he did not, the sultan could kill him with impunity and arouse no repercussions in Muslim society. In theory all Ottoman slaves were equal—all were equally the sultan's property—so that no slave was entitled to dominate any other. However, a favored slave might rise exceedingly high in the official hierarchy, even to the office of grand vizier. As such he presented no threat to his master, since he was not a member of the imperial family and could never himself aspire to the throne. To be the sultan's slave was considered an honor. Even the slaves of lesser men sometimes exercised important functions.

Most Ottoman slaves in the 14th century were prisoners of war, since according to Muslim law one-fifth of all captives taken in combat became the sultan's property. Slave markets supplied others. Apparently these sources proved inadequate, since in the 15th century the Ottomans began acquiring slaves in another way—through the system of child tribute known as devşirme. This was a tax on Orthodox Christian children from the Balkan lands of the empire. Assessed every three to seven years, it applied only to the sons of peasants, who were thought to be healthier physically and more malleable psychologically than town dwellers. Muslims and only sons were exempt from this tax, except in Bosnia among the families of converts to Islam. The tribute children could be between the ages of eight and twenty, although usually they were in their early teens. To be chosen, a boy needed good health, attractive physical appearance, and apparent intelligence. Initially most Balkan peasants sought to evade the tribute collectors, but after the news spread that devşirme offered career prospects inconceivable to Christian youths in any other manner, poor families sometimes welcomed it as a way of providing for their children's support. Occasionally Turkish recruiters were bribed to accept boys who would otherwise not have qualified.

The products of this child tribute, most of whom were trained for the army, filled the gaps left by the decimation of the old Turkish conquering class through constant warfare. The Ottoman Empire had become too extensive to be ruled and defended by Turks alone, who were spread ever more thinly throughout its territories. Moreover, the empire had come to include very heterogeneous and anciently civilized lands, which rough-hewn warriors were incompetent to govern. Thus a select few of the tribute children were sent to the palace school at Istanbul, converted to Islam, and trained for government or military service. They received a thorough education in Ottoman customs and the elements of Islamic high culture, but remained legally slaves. Afterward they entered the sultan's service and became eligible to attain high political and military posts—positions from which men born as Muslims were often excluded until the days of the empire's decline. The uniform education which these men received in the palace school provided them with a common frame of reference. Some joined the imperial government, while others entered the Janissary corps—an elite military unit comprised largely of men of devşirme origin. One advantage of this system was that it avoided nepotism: native Turkish officials would presumably feel the pull of family ties and succumb to pressure to find jobs for their relatives, whereas slaves were forbidden even to marry. Doubtless even more important was a well-founded fear that Turkish family loyalty might outweigh loyalty to the sultan. Men supplied by the child tribute were immune to both temptations. They had been torn at an early age from their relatives, who in any case were only poor Christian peasants without status. On the negative side was the fact that the Janissary slave corps soon became conscious of its power as the sultan's chief military support, and increasingly used its power to intimidate the government. The devşirme system also created resentment among native Turks. In many still-extant documents, old Turkish fighters complain bitterly at their exclusion from political power. However, a person born Muslim could not become a slave.

Another Ottoman technique of government was forced migration (sürqün). This could be either punitive deportation for individuals or the involuntary exile of whole communities. Transfer of populations was an ancient method of imperial control, recorded already in Biblical times. The Byzantine government had often resorted to this practice, for example after the reconquest of Bulgaria in 1018 when it exiled many Bulgarian boyars to Anatolia; or when it resettled Paulician heretics from Anatolia into Thrace. The Ottomans had too few Turkish subjects to populate all of their conquered lands with Turks. However, they could use enforced exile as a means of restoring regions devastated by war or providing labor power for Turkish warriors who had received estates in the European part of the empire. The presence of native-born Muslims among the Christian population also represented a safety factor. Accordingly, large numbers of Turkish peasants from Anatolia were moved into the Balkan Peninsula, especially into eastern Bulgaria. Similarly, Orthodox Christian families whose loyalty was questionable were forcibly transferred to Islamic centers like the fortress of Elbasan in Albania. The largest number of ethnic Turks transplanted into the Balkans probably consisted of tribal groups organized into military units. There they supplemented the activities of the regular cavalrymen, or sipahis, who were assigned to fiefs. Tribal strife in Asia Minor had produced a vast and mobile population of Turkic-speaking seminomads looking for new pastures for their herds. The Ottoman government moved many of these people into the newly conquered Balkan territories, thereby removing a disruptive element from within Anatolia. At the same time, the Turkic tribes in the Balkans became a valuable military resource close to the theater of military operations, particularly for the irregular hit-and-run warfare which was so much a feature of the Ottoman frontier in Europe.

A monarch's political advisers in the early medieval period usually constituted an informal group with fluctuating membership and no set rules of procedure. Later this body might become officially recognized as the royal Council. The functions of the Council were nowhere made specific; but in practice it exerted considerable influence on affairs of state. Members typically included the principal officials of the court (palatine, chancellor, treasurer, etc.), the bishops and archbishops, governors of important regions, and powerful magnates. Except for regular court personnel, most of these people would ordinarily not be present for meetings. Essentially the royal Council was an advisory rather than a legislative body; but the importance of its members, particularly the great landed magnates, meant that its advice was dangerous to ignore. However, as governmental functions gradually became more specialized, educated professional officials tended to displace the magnates in key positions. This development reflected the growing complexity of society, but was naturally not to the nobility's taste. Resentment at the nonnoble personnel in royal service motivated a group of Bohemian nobles in 1394 to hold King Wenceslas IV captive until he promised to establish a new royal Council consisting only of nobles and prelates. The nobles thus won their point in theory, but the king continued to run the government through his favorites from among the lesser nobility and the middle class. These were the people on whom he could rely for loyalty to himself or for professional competence.

A royal Council or its equivalent—a body of semipermanent advisers to the monarch—was a typical feature of medieval courts. The rulers of Serbia, for example, maintained a permanent entourage composed of their chief officials, as many as twenty-four in the 14th century under Tsar Stephen Dušan. In Hungary the royal Council apparently consisted largely of bishops and archbishops until the end of the 13th century, when various secular officials were added. No precise rules were observed as to who could belong, although the Council clearly represented the magnates rather than the lesser nobility. The king sought the Council's advice on questions of taxes, foreign affairs, and major appointments, rarely making any important decision without consulting it. In proclaiming a new decree he often used the stereotyped formula, "with the advice of the prelates and barons." In general, a royal Council extended its powers whenever the sovereign's position was weak. During an interregnum or when the king was out of the country, it operated as the government of the realm. Conversely, a strong king sought to undermine the Council's position. Thus King Matthias in the 15th century established new offices with jurisdiction which overlapped that of the older positions traditionally held by the barons of the Council. More often than not, he appointed men of modest social origin to the highest offices.

After Poland was reunified early in the 14th century, a royal Council took shape comprised of officials from the formerly independent appanages. No longer performing administrative functions, these men now defended the interests of their native regions at court. Just as in Hungary, the Council expressed only the attitudes and views of the great magnates. During the long reign of Jagiełło (r. 1386–1434) the Polish royal Council played a very decisive role, since this former grand duke of Lithuania was initially unfamiliar with conditions in his adopted country. Subsequently the Council acted as regent for his young son Vladislav VI, who came to the throne as a minor. Early in the 15th century the royal Council was transformed into the upper house (Senate) of the Polish Diet, or Great Sejm. After West Prussia joined Poland, a separate governing Council functioned for that province, convening several times a year to discuss taxation, trade, coinage, and legal matters. However, its concern to preserve Prussian autonomy made this body reluctant to meet jointly with either the Polish royal Council or the Great Sejm. The Prussians preferred to deal with the king separately.

In a development which paralleled the general increase in literacy and the use of written records, the sovereign's personal entourage gradually evolved into an organized administration with more or less clearly defined spheres of authority. In Bohemia, Hungary, and Poland the key office of central government became the chancellery. Its staff produced all necessary documents for the monarch, who in many cases was himself unable to write. The chancellor and his assistants not only drafted decrees and letters, copied documents, and wrote out royal privileges and grants, but also supplied the monarch with advice and proposals. The chancellor's principal sphere of activity was foreign affairs, since he was the person in charge of diplomatic correspondence. As custodian of the royal seal, which was essential for verifying documents, he held considerable power. The actual work of the chancellery office was done by notaries, who took part in discussions concerning the content of documents, participated occasionally in political missions, and often accompanied the sovereign on his journeys.

In Bohemia a royal chancellery existed from the early 12th century, with the chancellor as chief official of the royal court. Appointed by the sovereign, he was sometimes a foreigner, but always a high churchman. This was not only because of the Church's near-monopoly of education until the late Middle Ages, but also because possession of an ecclesiastical office obviated the need for a government salary. Lesser officials held benefices in the Church for the same reason. In Hungary a chancellery was first established in 1181 by King Béla III, who as former heir to the Byzantine throne had been educated at Constantinople. Indeed, the founding document expressly declared that the new office was established "after the model of the papal and imperial courts." Until that time, written records had seldom been required in Hungary, and the few which were produced usually dealt with church affairs. The chancellor, who became the king's most trusted adviser, was invariably the archbishop of Esztergom. The personnel of the chancellery office prior to the 14th century also consisted largely of clerics. In Poland the chancellor is first mentioned in sources of the early 12th century. As written records became more commonplace, an entire chancellery office developed to prepare them. Extensive documentation was required in connection with the extensive increase in immunity privileges for nobles (which they naturally wished to have formalized in writing), and with the founding of new towns according to German law. This role for the chancellery marked a departure from the earlier practice by which the recipient of privileges or immunities supplied the relevant documents himself and then submitted them for royal approval. Now the chancellor's office performed that function.

As government business became more complex, the necessary qualifications for chancellery officials also rose. In all Catholic lands a knowledge of Latin was indispensable. In the Orthodox countries of the Balkans Greek was used for certain purposes, but Old Slavic was more common. Chancellery staffs in Poland, Bohemia, and Hungary in the 14th century and afterward included many men with university degrees in arts or law. Initially they were usually clerics, but later laymen joined them. Such officials, who were valued for their expertise rather than for noble lineage, generally were willing co-workers of the monarch in promoting centralized authority. In Hungary the number of educated officials increased greatly under King Matthias (r. 1458–90), whose government was far better organized than its predecessors. Matthias was well aware of the advantages of a well-run tax system, and used his officials to assert prerogatives of monarchy that had fallen into disuse during the royal interregnums preceding his accession. A number of his new administrators came from the lower nobility or the towns and owed their positions to the king's preference for men with a humanist education. But even under Matthias the number of educated officials in Hungary remained small by the standards of Western Europe at that time.

Another official commonly found in the governments of medieval East Central Europe was the palatine, whose title means "count of the palace." Originally he was merely the supervisor of household affairs at court; but as the sphere of government widened he took on additional functions. In Hungary during the 11th century the palatine gradually became the king's second in command for judicial and military affairs. He managed the royal estates, supervised the commanders of the royal fortresses, and served as supreme judge for the nobility and for certain nomadic tribes living in the eastern territories—namely the Cumans, Iazygs, and Pechenegs. At first the palatine was the king's personal appointee, but by the end of the 13th century the occupant of this position had to be acceptable to the nobility. In Poland the office of palatine developed in analogous fashion. In the 11th century he was merely the director of court activities. Subsequently he served as the monarch's representative for other purposes, including judicial proceedings and leadership of the army—hence his alternate title of voivode, or "army leader." When Poland crumbled into appanages in the mid-12th century, a separate voivode functioned in each of the independent Polish provinces. However, the great magnates eventually combined to abolish the rank of palatine, which they considered excessively exalted. Henceforth the castellan—an official originally of lower rank—assumed first place in the governmental hierarchy at Cracow.

In the Ottoman Empire the closest equivalent to a palatine was the grand vizier, who was in charge of all lesser officials (also called "viziers"). He advised the sultan and represented him in secular matters. Laws of Mohammed the Conqueror refer to this official as the sultan's "absolute representative." The grand vizier might on occasion lead an army; but unlike a palatine, he had no judicial role. The functions of chancellor were carried out by the head of the state secretariat, who issued the sultan's commands and drew his signature on all decrees; and by the treasurer, who served as the highest financial authority. Justice was the province of the supreme judge of the empire, the kadiasker, who made final decisions in all legal matters and also appointed lesser judges for the provinces and towns. These four branches of government (policy; records; finance; justice) were known as the "four pillars of the empire," by analogy with the four poles which held up the sultan's tent. The most important collective organ of government was the imperial Council, or Divan, consisting of the sultan's highest officials. The sultan sometimes presided over this body himself, although in many cases the viziers conducted its business without him.

One unusual feature of Ottoman governance was the system which organized all the inhabitants of the empire according to religious affiliation. Since the Muslim religious law, or Shari'a, applied to all areas of life—in fact, no distinction between the secular and religious spheres was recognized—this law could not easily be applied to non-Muslims. Therefore each major religious community was organized into a separate administrative unit (known in the 19th century, although not earlier, as a millet). Each unit received a degree of legal autonomy; and the religious leaders of each faith held authority over their adherents even in secular matters. Christians in the Ottoman Empire were at first usually ruled by bishops who were answerable to the local Turkish authorities. After the conquest of

Constantinople in 1453, the entire Orthodox Christian community of the empire became subject to the Greek (or ecumenical) patriarch at the capital. A separate administrative department was organized for the Jews, and a third unit for the Armenians, who as Gregorian Christians were distinct from the Orthodox in religion. This Armenian millet also included any subjects of the sultan who were not otherwise classified. Since religious leaders were appointed by the sultan, they became in effect his officials. However, the system encouraged corruption. The patriarch typically owed his appointment to intrigue or bribery at the sultan's court; and his tenure of office was precarious. A prelate who could not produce the required sum in taxes from his flock was likely to forfeit his position.

Throughout all of medieval East Central Europe, governments on the local and regional level tended to resist control from the center. The oldest administrative districts perhaps originated as the settlement areas of various tribes, although this is uncertain. They may also have been purely political divisions created after tribal concepts of collective property had disintegrated. Whatever their origin, medieval Bulgaria, Serbia, and Croatia at an early date were divided into small districts called župas headed by chiefs known as župans, who were often the hereditary heads of their clans. The territory of the župa, which was basically an economic unit, coincided at first with that of the village. Typically it consisted just of a river valley surrounded by uninhabited forests or mountain zones, and it lacked fixed boundaries. The focal point of the župa was a wooden fortress, constructed either in the midst of a swamp or on an elevation. In Bulgaria the župa organization survived until the Ottoman conquest, although under different names, except during the interval of Byzantine overlordship (1018–1186), when the country was divided into themes on the Greek model.

In Serbia and Croatia the župas at first seem to have been territorial units subject to local chiefs, but subsequently became administrative divisions. The office of župan tended to become hereditary in the great families. The župas exercised considerable autonomy in local affairs. When Croatia joined Hungary at the end of the 11th century the župa system remained as the basis of local government. Eventually a dual power structure arose, whereby two župans sometimes functioned concurrently in the same district—one as territorial chief and another as the monarch's appointee. The relationship of the two župans to each other is difficult to assess, and probably was never clearly defined. Dualism of this type was likely to occur at a time when a central government was sufficiently powerful to begin imposing its own administrative structure, but had not yet succeeded in displacing the older, locally-based political units. A different sort of dualism developed in Serbia when King Stephen Dušan (r. 1331–55) overran the Byzantine-ruled territories in Macedonia. In these newly acquired lands Dušan retained most of the existing offices with their Greek titles, often without even replacing the officeholders. He then introduced a formal division between his Serbian and his Greek holdings, each with its own chancellery. He declared Serbia to be merely a "kingdom" with his young son Uroš as king; but the Greek lands (then known as "Romania," or "land of the Romans") he called an "empire," with himself as tsar (i.e., "emperor"). In fact, Dušan ruled both regions.

Hungary prior to the 13th century exhibited a type of administrative dualism derived from the circumstances of the "taking of the land" in 895–96. The descendants of the original invaders continued to hold the areas where their respective tribes had settled when they occupied the country, provided that they had never rebelled against royal authority; and the king did not rule them directly. However, all uninhabited areas (including forests and mountainous districts, as well as the confiscated land of tribes which had revolted against the king) were treated as royal property. During the reign of King Stephen I (r. 997–1038) this included perhaps two-thirds of all the land in Hungary. Stephen divided it into counties (i.e., districts around the royal fortresses), each subject to an appointed official called a count. The count's functions included providing the king with military service, provisioning the royal estates, and administering justice to the people. However, within a short time this fairly straightforward arrangement had evolved into an irregular mosaic of intertwined authorities, since some counts ruled parcels of land outside their own districts, while others held enclaves within counties governed by someone else. Subsequent developments gradually reduced both the functions and the territory of the royal counts. In the late 11th century the king's chief official, the palatine, replaced the counts as judge of all persons attached to the royal court. More and more estates belonging to the Church or the nobility received immunity from the authority of any count, especially from the mid- 12th century onward. In 1241 the Mongol onslaught struck a death-blow to the old county organizations. The Mongols' depredations destroyed many of the old county fortresses, while others were allowed to decay, since the military organization which was based on them had proved its inadequacy.

Hungary's eastern region of Transylvania was governed on semi-military lines because of its exposed position on the edge of the open steppe. Its voivode was above all an army commander, as well as chief executive and judge in the king's name. However, Transylvania in the Middle Ages was seldom treated as a single unit. The voivode's authority extended only over the royal counties,* while the Szekler, Saxon and Vlach lands were administered separately by their respective counts or knezi. The Transylvanian voivode controlled substantial private estates, but he could not grant lands, collect taxes and tolls, or coin money. These functions belonged to the king or the royal treasury. Nonetheless, in periods of weak central government he could often act quite independently, since he was generally a powerful lord in his own right and the monarch was far away. Transylvania's military forces often fought without help from the rest of Hungary—a circumstance which naturally tended to diminish

---

* Originally there were seven of these: thus the German name for Transylvania, "Siebenbürgen," or "seven fortresses."

the king's authority. In 1226 and again in 1260 the heir to the Hungarian throne, after leading an armed rebellion against his royal father, was allowed to rule Transylvania as a virtually autonomous province. While this particular arrangement proved to be temporary, some integration within the province did occur in the 15th century. In response to the peasant revolt of 1437, a Transylvanian assembly began meeting with some regularity to discuss common affairs; and after 1460 the king generally appointed the same person as both voivode and Szekler count.

Following the Mongol invasion of Hungary in 1241, King Béla IV encouraged his nobility to build stone fortresses capable of resisting another such onslaught. The castles which now arose made the major Hungarian landholders virtually independent of their king. In consequence, the second half of the 13th century witnessed an enormous increase in the nobility's political weight. The great nobles, or magnates, became able to monopolize the principal offices of state. Gradually they took over many royal estates as well as the lands attached to royal fortresses. In certain areas of the country they exercised almost unlimited control and forced the lesser nobles into their service. The power of these magnates was such that during the reigns of the last two Árpád monarchs (1272–1301), Hungary disintegrated into a collection of semi-autonomous provinces. More than twenty years would elapse before the first Angevin king, Charles Robert, could completely reestablish royal authority throughout the country, and even then he was impelled to remunerate the great magnates with "honors" (i.e., offices which entitled them to the income from royal lands and the right to govern extensive domains). The royal counts, although still formally appointed by the king, were now usually major landholders in the locality where they held office.

During the reign of King Sigismund (r. 1387–1437), who first had to fight for his Hungarian throne and after 1400 was often distracted by his other interests in Germany and Bohemia, the nobility again enhanced its influence. In his efforts to attract political support, Sigismund gave away large tracts of royal land. Powerful Hungarian magnates maintained their own courts, exercised quasi-governmental functions, and used tax money to hire their own mercenary forces. By the end of the 14th century, leagues of nobles controlled large areas of Hungary and exerted a decisive influence on the central government. In effect, the lay and ecclesiastical lords had become the king's co-rulers. Together with this ascendancy of the magnates the Hungarian counties were transformed from territory owned by the king into merely administrative units centered around a fortress. The old royal counties emerged in a new form as *noble* counties, the organs of the nobility's self-government. The king exercised only limited control over them; and indeed they provided a possible focus for resistance to him. While the count was still a royal appointee, though usually a local magnate, royal charters empowered the county nobility to elect their own magistrates, including judges and jurors, and to execute judgments.

The counties gradually assumed additional functions in local administration and peacekeeping. In times of civil war or weak central authority they became de facto the only real governments in Hungary. The counties were dominated by the middle nobility, whom some monarchs tried to enlist as allies against the magnates. King Béla IV, for example, in 1265 recognized as free noble properties the minor landholdings of soldiers in the royal garrisons. John Hunyadi as regent and his son King Matthias likewise confirmed the privileges of the lesser nobility. Béla IV also ordered each county to send two or three deputies to the royal legislative assembly, which marked the beginning of a regularly constituted national Diet. However, the county nobles were much more interested in local government, which affected their day-to-day existence, than in the affairs of the country as a whole. Their primary goal was to make county administration their own instrument, principally in order to restrain the power of the magnates, whom they greatly outnumbered. In Transylvania the lesser nobles had somewhat less success in gaining autonomy than their counterparts in Hungary proper. In theory they belonged to the same noble class; but in practice they were more closely controlled by the voivode, who resisted their attempts at self-government.

In Poland the oldest administrative unit was the opole, a judicial as well as a taxpaying district which antedated the foundation of the Polish state. It could include several villages or as many as several dozen. In the 10th and 11th centuries some of these districts were governed directly by royal officials, others by the lords of the great landed estates. Another type of district was the castellany (i.e., the area around a "castle"), which at that period meant merely an earthen fortress. The commander of a Polish castellany, who at first was entitled "count" and from the 12th century "castellan," was in principle the monarch's agent. This position was monopolized by great landed magnates, who waxed indignant if a nonnoble received the office. Thus in practice the monarch's right of appointment was greatly restricted. The castellan collected taxes, dispensed justice, and commanded the armed forces of his district. In return he was entitled to retain a portion of the locally collected revenue, including judicial fines and market tolls. From the local peasantry he received taxes in kind, both for his own use and to feed the monarch and his entourage when they stopped at the fortress on their tours around the country. Similarly in Hungary, castellans were important royal officials, eventually inheriting some of the earlier functions of the county counts. Both castellans and counts were appointed by the king, but by the 14th century most county land belonged to noble estates, leaving the count with a relatively small power base. The castellan's job was to defend the royal castle, collect the king's revenue, and judge the tenants on the castle estates. In some instances the same man served as both castellan and count. The distinction between the two offices is not always clear from surviving documents.

With the virtual disappearance of central government in Poland in the mid-12th century, offices multiplied in the semi-independent appanages. Even after reunification was achieved under Vladislav IV Łokietek about 1310, officials of the appanages continued to exercise considerable authority in their native districts. The king could appoint his own men only by agreement with the local nobility. Since a sovereign obviously needed subordinates loyal to himself, Łokietek began to appoint officials called starostas ("elders") to serve as counterweights to the nobles. Starostas were responsible to the king alone. They could not be natives of the region to which they were appointed, which made them useful tools of the central government. A starosta in his district exercised all the prerogatives of the monarch except for the right to grant royal lands or tax exemptions to private individuals. He prosecuted and judged criminal cases, collected taxes, summoned the nobles to war, watched that no one infringed upon royal property, and administered church lands during vacancies. Under Łokietek's son Casimir the Great (r. 1333–70), the starostas were powerful enough even to order great magnates beheaded without trial, probably most often for robbery.

In the Ottoman Empire the basic administrative unit was the sanjak, or district. The word means "flag" or "banner," thus testifying to the military character of the Ottoman state. The head of a sanjak, called the sanjakbey, was a military commander who led the troops of his district and collected its taxes. The primary purpose of Ottoman government was to provide resources for the sultan's campaigns. (The Turkish word for provincial administration, dirlik, literally means "livelihood," i.e., revenue-collection.) About half the land in the empire was assigned as fiefs (timars) to support the armed cavalry (sipahis) of the state, who together with their families were settled in villages throughout the Balkans. Since each fief holder owed service and loyalty directly to the sultan, subinfeudation was nonexistent, and everyone was equally subject to the central government. Like the nobility of Christian Europe, Ottoman military fief holders collected taxes from the peasants on their land and exercised jurisdiction over the peasants in minor cases. They also functioned as policemen in the countryside, applying the land laws. A sipahi could make arrests for minor infractions; but only a Muslim judge, or kadi, could set the appropriate punishment.

In contrast to the Balkan governments which it replaced, the Ottoman political system was strictly controlled from the center. Officials at the capital exercised close supervision over the sipahis and did not permit them to ruin the peasantry with excessive taxes. High officials of the districts and provinces were supported by revenues from the larger fiefs known as zeamets or hass. These often consisted of agricultural estates located near the towns where the officials in question resided, but might also include specified customs receipts or the yield from mining operations. Like the military fiefs, these estates remained the sultan's property, but differed from the timars in being separate from the office of their holder. A sipahi held authority only over his own timar, while an Ottoman official governed an entire district or region, not all of which constituted his fief. Despite a fairly tight centralized control, the Ottoman government in the provinces sought to adjust its style of rule to local conditions. After conquering a district, the Turks often allowed many of the Christian landowners to retain their property, converting only a portion of the land into timars for Turkish cavalrymen. Frequently the Ottoman authorities simply adopted the administrative arrangements already in force.

The high level of administrative centralization found in the Ottoman Empire was an anomaly in East Central Europe as a whole. Elsewhere the landholders in their districts often enjoyed considerable independence of the central power. A rudimentary governing apparatus, poor communications, and the poverty of medieval economies meant that a monarch possessed only limited control over outlying districts which theoretically were subject to him. Large portions of a country easily became semi-autonomous. Thus within the Bohemian kingdom the province of Moravia was governed by a semi-independent margrave. At times it was ruled separately from the other half of the realm, although the duke or king at Prague maintained his supremacy. Even when king and margrave were the same person, these two parts of one kingdom were treated as separate entities. Moravia possessed its own institutions and officials; and its nobility remained conscious of a distinct identity. This difference was reinforced in the 15th century, when the Hussite form of Christian worship became widely accepted in the Bohemian half of the realm, while Moravia remained mainly Catholic.

Hungary was so large (for medieval conditions) that its eastern province of Transylvania was able at times to become semi-autonomous. On occasion it became the power base from which a disgruntled group of lords could raise a revolt or exert pressure on the king. During the nearly half-century of semi-anarchy following the death of King Béla IV in 1270, Transylvania functioned virtually as an independent country. Its powerful voivode exercised quasi-monarchical authority, although without ever attempting to usurp the royal title. After Charles Robert consolidated his position as king (ca. 1310), the central government exerted more control over this eastern province. Nonetheless, the Transylvanian voivode remained a potent figure, usually a great landed proprietor who chose his subordinates from among his own personal retainers. A few such magnate families tended to monopolize this office. While in theory all royal decrees applied to Transylvania, in fact the king's wishes were often ignored there.

Certain areas of Transylvania enjoyed a unique legal status under the Hungarian crown. The districts occupied by Szeklers (a Magyar-speaking group with a distinct identity) were directly subject to a royal appointee known as the Szekler count. As county government increased its scope in the Hungarian kingdom in the 14th-century, the Szeklers created their own district assemblies and established a court of appeal for the entire Szekler land. Similarly, the Saxons constituted a separate entity in law, beginning with Andrew II's charter of 1224 (the "Andreanum") which placed their principal settlement areas under the authority of an official known as the Saxon count with his seat at Sibiu (Hermannstadt). In the 15th century all Transylvanian Saxons were recognized as belonging to the so-called Saxon Corporation (*universitas Saxonum*), a legal entity which may have been the first autonomous organization for an ethnic minority in European history. On both the Saxon and Szekler lands the Hungarian king's rights were comparatively limited, particularly with respect to the disposition of landed property. Saxons and Szeklers formed two of the three recognized "nations" of Transylvania—the third being the Hungarian nobility. The Vlachs or Romanians, who were certainly very numerous, and perhaps even a majority in the province, but Orthodox rather than Catholic in religion, lacked equivalent privileges. In the 13th century the Vlachs were organized into autonomous districts, each comprising several villages with a knez to head each one. This official collected taxes, judged minor disputes, and organized local defense in wartime. In Transylvania's exposed eastern borderlands the knez was a more important personality than in the interior of the province. Usually he was an independent landholder as well as a royal administrator.

Croatia maintained a separate legal status throughout the many centuries of its union with Hungary, which had occurred more by agreement than by force after the death without heirs of King Zvonimir in 1089. Following a period of considerable anarchy, a section of the Croatian nobility offered the throne to the king of Hungary. Hungarian troops entered northern Croatia in 1091, but no armed struggle took place. As a formerly independent country which had not been conquered, Croatia retained considerable autonomy. The agreement known as the Pacta Conventa, probably concluded between the two kingdoms in 1102, formally defined the conditions under which the Croat nobility accepted the king of Hungary as their sovereign. Its precise terms remain uncertain, since the document has survived only in a 14th-century version which may not be an exact copy of the original. In the 19th century some Hungarian nationalist historians challenged Croatia's special status by claiming that the Pacta Conventa had never existed at all. However, medieval Croatia's autonomous position with respect to Hungary is undeniable. The king of Hungary managed only its foreign affairs and acted as commander-in-chief of its army. The Croat nobles owed him military service only for defensive wars. If they crossed the Drava River into Hungary proper, the king was supposed to pay them for their services.

Union with Hungary brought no important changes in Croatia's internal administration. The old župa system continued in existence. Croatia maintained its own Diet, or Sabor, although its decisions became law only after confirmation by the Hungarian king—presumably the same prerogative which the kings of independent Croatia had exercised. Since the Croat landholders retained their hereditary property, the king of Hungary disposed of very little land in Croatia, which gave him only slight leverage over the local nobility. The king appointed a governor known as the ban to oversee his interests; but the ban was always a Croatian territorial lord, who combined the status of a great landed magnate with his royal office. He commanded the Croatian army, convened the assembly in the king's name and presided over its meetings, served as supreme judge of the country, and perhaps also supervised tax collection. In short, the ban exercised all the attributes of royal power except an independent foreign policy. In 1198 King Emeric created the position of "duke of Croatia and Dalmatia" to satisfy the desire of his rebellious younger brother (later king) Andrew for an appanage. After this the ban became second in command to the duke of Croatia, who was usually the son or younger brother of the reigning king of Hungary.

In theory all of Croatia south of the Drava River (the later Yugoslav-Hungarian border) was a unified territory subject to the ban or duke as personal representative of the Hungarian king. The reality was otherwise. The Petrova Gora hills southeast of Karlovac marked an important line of demarcation. To the north lay Slavonia, which in due time became divided into three large counties on the Hungarian model and was partially assimilated to Hungary proper. Here the Hungarian king was able to make land grants to his followers, creating large estates for favored nobles or for the Church. The division between the two parts of Croatia was further emphasized after the mid-13th century, when one ban was appointed for Slavonia and another for Croatia and Dalmatia. South of Petrova Gora the Croatian nobles enjoyed a greater measure of independence. They paid no direct taxes to the king; and no Hungarian ever received the gift of an estate there. Powerful Croatian noble houses possessed almost royal privileges within their own domains and remained virtually immune to the power of the monarchy.

Bosnia also maintained a special status under the Hungarian crown, and frequently escaped Hungarian control altogether. Prior to the 14th century, Bosnia was usually subject in theory to a governor (the ban) owing nominal allegiance to the king of Hungary. In practice the ban was often independent of Hungary, and the Bosnian lords for their part often ignored or resisted his authority. No administrative structure existed to enforce obedience, while a mountainous terrain multiplied all the normal difficulties of medieval communication. Bosnia's evolution into an independent state under its own monarch in the 14th century did not alter this situation. The country was in fact never more than a loosely knit federation, in which some of the nobles were as powerful as the Bosnian king. In their own domains they exercised all the usual powers of a sovereign, including justice, taxation, and even foreign relations. Their lands were considered inviolable (i.e., not subject to confiscation) whether they obeyed the king or not. On the borders of their estates the lords set up customs barriers and exacted dues from passing merchants. Even Tvrtko I (r. 1353–91), the strongest of the medieval Bosnian monarchs, had great difficulty in controlling his nobility.

Royal Prussia enjoyed considerable autonomy after it renounced the government of the Teutonic Knights in 1454 and became a province of Poland. Its leading men insisted, and the king conceded, that only natives of Prussia could hold office there (i.e., no more foreign knights). The Prussians themselves viewed their territory as united to Poland only through the king's person. They did not wish to participate in Polish campaigns or pay the same taxes as other Polish subjects. Only unwillingly did they join in meetings of the Polish royal Council, since participation would require them to execute its decisions. Social and ethnic differences reinforced this separateness. The towns of Royal Prussia possessed far greater economic strength than their counterparts in Poland and played a correspondingly greater political role. Representatives of the towns sat in the Diet of Royal Prussia and in the ruling Prussian Council. The same coinage circulated in both parts of Prussia, differing in weight and standard from that of Poland.

The joining of Poland and Lithuania under a single ruler by the Union of Krewo in 1385 similarly failed to produce a united Polish-Lithuanian state. Even after Grand Duke Jagiełło became king of Poland the next year, Lithuania under the rule of his cousin Witold behaved virtually as an independent country. It concluded treaties with the Teutonic Knights like a sovereign power and conducted its own wars. When Jagiełło died in 1434, his younger son Casimir became grand duke of Lithuania, while Vladislav, the elder, was elected king of Poland—a situation containing the elements of a renewed separation. However, Vladislav's death without heirs in 1444 at the battle of Varna opened the way for Casimir IV to become the ruler of both realms. Poland and Lithuania thus remained linked by personal union until that king's death in 1492. Briefly the earlier division was restored when one of Casimir's sons was elected king of Poland and another became grand duke of Lithuania, but this arrangement proved to be impermanent. The link between the two realms continued until the Partitions of Poland in the late 18th century.

After a brief period of uncertain independence in the 14th century, the two Romanian principalities were transformed into Ottoman vassal states. Walachia became tributary to the Turks shortly after Serbia was reduced to vassalage as a result of the battle of Kosovo in 1389. When the ruler of Walachia, Mircea the Old, handed over the Turkish tribute in 1393, he was apparently the first Romanian sovereign to do so; but these payments had not yet become a perpetual obligation. Farther north, Moldavia seems to have delivered its first tribute to the Turks in 1456. The rulers of the Romanian principalities, known as voivodes, were elected by their own boyar nobility from among the members of the two royal dynasties, although the sultans frequently interfered in the succession. Once elected, a voivode enjoyed considerable autonomy within his domain. He had to refrain from overt acts of hostility toward the sultan, supply him with troops upon request, and provide hostages as a guarantee of continued good behavior. As a sign of allegiance he was also required to pay the sultan a monetary tribute and periodically give him presents, particularly the falcons which he liked for hunting. However, Walachia and Moldavia were never directly included in the Ottoman administrative system. The Turks did not create new districts or establish military fiefs there.

As long as the two Romanian voivodes accepted their vassal status, their lands remained fairly immune from Ottoman military incursions and enjoyed relative peace. While their autonomy was violated in numerous minor ways, in internal affairs they were fairly independent. Initially no Muslims were allowed to settle in the Romanian principalities or build mosques there, although this restriction was abandoned after the Turks occupied central Hungary in 1541. The native Vlach nobility retained its former landed estates, and an independent Orthodox Church continued to function. Turkish military occupation was limited to the establishment of garrisons at certain strategic points. The two principalities maintained their own governments and legal systems and sent diplomatic representatives to Istanbul like independent states. However, Walachia was always more carefully watched and more tightly controlled than its sister principality, owing to its long boundary with the Ottoman Empire on the Danube.

The two small, poor, and mountainous lands of Albania and Montenegro (the latter known as Zeta until the 15th century) enjoyed a comparable independence from Turkish control. To forestall Ottoman conquest the Venetians captured the Montenegrin coast around the Bay of Kotor; but the interior was loosely governed by native princes of the Crnojević family. Montenegro merely paid tribute to the sultan and accepted his control in foreign affairs. Albania was initially conquered by the Ottomans in the 1420s. However, its warlike tribal society and independent-minded chiefs proved difficult to control. A serious uprising broke out in 1436 when the government confiscated some Albanian land for timars. The far more serious revolt led by Skanderbeg erupted in 1443 and continued intermittently for a quarter-century. Eventually the Turks acknowledged the difficulty of controlling the rugged Albanian countryside and concluded that the cost of subduing it far outweighed any conceivable profit from conquest. The tribesmen were permitted to live in their accustomed fashion in the mountains, and even to bear arms in return for payment of a small tribute. They enforced their own justice according to traditional codes of conduct, instigating many blood feuds. Altogether they enjoyed a large measure of autonomy. Many Albanians willingly became Muslims; and both Christian and Muslim landholders furnished auxiliary troops for the sultan's army. The Albanians ultimately proved to be the most loyal of all the sultan's European subjects.

An important adjunct to many medieval governments was the assembly of the land known as the Diet, Parliament, Sejm, or Sabor—a meeting of the principal nobles and prelates of a country, sometimes supplemented by representatives of the lesser nobility or the towns. This body was sometimes referred to as the Estates, since the right to participate was a function of the members' "estate," or social class. Essentially a medieval Diet was a larger version of the royal Council. Its function was to assist the monarch, not to serve as a legislative body. Usually it originated in those gatherings of notables whom the ruler himself had summoned to approve war or taxes, since in practice he could neither conduct a military campaign nor collect extra revenue without their consent. At a later period, the taxing power became the wedge through which the Diet extracted major concessions from the monarch. In all the countries of medieval East Central Europe such assemblies met on occasion, albeit irregularly.

Bulgarian documents mention a boyar assembly called the Sabor which gave advice to the monarch on questions of war and peace, proclaimed laws, or elected a new ruler if necessary. The large and small boyars met there together with the tsar, the princes, and the ecclesiastical hierarchy. Under the Second Empire three Bulgar sovereigns were elected by the Sabor (in 1258, 1323, and 1331), but only because no obvious heir was available. On three other occasions the Sabor was summoned to deal with heresy. The best-known assembly of this kind met at Tirnovo in 1211, convoked by Tsar Boril to pronounce anathemas upon the Bogomil heretics. However, such meetings were in no sense a real legislature. The boyars had a consultative voice, but the tsar was unquestionably the dominant party. Old Bulgar customs presumably contributed to this pronounced autocracy, since the Turkic steppe warriors who founded the Bulgar state were already accustomed to accept the supreme authority of a war leader. Moreover, the pagan Bulgar khans had made a practice of employing only Slavic officials and limiting the Bulgar boyars to army service or to military governorships. This Slavic officialdom developed into a nonhereditary court nobility, dependent entirely on the khan. Finally, Byzantine tradition was a strong influence in Bulgaria. No popular assembly had ever limited the authority of the Byzantine emperor, who was an autocrat governing through a nonhereditary bureaucracy; and the Bulgar sovereigns tried to follow this example.

By contrast, the Sabor in independent Croatia (before 1100) seems to have met fairly regularly at various locations in Dalmatia. The most important nobles and clerics appeared there in person, while the lesser nobility and the monastic orders sent representatives. Despite its upper-class character, the Sabor claimed to represent the entire nation; and it gave its decisions in the name of the whole Croatian people. While the king set the agenda, the Sabor decided whether to approve or reject a royal request for extraordinary taxes or for the levy of troops to serve abroad. Croatia's union with Hungary brought no essential change in the functioning of this assembly. By the Pacta Conventa of 1102, King Koloman agreed to recognize all of the Croatian nobility's traditional privileges and prerogatives, including the right of the Sabor to make laws for Croatia without reference to the laws of Hungary. In the 13th century the Sabor expanded its membership to include representatives from the free towns in addition to the nobility and clergy. Nonetheless, it continued to be dominated by the great landholders, both secular and ecclesiastical. A separate Sabor existed for Slavonia.

The Croatian Sabor always insisted on its separate sphere of competence, at times directly opposing Hungarian policy. On two occasions (in 1270 and 1272) it refused to recognize the king elected in Hungary because Croatian agreement had not been obtained beforehand. Conversely, the Croats acknowledged Charles Robert of Naples as their king long before the Hungarians did so. In 1385 the assemblies of Croatia, Slavonia, and Bosnia all declined to accept Louis the Great's daughter Maria as heir to the throne even though she had already been elected "king" in Hungary. (Ultimately this dispute was settled by force, and Maria's party prevailed.) In the 15th century, King Matthias made a practice of summoning Croat representatives to participate in sessions of the Hungarian Diet whenever Croatian affairs were being discussed. Reciprocally, Hungary sent delegates to the Croatian Sabor. However, despite sharing a monarch, the Croats made their own laws in their own Sabor; and the Hungarians on the whole respected Croatia's semi-autonomous status.

Popular assemblies among the Serbs date back to a very early period, when all the free men of a district met to discuss local affairs. The Sabor in Serbia included high and petty nobility as well as upper clergy; and the sovereign attended together with his high officials. This body convened at irregular intervals for certain fairly specific purposes. Some were purely ceremonial, such as the coronation of the king or the presentation of the heir to the throne. Others were more substantive, like issuing laws or settling internal disturbances. In recording new laws, Serbian documents of the 14th century invariably mention that the nobles and clergy had given their consent. Following the expansion of the kingdom in Stephen Dušan's time, the Sabor added representatives from the new Greek-speaking territories in Macedonia. In Serbia, as in Bulgaria, Byzantine influences tended to favor the central power at the expense of the popular assemblies. However, Serbia was also exposed to Western practices through its contacts with the free towns of Dalmatia. Even under the unsettled conditions of the 15th century, when the much-reduced Serbian Despotate was seriously menaced by the Turks, the Sabor continued to function.

For all the lands of the Bohemian crown jointly, as well as for the provinces of Bohemia and Moravia separately, an assembly of nobility and higher clergy functioned as early as the 11th and 12th centuries. The lesser bodies served as a forum for the lower nobility, who rarely held important offices at the royal court. As early as 1281 the Diet of (the province of) Bohemia added representatives from the towns, reflecting the fact that the royal towns of that region were larger and more prosperous than their counterparts elsewhere in East Central Europe. The Moravian Diet did not admit townsmen until after 1440, while the Silesian Diet apparently did so only in the 1470s. The original purpose of such assemblies was merely to take note of issues presented by the monarch. However, in the second half of the 13th century these assemblies assumed the character of genuine lawgiving bodies, discussing current affairs and passing laws. Admittedly, their meetings were very infrequent by modern standards. During the first half of the 14th century, the Diet of the Bohemian kingdom convened a mere half-dozen times, and at irregular intervals. King Charles I (r. 1346–78) attempted to gain its support for his centralization policy. In 1348 the Diet did accede to his wish that succession to the throne should remain with the Luxemburg dynasty, thus depriving the German emperor of his former rights of intervention. In effect this annulled Bohemia's status as a fief of the German Empire. However, when the Diet opposed Charles's proposed codification of the laws, he found it more expedient to rule alone. After 1356 neither he nor his successor Wenceslas IV summoned a national assembly during the remainder of the century.

Nonetheless, the tradition of representative assemblies survived in Bohemia, available as a vehicle for revolt during the Hussite upheavals. In 1419 the Diet met to defend the religious reform from the threat posed by Sigismund of Luxemburg, the rigid Catholic who had inherited the Bohemian throne. In 1424 the Diet laid down the conditions under which it would accept Sigismund as king—namely, a guaranteed legal status for the Hussite form of worship and freedom of lay communion. After waging five unsuccessful military campaigns into Bohemia in the attempt to assert his rights, Sigismund finally accepted these stipulations. Only after doing so could he enter Prague, the capital. From 1419 until 1436 the executive council of the Bohemian Diet, with Prague in the lead, functioned as the actual government of the kingdom. When Sigismund's successor Albert died prematurely in 1439, this failure of the dynastic line permitted the Bohemian Diet to dominate the political situation. First it elected George Poděbrady, the head of the Hussite party, as regent for the child Ladislas V "Posthumous" who had inherited the throne. When Ladislas in turn died in 1457, the Diet raised George to be king. This was a striking departure from dynastic legitimacy, unprecedented in European experience, since the new king lacked royal blood. The innovation was not perpetuated, either in Bohemia or in Hungary, where the similarly nonroyal Matthias Hunyadi was elected in 1458. In 1471 the Bohemian Diet elected a prince of the Polish Jagiellonian dynasty, Vladislav II, as George's successor.

In Hungary, King Andrew II (r. 1205–35) brought a popular assembly to life through his own ineptness. Andrew had given his subjects many causes for complaint. He conducted perpetual foreign wars at great expense and to little purpose. He maintained a lavish royal court, collected extraordinary taxes, debased the coinage, and showed gross favoritism to his palace coterie. The noblemen he had excluded from his circle felt threatened in their pocketbooks and deprived of the influence which they considered their just due. On the "court day" in 1222, when by tradition any Hungarian subject was entitled to complain to the king in person, a group of nobles and propertied freemen presented Andrew with their grievances. Intimidated by this armed and angry assembly, Andrew agreed to many of its demands. In his famous Golden Bull of 1222 he promised to hold a court day every year, guaranteeing the right of all nobles to attend. This measure had the effect of protecting the lesser nobility against arbitrary demands by the great landed magnates; and it created a recognized national Diet with political power. However, once this dangerous gathering had dispersed, Andrew proceeded to ignore his promises. Another assembly forced him to repeat most of them in a second Golden Bull in 1231. This recurrent pattern, whereby the king under pressure made promises which he afterward felt free to ignore, exemplified the limitations of medieval legislative bodies. Such a situation was hardly unique to Hungary. The nobility as a class could exert real influence only when it assembled personally in great numbers, which happened only occasionally. It could not influence the execution of its own decisions. The Golden Bull of 1222—Hungary's Magna Carta—is important chiefly as a legal precedent, not for any effect it produced in the 13th century. Largely forgotten for over a hundred years, it received a new lease on life in 1351 when King Louis issued a decree confirming its provisions. Every Hungarian king thereafter formally accepted the Golden Bull upon his accession to the throne.

Everywhere a weak monarchy favored the evolution of legislative assemblies. In Hungary the reign of King Ladislas IV provided an opportunity of this kind. Ladislas, known as the "Cuman," had inherited his throne as a minor in 1272. When he came of age, his heathenish behavior and unconcealed preference for his pagan Cuman relatives aroused great hostility among the Christian Hungarian nobility. In 1277 he could not prevent an armed assembly of nobles and clergy from transforming itself into a genuine Diet. When Ladislas died without heirs in 1290, the assembly stepped in to fill the vacuum. Since none of the contenders for the throne held a clear advantage in hereditary credentials, the monarch whom the Diet elected, Andrew III (r. 1290–1301), obviously owed his crown to that body. As it happened, Andrew had no objection to sharing power. Raised in Venice, he was familiar with the republican and aristocratic traditions of his native city. He made a practice of summoning the Hungarian Diet once a year, and convened a similar body for Transylvania. These meetings soon acquired a genuinely legislative character and became a regular feature of Hungarian government. As a consequence, the lesser nobility became a political factor of national importance. The Diet now met not only at the king's invitation, but whenever it wished, and presented its decisions to "the king and the barons" for confirmation. Admittedly, the economic dependence of many lesser nobles upon the magnates made them receptive to pressure. Nonetheless, the mere possibility that the lower nobility might take an independent line against the magnates served to some extent as a constraint.

On the other hand, a determined sovereign could still demonstrate the fragility of government by assembly. Constitutional development in Hungary was interrupted in the 14th century under the strong monarchs of the Angevin dynasty, whose French roots influenced them to copy Western models of royal absolutism. Although the Diet had elected Charles Robert of Naples to the throne, once he had solidified his position he insisted that he was king by hereditary right alone (through the female line). His ruling Council was composed of prelates and great secular lords who owed their lands and titles to his favor. Since he gradually dispensed with the Diet's approval for his acts, the lower nobility faded into the background politically. For a few years the Diet still met, but it was no longer the decisive factor in the Hungarian state. After 1323, Charles Robert ceased to summon it at all for the remaining nineteen years of his reign. His son Louis the Great called it only once, in 1351, in the aftermath of the failure of his Italian campaign. On that occasion he fulfilled a long-standing ambition of the lesser nobility by granting this class legal equality with the magnates, including exemption from all direct taxes not specifically voted by the diet. Louis found no occasion to summon the assembly again. While the nobility continued to dominate county government, the king's will was law in the kingdom as a whole.

During the long reign of Sigismund (r. 1387–1437), the lesser nobility sought to establish itself as a force in the central government as well as in the counties. Their leaders in this endeavor were typically the retainers, or familiares (literally: family members), of one of the great magnates. Many minor Hungarian nobles who had found it economically impossible to survive as independent landowners belonged to the extended household of one of these great lords. They managed estates or led troops on behalf of their more affluent fellow nobles. Occasionally they governed whole provinces. Such men occupied an intermediate status within the noble class and constituted an informal elite. Capable of influencing the magnates through close personal association, they also acquired a disproportionate authority over the lesser nobility to which they themselves belonged. These middle nobles became increasingly assertive in demanding a share in political decision making, claiming that their noble status entitled them to represent the entire Hungarian nation, including the common people. This self-assessment became so generally accepted that in ordinary Hungarian usage the word for "country" (ország) came to denote "nobility."

Representatives of the towns occasionally joined the nobility in the meetings of the Hungarian Diet, especially when the issue in question specifically concerned them. Townsmen were present in 1432, for example, when the chief item under discussion was regulation of the silver currency, which had lost some of its value through inflation. In 1435 the towns of Hungary officially acquired the right to representation in the Diet, although for a long time they failed to take much advantage of it, correctly suspecting that their participation was desired merely to extract more tax money from them. In any event, their dozen or so votes carried little weight against the overwhelming majority of nobles, sometimes numbering in the hundreds, who were entitled to attend in person. A further restriction on town representation was that the major urban centers in Hungary (as elsewhere in East Central Europe) were usually dominated by Germans, who often did not understand Hungarian, the language of the Diet. Economically the towns were far too weak to constitute a separate estate, and the townsmen's political effectiveness was hampered as well by their relative lack of social prestige. Town representatives finally began to participate in meetings of the Hungarian Diet in the 1440s, but the records usually fail to mention whether or not they assented to the decisions of that body. Obviously the political weight of the town class was vastly inferior to that of either nobility or clergy.

The Diet increased its role under King Sigismund (r. 1387–1437), a weak and vacillating personality who was frequently absent from Hungary after his disputed election as German emperor in 1400. This assembly became even more important in the years between 1439 and 1457, when royal authority was attenuated by dynastic conflicts, interregna, a child ruler, and the Ottoman threat on the frontiers, which demanded additional outlays for defense. The nobles naturally regarded all taxes on their peasants as levies on themselves. They insisted on being consulted in tax matters and reserved the right to reject royal proposals. Even after consenting to taxation, they were unwilling to let the king use the money as he wished. They sought to inspect the state expenses, either in the Diet or through the royal Council, which had meanwhile been expanded to include Diet representatives. After 1443 no one in Hungary seriously challenged the principle that the Diet's consent was required for all extraordinary taxes. This body became the forum in which all major political questions of the day were decided; and its agreement became indispensable to the validity of any law. From 1445 onward it met in every year except one, and in some years twice, replacing the royal Council as the main political decision maker. The king issued his decrees only with the Diet's consent. In this fashion the lesser nobility of the counties, meeting together with the magnates of Church and state, became a major factor on the national scene. However, the legal equality of all nobles did not mean that social rank was ignored. Records of the Diet's proceedings invariably identify participants as magnates, middle nobility, or county gentry. The last category was naturally most numerous.

The composition of the Hungarian Diet was never strictly regulated. In theory any nobleman was entitled to attend. The great nobles represented only themselves, whereas the counties often sent delegates. Sometimes just the county delegates assembled, whereas at other times the king ordered all nobles to appear in person. Election of a new monarch always required a meeting en masse. In 1447 the Diet stipulated that all nobles possessing at least twenty dependent households (portae, or tax units), should attend in person. At the same time, the lesser nobility recognized that it could assert itself against the magnates only by turning out in force at the sessions of the Diet, where its superiority in numbers could make itself felt. In the 15th century a large contingent began doing so. They met on the historic field of Rákos (now the eastern side of Budapest); and they came armed, which allowed the majority to intimidate their opponents. King Matthias, however, did not wish to deal with the entire nobility at one time, so that during his reign the counties were represented in the Diet only by delegates. After his death, mass meetings again became the rule. In the counties, assemblies of the lesser nobility became increasingly important during the 15th century as organs of county government. The monarchs generally supported county autonomy as a counterweight to the influence of the magnates.

Although meetings of the Hungarian Diet had a long tradition by the 15th century, King Matthias demonstrated that an able monarch could still successfully undermine that body's fragile authority. Starting his reign in a notably weak position, he nonetheless managed within ten years to create an absolute monarchy. Although in the early years he asked the Diet to approve new taxes, at the same time he augmented his income by transforming the tax system and insisting on his monarchical prerogatives. With funds acquired in this way, he created a professional standing army that made him independent of the nobility's military forces. The lesser nobles did not protest when he collected extraordinary taxes without authorization, doubtless in part because they viewed this king as the defender of their interests against the great magnates. Matthias did his best to weaken the system which turned many lesser nobles into retainers of the magnates, in practice favoring all elements in society which were too weak to challenge his power (i.e., the lesser nobility, the towns, and the peasant communities). All the same, after 1464 he rarely summoned townsmen to the national Diet; and townsmen failed to participate even in the provincial assemblies held during his reign. (The prosperous Saxon towns of Transylvania were the exception to this rule, retaining their seats in both bodies). After suppressing the rebellion of 1471, Matthias summoned the Diet of the realm only on rare occasions, exercising his authority by royal decree. He governed through a staff of professional officials, who were often of foreign origin and nonnoble lineage. The Diet was quiescent during his lifetime and neglected to challenge its exclusion from decision making.

The nobles of Transylvania were fully entitled to participate in all affairs of the Hungarian kingdom, although they also developed an identity of their own. The existence of a separate Transylvanian Diet is first noted in the records for 1288. On at least two occasions, 1291 and 1355, this body included representatives of all nationalities of the province, although subsequently the Vlachs (Romanians) were no longer invited. Their exclusion was a religious rather than a nationalist measure, since the Vlachs adhered to Eastern Orthodoxy, while the 14th-century Angevin kings pursued a zealous pro-Catholic policy. The activity of the Transylvanian Diet was mainly juridical in nature: the voivode summoned it once a year at Torda to elect judges. Through these meetings the three recognized Catholic "nations" of the province—Hungarians, Szeklers, and Saxons—gradually developed an awareness of shared privilege. During the Bobîlna peasant revolt of 1437, the Transylvanian Diet met on its own initiative for the first time, in order to decide on measures against the (largely Vlach) rebels. After the revolt was suppressed, that body convened once again to tighten the conditions of peasant servitude, hoping in this way to prevent further uprisings.

Assemblies of the free population are known to have existed as early as the 10th to 12th centuries in Polish Silesia, where decrees proposed by the king and the magnates were "confirmed by the commoners." Such assemblies existed also in the larger towns of Pomerania, like Wolin and Szczecin (Stettin), which were governed as oligarchic urban republics. In the semi-independent appanages into which Poland was divided in the 12th and 13th centuries, magnates and prelates met together with some regularity. During this period of disunion, the various appanage rulers were too weak to govern against the wishes of their nobles, but at most could hope to play off one faction against another. Assemblies of nobility were usually held once a year, although more frequently in the province of Little Poland. An appanage prince typically sought the assembly's approval for new laws, taxes, wars, marriage treaties, the conferral of offices or immunities, and the founding of new towns. Nevertheless, after Poland was reunified (ca. 1310), an assembly for the entire realm was slow to come into being. During the reign of Vladislav IV Łokietek (r. 1310–33), the restorer of the unified state, only four meetings of the Great Sejm have been recorded. Meetings were similarly rare under his son, Casimir the Great (r. 1333–70), since this able monarch preferred to govern alone. If Casimir needed to consult his subjects, he did so piecemeal. For example, in making peace with the Teutonic Knights in 1343, he ordered the chief provincial officials as well as representatives of the nobility, clergy, and towns to draw up separate documents guaranteeing the treaty. However, he did ask the assemblies of Great and Little Poland to approve his new law codes, thus demonstrating that even a powerful sovereign sometimes found it necessary to share his prerogatives.

The Great Sejm—the Diet of the entire Polish kingdom—was founded upon the custom of electing the king. At first this procedure was largely a formality by which the assembly gave its consent to the succession of the obvious heir and sought confirmation of the usual privileges of the nobility. However, in the 14th and 15th centuries the Sejm gained in importance from the failure of the ruling dynasty to produce legitimate male offspring. In each case the assembled nobility demanded additional privileges in exchange for assenting to a hitherto unprecedented order of succession. At Košice (Kassa) in 1374, King Louis asked the Sejm to accept one of his daughters as heir to the Polish throne, hoping thereby to reduce the likelihood of a challenge to her position after his death. In return he agreed to exempt the nobility from virtually all taxes. In 1386 a Great Sejm elected Grand Duke Jagiełło of Lithuania, husband of Queen Jadwiga, as king of Poland. Near the end of his life Jagiełło asked the Sejm to recognize Vladislav, his son by his fourth (but nonroyal) wife, as heir to the throne. After this young monarch's death in 1444 at the battle of Varna, the Sejm negotiated with his brother Casimir for three years before electing him as king, despite the absence of any other serious contender.

In the first half of the 15th century the Great Sejm of Poland consisted of the royal Council, certain high officials, nobles, and representatives of cathedral chapters or town councils if they chose to come, which frequently they did not. In principle all male members of the nobility were entitled to attend, including Lithuanian nobles after the Horodło agreement of 1413 had strengthened the ties between the two parts of the realm. Usually the Great Sejm convened once a year, ordinarily at Piotrków on the border between Little Poland and Great Poland. Exactly when the Great Sejm first met in two houses is not known, although certainly it had done so by 1493 and perhaps even earlier. The lower house represented the lesser nobility as well as the magnates, while the royal Council became the upper house, or Senate. In this respect the Great Sejm differed from the Diet in Hungary, where the lower nobility met separately from the magnates. However, in neither country did the clergy constitute a separate estate: bishops and abbots (who were usually of noble origin) belonged to the upper house. Distinctions in rank were carefully observed: at sessions of the Great Sejm the members of the royal Council sat on benches, while everyone else remained standing.

Assemblies of the nobility continued to function at the provincial and local level in all seven provinces of Poland in the 15th century. If the Great Sejm of the entire kingdom failed to meet, provincial sejms replaced it. District assemblies known as sejmiks also existed in some areas, consisting not just of delegates but of all nobles of the district, who came in person. The sejmiks imposed local taxes and served as courts of justice. They made possible a broad representation of the nobility on the local level, whereas the Great Sejm ordinarily was dominated by the magnates of the royal Council. Generally each sejmik sent two delegates to its provincial sejm and an additional two to the Great Sejm, although in principle no limit was set on the number. No hierarchical order governed the Polish system of national, provincial, and district assemblies, since none of these bodies was considered superior to any other. They acted in parallel fashion and sometimes alternately. It was a unique feature of the Polish legislative system that all were equally entitled to consider questions of national importance, and could conduct their deliberations and vote even in the absence of the monarch. When the king wished to levy extraordinary taxes, he sometimes preferred to summon the sejmiks separately rather than one of the larger assemblies, since the lesser nobility was more easily persuaded to accede to his proposals. He could then cite the agreement of one body as an argument to convince the others. Town representatives participated quite regularly in the Great Sejm from the end of the 14th century until the middle of the 15th, although rarely afterward, except in royal elections. The sole exception was Cracow, the capital, which always sent representatives to the Great Sejm.

This increased activity of provincial and district sejms, comprised exclusively of nobles, helped reduce the role of the towns, and corresponded to the growing political weight of the Polish nobility in the second half of the 15th century. The position of these assemblies was greatly enhanced by two privileges issued by King Casimir IV in 1454. At the beginning of the Thirteen Years' War, which was fought outside the boundaries of Poland, a group of nobles in the army extracted the king's promise not to undertake military expeditions in future without the consent of a general meeting. Not until he had conceded the point did the Polish troops move into battle—only to be thoroughly routed at Chojnice in the one major encounter of the war. This incident clearly demonstrated the king's dependence on his nobles, who feared that foreign conquests would add to the power of the monarchy. Casimir IV afterward summoned the entire Polish nobility to Nieszawa, a field near Toruń (Thorn), where he promised to convene either a sejmik or a provincial Sejm before imposing any tax or engaging in military action. A separate privilege-document was issued for each province, testifying to the survival of a strong regional consciousness dating from the appanage period.

Another way for the Polish nobility to exert pressure on the monarch was through the informal associations known as confederations. In medieval Europe it was not uncommon for a group of nobles to assemble on an ad hoc basis to promote some political objective. In Poland this became an accepted feature of political life. The nobles who joined a confederation bound themselves to act in common for some specific goal. Since they remained together only until the objective was either attained or abandoned, the association had a temporary character. Sometimes a confederation was formed to compensate for ineffective government, like the ones which the towns of Great Poland organized in 1302 and again in 1350 to ensure the security of the roads against robbers. Confederations typically appeared during interregna when the government had lapsed, as in 1382 after the death of King Louis. Their goal in such cases was to maintain law and order, keep the country united, and influence the selection of a new monarch. A confederation was organized in 1352 to demand a law prohibiting confiscation of noble estates by royal officials without a court judgment. In the 1420s and 1430s, confederations of both pro-Hussite and anti-Hussite forces sprang up. Two noble confederations met at Piotrków in 1406–7 to protest the Church's demands for tithe and for special clerical courts, to which the clergy responded by forming a confederation of their own. However, as the meetings of sejms and sejmiks became more usual, confederations became more rare. Their revival in the 17th century was a symptom of constitutional crisis and governmental breakdown.

The Polish middle nobility became increasingly active in politics in the second half of the 15th century. This class tended to regard the king less as the protector of the state than as a possibly hostile power and a competitor in taxing the peasants. In any case, the elimination of the Teutonic Knights as a serious threat to Poland after 1466 meant that the monarch's role as military leader was deemphasized. The nobility insisted not only upon being consulted on all important matters but that *only* nobles be so consulted, and did their best to cut off all avenues of social mobility for townsmen. By the statute of Piotrków in 1496 the Sejm restricted landholding to nobles alone, seeking in this way to prevent townsmen from gaining noble status through the purchase of estates. The same Sejm also forbade peasants to change their place of residence—an act which effectively instituted serfdom and cut off the principal source of population increase for the towns. These and other measures greatly hindered the development of an affluent urban class which might eventually have allied itself with the king against the nobility. The statute of 1505 entitled "Nihil Novi" (i.e., "nothing new") was the logical capstone of this process. In it the king promised not to issue any new laws without the consent of the Sejm, which would judge for itself what was really "new." Thus the royal Council could no longer enact decrees without the Sejm's approval, while the royal starostas—officials who were supposed to function as the king's agents—became tenured for life in their positions. After 1505 the sovereign was forbidden to create any new offices or officeholders whose primary loyalty would be to him. "Nihil Novi" definitively established the Sejm as the principal lawgiving institution in the country and fatally weakened the monarchy by depriving it of control over its own administrative apparatus. Thereby Poland became a true republic of nobles.

In Prussia, by contrast, noble representation in government arrived relatively late. There the Teutonic Knights maintained a total monopoly of political power, although as celibate monks and Germans they lacked organic ties with the country. Whenever the Knights elected a new grand master, they simply summoned Prussian representatives to Malbork to swear fealty to the new leader. At first these assemblies were purely passive; but from the 1390s onward they began actively to present proposals of their own. After about 1430 the Prussian Diet began to demand a permanent voice in the government of the country. The growing political weight of the nobility in neighboring Poland had evoked repercussions across the border, since many native Prussian families were linked by economic arrangements or marriage ties to the Polish nobility, and increasingly had come to resent their exclusion from political power. The defeat of the Knights' army during a war with Poland in 1410 compelled the Order to make concessions. In 1411 the grand master for the first time summoned an all-Prussian assembly to approve new taxes for carrying on the war. However, he still did not propose to modify any of the Order's administrative or judicial prerogatives, which effectively prevented this assembly from developing into a real governing institution.

By 1440 both the native Prussian nobility and the predominantly German townsmen of Prussia were sufficiently frustrated by the government of the Teutonic Order to join forces in forming the Prussian League. Led by Gdańsk, the most prosperous of the towns, the League's members swore to refuse obedience to the Order if it injured their rights and privileges. This accord, which reflected a realistic awareness of common interests, was nonetheless a rare instance of collaboration between two social classes which in medieval Europe were more often antagonistic. In 1453 the League formed a secret council—comprising an equal number of nobles and townsmen—and sought to escape the yoke of the Knights through alliance with Poland. The following year it began a military revolt, aimed at replacing the grand master of the Order with the king of Poland as sovereign of a largely autonomous Prussia. This objective was only partially fulfilled. At the end of the Thirteen Years' War (1454–66), western Prussia (henceforth known as Royal Prussia) was incorporated into Poland, while the rest of Prussia remained subject to the Teutonic Order, with the grand master owing fealty to the Polish king.

The Diet which now came into being in Royal Prussia was an extension of the assemblies of the Prussian League. The Prussian Council (the equivalent of a royal Council elsewhere) served as the upper house; representatives of the nobility, the towns, and some of the monasteries formed the lower house. Nobles and townsmen in the Diet met separately, although members of the Council sat with both houses and exerted a decisive influence. The king of Poland was represented only by nonparticipating observers. The Diet made all the most crucial decisions for Royal Prussia, especially those concerning taxation, and successfully asserted its right to meet without the king's consent. After 1459 it also elected the governor and other high officials of the province. Delegates from East Prussia, still ruled by the Teutonic Order, participated on many occasions in the meetings of the Royal Prussian Diet. Despite political separation, the inhabitants of both parts of Prussia retained an awareness of their common traditions and continued to feel that the two parts belonged together. Only the bishopric of Warmia remained a separate unit, represented in neither the Prussian Council nor the Diet until the end of the 15th century.

For medieval legislative assemblies generally, taxation remained the most crucial item of business and a frequent subject of dispute between them and the monarchs. Since government was rudimentary, the sovereign was expected (except in wartime) to finance it out of his personal income, which in turn was derived in large part from his so-called regalian rights. These entitled him to the profits from tariffs, customs, fines assessed by royal courts, and imposts on salt and wine. He was usually also entitled to dispose freely of any property not already claimed by private lords, including the lands tilled by the free rural population and any unplowed or uncultivable regions such as forests or swamps. Tariffs or tolls assessed on international frontiers provided important sums for the royal treasury. However, the process of collection required a large staff, while payment was relatively easy to evade. For this reason King Charles Robert in 13th-century Hungary abolished customs duties on the frontiers and instead taxed foreign goods at the markets where they were sold—a much easier task than policing the border zones. This market tax began at one percent of the value of the goods, but had increased to one-thirtieth by the 15th century, when it became the government's chief source of income. On the other hand, the profits from internal tolls, collected at strategic spots within a country, generally did not accrue to the monarch. Most tolls on roads, bridges, ferries, and markets belonged to private secular or clerical lords.

From the monarch's point of view, revenue derived from regalian rights possessed the considerable advantage of not requiring the consent of any representative body. Although treated as his personal income, the yield was differentiated only imperfectly from state property. Additional taxation was regarded as justified only for exceptional expenses, such as a royal coronation, the dowry or marriage of a princess, or a foreign war. Even if certain types of tax were assessed quite frequently, the fiction was usually upheld that they were "extraordinary" (i.e., occurring only in response to some specific and nonrepeatable situation).

Precisely on such occasions the Diet would be summoned to vote approval. On the other hand, any attempt to introduce a tax collectible at regular intervals always aroused enormous opposition. The nearly universal system of tax farming in medieval society, whereby collection was entrusted to private entrepreneurs, gave credence to the fiction that all general taxation was in fact "extraordinary." A permanent set of royal tax officials would have exploded this myth.

Tax farming had certain practical advantages as well. It was comparatively quick and efficient. The tax farmer received a lease permitting him to collect the revenue of a particular district in return for a specified sum of money. This arrangement produced a fixed sum known to the government in advance, since the amount was settled by contract between the monarch and the lessee. It avoided administrative expenses to the monarch and assigned the process of collection to persons experienced in financial matters. The disadvantage was that the lessees were largely independent of royal control. They treated their jobs as profit-making enterprises and often extorted far larger sums from the population than those to which they were entitled. The taxpayers were plundered; and many possible sources of royal income were exhausted in this way. On the other hand, it is unlikely that a system of official tax collectors would have functioned better. An honest fiscal administration would have required strict oversight and control from the center, which medieval governments were notoriously incapable of providing. Secular rulers were not alone in resorting to tax farming. The Church did likewise in collecting the tithe. Landowners sometimes became tax farmers with respect to their own peasants, thereby severing one more link between their dependents and any external authority. Even the Ottoman government employed tax farmers, highly centralized though it was by the standards of the time.

Profits from the mines were a major source of income for many rulers. Silver production in Bohemia during the reign of Charles I (r. 1346–78) amounted to one-third of the entire European yield. The Bohemian royal mint held a monopoly on coinage and the silver trade, with the king receiving an eighth of the profits. In Hungary all noble metals were considered state property, and delivered to the king at well below market prices: the rule was that between an eighth and a tenth of the yield from mining accrued to the royal treasury. Profits from the mines underwrote the military successes of many an ambitious monarch, among them Matthias of Hungary (r. 1458–90) and Stephen Dušan (r. 1331–55) of Serbia. The latter built up his ephemeral empire largely on the profits of the Bosnian silver mines. The enormous annual income which Despot George Branković drew from the mines of Novo Brdo was certainly a major factor in his otherwise amazing political survival in the vulnerable Serbian vassal state. The minting of coins provided additional revenue for any monarch controlling major supplies of ore, since debasement of a country's coinage was common practice. Salt was another important product of the mines, so indispensable in the human diet that no one could escape paying a tax on it. The rich salt mines of

Transylvania, like those near Cracow in Poland, produced great profits for their royal proprietors.

Quite frequently the monarch's chief official in charge of finance was an anomaly in his administration—a man of bourgeois origin when all other dignitaries of similar rank belonged to the nobility. The Serbian rulers, for example, routinely employed merchants from the Dalmatian coastal towns as treasury officials. Tax farmers likewise were usually townsmen who lacked noble status, since the incompetence of nobles in monetary matters was common knowledge. Military service, residence at court, or life on a rural estate did not prepare a noble to fill a position requiring administrative or technical expertise. Jews were particularly prominent as tax collectors and money changers because they often possessed business expertise. Inevitably, their employment aroused opposition in many quarters, especially from nobles (who were thereby deprived of a possibly lucrative concession) and from churchmen (fearing that contact with Jews might erode the faith of Christians). Muslims were much less numerous than Jews in East Central Europe outside the Ottoman Empire, but at times served a similar function. The Hungarian Golden Bull of 1222 expressly forbade the monarch to employ Muslims or Jews either as tax farmers or administrators of the coinage, the salt tax, or tariffs. In practice these stipulations were largely ignored. The Hungarian kings, like most of their fellow monarchs, needed the financial skills of these specialists and were not too pious to make use of them.

Neither the Church as an institution nor the clergy as individuals paid taxes as such to the state. Nonetheless, it was customary for them to offer gifts to a new sovereign when he took the throne; and later such presents became regular and obligatory. The Church tithe, amounting to one-tenth of a taxpayer's income, was assessed on the entire population. Christians paid it in addition to any other taxes they owed to a landholder or to the king, although by the 15th century the nobility was sometimes exempt. The tithe was the bishops' chief source of income, far more lucrative than the profits from even very large ecclesiastical estates. At times the king received a share of the tithe, often with the pope's express agreement, since papal agents needed the monarch's cooperation to collect it at all. Another tax having a confessional basis was the Ottoman poll tax, or jizya, paid by all non-Muslims. Although jizya in principle was calculated according to each taxpayer's income, in practice many villages paid it in a lump sum. Direct agents of the Ottoman government rather than tax farmers collected it; and exemptions were rarely granted. Jizya was regarded as politically untouchable because of the important religious distinction it embodied.

An additional source of a ruler's income was the tax on Jews, who frequently had to hand over sizable sums as protection money. This tax was included among the regalian rights. Since Jews were legally the monarch's servants, to kill or rob one was to commit a crime against the ruler personally. Kings, towns, and territorial lords quarreled over the right to exploit the Jews, who represented a rich source of revenue. For example, Bohemian nobles were usually forbidden to settle Jewish families on their lands, since this would deprive the monarch of some portion of the Jewish protection money. Hungary imposed a special tax on Jews (as on free immigrants and other "guests") in exchange for guaranteeing them personal freedom and exemption from military service. The Jews were also easy victims of extortion when the monarchs needed money, since they were quite helpless if deprived of royal protection. King John of Bohemia in 1336 financed his foreign military adventures in part by imprisoning affluent Jews and then demanding a ransom for their release. His search for hidden treasure in the Prague synagogue yielded a hoard of 2,000 marks. (Nondiscriminatory in his greed, John also confiscated valuables from the graves of Christian saints.) King Wenceslas IV of Bohemia ordered the imprisonment of many Jews in 1384 and 1389 so that he could more easily appropriate their property. Sigismund of Hungary forced the Jews to help finance the Council of Constance, a purely Roman Catholic endeavor. Irregular taxation of this type was in no way unusual.

The land tax was another source of state revenue, although powerful nobles increasingly won exemption for their estates. In Hungary the free folk living on royal land, especially the immigrant "guests" enjoying royal protection, paid a direct tax to the king based on the amount of land they held. In Serbia royal agents surveyed the countryside, marking the extent of everyone's fields by means of boundary stones or (in Dalmatia) with stone walls. Tax registers recorded the number of persons, fruit trees, and vines in each district together with children, slaves, and livestock. Extensive as this sounds, the Serbian tax books were nonetheless far less complete than the old Byzantine cadastral books. The Ottoman government often simply preserved the tax structure of its predecessors in the conquered lands. A tax commissioner appeared in every district soon after the conquest in order to assess possible sources of revenue. He recorded the names of the heads of village households, the extent of their land, and the total yield expected from existing taxes. This procedure was repeated every twenty to thirty years.

Personal services which subjects owed to their sovereign constituted a form of tax payable by every class of society. Early in the medieval era the monarch could demand labor services (corvée) from peasants directly, especially for purposes of defense. In Serbia, for example, all the inhabitants of crown lands were required to work for him, gathering and beating the grain, mowing hay, and cultivating vines. Villages belonging to monasteries were exempt from such services, and possibly the villages owned by high nobles were also. In general, as the nobility became more powerful, it came to resent any direct monarchical authority over the peasants on its estates as an infringement on noble rights. Thus the Hungarian nobility forced King Andrew II to agree in his second Golden Bull in 1231 that peasants from noble or ecclesiastical lands would not be used for work on border fortresses, entrenchments, or other royal projects. Another common grievance was quartering—the right of the monarch when traveling to demand that the nobles on his route provide hospitality for himself and his entire entourage of courtiers, officials, foreign ambassadors, and servants. This entailed food and lodging appropriate to a sovereign's high rank as well as an adequate supply of fresh packhorses, saddle horses, and forage. Resentful of the trouble and expense, the Hungarian nobility demanded in the Golden Bull of 1222 that the king refrain from quartering members of his retinue in their houses. Thus the Angevin kings in the 14th century collected a special tax from the population in lieu of quartering. In Serbia the obligation of supplying such services remained in force until the royal party reached either the next fortress or the frontier of the district. Moreover, if the monarch passed through a Serbian market town, the resident foreign merchants were required to offer him a present, although Tsar Stephen Dušan's law code eventually forbade this practice.

Taxes not rendered in labor services were generally paid in natural products. The underdeveloped monetary economy of the medieval period meant that coins were usually in short supply outside of major trading centers, so that in most cases a demand for payment in specie would have been wholly unrealistic. For example, in southern Bulgaria in the 11th century the peasants paid a tax of one bucket of wheat, one bucket of millet, and a jug of wine for each yoke of oxen that they owned. The towns of northern Dalmatia paid tribute to Venice in fox, marten, or rabbit skins. One Croatian tax continued to be termed the "marten tax" long after it had ceased to be paid in skins. Tsar Stephen Dušan's Serbian law code specified that the land tax was payable either as a bucket of grain or as one perper of silver. The Vlach herdsmen of Serbia paid in sheep and cheeses for the right to use pasturage. Annually they gave their sovereign four percent of their sheep. In Ottoman Bosnia at the end of the 15th century, each Vlach household paid a tax of one sheep with its lamb and one ram or the equivalent in money.

Indeed, nearly any product of value might be paid as a tax somewhere, sometime—olive oil and fish along the Dalmatian coast; wine, linen, or silk by the commercial towns; wax, honey, pigs, or chopped wood by forest dwellers. Peasants in the Ottoman Empire were required to deliver grain for the support of the army at designated camp sites, at a price somewhat below market value. By necessity, the yield of a tax in kind had to be consumed locally if transportation was impractical over any distance. Thus medieval lay and secular lords lived from the produce contributed by the tenants or serfs on their estates, while the monarch assigned the taxes of various regions to support his officials and military retainers. With the development of a money economy, taxes began to be paid in coin, although the extent to which this was done varied greatly according to circumstances. Tributes to foreign states had to be paid in money. For example, in the 15th century the despot of Serbia, as an Ottoman vassal, paid the sultan the enormous sum of 40,000 or 50,000 ducats annually. Since the despot was the owner of rich mines, this perhaps represented one-tenth of his annual income.

The principal revenue of the Ottoman Empire came from jizya, the head tax paid by each head of a non-Muslim household. However, if a place was strategically located in a frontier district, its inhabitants might receive a temporary exemption. By appointing the border dwellers to guard roads and mountain passes and keep the roads in repair, the Turkish authorities secured many types of services without direct payment. Muslims paid no taxes at all to the sultan unless military action took place in their area, which rendered them liable for a tax on one-tenth of their property. In addition, the Ottoman government realized important sums from the lease of government-owned lands and mines; from state monopolies, harbor duties, and customs; from debasement of the coinage; and from the tribute assessed on vassal states. Inevitably, the Ottoman sultans required more than the usual revenue of medieval governments just in order to finance their perpetual wars. Rarely was the empire at peace; and from the early 14th until the mid-16th century it continued to expand. This placed a heavy financial burden on the provinces, which doubtless greatly injured their prosperity. As long as the sultan's armies were victorious, the costs of war were partially offset by war booty, one-fifth of which automatically became the sultan's property to use "in Allah's name." In effect, all of the sultan's income was spent either on his own household or on the military establishment.

The Ottoman land tax was calculated according to the value of the land, not the status of the landholder. A vast bureaucracy existed to register each piece of ground together with its estimated annual yield. However, the Ottoman tax system was largely decentralized and in the hands of local fief holders. The income from an ordinary timar went entirely for the upkeep of the sipahi (cavalryman) to whom it was assigned, since its purpose was to free him to fight in the sultan's wars with his own equipment. Additional timars were set aside for the benefit of higher-ranking officers in the military establishment. The sipahi on his holding collected grain from his peasants in preference to the equivalent in money because grain had value both for consumption and exchange. However, in place of products which were difficult to store and not always marketable, such as fruit, vegetables, pigs, or sheep, he preferred cash. Frequently absent on campaign, he was in no position either to make use of perishable items or to sell them. He also collected taxes in cash on any water mills or artisan workshops on his property. The common people, or re'aya, in the Ottoman Empire were enlisted to serve the military and civilian establishment in a wide variety of occupations, for example, as oarsmen for the galleys, workers on construction projects, or as butchers, bakers, cooks, saddlers, shoemakers, tailors, and blacksmiths. These obligations, although never fixed in amount, at times could be very heavy. They took the peasant away from his farm for weeks or months, particularly during the summer campaigning season. Peasant labor service for the state was detrimental to the economic interests of the sipahis, but the Ottoman government was powerful enough to enforce it.

Towns everywhere were a more lucrative source of revenue than rural villages, owing to the opportunity they provided for the collection of market dues, port and bridge tolls, and taxes on artisans. When a town received the right to self-government, often by royal charter, it also accepted the obligation to pay a fixed yearly sum to the king in lieu of ordinary taxes. Local officials then decided how to distribute the burden. For example, the towns of the Dalmatian coast supplied tribute (i.e., a tax disguised as a gift) to their successive political overlords. Dubrovnik, the wealthiest of the lot, paid 2,000 perpers annually to the Serbian tsar in the 14th century, but 12,500 ducats to the Turks each year from 1481 onward. The funds came from customs revenues and the salt monopoly or occasionally from extraordinary contributions. Jewish communities were taxed by their own rabbis, who turned over the required amounts in a lump sum to a royal official. The entire Saxon district of Transylvania, which included a number of flourishing towns, received a lump sum assessement which the Saxons collected themselves. Royal towns, as the monarch's property, might even be sold or pawned. Thus in 1412, King Sigismund of Hungary pawned thirteen towns in the Zips district of Slovakia to the king of Poland in order to finance one of his campaigns against the Turks. Efforts to get them back proved unsuccessful until the first Partition of Poland in 1772.

Occasionally a tax which the population perceived as excessive gave rise to a major armed revolt. The stringent tax system which the Byzantines imposed on the recovered Bulgarian lands after 1018 helped incite two widespread rebellions, one in 1040 and another in 1072–73. Neither was successful. The first Albanian uprising against Ottoman rule was prompted by a census of village lands which people correctly viewed as the prelude to taxation. Albanian lords who had been deprived of parts of their estates to provide fiefs for Ottoman cavalrymen were disgruntled enough to revolt in 1432–33. This uprising dealt the sultan's army a major defeat in the Shkumbi valley and required two years to suppress. The Transylvanian peasant revolt of 1437 was ignited in part by the local bishop's demand that the church tithe be paid in coin, which was difficult for peasants to acquire in the undeveloped rural economy. Like its predecessors, this uprising ended in failure, serving only to worsen the legal position of the peasantry.

Ultimately a monarch's income from taxes provided a fair measure of his political effectiveness. One way for a ruler to increase his revenue was to improve the efficiency of tax collection and eliminate exemptions. Very successful in this respect was King Matthias of Hungary, who required large sums to finance his aggressive foreign policy. In 1467 he replaced the old Hungarian tax system, which was riddled with exemptions and immunities, with a new one that applied to everyone alike except clergy and nobility. Almost every year he convinced the Diet to approve an allegedly extraordinary war tax; and customs duties were collected more rigorously than ever before. Matthias also had at his disposal the vast private fortune of the Hunyadis. The effect was to more than double the royal income to a level approaching that of France or Burgundy at that time. Most of this revenue, however, still came from taxes on the peasantry rather than urban sources or customs duties—a clear indication that Hungary remained economically underdeveloped. Under the weak kings of the Jagiellonian dynasty who followed Matthias on the throne, the financial situation rapidly deteriorated.

The magnates in the Diet managed to get much of the state income under their own control. Moreover, as foreigners by origin, the Jagiellonians had no property of their own in Hungary. According to the reports of Venetian envoys, the income of the Hungarian crown between 1490 and 1526 totaled no more than one-fourth of the amount collected in Matthias's time.

In sum, the authority of even the strongest governments of medieval East Central Europe was very far from being despotic. The monarch could, and often did, behave autocratically toward his own entourage, especially toward servants and others of inferior rank. He might order heads to be chopped off or property confiscated, and he could inflict cruel tortures on people who aroused his wrath. But he could not expect to make his writ run throughout an entire territory without enlisting the cooperation of his leading men. At first this meant the tribal and clan leaders, and at a later period the landholding aristocracy. Moreover, the primitiveness of medieval communications made outlying areas difficult to control. No administrative structure existed which was capable of enforcing its decrees over an extensive land area in the absence of effective power at the center. In many instances the monarch lacked sufficient military strength to overawe the more powerful of his subjects, especially if several of the magnates joined forces against him. A sovereign who failed to fulfill adequately his role as war leader was likely to see portions of his kingdom break away. On the other hand, royal authority enjoyed the support of habit and tradition. The sovereign's position as military chief enhanced his power, since ordinarily he commanded the strongest military force in the country. The Church upheld his rule with the sanctions of religion. As time passed, central governments became better organized and assumed additional powers and functions.

Provincial administration inevitably reflected the constellation of power at the capital. A strong monarch was able to appoint his own officials in the various districts and replace them at his pleasure. Even so, he was frequently compelled to choose men from the leading families of a region, both in order to gain their cooperation and because he was not powerful enough to impose his own loyalists upon the countryside. Great lords who were also royal appointees tended to regard their offices as private sources of income and tried to make them hereditary. Usually they did not take charge of provincial administration personally, but delegated one of their retainers to do the actual work. When the monarchy was weak, local dignitaries became more or less autonomous, and the landed nobility tended to control the king. In cases of disputed succession or a very young ruler, great lords could virtually ignore the central government. Border regions tended to escape the sovereign's control altogether. In a frontier territory like Bosnia, even the strongest rulers rarely dominated more than a core area.

The growth of great landed estates and the increasing autonomy of the nobility as a social class in the 13th and 14th centuries led to a serious diminution in the power of central governments. Noble lords were often successful in obtaining

immunities from royal justice and taxation on their own estates. Some developed
into powerful autocrats within their own separate and private spheres. Great
magnates became largely exempt from royal control, while noble assemblies were
often able to challenge the monarch's authority. In this way the nobility became
in effect the monarch's co-ruler. Possession of extensive landed estates—the
principal source of wealth in the medieval era—could be translated into political
power. John Hunyadi became regent of Hungary in 1446 not only because of his
military reputation but because he was the richest landowner in the kingdom.
George Poděbrady parlayed his status as a great Bohemian landholder into
leadership of the Hussite party; and when the Bohemian Přemyslid dynasty
died out, the Diet elected him king. In Poland the nobility by 1505 was strong
enough to deprive the king of the power to control his own officials or to issue
laws without their consent. In this period of noble ascendancy, a sovereign could
usually make his will prevail only by enlisting the support of one noble faction against another. Sometimes this meant using the relatively numerous lesser
nobles against the magnates. However, no monarch in medieval East Central
Europe ever succeeded in concluding a solid political alliance with the leading
towns of his kingdom. With the partial exception of Hussite Bohemia or Royal
Prussia in the 15th century, the urban commercial class failed to transform itself
into a political factor capable of counterbalancing the nobility's influence.

During most of the medieval period in East Central Europe, the Diets or
Estates of the land were by no means full participants in political life. Their sessions were too infrequent to qualify them as genuine lawmaking bodies, or even
as a serious check on the sovereign's authority. They convened at the monarch's
request for some specific purpose and did not constitute an independent branch of
government. Nonetheless, on occasion they exerted a very considerable political
influence. The assembly's principal leverage came from its control over taxation,
since the sovereign needed the consent of the powerful men of his realm in order
to collect money from his subjects. In peacetime he was expected to finance the
costs of government from the revenues from his own lands and from exploiting
his regalian rights. Since these sources of income were inadequate for fighting
even a minor war, let alone a major one, he needed to summon the national
Diet to approve any extraordinary tax. Then the members could utilize the
opportunity to present grievances and extract concessions before acceding to his
proposals. In some cases—particularly if the old ruling dynasty had died out, or
if the succession was contested—the assembly actually selected a monarch from
among several possible candidates. Even when an obvious heir to the throne was
present and the Diet merely went through the motions of election, this procedure
was still necessary to give the sovereign legitimacy. It served to confirm the ancient
principle that the ruler was freely chosen by his subjects.

State power by the end of the medieval era was certainly less well developed
in East Central Europe than in Western Europe at the same period. The only
real exceptions were the government of the Teutonic Knights in Prussia and the

Ottoman Empire in the Balkans. A lower level of prosperity was certainly one reason for the difference. As compared to the states bordering the Atlantic, East Central Europe was much less favorably situated to take advantage of overseas trade to Asia or the New World. Meanwhile, Ottoman ascendancy had cut off the old overland routes to the Orient which were crucial to the welfare of many towns in the interior. Stagnant urban economies made it impossible for a middle class to develop the strength necessary to challenge monarchical power, or for monarchs to use the support of a town class to reduce the nobility's prerogatives. In Poland the prosperity of the towns was further depressed by legislative measures aimed at benefiting nobles at the expense of townsmen. Bohemia became largely isolated from the rest of Europe in the 15th century because of the Hussite religious revolt. However, the most significant political difference between Western and East Central Europe was the fact that the latter eventually became absorbed into enormous multinational empires. This had happened already in the late 14th and the 15th centuries in the Balkan Peninsula. In Hungary it occurred in the fifteen years which followed the battle of Mohács in 1526. Bohemia would experience a similar fate after the disaster of White Mountain in 1620, Poland at the Partitions of 1772, 1793, and 1795. The ultimate effect was to remove political authority over East Central Europe to a very few locations entirely external to the area—Istanbul, Vienna, St. Petersburg, or Berlin—where local interests or initiatives were unable to prevail against the overall policy of an imperial megastate.

CHAPTER 10

Laws and Justice

*E*verywhere in ancient times, law began with custom—the unwritten rules of social interaction developed within a community over many generations. In the young societies of early medieval East Central Europe all law was of this type, hallowed by tradition. The rights of persons and groups, together with the accepted penalties for violation of the rules, represented an approximate social consensus concerning what was just and right. Custom provided a complete juridical system for every aspect of life, quite independently of any confirmation or authorization in written law. It was viewed as part of the natural order, while the decrees of monarchs originally applied to a very small range of human behavior. Royal edicts normally did not supersede the ancient customs, but merely supplemented them.

Law as applied by the courts of medieval sovereigns thus consisted largely of traditional norms, based on memory rather than written texts. Indeed, judges often knew no other type of law. Monarchs who conquered new territories tended to leave local traditions and life-styles alone. In any case, custom was by definition a static system, resistant to change. Long after legislated law became common, important elements of the ancient customary law continued in force. Rulers often exercised their lawgiving function simply by confirming a particular custom, either by applying it in a specific instance or by issuing an explicit decree. Then the custom would be recorded in writing and communicated to the appropriate secular and ecclesiastical officials. Even in the later Middle Ages, when laws often originated in a representative assembly, they were usually proclaimed as royal decrees. Once issued, they acquired the force of precedent, which had considerable practical effect in determining future judgments. Since in principle the decision of a monarch did not bind his successors, or even himself in a subsequent case, the "old" laws had to be periodically reissued. The earliest medieval written law was primarily a record of custom, like the *Rožmberk Book* in Bohemia or the *Book of Elbląg* in Poland, both dating from the mid-13th century.

The law of ancient Rome, by contrast, had evolved as a unified legal system by which the Roman Empire ruled many diverse nations. Eventually it acquired a strong Christian coloring. As known to the European Middle Ages, Roman law was based on the 6th-century code of Emperor Justinian, originally compiled in Latin but soon afterward translated into Greek. It contained a systematic body of general principles, thus rendering it more suitable than native customary law to provide a framework for legal growth. Roman law laid particular emphasis on the authority of the ruler and the interests of the centralized state, a point which naturally appealed to the new national monarchies. Particularly influential were two variations of Justinian's code known respectively as the *Ecloga* and the *Procheiron*. The *Ecloga*, promulgated in 739, was an abstract of Justinian's code amended and rearranged to accord with contemporary Christian principles. The *Procheiron*, issued in 886, was a collection of the most important sections of that code. In addition, Byzantine jurists compiled, abridged, and arranged the civil and ecclesiastical laws on various subjects into systematic treatises called nomocanons. This Roman-Byzantine law not only provided the legal framework for Christian states, but also legitimized royal authority by its insistence that all monarchical power comes from God.

The earliest of the medieval states of East Central Europe to adopt some elements of Roman law was Bulgaria, which in this respect as well as others was a Byzantine successor state. Probably during the reign of Boris, its first Christian monarch (r. 852–89), Bulgaria produced the first translation of a Byzantine law code into the Slavic tongue. Known as the *Zakon Sudnyj Ljudem* ("Law for Judging the People"), it corresponds closely to the 17th chapter of the Byzantine *Ecloga*. Actually the *Zakon* is an adaptation rather than a direct translation. It fails to mention certain offenses, such as swearing false oaths or minting counterfeit coins, which either were not known in pre-Christian Bulgaria or not widespread there owing to the primitive economy. Other omissions are probably attributable to the translator's wish to retain certain old Bulgar customs. On the other hand, the *Zakon* prescribes punishments for some acts which the *Ecloga* ignores, such as pagan observances, incest, and polygamy. These became crimes in Bulgaria only after the advent of Christianity, whereas in Byzantium—already a Christian state for half a millennium—they cannot have been widespread. The very first article of the *Zakon* orders that villagers who practice heathen rituals and customs should be turned into serfs and sold for the good of the Church. The specific penalties it decrees for boyars who organize pagan religious ceremonies were probably directed at the group which revolted against Khan Boris in protest against his acceptance of Christianity. In some respects the *Zakon* is more lenient than the *Ecloga*. In cases of sexual transgressions for which the *Ecloga* prescribed death or amputation of limbs, the *Zakon* authorized merely ecclesiastical penalties. Apparently the translator sought to avoid giving offense to old Bulgar habits.

Particularly influential in the Balkans was the 9th-century Byzantine *Procheiron*, which was translated into Slavic in Bulgaria in the 11th century and later became widely employed in Serbia as well. In 1219–20 the energetic first archbishop of Serbia (and later saint), Sava, supervised the copying and/or translating of various versions of Byzantine canon law for the use of the Serbian Church. Included in his compilation of legal texts were the *Procheiron* as well as translations of two 12th-century Byzantine legal commentaries which treat the Church as an equal partner with the state. Probably by intention, Sava ignored other Greek legal writings like the *Ecloga* which regard the Church as subordinate to the emperor. An ecclesiastical synod in 1221 accepted portions of this collection as the legal foundation of the Church in Serbia. Known to the Slavs as *Kormčaja Kniga* ("Book of the Pilot"), Saint Sava's lawbook proved influential far beyond the boundaries of Serbia, becoming the basic constitution of both the Bulgarian and the Russian Church. The *Kormčaja Kniga* was applied as well to laymen under church jurisdiction: for example, Orthodox monasteries in the Balkans used it in exercising jurisdiction over the peasants on their estates.

Byzantine legal precedents also had considerable influence in Serbia in the areas of criminal law, contract, and inheritance. Tsar Stephen Dušan (r. 1331–55) continued the use of Byzantine law in the Greek territories he conquered, a practice which promoted stability and helped gain the favor of his new subjects. Ultimately he extended this law to his Serbian lands as well, which made it a unifying factor in his multinational empire. The Byzantine collection of laws known as the *Syntagma* ("Systematic Treatise"), compiled by Matthew Blastares in 1335, was translated into Slavic soon after its publication. The *Syntagma* was an encyclopedia of Byzantine secular and ecclesiastical laws arranged in alphabetical order. An abridgement of this work was prepared for the Serbian imperial court, carefully excluding those elements which tended to favor the rights of the Byzantine emperor and patriarch. In contrast to Bulgaria, where Tsar Symeon (d. 927) and his successors had followed a fairly consistent policy of Byzantinization, the laws of Serbia pay more attention to native customs. The Slavic version of the *Syntagma* was influential even in the Romanian principalities, since Slavic was the literary language there. Nonetheless, despite the availability of Roman law texts in the medieval Balkans, the lack of educated judges ensured that most disputes would continue to be settled according to local custom.

In countries subject to the Western Church, Roman law was introduced by way of Italy and the Italian law schools. However, the new states of East Central Europe did not adopt this imperial law wholesale. In Poland the influence of the nobility largely prevented its implementation, for fear that it would unduly strengthen the royal power. In Hungary some of the earlier laws show the influence of Frankish (i.e., Germanic) models. However, Roman law eventually came to have considerable impact. It first became influential at the turn of the 12th–13th century, when the initial group of Hungarians returned from legal studies abroad. It experienced a revival in the last decades of the 13th century, when university-educated lawyers filled all the important posts in the royal chancellery. The intellectual currents of Renaissance humanism which reached Hungary in the second half of the 15th century likewise encouraged the use of Roman law.

Although Roman law unquestionably tended to strengthen central authority, the judging of disputes had always been one of a monarch's main functions—perhaps his oldest one. As supreme judge over his subjects, the duke or king of a country superseded the chiefs of the old clans or tribes who had previously filled that role. No firm boundary divided the judicial from the executive or legislative power anywhere in medieval East Central Europe, including the Ottoman Empire. The reigning monarch conducted judicial proceedings at his capital (if he had one), or alternatively at various royal strongholds throughout the country. Sometimes alone, but more often in conjunction with the chief lords of a district, he decided when the customary or statutory law had been infringed and assessed the appropriate penalties. Specialized judicial organs did not exist in the early medieval period. In all serious cases the sovereign was expected to render judgment in person, or at least send a representative to act in his name. Judgment was personal in another sense also, in that the ruler could impose punishments or grant pardons without reference to any laws, merely as a consequence of his anger or partiality. In such cases the accused was not permitted to give explanations and the monarch was not obliged to give reasons.

Although the sovereign could judge any dispute at his discretion, the competence of the royal court normally extended only to the most serious crimes and to controversies involving the nobility. It heard cases in which important nobles quarreled over property or privileges, or were threatened with loss of life, honor, or possessions. This court also judged crimes affecting the royal income, such as embezzlement of tax revenues or falsification of the coinage. (The monarch reserved to himself the privilege of debasing the coin of the realm.) The supreme offense was always *lèse majesté*, or injury to the sovereign (i.e., an attempt on his life, freedom, or honor.) Almost equally serious was treason, which involved bringing an enemy into the country or surrendering a fortress without resistance. Disrespect for the royal person was a major offense even if directed against third parties, for example striking someone with a sword in the ruler's presence. In Serbia Tsar Stephen Dušan's law code prescribed strict penalties for "insulting a judge," which indicates the great importance he attached to the judicial function. According to this Serbian code, any noble who insulted a judge was condemned to lose all his property; a village which did the same would be "scattered and confiscated." In view of the close association of church and state, heresy was also considered an offense against the monarch. However, the range of crimes considered by the royal court depended to a great extent on the ruler's political strength and his capacity for making his will prevail.

Where the king was in theory accessible even to the common people for judgment, this fact held great symbolic significance. Stephen I, the first Christian king of Hungary, held a judgment day once each year at the coronation town of Székesfehérvár, and at an itinerant royal court at other times. In principle, any inhabitant of the country could appear before this court to present his grievances or requests in person. Stephen's successors continued this practice well into the

13th century. However, the practical importance of these court days cannot have been great. Ordinary folk were seldom in a position to be heard by the king himself, or even by one of his chief lieutenants. Roads were difficult of passage or nonexistent, and in many localities the king did not (indeed, could not) appear for years, even though at times he held court in the provinces. For most inhabitants of medieval Hungary the royal court was at best a place of final appeal, but more often simply inaccessible. The landed nobility naturally had easier access to the royal person, and generally preferred that their disputes be settled by the monarch himself rather than by his representative. Great lords and free royal towns were entitled to be judged by the king in person, or by the royal Council if the king was out of the country. The Golden Bull of 1222 forbade even the highest official of the royal household, the palatine, to sentence a noble to death or confiscate his property without the sovereign's knowledge. A law of 1267 forbade the king to judge a nobleman except in the presence of the barons. Characteristically, one of the concessions which the rebellious Hungarian nobility forced upon the hapless Andrew II in the Golden Bull was that he should hold a judgment day twice a year, not just once.

Vital pillars of any ruler's authority were the officials whom he named to give judgment on his behalf throughout the realm. In Hungary the count palatine exercised this function. After the government moved to Buda in the late 14th century, a chief justice (or justiciar) became responsible for judicial affairs, except in Transylvania, Dalmatia, Croatia, and Slavonia, which were separately administered. On the county level, a royal appointee with the rank of count originally served as judge in addition to his role as military governor. However, royal authority in the Hungarian counties declined considerably during the 13th century, thanks to the reckless generosity of King Andrew II (1205–35) in granting crown lands to his supporters; and after the Mongol invasion (1241–42) King Béla IV was far too dependent on his nobility to reverse this process. Thus in the course of the 13th and 14th centuries the county court became essentially an instrument of the local nobility, who elected its judges and participated in its sessions. Then as prominent lords increasingly secured immunities from royal justice for their own estates, the jurisdiction of the county court became restricted in effect to lesser nobles, who might have only a few peasant tenants or none at all. The great lords judged their own retainers (the so-called *familiares*, who performed military and administrative functions) as well as the peasants on their lands, while lesser nobles who were not in the service of any lord carried their disputes to the county courts. Important cases involving influential lords were heard either by the king in person or by an official designated by him. However, certain privileged groups stood outside of this system. The Szeklers, Saxons, and Vlachs were entitled to be judged by their own magistrates according to their own laws. Towns were not subject to the county courts. Gradually in the second half of the 13th and the 14th century many Hungarian towns received charters entitling them to judge their own affairs. This made them subject only to the king or to the royal official known as the tavernicus, the administrator of the king's income—unwittingly demonstrating that the government regarded towns chiefly as sources of revenue.

In the Ottoman Empire all judges came from the ranks of the ulema, the authorities on Islamic law, who were generally graduates of the theological schools called madrasas. From among the ulema the sultan appointed judges called kadis to serve as the chief religious officials of their districts. The kadis gave judgments on both secular and religious matters, while also exercising general supervision over the conduct of local governments. Only the written judgment of a kadi permitted an Ottoman secular official to carry out a sentence. Even on the landed estates, jurisdiction in theory belonged not to the sipahi (cavalryman) who held the land in fief, but to the kadi, who was supposed to settle any disputes arising between the landholder and his peasants. In principle even the sultan had to respect a kadi's decisions, although in practice the judges were not as independent as the theory said they should be. Local elites, or even the sultan's own officials, sometimes interfered with the judicial process by producing false witnesses or denunciations. In other cases the officials ordered punishments or executions without benefit of any judicial proceedings whatsoever. The sultan at times issued rescripts to correct the malpractice of provincial authorities. Since all Ottoman judges were directly responsible to Istanbul, no system of higher and lower courts existed. In civil and commercial cases the courts applied Islamic religious law, and in criminal cases the sultan's decrees. However, most disputes never reached a kadi's court at all. Usually each village, guild, or social group preferred to arbitrate its own disputes with the aid of the local ulema. Violations of social mores were normally punished without official intervention, particularly in cases of unchastity or adultery.

The theocratic Islamic concept of society meant that the religious law also became the law of the state. However, because Muslim jurisprudence was obviously unsuitable for non-Muslims, the Christians and Jews of the Ottoman Empire were left to be judged by their own religious leaders and their own laws. After the Turks conquered Constantinople in 1453, the Orthodox ecclesiastical hierarchy exercised considerable civil as well as religious jurisdiction over the Christians. In cases of conflict between Christian and Ottoman legal institutions, or between Christian and Muslim litigants, the Islamic law prevailed. In Muslim courts it was taken for granted that evidence given by non-Muslims was untrustworthy, except where the matter at issue concerned wills, family relationships, or inheritance. This meant that in the Balkan lands of the Ottoman empire, despite their overwhelmingly Christian population, the testimony of Christian witnesses against Muslims could not be accepted.

The sultan himself was both a secular and an ecclesiastical ruler. His decrees, called firmans, frequently reiterated that he was duty-bound to lead his subjects, both Muslim and non-Muslim, along the path of God's law. Despite his status as a despotic monarch, he was bound in conscience by the law of the Koran, or

Shari'a, which God allegedly had revealed directly to the Prophet Mohammed. The basis of Shari'a was ethical, appealing to the religious duty of the believer. Only rarely did it prescribe specific penalties. Interpretations of this law were established through the consensus of the ulema, a process in which the state played no part, but was nonetheless obliged to accept. Although four distinct schools of Shari'a existed, all of which were considered orthodox, the Ottoman sultans chose to appoint as kadis only ulema of the Hanefi school. According to some Islamic jurists, Shari'a sufficed to answer all legal questions. In practice the sultans found that they needed additional laws for situations which the Koran did not cover. To supplement Shari'a they issued decrees called kanuns, which unlike Shari'a could be changed as circumstances required. Kanuns, of course, could contain nothing contrary to Shari'a. They were supposed to conform to some generally accepted Islamic principle that provided a basis for analogy. But whereas all kanuns lapsed at the end of each reign unless confirmed by the next sultan, Shari'a was permanent and unchangeable. In theory the state existed merely to execute it.

In Christian Europe likewise until the end of the 12th century, no real separation existed between secular and ecclesiastical law. Spiritual and lay lords were equally subject to the king as supreme judge, while churchmen cooperated with secular officials in capturing guilty persons and bringing them to justice. This situation continued down to the end of the Middle Ages in the Orthodox lands of the Balkans, as well as in the Byzantine Empire. Very little legal distinction existed between church and state. The Byzantine emperor and the patriarch of Constantinople could never be at loggerheads for long, since the emperor appointed and dismissed the patriarch virtually at will. Emperors issued imperial decrees which referred certain types of cases, particularly those involving betrothal, marriage, or adoption, to the judgment of the bishops. Whether the bishops' jurisdiction was optional or compulsory in such cases is uncertain. In any event, little or no distinction seems to have existed between the ecclesiastical and civil courts of Byzantium.

In the Latin West, by contrast, canon law gradually came to occupy a sphere all its own. This religious law evolved as a direct consequence of papal claims to ascendancy over the national monarchies. Beginning in the second half of the 11th century, a series of strong-willed reformer-popes attempted to exercise authority over lay rulers. (The Greek patriarch never dared go as far as this, even in the centuries of Byzantine decline.) As a corollary, the Roman ecclesiastical hierarchy insisted that a separate law and law courts were essential to protect the integrity of the Church from the corrupting influences of secular life. Monarchs desiring good relations with the Church found it necessary to accept this, although canon law undermined the law of the state by being on the whole less severe and removing large numbers of people from royal jurisdiction. Persons claiming clerical status, who were very numerous, insisted on their right to be tried by church courts for offenses of every type. Poland, Hungary, and Bohemia all followed the example set earlier by West European states in permitting clerics to resort to ecclesiastical courts.

"Benefit of clergy" was the privilege enjoyed by anyone with clerical status, which encompassed people in minor orders who were free to return to secular life (including university students and persons holding subordinate church offices) as well as priests or monks. It applied no matter what the alleged offense; and it placed laymen at an automatic disadvantage. A law of 1222 in Hungary, for example, specified that a layperson in a secular court must automatically lose a case involving a cleric, which had the effect of forcing all such mixed cases into the church courts. The only exceptions concerned disputes over landed property, which was so important to the nobility that the Church was unable to monopolize judgment even when its own holdings were at issue. However, the clergy did seek to exercise jurisdiction over all cases in which either the Christian faith and doctrine or the Church as an institution might be harmed. Into this category fell questions of marriage, oaths, breach of promise, or usury as well as tithes, wills, and inheritances, particularly because the Church often stood to inherit property.

Since ecclesiastical justice completely bypassed the royal courts, this dual judicial system inevitably created conflicts between the Church and the state. Secular authorities often resisted turning cases over to the church courts, which they considered excessively lenient, partial to clerical interests, and an infringement on their rightful authority. In Hungary, noble landowners successfully defended the jurisdiction of their estate courts against the Church, while the town of Buda in the course of the 14th century increasingly curtailed the rights of ecclesiastical courts. In general, church courts had few remaining powers in Hungarian towns by the second half of the 15th century; and King Matthias in 1481 assured the magistrates of Pest that such courts would not be allowed to infringe upon municipal liberties. Sometimes a powerful monarch took specific steps to restrict the scope of ecclesiastical justice. In Poland, King Casimir III decreed by a law of 1359 that secular persons could not appear before church courts in cases of debt and other civil matters, except where questions of faith or the tithe were concerned. However, King Vladislav V (Jagiełło) reversed this policy in 1424 by placing royal and town courts at the Church's service. He also issued an edict which authorized all courts to hunt down persons accused of the Hussite heresy—a spiritual offense. Jagiełło was particularly vulnerable to ecclesiastical pressure because as grand duke of Lithuania he had formerly been pagan, and now needed to demonstrate his Christian orthodoxy.

Particularly striking evidence of the Church's judicial power comes from the courts of the Inquisition. These were special ecclesiastical tribunals staffed chiefly by Dominican friars, which functioned for the specific purpose of identifying and punishing heretics. Until late in the 12th century, Catholic rulers had sometimes caused heretics to be burned at the stake, while the official Church opposed capital punishment. Then in the 1180s the situation was reversed, since the spread of heresy had begun to threaten Rome's monopoly of religious life. The Church now assumed the task of actively seeking out heretics and bringing suspected persons to trial. Anyone who failed to appear either for confession or communion at least three times a year automatically fell under suspicion. No one was allowed to possess the Bible, psalters, or breviaries in a vernacular language, since an interest in such items suggested a wish to interpret these texts for oneself. The condemned books were publicly burned to emphasize that their contents were sinful and that reading such books endangered a Christian's eternal soul. The Inquisition used procedures forbidden by other tribunals, such as bringing charges on the word of anonymous informers, withholding the names of hostile witnesses, and using the evidence of criminals, heretics, children, and accomplices whose testimony would have been prohibited in secular courts. The accused was denied the right of defense or a defense lawyer; and from the sentences of Inquisition courts no appeal was permitted. A person accused of heresy rarely escaped conviction, the usual sentence being life imprisonment. At the same time, the Inquisition took care to uphold the fiction that the Church did not kill. Church courts gave out only ecclesiastical punishments like excommunication or penance. People convicted of heresy by a court of the Inquisition were merely "deprived of the protection of the Church"—a euphemism which authorized the secular power to burn them at the stake without committing a mortal sin. The corpses of the condemned could not be buried in consecrated ground, but instead were dragged through the streets and thrown into refuse pits.

Although the Inquisition is best known for its activities in southern France, northern Italy, and Spain, where it served to enhance the power of the national monarchies, it functioned in Bohemia and Poland as well. In Bohemia it flourished during the first decades of the 13th century and was revived again after 1315, following a pause in its activities of some fifty years. Originally the bishop of Prague named inquisitors for specific trials only; but after 1318 the pope appointed others on a permanent basis. Until the middle of the 14th century both types of inquisitor worked continuously in Bohemia and Moravia. Their chief targets were the Waldensian heretics, although a wide spectrum of other suspects likewise became subject to investigation and persecution. The Inquisition came into conflict both with the normal ecclesiastical courts and with the town courts, which attempted to limit its operations. In Poland the Inquisition functioned from 1237 onward, with the "secular arm" placed at its disposal. The royal courts were ordered to cooperate with it on pain of incurring the monarch's displeasure.

The great influence of the Church upon secular governments is evident in the legal restrictions placed on Jews in both Catholic and Orthodox countries. As the object of special regulations the Jews were hardly unique in the Middle Ages, inasmuch as many ethnic and religious groups occupied a separate status of some sort. Nonetheless, the laws pertaining to Jews reveal a hostility far beyond just the typical medieval tolerance of different laws for different peoples. Anti-Semitic legislation was a consequence both of religious fear and of popular prejudice, namely apprehension that the Jewish presence might cause Christians to waver in their faith, mixed with resentment that the Jews refused to accept Jesus' message and become Christians. Roman law had accorded Jews the rights of citizenship (granted by Emperor Caracalla to all free inhabitants of the empire in the year 212); and it had recognized Judaism as a legal religion. These general principles remained effective well into the Middle Ages, despite many specific restrictions. Jews were tolerated in the Byzantine Empire, although both law and practice banned them from occupying any public offices. Byzantine law forbade the erection of new synagogues, but also prohibited violence against existing ones. Intermarriage between Christians and Jews, or the conversion of adult Christians to Judaism, were punishable offenses. Nonetheless, not all of Byzantium's anti-Jewish laws were enforced, and perhaps were not meant to be. For example, the edict of Emperor Leo VI the Wise (r. 886–912) decreeing that the Jews must either accept Christianity or be expelled from the empire, may have been intended chiefly to please the pope and help bridge the widening schism between the Eastern and Western Church, since it seems never to have been applied.

The status of the Jews in medieval Europe gradually declined through new legislation. Jews typically fell into the category of *servi camerae* ("servants of the [king's] Chamber"), who paid special taxes to the royal treasury in return for protection of their lives and property. This "servant" concept was basic to the decrees regulating their status in Central and Eastern Europe from the 13th century onward. Jews were treated not merely as sources of royal income, but in some respects as the actual property of the monarch, who therefore held title to all their possessions. When a Jew died his property could revert to the king, although in practice the heir was usually allowed to buy it back. Governments might issue charters of Jewish privileges, but these in no way surrendered the sovereign's ultimate rights. All Jewish privileges could be rescinded without notice, and sometimes were. The only way for Jews to protect themselves was by offering bribes to the ruler and his officials, paying hard cash for whatever sufferance they enjoyed. If a monarch decided that the political fallout from tolerating "Christ's enemies" was excessive, or that the expense of protecting the Jews outweighed the sums they provided in taxes and bribes, he had no compunction about expelling them from the country. Neither in law nor practice did Jews have any rights, although occasionally they were given privileges.

The model for all major grants of privileges to Jews in medieval East Central Europe was the charter issued by Duke Frederick of Austria in 1244, apparently with the aim of gaining Jewish support in his conflict with the German emperor. Its provisions were repeated with few changes and additions in documents subsequently issued in Hungary and Bohemia in the 13th century, as well as in Poland and Bohemia in the 14th. Frederick's charter did not specifically define Jews as the ruler's servants, but this was essentially their position. Jews stood under the direct and exclusive protection of the duke and his officials, which meant that no one else was entitled to tax them. They were allowed to travel freely throughout the realm, presumably on business; and local authorities were forbidden to impose tolls on them. No one was permitted to disturb Jewish synagogues and cemeteries or kidnap Jewish children for baptismal purposes. The largest number of provisions in the charter served to protect the security of Jewish financial activities and settle disputes relating to loans. If a Jew lent money to a noble on the security of land or documents, he was entitled to repossess the pledge if the sum was not repaid. A Christian bringing suit against a Jew had to support his claim with evidence from both a Jew and a Christian. A Jew could be tried only by the duke himself or by a ducal official. The maximum interest rate on loans was set at about fourteen percent monthly. A scale of penalties was set for violence against Jews. Murder was punishable by death and confiscation of property, serious wounding with a moderate fine paid to the duke (not to the victim).

The charters issued for the Jews of East Central Europe usually permitted them to adjudicate without outside interference any legal matters affecting only themselves. They received full autonomy in communal affairs, including the right to employ their own system of jurisprudence in legal cases in which no Christians were involved. Their rabbis functioned as judges, applying Talmudic law. In serious cases the Jewish judge turned over the guilty person to royal or town authorities for punishment, perhaps for a beating. Ordinarily the most serious penalty inflicted by a Jewish court was excommunication and expulsion from the community. Christian monarchs established their own courts to try certain types of Jewish cases, most of which presumably concerned suits for repayment from a defaulting debtor. The Jew took his oath on the Ten Commandments or the Pentateuch, just as the Christian swore on the Bible. Accusations by Christians against Jews typically were brought in a Jewish court; and in mixed cases each party had to support his claim with evidence from persons of both faiths, although a Christian could not be compelled to appear in a Jewish court. The principle of communal responsibility was frequently applied to the Jews, meaning that the entire Jewish population of a town could be held liable for a crime committed by one of its members; and mass arrests might occur to extract payment.

The Church and the sovereign often had diametrically opposed objectives with respect to Jews. The Church wished to convert them, while the monarch wished to profit from their activities. Consequently, anti-Semitic decrees were periodically issued but not consistently enforced. Because in canon law "usury" was a crime just like sorcery, blasphemy, and heresy, the Church claimed jurisdiction over Jews for this offense. However, secular rulers were usually unwilling to let the Inquisition do more than point out Jewish culprits, since actually punishing them for usury might affect the royal revenue. Charters of privilege for Jews regularly allowed them to be judged in royal courts rather than ecclesiastical courts. Just as regularly the bishops protested such provisions, although it was obvious that a Jew facing an ecclesiastical court would stand at a grave disadvantage. The

Church was equally concerned to prevent situations in which Jews held authority over Christians. Laws which forbade Jews from marrying Christians, buying or selling Christian slaves, or employing Christian servants were standard in both Eastern and Western Christendom. Jews were required to stay indoors on Christian holidays, since their presence might cause offense to Christians participating in religious processions. For his part, the sovereign attempted to ensure that legal contracts between Christians and Jews were enforced, since the Jews' ability to pay taxes would be affected if Christians were permitted to rob them with impunity. He directed royal officials to register the loans made by Jews and record the amounts involved. On the other hand, rulers rarely interfered with the decrees of church synods that sought to prevent personal contacts between Christians and Jews.

In early medieval Hungary, Jews were permitted to hold landed property, but not to marry Christian women, keep Christian servants, or buy or sell Christian slaves. They could reside only in towns which were the seats of bishoprics, thereby enabling the bishops to keep them under surveillance. King Koloman I (r. 1095–1116) specifically allowed Jews the freedom to sign contracts and testify in court. To protect Jewish commerce he decreed that loan contracts between Jews and non-Jews must be witnessed by men of both faiths. On the other hand, the pious King Ladislas I (r. 1077–95) ruled that markets must be held on Saturday, the Jewish Sabbath, but that anyone conducting business on Sunday would be subject to punishment. Merchants (meaning mostly Jews) were required to pay a double market tax. King Béla IV in 1251 issued the first Hungarian charter of privileges for Jews and placed a Jew in charge of the royal mint. However, he required Jews to wear pointed hats distinguishing them from Christians, and forbade them to sell their goods on regular market days. In 1376 the strongly pro-Catholic King Louis I loaded the Jews of Buda onto barges on the Danube and expelled them from Hungary, causing some of them to settle in Bulgaria.

In Bohemia the first charter of privileges for Jews was issued by King Ottokar II in 1254, a paraphrase of the Austrian decree of 1244. Although King Charles I renewed it in the following century, he did nothing to protect the Jews in Germany, where he was emperor, during the pogroms connected with the Black Death of 1348–49. In Poland the Jews seem to have suffered few legal disabilities prior to the late 12th century, when larger numbers of Jewish immigrants from Western Europe began seeking refuge in the country. Only then did the need for special protective measures arise. Duke Boleslav the Pious of Great Poland issued the first Polish charter of Jewish privileges in 1264, based on the Austrian model. This document gave the Jews religious and judicial autonomy and authorized them to carry on trade under the same laws applying to everyone else. It further stipulated that no Jew could be accused of using Christian blood for a religious ritual, "because their law prohibits the use of any blood"; and it prescribed a fine for any Christian who witnessed a violent attack on a Jew and failed to come to his aid. This charter was later extended to various principalities in Silesia; and King Casimir the Great (r. 1333–70) subsequently confirmed it.

Casimir showed particular friendship toward the Jews. He permitted them to reside anywhere in Poland, to travel and trade freely, and to lend money at interest. He also proclaimed the death penalty for anyone making unfounded accusations against Jews, especially the commonly heard canards that Jews used Christian blood in their Passover ceremonies and desecrated the host (wafer) used in the Catholic Eucharist. He ordered his officials to prevent the Christian clergy from molesting Jews. Casimir's attitude caused Poland in his day to be known as "the Jewish paradise." Even so, the influx of Jews into Polish towns in the 15th century created commercial antagonism between them and their Christian competitors, leading to various restrictions on Jewish activities. In 1495 the town government of Cracow forbade Jews to participate in commerce, except for pawnshops; and other Polish towns followed suit. However, official decrees could not alter the fact that many Christian nobles still required the services of Jews as moneylenders, estate managers, or merchants. Since nobles held all high government posts, the anti-Jewish laws in 15th-century Poland remained essentially a dead letter.

Even where no religious differences existed (as with the Catholic Saxons and Szeklers of Hungary), medieval states typically took into account the different legal traditions of minority groups. The Armenians and Tatars of southeastern Poland and Moldavia, like the Saxons, Szeklers, Vlachs, and Cumans of Transylvania, were recognized as separate nationalities entitled to live under their customary laws. In the Byzantine Empire the Venetians (from 1199) and the Genoese (after 1261) enjoyed rights of extraterritoriality and religious freedom. So did the merchants of Dubrovnik in the Balkan interior under both Serbian and Turkish rule. Ottoman officials in the Balkans tolerated any local practices which they did not regard as contrary to the Koran or to Islamic legal principles. They applied separate regulations to various districts, experience having demonstrated that drastic changes invited political unrest as well as an unfortunate decrease in tax revenues. This coexistence of different legal systems within a single territory naturally created jurisdictional conflicts. However, medieval regimes were willing to accept that inconvenience. The class structure of society and the division of the world into separate ethnic units were both regarded as God-given and immutable.

Vlach law (*jus valachicum*) furnishes an example of a legal system with an ethnic rather than a territorial basis. Documentary sources from medieval Transylvania, Serbia, and Poland attest that certain villages were founded according to "Vlach law," which was regarded as a guarantee of Vlach liberties. Typically the Vlachs enjoyed the right to be commanded in war by their own military leaders and to be judged in peacetime by their own chiefs and judges, the knezi. In the Ottoman period the term "Vlach" actually acquired a legal connotation quite apart from its original ethnic basis, since "Vlach status" (unlike the condition of peasants or slaves) entitled a person to free migration out of his native district. For this reason it is not always clear in the documents whether the persons benefiting from this status were ethnically Vlach or not. In any event, the exact provisions of medieval Vlach law are imperfectly known, since it was first codified in the mid-17th century in the independent principalities of Walachia and Moldavia. The Saxons of Transylvania also benefited from the special rights originally granted in 1224 to settlers in the Sibiu district. Saxon communities were permitted to elect their own mayors and priests; and only the king or his appointed judge had jurisdiction over them. Saxon merchants were exempt from taxes, and their markets were free of tolls. Apparently the king's objective in granting such rights was to create a counterweight to the power of the Transylvanian landed magnates. In subsequent years—1318, 1393, 1422—Sibiu's privileges were extended to all the regions inhabited by Saxons, which collectively became known as the *universitas Saxonum* or "Saxon corporation."

Great nobles formed an important part of the judicial process everywhere in medieval East Central Europe outside of the Byzantine and Ottoman empires. Court proceedings held in the presence of the assembled nobility were essentially an updated form of the old tribal meeting; and a great deal of medieval justice was conducted in this way. The assembly usually met under the open sky, with great crowds of nobles and prelates present. There the monarch heard the opinions of the chief men of the realm; and normally the group consensus prevailed. In Hungary, for example, matters regarded as too important for the regular county court might be handled by a general meeting of the local nobility. Even more important was the judicial assembly held by the king's chief official, the palatine, which normally met once a year, sometimes for several counties at once. The palatine's assembly was the usual court for serious cases involving either nobles or ordinary freemen. In theory even a serf could attend to present his complaints, although this must rarely have occurred. The most common cases concerned robbery and theft. The assembly gave its opinion on the matter in question; and if the accused was found guilty, he could be punished by imprisonment, death, or confiscation of property. In Poland the noble-dominated sejm, or parliament, could sit as a court during its legislative sessions, thus duplicating the authority of the king's court. The sejm was entitled to handle cases in which nobles were threatened with sentences of death, imprisonment, loss of honor, or confiscation of goods; or where officials were accused of crimes.

The Bohemian kingdom likewise maintained "courts of the land" where the nobility gave judgments four times a year. Originally convening at a variety of locations, these assemblies met exclusively at Prague from the mid-13th century onward. Just as in Hungary, they considered only the cases of nobles or property-holding freemen; and higher nobility dominated the proceedings. In the province of Moravia, which maintained its own separate institutions, five separate judicial assemblies existed for the various regions until the 14th century, when all of them came together at the Moravian capital of Olomouc. When the Polish kingdom was reunited in the 14th century, the former provincial assemblies retained their functions as local courts. Their importance was enhanced by the privileges of Nieszawa in 1454, whereby King Casimir IV abolished the authority of royal courts over the nobility and limited the authority of royal officials (the starostas) to cases of arson, highway assault, burglary, and rape.

Justice for the peasants on private estates became increasingly subject to the lords' sole discretion. Even a powerful monarch might be unable to resist the nobles' demands for complete judicial authority over the people living on their property, though this obviously infringed upon royal prerogatives. Not all landholders in a country enjoyed identical judicial rights, however. Generally speaking, only the great magnates exercised rights of high justice over their dependents, while less influential nobles did not. The landholders appointed judges for the villages on their estates, and peasants could in theory appeal the judges' decisions to the county court. However, since nobles and their retainers controlled the courts, a peasant stood little chance of winning a case against his lord. One corollary of this system was that dependent peasants were no longer considered responsible for their own acts. To mutilate or kill a serf became an offense not against the victim but against the lord, who was thereby deprived of the serf's labor. An injured serf received no compensation; and any penalty due him was paid to his lord. Conversely, the perpetrator of a crime against a serf paid a fine to the serf's lord, but suffered no bodily punishment himself. A few efforts were made to limit the arbitrary authority of nobles over serfs, but with slight effect. The Church occasionally required an offender to do penance for injuring a serf. A strong monarch might seek to protect the serfs against illegal acts of their masters, as the Serbian Tsar Stephen Dušan did in his laws stating that "Every serf is free to lay plaint against his master," and "No man is free to withhold a serf from my imperial court; only the judges shall judge him." Whether these stipulations were observed in practice is uncertain. However, if a serf somehow became free his legal status changed accordingly; and he would be judged by the laws applying to freemen.

In Bohemia during the 13th and 14th centuries the nobility gradually acquired the right to judge all legal cases involving the persons residing on their lands. Some of the larger Bohemian estates even maintained two courts: one for minor crimes, with the lord's deputy presiding; and another for capital crimes, where the lord officiated in person. Punishments might include flogging, the stocks, or monetary fines, the latter comprising an important part of the lord's income. In Hungary by the 14th century private lords held virtually complete judicial power over their peasants and sometimes even condemned them to death, though this was prohibited by law. Serfs were not entitled to wergild (the fine paid by a murderer to a victim's family to avoid blood revenge), although if a lord had to pay a fine on a serf's account he might demand recompense. Landowners who thus exercised justice over their peasants were themselves exempt from the competence of all courts except that of the king himself. Initially this private jurisdiction did not transform the Hungarian peasants into serfs. Laws of King Matthias (r. 1458–90) confirmed their freedom to migrate, a right rescinded only in 1504. However, after the great peasant revolt of 1514, the Hungarian lords in the Diet decreed that peasants henceforth would be tied to the land forever.

In Poland by the 14th century the landholdings of the nobility enjoyed virtually complete immunity from the jurisdiction of the royal and county courts. Nobles were free to ignore any complaints which ordinary knights or commoners might bring against them. This privilege was known as "nonresponse" (i.e., freedom to disregard a summons from local judicial authorities). No officials of the crown were entitled to set foot on the property of a landowner holding immunity rights. A noble lord could not be arrested prior to judgment no matter how grave the crime of which he was accused, including treason. He could not be imprisoned or condemned until sentence was passed on the matter at issue unless he had been caught in the act of committing the crime. Fugitives from justice were safe with him, while he himself could be judged only by a court of his peers. Furthermore, a Polish lord could mistreat his peasants with impunity and exercise justice over them without interference. By laws of 1496 and 1501, town and castle (i.e., royal) courts were forbidden to judge peasant cases, which placed the peasants entirely at the lords' mercy. In practice the lords often referred the more serious cases to these courts anyway, in order to let the odium of a heavy punishment fall on the government rather than on themselves. However, each noble estate had become a legal entity in itself, with the lord able to set the rules as he wished. In practice he often followed the customary law. Nonetheless, peasants could appear in court or bring accusations against a lord only if their lord consented. Except in a jurisdiction which applied German law, the lord or his appointee made all judicial decisions and carried out all sentences other than those involving the death penalty.

The authority of nobles over peasants should not obscure the fact that a great deal of medieval justice was handled by the peasants themselves. Village headmen rendered decisions at a purely village level for free farmers, sometimes even for serfs. A noble landowner usually did not wish to be bothered with peasants' disputes—he merely wanted to retain overall authority and prevent the monarch's agents from interfering with him. Often he permitted the village headman and his assistants to dispense justice in lesser matters, reserving for himself only the right to judge serious crimes like murder, arson, robbery, and assault. Depending on the locality, these headmen bore a variety of titles—judge, mayor, knez, burgrave. In free villages they were either elected or chosen by an informal consensus of the inhabitants, while in villages belonging to a noble's estate the lord might impose his own candidate. The headman adjudicated minor disputes between villagers; and the lord acted as a court of appeals when necessary.

Punishments for contravening the law conformed to medieval notions of class distinction by recognizing the social rank of both offender and victim. Examples of this unequal justice are legion. The amount of wergild was set higher for noble perpetrators of crimes. In 11th-century Hungary the wergild for murder was fifty gold pieces (or alternatively: fifty oxen) when the guilty party was a count, ten if he was a knight, but only five if he was a freeman. The reasoning seems to have been that persons of higher status could afford to pay more. In the Ottoman Empire a non-Muslim, a female, a slave, or an unmarried person paid only half the penalty assessed on a Muslim, a male, or a free or married person. For adultery a rich man was fined 300 Turkish akçes, a middle-income man 200, and a poor one merely 100. At the same time, a transgression against someone of a higher class was considered more serious than the identical deed committed within one's own class. Polish law provided that a noble who killed another noble was allowed to go free by paying monetary compensation to the victim's family, whereas a townsman or peasant committing the same crime automatically received the death penalty. According to the Serbian law code of 1349, if a great lord insulted a lesser one he paid a fine of 100 perpers; but a lesser lord doing the same to a great noble would be beaten with sticks in addition to paying the fine. A lord who killed a commoner paid 1,000 perpers, but a commoner who killed a lord paid 300 and had both his hands cut off. A noble who "utters heretical words" paid 100 perpers, but a nonnoble paid twelve for the same offense and was also "flogged with sticks." However, in particularly outrageous cases even a noble might incur physical punishment. According to the Serbian code, a nobleman who captured a noblewoman by force should have both his hands cut off and his nose slit. A commoner committing the identical crime was hanged.

Laws protecting a nobleman's "honor" illustrate the importance which the noble attached to his person. Preservation of honor (i.e., reputation) was a serious matter, essential to ensure that society would respect noble rank. Honor was a distinguishing mark which set nobles apart from commoners, since townsmen and peasants were not thought to possess it. Offenses against honor included insulting the noble personally, charging him with a crime, or calling into question his own or his mother's legitimate birth. If the antagonist could not prove his charges, he was punished at law. According to King Casimir III's statute for Little Poland, a person who impugned the honor of a noble had to pay a fine and retract his insult in court, repeating "with a dog's voice" the words: "I lied like a dog in what I said." King Charles Robert of Hungary (r. 1310–42), who sought to imitate the customs of the French nobility, set up a special "military" court to deal with offenses against honor. It monitored the manners and morals of the king's retainers, with Charles Robert in person sometimes acting as judge. All questions involving the knightly code of behavior—which included the requirement of faithfulness to the sovereign, physical courage, and politeness—came before this court. Proof was established by a judicial duel. The penalty for the loser was loss of honor and exclusion from the society of the royal court and household. In Poland a judgment of infamy, or loss of honor, was prescribed for certain crimes. It barred the guilty person from holding any public office which required noble status (which meant most offices). A still more serious penalty was banishment, which forced the offender to leave the country and usually also involved confiscation of his estates.

In medieval law, hostile acts against individuals, even assassination or physical mutilation, were generally considered private matters rather than crimes against the state. The murder of a noble created a condition of enmity between the family of the victim and that of the murderer. Since revenge was a recognized legal principle, the laws merely specified the type and degree of the revenge to which the injured party or his relatives were entitled. All the same, no monarch willingly allowed his subjects to disturb the peace with unregulated blood feuds. Wherever possible, rulers insisted that the victim or his family could take revenge only as specified by a court judgment. They forbade the injured parties to decide on the punishment themselves. Lawgivers also took measures against dishonest witnesses, whose testimony could lead to feuds. King Koloman in Hungary punished false accusers as harshly as he did thieves, having them branded on the face with the sign of the cross.

Various laws set limits to the amount of permissible revenge. For instance in Mazovia (an independent Polish principality until 1529), the laws specified that revenge was permissible only against a murderer himself, not against his relatives, and only within the twenty years following the crime. In 15th-century Poland a person desiring revenge was required to make formal announcement of that fact to the government within six weeks after a murder had been committed. The accusation had to be written down in a court record and announced three times by a messenger in the marketplace. The accused person then appeared in court. The law encouraged conciliation by means of a monetary payment, inasmuch as the old law of talion ("an eye for an eye," etc.) was a never-ending source of blood feuds. According to a decree of Louis the Great in Hungary, the victim or his representative was permitted to "deliver the appropriate punishment to the offender" only if a judge was unable to get the parties to agree on appropriate financial compensation. When a noble injured someone of equal status in the social hierarchy, reconciliation might require that the offender humble himself publicly. In Poland this occurred at a ceremony in which the guilty noble, stripped to the waist, came forward together with his retinue to beg forgiveness from the murdered man's relatives.

Ascertaining the truth of an accusation was always a problem for medieval courts, especially when witnesses and physical evidence were lacking. Religion was employed to fill the gap, on the assumption that God was a just God who would not let the innocent be punished or the wicked go free. Thus sworn oaths frequently took the place of evidence. The validity of an oath was based on the belief that false swearing would bring divine punishment, either in this life or the next. A semimagical quality was attributed to the words of the oath, making its efficacy dependent on absolutely exact repetition. In early medieval

Poland, for example, the oath itself was considered invalid if the swearer stumbled in pronouncing it. Nor did the oath of a single witness suffice. Several persons of good reputation had to testify to the uprightness and honesty of the contending parties. Polish law required between two and twelve co-swearers, depending on the seriousness of the crime. Only nobles could testify on behalf of other nobles. In sharp contrast to modern judicial practice, these oaths concerned only the character of the accused, and had no bearing on the facts of the case.

Another favorite mode of establishing guilt or innocence was the ordeal, also known as the "judgment of God." This might consist of a trial by hot water, cold water, red-hot iron, or judicial duel, and again was based on the belief that God would determine the outcome. Ordeals were generally carried out only in trials conducted by the monarch or his representatives, although a few noble magnates also used them in their estate courts. The ordeal by cold water was perhaps the least painful of the lot. The accused was thrown into water with his hands tied under his knees and the end of a rope around his waist. If he sank he was pulled out and won the case, since water was supposedly a pure element which would refuse to accept a guilty person. Trial by hot water required the accused to retrieve an object from a kettle of boiling water in order to test whether his hand would be burned. Trial by hot iron involved taking three steps on burning coals, or while holding a red-hot piece of iron. The accused was considered innocent if after three days he showed no burns on his hands or feet. In a Serbian variant on this procedure, an accused thief or brigand was ordered to remove a red-hot iron from a fire at the church door and place it on the altar. A popular form of the "judgment of God" was the duel, in which the winner of the combat was declared innocent of the crime and the loser guilty. Nobles fought their duels with swords; but peasants used sticks. If a peasant summoned a knight, the latter assigned a representative to replace him, since it would be undignified to fight with someone beneath him in status. The clergy also used substitutes in duels, since they were not supposed to fight in person.

As society became more sophisticated, proofs resting on the alleged judgment of God no longer appeared so convincing. The Polish Sejm in 1215 forbade clerics to participate in duels, although this failed to halt the practice. After all, many churchmen were themselves nobles by origin, trained in the use of arms. King Béla IV of Hungary in the mid-13th century forbade trials by "judgment of God." His 14th-century successor, King Charles Robert, adopted the modern French judicial procedures for his royal courts. Instead of using co-swearers who testified merely to the character of an accused person, he ordered that cases actually be investigated. This new method was supposed to include the furnishing of material proof, hearing of witnesses to the facts, and providing documentary evidence. But even Charles Robert continued to permit duels in his knightly courts, presumably because the nobility desired them.

Medieval punishments were often barbarous in their severity, in part because the violent nature of medieval life evoked correspondingly harsh efforts at keeping the peace. The death penalty was imposed for relatively trivial crimes. The law code of King Stephen I in Hungary (early 11th century) ordered the death penalty for any free person found guilty of theft for the third time. King Ladislas I of Hungary (late 11th century) ordered that anyone who stole an object worth more than a chicken should be hanged and his children enslaved. Arsonists and counterfeiters were sentenced to die at the stake. Tsar Stephen Dušan's law code for Serbia established the death penalty for counterfeiting and for highway robbery. In Poland in the 14th and 15th centuries death sentences were imposed for robbery and theft, counterfeiting of coins, dealing in foreign currency (which damaged the royal treasury), and even for failing to inform the king's officers of such offenses. The execution itself was often carried out in the most painful way possible, for example by quartering, burning at the stake, or cutting off limbs, as Duke Boleslav II of Poland (to his subsequent regret) decreed for his opponent, Bishop (later Saint) Stanislas. Death by burning was the favored punishment for heretics, an indication of the seriousness with which religious deviation was regarded. Prior to death the condemned heretic might also be tortured, perhaps by breaking on the wheel, which involved tying him horizontally to a large wagon wheel and breaking his limbs.

Many punishments involved physical mutilation. In Poland the cutting off of ears or hands could be the penalty for theft. The tongue or nose might be severed for crimes perpetrated through speech. Stephen Dušan's code specified that a thief should have his eyes gouged out. In fact, mutilation by blinding or loss of limbs was considered a relatively humane punishment, since it often replaced the death penalty. Rebels against a sovereign often received this punishment, which usually prevented them from seeking the throne again but avoided the stigma of killing a royal personage. Punishment through loss of hand, eye, nose, ears, or tongue, as well as branding and the burning of beard and hair are all prominently mentioned for a variety of crimes in the 14th-century Serbian law code. Medieval Byzantium, where the death penalty was rare, employed similar penalties. Perhaps owing to this example, Serbia rarely invoked the death penalty, which was imposed only on counterfeiters, highway robbers, and the murderers of bishops, priests, or monks. The Ottoman Empire sometimes exacted the death penalty for serious crimes, but also imposed punishments like amputation of a hand or leg or condemnation to the galleys. For minor crimes like wine drinking (forbidden by Islamic law), a beating might be deemed sufficient.

Occasionally an accused person was able to gain asylum, which saved him from being brought to trial, or if sentence had already been imposed, prevented the carrying out of judgment. Either the cathedral church or the monarch's court might grant this privilege if it saw fit to do so. Asylum might also protect a person from private revenge or from an arbitrary judgment pronounced by the king. In Poland this was known as "voivode's asylum," and only nobles could invoke it. It evolved in the 14th century under King Casimir III, whose attempts at strengthening royal power frequently involved confiscation of nobles' goods or death sentences without trial. Voivode's asylum permitted the chief military authority of a region to offer temporary refuge to an accused noble for one or two months, during which time his relatives could seek assurances that he would receive a fair trial. If they failed in this, the voivode helped the accused to leave the country. After a year had passed the relatives could again seek to arrange a trial, provided that the accused person had not committed treason while abroad. Voivode's asylum disappeared in Poland in the first half of the 15th century, having become an irrelevance. By that time the Polish nobility had gained privileges which adequately ensured them against arbitrary royal judgment, specifically prohibiting the confiscation of estates without a court judgment or due process of law.

Responsibility for a criminal act did not always rest exclusively with the perpetrator. Medieval law knew many instances of joint responsibility for crimes. For serious offenses against the state like treason, the entire family of a condemned person might be punished with exile, confiscation of property, or even death. Common responsibility was most often a means of exerting pressure on people to reveal the identity of a culprit. Thus in 11th-century Hungary each community was made responsible for law and order, so that when the king's itinerant justice arrived in a place, all local offenders could immediately be turned over to him. In medieval Poland the population of each district was expected to pursue any criminal in its midst as far as the boundary of the next jurisdiction, which then assumed the obligation. If a corpse was found and the murderer could not be located, the entire district was punished. On a landed estate the lord was responsible for offenses committed by his farmhands or serfs. However, Casimir the Great's law code for the province of Little Poland departed from the principle of joint responsibility by stipulating that a father was not required to answer for the crimes of his son or other relatives, or they for his. According to the Serbian code, if a theft or robbery occurred on the territory of a village, the lord of the place was personally liable and might suffer confiscation on his land. If a fine was assessed upon a peasant, his household, his village, and the village lord were jointly responsible. Similarly in the Ottoman Empire, if a criminal could not be located his whole village was subject to punishment. Common responsibility existed because medieval governments lacked organs of their own for hunting criminals, leaving them no choice but to rely on local districts and communities. However, since joint liability for crimes was obviously burdensome to all concerned, specific villages or districts were sometimes exempted from it. Governments could not apply this principle to noble estates possessing judicial immunity, since in such cases all direct connection between the peasants and the royal power had been severed.

Other types of legal accountability as practiced in the Middle Ages strike the modern mind as even more curious. Medieval law did not concern itself with intent, but merely with the results of an act. Judges or jurors could be considered culpable if their verdict in a case later was proven incorrect, even where no fraud or bribery was involved. A law of 1078 in Hungary specified that judges who were either too lenient or too strict with thieves should be punished together with the thieves. The Serbian code provided that if the jurors in a case acquitted someone who was afterward shown to be guilty, they should each be fined 1,000 perpers—a considerable sum—and would all henceforth be forbidden to marry. Another type of joint responsibility involved crimes committed by foreigners, whereby anyone at all from the foreigner's country could be arrested if the real offender was unknown or unavailable. The independent republic of Dubrovnik protested from time to time that the Serbian authorities had unjustly detained one of its citizens for this reason. Various edicts of Serbian rulers attempted to halt the practice, but without success.

Very significant in medieval East Central Europe was the so-called German law, which spread into Poland, Bohemia, Hungary, and Serbia during the wave of eastward migration in the 12th–13th centuries. This term is somewhat misleading, since it did not refer to any legal system valid for Germany as a whole. (Nothing of the sort could possibly have existed in the fragmented German Empire of that time.) Although the medieval immigrants into East Central Europe were in fact largely German by origin, German law was not designed specifically for them. Rather it resembled the privileges which had long since been granted to the so-called free guests or hospites (i.e., foreigners in a country who were free people and not serfs). German law was a colonists' law, originally designed to facilitate immigration into eastern Germany by allowing newcomers to retain their customary way of life. In any event, the right of a free person to his language and customs was taken for granted in that prenationalistic age, while the embryonic judicial systems of East Central Europe were themselves unprepared to deal with the special requirements of foreigners. Thus as early as the first half of the 12th century, documents describe the Germans of Prague as free people, entitled to choose their own judges and elect their priests. Only in cases of murder, theft, or disturbance of the peace should the duke's officials intervene. The Prague Germans were exempt from military service outside Bohemia and from the quartering of troops; however, in wartime they were required to supply twelve armed men for each of the city's gates.

German law was emphyteutic law, which meant that legal title to a piece of land remained with the lord, but the right of use was fully heritable and salable. Tax assessments under German law were fixed "for always," so that the peasant cultivator need not fear an arbitrary increase, and the landlord could expect a fixed income. Towns or villages subject to German law were organized into separate judicial districts, each possessing its own court, which freed them from the law applying to the surrounding countryside except in military matters. A place receiving German law thus enjoyed some degree of self-administration, including "low justice" (i.e., jurisdiction over crimes not involving the death penalty). In fact, many new settlers came from regions where some elements of emphyteutic law already existed. However, it cannot be said that they carried their native law with them, since it was normal for colonists to receive the maximum rights allowable in their new country. The promise of German law was an inducement for people to immigrate into East Central Europe precisely because it represented an improvement over their situation back home. It guaranteed the new settlers several initial years of tax exemption, a modest fixed tax in subsequent years, and personal freedom with no obligation to perform services for a lord. Frequently it also included exemption from military service.

A town acquiring German law received a municipal charter granting it the status of a commune. The lord of the town (in royal towns the monarch, otherwise the lord of the estate) issued a formal document specifying the inhabitants' rights to self-government and tax exemptions. Despite local variations, the basic pattern was everywhere approximately the same. The townsmen were legally free people subject directly to the sovereign, not to any of his officials. Citizens of the town (as opposed to mere residents) could elect their own judges and "sworn men," or jurors. The town court exercised original jurisdiction, although occasionally royal judges preempted this right. German-law towns also enjoyed important economic advantages, such as permission to hold a weekly market and annual fair. At first the municipal government was headed by a Vogt, who combined the functions of mayor and judge and whose office was for life and heritable. In the larger towns elected councils sprang up in the second half of the 13th century to share in governmental authority. Usually these were formed by members of the wealthy merchant class who wanted more independence from the Vogt and the territorial lord. A typical town council consisted of a dozen or so members with a mayor at its head, adding new members by cooptation.

Villages located in the vicinity of towns sometimes received German law as well. Such grants, intended to promote immigration, became a large-scale phenomenon in Poland in the 13th and 14th centuries. Most native peasants did not receive equivalent privileges. They remained subject to Polish law, as did the native Balts and Slavs who inhabited the territory of the Teutonic Knights in Prussia. The fortunate peasants who lived by German law were relieved of many burdensome taxes and services, paying a single fixed tax instead. They were not tied to the land, although rights of migration were usually subject to prior restrictions such as discharging tax arrears or finding substitute settlers. If the village was part of a town's property, it often enjoyed self-government as well. Otherwise it was subject to the authority of a noble landowner. While this system permitted disputes to be settled expeditiously at the local level, it also deprived the peasants of access to the royal courts. Royal protection for peasants gradually became a dead letter in Poland. By the 16th century, a Polish noble who owned a village or a town could alter its law whenever and however he wished.

German law existed in a number of variants. In Bohemia and Poland it was largely modeled on the law of Magdeburg in eastern Germany. The commercial towns of the Baltic coast which belonged to the Hanseatic League generally adopted the law of Lübeck, chief town of the League. As befitted the Hansa's independent spirit, Lübeck law from the outset provided for a municipal council with important powers of governance, whereas towns which adopted Magdeburg law usually formed such councils only later. The law of Chełmno (Kulm) supplied the model for many towns in the Teutonic Knights' Prussia, and was widely applied also in Mazovia. It was based on Flemish law, from which the Magdeburg law had earlier been adapted. However, it differed from Magdeburg law in permitting inheritance through the female line. In Hungary the law applying to colonists was similar to the type known elsewhere as "German," although usually it was called by some other name. Nonetheless, German influences upon it are obvious. This law was most often applied in its Viennese form, since many of the inhabitants of Hungarian towns had roots in Austria or southern Germany.

Mining law had its own special features. It set guidelines for the demarcation of territory, regulation of drainage, ventilation in the pits, and the division of expenses and profits among entrepreneurs. The oldest mining law in Central Europe stems from the town of Jihlava (Iglau), a rich silver producer in the Moravian highlands. Some variant of Jihlava law was ultimately adopted by most other mining centers in Bohemia and Hungary. For the important silver producing town of Kutná Hora, the Bohemian King Wenceslas II (r. 1278–1305) issued four books of law modeled on the legal system of Jihlava. Another variant of Jihlava law, that of Banská Štiavnica (Schemnitz) in Slovakia, served as the model for many Hungarian mining towns. The principal Hungarian gold mining center, Kremnica (Kremnitz) in Slovakia, took its law from Kutná Hora. In the 16th century Wenceslas's mining-book was even translated and adopted for use in Spain and Spanish America, thus attaining an unexpectedly wide diffusion far beyond its place of origin.

The adoption of German law in East Central Europe created a dual legal system at the highest governmental level. It was clear that appeals from the judgments of German-law courts could not adequately be settled by judges applying the older native law. For a long time litigants in Bohemia or Poland could appeal the decisions of local courts to the high court of Magdeburg in Germany. Eventually this procedure became offensive to national pride, with the result that such appeals were discouraged or prohibited. In 1337, King John of Bohemia founded a high court specifically for his royal towns, staffed by judges who were themselves town citizens. John granted identical rights to all his towns, spelling out their financial obligations in order to protect them from excessive claims. In 1356, King Casimir III of Poland forbade his subjects to patronize foreign courts of appeal. As a substitute he created a high court in Cracow to hear German-law cases, though even this did not entirely stop the practice of appeals to Magdeburg.

In Hungary a right of appeal to foreign courts seems never to have existed,* probably because of the country's relatively strong monarchy. In the 14th century the larger Hungarian towns carried their legal appeals either directly to the king or more often to the royal official responsible for towns, the tavernicus. The tavernicus' court held its sessions at various locations throughout the kingdom, aided by jurors representing the various towns who were knowledgeable about local customs. Gradually this tribunal evolved into a court of appeal that derived its competence not from the king but from the charters of the towns themselves, although the tavernicus himself continued to be a royal appointee. The law of Buda, for example, provided that the tavernicus' court could handle cases concerning land and other property but not those where the spilling of blood was involved. Smaller towns often appealed their cases to courts in the larger centers, such as Buda and Sopron, or to Krupina (Karpfen) in Slovakia, which caused some overlapping of jurisdiction with the tavernical court. However, by the second half of the 15th century specific regional courts of appeal had been established for various parts of Hungary, while the seven chief commercial towns of the kingdom took their appeals to the tavernical court (or on occasion directly to the king). The town charters of all but one had been modeled on that of Buda; and the common lawbook they issued, *Laws and Customs of the Seven Towns*, was likewise closely modeled on Buda law.†

During much of the medieval era in East Central Europe, no attempt was ever made to collect and systematize the royal decrees and legal customs of a country. Copies of laws and judgments were retained by various secular and ecclesiastical authorities, but these were insufficiently accessible to lawyers and judges. By the 14th and 15th centuries, however, the increasing professionalization of the law had created a clear need for some form of systematization. Accordingly, several monarchs made attempts at collecting and ordering the laws, with the object of harmonizing existing customs and decrees with one another. Legal codification would naturally tend to favor the royal power by resolving contradictions and deciding questions of disputed jurisdiction in the king's favor. Therefore the nobility usually opposed the process. Only the most powerful sovereigns even made the attempt to codify their country's laws.

In Bohemia King Wenceslas II (r. 1278–1305) was the first ruler to propose codification. He hired an Italian professor of Roman and canon law to undertake this work; but nothing came of it. The Bohemian nobles feared that the promonarchical emphasis of Roman law would serve to curtail their privileges; and they forced the king to abandon his plans. Even a century and a half later

---

* The one minor exception to this rule, the small town of Žilina (Sillein) in Slovakia, referred cases to Těšín (Teschen) in Bohemian Silesia just across the border.

† The seven were Buda, Košice (Kassa), Pozsony (Bratislava), Sopron, Nagyszombat (Trnava), Eperjes, (Prešov), and Bártfa (Bardejov). The charter of Nagyszombat antedated that of Buda.

the much more powerful Charles I (r. 1346–78) had no better success with his proposed *Maiestas Carolina*. Charles ordered the collection of all the laws valid up to his time, to be supplemented as needed by Roman legal decisions. This code was designed to apply to all the lands of the Bohemian crown, except where German law or the legal immunities of noble estates were in force. Charles submitted this code for approval to the Bohemian Diet at a particularly favorable moment, when he had just returned from his coronation as Holy Roman emperor in 1347. Although he then stood at the summit of his power and prestige, the nobility overwhelmingly rejected the project, fearing competition for judicial positions from university-trained lawyers. Ultimately Charles abandoned his efforts at formal codification and established his own royal courts without asking the nobility's consent. He appointed officials of his own throughout Bohemia to judge cases of theft, burglary, arson, plunder, and breaches of the peace. Frequently he held court in person, judging the excesses of the great men of the kingdom with particular severity. By centralizing judicial authority, these measures largely accomplished the same purposes as a formal code. The judges were royal appointees often having strong ties to Charles himself.

Tsar Stephen Dušan's law code for Serbia, first issued in 1349 and expanded in 1354, was a rather unsystematic collection of laws evidently meant as a supplement to the statutes of Byzantine provenance that already existed in Serbia. The extant manuscripts of the code usually include Slavic-language abridgments of the 14th-century Byzantine *Syntagma* (comprising four-fifths of that document) together with the Byzantine *Nomos Georgikos* ("Agrarian Law"). Dušan's contributions form the third section. His additions pertained to matters not covered in the Byzantine codes, for instance provisions regarding dependent peasants, which the Byzantine agrarian law does not mention. The Serbian code contains many rulings concerning legal procedure, town administration, and the rights of nobles and peasants. Byzantine influence is obvious, since the work often employs Greek legal terms unaltered; and its property law also suggests Greek models. Dušan's code followed Byzantine examples in prescribing bodily mutilations in lieu of the death penalty, which was imposed only rarely. Despite many such borrowings, most laws in the code were still based on previous decrees of the Serbian kings, which in turn had originated in customary law. Officially Dušan's code continued in use in the Serbian Despotate of the 15th century, although customary law replaced it for most purposes. The code survived as a point of reference for Serbian communities under Turkish rule, which exercised considerable legal autonomy in civil cases.

Another famous medieval law code was issued by King Casimir III of Poland (r. 1333–70), and ranks high among his claims to be called "the Great." Casimir initiated and oversaw the preparation of statutes drawn up by the most eminent jurists of his court. To be sure, the divergent customs prevailing in various parts of Poland at that time made it impossible to unify the law throughout all of his territories, which no doubt he would have preferred. Accordingly he issued separate codes for his two chief provinces, Little Poland and Great Poland. The former collection contained one hundred articles, the latter fifty; and they differed in other respects as well. For example, the code for Little Poland permitted peasants to change their residence if only one or two on an estate did it at any one time, whereas the law for Great Poland forbade any migration whatsoever except in unusual cases. The statutes thus took into account the considerable differences between the two provinces, which had only recently been reunited after nearly two centuries of separation. Casimir's interest in the law was attested also by his concern to introduce a law faculty at his newly founded university in Cracow.

The basis for both of Casimir's codes was Polish customary law, supplemented by borrowings from Bohemia and Hungary and from canon law. These statutes were promulgated in or about 1347, probably at a separate assembly for each province, and required Polish courts to judge according to the written law rather than by the usual reference to oral tradition. Later both Casimir and his royal successors issued additional articles known as concurrences, which sought to harmonize various features of the codes of Great and Little Poland. These supplements included statutes voted by the Sejm as well as privileges issued by Casimir and subsequent kings. Links of this kind functioned as a substitute for the all-Polish code which was never issued, while the concurrences tended to reduce differences in the legal systems of the formerly separate provinces. Casimir's two statutes were never entirely replaced, but served as the foundation of Polish law for centuries afterward. Analogous to these secular statutes was the codification of Polish ecclesiastical law carried out in 1420 by Archbishop Nicholas Trąba and supplemented in 1523 by Archbishop John Łaski. This project unified the decrees of various synods, bishops, and cathedral chapters, and tended to increase the independence of the Polish Church vis-à-vis the Holy See.

Entirely separate were the judicial systems of the various territories which joined the Polish kingdom only in the 15th and 16th centuries. Until its incorporation into Poland in 1529, Mazovia remained an autonomous province with its own customary laws, statutes, and privileges. Similarly, the Polish-Lithuanian union of 1385 left untouched the (still largely customary) laws of Lithuania, which gradually were supplemented by the decrees of its own grand dukes. When King Casimir IV issued his lawbook for Lithuania in 1468, this was in his capacity as grand duke, not as king of Poland. Likewise the laws of Prussia remained unaffected when the area west of the Vistula exchanged the government of the Teutonic Knights for the suzerainty of Poland in 1454. The Knights had seen to the codification of native Prussian law as early as 1340. Then when West Prussia (afterward called Royal Prussia) became subject to Poland, it retained its former judicial system. At first its laws varied even from district to district, although greater internal uniformity was achieved in 1476 when Chełmno (Kulm) law was extended to the entire Royal Prussian nobility.

In Hungary the unwritten laws of the realm were put into writing in the 14th and 15th centuries, although the lack of any systematic law code permitted judges to exercise considerable discretion in rendering decisions. The prevailing view was that a new law did not necessarily annul a previous one unless it explicitly did so, thus adding to the legal confusion. Finally, a mere dozen years before the destruction of the kingdom in 1526, a code of Hungarian law was produced by Stephen Verböczy, a practicing lawyer and judge who was also the leader of the lower nobility in the Diet. His code, completed in 1514 and known as the Tripartitum, was essentially a summary of Hungarian customary law as it had developed over the centuries, though it also incorporated some elements of Roman law. Significantly, it embodied the fondest wishes of the lower nobility by stating explicitly that all Hungarian nobles, whether great magnates or impoverished squires, were free men and absolutely equal in law. It specifically exempted members of the nobility from taxation and obliged them to go to war only to defend their country, not on campaigns abroad. Imprisonment of nobles without warrant and judgment was forbidden. If the king violated any of these stipulations, which dated back to the Golden Bull of 1222, the nobility was entitled to resist him. Verböczy's code also legalized the nobles' class prejudices, which had recently been sharpened in reaction to the great peasant revolt of 1514. While insisting on the rights of nobles, it consigned the peasantry to perpetual serfdom. The Tripartitum never became law in a formal sense, since it was never promulgated by any ruler. Nonetheless, it was generally regarded as the law of the land until the revolutionary year of 1848; and it put a strongly legalistic stamp on Hungarian political life. For many centuries it served the Hungarian elite as a constant point of reference.

The Ottoman government produced a collection of laws known as the *Kanun-i-osmani*, reflecting the high degree of control exercised by the center over the provinces. Usually assigned to the 16th century, it was actually promulgated by Sultan Mohammed the Conqueror in 1453 and 1476. The overriding principle of this pan-Ottoman code was that "the people and the land belong to the sultan" (i.e., that all governmental authority was derived from the sultan and from no one else). This principle in operation led to the elimination of all forms of noble landowning in the Balkan provinces of the empire and permitted the Ottoman government to establish the timar system of conditional landholding. The *Kanun-i-osmani* replaced peasant labor services with cash payments and introduced a graduated system of taxation calculated according to the ability of the taxpayer to pay. Ottoman officials were ordered to buy necessary provisions from the peasants at market prices and not resort to confiscation, except in emergencies. Concerned as always to ensure sufficient supplies for the cities and provide for the army, the central government at Istanbul did not wish to discourage agricultural productivity or permit local power holders to appropriate the sultan's property. Although each district of the empire retained its own regulations based on local custom, all had to conform in essentials to the *Kanun-i-osmani*.

In sum, orally transmitted customary law was gradually reduced to writing throughout all of East Central Europe, becoming intertwined with legal norms derived from the old Roman and Byzantine empires. Customary law was certainly the prevailing type throughout most of the medieval era, especially in provincial and village courts. Judges cited it in their decisions and used it as precedents. On the other hand, as central governments became more powerful, the monarchs increasingly came to favor Roman-Byzantine law, which stressed state power and the divine origin of royal authority. The ability to apply Roman-law principles was in itself a direct function of enhanced centralization. Where codification of the laws proved successful, it further strengthened this tendency. Nonetheless, by the close of the Middle Ages the legal systems of the various kingdoms of East Central Europe were still far removed from being either centralized in theory or systematized in practice. National and religious groups continued to live by their own traditional norms. The nobles on their private estates typically resisted both Roman law and the codification of native customary law. The overall legal picture is a mosaic of enormous diversity.

CHAPTER 11

Commerce and Money

Commerce has everywhere begun along the natural pathways provided by valleys, rivers, and seas, so that centers of exchange grew up at places suitable for communication. This close link between commerce and geography meant that trade in medieval East Central Europe still followed many of the same itineraries used in Roman times, while towns continued to exist on many of the identical sites. South of the Danube line a number of the most frequently traveled roads were already well established in the Greek and Roman period, and even in the Middle Ages the road network left by the Romans greatly facilitated communication. The most direct overland route from Belgrade (Roman Singidunum) to Constantinople, known simply as the Diagonal, followed the basins of the Danube and Morava rivers, struck eastward across the Sofia plateau, and continued along the basin of the Maritsa to Constantinople, the route of today's Orient Express. All other roads in the Balkan Peninsula connected with this main artery, except for the coastal routes and the Roman Via Egnatia, which led overland from Durrës in Albania to Salonika and Constantinople. West of Belgrade the main road followed the Sava River across what later became Yugoslavia. One branch turned southward at Sisak and led into Italy; another struck northward in Slovenia and continued as far as Buda (Roman Aquincum). Farther eastward the overland trade between Constantinople and Kievan Rus passed either through the Bulgar capital of Preslav or followed the coastal road along the Black Sea. In Roman times these various arteries were subject to a single government; but in the Middle Ages they were divided among a number of independent states and no longer were maintained in good repair.

The miserable condition of the roads meant that long-distance commerce in the medieval era was usually practicable only via the waterways. The Vardar-Morava route permitted fairly easy access from the Mediterranean into the heart of the Balkans. Salonika owed much of its prosperity to its location at the mouth of the Vardar River, which cuts through Macedonia southeastward before entering the Aegean Sea. A short overland crossing leads from the Vardar to the Morava, which flows northward to enter the Danube near Smederevo southeast of Belgrade. The Vardar-Morava valley is broader, and its mountain passes lower and shorter, than any other routes leading inland from the Aegean. On the other hand, the rivers of Albania flow from east to west, making that country a natural point of departure for overland communication across the southern Balkans. Whether political circumstances in the medieval era permitted trade to follow the ancient route of the Via Egnatia is not certain; but other trans-Albanian axes were definitely in use (e.g., through the Devolli valley).

For exchanges over shorter distances it was the river basins, rather than the rivers themselves, which created the communication routes. Even in medieval times most waterways in the Balkans had little importance for navigation because of their steep descent, although a significant local trade with boats and rafts existed on some of them. The Danube was navigable for most of its length, even for large vessels; and the rapids at the narrow gorge known as the Iron Gates (on the Serbian-Walachian border) seem not to have created major problems for medieval shipping. Commerce flourished along the Maritsa River, which flows eastward through the entire plain of Thrace and was largely navigable prior to the 19th century. On the banks of the Maritsa lay Plovdiv (Philippopolis) and Edirne (Adrianople), already important in Roman times as bases for Roman military fleets. Likewise navigable for small boats and rafts were the lower Drin in Albania, emptying into the Adriatic; the Drina and the Morava tributaries of the Danube; and the Vardar and Struma rivers, which flow southward into the Aegean. Canals suitable for shipping did not exist in the medieval Balkans, since the terrain was unfavorable.

Whether on the rivers or the seas, medieval ships were propelled both by oars and by sails. Their average speed was between five and seven miles per hour, although this varied according to the number of rowers, the direction of the wind, and the velocity of the currents. Since voyages lasted for so many days, frequent stops in port were necessary to restock foodstuffs, repair sails, and seek protection against storms. Navigators could orient themselves much more easily with land in sight than with only the stars as a guide. These factors all contributed to the importance of the Adriatic as a communications artery, even aside from the fact that it provides the shortest water route between Europe and Asia Minor. In both the Adriatic and the Mediterranean seas, currents are weak and fog is uncommon, although winds can be dangerous at some seasons. Freezing is virtually unknown, but the strong winds prevent navigation during the winter.

Until quite recent times most routes from the Adriatic Sea inland were little more than mountain trails, better suited to beasts of burden than to wheeled vehicles. Several important passages of this type linked the Adriatic coast with the hinterland. One led from Split to the Sava River, another from the mouth of the Neretva into the valley of the Bosna River and from there eastward. Geographically easiest was the passage from the Adriatic via Lake Shkodër and the mountain passes of northern Albania into central Serbia. However, the most traveled route began in Dubrovnik, crossing the mountains of Hercegovina to the Drina and beyond, making Dubrovnik the principal commercial entrepôt on the Adriatic Sea. To ply this route, professional captains in the Adriatic coastal towns organized caravans which sometimes included as many as 250 to 300 horses. The horses were often rented from shepherd chiefs who pastured their flocks in the highlands. Merchants loaded their goods on wooden packsaddles in bales, sacks, or leather saddlebags secured with padlocks. En route they camped in tents or in inns if available. They, their servants, and their guides all traveled well armed with bows and arrows, swords, and shields, since this overland trade was perpetually endangered by the vicissitudes of warfare and the plundering of caravans by the many petty lords of the region.

Already in Roman times sea commerce was an important activity along the eastern Adriatic coast, where the towns furnished sailors both for merchant ships and for the Roman and Byzantine war fleets. Then in the 7th century the Slavic and Avar invasions seriously disrupted this activity. The major Roman ports on the Dalmatian shore were destroyed by these intruders about A.D. 614, although several smaller settlements survived. Gradually the Adriatic commerce revived, but few details of the process are known. The configuration of the eastern Adriatic coastline, which is rich in bays, gulfs, and ports, was highly favorable to navigation. Hundreds of islands and rocky islets lie offshore, offering many possible routes to sailors through the intervening channels and between the numerous natural harbors in the bays which interrupt the shoreline. By contrast, the west (Italian) coast is low and stony, with water too shallow to permit ships to approach the shore. The eastern coast is also richer than the western in the fish and rainfall essential to provide food and water for the sailors. In the days of independent Croatia (9th–11th centuries), a wide-ranging commerce flourished on the Adriatic. Venice paid the rulers of Croatia a yearly tribute to ensure her ships free passage through the sea-lanes. Nonetheless a pirates' nest flourished at the mouth of the Neretva River until about 1420, when Venetian hegemony was established over Dalmatia.

Commerce continued between the Balkan peoples and the Byzantines even after Constantinople lost political control over large portions of Balkan territory. In 716 the Bulgars concluded a trade treaty with Byzantium which guaranteed free movement to merchants from both states on condition that they show proper passports and seals at the border crossings. This allowed the Bulgars to carry their merchandise to Constantinople, where they distributed it to Greek merchants in a quarter of the city specifically reserved for the Bulgar trade. Bulgaria lay on the overland transit route between Kievan Rus to Constantinople, which led either through Preslav and Adrianople or followed the coastal road along the Black Sea. The Preslav option allowed travelers to circumvent the dangerous Tatar country along the lower Dnieper river in Ukraine, although the Kievans more commonly followed the coastal route, presumably because it passed through the flourishing Greek maritime towns. Sviatoslav, the ruler of Kiev, praised the wealth of these towns when he invaded the Balkans in 967–68, reporting that the ports of the Danube delta contained "gold, fine fabrics, wine, and various fruits coming from Greece, silver and horses from Bohemia and Hungary, furs, wax, honey, and slaves from Rus."

In the more northerly regions of East Central Europe, where states took form considerably later than in the south, commerce for a long time remained much smaller in scope than in the former territories of the Roman Empire. Precise information is unattainable, although archaeologists have unearthed evidence of long-distance trade existing from a very primitive period. Objects of Frankish origin dating from the 8th and 9th centuries have been found in Bohemia and Moravia. According to the Jewish traveler Ibn Jakub, who journeyed through Bohemia in 965, Prague at that time was the largest marketplace in all the Slavic lands, visited not only by Slavic merchants but also by Muslims, Jews, and Turks. In Bohemia these traders sought slaves, tin, and various animal skins which they purchased with gold and silver bars, coins, or jewelry. By the 11th century Bohemia could boast a growing number of markets and roads, but bridges still were rare and brooks and rivers generally had to be forded. Burial finds from Poland in the 10th century show imports from Kievan Rus and even from the more distant Turkish-Tatar lands, although the route by which they arrived is not known for certain. Along the southern coast of the Baltic Sea a significant commerce began to develop in the 9th century, apparently via the island of Gotland, although the effects probably did not extend far inland. Early in the 10th century trade became more active in this region, centered on the island of Wolin near the mouth of the Oder River.

Security of their persons and goods was always a prime concern of medieval merchants. For this reason markets were often situated near the residence of a king or lord, who offered protection as well as an established clientele for resident artisans. Since a monarch's authority extended farther than that of local lords, royal settlements from the outset enjoyed greater possibilities for development than those dominated by mere nobles. Nonetheless, a king's guarantees of safety were not always sufficient to protect travelers, so that merchants usually formed armed convoys and journeyed together. In medieval Serbia the rule was that if merchants were robbed or ships disappeared, the town or village closest to the scene of the crime had to pay an indemnity (apparently on the assumption that the town had either been lax in providing security or that the culprits were local people). If the town could not find the money, the monarch paid. In perpetually insecure regions like Walachia and Moldavia, the roads remained exposed to every sort of attack by outlaws throughout the Middle Ages and afterward.

Pirates were an ever-present danger at sea unless a major naval power intervened to enforce the peace. At various periods Arab sea-raiders endangered shipping along the coasts of Italy and Dalmatia as well as in the eastern Mediterranean. In the 9th century the pirates domiciled at the mouth of the Neretva River in

Dalmatia were famous for their daring attacks on ships in the Adriatic. However, during the period of Venetian hegemony in Dalmatia in the 15th century, the Adriatic became relatively safe, since a permanent Venetian war fleet cruised there. The Aegean was more dangerous, since Italian, Greek, and later Turkish pirates were numerous in its waters. By contrast, the Adriatic was bothered mostly by petty privateers who attacked small trading vessels and in turn were chased by ships from Venice or Dubrovnik. Captured pirates were shown no mercy: either they had their eyes gouged out or were hanged.

Maritime commerce in the Black Sea was a Byzantine monopoly until the 12th century. Control of the narrow Straits which constituted the only opening from the Black Sea into the Mediterranean enabled Constantinople to exclude all competitors in the enormously lucrative exchanges between East Asia and Europe. Customs duties assessed on the East-West trade provided a significant share of the imperial revenue, while the subsequent loss of this commercial monopoly heralded the eventual fall of the Byzantine state. Venetian merchants gained access to a portion of Byzantine territory by decrees of the emperor in 992 and 1082 which exempted them from the usual customs duties. However, despite various concessions to the assertive Italians, the government at Constantinople insisted on closing the Bosphorus to all foreign ships. In this way it retained control of all vital centers of trade along the Black Sea coast and maintained its monopoly over the lucrative trade between the Far East and the lands of the Mediterranean. The first breach in this centuries-old system occurred in 1169. To better resist Venetian pressures, Emperor Manuel Comnenus granted the Genoese free access to all the empire's territories, with only minor exceptions. Evidently the Genoese at that time failed to comprehend the profit-making potential of the Black Sea trade, since they failed to utilize their newly won privilege to penetrate that region to any extent. However, the mere fact that this concession was granted indicates that Italian competition already was undermining one of the chief pillars of Byzantine strength—its commercial position in the eastern Mediterranean.

The situation changed abruptly in 1204 when the men of the Fourth Crusade captured Constantinople and established the Latin Empire. The leading role which Venetians had played in this Crusade placed them in a key position to dominate the commerce of the new state. Almost immediately they secured a treaty allowing them to close the Straits to any powers with which Venice was currently at war. Even so, they showed little initial interest in engaging in the Black Sea trade themselves; and they did not found any settlements in its ports. Their principal concern at this point was to protect the Latin Empire—and with it their commercial privileges—from the efforts of the exiled Byzantine government at Nicaea to retake its former capital. They not only employed their fleet for this purpose but also arranged a treaty with the Genoese—ordinarily their archrivals—by which the latter were permitted to establish a settlement at

Constantinople in exchange for a promise to refrain from aiding the Nicaeans. Both Venetians and Genoese now became active in the Black Sea trade, particularly in the lucrative traffic in slaves. In the late 1230s their opportunities for profit increased when the regions north of the Black Sea became part of the vast Mongol (Tatar) Empire—an enormous free-trade zone.

The unaccustomed friendship between Venice and Genoa could not indefinitely stand the strain of their commercial rivalry. Disputes in Palestine led to the breakup of the alliance in 1256 and prepared the ground for the fall of the Latin Empire. Aided by Genoa, the Nicaeans recaptured Constantinople in 1261. Venice's earlier support of the Latin Empire was held against her, with the effect of excluding her merchants from the Black Sea for the next forty years. The Genoese now became the chief beneficiary of Byzantine commercial concessions. To further their trade in the Black Sea they established a colony at the port of Vicina along one of the mouths of the Danube. This strategically located town, politically autonomous although theoretically a Byzantine possession, served as the terminus of the major land route from the Baltic Sea as well as the main emporium for the sale of wheat and salt from its own hinterland. Subsequently the Genoese expanded their Black Sea operations by concluding a trade treaty with the Tatars of the Crimea, offshoots of the great Mongol Empire. In 1290 they built the town of Kaffa in the Crimea on land granted to them by the Tatar khan. Competition returned to the Black Sea after 1302, when the Venetians secured a new treaty with Constantinople which terminated their banishment from Byzantine territories. However, in 1351–52 Genoa defeated Venice in one of their intermittent trade wars, so that Venetian merchants again lost access to the region. The Byzantines, as allies of Venice in that lost war, were forced to renounce altogether their control over the Danube delta. At about this time the Genoese moved their Danubian operations downriver to Kilia. The new location was closer to the sea and less vulnerable than Vicina to interference from the Bulgars who controlled inland shipping on the Danube. Vicina decayed economically, and eventually was abandoned so thoroughly that even today the exact spot where it stood cannot be identified with certainty.

Commercial activity increased greatly in East Central Europe from the 13th through the 15th century. Hungarian merchants, for example, had already been active at trading spots in southern Germany, Bohemia, and Bulgaria in the 10th century, but by the end of the 13th had branched out to reach Venice, Silesia, and Little Poland. Financiers from Italy, southern Germany, and Flanders settled in Hungary because of the easy availability of gold from the country's rich mines. On the other hand, a lack of both capital and business experience meant that the native Hungarian merchants usually did not travel far afield. No organization existed in Hungary analogous to the Hanseatic League which flourished in Germany and along the Baltic coast, offering mutual aid and protection to its members abroad. Thus the merchants of Buda, Bratislava, or Sopron rarely ventured farther from home than Vienna or Brno in Moravia.

Bohemia lay aside from the main long-distance routes through Central Europe, which in medieval times were linked to the Rhine or the Danube and their tributaries. This meant that its foreign trade was largely regional in scope; and Prague lacked the commercial importance of Vienna, Nürnberg, or Regensburg, where transit trade played a major role. The foreign goods which arrived in Bohemia—cloth in particular—were largely for internal consumption. A "cloth route" reached Prague from Flanders via Cologne, Frankfurt, and Nürnberg; or from Italy through Regensburg or Vienna, the latter being less frequently traveled owing to the restrictive Viennese trade policies. Links to Nürnberg and Regensburg in southern Germany constituted Bohemia's most important foreign connection. A less-used thoroughfare ran from Prague to Wrocław in Silesia or to Cracow. Then in the 15th century Bohemia's international trade contracted severely, owing to the Hussite wars and the country's reputation for heresy.

Important commercial routes which linked German and Prussian lands with the Black Sea ran through Poland in the early 13th century. Lvov in southeastern Poland (now Ukraine) functioned as the major entrepôt of this trade. The more northern of the Polish routes ran from the Baltic Sea through Toruń and Lublin or Sandomierz, while the southern one led from Leipzig through Wrocław and Cracow. From Lvov, caravans continued toward the southeast along the so-called Tatar route north of the Dniester River to the Crimea. Then near the end of the 14th century, warfare in the Crimea caused this route to be abandoned in favor of a safer one running lengthwise through Moldavia. This "Moldavian route" connected Lvov with Suceava, the Moldavian capital, and led via Iaşi to the Black Sea ports of Cetatea Alba at the mouth of the Dniester or to Kilia and Vicina on the Danube near the sea. It competed with the "Danube route" terminating at Kilia, which the 14th century Hungarian kings sought to develop. The Lvov merchants held a quasi monopoly on commerce along the Moldavian route, dealing particularly in cloth and metal wares which could be exchanged for Oriental silk, spices, and fruits. From Cetatea these goods traveled by sea to Constantinople, Asia Minor, and Cyprus, or northward along the coast of the Black Sea to the Tatar country. This track through Moldavia, which is first mentioned in the sources in 1382, was the so-called golden artery for Lvov until the second half of the 15th century, when the advance of the Ottoman Turks gradually severed Lvov's ties with the Near East.

Poland's trade with Lithuania also became more active in the 15th century, greatly enhancing the importance of eastern towns like Warsaw and Lublin which hitherto had been comparatively insignificant. Furthermore, victory over the Teutonic Knights in the Thirteen Years' War (1454–66) gave Poland control of Gdańsk at the mouth of the Vistula River. Gdańsk (Danzig) was a major port, which in the mid-15th century could count some 500 ships of varying types flying its flag. Possession of Gdańsk transformed the Vistula and its tributaries into the vital artery of an extensive Polish wheat trade to Western Europe. As a result, commercial routes through the Baltic Sea became increasingly important for Poland in the 15th century. The Baltic is friendly to navigation despite its northern latitudes, since it generates neither large tides nor high waves.

Shipping in the Adriatic also expanded in the 14th century, accompanying the development of larger sailing ships. Here the most important center was Dubrovnik (Ragusa), linked to the Balkan hinterland through mountain passes and distant enough from Venice to avoid domination by that powerful Italian republic. Dubrovnik's most flourishing period occurred between 1480 and 1600, when seventy or eighty large ships with full-rigged masts were domiciled in its port—an exceptionally large number for that era. These ships had to be well armed and strong enough to defend themselves against the North African pirates who infested the Mediterranean. By means of judicious tribute payments, Dubrovnik's prosperous merchant class managed to keep the town independent of all its powerful neighbors: Hungary, Venice, and the Ottoman Empire. At the same time, Venetian commercial regulations seriously hampered the maritime activity of Dubrovnik's competitors farther north along the Adriatic coast. Venice dictated what products those towns could sell, monopolized the sale of others, and insisted that a number of goods must be sold to Venice alone.

In the towns and markets of Albania's river valleys, Venetian traders were already active in the 13th and 14th centuries. However, their interest in that country was more strategic than commercial—to ensure that the narrow sea passage from the Adriatic into the Mediterranean would not be blocked by any hostile power. The Ottoman advance into the Balkans prompted Venice to preempt the enemy by occupying the major Albanian coastal towns: Durrës in 1392, Lezhë in 1393, Shkodër in 1396. This last move caused armed clashes with the Turks, who had briefly held Shkodër from 1393–95 and now regarded it as theirs. In accordance with their usual policy, the Venetians maintained a monopoly of wheat exports in those portions of Albania that they controlled. Otherwise their commercial interests in the region were fairly limited in scope, to the point where they permitted ships from Dubrovnik to conduct a triangular trade between that Adriatic town, the Albanian ports, and Venice itself. Since Venice's richest profits came from commerce with the distant Orient, its fleet was mainly reserved for this purpose. Venetian hegemony over the northern Albanian coast, however, had the effect of cutting off the towns from contact with the hinterland, causing their commerce to decline.

Smaller settlements developed along the Albanian coast in the 15th century to handle the traffic in local products—particularly grain, wood, and salt—while Durrës forfeited most of its former importance and the Balkan transit trade ceased altogether. Then in 1417 the Turks captured Vlorë, which thus acquired free access to the Turkish-controlled Balkan interior. Commerce flourished at Vlorë under the Ottoman regime, conducted largely by Greek and Jewish merchants. Much of this was transit trade between Italy and the Balkan interior, since Albania itself was too poor to purchase expensive foreign products. However, the prosperity of Vlorë was exceptional, since on the whole the Albanian coastal towns saw their commerce decline during the Ottoman period. Turkish conquest caused many of the inhabitants to emigrate, while the introduction of military fiefs in the countryside tended to inhibit commodity production for the market.

Commerce between Hungary and southeastern Europe was negligible prior to the founding of the two Romanian principalities in the 14th century. Merchandise reached Hungary from the Orient not via the Danube waterway, but from Venice or the ports of Dalmatia. Not only was the lower Danube unnavigable for the larger galleys; it also traversed a wild and dangerous region loosely dominated by Cumans or Bulgars. Merchants rash enough to use the Danube route to the Black Sea before the 14th century would have incurred not only the expense of frequent unloadings and reloadings but also the risk of marauders while on shore. However, the establishment of a Walachian and a Moldavian state structure in this formerly anarchical country created safer conditions which made possible an extensive trade through southeastern Europe. The Danube route began to function between central Hungary and the Black Sea, while an overland trail connected the Black Sea ports with Transylvania. In the latter region the new commercial links brought prosperity to the Saxon towns, especially Brașov, Sibiu, and Bistrița, which now sent their wares through the Carpathian passes southeastward. Brașov (Kronstadt), located near the exit of several passes over the southern and eastern Carpathians, became the most important entrepôt in this trade.

In the early medieval period the commerce of East Central Europe functioned without much use of money. Bohemia in the 10th century produced finely woven cloth which could be used as a means of exchange. Marten pelts served the same purpose in Croatia in the 10th–11th centuries. In Poland animal hides and salt functioned as means of payment. Neither the First Bulgarian Empire at its height in the 10th–11th centuries nor the rising Serbian state of the 12th century possessed any coinage of its own. In the Balkan peninsula during this period, metal coins rarely circulated except in the territories under direct Byzantine control (i.e., along the western coast of the Black Sea). There the political boundary between Byzantium and Bulgaria marked a pronounced economic contrast, exemplified by the wall which stretched across Dobrudja south of the Danube mouths and divided the two realms. Numerous coin deposits from the 9th century have been unearthed north of this line on what was then Byzantine territory, whereas south of the wall in Bulgaria such finds are generally absent.

The Byzantine government fostered a monetary economy throughout its Empire by decreeing that all taxes, even the hearth taxes assessed on rural serfs, must be paid in cash. This practice stimulated the circulation of money even in remote districts and minimized the usual tendency of people in poor areas to hoard rather than spend their cash. By contrast, barter was the prevalent method of exchange in the interior (unlike in the coastal towns) of the Balkans. Sheep, cows, and marten skins were the usual substitutes for money; but wheat, wine, oil, salt, cheese, bread, hogs, and goats served this purpose also.

Barter remained widespread as late as the 14th century, even in an active trading port like Dubrovnik. Within the town itself, horses, mules, and slaves were exchanged for cloth, while merchants from Dubrovnik traveled into the hinterland to buy small animals or cheese from the mountain herdsmen in exchange for salt. A salient feature of Balkan monetary history is the fact that coins entering an area where they were not needed for purposes of exchange—the result, for example, of a military expedition or Byzantine tribute payments—seem simply to have accumulated as treasure hoards (i.e., stagnant reservoirs of currency). Unless supplemented by a petty coinage, gold pieces only rarely functioned as money, sometimes finding their chief use as jewelry or grave decorations.

Almost everywhere the coining of money began very soon after the establishment of a state. Possession of a separate coinage was a matter of political prestige quite aside from its value to commerce, and might also be necessary for paying soldiers. In Bohemia the first silver coins were issued in the mid-10th century, stamped from imported rather than native silver. Poland struck a few coins in the 10th century, apparently only for small transactions. It soon abandoned the practice, probably because imported silver satisfied the demand for metal currency. Hungary produced its first coins early in the 11th century. These initial issues were chiefly employed in international trade, because merchants traveling abroad needed to carry a considerable supply of gold and silver on their persons. Coins were not required on the inland market, so the fact that a country minted them did not necessarily indicate the existence of a local money economy.

Bohemia and Hungary, which both possessed important silver mines, were the first states in East Central Europe to establish their own coinage on a significant scale. Bulgaria issued its first metallic money only in the 13th century. Both Bulgaria and Serbia minted a gold coin modeled on the Byzantine hyperperon, which they supplemented with an extensive silver currency. Serbia issued its earliest silver coinage in the late 13th century, concurrently with the onset of silver mining in that country. Judging from the large quantity of Serbian money discovered at various sites throughout the Balkans, silver coins were produced on a massive scale in that country for the next two centuries. Over 800 different types have been identified. The Ottoman government began minting the small round silver coin called the akçe in the reign of Sultan Orkhan (r. 1326–61), and issued its first gold coins following the conquest of Constantinople in 1453. The akçe remained the standard for Ottoman government accounting down to the end of the 17th century. Even states which lacked their own gold and silver supplies often found it helpful to establish an independent coinage. Walachia began doing so in about 1365 and Moldavia in 1377, the latter less than two decades after its founding as a state. Mines providing valuable yields of raw gold and silver became frequent bones of contention. The rich silver producing town of Srebrenica in eastern Bosnia is an extreme example, but nonetheless indicative. During one particularly troubled half-century (1411–63) it was once Hungarian, five times Serbian, four times Bosnian, and three times Ottoman.

A town or a kingdom which began to mint its own coins typically copied the design from neighboring regions where a money economy was better developed. Thus the earliest Serbian silver coins imitated those of Venice, both in the design and the legend appearing on the face, but weighed somewhat less, which precipitated complaints from Venice. Hungarian gold coins were modeled upon the Florentine gold florin, with the result that the Hungarian monetary unit even today is called a forint. King Casimir the Great of Poland issued coins modeled on those of Bohemia, but containing less silver. The earliest Walachian coins (14th century) were patterned after the deniers and obols of neighboring Hungary, whereas Moldavia's coins copied those of Lvov, the great emporium of southeastern Poland. The first Ottoman gold coins were modeled upon the Austrian ducat. In part this imitation was caused by the need to employ foreign experts to design a new coinage. For example, King Wenceslas II of Bohemia in 1300 imported Florentine mint masters to produce his new coins, while later in the same century Charles Robert of Hungary used Bohemian Germans for the same purpose. Experience also demonstrated that the population more readily accepted familiar-looking new coins than entirely strange models. As a new type of coin became better known, it tended increasingly to diverge from the earlier pattern in design and value. This evolution can be traced in Serbia, for example, where the oldest coins reproduced quite faithfully the details of their Venetian models, whereas later ones adopted a more distinct style.

Rarely in the early Middle Ages was the right to mint coins the exclusive prerogative of a monarch. In many cases powerful territorial lords, towns, or even monasteries shared in this privilege, which was highly valued for its profit-making potential. Most coins did not bear the name of their country of origin, but rather of the place where they were minted or which served as their model. Medieval sovereigns could not always prevent powerful nobles or semi-independent towns from issuing their own money. On the Adriatic coast, for example, even small towns like Kotor, Shkodër, Ulcinj, and Bar minted silver or bronze coins. Hungary was quite exceptional in successfully reserving the right of coinage to its monarch at an early date. The 12th-century chronicler Otto of Freising noted with astonishment that in Hungary no one but the king was permitted either to coin money or establish tolls. (These restrictions of course did not extend to Croatia, which insisted on its special status under the Hungarian crown and minted its own coins.) Enforcement of a standard currency was beyond the powers of most medieval governments. Prussia was an exception in the 13th–14th centuries—a unified economic region with no internal tariffs and a single silver coinage, owing to the unusually well-organized government of the Teutonic Knights.

Most coins had a comparatively limited circulation. Those issued by towns, lords, or bishops normally were used only within a radius of 50 to 100 miles from their place of origin—sometimes less. The Adriatic coast, for example, was so mountainous that each small town tended to become the focus of a circulation area extending no farther than its own immediate hinterland and the offshore islands. The coins in question bore a low face value. Even after a country had established its own currency, foreign money often continued to be favored in some parts of the realm. Coins of good quality—which meant that they contained a high proportion of silver or gold and enjoyed a reputation for honest weight—were willingly accepted far beyond the place where they were issued. In contrast to the standard practice of modern states, rarely in medieval East Central Europe did a country's own currency circulate to the exclusion of all other types. However, it did not happen that a confusing and haphazard variety of coins was in use in a particular locality. Money changers doubtless established exchange rates between the different types of coins they were offered; but at any specific place and time, payments were normally made in a single currency only. In the treasure hoards it is unusual to find coins of more than one kind, except for the occasional stray piece. The type of money actually employed in a particular area depended chiefly on economic factors and proved resistant to political regulation. The attempts of monarchs to promote their own coinage by forbidding the use of foreign money usually proved futile.

Until the end of the 12th century the influence of Byzantine currency on the monetary systems of the Balkans was enormous. The Byzantine gold hyperperon, which was issued from the 4th through the 11th century without ever being depreciated, was gladly accepted throughout Europe. Within the Greek empire itself, immense quantities of coins were in circulation, including an abundant supply of copper coins as petty cash. The quality and availability of Byzantine money probably explains why in Bulgaria no independent coinage appeared until the early 13th century under the Second Empire. Byzantine coins circulated in Croatia and Serbia and in parts of Dalmatia even as late as the 14th century. In Serbia the Byzantine monetary standard continued to be used for accounting purposes even after actual Byzantine coins disappeared from active circulation. However, political weakness ultimately impoverished the Byzantine economy and weakened its currency. Venice, Genoa, and Dubrovnik, applying pressure at Constantinople, extorted tax concessions and customs exemptions on behalf of their merchants. The throne conflicts after 1180 and the establishment of the Latin Empire in 1204 proved especially disastrous. By the second half of the 14th century the Byzantine Empire was in effect a vassal state of the Turks, unable to maintain its own fleet and subject to increasing Ottoman pressure. Not surprisingly, the circulation area of its currency greatly contracted. In the eastern part of the Balkan Peninsula the Byzantine gold hyperperon continued in general use until about 1340. Its name survived even longer in the Bulgarian and Serbian word for this unit of value: perpera.

Very few Byzantine coins dating from after the mid-14th century have been found in the Balkans. The famous gold currency which had survived for so long was now replaced by silver and copper, while a variety of foreign coins came to replace the Byzantine types which had vanished. Bohemian or Hungarian coins predominated in the north of Moldavia, whereas in the south the so-called Tatar coins of the Mongol Golden Horde were more commonly in use, especially the copper ones, which were issued in small denominations. In the second half of the 15th century these Tatar coins were replaced with Ottoman ones, although for internal circulation Moldavia retained its own silver money. When the influence of Venice superseded that of Byzantium in Dalmatia, the Venetian gold ducat also supplanted the Byzantine hyperperon. However, the circulation area of the ducat was largely limited to the Adriatic coastal districts, while the Florentine gold florin, which was minted in much greater quantities, became more popular overall. In the 14th century, Bohemian silver coins were employed extensively in Central Europe for international transactions, owing to their high quality and plentiful supply. The groschen of Vienna circulated for many centuries in western Hungary.

Uncoined silver (valued by weight) was a major means of exchange throughout all of Europe outside Italy until the end of the 12th century. This preference for bullion over coins was a response to the unreliable metal content and erroneous valuation of much of the legal coinage. Since the price of silver fluctuated according to the current supply on the European market, governments should have adjusted the legal value of their coinage accordingly. Frequently they failed to do so, with the result that the use of silver bullion created serious difficulties in international trade. Moreover, as commerce became more active in the 13th and 14th centuries, heavy silver bars became too unwieldy for large-scale transactions. Gradually gold bullion replaced them. Gold was less widely available than silver, but its supply was far more consistent, so that the value of gold currency varied much less than that of silver. Gold was more valuable than silver per unit of weight and also more stable in price because of its comparative scarcity.

Prior to the mid-13th century, international gold payments in Europe were made either with Byzantine or Arabic gold coins or with gold bullion. As the Italian towns became more active in Near Eastern trade, they found it necessary to mint their own coins. In time the Florentine gold florin and Venetian gold ducat became the most popular currencies throughout Europe on account of their stable value and the preeminence of Florence and Venice in international trade. In East Central Europe only Hungary could supply gold coins on a comparable scale. In the 1320s the Hungarian and Bohemian mines together accounted for more than half the silver production of Europe and over 90 percent of its gold production. Hungary held a near monopoly of gold in the 14th and 15th centuries—a vital factor in its military and political power, which reached its greatest height precisely at this time. Bohemia enjoyed a commanding lead in silver production, with Prague silver groschens circulating widely throughout Europe. In 1327 the two kingdoms experimented with establishing a joint currency and set the ratio of gold to silver by treaty. However, within the decade a sharp rise in the price of gold had caused this arrangement to founder. Accordingly, King Charles Robert in 1337 cut the link between the two currencies and made the gold gulden the sole monetary standard in Hungary.

Since the value of all medieval coins, even of small pieces, depended on the actual quantity of metal they contained, some depreciation inevitably occurred through wear. Far more serious, however, was the fact that very few monarchs could resist the temptation to debase their coinage. A tidy profit could be realized by reducing the amount of gold or silver in a coin, claiming all the while that its value remained the same as before. On the other hand, the notorious unreliability of most medieval coinage caused the public to lose confidence in it, making its value decline faster and farther than it might otherwise have done. The kings of Hungary found currency debasement particularly profitable, owing to the country's rich complement of gold and silver mines. However, many other monarchs also engaged in this practice. The Ottoman Sultan Mohammed II (r. 1451–81) several times ordered what was euphemistically known as "recall" of the coinage, although prior to his time the weight and standard of the silver akçe had been fairly well maintained. Before issuing new coins, he sent his officials throughout the empire to collect all old silver coins and privately owned silver. He even authorized the search of travelers' rooms and baggage.

In Hungary from the mid-11th until the 14th century, debasement of the coinage became a kind of permanent tax on the realm. The attempts of several monarchs to correct the situation met with limited success, since the royal court had become excessively dependent on this source of revenue. The process reached such extremes that after the mid 12th century the government was issuing new coins every year. The debased money depreciated rapidly on the market, until at the end of each year it was recalled by royal decree and forcibly exchanged at half its nominal value. This pernicious system was finally corrected by King Charles Robert (r. 1310–42), who had grown up in the more commercially oriented milieu of southern Italy and understood the need for a stable currency in international trade. In 1323 he ordered the minting of new gold guldens with a metal content equal to that of the Florentine florins. Resembling the florin in both weight and appearance, these new coins became a permanent issue in Hungary. The Hungarian gold gulden soon gained an excellent reputation and came to be used extensively in international exchanges. No longer was Hungarian coinage treated as a source of profit for the royal treasury, but henceforth served its natural purpose of facilitating commerce.

The gold shortage which occurred in Europe in the early 14th century caused an international financial crisis which greatly enhanced the importance of Hungarian gold on the European market. Until that time the Islamic states of Africa and the Near East had supplied most of Europe's uncoined gold. However, in preparation for a new Crusade to the Holy Land, a series of papal bulls now forbade Christians to trade with Muslims. These prohibitions, while meant only to harm the Islamic states, had the unintended effect of enriching Hungary at the expense of the rest of Christendom. Since Hungary was the chief producer of gold on the European continent, King Charles Robert took advantage of the situation to make windfall profits. In 1325 he totally banned the export of bullion from Hungary and established a state monopoly of gold and silver mining. These orders were rigorously enforced. Foreign merchants could no longer exchange their goods for uncoined metal in Hungary, but instead were required to accept Hungarian gold and silver coins in payment. Foreign silver money had to be exchanged in the royal exchange offices at a price which brought the king's treasury great profit. Gold was traded against silver at double the normal rate. This artificially induced gold shortage reached its height in 1343–44, when a chance event abruptly brought the crisis to an end. In 1343 King Charles Robert's widow transported an enormous fortune in gold and silver from the Hungarian royal treasury to Naples in hopes of using it to promote the claims of her youngest son to that Italian throne. At one stroke a quantity of gold equivalent to two years' supply for the entire world began to flow onto the Italian market. The price of gold quickly fell back into its old ratio against silver of 1:11 or even 1:10. At this level it remained stable during the second half of the century, as expectations of a new Crusade slowly faded and trade with the Near East resumed.

Paradoxically, a country's possession of rich gold and silver mines might easily result in impoverishment over the long run. Medieval rulers who controlled a sizable supply of these metals saw no harm in spending it on the purchase of luxury goods abroad, with the inevitable tendency of discouraging artisan work at home. Both Bohemia and Hungary incurred a huge imbalance of imports over exports, financed by sending gold and silver out of the country. The usual stimulus to produce for export was lacking when so much money was available at home. Thus Bohemia's craftsmen served an essentially local and regional market in the 14th century, while the country's negative trade balance was financed by the export of silver coins. Similarly the Hungarians neglected native crafts in the 15th century and incurred an enormous trade deficit, also defrayed by the export of coinage. The situation of both kingdoms invites comparison with 16th-century Spain—a country likewise temporarily enriched by gold and silver treasure (from the New World) but ultimately harmed by the resulting industrial stagnation.

Medieval monarchs typically exerted direct control over gold and silver mines for the benefit of the royal exchequer, while private initiative was more common in the extraction of other ores. Hungarian copper is a case in point. This metal was much in demand for producing the thin copper sheets which covered the roofs of the better-quality houses. Throughout the 15th century, Hungary was an important copper exporter. However, after the mines had been worked for some time, deeper penetration into the earth caused an upsurge of ground water which could not be controlled with the primitive techniques of the period. By the end of the century, Hungary's copper mines were on the verge of ruin. The situation was saved by a certain John Thurzó, a native of the Slovak mining district, who discovered a technical solution to the problem of ground water. Buying up abandoned mines cheaply, Thurzó restored them to production, thus becoming the first important Hungarian private entrepreneur. Eventually he forged a partnership with the south German banking house of Fugger, creating in this way a major industrial enterprise which exported copper throughout Europe.

Venetian and Dalmatian merchants conducted a very large part of the long-distance trade in medieval East Central Europe. Superior in their mastery of commercial techniques, they also possessed far more extensive capital resources than the natives of other regions could muster. Their relations with the host countries were regulated by treaty. Venetian traders were prominent at Varna, Bulgaria's principal port on the Black Sea, and in various towns of Macedonia, from which they sent caravans overland to the Adriatic coast or eastward into Ukraine. Merchants from the coastal towns of Dalmatia—chiefly Dubrovnik, but to a lesser extent Kotor and Bar—dominated the trade between the Adriatic and its Balkan hinterland. Especially active in Bosnia and Serbia, they extended their activities also into Hungary, Bulgaria, and Albania. By paying tribute to local rulers, Dubrovnik was able to establish colonies with extraterritorial privileges in the interior of the Balkan Peninsula, where its citizens were entitled freely to reside and trade. There the merchants of Dubrovnik maintained warehouses, while their fellow townsmen worked as tailors, clothiers, goldsmiths, or stone-masons. These expatriates remained answerable only to the judicial authority of consuls appointed by the home government, who rendered decisions based on Dubrovnik's own law. When a looser Hungarian overlordship replaced Venetian suzerainty over Dubrovnik in 1358, these consuls gained additional powers as diplomatic representatives of their home city.

Farther north in East Central Europe the role of the south German traders was analogous to that of the Venetians and Genoese in the Black Sea. The merchants of Nürnberg had been particularly hard hit by the shortage of silver money in Europe, caused by the exhaustion of many older mines. Since metal currency was indispensable for their wide-ranging international transactions, they sought additional silver in Bohemia. In 1321 King John of Bohemia granted them full freedom to trade in Prague as well as protection for their commerce throughout Bohemia. In their search for silver the Nürnbergers gradually took over the entire Bohemian metal trade, not only in silver but also in the copper and tin needed by their artisans at home. Subsequently their connections with Prague were interrupted by the Hussite wars, causing them to establish new commercial bases in Catholic Plzeň on Bohemia's western border. Meanwhile the Fugger banking interests of Augsburg had acquired a major share in Hungarian metal exports through their partnership in the Thurzó enterprises. John Thurzó himself, despite his ownership of many copper mines, lacked sufficient capital to finance distribution of the metal on a broad international market.

Shortage of credit was frequently a serious hindrance to medieval commerce. Here Jewish moneylenders proved highly useful. Prohibited by law or custom from owning land or engaging in various other occupations, Jews from very early times had gravitated toward urban commercial and artisan activities. After the First Crusade had made travel unsafe for them, many Jews took advantage of the growing demand for money in European society and shifted their emphasis from commerce into moneylending. Thus they avoided being caught on the roads with bulky merchandise; money or precious objects could more easily be hidden or carried away. Jews stood ready to lend money at interest to Christians—an activity vital to the developing trade of the period, but which the Church stigmatized as "usury" and forbade Christians to practice. In addition, Jewish financiers served as tax-farmers for kings, paying large sums for the right to collect customs duties and state taxes. In some cases Jews administered the royal mint, as they did on occasion in Poland in the 12th and 13th centuries. A few medieval Polish coins were actually engraved with Hebrew characters, apparently because some Jewish mint masters were unfamiliar with Slavic alphabets.

The markets of East Central Europe handled a surprising variety of commodities even in the early medieval period. Despite the primitive rural economy with its overwhelmingly local orientation, self-sufficiency was never total. Certain vital supplies could be acquired only through exchange. Salt was a product of this kind—indispensable for the human organism but present in nature in just a few localities. Available only along the seacoasts or where salt springs or salt mines existed, it had been an important article of commerce since ancient times. In East Central Europe the major sources of salt were located near Cracow in southern Poland, in the mountains of Transylvania, and near the town of Tuzla in Bosnia, where salt mines had existed already under the Roman Empire. Bohemia acquired most of its salt from Salzburg across the border in Austria. For the southern Adriatic region, mines in the neighborhood of Durrës and Vlorë in Albania were the principal sources. At Dubrovnik salt was considered so essential that the town government assumed responsibility for ensuring an adequate supply, hiring a ship and ship's captain from time to time to sail to Durrës to buy it at a fixed price. In fact salt made the fortune of Durrës, which had little else to sell but found permanent markets for this commodity in the Balkans.

On the whole, East Central Europe supplied the international market with products of agriculture and mining rather than manufactured goods. Chief among Hungary's exports were cattle, horses, sheep, and pigs, which could be driven on the hoof rather than transported. By the end of the 14th century the demand for meat at the courts of kings and in the town houses of prosperous merchants in Western and Central Europe had grown to a point where the surrounding rural districts could not provide adequate quantities. As a result, it became worthwhile for traders in Germany to import beef from a considerable distance. Hungary, with its rich and abundant grazing lands, was the single most important source. Serbia too exported horses and livestock together with all the products of stock raising, such as skins, wool, and cheese. Moldavia and Walachia supplied large herds which were driven via Lvov, Cracow, and Wrocław to Nürnberg and Frankfurt-am-Main. German merchants in the two Romanian principalities and the towns of Transylvania were the chief middlemen in the trade through Nürnberg.

Grain was a major article of export for the regions of East Central Europe having access to the Baltic Sea. The population of the growing towns of Western Europe had to be fed; and for the majority of medieval people, bread was the central component of the diet. In Prussia the Teutonic Order of Knights became a great trader in wheat and rye, using the profits from this activity to finance its various enterprises. Canon law forbade members of the Order to trade but did not define "trade" very precisely, enabling the Knights to argue that only profit-making trade was prohibited. Clearly the cloisters needed to sell some of their products in order to maintain their operations, although the Order expanded its trading operations far beyond its own needs, irritating the native Prussian merchants as they did so. After Poland acquired access to the sea in 1466, a flourishing wheat trade developed via the port of Gdańsk, where the Vistula empties into the Baltic Sea. Now for the first time, grain from the estates of the Polish nobility could be transported to the seacoast via the Vistula and its tributaries. Each year a hundred-odd ships left Gdańsk bound for Western Europe, carrying wheat and other agricultural and forest products. This trade created large profits for many Polish nobles, driving them to require heavier labor services from their peasants, which in turn accelerated the decline of the peasantry into the "second serfdom." Other bulk articles, too heavy to be moved overland, were similarly transported by water, such as the wool, leather, and hemp of Poland. Polish wool was exported in such large quantities in the second half of the 15th century that too little remained for native cloth weavers, evidently because foreigners bought up the supply at higher prices. Large quantities of lumber, wax, and honey were exported from the forests of Poland and Lithuania in the 14th and 15th centuries, thus contributing to the growth of Warsaw, the future Polish capital. The forests which covered large sections of East Central Europe at that period provided furs as well as lumber for export from Poland, Bohemia, and Serbia. Dubrovnik, situated in a region with few trees, relied on wood from the Albanian estuaries for construction of its houses as well as its ships. Fish from the Baltic and Adriatic seacoasts was transported into the hinterland. In addition to wheat, Bulgaria shipped barley, leather, forest products, and especially the famous Zagora cheese from its Black Sea ports. Wine was a major article of export from both the Adriatic coast and Hungary.

The commodity most often imported into East Central Europe from abroad was textiles, since locally produced cloth was inferior in quality to the sort available in Italy or Flanders. Clothmakers were quite numerous in 14th-century Prague, for example, but did not have access to high-grade wool. For Hungary in the mid-15th century, textiles comprised 75 percent of all imports from Western Europe. Certain imports came from as far away as the Far East or India (e.g., cloth, spices, wine, dye, perfume, salve, and ornaments of gold and silver). In general, East Central Europe exported agricultural products and imported manufactures—a pattern partly due to its relative lack of investment capital as compared to the more developed regions of Italy or Flanders. Scarcity of capital made the organization of large-scale production for the market impossible, with the result that artisan work frequently stagnated at the stage of small-goods production by the guilds. One exception to this general rule was weapons manufacturing. The town of Braşov in Transylvania, located near the theater of the Turkish wars, became a major weapons supplier to 15th-century Europe. As chief armorer of the Hungarian lands, Braşov originally produced bows, arrows, and shields, and at a later date firearms, cannons, powder, and rifles. Among its best customers were the Hungarian general John Hunyadi and Voivode Stephen the Great of Moldavia, successful commanders against the Turks.

No discussion of medieval commerce would be complete without reference to the lucrative slave trade. The capture of human beings for profit was a primary aim of warfare throughout the medieval period. Since in theory Christians should not buy or sell other Christians, Jewish merchants often served as middlemen in this trade. Similarly for religious reasons, the pagan north served as a great reservoir of human merchandise until the conversion of the region to Christianity. East Central Europe was a major source of captives for the great slave markets of Venice. Important centers of slave trading functioned at Dubrovnik and Kotor, and later at the mouth of the Neretva River in Dalmatia. Particularly desirable as slaves were the alleged Bogomil heretics from Bosnia, since their sale did not offend the traders' moral scruples about enslaving fellow Christians. The Church raised no objections to the slave trade, except occasionally to register discomfort at the spectacle of Jewish merchants buying Christians, or of Christians being sold to "Saracens" (i.e., Muslims). Sometimes even ecclesiastical institutions bought slaves. Extant purchase records show, for example, that Catholic monasteries in medieval Croatia bought human beings from overseas traders and pirates for eight to ten gold solidi apiece. Finally, Turkish soldiers in the Balkans in the 14th–15th centuries abducted many men, women, and children for sale. In theory all residents of the Ottoman Empire were entitled to the sultan's protection and could not legally be enslaved; but this prohibition did not apply to persons captured on raids beyond the frontiers. When the Turks first entered Europe in the 14th century, they enslaved mainly Greeks and Bulgarians. In the 15th century they did the same to Serbs, Albanians, Walachians, and Bosnians according to the current location of the border.

Perhaps motivated by piety, a few rulers saw fit to place restrictions on the slave trade. King Tomislav of Croatia in the early 10th century supposedly prohibited the sale of slaves except as rowers for his war galleys, where no doubt they were considered indispensable. In Hungary, King Koloman (r. 1095–1116) forbade the sale of Hungarian slaves abroad and freed his own slaves. The Hungarian Golden Bull of 1222 specified that Jews were not permitted to keep Christian slaves; and in the 14th century King Louis I freed the slaves in all his lands—an action probably more applicable to Croatia than to Hungary, where large-scale commerce in slaves had never existed. From about the year 1400, Dubrovnik began issuing laws against the slave trade. The original prohibition applied only to the enslavement of Catholics, while commerce continued in black slaves from Africa, who were much esteemed in the Mediterranean world for their exotic appearance. Even in the 15th century the merchants of Dubrovnik dealt quite openly in slaves. They merely refrained from bringing them into town, where blatant offenders against the antislave laws were sometimes punished. The citizens of Dubrovnik, accustomed to using slaves for domestic labor, were still permitted to buy them for personal use, although not for resale. This exception ensured that slavery would be perpetuated in the town for many decades more. In any case, mountaineers living just beyond Dubrovnik's borders continued to buy and sell human beings in their accustomed fashion.

Whether the merchants were natives or foreigners, Christians, Jews, or Muslims, all medieval rulers of East Central Europe sought as far as possible to regulate commerce. Many international treaties contained clauses dealing with this subject. The monarchs' interest in trade was largely fiscal, since internal tolls and river taxes together with customs duties on the frontiers produced considerable profit. Hungary's border tariff in the late 12th century amounted to one eightieth of the value of all merchandise. By the 15th century this had risen to one-thirtieth, and was assessed at the markets where the goods were actually sold rather than on the border. Serbia collected a tax of ten percent at its markets, the same rate as the Byzantine Empire, although administration of the Serbian tolls was entrusted not to state officials but to private commercial societies based in Kotor or Dubrovnik. From the perspective of merchants, the frequent unloading and examining of goods at the various checkpoints constituted a serious hardship. Thus Polish towns at the end of the 13th century sometimes purchased the tariff stations on nearby roads from the king and abolished customs duties there for their own citizens, while continuing to exact payment from foreigners. In Bohemia the rivers and roads which crossed the border were provided with customs stations; travelers found them difficult to avoid, since the most practical routes led through mountain passes which were easy to watch. Similarly in Hungary, traders were supposed to keep to the paths designated by the government, which was able to guard only the main arteries. Merchants who used other "secret routes," if caught, were punished by confiscation of their goods. In addition to the official tolls charged by monarchs, nobles who controlled large territorial estates often imposed their own fees.

In Poland the influence of the nobility on government eventually led to the ruin of the native merchant class. Nobles looked with distaste upon townsmen, whom they despised as their social inferiors, blamed for the high price of imported goods, and resented for their wealth. On various occasions in the 15th century the noble-dominated Great Sejm, or Diet, ordered the government to fix prices on artisan goods, although this was still rarely done. Then in 1496 the Sejm passed a crucial law abolishing the tariffs on goods exported "from the household" or imported "to the household," meaning that no charges could be assessed either on grain exported directly from a noble's estate or on foreign goods purchased for a noble's personal use. The object was to exclude the town class from participation in the import-export trade, since town residents would still be required to pay the tolls. Elimination of the urban middleman's fees was supposed both to maximize the noble landowner's profit from grain sales and to reduce the price of the wares he bought from abroad. Only gradually during the 16th century did the harmful consequences of this self-serving and shortsighted policy become evident. The new regulations encouraged the nobles, through their agents, to export the products of their estates directly. The results were other than anticipated. The cost of imports did not go down; native Polish industry and trade were severely damaged; and the towns became impoverished. In the meantime, foreigners not only flooded the Polish market with duty-free goods but also managed to profit from the export trade.

The Ottoman government, faithful in this respect to Byzantine and Oriental tradition, adopted a policy of strict state control of the economy. All its Balkan lands became subject to detailed commercial regulation. Aware that bread was essential to the survival of Istanbul and the towns of Thrace, the Ottomans prohibited the export of grain from the empire except with permission from the grand vizier, which was rarely granted. Even the vassal states of Moldavia and Walachia in the 15th century were obliged to export their grain exclusively to the Ottoman Empire, although this monopoly proved impossible to enforce completely. Merchants were not at liberty to sell grain wherever they chose: Ottoman officials designated the places to which it must be delivered. The purpose was to ensure a regular supply to the towns, prevent the smuggling of grain abroad, and forestall grain speculation. Although private merchants handled the buying and transport of the grain, they needed a permit to do so from the chief judge of Istanbul. The Ottoman government set the price of both purchase and sale, taking into account the costs of transportation. A profit margin was calculated into this price, usually amounting to about ten percent. Where large quantities of grain were involved, a guard accompanied the shipment to make sure that it reached its proper destination. Subject to similar regulation were other commodities which the Ottomans considered particularly important, such as salt and rice. Penalties for infringement of the economic directives included public ridicule, flogging, mutilation, and even death.

A technique employed by many medieval governments to control commerce was the granting of staple rights. A town possessing such rights was entitled to demand that all passing merchants stop, lay out their wares, and offer them for sale to local people for a specified length of time. Commercial travelers were required to sell their goods only in bulk quantities and forbidden to trade among themselves. The precise meaning of "bulk" was prescribed for each type of merchandise. After a fixed period had elapsed the merchant could usually carry away his unsold goods, although in certain cases even this was prohibited. Traders failing to respect the regulations were subject to severe punishment. Staple rights were directed not only against merchants from other towns or foreigners, but even against residents of the town itself who lacked rights of citizenship. Medieval people assumed as a matter of course that commerce represented a fairly static quantity of exchanges, not an infinitely expandable one. Staple rights were openly aimed at enhancing the importance of the staple town (usually at the expense of neighboring localities), enriching its privileged citizens, and facilitating the collection of tolls for the monarch's benefit. It would scarcely have occurred to anyone that such regulations might restrain the total volume of commerce and lessen the overall prosperity of the state.

The staple system worked best when applied to large towns on major trade routes, where the disadvantage of the restrictions would be offset by the convenience of the route and a large local market. For this reason the smaller towns usually possessed only limited staple rights or none at all. On the other hand, staple privileges which initially were favorable to a town's prosperity tended to have the longer-term effect of discouraging local enterprise. While details varied greatly from place to place, staples were quite common in the towns of medieval East Central Europe. In some cases they applied only to certain products, or to merchants traveling in a particular direction. If a town sponsored an occasional trade fair, it usually suspended the regulations during that time. To attract business to the fair, foreign merchants would be given temporary rights to buy and sell without restriction, and could even bypass the local people by dealing directly with each other.

The Vienna staple was particularly strict, and naturally affected the trade of neighboring Hungary and Bohemia. Originally established in 1221, it required itinerant foreign merchants to offer all their wares for sale on the spot. Only citizens of Vienna were permitted to carry these same goods out of town, so that the entire profit of the transit trade fell to the Viennese. Any wares which found no buyers in Vienna had to be carried back home—a regulation which doubtless prompted many foreign merchants to sell cheaply or at a loss rather than incur the further costs of return transport. Vienna was difficult to bypass because of its strategic location on the Danube waterway—the easiest and cheapest transit route through Central Europe. Nonetheless, foreign traders sought to circumvent it. An alternate route from Hungary into Germany which avoided Vienna led from Buda northward via Brno in Moravia. At a conference in 1335 at the Hungarian royal castle of Visegrád the three sovereigns of Bohemia, Hungary, and Poland agreed to cooperate in regulating trade on this northern artery, since all three shared an interest in escaping the Vienna staple. Ultimately the Viennese themselves suffered from the harmful effects of staple rights. Secure in their monopoly position, they became accustomed simply to sit back and wait for the Germans to arrive with their wares and Hungarians to come to buy. They lost any incentive to promote their own artisan products for export. Once the Germans ceased coming, the Viennese had nothing to sell. Vienna abolished its staple in 1515.

The Hungarian kings issued staple rights to some of their own towns. In 1244, Buda received the right to intercept all passing ships and wagons and force traveling merchants to lay out their wares for sale. No foreign tradesmen were permitted to continue their journey beyond Buda, which was strategically located downriver from Vienna on the Danube. Later in the 13th century Győr in western Hungary acquired its own staple rights, as did Košice and Bratislava in Slovakia. Esztergom also sought staple rights, but its location only 27 miles north of Buda was a disadvantage; and the citizens of Buda successfully protested. In the 14th century Buda was the favored market within Hungary for goods from Italy or Germany, as well as the principal spot from which Hungarian exports left the country, although Košice dominated the trade between Hungary and Poland. Then in 1402 King Sigismund granted a staple to five Hungarian border towns, thereby abolishing the rights of the Buda merchants in those localities. As a consequence, many merchant enterprises gravitated from Buda to Bratislava (Pozsony). Staple rights contributed strongly to the prosperity of both Bratislava and Sopron during the first half of the 15th century, whereas Buda's role in long-distance commerce declined.

In the 14th century the Saxon towns of Transylvania acquired staple rights aimed at promoting trade between Hungary and the newly established Romanian principalities. Brașov in 1369 and Sibiu in 1382 received staples with respect to the trade in cloth from Poland or Germany, giving their merchants a monopoly on its sale in Transylvania, Walachia, and Moldavia. By a decree of 1378 all persons from outside Transylvania were forbidden to engage in commerce in these two towns except for small items sold at the fairs. Hungary's partial suzerainty over Walachia rendered these Transylvanian staple rights exceedingly valuable. For example, King Matthias could order the Walachian prince Vlad III to protect the Saxon merchants in that country against Turkish raids and not to harass them. In this way the Saxon towns were shielded from competition in several directions. Their merchants could dominate the trade between Transylvania and the regions to the southeast, where they sent cloth, arms, metal products, and household utensils in exchange for animals, hides, cotton, wax, and honey.

The rerouting of the Lvov-Black Sea transit trade from the old "Tatar route" to the alternative "Moldavian route" occurred only after an embryonic state structure had been created in Moldavia, thus enhancing the security of travel. The new principality, located at the junction of roads leading eastward from both Transylvania and Poland, profited greatly from this international traffic. Poland's efforts in the 14th and 15th centuries to dominate Moldavia were prompted in large part by the importance of the Moldavian ports of Kilia and Cetatea Alba, where this route terminated. However, the inland towns of Moldavia suffered from the staple regulations in effect at Lvov and in the Saxon towns of Transylvania, particularly with respect to cloth—the chief article in international commerce. In 1368, Braşov forbade foreign merchants to carry cloth out of town eastward, thus reserving to her own citizens the profits of this trade with the Romanian principalities. When Hungary's suzerainty over Walachia and Poland's over Moldavia weakened in the 15th century, the Romanian rulers were able to grant staple privileges to some of their own towns. Walachia enforced such regulations by stringent methods, including impalements and decapitations of Saxon traders who tried to bypass the staple towns. As a consequence, merchants from Braşov or Sibiu were almost totally excluded from the trade with Walachia, enabling Walachians to replace them. Moldavia's staple regulations had a similar effect in eliminating the Genoese and diminishing the role of Lvov in the long-distance trade through the principality.

The kingdom of Bohemia was unfavorably situated to profit from staple rights, since the most important medieval transit routes bypassed its territory. The chief international thoroughfares which crossed in Prague— those from Nürnberg into Hungary and from Regensburg to Wrocław—were of only secondary importance. Accordingly, foreign merchants traveling through Bohemia were not required to offer their wares for sale there. A royal edict of 1304 provided that foreigners who stayed for fewer than five days in any Bohemian town without unpacking their goods were entitled to carry them elsewhere. In 1393, King Wenceslas IV sought to strengthen the position of his capital by decreeing that foreign merchants entering Bohemia must travel via Prague and sell their wares only to citizens of Prague Old Town. Nevertheless, Prague never received complete staple rights, since its geographic position did not promise advantages from such a policy. A strict staple system would probably have caused the transit trade to avoid Bohemia entirely.

In Poland, by contrast, staple rights in one form or another were widespread. By the early 14th century all of the larger towns possessed them, albeit usually subject to various limitations. The period after which unsold goods could be carried elsewhere varied from three to eight days. Altogether 48 Polish towns gained staple rights of some kind in the 14th and 15th centuries. Most stipulated that foreign goods must be offered for sale in the town for at least a few days. Wrocław's staple was the oldest in Poland, dating from 1274, and required that all merchants arriving from the east must either sell or exchange their wares in Wrocław itself. Cracow's staple in the 14th century enabled it to dominate the east-west trade across southern Poland. Until about 1400 the staple privileges of Toruń on the lower Vistula allowed it to dominate trade with the regions farther upriver. Lvov, the starting point for both the "Tatar route" and the "Moldavian route" to the Black Sea, received extensive staple rights in 1444. Traders from the West arriving in that town were forbidden to proceed onward to the ports of the Black Sea, whereas merchants from the East were prohibited from traveling westward. All were obliged to buy and sell in Lvov alone. The effect was to exclude Cracow from the lucrative Oriental commerce.

The Ottoman conquest of the Balkans in the 15th century wrought major changes in the trade patterns of the region. The Turks eliminated many former political borders and tariff barriers and created an enormous free-trade zone within their vast empire. Reduction of brigandage made the highways of the Balkans much less dangerous than formerly. The Ottoman government was favorably disposed toward trade and understood its potential for creating profit. Since the Turks themselves had not developed an extensive commercial economy or a wide-ranging network of trade and credit, they permitted non-Muslims—in practice mainly Armenians, Jews, and Balkan Christians—to trade freely in their empire on condition of paying specified taxes to the sultan's treasury. Some of these people were Ottoman subjects, but many were foreigners. Subjects of Dubrovnik as well as a few Italians residing at Sofia, Vidin, or Tirnovo were prominent in the commerce of Ottoman-controlled Bulgaria in the 15th century. The Romanian vassal states were drawn into the orbit of the Ottoman economic system as major sources of raw materials as well as tribute. Peace with the Turks proved to be a catalyst for Romanian commerce in the Balkans and Asia Minor. The resultant wealth constituted a powerful source of support for the Walachian and Moldavian princes.

Conversely, Ottoman expansion proved detrimental to Polish trade. The fall of Constantinople in 1453 was followed by the Turkish conquest of Kaffa in the Crimea in 1475 and Kilia and Cetatea Alba on the Dniester and the Danube in 1484. These events marked the gradual blocking of both the "Tatar road" and the "Moldavian road" to the Black Sea, on which the prosperity of Lvov was based. Oriental goods now arrived in Poland chiefly from Western Europe via the new ocean routes to the East Indies. In the 15th century Venice and Genoa lost their former position of dominance in the Black Sea trade, as the Turks captured their colonies one by one. The main commercial routes to Persia and India now passed through Ottoman territory, so that Istanbul became the chief entrepôt for exchanges between Europe and the East. Although Venice and Genoa still conducted some trade in the Balkans, their bitter struggles over markets not only had exhausted their forces and sapped their prestige but also provoked Ottoman animosity.

Part of the role formerly played by Venice and Genoa in the Balkan and Black Sea trade fell to Dubrovnik as a result of its success in gaining the Turks' good will. In 1399, only three year after the fall of Bulgaria, Dubrovnik obtained permission from Sultan Bayezid I for its citizens to trade freely in any part of the Ottoman Empire. Sultan Murad II issued a similar order in 1430. Nonetheless, as long as the possibility existed that the Turks might be expelled from the Balkans, Dubrovnik loyally supported the Christian side in the anti-Turkish wars. The renewed Ottoman incursions into Serbia in 1454–55, followed by the collapse of the Serbian Despotate in 1459, finally convinced the town's rulers of the need to make terms with the sultan. An embassy to Istanbul in 1458 brought back a highly favorable tariff agreement, which remained largely unchanged thereafter. The town agreed to pay the sultan a heavy tribute, in return for which its merchants acquired a favored position in the Ottoman Empire in the Balkans. Goods sent from Dubrovnik into Ottoman territories would pay a customs duty of only two percent, as opposed to the five percent paid by others. These concessions were in fact very similar to those which Dubrovnik had formerly obtained from Serbia, except that now its consuls in the Balkans were replaced in most cases by Ottoman officials. The government of Dubrovnik accepted responsibility for any misdeeds committed by its merchants on Ottoman territory, including unpaid debts. Despite numerous difficulties arising from the new situation, the town not only retained its Balkan markets but actually increased them during the Ottoman period. Dubrovnik's foreign connections proved exceedingly useful to the Turks, who possessed few commercial links of their own with the Western world. Moreover, trade in general benefited from the disappearance of internal customs barriers and the establishment of peace within the Ottoman Empire.

Bohemia's commercial position in the 15th century, although largely unhurt by the Ottoman advance in the Balkans, was seriously damaged by the Hussite wars. The hostility which many Europeans felt toward "heretic Bohemia" created strong pressures upon loyal Catholics to avoid dealing with the Czechs. Furthermore, intermittent religious strife threatened the safety of transport in the kingdom. Social changes in the Hussite-dominated towns undermined credit and interrupted production in the silver mines. Shortages of essential imports occurred; and Prague's central role in the commerce of Bohemia was largely destroyed. Those Bohemian towns which remained faithful to the Roman Church forged their own links with Catholic towns abroad and ceased to work through Prague. The old trade route from Germany through Prague to Silesia lost its importance, since the Germans now sent their goods through Saxony instead. Bohemia's former trading partners, the towns of southern Germany, stood decisively on the anti-Hussite side, fearing not only the power of the German emperor and his allies but also the spread of Hussite doctrines among their own citizens. Nevertheless, commercial interests did not always go hand in hand with religious conviction. German merchants retained their interest in Bohemian silver and grain, despite priestly fulminations against persons who dealt with heretics. The Nürnbergers continued to trade with Bohemia despite their consistently hostile attitude toward Hussitism; and individual merchants from other localities did likewise. This commerce involved some risk, since the home towns of these merchants had to conceal or publicly condemn such activities in order to preserve the appearance of loyalty to Catholicism and the emperor. As a consequence, Czech towns near the German border like Plzeň and Domažlice assumed a leading

position in Bohemia's foreign trade, since transactions along the frontier were
naturally less dangerous than those with the interior.

Commerce thus continued, regardless of political changes. Monarchs normally
regarded it as a source of profit and sought rather to promote than impede it.
Nonetheless, from a purely economic standpoint their regulatory measures were
often self-defeating. Seeking short-term advantage rather than long-term prosperity, they were tempted to impose high taxes which made commerce unprofit-
able. Tariffs and internal tolls diminished the total quantity of trade in the interest
of benefiting the royal treasury or powerful individual lords. Debasement of the
coinage produced recognizably pernicious effects. Moreover, from a monarch's
standpoint commerce was not merely a source of tax revenue, important as this
undoubtedly was, but also an activity to be managed in the interest of maintaining his authority over the population. Ottoman economic regulations—extending far beyond anything attempted by the comparatively rudimentary Christian
states—undoubtedly had this intent. As inheritor of the Byzantine Empire's
trade policy as well as its great cities, the sultan's government took it for granted
that economic controls were essential to ensure supplies to the cities and prevent urban unrest. In the long run, however, state management of the Ottoman
economy impeded the development of the productive forces which mark the
beginning of the modern age.

The relative backwardness of commercial life in East Central Europe vis-à-vis
Western Europe in the Middle Ages invites a variety of explanations. Among
the relevant factors were undoubtedly the sparse population of the region, the
devastation caused by the Mongol attack, the relatively unfavorable climatic
conditions in the northern sector, and the long-standing conflict with the Turks
in the south. Still in the future lay the shifting of trade routes westward to the
Atlantic, which in the 16th century would lead to commercial stagnation both in
Germany and in East Central Europe. The gold and silver production of Bohemia
and Hungary undermined the position of their own artisan classes, since many
goods could more easily be purchased abroad than produced at home. In Poland
the nobility utilized its political dominance to enact measures detrimental to
townsmen, although most such laws bore their bitter fruit only in the 16th century
and afterward. Regulation of trade by monarchs and towns—a situation hardly
unique to East Central Europe—certainly contributed to reducing the overall volume of exchanges and limiting the resources available for commercial activity.

Much more than just material prosperity was involved in this relative underde-
velopment of commerce in East Central Europe. Only the exchange of surplus
products could provide sufficient wealth and tax revenue for a central government to maintain internal peace and defend a country against external enemies.
Without a strong army under centralized control, a kingdom tended to fall apart
or become an easy prey for its neighbors. Moreover, commerce was the lifeblood
of the towns, which in turn were essential to the development of civilization.

Aside from the courts of kings and nobles (in whose life few could share) or the fairly restricted world of the monasteries, towns formed the most favorable milieu for the creation and dissemination of literature, art, philosophy, and all other achievements of high culture. Only commerce combined with active artisan production could provide the economic surplus which allowed the leisure for creative activity to even a small segment of society. Only towns could supply the multiplicity of human contacts necessary for intellectual stimulation. The weakness of the towns and of commercial life certainly contributed to the fact that East Central Europe lagged well behind Western Europe in the achievements of medieval civilization.

CHAPTER 12

Foreign Affairs

The history of interstate relations in medieval East Central Europe necessarily begins in the southernmost sector, namely in those lands which subsequently became Albania, Bulgaria, Romania, Hungary west of the Danube, and the Yugoslav successor states. All these territories belonged at one time to the Roman Empire; and along the Adriatic, Aegean, and Black seas the first medieval states of the region took form. Not surprisingly, our earliest documentary evidence about them is supplied by authors writing in Greek who reported on the foreign relations of the Byzantine Empire. With respect to the more northerly territories which became Hungary, Poland, the Czech Republic, and Slovakia the historical records for the 7th through 9th centuries consist largely of blank space. Archaeology can tell us something about the material culture of the inhabitants; but extant documents provide information concerning only those regions falling within the field of vision of the great powers of the time—the Byzantine Empire and, to a much lesser extent, the empire of the Franks.

The Slavic and Bulgar invasions of the 5th to 7th centuries eroded Byzantine authority in most of the Balkan Peninsula virtually to the point of extinction. Toward these intruders the government at Constantinople adopted a flexible policy, employing sometimes the army, at other times bribes ("tribute"), peace treaties, or the grant of honorific court titles to the tribal leaders. Much of the empire's remaining power rested on its navy. Greek ships still plied the Danube; and Byzantium controlled access to the Adriatic Sea through its possessions in lower Italy and Albania. Territorial losses had not yet seriously undermined the old Roman theory of the empire as a universal state, headed by an emperor who was Christ's representative on earth. Whatever the actual political situation might be, the Byzantine emperor still claimed as his inheritance the lands settled by the South Slavs, and treated their leaders as his subordinates.

The extraordinary expansion of Arab power in the 7th century under the impetus of the new religion of Islam placed an enormous military strain on the Byzantine Empire. The result was the loss of huge territories in Asia Minor,

Syria, and North Africa. In the 8th century, Byzantine power was challenged by Turkic-speaking Bulgars from the Ukrainian steppe who carved out a tribal state from the empire's Balkan lands. In the year 681 Byzantium was forced to recognize the existence of an independent Bulgaria in the Balkan Peninsula and pay the Bulgars an annual tribute, on condition that they refrain from further conquests at the empire's expense. By a further treaty of 716 the boundary between Bulgaria and the empire was set along a line bringing Bulgar power perilously close to Constantinople itself. The Byzantine government promised to pay the Bulgar khan the equivalent of 30 pounds of gold each year. Similarly along the eastern shore of the Adriatic, Byzantium's role was minimal in the 7th–9th centuries, so that the Arabs were able to endanger Constantinople's control of the Adriatic Sea.

Clearly the Byzantines were unwilling to regard their military and political reverses in the Balkans as final. Particularly in the case of Bulgaria, they could not acquiesce in the existence of a barbarian state so close to their capital, on land which had been imperial Roman territory ever since the first century B.C. The loss of the Black Sea coast severely damaged their trade as well. For this reason they invariably directed their future wars against Bulgaria toward the region of Varna and the mouths of the Danube. However, the temporary successes of Byzantine armies merely led to new rebellions, after which the Bulgars would replace a pro-Byzantine puppet ruler with one of the opposite persuasion. After a century of intermittent conflict, a new treaty in 816 established the frontier between the two states along approximately the same line as in 716. This agreement left Byzantium with a strip of land some 40 miles wide on the northern shore of the Aegean. Along this border the Bulgars built an extensive line of fortifications—a great ditch with a high rampart on its northern side, along which soldiers kept constant watch. The Greeks termed this the Great Fence of Thrace.

Bulgaria indubitably became a major power in the 9th and 10th centuries, the chief threat to Byzantine hegemony in the Balkans. Its brilliant Emperor Symeon (r. 893–927) seriously aspired even to the Byzantine throne. Several times he invaded Byzantine territory with the aim of capturing Constantinople, supplementing his threats with diplomatic methods. Advancing with his troops to the walls of the imperial capital in 913, he intimidated the Byzantines into agreeing that his daughter could marry their young Emperor Constantine and he himself would become co-emperor. However, as soon as the Bulgar armies withdrew, the Byzantine government reneged on this agreement. Certainly the powerful Bulgar emperor was hardly unique in wishing to possess Constantinople (nor in being outwitted by Byzantine diplomacy). The magnificent Greek city on the Bosphorus, together with the high civilization it embodied, exercised a powerful attraction upon all the neighboring lands. Symeon's ambition to rule there was not without foundation, considering that he had at his disposal the resources of a major Balkan state. His Bulgar ancestry was not an insuperable barrier either, since a number of previous Byzantine emperors had begun life in notably humble circumstances. Moreover, Symeon himself was well versed in the Greek language and culture, having spent much of his youth at Constantinople. Unfortunately for his ambitions, the mother of the Byzantine child-Emperor Constantine VII* adamantly refused to approve a marriage between her son and the daughter of a "barbarian."

Tsar Symeon's peace-loving son Peter (r. 927–69) sharply reversed his father's expansionist policy. Early in his reign Peter fought the Byzantines long enough to secure a favorable treaty reestablishing the old boundary along the Great Fence and recognizing the independence of the Bulgar Church. These arrangements, concluded in 927, preserved the peace for nearly forty years. Then in 967 the Byzantine government, provoked by an ill-considered Bulgarian demand for tribute, stirred up an attack on Bulgaria by Sviatoslav, the ruler of Kievan Rus. Sviatoslav was so pleased with what he found in Bulgaria that he wished to remain there. When he invaded the country a second time and moved uncomfortably close to Constantinople, the Byzantines took fright and sent an army against him. In a brilliant campaign in 971, the regent (and future emperor) John Tzimiskes not only defeated the Rus but in the process restored Bulgaria to the Byzantine Empire. Nonetheless Byzantium's hold on Bulgaria was not yet complete. After the death of Tzimiskes in 976, the four brothers known as Comitopuli (i.e., "the count's sons") organized a rebellion in western Bulgaria (now Macedonia). One of them, Samuel, became sole sovereign and succeeded in recovering all of the territories once ruled by Symeon. However, this restoration was brief. In 991 the Byzantine Emperor Basil II (afterward known as Basil the Bulgar-slayer) began an extensive series of campaigns against Bulgaria. Samuel valiantly resisted until his death in 1014; but the tide of battle increasingly turned against him. His weak successors were utterly unable to master the situation; and by 1018 independent Bulgaria had ceased to exist. Once more the Byzantine Empire's northern boundary stood on the Danube.

Byzantium Dalmatia, by contrast, was too distant from Constantinople to be adequately controlled. The Byzantine government's inability to exercise effective sovereignty there enabled the Croats to establish an important coastal state. Under King Tomislav (r. 910–28), Croatia developed into a major Adriatic power, reportedly possessing a fleet only slightly inferior to that of Venice or Byzantium at that time. Unable to prevent Tomislav from taking over the northern Dalmatian coast, and apprehensive that he might ally himself with Bulgaria, the Byzantine government sought to win him over with honors. To legalize the de facto situation, it granted him the court title of proconsul—a rare distinction for a foreigner—as well as official permission to take over the administration of Byzantine Dalmatia. In 986 it bestowed the same rights and an appropriate imperial title on another Croat king, Stephen Držislav. A dozen years later still, doubtless responding to changes in the local power configuration, the Byzantines permitted Venice to

* This was the future Byzantine historian, Constantine Porphyrogenetos.

exercise suzerainty over Dalmatia in the emperor's name. However, the government at Constantinople refused to renounce its formal rights even when it could not exercise them. The Adriatic towns were important both for their commercial wealth and for their strategic position along the sea-lanes between Italy and the eastern Mediterranean. Moreover, Dalmatia was valuable territory simply by virtue of its topography. Its protected harbors were surrounded by islands which could shelter ships in bad weather, while its rough landscape provided mariners with landmarks easily visible as navigational points of reference. These characteristics were almost entirely lacking on the Italian side of the Adriatic, which was flat and lacked good harbors. As a consequence, the Dalmatian littoral frequently changed hands.

The late 9th century marked the final time that a seminomadic confederation from the steppes of Ukraine established itself in the heart of Europe. The Magyars who arrived on the Central European plain in 895–96 conducted plundering raids as their chief source of wealth. Their campaigns took them into the heart of Germany all the way to the North Sea as well as into eastern France and central Italy, where on several occasions their horsemen reached the gates of Rome. In 938 and 943 the Magyars invaded Byzantine territory as far as southern Greece and the outskirts of Constantinople, retreating only after the Greek patriarch bought them off. Most of these campaigns had no apparent political purpose. Certainly they were not necessary for securing possession of the Hungarian plain, which at the time was half-empty territory controlled by no major power. Rather the Magyars' raids were the typical reaction of seminomadic herders when confronted with the comparative wealth of a settled society, particularly the gold and silver treasures preserved in Christian churches. Especially vulnerable, because nearest at hand, was the German Empire. Only after the Germans themselves had learned the effective use of cavalry tactics could they successfully resist the Magyar attacks. First at Merseburg in 933 and then at Lechfeld near Augsburg in 955, a coalition of forces from the various German dukedoms dealt the Magyars annihilating defeats which broke their military power and pushed them back into Hungary.

The defeat at Lechfeld was merely the initial step toward integrating these steppe raiders into the European political system. Genuine acceptance required first of all that the Magyars give up nomadry and organize a state, and secondly that they become Christian. Failing this, they might well have suffered the fate of other nomadic peoples who had formerly ruled empires in the heart of Europe. The Huns, Gepids, and Avars had all once held such transitory hegemony, only to disappear afterward from the stage of history. For defense against neighboring states the Magyars required an organized political structure, whereas adoption of Christianity was the inescapable act of legitimation enabling them to become a full partner in the Christian community of nations. Conversion also deprived foreign Christian rulers of an excuse to attack the Magyars as heathens, while it qualified the Hungarian ruling dynasty for intermarriage with the other royal houses of Europe.

The turning point came when the Magyar overlord Géza arranged the marriage of his son Stephen with the Christian princess Gisela of Bavaria. This dynastic link gave Hungary a distinctly Western orientation and irrevocably set the course of future Hungarian history. In agreement with both the pope and the German emperor, King Stephen I in the year 1000 formally ordered the conversion of all Hungary. His decision to accept Christianity in its Latin form was doubtless influenced by the generous attitude of the young Emperor Otto III, who abandoned his predecessors' claims of hegemony over all Christendom by demonstrating that the conversion of a country need not entail subjection to the Church of the German empire. Stephen I took the lead in converting his countrymen to the new religion. Despite the more predatory attitude of Otto III's imperial successors, the kingdom of Hungary thereafter remained firmly attached to the Latin Church and politically independent of the German empire for all but a brief period in the 11th century. This was due to the strength of the kingdom, not to any lack of imperialist ambition on the part of the German emperors, since the Hungarians turned back several German invasions in the 11th century.

Bohemia, the westernmost major territory inhabited by Slavs, was less favorably situated than Hungary to avoid political dependence on the German Empire. Although protected on the north, west, and south by mountains, it also was surrounded on three sides by imperial lands. Territorially smaller and militarily weaker than Hungary, Bohemia usually was forced to acquiesce in some degree of subjection. As a consequence of German military pressure, the Bohemian Duke Wenceslas* became a vassal of the German emperor in 929. His successor, Boleslav I, after years of fighting the Germans, finally concluded that perpetual warfare was the only practical alternative to vassalage, and that the latter was preferable. During the following centuries, several Bohemian rulers sought without success to shake off German overlordship. Duke Břetislav I (r. 1034–55) made particular efforts to do so. After defeating the Germans in battle in 1040, he requested that Emperor Henry III recognize Bohemia's "own laws" and renounce its yearly tribute to the empire. Henry refused. The following year he forced Břetislav to give up the lands he had recently conquered in Poland on the ground that both countries should not be governed by a single ruler. Břetislav had to humble himself barefoot before Henry's throne, swear a vassal's oath, and renounce all his Polish conquests except those where his legal title was unchallenged. His further efforts at independence proved equally futile. However, for the most part the rulers of Bohemia accepted the inevitable and maintained friendly relations with the German Empire.

The fundamental obligations of vassalage, as this status was understood in medieval Europe, included loyalty to the overlord, military aid and support against the lord's enemies, attendance at the lord's court, and the payment of

---

* This is *Duke* Wenceslas, not to be confused with the later *King* Wenceslas I of Bohemia (r. 1230–53).

tribute. The person recognized in Bohemia as sovereign had to seek confirmation and enfeoffment from the emperor, who bestowed the title of duke in a solemn ceremony of homage. The ruler of Bohemia did not enjoy the option of allying himself with any of the empire's enemies. This was clearly demonstrated in 1031 when a duke who had taken sides with Poland against the empire was tried in a formal imperial court process, found guilty, deprived of his duchy, banned, and imprisoned. The Bohemian monarch participated in sessions of the imperial court of justice, at which the emperor wished to be surrounded by all his vassals. These court days were held at various towns throughout Germany concurrently with the meetings of the Reichstag, the assembly of the German princes and prelates. The period of required attendance was probably about six weeks, although this was not formally specified until 1212; and the meetings occurred on the average about once every three years. On occasion the Bohemian duke sent a representative or presented an excuse; but only two instances have been recorded in which he actually refused to go.

Vassalage did not prevent the Bohemians from managing their own internal affairs. Throne conflicts sometimes permitted the German emperor to interfere in the Bohemian succession, but he could not ignore the hereditary claims of the Přemyslid dynasty or the well-established right of the Bohemian nobility to elect their own sovereign. The German emperors exercised no judicial power in Bohemia and held no lands there. Moravia, initially a borderland directly subject to the empire, became subordinate to Bohemia after 1197. Moreover, Bohemia's rulers gradually increased their own political standing. Several received the emperor's permission to call themselves "king," even though most were simply entitled "duke" until the early 13th century. Originally the rulers of Bohemia were not allowed to participate in the elections for German emperor, because the Přemyslids were regarded as a Czech dynasty, not a German one. Later this restriction was dropped. After the Bohemian ruler was officially designated "king" he held the highest rank among the seven recognized electors of the empire.

In the course of the 10th century many nations of northern and eastern Europe accepted Christianity. This period saw the baptism of the Czechs, the Rus, and slightly later the Hungarians, Swedes, and Norwegians. Ultimately the only remaining pagans in Europe were the Baltic peoples—Prussians, Lithuanians, and Finns—and the Slavic tribes living between the Elbe and Oder rivers. In Poland's case the military threat from Germany provided the immediate impetus for conversion. Otto I the Great, the German king whose coronation by the pope in 962 revived in theory the Roman Empire in the West, used Christianity as a means of extending his rule over the pagans on his eastern frontier. Missionary work and territorial acquisition went hand in hand, so that where baptism was not received voluntarily it was imposed by the sword. Between 938 and 950, Otto I conducted a series of brutal campaigns against the Slavic peoples who then resided in large numbers east of the Elbe River. He appointed his own officials to govern Germany's eastern borderlands, or marchlands, and in 948 he founded three missionary bishoprics for them. In the year of his coronation as German emperor he established a new archbishopric at Magdeburg for the express purpose of proselytizing in the East. The political implications of these activities were surely not lost upon the Polish duke.

Thus the Polish state which arose in the 10th century in the region around Gniezno and Poznań (the later province of Great Poland) was obliged to establish a modus vivendi of some sort with the German Empire. The earliest reference to Poland in a historical document occurs precisely in the context of its relations with Germany. The date is 963, when the Polish Duke Mieszko I was twice defeated in war by the German count of Saxony. Subsequently Mieszko accepted some type of dependency relation to the German Empire, which required him to pay tribute for his lands west of the Warta River. Although still a pagan, he arranged to marry a Christian princess, Dobrava of Bohemia. Doubtless this action was accompanied by his own promise to accept Christian baptism, as well as by the implicit or explicit understanding that all his subjects would be required to do the same. The initiative for this turn of events evidently came from Mieszko himself, who recognized that acceptance of Christianity was the indispensable prerequisite for attaining equal status with the other European ruling dynasties. In 986 he formally recognized the German emperor as his overlord.

In accepting Christianity of his own free will, Duke Mieszko parried the threat of a possible Christian crusade against "heathen" Poland. He also emphasized his independence of the Germans by making his realm a direct fief of the Holy See and himself becoming a vassal of the pope. While remaining politically in vassalage to the German emperor, he concurrently accepted submission to Rome. The exact meaning of this act has been much discussed by historians, although no consensus has emerged. Presumably Mieszko's motive was to gain political leverage against the emperor. However, the document recording his agreement with the pope, the so-called "Dagome iudex," presents so many riddles that the precise nature of the original understanding (if indeed it was clearly defined) cannot be ascertained. Despite his vassalage to both pope and emperor, Mieszko retained great freedom of action, and left to his son Boleslav I a much larger state than he himself had inherited.

The claim of the German emperors to supremacy over the other Christian rulers of Europe was a source of perpetual tension with neighboring states. Ever since the imperial coronation of Otto I in 962, he and his successors had regarded their status as vastly exalted above that of mere kings. They viewed themselves as the political heirs of Charlemagne, whose coronation by the pope at Rome in the year 800 had allegedly given him the same powers and rights as the ancient Roman emperors. Young Otto III, son of the Byzantine princess Theophano, viewed his Roman heritage with extreme seriousness. Creatively modifying Byzantine political theory, he regarded the German Empire as a confederation in which he as emperor was the supreme head, but would refrain from direct interference in the internal affairs of the associated states. According to this concept, all Christian lands should form a single entity, subject in religion to the pope but in secular matters to the "Roman" Emperor. Otto III offered alliance to the neighboring princes as an ally or "brother," not as a sovereign or conqueror.

The fruit of this policy for Poland was his stunning visit in the millennial year 1000 to Gniezno, then the Polish capital and burial place of the martyred Saint Adalbert. The Polish Duke Boleslav I received him there with great pomp and ceremony. Otto placed a crown upon Boleslav's head and honored him with the titles "Friend and Confederate of the Roman People" and "Patrician." Whether this act should be seen as a formal coronation is not entirely clear. Poland and the empire concluded an alliance at that time which included an obligation on the part of Poland to pay tribute. In the end, this unusual fraternal relationship of the two sovereigns proved to be short-lived, since Otto III died prematurely in 1002. Nonetheless, it brought concrete advantages to Poland. Otto renounced the tribute which the Poles hitherto had paid to the empire for their land on the left bank of the Warta River. He also agreed—contrary to the wishes of his own German bishops—to found an independent Polish archbishopric at Gniezno.

Whether Otto III's imperial policy could have retained its idealistic outlines in the long run is a matter for speculation. In fact, Poland's relationship to the empire deteriorated almost immediately after his death. Duke Boleslav I (r. 992–1025) fought three wars with Otto's successor, Emperor Henry II. He conquered Bohemia, which Henry proposed to let him keep only on condition of receiving it as a fief of the empire. When Boleslav refused these terms, Henry drove him from the country and installed a member of the Czech Přemyslid dynasty in his place. (Subsequently the Přemyslids did accept Bohemia as a fief of the empire.) Throughout his reign Boleslav I, known as "the Brave," was almost continuously at war somewhere and achieved military successes which raised Poland's international prestige. He gained territory between the Oder and Elbe rivers, and twice placed his son-in-law on the throne of Kiev in Rus. Except for some newly acquired territory on his western border, he avoided vassalage to the German Empire and ended his career with a royal coronation in which he assumed the title of "king." Boleslav the Brave of Poland was undoubtedly an energetic and courageous soldier, whose conquests subsequently made him a national hero. Polish historians have sometimes interpreted his campaigns either as national struggles against the Germans or as part of an overriding scheme to unify the Slavic peoples. No evidence exists that Boleslav himself entertained such notions. His campaigns into Bohemia and Russia are easily explainable by quite ordinary dynastic and expansionist motives; and he had many Germans in his family and among his advisers.

In reality, the Polish state in the 11th century was militarily much weaker than the German Empire, able to avoid a dependent relationship only under an exceptionally able monarch. Boleslav the Brave was an incessant campaigner, although he did nothing to establish permanent institutions which might have consolidated his conquests. As a result, most of his territorial acquisitions were lost to Poland after his death. During the greater part of the 11th century the rulers of Poland were vassals of the German emperor. One duke came to power only with German aid; another remained an imperial vassal despite pursuing his own expansionist policy; and a third, who was married to the emperor's sister, was openly a German ally. The political weakness of Poland was illustrated even more graphically after 1138, when the entire state disintegrated. Only its reunification after 1310 forced the empire finally to drop its claim to supremacy over Poland.

In addition to the German threat, Poland and Hungary in the 11th and 12th centuries faced danger from the steppe horsemen on their eastern and southern frontiers. The grasslands north of the lower Danube, geographically an extension of the great Eurasian plain, lay wide open to invasion by seminomadic tribes from Ukraine. This territory, which much later formed the principalities of Walachia and Moldavia, was the domain of various pastoral peoples. Richly supplied with the fodder indispensable for horses and cattle, it constituted an open invitation to whatever migratory group currently sought refuge from its enemies by fleeing westward. Obscure movements of tribes on the northwest borders of China found echoes at various removes in the invasions of mounted warriors into southeastern Europe. Each new group of intruders behaved much the same as its predecessors, adding to its wealth by raids into settled areas in order to collect plunder and tribute. These steppe warriors were also available for hire as mercenaries by one or another of the more civilized neighboring states. The swift attacks of these skilled horsemen nearly always caught the agricultural populations by surprise and caused great destruction.

The plains of the lower Danube were held in succession by several pagan Turkic-speaking tribes from the steppe. The Pechenegs occupied this territory in the 10th and 11th centuries, only to be pushed out by their near relatives, the Iazygs (or Uzes). The Iazygs in turn were destroyed by a Hungarian army when they invaded Transylvania in 1068. Cuman tribes then moved into the gap caused by the Iazygs' defeat. The Cumans eventually created an empire which reached from the mouth of the Don River to the lower Danube. From their vantage point north of the Danube they harassed the settled peoples of Transylvania, the Byzantine lands, and Rus for 170 years. The Byzantine government sought to contain this Cuman threat by maintaining a military presence at the mouth of the Danube and cultivating friendly relations with the Rus princes. However, in 1185 the Asen brothers' revolt in Bulgaria freed the lands south of the Danube from Byzantine rule. Fear of the Tatars (i.e., Mongols)—a still more powerful nomad confederation—drove some of the Cumans to seek asylum in Hungary in the 1230s. Others remained along the lower Danube, where their relations with the Bulgars were generally friendly. "Cumania," as their vaguely defined territory was then known, nonetheless remained a danger to its neighbors until the 14th century, when new states were organized in Walachia and Moldavia which pushed the frontiers of civilization eastward.

The prestige of the Byzantine Empire stood high in the Balkans during much of the 11th and 12th centuries. By 1018 Emperor Basil II had completed his conquest of Bulgaria and reintegrated its former territories into his realm. This brought Byzantine rule in the Balkans north to the Danube and west to a line beginning about 40 miles west of Belgrade and ending on the coast of Albania. The effect was felt immediately in Serbia (the old Dioclea along the Adriatic). Whereas previously the Serbian princelings could count on Byzantine support against the Bulgars, now the Empire's territory surrounded them on three sides. The Serbian princes became dependent for their positions on Byzantine good will; and any who were suspected of disloyalty had to send hostages to Constantinople. The Byzantine government reinforced its authority when necessary through military expeditions. Pretenders to the various Serbian thrones were generally available to replace any ruling princes who appeared unreliable. Despite these controls, the Serbs continued to give trouble with their numerous raids; and Byzantine attempts at retaliation were not invariably successful. The drastic weakening of Byzantine power after the death of Emperor Manuel Comnenus in 1180 soon had its effect in the Balkans. In the interior of the peninsula between Belgrade and Skopje, Serbian tribes began making themselves independent.

In Dalmatia, Byzantine sovereignty had largely ceased to exist by the early 11th century. When the coastal towns came into conflict with neighboring Croatia, they sometimes called upon Venice for help. In the year 1000 the doge of Venice led a naval expedition to Dalmatia, receiving oaths of loyalty from its principal towns without troubling to ask the consent of Byzantium, their nominal overlord. However, Byzantine authority in the Adriatic increased after Emperor Basil II's triumph over Bulgaria in 1018. For the next six or seven decades Venice and Byzantium alternately claimed sovereignty over Dalmatia, while the towns of the littoral began to behave more independently. In 1074 a third competitor for the region appeared in the form of the Normans of south Italy, who captured and briefly held some of the towns. At times the Byzantine government authorized the Normans to rule Dalmatia in its name.

Possession of Dalmatia was disputed almost continuously in the 12th century among Byzantium, Hungary, and Venice. The Byzantines had never renounced their claims to this portion of the old Roman Empire, whereas Hungary's rights were derived from her position after 1102 as heir to the extinct Croatian royal dynasty. Venice, though a relative newcomer, was mistress of a large commercial and military fleet in the Adriatic and held colonies throughout the eastern Mediterranean. These competitors had very divergent interests in Dalmatia. As a land-based power, Hungary viewed the coastal towns chiefly as sources of revenue and prestige. Byzantium and Venice valued them for their strategic location on the maritime routes, as way stations along the narrowest section of the waterway between Italy, Greece, and Asia Minor. Security of the sea trade was vital to the prosperity of both states. Moreover, since Venice was a city built on islands, it needed to import much of its food supply, in part from the Dalmatian hinterland. The towns themselves generally preferred Hungarian to Venetian control. Venice's monopolistic trade policies threatened their livelihood, whereas Hungary was primarily a continental state. Dubrovnik, too, resisted Venice and preferred Norman protection. However, regardless of which power held de facto authority in Dalmatia, the Byzantine government always insisted on its legal rights. Even if unable to exert direct hegemony, it was often able to play off its opponents against one another.

The Byzantine warrior-Emperor Manuel Comnenus (r. 1143–80) exerted pressure on the Adriatic coast with a series of campaigns against Hungary. After a victory in Dalmatia in 1163, he proposed to neutralize further opposition through an imaginative dynastic scheme. Prince Béla, younger brother of the Hungarian King Stephen III, had earlier been made Duke of Croatia and Dalmatia. Manuel, who at that time had no male offspring, offered Béla the hand of his daughter Maria and recognition as heir to the Byzantine throne. Reluctantly the Hungarians accepted this proposal, which threatened permanent loss of Croatia, but would also remove the immediate military threat from Byzantium. Above all, it offered the prospect that a member of the Hungarian Árpád dynasty might become Byzantine emperor. Accordingly the thirteen-year-old Béla was sent to Constantinople, where he received the newly created title of "despot" and full honors befitting the heir to the throne. Although as duke of Croatia Béla was not an independent ruler, his status as the emperor's future son-in-law permitted the Byzantines to claim Croatia as their own. In 1165, Manuel forced the Hungarian government to cede him the region of Syrmia (Srem) on the Danube and all of Dalmatia, ostensibly as Béla's future inheritance. By 1168 nearly the whole of the eastern Adriatic coast lay in his hands. However, two unforeseen dynastic events drastically altered this situation. In 1169, Manuel's young wife gave birth to a son, thus depriving Béla of his status as heir to the Byzantine throne (although Manuel did not thereby renounce the Croatian lands he had taken from Hungary). Then in 1172 Béla's elder brother, the king of Hungary, died childless, and Béla went home to take his throne. Before leaving Constantinople, he swore a solemn oath to Manuel that he would always "keep in mind the interests of the emperor and the Romans [Byzantines]." He also kept his word. As long as Manuel lived, Béla III made no attempt to retrieve his Croatian inheritance, which he only afterward reincorporated into Hungary.

The death of the powerful and energetic Emperor Manuel in 1180 marked the last time that Constantinople held any effective authority over Dalmatia. Even during his lifetime this attempted dominance represented an overextension of imperial resources. Manuel's reign marked Byzantium's final appearance as a first-class power on the European scene, although the shell of Empire would survive for nearly three centuries more. Manuel was also the last Byzantine emperor daring to call himself "ruler of Dalmatia, Bosnia, Croatia, Serbia, Bulgaria, and Hungary." The power vacuum produced by his death evoked enormous repercussions in the Balkan Peninsula. Bulgaria was lost to the Byzantines as early as 1185 through the uprising led by the Asen brothers, which restored that country's independence. When the Third Crusade passed through Bulgaria in 1189, the Asens even sought to enlist its support for a joint attack on Byzantine territories. Since the leader of the Crusade, the German Emperor Frederick Barbarossa, hoped for Byzantine cooperation in reaching the Holy Land, he did not rise to the bait.

Venice became Hungary's chief rival for Dalmatia after Byzantine power passed from the scene. For ten years (1181–91) the Venetian fleet sought to capture the port of Zadar (Zara), but the town's Hungarian garrison nullified its efforts. Another opportunity presented itself during the planning for the Fourth Crusade, sponsored by Pope Innocent III in hopes of adding glory to his papacy by the conquest of Jerusalem. However, owing to the decline of Byzantine authority in the Balkans, the land route from Western Europe was no longer safe. The Crusaders would have to travel to Palestine by sea; and only Venice possessed sufficient ships for such an enterprise. Accordingly, the leaders of the Crusade drew up a contract with the Venetians, who agreed to provide transport and one year's provisions for 33,500 soldiers in exchange for 85,000 silver marks. Ultimately fewer Crusaders than expected arrived in Venice, so that insufficient funds were available to fulfill the contract. The Venetians refused to supply the ships unless they were paid; and, as an alternative, suggested that the Crusaders capture the Dalmatian port of Zadar. Under considerable pressure from their restless followers stranded in Venice, the leaders of the Crusade agreed. But when they actually occupied the town (November 1202), an enormous outcry ensued. Pope Innocent III, furious at this perversion of the Holy War he had sponsored, threatened to excommunicate the whole army. This frightened the Crusaders into abandoning the town, after which the Venetians found their position there untenable. Zadar returned to Hungarian possession.

This episode was a portent of worse to come, for a taboo had been broken. Zadar was the first Christian town to be captured by Crusaders; Constantinople would be next. Undeterred by the fiasco at Zadar, most of the Crusaders remained avid for conquests and not unduly troubled about principles. The Venetians had little interest in recovering the Holy Land from the Turks, but wished to destroy the commercial power of Constantinople, a rival far more serious than Zadar. A dynastic conflict provided the occasion. The current Byzantine emperor, Alexius III Angelus, had gained his title some years previously by deposing and imprisoning his brother Isaac and Isaac's son Alexius. In 1201 this younger Alexius escaped from prison, sought out the leaders of the Fourth Crusade, and proposed that on their way to Palestine they stop off at Constantinople and place him on his uncle's throne. If the venture succeeded he promised to pay all their debts to the Venetians, provide supplies for a year of campaigning, and ensure the submission of the Eastern Orthodox Church to the pope. The offer was tempting. While a few Crusaders protested that the Holy Land was their real objective, many of them already blamed the Byzantine government for the failure of previous Crusades. This proposed diversion looked like a way to enforce Byzantine cooperation. The more cynical Crusaders also looked forward to the prospect of looting the richest city in Christendom.

The fatal agreement was made; and in June 1203 the army of would-be Crusaders arrived on Venetian ships on the outskirts of Constantinople. The soldiers successfully made a breach in one of the city walls, while Alexius III fled. The ex-emperor Isaac II was released from prison and enthroned as joint ruler with his son, now Alexius IV. However, the new rulers could not pay the promised reward, since Alexius III in flight had taken with him most of the gold from the imperial treasury. The Crusaders remained encamped outside the walls of Constantinople, rendering life in the suburbs unsafe with their rowdiness and pillaging. The two emperors sought to raise funds by decreeing new taxes and confiscating gold plate from the churches. In response, the inhabitants of Constantinople revolted and overthrew Isaac and his son, whom they accused of betraying the empire. At this point the exasperated Crusaders saw no prospect of receiving any Byzantine treasure unless they took it themselves. Urged on by the Venetians, in April 1204 they began a new attack on Constantinople, capturing it from a weak garrison already demoralized by the recent upheavals. The victors now abandoned all thought of proceeding to the Holy Land as they sought to consolidate their hold on this unexpected prize, while the Byzantine government fled to the nearby town of Nicaea. Thus was founded the so-called Latin Empire, ruled by Western Europeans of the Catholic ("Latin") faith. Despite its grandiloquent name, the new state actually consisted of little more than the city of Constantinople with a small adjacent territory.

From 1204 to 1261 the Latin and the Nicaean Empires stood to each other as political as well as religious rivals, with the Balkan states frequently enmeshed in their conflicts. For Bulgaria the fragility of the Latin Empire constituted an invitation to territorial expansion. The new Latin government, disregarding military realities, claimed title to all the former Byzantine lands and rejected Bulgaria's offers of friendship. Grandiloquently it informed the Bulgar Tsar Kaloyan that he was not the equal, but merely the servant, of their newly elected Latin emperor. Kaloyan put a quick end to such pretensions in 1205 by decisively defeating the Latins in battle at Adrianople, enabling him to extend his rule over imperial territories in western Macedonia and Thrace. At the same time the Latin Empire's religious policy introduced a jarring new note of discord into the Balkans. Urged on by successive popes, the new rulers of Constantinople asserted a militant Catholicism. Their attempts at imposing Catholic worship on their Orthodox subjects inevitably alienated the population. As a result, the Balkan peoples on the whole preferred the rule of the Orthodox Bulgar tsar, although special circumstances sometimes caused a temporary change of attitude.

Alliances shifted with bewildering rapidity in the Balkans during the 13th century. The major contenders for power were the Latin and Nicaean empires, Bulgaria, Hungary, and the newly formed despotate of Epirus in western Greece. However, several unbroken threads run through this confusing warp of changing allegiances. The Latin and Nicaean empires were permanent enemies, since both claimed Constantinople and (in theory) all territories which had ever belonged to Byzantium. The hostility between the Catholic and Orthodox churches intensified this antagonism. The pope invariably supported the Latin Empire, which had imposed a Roman ecclesiastical hierarchy upon a sullen Eastern Orthodox population. Hungary was a consistent ally of the pope, and thus of the Latin Empire as well. However, the Bulgars were free to shift allegiances as they pleased, and in fact did so with considerable frequency. Kaloyan's successor, Tsar Boril (r. 1207–18), fought many battles against the Latins in Macedonia and Thrace, although for a brief period he was their ally against Serbia. A Hungarian attack on the Danubian town of Vidin in 1230 blocked any further expansion of Bulgaria toward the west. Nonetheless, in the time of Tsar John Asen II (r. 1218–41) Bulgaria covered a large part of the Balkan Peninsula, including Macedonia, Thrace, Thessaly, and parts of Dalmatia and Albania.

Since the Latin Empire of Constantinople lacked any real legitimacy and its military weakness was evident, the rulers of Bulgaria and Epirus as well as Nicaea—whose rulers insisted on their status as the true Byzantine emperors—entertained visions of supplanting it altogether. Between 1204 and 1235 the Bulgars often joined the Nicaeans to fight the Latins, thereby contributing to Nicaea's survival. Occasionally Bulgaria allied itself with the Latins and cooperated with Hungary, although Hungary's designs upon Bulgar territory usually made it an enemy. Epirus ceased to count as a major Balkan contender after 1230, when its ambitious Despot Theodore made a classic miscalculation and attacked Bulgaria, with which he had recently concluded an alliance. Incensed at this treachery, the Bulgar Tsar John Asen II marched into battle holding aloft a copy of the broken treaty and roundly defeated the Epirotes at Klokotnica. Theodore's reasons for this betrayal remain obscure, but probably were linked to the aspirations of both Bulgaria and Epirus to control the city of Constantinople. The Latins had recently proposed to marry their young emperor to John Asen's daughter, with John to serve as regent of the empire. This offer perhaps was intended merely to break up the Bulgar-Epirote alliance. In any event, the Bulgarian princess did not marry the Latin emperor; and John Asen II never ruled in the imperial capital on the Bosphorus.

Bulgaria's association with Nicaea reached its high point in 1235, when John's daughter married the heir to the Nicaean Empire and the two states collaborated in an unsuccessful attack on Constantinople. With better luck, this ambitious Bulgar tsar might conceivably have gained the imperial title which his predecessor Symeon had so avidly sought three centuries previously; but military failure decided otherwise. Over the next dozen years the configuration of Balkan politics changed several times more. In 1237, John renounced his Nicaean alliance in hopes of a marriage arrangement with the Latins. When this prospect faded he returned to the Nicaean allegiance. His death in 1241 marked the end of an era, for John Asen II was the last really powerful ruler of Bulgaria. In 1246 a child inherited the Bulgar throne, and the Nicaeans began to occupy portions of Bulgarian territory. In 1261 their capture of Constantinople altered the entire picture of Balkan politics by restoring the Byzantine Empire and removing the Latin enemy altogether. Thereafter Bulgaria and the Byzantines generally faced each other as opponents. When a major rebellion broke out in Bulgaria in 1277–80, the Byzantine government on three occasions sent troops to help the cause of a pretender.

The occupants of the papal throne after 1261 refused to accept the return of the Byzantine government to Constantinople as final. Seeking a suitable instrument for restoring the Latin Empire, they found it in Charles of Anjou, the ambitious and warlike younger brother of the saintly King Louis IX of France. As a preliminary measure, Pope Clement IV authorized Charles to expel the Hohenstaufen ruler of the Two Sicilies (i.e., Naples and Sicily) from his kingdom. The pope's objective was twofold: to give Charles a base for further conquests; and to rid Italy of this German imperial dynasty, the traditional opponent of papal policy. At the battle of Beneventum in 1266, Charles of Anjou won the crown of the Two Sicilies by defeating the last scion of the Hohenstaufens. In preparation for his planned reconquest of Constantinople, he signed a treaty with the exiled Latin Emperor Baldwin II, transferring most of the latter's rights to himself. As a steppingstone to the East he seized several fortresses in Albania, most notably Durrës, and began calling himself "by Grace of God King of Sicily and Albania."

The Byzantine Emperor Michael VIII Paleologus fought back with diplomacy as well as with arms. Playing for time, in 1274 he accepted the Union of Lyons, an agreement to unite the Eastern and Western Churches on terms favorable to the pope. (Back home Michael took care to conceal the exact provisions of this merger, knowing perfectly well that neither the Orthodox hierarchy nor the Greek population would ever willingly accept it.) By fulfilling a long-standing objective of papal policy, the accord reached at Lyons temporarily restrained the pope from authorizing an invasion of Byzantine territory. Aware that papal supremacy had been resented enormously during the existence of the Latin Empire, the pontiff imagined that a union imposed by a Greek Emperor would bring better success. Michael VIII repeatedly assured the pope that he was doing his best to comply with the Union of Lyons. To demonstrate his good faith he even persecuted some of its opponents. However, this deception could not continue indefinitely. After some years the pope became convinced that Michael was not sincere about promoting church union. He gave Charles of Anjou the long-awaited permission to invade the Byzantine Empire.

Initially Charles attempted to enter Byzantine territory from Albania, sending an army inland to besiege the great fortress of Berat, gateway to Macedonia.

There in 1281 the Byzantines defeated him in a landmark battle—the earliest major triumph of light infantry over heavy cavalry. Charles next began negotiations with Venice for naval transport to take his army to Constantinople. However, the defeat at Berat had severely shaken his position; and on his home territory the great rebellion of 1282 known as the "Sicilian Vespers" frustrated his plans. The Sicilians hated Charles's harsh regime and the heavy taxation he had imposed to finance his ambitious wars. Byzantine gold apparently encouraged their disaffection. The rebels destroyed Charles's fleet, while King Peter III of Aragon, a relative of the deposed Hohenstaufens, took possession of Sicily. Despite this setback, Charles did not renounce his plans to conquer Byzantium, but died in 1285 before renewing the attempt. At his death he ruled only the kingdom of Naples and residual lands in Albania, remnants of which his descendants retained for another seventy years.

Early in the 13th century the region of Galicia (Halicz) became an object of contention between Poland and Hungary. The rulers of both Little Poland and Mazovia, two of the independent appanages established in the 12th century after the disintegration of the Polish state, sought to extend their lands to the east. King Andrew II of Hungary cherished designs on the same territory, which he justified with some tenuous legal claims. Obsessed with acquiring Galicia, he campaigned there virtually every year between 1204 and 1216, meanwhile ignoring the more serious threats to his borders in Dalmatia and Transylvania. Andrew's frequent and expensive military expeditions brought slight profit to himself and irritated his nobles, who ultimately rebelled against him. In the end neither Poles nor Hungarians managed to prevail in Galicia, which was annexed about 1238 by Rus princes from neighboring Volhynia. After the Mongol invasion of Europe in 1241, the Hungarian King Béla IV sought to forge closer relations with Galicia, which by its geographical position stood as a barrier against the Mongol Golden Horde in Ukraine.

On its southern frontier Hungary faced increasing competition from Venice. The elimination of Byzantine power from the Adriatic enabled that island republic to dominate northern Dalmatia in the 13th century. Farther south, Venice held Zadar also and exercised strong influence over Dubrovnik during most of that century, while Hungary retained several important towns (Split, Trogir, Šibenik) in central Dalmatia. The Venetians were interested chiefly in securing the sea route to the Levant. They made no effort to penetrate the Dalmatian hinterland, nor did they interfere in the governments of the coastal towns, which continued to be ruled by local councils and laws. The towns' obligation to Venice was limited to paying tribute, observing Venetian commercial regulations, and providing military aid when requested. However, the Venetians' insistence upon monopolizing the Adriatic trade encouraged Dalmatian merchants to direct their activities toward the hinterland. As a result, Dubrovnik became the major commercial power in the Balkan Peninsula. In 1358 it recognized Hungarian supremacy, but retained its internal autonomy. No Hungarian garrison was ever stationed there.

The formerly Byzantine possessions in Albania likewise became pawns in Mediterranean politics during the 13th century. Small and very mountainous, this country nonetheless possessed a double strategic value—positioned as it was not only at the narrow entrance to the Adriatic but also at the western end of the Via Egnatia, the road leading overland through the mountain passes to Salonika and Constantinople. In 1205 the Venetians captured the most important of the Albanian towns, Durrës (Durazzo), which in the hands of a hostile power might seek to prevent their ships' passage from the Adriatic into the Mediterranean. Eight years later Durrës, together with most of Albania, came under the hegemony of Greek Epirus, with which Venice preserved good relations. Then in 1256–57 the Nicaean Empire annexed parts of the central Albanian coast. After the Nicaeans recaptured Constantinople in 1261, Albania acquired renewed importance in the pope's plans for restoration of the Latin Empire.

Farther north in East Central Europe the Mongol invasion was the most traumatic event of the 13th century. In 1237–40 these Asiatic horsemen—known to Europe as Tatars—conquered southern Russia and Ukraine. In 1241 they swept into Poland and Hungary in several coordinated columns. Their attack was sudden in its onset and enormously destructive to all the lands it touched. Aided by speed, surprise, and an amazingly swift system of communication, the Mongols won every battle they fought. The Hungarian King Béla IV fled to the Adriatic coast and barely escaped capture, while the states of Western Europe failed to provide any aid. The German Emperor Frederick II continued his campaign in Italy, while Duke Frederick of Austria took advantage of Béla IV's distress to occupy several counties in western Hungary. With such disunited opponents, an Asiatic hegemony over Europe might well have lasted indefinitely. The early retreat of the Mongols was a stroke of luck that owed nothing to any European efforts. For decades afterward the Europeans were terrified at the prospect of their return.

In 1252 the news reached Hungary that the Mongols were preparing another attack on Europe. No military aid could be expected from the West, where the German Empire had lapsed into anarchy since the death of Emperor Frederick II in 1250. Instead King Béla looked for support to the Cumans, the seminomadic Turkic tribesmen who had long controlled the grasslands of Walachia and Moldavia. In the 1240s a large contingent of these primitive pastoralists had entered Transylvania with his permission. Predominantly pagan, the Cumans were uncivilized even by the undemanding European standards of that time. The Hungarians deeply resented their king's acceptance of help from such a source. Nonetheless Béla IV apparently felt he had little choice. The Cumans stood directly in the Mongols' probable line of advance through the Transylvanian mountain passes; and their light cavalry knew how to fight in the style of the steppes. Béla needed an ally both willing and able to offer resistance to the Mongols; and no European ruler stood ready to oblige. In hopes of ensuring the Cumans' loyalty, he even betrothed his son Stephen, heir to the Hungarian throne, to the Christian daughter of one of their chiefs. This unlikely marriage actually took place in 1252. The mere fact that the proud king of Hungary, scion of one of Europe's most ancient dynasties, consented to this humiliating alliance offers eloquent proof of his desperation.

The Mongol danger seemed to have materialized in 1254 when the khan of the Golden Horde in Russia sent threatening letters to the rulers of both Galicia and Hungary. From Prince Daniel of Galicia he demanded total obedience and the payment of tribute in wheat and animals; failing this, he declared his intention to destroy Daniel's lands. From Béla IV of Hungary the khan sought a marriage alliance and substantial military aid for the campaign he planned to undertake via Poland into Western Europe. If this offer was accepted, he promised to refrain from invading Hungary and to exempt it from tax payments; otherwise he would destroy the country. Previous experience warned both rulers that this was no idle threat. In 1259 and 1264 Béla received further ultimatums, which he managed to sidestep by diplomatic procrastination. In 1259 a Mongol expedition entered Lithuania and Poland, where it massacred the local inhabitants and ravaged the countryside. However, it advanced no farther, and after three months went home with its booty. Once again Europe was saved not by its defenses, but by the Mongols' own priorities. The unified Mongol empire of former years had already begun to disintegrate; and after Kubilai became great khan in 1260, he directed his major efforts toward the conquest and rule of China. After his death in 1294 the link between the Mongol princes in Russia or Ukraine and the great khan in Mongolia became purely nominal. The Golden Horde survived along the lower Volga and Don rivers for a total of nearly two and a half centuries, controlling the Muscovite princes from a distance. Most of East Central Europe escaped this subservience, but just barely. The region directly north of the Danube mouths remained a frontier zone, where semi-independent Mongol princes (here usually called Tatars) ruled for the remainder of the 13th and most of the 14th century. About 1280 the Tatar chief Nogai made himself independent of the khan of the Golden Horde and repeatedly interfered in Balkan affairs. Tatar princes also dominated Galicia and Volhynia, just beyond Poland's southeastern border, from which vantage point they conducted raids into Walachia, Moldavia, Poland, and Lithuania.

In particular the Tatar presence in Ukraine affected the Bulgars. Too weak to prevent intermittent raids from across the Danube, Bulgaria became a protectorate of the Golden Horde. Its situation deteriorated still further after khan Nogai became the de facto ruler of the Horde's western territories and encouraged various Bulgarian boyars to establish their own petty principalities. The supreme khan of the Horde proved unable to control Nogai or protect Bulgaria from his depredations. Finally in 1285 the Bulgar Tsar George Terter abandoned his allegiance to the Horde and accepted that of Nogai. Even this did not put a stop to the Tatar raids and political interference in Bulgaria, which became especially oppressive in the last two decades of the 13th century. After Nogai was killed in 1299, Bulgaria resumed its former tributary relationship to the main body of the Horde. Thereafter the Tatars exercised only a very loose overlordship over Bulgaria. Their raids became less frequent and smaller in scale; and the usual object was only plunder.

Finally the Poles and Hungarians put an end to Tatar provocations. In 1340 the Polish King Casimir III, aided by Hungarian troops, campaigned against the Horde in Galicia. A further offensive in 1349 permitted him to annex Volhynia, giving Poland a common boundary with Moldavia. The peace treaty with the Tatars required Casimir to pay them an annual tribute for Volhynia, just as the princes of Galicia formerly had done. In 1345 and 1346 the Hungarian King Charles Robert sent his Szekler troops against the Tatars—an expedition which produced many Tatar captives and considerable booty in gold and silver objects. Ultimately Tatar dominance over Moldavia would last for another quarter-century, although by this time the decline of the Golden Horde was undeniable. King Louis of Hungary continued his wars against the eastern "schismatics and infidels" (i.e., Orthodox Christians and Muslims), for which purpose the pope allowed him to appropriate the papal revenues due from the Hungarian kingdom. In 1363 the Lithuanian prince Olgerd penetrated farther into Tatar territory than any European army hitherto had done, winning a major victory over the Tatars on the Dnieper near the Black Sea. However, the Tatars continued to hold large portions of southern Ukraine until late in the 14th century.

Fear of the Mongols understandably affected the Bohemians less than their neighbors whose territories bordered directly upon the Golden Horde. The crucial foreign issue for Bohemia in the 13th century was its effort to avoid vassalage to the German emperor. The powerful and ambitious Duke Ottokar I (r. 1198–1230) intervened with success in the conflicts then raging over the imperial throne and supported the ultimate victor, Frederick II. In return Emperor Frederick in 1212 issued a decree very favorable to Bohemia, known as the "Sicilian" Golden Bull because it bore the seal he used as king of Sicily. This edict in effect renounced the emperor's legal (although rarely exercised) rights to appoint the rulers of Bohemia or the bishops of Prague and Olomouc (Olmütz). It confirmed Bohemia's independent status within the empire, declared its boundaries inviolable, recognized its monarchy as hereditary, and authorized Ottokar and his descendants to call themselves "king" (a title already borne by several of his predecessors on a personal rather than a hereditary basis). By recognizing the right of the Bohemians to choose their own monarch, whose election the emperor could merely confirm, this decree placed strict limits on the latter's authority to interfere. It also defined more precisely Bohemia's obligations toward the empire. For example, its king could decide whether he preferred to accompany the emperor to his coronation in Rome with 300 companions or pay 300 marks in silver. He would be required to attend the imperial Reichstag, or Diet, only when it met at Nürnberg or Bamberg near the Bohemian border (although in fact he often chose to attend at other locations). The Sicilian Golden Bull created nothing really new, but legalized approximately the existing political situation.

In the mid-13th century a ruler of Bohemia became briefly the most powerful man in the German Empire. King Ottokar II (r. 1253–78), known as "the Golden King" or "Ottokar the Great," aspired to create a large kingdom for himself in Central Europe. Taking advantage of some doubtful legal claims, he added the German lands of Upper and Lower Austria, Styria, Carinthia, and Carniola to his Bohemian inheritance. Predictably, his rapid rise aroused jealousies and also made him arrogant. Since his legal rights to Carinthia and Carniola were questionable, the high court of the empire, composed of German princes, conducted a formal trial and declared that he held these lands contrary to imperial law. Aware that his political support had eroded, Ottokar in 1276 formally renounced all his holdings except for Bohemia and Moravia, where his hereditary rights were indisputable. Nonetheless, his ambition could not so easily be squelched. Within two years he had raised another army for an attempt to reconquer the lost provinces. The issue was decided in 1278 at the battle of Marchfeld north of Vienna, fought between Ottokar and his German rival, Rudolf of Habsburg. Marchfeld was one of the decisive military encounters of the Middle Ages. The Bohemians were defeated and Ottokar himself was killed, apparently not by the enemy but by a treacherous relative. This outcome forced Bohemia back within its previous boundaries and prevented the creation of a territorial link between the Western and Southern Slavs. Moreover, it helped unify the Austrian principalities under the Habsburg dynasty, laying the groundwork for its future role as one of Europe's leading royal houses.

Bohemia's monarchs continued to play a major role in the wider sphere of European politics. King Wenceslas II took advantage of Poland's disunity to conquer Little Poland in 1300. His son, the future Wenceslas III, was elected as king of Hungary in 1301 by one faction of the Hungarian nobility, but proved unable to prevail militarily and subsequently withdrew. His death in 1306 brought to an end not only Czech rule in Poland, but also the male line of the Přemyslid dynasty. The next king of Bohemia was John of Luxemburg (r. 1310–46), who married the Přemyslid heiress. A passionate knight-errant, John could not resist a battle, and fought all over Europe for causes having little connection with Bohemia. He took the Crusader's vow, which he fulfilled by joining the Teutonic Knights in several of their wars against pagan Lithuania. King John also campaigned in Italy, where for a few years in the 1330s he ruled western Lombardy and Tyrol. He died in 1346 in the Hundred Years' War, fighting for France in the famous battle of Crécy. On the diplomatic front John succeeded after twelve years of negotiation in arranging the election of his son Charles as German emperor. Although the empire by this time was little more than an association of independent states, the title retained great prestige. Charles, who was king of Bohemia as well as emperor, sought to make Prague the leading city of the Empire. His imperial Golden Bull of 1356 confirmed Bohemia's semi-independent status by providing that if the ruling Luxemburg dynasty died out, Bohemia would not revert to the German Empire like other imperial fiefs. To avoid future disputes, the Bull identified seven permanent electors—four secular princes and three prelates of the Church—who would henceforth elect the emperor. Charles also acquired the margravate of Brandenburg for his house, which in 1374 he united with the crown of Bohemia.

Favorable external circumstances between 1306 and 1320 facilitated the transformation of Poland from a collection of often quarreling principalities into a single state. Since both Muscovy and the German Empire at that time were either weak or inactive, the energetic and stubborn Piast prince Vladislav "Łokietek" was able to add to his hereditary lands without serious foreign complications. Łokietek fought against rival Polish princes, the Teutonic Knights, and the Bohemians, who still claimed title to the province of Little Poland. Military operations consumed most of his reign; but when he died in 1333 he ruled an extensive Polish territory. By contrast, his son Casimir III "the Great" proceeded more by diplomacy than by war. Casimir took care not to assert unrealistic claims. For example, the formerly Polish region of Silesia now consisted of numerous small principalities under Bohemian suzerainty. Regaining them would have demanded a major military effort, quite possibly beyond Poland's resources. Therefore, at the outset of his reign Casimir concluded an agreement with Bohemia by which he renounced all of Poland's legal rights to Silesia. He also paid the Bohemian King John a substantial sum of money, in exchange for which John abandoned his rights to the Polish throne.

Casimir also succeeded in breaking up the dangerous alliance between Bohemia and the Teutonic Order. In 1343 he concluded peace with the Order by a mutual adjustment of territorial claims—a peace destined to last for sixty-six years. Having thus renounced an active policy in the west and north, he recouped these essentially theoretical losses by an expansionist policy in Galicia, where the competition for territory was less fierce. Here too he proceeded carefully, citing legal claims and neutralizing possible opposition through an alliance with Hungary. He enlisted the aid of the pope, who permitted him on several occasions to appropriate the papal tithes for his campaigns. Papal bulls in 1352 and 1355 officially identified these wars in the East as crusades. Poland's opponent in this eastern-oriented policy was Lithuania, a enormous but loosely organized multiethnic confederation with which relations were hostile for over two decades. In 1352 Casimir was able to incorporate most of Galicia into Poland, including the important town of Lvov. These conquests for the first time gave Poland a substantial population professing the Orthodox faith.

The Teutonic Knights' frequent and destructive campaigns into Lithuania led to a military stalemate. The Knights could not conquer that vast country, nor could either Poland or Lithuania alone dislodge them from Prussia. Mutual hostility to the Teutonic Order was a major impetus for the Polish-Lithuanian union in 1385, which was sealed by the betrothal of the Polish Queen Jadwiga with Grand Duke Jagiełło of Lithuania. Prussia was now enclosed on three sides by a much larger and more powerful opponent than before. Furthermore, a key condition of the marriage between the Polish heiress and the still-pagan Jagiełło had been that he not only receive baptism himself but also agree to Christianize Lithuania. Henceforth the Teutonic Order could no longer cloak its territorial aspirations with the claim that conversion of the heathen was its motive. The Polish-Lithuanian union also served notice to the duke of Mazovia that his semi-independent position was doomed, bringing him to swear allegiance to the king of Poland. Finally, the union facilitated an extension of Polish power southward into the Romanian lands, where Moldavia (albeit temporarily) accepted Polish hegemony in 1387.

Hungary under its Angevin kings was the most powerful state of East Central Europe in the 14th century, wealthy enough to provide the armed strength necessary for an activist foreign policy. King Charles Robert (r. 1310–42) directed his ambitions chiefly toward his southern frontier, where he asserted firm rule over Croatia, Dalmatia, and Bosnia and sought conquests in Serbia and Bulgaria. He also tried unsuccessfully to make good his hereditary claims to the kingdom of Naples. His son Louis the Great (r. 1342–82) conducted a similarly energetic foreign policy. With intermittent success Louis attempted to assert Hungarian sovereignty over Walachia, led several campaigns against the Serbs, and drove the Venetians from Dalmatia. His war with Venice, ending in 1358, established Hungarian suzerainty over the entire east coast of the Adriatic except for Dubrovnik. Dalmatia remained Hungarian for the next half-century. Louis also demonstrated extensive territorial ambitions in the Balkans, where in 1365 he occupied Vidin in northwestern Bulgaria. There he undermined his own aims with an aggressive Catholic missionary policy which contributed to his expulsion from that principality in 1369. Louis's Bulgarian wars had the effect of weakening the resistance of the Christian powers to Ottoman encroachments. In 1371 the Turks won their most significant victory in the Balkans up to that time at Černomen (near Plovdiv) on the Maritsa River. Despite these military efforts, Louis gained his largest territorial acquisition—Poland—peacefully in 1370 through inheritance from his uncle, Casimir the Great.

The rise of Serbia to prominence in the Balkans was the direct result of weak government at Constantinople. The Latin emperors in the 13th century could not prevent the Serbs from moving into what was essentially a military vacuum. Serbia's center no longer lay near the Adriatic, but rather in the interior of the peninsula around the town of Raška on lands formerly claimed by Bulgaria. In 1330 the victory of King Stephen Dečanski over the Bulgars at the decisive battle of Velbužd (now Kyustendil in western Bulgaria) opened the way to Serbian hegemony in Macedonia. Tsar Stephen Dušan (r. 1331–55), driven on by his land-hungry boyars, conducted an active expansionist policy. While exercising a powerful influence over Bulgaria, he directed his principal attacks southward into the Greek-held territories in Macedonia, where the potential booty was richest. The civil war then in progress in the Byzantine Empire provided favorable opportunities. Constantinople abandoned western Macedonia to its fate and Dušan soon overran it.

Amazingly, Serbia's expansion at Byzantium's expense proceeded without a single major battle. Dušan simply blockaded the Greek fortresses in the Balkans, which the government at Constantinople was too weak to defend. Internal warfare had caused such disruption in the Byzantine Empire that many of its garrisons simply deserted to the Serbs. At the height of his career Dušan controlled large parts of Macedonia, northern Greece, and most of Albania. In 1345, shortly after capturing the important town of Serrai (northeast of Salonika) in Macedonia, he proclaimed himself "Emperor of the Serbs and Greeks." Nonetheless, the outward brilliance of his achievements was deceptive. During his heyday neither Bulgaria nor Byzantium was powerful enough to challenge him; and the Turks had not yet invaded Europe. Dušan's policy strongly suggests that he viewed himself as a possible successor to the Byzantine emperors. Serbian folk poetry gives voice to this impression by depicting him as dying on route to Constantinople. However, no real evidence indicates that Dušan ever undertook such a campaign, and various objective factors speak against it. At the time of his death in 1355 he still possessed no fleet, while the Turkish presence near the city would have created complications. The Ottomans themselves, with far greater resources, failed to capture Constantinople until 1453. Soon after Dušan's premature death the Serbian Empire disintegrated. Ottoman victories in 1371 and 1389 reduced the country to a remnant of its former self known as the Serbian Despotate, which survived as a small independent principality until 1459.

By contrast, the commercial town of Dubrovnik never became subject to direct Turkish control, instead paying tribute to the sultan while retaining its independence. Its citizens received full liberty to trade wherever they wished in the Ottoman Empire or its vassal states. This concession—commercially very valuable—was nonetheless offset by the unfavorable impact of Turkish restrictions. Merchants of Dubrovnik were now forbidden to export raw silver, which had previously been a major article of their commerce with Serbia and Bosnia. Dubrovnik's consuls in the Balkans lost their former judicial autonomy. As a result, until the Turks became firmly entrenched in the Balkans, the town's government stood ready to take part in any anti-Ottoman military efforts which showed promise of success. In 1441 it participated in the defense of Novo Brdo in Bosnia, the principal source of Serbian silver; and twice it gave asylum to the Serbian Despot George Branković when Turkish pressure forced him into exile. In 1444 Dubrovnik's fleet participated in a Christian attack on Gallipoli at the entrance to the Straits. However, the abysmal failure of the Varna crusade that same year put an end to any hope of permanently expelling the Turks from Europe.

Ultimately both Dubrovnik and the Ottoman Empire perceived the advantage of good relations. Lacking any broad commercial network of their own, the Ottomans sought to profit from Dubrovnik's many colonies in the Balkan Peninsula. In 1442 Dubrovnik accepted the obligation to send a silver vessel worth 1,000 Venetian ducats to the sultan each year. In 1458 and again in 1462 the sultan confirmed Dubrovnik's trading privileges, which underwent little change thereafter except for an enormous rise in the amount of tribute demanded. Actually the merchants of Dubrovnik enjoyed an exceptionally favorable position vis-à-vis the Ottoman Empire, paying a customs duty of only two percent on their exports to its territories, whereas other foreigners paid five percent. Concurrently the town maintained its tributary obligations to King Matthias of Hungary, while concealing from him as far as possible its relations with the Turks. The internal peace and lack of customs frontiers within the Ottoman state promoted Dubrovnik's commercial prosperity. The town was even able to increase its land area by exploiting rivalries among the territorial lords in its own neighborhood. By 1472 it controlled an area extending some 50 miles along the Adriatic coast.

The Ottoman Empire in the 14th century was in a phase of rapid expansion, driven on not only by the lure of plunder and conquest but also by the vision of holy war (jihad) against non-Muslim peoples. Probably in 1369, Turkish troops captured their first major city in Europe, Adrianople (henceforth called Edirne). The sultan moved his capital there long before the fall of Constantinople in 1453, thus revealing his intention to advance still farther into Europe—potentially a far more lucrative source of revenue than Asia. Ottoman expansion was facilitated also by the quarrels endemic among the minor princelings and lords of the Balkans. Many Christian princes were in no way averse to enlisting Turkish aid against their enemies, despite the religious gulf between Islam and Christianity. In fact, the hostility between Catholics and Orthodox was often just as profound as that between Christians and Muslims. Many Orthodox rulers felt more threatened by Catholic Hungary than by the Turks. With deplorable lack of foresight, most of the Balkan princes failed to see that the Ottoman Empire was a powerful expansionist state whose activities in the long run threatened themselves.

The Ottomans took a giant forward step into the Balkans with their victory in 1371 at the battle of Černomen on the Maritsa River, where their army overwhelmed a coalition of Serbian princes. As a consequence, many regional lords in Macedonia, Greece, and Albania were forced to pay tribute to the sultan. No major state then existed in the peninsula which might have blocked the Turks' progress. Ottoman troops took Sofia from the Bulgars in about 1382 and then advanced into Albania, winning a decisive victory against a coalition of local forces on the plain of Savra in 1385. Most of the Albanian lords now became vassals of the sultan, paying him tribute and supplying soldiers for his wars.

In 1386 the Turks captured Niš in eastern Serbia and appeared also in Bosnia, causing a mass flight of the inhabitants. In 1388 eastern Bulgaria recognized Ottoman overlordship, the prelude to its complete loss of independence. In 1389 occurred the famous clash at Kosovo ("Blackbirds' Field") in Serbia, immortalized in folk poetry as the crucial event in the country's destruction. Turkish armies captured the Bulgar capital of Tirnovo in 1393 and incorporated eastern Bulgaria into their empire. In 1395 their victory over the Vlachs at Rovine in Walachia enabled them to annex the remaining semi-independent principalities of southern Serbia. Finally, the failure of the Nicopolis crusade in 1396—a major anti-Ottoman expedition organized by Hungary—opened the way for Sultan Bayezid I to annex the principality of Vidin, transforming this last remnant of independent Bulgaria into an Ottoman province.

Meanwhile the Venetians took steps to protect their interests along the eastern Adriatic. To prevent Ottoman occupation of the Albanian coast, they assumed the defense of Durrës in mid-1392, retaining control over that major port for over a hundred years thereafter. The Dalmatian towns, newly vulnerable to Ottoman attack, chose submission to Venice in preference to conquest by the Turks. Between 1412 and 1420 Zadar, Šibenik, Trogir, Split, and Kotor all became Venetian possessions. Later the offshore islands from Krk to Korčula followed suit. Thus Dalmatia was split threefold, with its northern portion still subject to Hungary, a Venetian sector in the center and south, and Dubrovnik as a case by itself, retaining considerable local autonomy. Venice provided her Dalmatian towns with money and arms, sometimes also with troops and ships, and assisted them in building fortifications. The towns for their part supplied crewmen for the Venetian fleet. These efforts succeeded in keeping the Adriatic maritime routes open and prevented the Turks from gaining a serious foothold on the Dalmatian coast.

The Ottoman vassal states occupied an intermediate position between complete independence and direct Turkish administration. The autonomy which they enjoyed was bought at the price of heavy tribute payments. These sums were demanded not merely for the Turks' own enrichment, which was naturally an important motive, but also as a symbol that the payer recognized the sultan's supremacy. The amount was never set by treaty, which would have implied at least formal equality between the two signatory parties, but rather by a "privilege" or act of grace issued by the sultan. Faithful rendering of tribute usually spared the vassal states from large-scale Turkish plundering and ravaging, although even this was never assured. Venice and Dubrovnik, both of which were tribute-paying, self-governing republics, received commercial rights in the Ottoman Empire only after delivering the required sums. Dual loyalty was possible: thus the Serbian Despotate maintained an equivocal status between Hungary and the Ottoman Empire for the seventy years following the battle of Kosovo (1389). Dubrovnik paid tribute to both the sultan and the king of Hungary. Bosnia and Walachia in the 15th century were vassals concurrently of the Ottoman Empire and Hungary, though their obligations to the Turks were heavier; and Hungary was unable to protect them from additional Turkish demands.

Any vassal ruler who delayed or declined payment of the tribute could expect Ottoman military intervention in short order. This threat was always implicit and sometimes explicit. For example, an entry in the Moldavian Chronicle for 1455 reports Turkish envoys as stating that annual rendering of the tribute would bring peace: "Otherwise, you know [what will happen]." At times the Turks took hostages as a guarantee of payment. Refusal to deliver the assigned sum was invariably a signal that the vassal state was revolting against Ottoman authority. After the victorious Hungarian-led Long Campaign into the Balkans in 1443, many vassals stopped paying the Turkish tribute; but in 1444 after the failure of the Varna crusade they were forced to resume this obligation. The tribute in itself carried no guarantees. Even faithful payment and unswerving loyalty to the sultan did not save the vassal states from eventual or even imminent incorporation into the Ottoman Empire. When he so chose, the sultan attacked and destroyed his loyal vassals just as surely as he subjected those who attempted to resist him.

Tribute constituted a serious burden upon the vassal states. The native rulers were responsible for collecting it, which placed them in the unenviable position of oppressing their own subjects for the sultan's benefit. Whenever a new sultan came to the throne, an additional amount had to be remitted as congratulations. Then the vassals' status was reviewed, and frequently the payments were increased. The sultan did not care by what means the tribute was collected as long as it was forthcoming. No one escaped this Turkish taxation, not even religious organizations which were otherwise tax-exempt. In the documents issued by Christian vassal princes recording their gifts of lands and villages to monasteries, we frequently read that the properties were freed from all taxes "except the Turkish tribute."

The amount of the tribute naturally varied according to Ottoman estimates of each vassal's ability to pay. In the 14th century the Byzantine government paid the sultan the enormous sum of 30,000 gold pieces every year, which was still decidedly cheaper than a military campaign. When the Walachian Voivode Mircea the Old first became subject to the Turkish tribute in about 1393, he apparently paid 3,000 ducats yearly. By 1462 the amount had been raised to 10,000 ducats—this at a period when 45 ducats sufficed to purchase an entire village. Moldavia paid tribute for the first time in 1456, with the annual amount fixed at 2,000 ducats. On the other hand, Bosnia's tribute amounted to 50,000 ducats a year; and the Serbian despot paid even more, which he could afford on account of his rich silver mincs. In the 20 years between 1458 and 1481, Dubrovnik's tribute rose from 1,500 to 12,500 ducats annually. These contributions represented a substantial portion of the sultan's total income.

Another type of tribute was military aid. All the vassal princes sent troops to the sultan upon request, and usually were required to lead them in person. As a result, Christian soldiers from the Balkans contributed to many Turkish victories in the battles of the 14th and 15th centuries. Conversely, pretenders to the Byzantine throne often fought each other with Turkish assistance. Bosnian lords and certain rulers of Serbia, Bulgaria, and Walachia did likewise. Many Balkan princes were evidently quite devoid of religious scruples where military matters were concerned. No feeling of Christian solidarity against Islam animated them even in the 15th century, when the Ottoman threat was unmistakable. Still less was any such attitude evident in the 14th century. To be sure, the honor of a soldier demanded that he fight bravely for his lord, whoever that lord might be. Princes who later became celebrated in folk epics as intrepid warriors for Christianity had sometimes spent most of their actual careers fighting for the Turks. A striking example of this phenomenon was Marko, the Christian protagonist of many Serbian heroic ballads, who in reality died fighting in Ottoman ranks at the battle of Rovine in 1395.

The deteriorating political situation in the Balkan states which began in the latter half of the 14th century had no counterpart farther north in East Central Europe at that time. While the Ottoman advance first undermined and then destroyed the independence of Bulgaria, Serbia, and Bosnia, and forced Walachia and Moldavia to become tribute-paying vassals, Poland-Lithuania grew appreciably in power and influence. Admittedly, the fact of union did not automatically create an identity of interests between the two parts of the dual state. The Poles at first remained aloof from Lithuania's conflicts with the Teutonic Order. The Order for its part sought to justify its continued existence as a crusading organization by claiming that Lithuania's conversion to Christianity had been superficial. It encouraged separatist tendencies in Lithuania and conducted armed incursions into its territory. Nonetheless, in 1401 Poland and Lithuania struck another blow at the Order's ambitions by concluding the Radom-Vilnius accords, strengthening their union by stipulating that in the future nothing should be decided without mutual consultation between the Polish and Lithuanian nobilities.

In 1404 the Teutonic Knights seized Samogitia (the small territory wedged in between Prussia and Livonia) at a time when the Lithuanian army was temporarily occupied on its eastern frontier. Five years later the Lithuanian grand duke incited an uprising in Samogitia; the Order declared war; and this time the troops of both Lithuania and Poland responded. At the battle of Tannenberg in 1410 the grand master of the Order and all its principal landholders perished. This was a landmark victory, which marked the beginning of the Teutonic Order's decline as a military power. Many Prussian towns now opened their gates to the Polish-Lithuanian army, although the Order tenaciously resisted the siege of its fortress capital, Malbork (Marienburg). For Poland the political consequences of Tannenberg were remarkably meager. In the month after the battle the Lithuanian army went home, thus nullifying most of the advantages of victory. Lithuania's grand duke showed no interest in territorial acquisitions which by the dictates of geography could only accrue to Poland. At the peace concluded at Toruń in 1411 the Order renounced nothing except the recently acquired Samogitia. However, its reputation as the most powerful military force in northeastern Europe had been irrevocably shattered. The customary flow of foreign knights into Prussia for the campaigning season declined. Two more short but unsuccessful wars in 1422 and 1430 marked the Teutonic Order's final, futile attempts to break up the Polish-Lithuanian union.

In Bohemia the Hussite religious reforms evoked major foreign repercussions. On one level this was a conflict between an older tradition of Christian unity, represented by the pope as head of an allegedly universal Church, and newer aspirations for a purer spiritual life which tended to shatter that unity. However, European opinion in the 15th century was still very far from accepting religious differences as either legitimate or tolerable. The Hussite movement transformed Bohemia into an international outcast. Initially Hussitism was a purely religious phenomenon stressing spiritual renewal and the preaching of the gospel in the Czech vernacular. Nonheretical in intent, it soon ran afoul of the Roman Church's demands for total conformity. At the Council of Constance in 1415, Emperor Sigismund submitted to pressure from the cardinals and bishops and permitted John Hus to be burned at the stake. The outrage which swept Bohemia as a consequence meant that when Sigismund himself inherited the Bohemian throne in 1419, the Hussite party refused to accept him. Against all odds, the Czechs defeated five armies which he sent into Bohemia and sought another prince to rule them. They offered the throne first to Jagiełło (King Vladislav V) of Poland, who was tempted; but clerical influences at home prevented him from accepting. Then in 1424 the Czechs elected the Lithuanian prince Sigismund Korybut, who promised to respect the Hussite articles of faith. Korybut reigned in Bohemia without much real authority until 1427, when he was found to be negotiating secretly with the pope and the Czechs expelled him. Finally even Emperor Sigismund realized that he could not prevail militarily against the Czechs and reached a compromise with the Hussite party. He accepted the so-called Basel Compacts, which recognized both Catholicism and a moderate form of Hussitism (Utraquism) as legal faiths in Bohemia. In 1436, seventeen years after inheriting the Bohemian throne, he finally took possession of Prague.

The election of the "Hussite king" George Poděbrady by the Bohemian Diet in 1457 led to further foreign complications. King Matthias of Hungary, who similarly lacked hereditary rights to his throne, nonetheless possessed faultlessly orthodox religious credentials. He viewed the Bohemian situation as an opportunity to add to his lands and enhance his European reputation by means of a religious crusade against "heretic" Bohemia. King George did not consider himself a heretic and sought to reach an accommodation with the pope, but refused to submit to the latter's demand for unconditional obedience. To renounce the cup for the laity at Mass—the minimum demand of even the most conservative Hussites—would forfeit his political support within Bohemia. Indifferent to this internal problem, Pope Paul II in 1466 placed George under the ban of the Church and released the Bohemians from their oath of loyalty to him as king. In the guise of religious war, Matthias attacked the Bohemian kingdom and succeeded in conquering Moravia. Since no other Christian monarch was willing to alienate the pope by aiding Bohemia, the Czechs found themselves utterly alone.

The cumulative effect of this isolation combined with Hungarian and papal hostility finally convinced the Czechs to make concessions. Bohemia had become a pariah in Europe, shunned by its Catholic neighbors as a source of religious contagion, vulnerable to attack by any monarch claiming to be a loyal Catholic in good standing. The pope even undermined Poděbrady's efforts to organize a league against Turks (a project which Rome normally supported), considering it more important to humble the disobedient king. Ultimately the Czechs became weary of the unending religious troubles. When King George died in 1471, the Diet elected a king whose religious orthodoxy was beyond question—Vladislav, the son of King Casimir IV of Poland. Although Vladislav was required to accept the Basel Compacts as a condition of taking the throne, Catholics could now hope that his accession was the first step toward Bohemia's return to papal obedience. Instead, the Bohemian Diet in 1485 passed the statutes of Kutná Hora, which established freedom of choice between Utraquism and Catholicism as the law of the land. This religious toleration remained in effect until abolished by a later foreign intervention—the victory of a Habsburg-led Catholic army over the Czechs at White Mountain in 1620.

Meanwhile in the Balkans the Serbian Despotate survived as a much-reduced buffer zone between the Ottoman Empire and Hungary. Rule over Serbia was disputed between the two rival princely houses of Lazarević and Branković, whose quarrels were compounded by Turkish interference. Despot Stephen Lazarević (r. 1389–1427), son of the Serbian Prince Lazar who had died fighting the Turks at Kosovo in 1389, was an Ottoman vassal who paid tribute to the sultan and supplied him with auxiliary troops. Stephen was obliged to permit free passage of the Ottoman army through his domains and tolerate Turkish garrisons in his fortresses. He participated on the Turkish side in many important battles, including Rovine in 1395, Nicopolis in 1396, and even Ankara in central Anatolia. As a reward for his services at Rovine, the sultan allowed him to appropriate additional lands in Serbia, confiscated from a relative who had not joined the battle.

Civil war broke out in the Ottoman Empire following the defeat and capture of Sultan Bayezid I by the Mongol conqueror Timur (Tamerlane) at Ankara in 1402. For more than a decade (1402–13) Bayezid's three sons, each at the head of an army, battled for the succession. At this point the European states might well have seized this chance for a renewed attempt to expel the Turks from Europe. The fact that they did nothing was striking proof of their demoralization, as well as their inability to cooperate. Neither Byzantium, Bulgaria, nor Serbia alone possessed sufficient strength to defeat even one of the contending Ottoman princes. The Hungarians were chastened by their recent loss to the Turks at

Nicopolis (1396) and governed by the indecisive King Sigismund. Neither they nor any other European power now made the slightest effort to organize an anti-Turkish coalition.

The Ottoman civil war did prompt the Serbian Despot Stephen Lazarević to assume a more neutral stance between Hungary and the Turks, maintaining a delicate balance as the vassal of both simultaneously. To avoid the appearance of favoring either of his overlords, he fought for both of them. Stephen aided the Hungarian King Sigismund in the latter's Balkan campaigns, his attacks on Bosnia, and his wars against the Czech Hussites. At other times he sent troops to fight with the Turks against Hungary, although without renouncing his Hungarian connection. This dual political allegiance, intolerable in the light of modern nationalism, reflected the reality that neither the Ottoman Empire nor Hungary was in a position to conquer Serbia completely. Such double loyalty demanded uncommon political skill on the part of the Serbian despot, since both of his suzerains perpetually suspected his intentions. Occasionally the arrangement broke down, as in 1425 when the Ottomans accused Stephen of becoming too friendly with Sigismund and launched an attack on Serbian territory. In this case the Hungarians intervened, the Turks withdrew, and peace was restored.

The next Serbian despot, George Branković (r. 1427–56), was even more adroit at maintaining Serbia's equivocal position between its two more powerful neighbors. George was an outstanding diplomat as well as an experienced general and able administrator. He was not only one of the richest magnates in Hungary but also the sultan's vassal, paying him 50,000 ducats annually in tribute and sending 2,000 knights each year into the Ottoman army. He strengthened his position by family ties in both realms, marrying his elder daughter Mara to Sultan Murad II and the younger daughter to the powerful Count of Celje in southwestern Hungary. Yet in the final reckoning, all of the despot's wealth and political skill could merely postpone the ultimate catastrophe. In 1427, the first year of his reign, Ottoman armies took an additional bite from Serbian territory, clearing the way for future advances into the Balkan interior. Since the Turks now occupied all the major towns of Serbia and the Hungarians held Belgrade, George built himself a new capital at Smederevo (Semendria), farther east along the Danube.

The Ottoman army captured Smederevo in 1439 after a bombardment of three months which placed almost the entire Serbian Despotate in their hands. At this point, the last vestiges of Serbian independence seemed about to be extinguished. Then in 1443 the success of the Hungarian Long Campaign, led by the veteran general John Hunyadi, prompted the sultan to propose a truce. His terms were surprisingly generous: a ten-years' armistice, the return of Serbia to the despot, and a tribute of 100,000 gold pieces to the king of Hungary. In June 1444, the two sides agreed upon a preliminary truce. The sultan then sent his envoys to Szeged in southeastern Hungary to have the agreement ratified by Hunyadi and the king. Whether a formal accord was concluded at this time is not entirely clear, since no document to that effect is extant. Perhaps none was drawn up, inasmuch as the sultan on principle never signed any agreement which implied his equality with infidels. But clearly some understanding was reached, because soon after this the Ottoman army retreated from Serbia and evacuated the Serbian fortresses.

This whole affair has long puzzled historians, since within a short time after the meeting at Szeged the Hungarians resumed the war. To all appearances, the renewed hostilities involved a breach of faith. The sultan's envoys obviously believed that a truce had been concluded, because the Ottoman army withdrew from Serbia and the sultan himself soon crossed into Asia. The most likely explanation is that the final peace agreement was an elaborate farce staged by Hunyadi and King Vladislav, aimed at deceiving the sultan into restoring Serbia to the despot and perhaps also at buying time. The pressures were heavy upon the young king to renew the war, which many Europeans viewed as a holy crusade to expel the Turks from Europe. The striking success of Hunyadi's Long Campaign the previous year had encouraged many Christians to believe that such an outcome was possible.. The pope and his legate, the wily canon lawyer Cardinal Cesarini, also cherished hopes that a victorious Christian advance to the Straits might make possible a union of the Orthodox and Catholic Churches, by force if need be. Accordingly, Cesarini persuaded the king that promises made to infidels were not binding.

On August 4, 1444, King Vladislav took a formal public oath at Szeged that he would continue the crusade that year, irrespective of whether or not he concluded peace with the sultan. The oath was cleverly constructed, doubtless by Cesarini, whose experience with canon law had made him fully conversant with the technicalities of true and false oaths. By disavowing in advance any oath he might subsequently make, Vladislav sought to avoid the sin of oath breaking. This solemn ceremony, which was probably meant to reassure the allies, indicates that the young king never had the slightest intention of forgoing the much-desired crusade. A week and a half later at Várad, where the royal court had since moved, he and Hunyadi met with the sultan's envoys and accepted the truce. Hunyadi swore to it personally, while the more cautious Vladislav simply acquiesced. Presumably neither of them would have dared to risk the salvation of their immortal souls by breaking a sworn oath without the benefit of the Cardinal's expert advice. Why a peace was signed with the Turks at all is not immediately obvious. However, from the standpoint of the despot, George Branković, an armistice which restored Serbia to him (even though as a vassal state) was preferable to taking his chances on the outcome of a further campaign. Probably at this time he concluded a secret agreement transfering half of his extensive estates in southern Hungary to Hunyadi in exchange for the latter's support for the truce. Documentary evidence shows that prior to 1445 Hunyadi indeed took possession of many of the despot's Hungarian properties, and that at a later date the status of these lands became a bone of contention between them. Thus it was necessary to deceive the Turks into restoring Serbia, after which the Hungarians would be free to renew the war. Branković naturally refused to participate in the Varna crusade later that year, which (as he may have anticipated, in view of the inadequate preparations) ended in a catastrophic Christian defeat. Meanwhile, John Hunyadi had become the richest lord in Hungary.

A rare example of successful Christian resistance to the Turks in the 15th century, although in a fairly remote part of Europe, was provided by Skanderbeg, the Albanian mountain chieftain who became the leader of a national revolt. For over a quarter-century until his death in 1468, he led the Albanians in surprisingly effective guerrilla warfare against the Turkish occupiers of his country. Despite this exemplary record, he received slight aid from the rest of the Christian world. A succession of popes sent him encouraging words, but minimal financial help. At times the Venetians provided him with funds, most notably in 1464 during their own war with the Turks; but usually they found it more advantageous to pay tribute to the sultan. For the most part, the Venetian authorities viewed Skanderbeg as a threat to their control of the Adriatic coastal towns, and purposely undermined his position by promoting discord among the Albanian territorial lords. Admittedly, Skanderbeg's victories in this minor theater of war failed to shake the overall Ottoman position in the Balkans. Nonetheless, as long as he lived the Turks were unable to control Albania, which became an Ottoman province only in the 1480s.

The inability of the Christian states to join forces against the Ottomans was equally well illustrated in 1448 during Hunyadi's campaign into Serbia. The recently restored Despot George Branković, conscious of his exposed position vis-à-vis the Turks, had no wish to risk his political survival in a possibly fruitless campaign. He not only remained neutral, but actually informed the sultan of the direction of Hunyadi's march and occupied the mountain passes on the Serbian-Albanian border to prevent Skanderbeg's arrival. In return, Hunyadi treated Serbia as enemy territory, plundering and devastating the countryside. No Serbian troops were present on the field of Kosovo in 1448, where a Christian army for the second time met defeat in a major encounter with the Turks. Meanwhile, a Venetian attack on northern Albania delayed Skanderbeg in coming to Hunyadi's aid. Branković retaliated for the damage perpetrated by the Hungarian army in Serbia by capturing Hunyadi on his retreat and having him imprisoned. This pattern of noncooperation was only too typical of the period, as short-range objectives caused the Christian states to overlook their common interest in preventing Ottoman expansion.

Although Branković managed to prolong Serbia's autonomous existence by clever diplomacy and by standing aside from the anti-Turkish campaigns led by Hungary in 1444 and 1448, this reprieve was short-lived. The fall of Constantinople in 1453 put an end to the Byzantine Empire and sealed the fate of the Serbian Despotate. Ottoman troops attacked Serbia in 1454 and mounted a major effort in 1456 to capture Belgrade, the key fortress at the junction of the Sava and the Danube. Belgrade resisted successfully—it would remain in Hungarian possession until 1521—but the Turks encountered few obstacles when they overran the remainder of Serbia. In 1459 they captured the fortress of Smederevo without a battle. Serbia now became an Ottoman province, while Hungary in the following seventy years was reduced to an essentially defensive stance vis-à-vis the Ottoman Empire.

Walachia and Moldavia, protected to some extent by the natural barrier of the Danube, stood aside from the main line of Ottoman advance. Their relationship to the sultan was often a tributary one, although they were never directly incorporated into the Ottoman Empire. Despite frequent Turkish intervention in their dynastic quarrels, the two principalities retained considerable internal autonomy. However, they suffered the usual misfortune of small countries squeezed in between contending great powers—namely, perpetual instability combined with outside interference. Poland, Hungary, and the Ottoman Empire all regarded the Romanian principalities as their natural zone of influence. Rarely were any of the three content for long with a Romanian voivode allied with a rival power.

This situation was made to order for a pretender—in principle, any prince from the Walachian or Moldavian dynasty—who might seek to gain the throne of his country by enlisting the aid of one of the neighboring powers. In the event of success, he was expected at minimum to behave as the client and ally of his benefactor, and usually also to become a tribute-paying vassal. However, the loyalty of a Romanian voivode often wavered. More than once a prince installed by the Hungarian army found himself soon afterward paying tribute to the sultan, perhaps simply to reduce the number of Turkish raids into his lands. Conversely, when Ottoman forces installed a voivode, they expected him to join them in attacking Transylvania. This would prompt the Hungarians to reappear in turn with a new pretender. Occasionally a Romanian voivode sought to become independent from all foreign control; but such efforts were rarely successful for long. The struggle was permanently unequal, since neither Walachia nor Moldavia was a match for its larger neighbors in overall resources and population. Nor did the two principalities often aid each other.

Illustrative of the difficult position of a Romanian ruler sandwiched between Hungary and the Ottoman Empire was the career of Vlad II Dracul, voivode of Walachia. His cognomen "Dracul," which means "dragon" or "devil," was presumably derived from his membership in a typically medieval knightly association known as the Order of the Dragon, founded by King Sigismund of Hungary and ostensibly aimed at fighting the infidel. Vlad apparently spent much of his youth at the Hungarian court, and began his reign in Walachia in 1436 with Sigismund's blessing. Initially he refused to pay tribute to the sultan; but the prompt appearance of a Turkish army in Walachia soon changed his mind. In 1437 he became the ally of Sultan Murad II, to whom he made formal submission. When the Hungarians chased him off his throne, Vlad Dracul took refuge with the Turks, who in 1443 restored him to power. This time he was forced not only to promise allegiance to the sultan and pay tribute, but also to give his two young sons to the Turks as hostages. The Varna campaign in 1444 brought him further embarrassment. As a Christian, he hardly dared to sit out a war proclaimed as a holy crusade. At the same time, conscious of his sons in Turkish capitivity, he gave the Hungarians as little aid as he dared. In 1447 he concluded a final alliance with the Turks, and died in the same year in battle against the Hungarians.

The tangled career of his son Vlad III, known as the Impaler, shows a similar pattern of shifting allegiances and lack of scruples. Noted for a cruelty considered excessive even in that hardened age, Vlad III subsequently passed into European legend as the vampire Dracula (in Romanian: Draculea, or son of Dracul). In his youth a Turkish hostage, Vlad afterward became an officer in the Ottoman army, and with Turkish aid ascended the Walachian throne in 1448. After holding this position only briefly, he was expelled and fled to the court of Moldavia. In 1456 he again entered Walachia, defeated the reigning voivode, and began his longest tenure of power, this time lasting about six years. While supposedly an ally of Hungary, he also paid tribute to the Turks. However, when the sultan demanded personal homage from him, Vlad not only refused but ordered the impalement of the Turkish envoys who arrived to collect the customary tribute. He followed up this provocation by crossing the Danube into Ottoman Bulgaria with a large army early in 1462 and destroying a number of Ottoman border fortresses. That summer he annihilated a numerically superior Turkish army which had penetrated north of the Danube into Walachia. Despite these important victories, he was deposed soon afterward and fled to Hungary, where King Matthias for reasons unknown had him imprisoned. Apparently it was at this time that tales of the cruelty of "Draculea" received wider European currency, perhaps at Hungarian instigation to justify Matthias's imprisonment of this successful anti-Turkish warrior. In 1475, Vlad the Impaler came to power one final time with Matthias's blessing, but soon afterward met his death at the hands of some pro-Turkish Walachian lords.

Moldavia's international position was in some ways even worse than Walachia's, requiring its voivode to balance among three great neighbors instead of just two. As the more northern of the two Romanian principalities, it first acquired a common boundary with Poland in the 1350s through King Casimir III's acquisitions in Galicia. The Poles subsequently sought to make it a vassal state; and in 1387 the Moldavian voivode was forced to do homage to the Polish king. However, at intervals the Hungarians were able to detach Moldavia from Poland in order to align it with themselves. In the quarter-century prior to the accession of Stephen the Great as voivode in 1457, a series of separate Polish and Hungarian interventions occurred in Moldavia, with the result that its throne changed occupants with exceptional frequency. On the whole, a Polish alliance best suited Moldavia's interests, since a Hungarian orientation almost inevitably involved the principality in war with the Turks. Conflict with Poland concerned chiefly the lesser question of Pokucie, a frontier district on the upper Pruth River claimed by both states.

Moldavia's continued independence from the Turks in the second half of the 15th century was largely the achievement of its determined Voivode Stephen the Great (r. 1457–1504). This prince would stand out in the troubled history of the Romanian principalities if only for the unusual feat of maintaining himself on that insecure throne for forty-seven years. His real greatness lay in the skill and tenacity with which he upheld Moldavia's autonomy against far more powerful neighbors: Hungary, Poland, and particularly the Ottoman Empire. Maneuvering between Poland and Hungary, he managed to avoid permanent vassalage to either one. Early in his reign, when his chief opponent was Hungary, Stephen agreed to pay homage to the Polish King Casimir III and aid him against the Tatars. In 1467 he fought the Hungarians to prevent King Matthias from replacing him with a pretender. This latter campaign marked Hungary's last attempt at conquering Moldavia by force. By the early 1470s Stephen had come to view the expanding Ottoman Empire as his chief enemy. His refusal in 1473 to pay tribute to the sultan was in effect a declaration of war. Then to the astonishment of Europe, he led the Moldavians in 1475 to a decisive victory over a major Ottoman army near Vaslui. Ultimately a lack of allies forced him to make peace with the sultan in 1478 and resume tribute payments. In 1484 he suffered the greatest setback of his career when the Turks captured his ports of Kilia and Cetatea Alba on the Black Sea. Still defiant, in 1497 he repulsed a Polish attack which was probably aimed at placing a Polish prince on the Moldavian throne. Finally in 1500–1501 he joined his last anti-Ottoman coalition, this time together with Hungary and Venice.

Stephen the Great of Moldavia surpassed all other medieval Romanian princes in the persistence as well as the success of his resistance to foreign control. Albeit on a small stage, he was indubitably one of the outstanding European personalities of his time. Statecraft rather than religious zeal motivated his policy. Most notable as a Christian opponent of the Turks, he did not hesitate to join with them in 1497 when danger loomed from Poland. In view of his frequent lack of allies, Stephen's long ability to resist Ottoman pressure is astounding. Partly this was because he could call to arms nearly all the able-bodied men of his country. As long as he held Cetatea and Kilia he could obtain supplies by sea. Thus the Turkish capture of these ports in 1484 meant the loss of an important resource and the establishment of Turkish garrisons on Moldavian soil. Nonetheless he continued the struggle, despite the apparent invincibility of the Ottoman colossus. Together with Hunyadi and Skanderbeg, Stephen the Great stands out as the only Christian commander of the 15th century able to win major victories over the Turks. In the process he put Moldavia on the map—a country whose very existence had been virtually unknown to Western Europe until his time.

Hungary was in fact the only European state which was both strong enough and sufficiently threatened in the mid-15th century to have organized success-ful resistance to Ottoman power. During the period when John Hunyadi domi-nated Hungarian politics (i.e., from the early 1440s until his death in 1456) the anti-Turkish wars were conducted with some degree of success. The Turks were kept from seriously violating Hungary's borders, while Serbia, Bosnia, and the Romanian principalities served as buffer states. By contrast, Hunyadi's son King Matthias (r. 1458–90) largely ignored the Ottoman danger. Elected on the strength of his father's enormous wealth and military reputation, which promised further successes against the Turks, Matthias nonetheless paid little attention to the threat on his southeastern frontier. In many respects he was an outstanding monarch; but his gaze was turned chiefly toward Italy and Western Europe. To establish a royal dynasty of his own he needed recognition from the traditional ruling houses of Europe, not the addition of new lands in the Balkans. Therefore he employed his army for his wars in Central Europe. Matthias's intervention in the Hussite conflict in Bohemia left him in possession of much of Moravia; and in 1485 he became the first Hungarian king ever to capture Vienna. At the time of his death he ruled Silesia, Moravia, and Lower Austria, and had made Hungary the chief power in Central Europe. However, he had not founded a royal dynasty; and soon after his death in 1490 all his conquests were lost.

Matthias made little progress against the Ottomans. After capturing the Bosnian fortress of Jajce in 1463, he took merely defensive measures against them. Although Venice and the pope gave him huge subsidies to finance further anti-Turkish wars, his dilatory behavior while on campaign raised justified doubts as to his seriousness of purpose. He did not energetically oppose the increasingly numerous Turkish attacks on his Croatian lands. Serbia was incorporated into the Ottoman Empire in 1459, most of Bosnia in 1463, while Turkish irregulars intermittently passed through Hungary to plunder in Styria and Carinthia (present-day Austria). However, the Habsburg Emperor Frederick III was Matthias's most consistent enemy. Frederick suspected him of secret deals with the Turks, while Matthias in turn blamed Frederick for failing to join an anti-Turkish crusade, which he had promised repeatedly to do. The animosity was such that Matthias feared, with good reason, that if he moved against the Turks Frederick would attack Hungary in his absence. Amid these competing ambitions and suspicions, all possibility evaporated of a successful combined attack on the centralized Ottoman Empire.

Hungary between the time of Bosnia's fall in 1463 and the final disaster of Mohács in 1526 occupied an unenviable position as a bone of contention between the Habsburg and Ottoman power blocs, each of which wished to use it as a buffer against the other. Within Hungary itself until 1526 a Western orientation was paramount. The Hungarians were conscious of belonging to Christian civilization and hostile to Islam. They did not wish to offend Venice or the pope, both of which supplied indispensable, although never sufficient, financial aid for the defense of the southern frontiers. On the other hand, Ottoman power was growing, which might have suggested the need for a more pro-Turkish policy. Officially a truce was in effect between Hungary and the Ottoman Empire between 1463 to 1499, but this brought no genuine peace. Quite the contrary, it was accompanied by incessant and often devastating incursions by Turkish irregulars along Hungary's southern borders. Apparently the Hungarians by 1499 had had their fill of this situation, since in that year they refused to extend the truce. Thus freed to join an anti-Ottoman coalition formed by France, Poland, and Venice, they conducted military operations into Ottoman territory in the Balkans in 1501–2. Then the European alliance collapsed and peace was restored. Similarly, collaboration with Pope Leo X in his plans for an anti-Ottoman crusade in 1514 produced no positive result, but instead led to a major peasant rebellion that year.

From the perspective of Istanbul, the European situation changed significantly for the worse in 1519 when the heir to the extensive Habsburg territories in the Low Countries, southern Germany, Austria, Italy, Spain and Spanish America was also elected German emperor as Charles V. Now that Serbia and Bosnia had fallen, the Habsburgs stood as the principal obstacle to further Ottoman expansion in Central Europe; and Charles's new dignity increased the resources at his disposal. In 1520 the death of Sultan Selim I and the accession of Suleiman I (later known as "the Magnificent") presented a natural opportunity for a new accord with Hungary, since according to Turkish custom all the laws of a former sultan lapsed with his death. The terms which the Turks offered Hungary in 1520 are not known for certain; but apparently they were more severe than the previous arrangements, since the Hungarian government rejected them. Instead it sent emissaries to ask for aid from the Catholic West, despite the insufficient assistance it had received from that quarter in the past.

Whether Sultan Suleiman's ultimate aim was the conquest of Hungary remains a disputed point. As of 1526, it appears that he regarded the Danube-Sava line as the natural northern boundary of his empire. Hungary might be conquered, but it was arguably too distant from the main theater of Ottoman military operations to be held. Much evidence suggests that the sultan's preferred course would have been to make Hungary a vassal state like Walachia and Moldavia, not to destroy its independence altogether. Unquestionably he was also aware of the treaty of 1515 which permitted the Habsburgs to inherit Hungary if King Louis II died without heirs—so he can scarcely have desired the death of the young and still childless king at Mohács. Suleiman's intention was obviously to bring Hungary within the Ottoman orbit, but not necessarily to make it an Ottoman province. Hungary's rejection of the Ottoman peace offer meant war; and the Ottoman Empire's overwhelming military superiority left the outcome scarcely in doubt. Belgrade fell in 1521, rendering Hungary's southern border largely defenseless. Although the final blow was delayed for five years while the Turks were occupied elsewhere, in 1526 a massive Ottoman army invaded southern Hungary. The objective was probably to coerce King Louis into accepting the Ottoman terms. Instead the Hungarians were utterly defeated and the king died, bringing the Habsburg inheritance treaty into effect. Not until 1541 was the situation in Central Europe stabilized, with the Habsburgs retaining Slovakia and portions of western Hungary and Croatia. Transylvania became an Ottoman vassal state, while the central region became an Ottoman province—and so they both remained until 1699.

Poland's most important foreign involvement during the 15th century was the Thirteen Years' War (1454–66) with the Teutonic Order of Knights. This conflict originated neither with the Knights nor the Poles, but with the towns and nobility of Prussia, frustrated with the Knights' government. The Teutonic Order still functioned as a medieval monastic organization, autocratically ruled by its grand master, although commercial towns of a more modern type had begun to flourish in its territories. The urban merchants complained of the many restrictions that the Order imposed upon their trade. Similarly disgruntled were the indigenous Prussian nobles, who resented the Order's political monopoly. These grievances brought the townsmen and nobility to join forces in organizing the Prussian League, which revolted against the Order in 1454 and requested assistance from the king of Poland. When the king accepted this challenge, an armed struggle became inevitable.

The ensuing Thirteen Years' War demonstrated that medieval chivalry as represented by the Teutonic Knights was no match for prosperous towns which could afford to hire mercenary soldiers. After one significant victory by the Knights, the war became one of attrition. Ultimately the Order conceded defeat. In 1466 by the second Peace of Toruń (Thorn), it ceded all its territory west of the Vistula (i.e., West Prussia) to Poland as an autonomous province. The rest became legally a Polish fief, although for all practical purposes it remained subject to the Order. The treaty of 1466 required that the grand master of the Teutonic Knights swear an oath of loyalty to the king of Poland as his overlord. In reality, all future grand masters did their best to avoid this humiliating ceremony, which was performed for the last time in 1489. Relations between Poland and the Order remained antagonistic. However, this war brought Poland the double benefit of substantial tax revenue from the flourishing Prussian towns and a significant weakening of the Teutonic Order as a military rival.

A portent for the future appeared in the relations of Poland-Lithuania with Muscovy, although during the 15th century the threat from that quarter did not seem overly grave. Ivan III the Great, tsar of Muscovy (r. 1462–1505), was an able and activist ruler; but he needed to subjugate the Russian principalities to the west of his hereditary lands before he could touch Lithuania. Muscovy's expansion at Lithuania's expense began only toward the end of the century. In 1480, Ivan shook off the yoke of the Golden Horde forever, freeing him to turn his attention westward. His first full-scale war with Lithuania in 1486–94 gained him important territories at Lithuania's expense. Again in 1500 Muscovy defeated Lithuania in a major battle, for which the Poles sent no aid.

Despite these reverses, Poland-Lithuania at the end of the 15th century remained the largest state in East Central Europe. Its territories reached far into Ukraine, allegedly "from sea to sea" (i.e., from the Baltic to the Black Sea), although in reality Lithuania held only indirect authority over a small portion of the Black Sea coast. In 1466 the acquisition of West Prussia (henceforth known as Royal Prussia), with its flourishing port of Gdańsk, provided access to the Baltic Sea. However, until the end of the 15th century Poland still functioned essentially as a land power, hardly utilizing its maritime potential. Only in the 16th century did it become a major grain-exporting state. Tatar attacks on the outlying Ukrainian territories subject to Lithuania still occurred nearly every year. Nonetheless, the Polish-Lithuanian state held its own. In 1487 the Poles won an impressive victory against the Tatars in Ukraine, and in 1497 conducted another major campaign deep into the interior of Russia. They also attempted without success to establish sovereignty over Moldavia. Losses of territory in the east to Muscovy were not yet severe. In 1500 Poland was poised on the threshold of a cultural renaissance which would come to fruition during the 16th century.

In the southeast, by contrast, Ottoman hegemony had created a fateful split in the body politic of Europe. By sheer coincidence, this demarcation line conformed quite closely to the ancient division between the Western and the Eastern Roman empires, perpetuated now in the conflicting spheres of Catholicism and Orthodoxy. Christianity and Islam remained enemies, despite the practical accommodations sometimes reached between Christian and Islamic states. Cultural contacts across this Muslim-Christian religious frontier were few and far between. The intellectual and spiritual ferment of the Renaissance and Reformation in 16th-century Europe, like the dynamism of the Commercial Revolution and Age of Exploration, would find few echoes on the Ottoman side of this religious and political divide.

CHAPTER 13

Ethnicity and Nationalism

Nationalism as a form of self-identification—the consciousness of belonging to a distinct ethnic group with its own language, culture, and traditions—has been an enormously powerful factor in modern history. The mystique of one's own nationality as the bearer of unique and superior qualities has profoundly affected much of the present-day world. This was an attitude rarely existing in the Middle Ages. Although sentiments of a nationalist type can occasionally be found as long ago as ancient Egypt or classical Greece, nationalism was not then a large-scale phenomenon. In both ancient and medieval Europe, the distinctions of social class, rank, and religion were vastly more significant. No one in those days regarded the lower classes as bearers of a national tradition worth preserving, or thought that peasant customs and folktales should be taken seriously by educated people. Nationalism as an emotional force capable of binding together all social classes, submerging even religious differences and creating loyalty to an ethnic group or to an impersonal entity called a state, had yet to be born.

Even the word "nation" (the Latin *natio*) in medieval Europe did not refer to people of similar language and cultural heritage. A "nation" was a group possessing certain legal privileges. At medieval universities, for example, teachers and students were assigned to a "nation" according to the directions of the compass, not by ethnic identification. Nonetheless, ethnic groups did exist; and medieval nationalism arose out of the cognizance of such differences by persons living in areas of ethnic diversity. Frequently this national awareness was accompanied by feelings of solidarity with one's own ethnic community and hostility toward others, particularly where competition for place and position entered the picture. However, with the partial exception of 15th-century Bohemia, national consciousness was not a mass phenomenon in the Middle Ages. Its chief bearers were precisely those individuals whose interests and mental horizons extended beyond a single locality or ethnic group. Among them were the higher nobles and prelates of the Church, whose identity was linked to the state and the monarchy;

and town dwellers associated in some fashion with long-distance commerce. The towns of East Central Europe were unusual in that most of the major ones were dominated politically and economically by foreigners (usually Germans, although in some parts of the Balkans Greeks or Italians). On the other hand, village dwellers ordinarily had very little contact with the outside world and were only vaguely aware of their relation to it. Medieval peasants identified themselves not by nationality, but as belonging to a certain family, religion, or locality. In the rural, isolated, fragmented, and overwhelmingly illiterate society of the Middle Ages, most people were quite unable to relate their own language and customs to those of a similar but more widely diffused group beyond their own experience.

Political loyalty in the medieval era was most often an expression of fidelity to a sovereign's person, not an emotional attachment to a cultural or linguistic community. Governments were the creations of reigning dynasties and their associated nobilities, not the products of national feeling. Medieval monarchs typically assumed a supranational attitude, since their allegiance belonged to the dynasty, not the ethnic group. A king's exalted status usually required him to seek a consort abroad, since no conceivable marriage partner within his own country held sufficiently high rank. This meant that many of his closest relatives (through his mother as well as his wife) were foreigners. Furthermore, most monarchs gladly utilized the services of men with specialized skills in warfare or (after government became more complex) a good knowledge of Latin, whether or not they were natives of his realm. Such outsiders frequently lacked close ties to indigenous society and were thus more reliably loyal. King Stephen I of Hungary in the 11th century exemplified an attitude not uncommon in the medieval upper classes when he emphasized the usefulness of diversity. In his often-cited advice to his son Emeric, he advocated the employment of foreigners in the royal service precisely because their different languages, habits, laws, and weapons would add to the strength of the realm.

Language could not give rise to ethnic awareness in any serious way while literacy remained essentially the preserve of clerics schooled in an ancient foreign tongue. As long as Latin remained the only medium of serious communication in Bohemia, Poland, and Hungary, ethnic distinctions necessarily remained subordinate to a broader feeling of Catholic unity. In Bulgaria, Serbia, and the Romanian principalities Old Slavic played a similar role for Eastern Orthodoxy. The continued use of these old languages, which had ceased to be the vehicle of common speech, inhibited the growth of a national consciousness. Moreover, by the 12th and 13th centuries the formerly unified Slavic tongue had evolved into numerous dialects which shaded almost imperceptibly into one another. Thus the growth of ethnic consciousness was inseparably linked to the growth of separate vernacular literatures. These in turn reflected major changes in society. By the 13th century the expansion of towns and trade had created a small middle class of lay persons who lacked training in the ecclesiastical language, but nonetheless aspired to literacy. The art of writing had become necessary for the keeping of business accounts; and the increased availability of leisure time gave rise to a desire for higher culture. This situation encouraged literary creativity in the language of ordinary speech. Nonetheless, down to the end of the Middle Ages the written vernaculars occupied a very modest place beside the ancient tongues.

Amid the various ethnic groups of East Central Europe, the Albanians have resided longest on their present territory and speak the most archaic tongue. Prior to the 13th century they were almost certainly more numerous in relative terms than they have been since. After that time many of them became assimilated to Greek or Slavic culture in northern Greece, Macedonia or Montenegro. The rest remained confined in large part to the mountainous territory of their present homeland and the neighboring region of Kosovo to the east. Their history is difficult to disentangle from that of the other nationalities—Greeks, Italians, and Slavs—which have lived at one time or another in the same area. During the medieval period, when the small territory now called Albania was a major outpost of the Byzantine Empire, its upper stratum of nobles and townsmen was Greek by culture and language. Its towns contained a population of mixed ethnic character, with the proportions varying from place to place. The earliest known references to Albanians stem from Byzantine sources of the 11th century. Even then the term applied not to speakers of the Albanian language as such, but only to the inhabitants of the small province known as Arbanon.

National distinctions cannot have been of crucial importance in medieval Albania, since the documents of the period so rarely take note of them. It is clear nonetheless that as the Byzantine position in Albania weakened in the 13th century and after, ethnic Albanians became increasingly dominant throughout the country. Of the major towns, Durrës probably held an Albanian majority by the end of the 13th century, although Vlorë seems to have followed suit only in the 15th. In rural areas the proportion of Greek or Italian inhabitants gradually declined during the 13th century, with ethnic Albanians taking their place. According to travelers' reports, the rural districts were wholly in the hands of Albanians by the early 14th century. On the other hand, the pressure of Turkish raids after about 1350 combined with warfare among the local lords to prompt a considerable exodus of Albanians to southern Italy, Venice, or Dubrovnik.

Like the Albanians, the Vlachs (Romanians) are an ancient nationality in East Central Europe. Their ancestors were the Latin-speaking inhabitants of the Balkan sector of the Roman Empire; and all their dialects are offshoots of Latin. During the Middle Ages the Vlachs nearly always lived as stock raisers in the hilly portions of the Balkan Peninsula, migrating between winter and summer pastures, so that it is difficult to associate them with a specific territory. However, several distinct Vlach groups were known in the late Middle Ages, each with its own linguistic peculiarities. The Aromanians, or Macedo-Romanians, lived chiefly on the slopes of the Pindus Mountains in Macedonia and Thessaly. They were so numerous in Thessaly that documents of the 11th century refer to the entire region as "Vlachia." The Megleno-Romanians were a smaller group residing in Bulgaria south of the Rhodope mountains. Apparently they were politically influential in medieval Bulgaria, since the Second Bulgarian Empire, founded in 1185, was officially known as the Empire of the Bulgars and Vlachs. A third group were the Istro-Romanians inhabiting the mountainous districts parallel to the Dalmatian coast. In the Balkan interior the Vlachs were much less numerous, and eventually the Slavic majority absorbed them.

A significant Vlach population also resided in Transylvania, at least from the 12th century onward, when historical sources first mention them. It is less clear whether a Vlach presence was continuous in Transylvania from the year 270, when the Romans abandoned their province of Dacia. In Hungarian-ruled Transylvania the Vlachs were a socially subordinate class, though certainly a numerous one. The Hungarian nobility (either native Magyar or Magyarized) played the leading political role, while Saxons and Szeklers enjoyed legal rights that others did not. The constitutional document known as the "Union of the Three Nations," adopted by the Transylvanian Diet in 1437, ignored the Vlachs as though they did not exist. Herders and peasants by occupation, the Vlachs occupied the lowest rung of the social ladder, superior only to slaves. They suffered the additional disability of adherence to Eastern Orthodoxy, which in predominantly Catholic Hungary was considered a deviant and sometimes even a heretical form of Christianity. However, no merely ethnic prejudice prevented an ambitious Vlach from acquiring land and joining the Hungarian noble class, provided that he accepted Catholicism and adopted a noble life-style. The outstanding example of this is John Hunyadi, who became the leading military commander, the richest lord, and ultimately the regent in Hungary, but whose Vlach father had risen from obscurity into the Hungarian petty nobility through marriage. At the same time, the fact that upward mobility required the renunciation of Vlach identity clearly hindered this group in developing a sense of ethnic solidarity.

In the southernmost part of the Balkans the Greek tongue had always predominated over Latin even under the Roman Empire, although Latin remained the official language of the army and most of the government until the 7th century. Greek-speaking enclaves continued to exist in the Balkans even as late as the 9th and 10th centuries, particularly around the town of Sofia and along the lower reaches of the Danube. These Greek minorities exerted a strong cultural influence on the Turkic-speaking, pagan Bulgars who settled in that region beginning in the late 7th century. Nonetheless, the Greeks were too few in number to impose their native tongue upon either the Bulgars or the even more numerous Slavs who had infiltrated the region from about the 4th century onward. By the 9th and 10th centuries the Bulgars had become Slavicized; and the flourishing First

Bulgarian Empire was a Slavic state. Pride in this empire is evident in early Old Slavic literature. The Bulgarian "Apocryphal Chronicle," for example, which probably dates from the second half of the 11th century, ascribes the foundation of the Bulgar state to an act of God. It lists quite accurately the rulers of Bulgaria over a period of several centuries and lauds their deeds as builders of towns and villages and as leaders of their people. The "Legend of Salonika," from that same era, describes the Bulgars as the nation selected by God to disseminate the Slavic alphabet.

The 11th-century Bulgar revolts against Byzantium, although spurred by immediate grievances over taxation, certainly owed something to the memory of former years when independent Bulgaria was a great power in the Balkans. Byzantine rule had been reimposed upon Bulgaria in 1018. The uprising led by Peter Delyan in 1040 was a conscious attempt to restore the dynasty of Tsar Samuel (d. 1014), who had heroically defended the Bulgar state for nearly a quarter of a century against the Byzantines. Delyan, whom the insurgent Bulgars proclaimed as king, was allegedly Samuel's grandson. The successful rebellion of the Asen brothers against Byzantine rule in 1185 evidently owed some of its popular support to a widespread awareness of the former Bulgarian dominance in the Balkans. Folk tradition clearly identified Byzantium as the national enemy. The Bogomil religious heresy which flourished in Bulgaria in the 11th century also carried obvious anti-Byzantine overtones. The dualist Bogomils claimed that Satanael (Satan), the force of Evil in this world, made his home in Hagia Sophia, the principal Christian church in Constantinople.

In the late 9th century when the people known to Western Europe as Magyars or Hungarians entered the land which became the kingdom of Hungary, they were a multiethnic and multilingual confederation. Their supreme leader was Almus, the chief of the Turkic-speaking Onogurs, while the Finno-Ugric Magyars constituted just one of the eight component tribes. Byzantine writers of the 9th and 10th centuries—long accustomed to the Onogur presence along the lower Danube—referred to all members of the confederation without exception as "Turks" and their country as "Turkia." However, in the famous "Covenant of Blood" the Magyar tribe had accepted Almus's son Árpád as the military commander who would lead them into Hungary; and Árpád subsequently became the founder of the Hungarian royal dynasty. When he succeeded his father Almus as head of the confederation, the Magyars—his principal power base—automatically became the leading tribe; and their Finno-Ugric language eventually became dominant throughout the Hungarian kingdom. Medieval Western sources treat the mounted warriors from Hungary who terrorized Europe in the first half of the 10th century as if they belonged to a single "Magyar" ethnic group. In physical appearance these predators must have differed noticeably from the European norm. Chroniclers of the time, doubtless with malice, describe them as monsters and malformations of humanity.

Closely related to the Finno-Ugric members of the Hungarian confederation were the Szeklers, a people of purely Magyar speech but a distinct identity. In the late Middle Ages, popular opinion regarded their dialect as the purest form of the Magyar tongue in existence. However, the origins of the Szeklers are obscure. According to one view, they originated as a Turkic-speaking tribe (the Szikül) which joined and fused with the Magyars during the latter's wanderings in Russia or Ukraine and entered Central Europe together with them in 895–96. Conversely, medieval Hungarian documents (doubtless based on folk tradition) describe the Szeklers as already present in Hungary at the time of Árpád's arrival. If so, they were probably former subjects of the Avar-led empire destroyed by Charlemagne. Unquestionably the Szeklers were closely associated with the Magyars at an early date, serving as military auxiliaries. Their "pure" (perhaps old-fashioned) speech patterns are likely to have been the consequence of a relatively isolated life-style.

While traditionally regarded as an ethnic group, the Szeklers perhaps owed their distinctiveness (at least in part) to their role as military guardians of the frontier. According to this hypothesis, the term "Szekler" originally carried an occupational as well as an ethnic connotation. The medieval Szeklers were noted for their fighting skills and formed an advance guard of the Hungarian army. This life-style was reflected in the pattern of their settlements, of which the vast majority were located in the exposed borderlands of the Hungarian kingdom, either in Transylvania or along the western frontier with Austria. At a later period, well after most Hungarian nobles had adopted the heavy cavalry style characteristic of Western knights, the Szeklers continued to fight as light cavalry archers in the manner of the steppe. Even in modern Hungary their descendants remain conscious of a distinct identity. Today approximately every tenth Hungarian is a Szekler; and the question of their origins arouses considerable interest among the Hungarian public.

The Turkic-speaking Cumans, who played so important a role in the history of medieval Hungary, ultimately disappeared altogether as a separate ethnic group. Seminomadic and uncivilized, many of them had settled in the lowlands of Walachia and Moldavia in the early part of the 13th century. There in the year 1227 some 15,000 of them were baptized under Hungarian sponsorship. The Mongol (Tatar) invasion of Europe in 1237–40 pushed still other Cumans from Ukraine into the Balkan Peninsula; and the Hungarian King Béla IV allowed some of them to take refuge on the half-empty Danube-Tisza plain. Conflicts with hostile lords in the Hungarian army at the time of the Mongol attack in 1241 caused them to move into Bulgaria, where their leaders ultimately became integrated into the Bulgar boyar class. After the Mongol retreat, King Béla renewed his overtures to the Cumans, whose cavalry represented a valuable military asset. Once again Cumans came to settle on the Hungarian plain, where they continued their pastoral life-style. Quarrels were endemic between them and the native Hungarians, especially in the time of King Ladislas IV, who sympathized with them. For decades the Cumans were a disruptive influence in the kingdom; but slowly they turned Christian, became absorbed into Hungarian society, and lost their ethnic identity.

Gypsies too were an alien element in medieval Hungary. A darkskinned people of north Indian ancestry, they spoke a language called Romany, which was likewise of Indian origin. Their wanderings took them as far as Persia by the 11th century; and by the 14th century they had reached Central Europe, with Transylvania often serving as their gate of entry. Hungarian documents first mention gypsies for the years 1416 and 1417, when a group of them entered Transylvania in flight from the Ottoman Turks. King Sigismund gave them permission to remain. Some of them went on to Germany and Bohemia in the 15th century, but certain Hungarian words remained in their vocabulary. In the late Middle Ages gypsies were often welcomed in Europe as tinsmiths or weaponsmiths, receiving letters of privilege from various rulers. Everywhere comparatively few in total numbers, they were more numerous in Hungary than elsewhere in Europe. Even in the 20th century most of them have not become assimilated, but retain their distinctive character.

Transylvania remained an ethnic mosaic throughout the medieval era, populated by Germans (popularly known as "Saxons"), Szeklers, and Vlachs as well as Hungarians. The first Saxon settlers in the province were peasants from the Rhineland, invited by King Géza I in the mid-12th century as part of a policy aimed at safeguarding the Carpathian frontier. A second wave of immigrants followed in about 1160 and a third in 1180–90. Originally peasant cultivators, the Saxons developed important urban communities only from the 14th century onward. Because this flow of German immigrants into Transylvania produced conflicts with the Szeklers, whose life-style had remained seminomadic, King Andrew II in about 1225 separated their respective settlements. He relocated the Szeklers along the eastern border of the province, where their military skills could be useful against the steppe raiders, and granted the former Szekler territories in the interior to the Saxons. The lands assigned to each group were reserved to them alone; and a royal governor was appointed for each region (the Szekler count and the Saxon count). This separation of nationalities became a permanent feature of Transylvanian life in the Middle Ages. The Saxons continued to speak their German dialect and defined themselves as a distinct nationality. Smaller but equally separate groups of Saxons and Szeklers lived in the Zips region of northern Hungary (Slovakia).

The eastward migration of Germans in the Middle Ages was a large-scale phenomenon encompassing all of East Central Europe from northern Poland to southern Serbia. As early as the 10th and 11th centuries, but particularly in the 12th, the boundaries between German and Slavic settlement began to shift significantly. Regions which were once overwhelmingly Slavic in character, such as Holstein, Mecklenburg, Brandenburg, and Saxony, now became primarily

Germanic, as they have since remained. Still farther to the east, German enclaves were created in primarily non-German regions. The movement of German peasants and artisans spilled over on a large scale into Poland and Bohemia, but also reached into Hungary, Slovenia, and the mining districts of Serbia. Many of these immigrants had been persuaded to migrate eastward by the professional colonizing agents known as "locators," whom the monarchs or great magnates empowered to establish new settlements or augment older ones. The objective was to open up underpopulated regions, create new taxpaying residents, and promote the development of urban artisanry and trade.

Modern historians examining this eastward migration have often interpreted it in a nationalist sense. German authors have praised it as bringing the gift of German medieval civilization—advanced agricultural techniques, urban artisanry, and municipal self-government—to previously underdeveloped regions. Polish, Czech, and Hungarian writers have treated it as sinister evidence of an allegedly consistent German ambition to establish hegemony in the East (the so-called *Drang nach Osten*). Neither interpretation is valid, because medieval people did not employ this nationalist frame of reference. Prior to the age of modern nationalism, no one supposed that the ethnic identity of ordinary folk bore any relevance to the question of who should govern them. Sovereigns happily annexed lands inhabited by people alien in language and customs both to themselves and to the majority of their other subjects. Furthermore, no evidence exists to suggest that the rulers of medieval Germany promoted this eastward colonization. Alone on a priori grounds they are unlikely to have done so, since no monarch would wish to lose taxpaying subjects. From the eastern perspective, the immigration of German peasants or craftsmen was certainly not viewed as a prelude or adjunct to imperialist expansion, since otherwise the rulers of the target countries would have tried to prevent it. In actuality the monarchs of East Central Europe facilitated the colonization by granting exceptional privileges to the new settlers, including the so-called German law.

This eastward migration involved members of every social class—clerics, knights, tradesmen, artisans, and peasants. While Germans were decidedly in the majority, some of the newcomers hailed from even farther afield—Flanders, France, or Italy. Educated churchmen were welcomed for their knowledge of Latin and employed as clerical staff for the royal courts. Knights were useful for their military expertise, and often won advancement through the personal favor of native princes or lords. As foreigners lacking family connections in a strange land, immigrants were highly dependent on their patrons and likely to be loyal. Inasmuch as town development was more advanced in Western than in Eastern Europe, the skills of foreign merchants and artisans were greatly valued. Clergy from the West found plenty of work to do in the churches and monasteries of Poland, Bohemia, and Hungary, where in the 11th and 12th centuries Christianity was a new faith. Native priests and monks were few in number and entirely insufficient for Christianizing an entire country. Employment of foreign priests was the only realistic option; and geographical proximity ensured that a high proportion of these men would be Germans. Nonetheless, particularly in the early years of the eastward movement, the majority of German immigrants were simple peasants whose task was to turn untilled and uninhabited territory into farmland.

The Church became an important instrument of Germanization in the Catholic sector of East Central Europe. German clerics were especially prominent in Bohemia, which was surrounded on three sides by German-speaking lands and belonged to the German Empire. Until the 14th century, Bohemia did not even constitute a separate church province, but formed part of the metropolitanate of Mainz. Even in the 15th century many of the Bohemian upper clergy—canons, archdeacons, abbots, and priors as well as bishops—were German-born and spoke German as their native language. The Czechs' resentment at this situation ultimately played an important part in provoking the Hussite upheavals. Some monastic orders in Poland were exclusively German and excluded Poles altogether. The great Catholic brotherhoods of Cistercians, Dominicans, and Franciscans all maintained headquarters in Western Europe and sent foreigners of many nationalities into their monasteries in the East. The Latin civilization which these monks carried with them naturally became known primarily in its German form.

Prussia remained unique as the only complete state in East Central Europe to be ruled by Germans. Until the Teutonic Knights began conquering it in 1230, this was a wild and pagan land lying on the northeastern frontier of European civilization. The native Prussians spoke a Baltic language closely related to Lithuanian. (Only at a much later date did "Prussian" refer to a German, not a Baltic, nationality.) In the heyday of the Knights' activities in Prussia—the 13th and 14th centuries—its flourishing towns attracted numerous German immigrants. As Christianity gradually took hold among the Baltic Prussians, they eventually became absorbed by either the Germans or the Poles. Nonetheless, much of the rural population retained its Baltic (i.e., "Old Prussian") character down to the end of the Middle Ages. On the other hand, the Teutonic Order consisted largely of ethnic Germans and managed its lands in essentially colonial fashion—that is, as foreigners dominating a native population. At one time scholars believed that the Order excluded non-Germans on principle, although subsequent research has indicated otherwise. During the 14th century, certain nobles of Baltic stock joined the organization and occasionally even rose to the rank of commander, although their small numbers scarcely altered its overwhelmingly German character. Immigrant German knights formed the Order's main component. For reasons of geographical proximity, most came from northern Germany; and the usual route to Prussia ran overland. The Teutonic Order was a prime source of employment for the impoverished petty nobility of the German Empire.

The Poles resented the German domination of Prussia—a land which many regarded as rightfully part of Poland. Military clashes with the Teutonic Knights led Poles to think of Germans as the national enemy; and the pope's almost invariable support of the Knights in any conflict became a standing grievance. This accumulated ill-feeling came into the open after the Polish victory over the Teutonic Knights at the battle of Tannenberg in 1410. The Peace of Toruń (Thorn), signed the following year, stipulated that henceforth up to half the members of the Teutonic Order must be Polish subjects. Actually this rule never went into practice, since the Knights strongly resisted it; but Polish feelings on the subject were unmistakable. While the nationalists of a later age interpreted Tannenberg as a conflict between Germans and Slavs, no one at the time viewed it in that light. The troops which fought for the Teutonic Order were by no means exclusively German; and the Polish-led force was similarly multi-ethnic. The conflict concerned political power, not nationality rights.

The prominence of the German element in many towns of East Central Europe sometimes led to conflicts along ethnic lines. In all self-governing towns voting was subject to a property qualification, which meant that the German element—even if a numerical minority—often monopolized the chief positions in the local administration and courts. Occasionally the natives of the country rebelled against this situation. The loss of Buda's staple rights, for example, led to a decrease in the German population and an increase in Hungarian assertiveness. In 1439 major riots broke out between German and Hungarian factions, in which the properties of German merchants and even the royal treasury were looted. The ethnic tension eventually produced an agreement that half the members of the Buda town council must be Hungarians. At Cluj in Transylvania, a rule was established in 1458 that municipal offices must be shared equally between Germans and Hungarians. Where the Germans monopolized membership in the craft guilds, groups of indigenous artisans sometimes organized parallel guilds, especially after the virtual cessation of foreign immigration in the 14th century had caused the proportion of Germans to decline. The Germans themselves occasionally enforced restrictive measures: thus at Olomouc in Moravia as late as 1415 a local law excluded non-Germans from membership on the town council. In many towns of Prussia, only Germans were permitted either to become citizens, assume town office, or engage in trade, artisanry, crafts, or hotelkeeping. Where Germans comprised the ruling class, non-Germans who desired full citizen rights were obliged to adopt German language and culture.

Massive as it was, the eastward migration of Germans in the Middle Ages failed to produce long-term ethnic changes in East Central Europe. Except in Prussia, where the rule of the Teutonic Order caused the native upper class to become Germanized, foreign knights usually did not preserve their German identity for long. Rather they aspired to join the local nobility and soon were absorbed by it. Urban migrants kept their German ethnic character longer than knights did because they retained commercial links with the homeland. Merchants utilized family and business connections in their native region to encourage new immigration. However, if no Germanic rural hinterland existed from which the towns could draw new residents, a decline in foreign immigration inevitably caused a reduction in the proportion of Germans. The chief reason for this was that medieval towns were notorious breeding grounds of disease, dependent upon a steady influx of new settlers to maintain a constant population. Moreover, the Black Death (bubonic plague) which struck Western Europe in 1347–50 opened up many opportunities for the survivors in their home districts. The result was that immigration into East Central Europe virtually ceased after 1350. Many long-established German families in Poland, Hungary, or Bohemia gradually adopted the language and customs of the surrounding region, eventually becoming indistinguishable from the natives.

Some members of the German upper class in the towns managed to join the local nobility, a move which likewise involved the loss of their German identity. German townsmen of lesser rank were overwhelmed by the flow of peasants from the surrounding countryside. De-Germanization was well under way in Bohemia in the 15th century even before any fears of Hussite violence prompted the out-migration of many German inhabitants. In Poland the proportion of Germans declined earlier in the western than in the eastern regions, where Germans had settled at a later date; the process of Polonization took time. Major trading centers like Cracow and Lvov retained German municipal governments until the 16th century, owing to their extensive international connections. The principal towns of Prussia, especially Gdańsk, kept their German character longest because they were centers of the international wheat trade in the Baltic Sea. (The large German element in many towns of East Central Europe in the 19th and 20th centuries reflects a much later immigration.)

A permanent change in the ethnic character of a region from Slavic to German, such as had occurred already in Brandenburg or Mecklenburg by the 12th century, came about in the 13th century solely in regions of peasant immigration. This meant chiefly the western borderlands of Bohemia and Poland, geographically closest to areas which were already overwhelmingly German in population. The influx of German peasant colonists into western Bohemia created solidly German districts which maintained that character well into the 20th century (thus bequeathing a Sudetenland problem to the new state of Czechoslovakia). Silesia in the 14th century became ethnically and culturally German to a great extent. Peasants much more than townsmen or knights were likely to resist changing their ethnic affiliation. Illiterate and relatively isolated in their villages, they tended to be conservative in life-style. Only in regions of very mixed population, for example in parts of Bohemia in the 14th century, did peasant settlers sometimes adopt the local nationality through intermarriage and participation in the life of the older villages. Once again Prussia was a special case, since there the Old Prussian (i.e., Baltic) peasantry gradually did adopt the German language and culture.

Concurrently with the German colonization in East Central Europe came an influx of Jews. Customs and (often) language as well as religion distinguished them from Christians, making them an ethnic group with a particularly marked identity. Their presence in the area was not new. Jews had lived in the Balkan Peninsula in the time of the Roman Empire and continued to do so in the early Balkan states. Communities of Greek-speaking Jews flourished in the chief towns of Bulgaria in the 10th century. At first they engaged chiefly in barter and handicraft production, but afterward took over much of the international trade of the region, replacing the Tatars who previously had dominated that activity. Ashkenazi (i.e., German-speaking) Jews arrived in Bohemia, Poland, Hungary, and Dalmatia in the 10th century. However, the principal wave of Jewish eastward immigration began in 1096 in connection with the First Crusade, which had aroused Christian fanaticism and outbursts of murderous sectarian zeal. Irregular bands of armed men en route to the Holy Land were susceptible to the suggestion that they deal first with "infidels" closer to home. Many Jews abandoned Germany in response to this new danger. The 12th century witnessed a large Jewish eastward movement, especially into Poland, an area the Crusaders did not touch. At the time of the Mongol attack on Poland and Hungary in 1241, fearful mobs in Bohemia often threatened the Jews, prompting another exodus. Then in 1347–50 when the Black Death struck Western Europe, rumors began to circulate that Jews had caused the disease by poisoning the wells. This canard provoked large-scale massacres which set off still another surge of Jewish eastward immigration.

The history of the Jews throughout all of medieval Europe reflects a periodic alternation between tolerance and persecution. Their adherence to a non-Christian religion made them natural victims in the medieval age, which was utterly dominated ideologically by religious modes of thought and feeling. The Christian majority found Jews highly suspect. Whether the established Church was Catholic or Orthodox, priests and monks generally stood in the forefront of efforts to discriminate against these outsiders. Clerics regarded them as contumacious for their failure to accept Jesus as Savior. Church synods prescribed social barriers between them and the Christian population. Popular preachers sought to strengthen Christian self-awareness by engaging in anti-Semitic tirades. Moreover, the Roman Church claimed a theoretical supremacy over the Jews as part of its asserted right to deal with all matters impinging upon religion. Papal bulls defined the Jews' status as "perpetual servitude"—allegedly the penalty for their role in Jesus' crucifixion. The Church thus gave its blessing to social discrimination and legal restrictions upon Jews. Particularly active in inciting anti-Semitic feeling were the mendicant friars, who proclaimed that Jews represented a danger to Christianity and ought to be segregated from Christian society. The well-known friar John of Capistrano, who traveled through Bohemia and Poland on a preaching tour in the 1450s, urged violent action against the Jews. In Cracow in 1452 only the direct intervention of King Casimir IV prevented him from arousing a pogrom.

An additional component in Christian-Jewish hostility was commercial competition. Unlike the vast majority of medieval Christians, the Jews were largely town dwellers, who at an early date had developed many of the skills essential to urban life. Though Jews might be disliked, their competence in trade and finance proved highly useful to the new towns and the rising monarchies of medieval Europe. On the other hand, once Christians had begun to invade these fields, the Jews could easily be thrust aside without serious damage to the wider community. Then the preexisting hostility against them bore fruit in persecutions and expulsions. At such times many Jews moved eastward into Poland, Bohemia, or Hungary, where town life was relatively undeveloped and their skills were more needed. However, at the same period a very different atmosphere prevailed in the Byzantine Empire. Urban communities had existed there since the classical age of Greece, while expertise in business, trade, and moneylending was widely disseminated among Christians. At Byzantium the Jews never aroused the type of resentment which elsewhere was evoked by their supposed wealth and near-monopoly of many occupations. From the 7th through the 11th century, Jews handled most of the Byzantine trade with Europe, where they had many useful connections. Only after that time did they turn primarily to moneylending. No large-scale massacres of Jews are known ever to have occurred in the Byzantine Empire, although various forms of discrimination persisted. Byzantine legal codes uniformly denied the Jews entrance into the government and army and forbade them to hold public office. These provisions seem to have been strictly observed, since extant documents reveal no names of Jewish officials in the empire—not even in the 11th and 12th centuries, when public offices were frequently sold to the highest bidder.

Everywhere in medieval Europe the Jews were treated as a special class, outcasts from Christian society and subject to laws applying to themselves alone. Admittedly, separate status was not prejudicial per se. The notion of a uniform law applicable to all inhabitants of a country is a modern idea quite alien to the medieval mind, which regarded the hierarchical order of society as part of God's plan for the universe. Continuing the tradition established earlier by the Roman and Byzantine empires, Jewish communities in the towns of East Central Europe functioned as legally recognized, autonomous entities. Jews were excluded from participation in the regular municipal governments, but at the same time were exempted from the competence of municipal courts. They stood under the monarch's direct protection; and only a designated royal official or Jewish judge was entitled to judge them. The Jews turned their districts into enclaves resembling the prevailing urban model, with the rabbi serving as chief. They elected elders and settled their own internal conflicts unless non-Jews were involved, in which case the matter was referred to the appropriate royal official. The Jewish quarter of a town maintained its own administration, laws, hospitals, and guilds. In Poland the rabbis imitated the example of the nobility by meeting in district, provincial, or even national assemblies, where they discussed religious matters and the apportionment of taxes.

Nonetheless Jews occupied the lowest rung on the social ladder, ranking only slightly above serfs. A number of legal restrictions applied to them, varying from place to place. Typical was a prohibition against carrying weapons, which rendered Jews largely defenseless against the occasional violent attacks upon their persons and property. In towns Jews were excluded from the craft guilds and forbidden to employ Christian workmen. The sole occupation always open to them was usury—the lending of money at interest—which the Church forbade Christians to practice. Thus Jews often took up this trade and accordingly were despised for it. Often they were assessed a special "Jewish tax," which was actually protection money; and sometimes they suffered arbitrary confiscation of property. Whatever favor they enjoyed was viewed as a privilege, not a right, and could be withdrawn without notice at any time. Certain rulers found it advantageous to grant privileges to Jews because of the valuable role they played in commerce and finance. The Polish monarchs, for example, sometimes served as mediators in disputes between Christians and Jews and generally sought to protect the Jews from violence. Indeed, rulers tended to regard Jews as a valuable resource, a source of tax money and loans, and sought to monopolize their services. For this reason the Bohemian kings in the 14th century carefully restricted the number of Jews which particular towns or nobles were permitted to acquire. Other sovereigns, more susceptible to ecclesiastical pressures, turned a blind eye to anti-Semitic violence and acceded to the demands of Christian clerics that the Jews be banished.

Medieval Bulgaria furnished a refuge for Jews under both the First and the Second Empire. During the "Golden Age" of Tsar Symeon (r. 893–927), Bulgaria offered the Jews prosperity and freedom from religious persecution at a time when the Byzantine emperors had issued orders for their forcible conversion. During the Second Empire, Tsar John Asen II (r. 1218–41) permitted Jews to reside in his country, trade freely, and form commercial partnerships with anyone they wished. Bulgaria witnessed even the anomaly of a Jewish-born queen named Sarah, who after her Christian baptism was known as Theodora and became the wife of Tsar John Alexander in 1335. She was reputedly a woman of exceptional intelligence and political shrewdness. However, the Church apparently viewed with alarm the tsar's intention to bequeath half of his realm to his son by her, John Šišman, thus partially disinheriting an elder son by a prior marriage. Precisely at this juncture, in 1355 and 1360, a Holy Synod met at the Bulgarian capital of Tirnovo and passed decrees condemning both Jews and heretics. However, these measures seem to have had little practical effect. Various Danubian towns in both Bulgaria and Walachia provided refuge to Jews who were expelled from Hungary and some parts of Germany at that time.

A new chapter opened in the history of Bulgarian Jewry with the edict of 1492 by which the Spanish sovereigns Ferdinand and Isabella expelled the Jews from all their lands. Spain for centuries had been a major center of Jewish civilization. Many of these Sephardic, or Spanish-speaking, Jewish refugees found new homes in Bulgaria, which had meanwhile become part of the Ottoman Empire. They arrived in sufficient numbers to overwhelm the Ashkenazi and Greek Jews already present, with the result that most Bulgarian Jews eventually became speakers of Ladino, a variant of medieval Spanish. They formed a uniform, well-organized community and maintained a high level of culture quite different in character from that of their adopted country. Indeed, the position of the Jews was decidedly more favorable in the Ottoman Empire than in Christian Europe. Unlike Christians, Jews could not be suspected of sympathizing with the sultan's European enemies. The influx from Spain was so large that Sephardim came to outnumber all other Jews in the Ottoman realm. However, even before the Spanish expulsion of 1492 the news had spread that Jews were welcome in the sultan's domains. Jewish doctors from the medical school of Salamanca were very much in demand. Sultan Murad II (r. 1421–51) employed Jews as his personal physicians and gave other Jews important positions at court. Sultan Bayezid II (r. 1481–1512) was known to regard Jews with special favor. In the cities of the Ottoman Empire many Jews worked as merchants and artisans, belonged to the guilds, and engaged in long-distance trade. Others served as interpreters. The largest single community of Jews in all Europe could be found at Istanbul.

Foreigners in general were often the object of suspicion and hatred, regardless of their religious allegiance. Occasionally such sentiments find expression in historical records. The Bohemian chronicler Cosmas of Prague, for example (d. 1125), was an outspoken opponent of Germans, whom he accused of arrogance and contempt for the Slavs. His polemics apparently reflected the attitude of the native Czech clergy, which looked upon Germans as competitors for positions in the Church. Even more xenophobic is the anonymous Czech chronicle attributed to a certain Dalimil and written in about 1310. Betraying an intense nationalism unusual in the medieval age, the author was a fervent adherent of old Czech customs and full of hatred for Germans. He judged past Bohemian sovereigns largely on the basis of this single factor—very simply, those who showed favor to Germans were evil monarchs. Strongly critical of foreign knights and foreign influences in general, he sharply opposed granting any privileges to foreigners. Surprisingly for so early a writer, Dalimil advocated an independent Czech state with its own language. His polemics have an astonishingly modern sound.

The major chroniclers in medieval Poland similarly took an antiforeign stance. One of them was Gallus Anonymous, a monk of presumably French extraction who worked in the ducal chancellery in the early 12th century. Although a foreigner himself, Gallus evidently had absorbed the prejudices of the Polish court—namely, hatred of Czechs, scorn for the Rus, and hostility toward Germans. A similarly nationalistic tendency appears in the work of Vincent Kadłubek (d. 1223), a native Pole and bishop of Cracow, who sought to enhance Poland's prestige by embellishing its history. Kadłubek disliked Germans in particular and criticized Polish princes who took foreign wives. However, the most distinguished of the medieval Polish chroniclers, John Długosz, worried far more about Czechs than about Germans. His dislike for Czechs is doubtless partly attributable to his official position at the court of the bishop of Cracow in the 15th century, when the Hussite heresy was spreading from Bohemia. Other antiforeign sentiment in Poland was clearly related to military threats from abroad. Efforts of the German Empire in the 12th century to reduce Poland to vassalage, followed by bitter conflicts with the Teutonic Knights in the 13th and 14th centuries, made many Poles feel that Germans were their principal enemies. Czechs were similarly unpopular, although usually perceived as less dangerous. To be sure, the Bohemian King Wenceslas II overran most of Poland, which he governed briefly (1300–1305); and his successor, John of Luxemburg, definitively incorporated Polish Silesia into Bohemia. Nonetheless, while Poles often disliked Czechs, they generally felt an even stronger aversion for Germans.

The many high officials of foreign origin at royal courts in medieval East Central Europe provoked considerable hostility among the native nobility. In part this was due to competition for position and favor. The Polish nobility strongly resented the foreigners in the entourage of King Louis of Hungary, who reigned in Poland after the death of his uncle, Casimir the Great (i.e., 1370–82). Partly for this reason, when he died they declined to continue the union between the two countries. Sigismund of Bohemia, elected co-ruler of Hungary in 1387 after his marriage to Louis's daughter Maria, was required to promise that he would not give any offices in the Church to non-Hungarians. When this same Sigismund inherited the Bohemian throne in 1419, the Hussite party included among their conditions for accepting him as king that: (1) no foreigners would be appointed to any office for which qualified Czechs were available; (2) judicial proceedings would henceforth be conducted in the Czech language; and (3) Czechs would have the "first voice" throughout the realm. Such promises notwithstanding, the temptation for a monarch to appoint foreigners to high office was often overwhelming. Aliens by definition were more likely than natives to be loyal to the sovereign, since usually they were strangers without important local connections. Moreover, the monarch enjoyed a freedom of choice in making such appointments which did not apply with natives, who invariably had local political ties.

Despite all protests, many kings continued to employ significant numbers of foreigners in high office as well as in more modest positions. The Germans at the courts of various appanage princes in 13th-century Poland often felt no need to learn the Polish language, since they found so many of their German compatriots already in residence. Similarly within the Church the prominence of foreigners caused resentment. Many of the lower clergy in Poland were ethnic Germans who held benefices, carried out parish duties, and conducted schools. Not all of them took the trouble to learn Polish. A letter sent to Rome by a synod of the Polish Church held at Łęczyca in 1285 expressed the unhappiness of the native Poles at this situation and blamed the papacy for it. This same synod approved a statute ordering the clergy to pray for the Polish Church, monarch, and homeland and to sing songs honoring Poland's patron saint. Another paragraph stated that only persons fluent in the Polish language should be allowed to teach boys. Finally, the synod asked the bishops to take punitive measures against monastic orders which excluded Poles from membership.

The extensive immigration of foreign peasants and townsmen into East Central Europe in the 12th and 13th centuries might well have created ethnic tensions. Yet extant documents bear witness to few local confrontations. In Poland no records survive of any important conflicts between German settlers and natives. No doubt this was partially due to physical isolation, since immigrant peasants settled largely on uninhabited lands rather than in established villages. In towns the authorities tried to separate newcomers from the local population by treating them as a special group. The kings of Bohemia, Poland, and Hungary all sought to attract foreign immigrants by allowing them a privileged legal status (i.e., German law or its equivalent). Predictably, this favoritism aroused jealousy among the natives. However, the usual result was not to deprive foreigners of their privileges but rather to apply German law more widely, even to communities containing few actual Germans. Hungary contained so many different nationalities that only those persons who themselves had immigrated from abroad were considered real foreigners. Long-established residents of the country whose native language was not Hungarian did not count as foreign.

Most medieval inhabitants of East Central Europe regarded religion, not nationality, as the primary characteristic of any group. Language existed as either a barrier or a means of communication; but nationality as defined chiefly by language had yet to become a major focus of loyalty. Bohemia in the 15th century was a partial exception to this rule, since the Hussite revolt both drew upon and contributed to a growing sense of Czech identity. This degree of national feeling, while still medieval in its powerful religious substrate, remained highly unusual for that era. Its development was enhanced by the increasing economic importance of the Bohemian towns, especially Prague, where Czechs and Germans lived in close proximity. On the other hand, the Czech-speaking nobles felt no particular animus against Germans, who did not threaten their position: no German nobility of any importance existed as yet in Bohemia. In the Bohemian villages very little antagonism seems to have existed between Czechs and Germans prior to the Hussite period.

Czech national consciousness was clearly on the upswing in the towns of Bohemia in the 15th century. As Czech speakers became proportionately more numerous in the urban population, they increasingly resented the Germans' political and economic predominance. Germans tended on the whole to be more affluent than their Czech fellow townsmen and played the leading role in the more important guilds and in town government. The Czech middle classes began to demand representation on the municipal councils. As early as 1356, Czechs gained a majority on the council in Prague New Town, although Germans remained dominant until the first years of the 15th century in Old Town, where Czechs comprised some two-thirds of the population. In response to Czech protests, King Wenceslas IV decreed in 1412 that at least half the members of the council in Prague Old Town must be Czechs. This order aroused vehement resistance among the Germans, leading even to bloodshed.

Literature in the Czech language also contributed to the growing Czech national feeling. Originally oral in nature, it assumed written form with ever-greater frequency in the 14th century. Toward the end of the century Czech began to replace Latin in official Bohemian documents. Voices were raised to demand that all officeholders in Bohemia must be fluent in Czech. The Hussite movement for religious reform soon assumed a Czech cast, in part because it criticized the existing church hierarchy and because so many of the leading prelates in Bohemia were Germans. Reformers founded the Bethlehem Chapel in Prague in the 1390s as a place for preaching exclusively in the Czech tongue. John of Jesenic, a legal scholar, argued that each nation should be supreme in its own land because the dominance of foreigners over natives was unnatural. John Hus and his followers promoted the use of Czech and the rights of Czech speakers within Bohemia. Hus's colleague and fellow reformer Jerome of Prague was a passionate Czech patriot who interpreted the accusations of heresy hurled at the Hussites as insults to the Czech nation. According to Jerome, "no pure Czech can be a heretic." The news that the Council of Constance had burned Hus and Jerome at the stake was received in Bohemia as an affront to the Czech nation.

As it gradually became clear that the majority of Germans in Bohemia would not support the Hussite reform, national antagonisms intensified. The control by Germans of three of the four so-called nations at the university in Prague drew increasing criticism from the growing number of Czech degree holders, who persuaded King Wenceslas to change the rules. The king complied in 1409 with the decree of Kutná Hora, whereby the Bohemian nation received three votes against just one for the three foreign nations taken together. The response was a large-scale exodus of German teachers and students from the university. In 1419 the Bohemian Diet decreed that no foreigners in Bohemia could receive either spiritual or temporal offices, and that no Germans could hold offices in the towns if Czechs were able to fill them. All court indictments and sentences must be presented in Czech (previously the king's affairs had been handled either in German or in Latin). Czechs were to have the "foremost voice" in the kingdom. When the need for defense against foreign invasion became evident, Hussite propaganda emphasized the Czechs' determination to prevail against all enemies. Then in the 1450s and 1460s the hostility of Catholic Europe toward "heretic Bohemia" forced the Czechs into greater isolation. As a consequence their expressions of intolerance and hatred of foreigners became more frequent.

Despite its strongly Czech character, Hussitism remained in essence a religious movement rather than a nationalist one. John Hus had declared explicitly that he preferred a good German to a wicked Czech, even if the latter was a blood relative. Warning his followers not to set the wrongs of Bohemia above "God's cause," he placed the aims of faith above those of the Czech nation. The widespread popular demand that Czech, "the language of the common people," be made equal to Latin in church services arose less from nationalist sentiment than from the desire of simple believers for closeness to God with a minimum of priestly intervention. Prior to the wars of 1421–24 the Hussites had thought of themselves as propounding a universalist message; and some of the Bohemian Germans had supported them. Nationality was not the determining element in the Hussites' attitude toward Germans, even after the German emperor proclaimed a crusade against Bohemia and led German and Hungarian troops into the country. The decisive factor was a person's attitude to the "cup" or "chalice"—the symbol of the Hussites' belief in communion for lay believers in both bread and wine.

Nonetheless, the Hussite revolution greatly promoted the polarization of Bohemian society along national lines. Adherents of the chalice successfully resisted the Catholic-supported German and Hungarian invasions and rejected the pope's imprecations. The Germans of Bohemia were quick to identify the reform movement with Czech speakers, which it largely was in practice, although in theory it was simply Christian. Hussite manifestos after 1419 refer frequently to "the Czech tongue" (český jazyk), never to a Bohemian "nation," which would have meant something quite different. This indicates that in 15th-century Bohemia the word jazyk had come to mean "nation" in the modern sense, with language understood as the principal component of national identity. The specific circumstances of the Hussite revolt contributed to this view of the importance of language. In Bohemia, unlike most countries at that period, the monarch could not embody the spirit of the nation or serve as a focus of national loyalty. King Sigismund was Czech by birth, a younger son of the great Charles I (Emperor Charles IV); but when he inherited the Bohemian throne in 1419 he already had enjoyed a long tenure as German emperor and king of Hungary. This in itself made it impossible for him to serve as a symbol of Bohemia. However, the crucial issues for the Hussites were his opposition to their religious reform, his role in the execution of John Hus at the Council of Constance, and his unwillingness to guarantee the free practice of religion in Bohemia. The Czech Hussites prevented Sigismund from occupying the Bohemian throne, while he in turn led foreign armies into the land of his birth. Since this king could not represent the Czech nationality—český jazyk—the Czechs sought other symbols of unity, the chief one being language itself. Another major symbol was the chalice, by which every Hussite publicly acknowledged his adherence to the religious reform.

Thus 15th-century Bohemia was the only kingdom in medieval East Central Europe where a movement resembling modern nationalism came into being. Nowhere else did national feeling assume a mass character, despite occasional outbreaks of antiforeign feeling in other times and places. The Bohemian exception arose from the unique set of circumstances which linked a typically medieval movement for religious reform to a specific language group. A tendency toward nationalist polarization, already present in the larger towns, received powerful reinforcement when the Hussite wars pitted Czechs against foreigners who invaded and ravaged their country. The inevitable effect was to strengthen the Czechs' awareness of themselves as a separate people with their own distinct language and characteristics. Bohemia's experience in the 15th century was a forerunner of that mass nationalism which in the 19th and 20th centuries would create enormous political and moral pressures on a European and worldwide scale.

CHAPTER 14

Languages and Literatures

*L*inguistic and cultural diversity is perhaps the most salient feature of East Central Europe in recent times. No major world language is native to the region; and for the most part its literature is accessible to outsiders only in translation. Aside from the Yugoslav successor states of Croatia, Bosnia-Hercegovina, and Serbia, which share the use of Serbo-Croatian (a single tongue with certain dialectical variants), all the other national states into which this territory is divided have different official languages. Until the early 1990s two of them had more than one: Czech and Slovak in Czechoslovakia, and Slovenian, Serbo-Croatian, and Macedonian in Yugoslavia. A significant political factor in several of these countries is the existence of important national minorities: particularly the Hungarians and Germans of Romania, the Albanians of Serbia, and the Turks of Bulgaria. Moreover, nationalism stresses the distinctiveness of each culture and tends to set boundaries between it and all others. National diversity within East Central Europe is not only an internal problem but also an obstacle to cultural communication with the rest of the world.

Until nearly the end of the Middle Ages, East Central Europe knew a countless variety of spoken dialects, but just three literary languages—Greek, Latin, and Old Slavic. The first two date back to the classical period of European history, when Greek served as lingua franca in the eastern half and Latin in the western half of the Roman Empire. The boundary between them ran from west to east through the Balkan Peninsula. This fault line, which can be traced with some precision from the language of inscriptions, milestones, and coin finds, ran roughly from the Adriatic coast of central Albania eastward through Macedonia south of Skopje, then followed the northern slopes of the Balkan (Stara Planina) range to end at Varna. Most of present-day Bulgaria and Macedonia lay in the Greek sphere, while the greater part of Serbia and all of Croatia belonged to Latin. However, a very different linguistic division came into existence after the Slavic invasions of the 5th to 7th centuries. Old Slavic replaced both Greek and Latin as the common speech of much of the Balkan Peninsula; and in the 9th century it acquired written form. Throughout the Middle Ages the Roman Church held fast to the Latin language, which also had deep roots in administrative and legal practice. Except for a while in Croatia, the Slavs who adhered to Latin Christianity adopted the Latin script when they began putting their vernacular speech into written form. However, Old Slavic soon replaced Greek among the Eastern Orthodox peoples—the Serbs, Bulgarians, and Vlachs (Romanians).

The Slavic invasions were sufficiently massive to cause major population transfers which drastically altered the linguistic pattern of the Balkans. The Slavs tended to settle on the plains and along the rivers, often forcing the old Roman or Romanized inhabitants into the hills. Thus in the Balkan interior many speakers of Latin or its derivatives gave up farming and transformed themselves into the migratory herders known throughout the area as "Vlachs." On the other hand, in the Adriatic towns and on the offshore islands Latin survived much longer. Coastal settlements were more defensible than villages in the interior, both because of their greater size and because the early Slavs possessed no ships capable of attacking from the sea. Furthermore, the invaders were interested in towns only for purposes of plunder and usually declined to live there. Precisely at what point Latin ceased to be a spoken language along the Dalmatian coast is difficult to say. At Dubrovnik it lasted into the 16th century (although definitely not in its classical Roman form), and on the island of Krk until the end of the 19th. At a much earlier date, however, the lower classes of the Dalmatian towns spoke Slavic exclusively. Latin was used only in public life and for business purposes, while Italian in its Venetian form also had wide currency.

Since the medieval Vlachs lived mostly in the hills where they had little contact with civilization, the Latin they spoke underwent comparatively minor changes over time. Thus Romanian, its modern descendant, retains many archaic Latin inflections and sound changes. At the same time, the wandering life of the Vlach herdsmen caused their speech to develop unusually few local peculiarities. In this respect it differs from Slavic, since the Slavic peasantry lived a more sedentary and isolated life. The late imperial Latin of the Balkan Vlachs was spoken over a very large territory, extending from Istria on the border of Italy into Thrace and Transylvania. The derivative form of this Latin known as Daco-Romanian, which was spoken north of the Balkan Mountains, subsequently gave rise to the modern Romanian language. Romanian today is the only major vernacular of East Central Europe which is structurally derived from Latin. In vocabulary, although not in grammatical structure, it owes a considerable debt to Slavic influences. Its morphology, syntax, and phonetics make it a true Romance language despite its numerous Slavic words and suffixes.

The Albanian language likewise betrays strong Latin influences, although structurally it does not belong to the Romance type. The oldest elements in Albanian are probably derived from the speech of the Illyrian tribes who lived in the southern Balkans prior to the age of classical Greece, although too few examples of this ancient Illyrian survive to permit certainty. Possibly Albanian also contains elements of Thracian, a related and equally archaic language spoken farther to the east. Certainly at one time the Albanian language was quite widely diffused throughout the Balkan interior, far more so than its present diminutive homeland would suggest. Its very extensive vocabulary of Latin derivatives indicates long contact with Latin speakers. The Latin in question was of the type employed along the Danube, whereas fewer Albanian words are derived from Dalmatian Latin and almost none from the Latin of the Italian peninsula. Slavic influences are much more recent, indicating that the basic grammatical structure of Albanian was well established prior to the Slavic invasions. Furthermore, all Balkan languages show affinities of a type almost never found elsewhere in Europe. To cite only two examples: Albanian, Bulgarian, and Romanian all place the article after the noun; Greek, south Albanian, Old Romanian, and (at times) Serbian form the future tense with the auxiliary verb "to want." Certain characteristics of these languages which have no counterparts elsewhere suggest possible influences from the speech of the ancient Thracians and Illyrians. Linguistic evidence thus indicates widespread contacts among the Balkan peoples at an early date.

A language which became dominant at a fairly late period in important areas of East Central Europe was German. The massive eastward colonization movement of the 12th and 13th centuries which had brought so many German-speaking peasants and townspeople into the region created large islands of German speech, especially in western Bohemia and western Poland. In Prussia, the conquest of the country by a strictly Germanic organization—the Teutonic Order of Knights—naturally also fostered the spread of various German dialects. The official language of the Order was a type of Middle German which all Germans of that period could comprehend; and under the Knights' protection, many German-speakers migrated into Prussia. However, the conquered native population of the country spoke the Baltic tongue known as Old Prussian, which belongs to the same family of languages as modern Lithuanian and Latvian. The Teutonic Order in its capacity as the government of Prussia conducted a conscious policy of Germanization, for example by forbidding Germans to speak Prussian to their servants. An important agent of this language policy was the Church, with its German-speaking hierarchy and missionaries. By the beginning of the 14th century the indigenous language had already disappeared from large areas of Prussia; and by the mid-16th century it had become virtually extinct. Nevertheless, even at this late date some parish churches found it necessary in their worship services to translate the sermons into Old Prussian; and natives were allowed to confess to a priest with the aid of an interpreter.

When the Slavic peoples entered East Central Europe in the 5th to 7th centuries, they spoke what was essentially a single language. Until about the year 1000 the differences among the various forms of Slavic speech were negligible, certainly too slight to inhibit mutual understanding to any significant degree.

The 9th-century translations made by the apostles Cyril and Methodius into the language now known as Old Slavic, Old Slavonic, Old Church Slavic, or occasionally Old Bulgarian were easily comprehensible to all the Slavic peoples. With certain modifications, this now-extinct language is still employed in the liturgy of the Orthodox Church in Slavic countries. Like any living tongue, Old Slavic underwent numerous modifications in the course of time; and the dispersion of the Slavs across a wide geographical area ensured that these changes would not be uniform. As early as the 10th century the texts in Old Slavic began to reflect these linguistic differences. By the 12th century new groups of consonants had entered some variants of the language, so that the speakers of one Slavic dialect could no longer easily understand the speakers of another.

Geographically the area dominated by Slavic-speaking peoples has remained remarkably constant ever since the 7th century, with two major exceptions. The Magyars who invaded Central Europe in the final years of the 9th century drove a wedge into the area of Slavic settlement. Geographic separation thus widened the developing linguistic gap between the Western and Southern Slavs. Then the Slavs who had penetrated westward as far as the Elbe River gradually became absorbed or pushed aside by the eastward migrations of Germanic peoples. Only the small, relatively isolated groups of Slavic speakers known as Wends, Sorbs, or Lusatians (virtually equivalent terms) live now in eastern Germany. Their survival as a distinct ethnic group was doubtless facilitated by the fact that Lusatia (today part of Saxony) belonged to Slavic Bohemia in the 14th to 17th centuries.

On the other hand, the 7th-century migration of Turkic-speaking Bulgars into the region now known as Bulgaria failed to alter its predominantly Slavic character. The Bulgar ruling class eventually abandoned its Turkic language and adopted Slavic so completely that no trace of Turkic speech patterns can be found in any Old Slavic texts. Nonetheless the Bulgars were able to preserve their native language and customs for about two hundred years. The 9th and 10th centuries marked an interval of bilingualism, after which the descendants of the original Bulgar conquerors gradually forgot their original Turkic vernacular and became entirely Slavic in speech. By the 12th century the proto-Bulgar language had utterly died out in the southeastern Balkans, so that "Bulgarian" henceforth denoted a purely Slavic tongue. Nothing of the sort happened in Hungary, where the descendants of the Megyeri—the leading tribe among the new immigrants to the land in the late 9th century—preserved the speech of their ancestors. Unlike the Bulgars, who had settled in a region liberally populated with Slavs, the invading Magyars occupied an area only sparsely inhabited by remnants of the Avars and Huns and by a scattered Slavic peasantry. Their language remained without serious competitors in the new Hungarian state, except perhaps for the Turkic dialects of other tribes in the confederation to which they belonged.

Unlike most European vernaculars, Hungarian (known to its native speakers as Magyar) does not belong to the Indo-European family of languages, but rather to the group which linguists call Finno-Ugric. A unique phenomenon in the heart of Europe, it has no close European relatives except Finnish. Structurally, Hungarian is quite different from the Slavic or Germanic languages: for example, it employs suffixes to express ideas for which the Indo-Europeans use prepositions or articles. Its rules concerning vowel harmony correspond to those of many Asiatic languages. (Thus Hungarian words may contain either the "high" vowels a, o, and u or the "low" vowels e, ö, and ü, but never a combination of the two, so that suffixes must change their vowels to agree with the word stem.) Except for occasional borrowed words, the vocabulary of Hungarian is likewise not derived from Indo-European roots. These dissimilarities tend to isolate the speakers of this language from all their European neighbors, who find Hungarian difficult to learn and rarely attempt to do so.

The Megyeri, or proto-Magyars, who invaded East Central Europe in the late 9th century spoke a Finno-Ugric tongue consisting of a mixture of elements acquired in the course of many wanderings in Russia and Ukraine. The earliest of their known forebears lived in the forests along the middle Volga, where probably in about 2000 B.C. they split into a western (Finnic) and an eastern (Ugrian) branch. Subsequent migrations brought the latter group into contact with the Turkic Onogurs, from whom their name in many European languages is derived (i.e., "Ungr-," "Ungar," "Hungarian"). Numerous word borrowings bear witness to the many-sided Turkic and Iranian influences on these Finno-Ugric speakers, who eventually became part of a multi-ethnic confederation loosely called Magyar after the name of its leading tribe. Indeed, many of the prominent personal and clan names found among the 9th- and 10th-century Hungarians are of Turkic origin, indicated that part of their leading class was of Turkic (Onogur) descent. However, the Finno-Ugric language of the Megyeri—enriched with many Turkic elements—ultimately prevailed in Hungary, and the Turkic tongue of the Onogurs died out.

Neither the Bulgars nor the Slavs possessed an alphabet of their own when they settled in East Central Europe. Nor did their primitive life-style really require one. Despite this deficiency, the Bulgars of the 8th and 9th century produced stone inscriptions in Greek letters, nearly a hundred of which have since been found in northeastern Bulgaria near the old capital of Pliska. Some employ the Turkic language of the original Bulgar conquerors; others contain Slavic terms; but all use the Greek alphabet. These inscriptions are essentially official in nature: chronicles of events, names of fortresses and battles, records of titles and buildings, military regulations, and peace treaties. Neither the use of Greek letters nor the custom of engraving in stone can be ascribed to Byzantine influences, since Greek was an international language in the Bulgars' earlier home along the Sea of Azov; and the inscriptions resemble Iranian models of the Sassanid period. Like the Bulgars, the Magyars originally learned to write during their residence in southern Ukraine. Their scribes at first used the Turkic alphabet, augmented by the needed vowels missing in Turkic. They carved these letters with knives onto wooden sticks, although apparently only for inscriptions, not for more ordinary purposes. Long after the Latin alphabet had come to prevail in Hungary, remnants of this ancient notched writing still survived in Transylvania. In some localities it could be found even as late as the 16th century among the Szeklers, a Magyar-speaking people who lived along the eastern frontier.

The first complete alphabet created specifically to express Slavic sounds is Glagolitic (so named from the Old Slavic verb for "to speak")—a script of somewhat uncertain provenance which never attained more than a limited diffusion. It has been held to resemble both Carolingian minuscule writing and a form of Greek cursive. Early forms of Glagolitic dating from the 8th century have been discovered in northeastern Italy and in the Salzburg diocese of Austria, where they probably were used in connection with missions to the local Slavs. Apparently these letters were adapted and refined in the 860s by the famous Greek scholar and apostle to the Slavs, Constantine (later canonized under his monastic name of Cyril), although this is not entirely certain. The Glagolitic alphabet demonstrates a sophisticated phonetic analysis of Slavic and includes at least one sign derived from Hebrew, a language well known to Saint Cyril, who had previously translated a Hebrew grammar. Glagolitic was called Cyrillic after its presumed inventor even as late as the 11th century, whereas the term Glagolitic apparently became current only in the 19th century.

At the end of the 9th century a simpler Slavic script appeared which was based on the Greek uncial, or capital letters. This is the alphabet now known as Cyrillic, in which all East Slavic languages are written, including Bulgarian, Serbian, and Russian. Since intermediate forms of this second alphabet are extant, no single person is likely to have invented it. Recent scholars have largely discarded the traditional view that Constantine-Cyril was its creator. Cyrillic probably developed in the First Bulgarian Empire, which became the earliest major center of Slavic literacy. Undoubtedly the Bulgars preferred an alphabet closer than Glagolitic was to Greek. They already used Greek for official documents and inscriptions, so that educated Bulgars were familiar with its script. The Bulgarian Diet (Sabor) of 893 which established Tsar Symeon on the throne proclaimed this simpler alphabet as the official one for both secular and religious purposes in Bulgaria. At the Bulgar capital of Preslav all Slavic texts previously written in Glagolitic were transcribed into Cyrillic. New translations used that script exclusively.

Cyrillic gradually drove out Glagolitic among all the Slavic peoples who adhered to the Eastern Orthodox Church. Literacy arrived in Kievan Rus in Cyrillic form. The Serbs adopted Cyrillic in the 12th century; and in the 13th century a cursive form of it came into use. The medieval Bulgarian and Serbian kings issued their official documents in Cyrillic. This same script was employed for medieval Ruthenian, the ancestor of modern Belarussian and Ukrainian, which was spoken in the Grand Duchy of Lithuania in the 15th and 16th centuries. In the areas of Croatia in closest proximity to the Orthodox lands a hybrid form of Cyrillic developed which began to replace Glagolitic. Containing elements from both the

Glagolitic and the Latin scripts, it is unintelligible to readers familiar only with standard Cyrillic. This so-called Croatian, or Bosnian, Cyrillic constituted the main alphabet used for official purposes in Bosnia, Hercegovina, and Montenegro from the 12th until the 14th century, when the Latin script gradually replaced it. The chancelleries of the Dalmatian towns, which used Latin letters for writing in their own Slavic vernacular, employed both forms of Cyrillic as needed for correspondence with foreign Slavic princes. Even in Walachia and Moldavia, where a Romance language was spoken, Old Slavic in Cyrillic letters remained the medium for diplomatic and religious purposes.

Despite Cyrillic's wide acceptance, Glagolitic died out only slowly, and in some places not at all. Many of the early manuscripts produced by Saint Clement's school at Ohrid in Macedonia (western Bulgaria) were written in Glagolitic, perhaps because Saint Cyril had been Clement's teacher. The two alphabets existed side by side in Macedonia and in Serbia until about the 14th century. Glagolitic survived longest among the Roman Catholic Croats, particularly in northern Dalmatia, the islands of the Quarnero Gulf, and Istria. There it acquired political significance, symbolizing the resistance of the Slavic-speaking lower clergy to the efforts of the Roman ecclesiastical hierarchy to impose a monopoly of Latin in church services. Croat folklore ascribed the invention of Glagolitic to a revered native son of Dalmatia, Saint Jerome, the 4th-century Church Father and translator of the authorized Latin Bible, the Vulgate. This erroneous attribution apparently originated in the 12th century with Croatian Glagolitic priests seeking to protect themselves from charges of heresy. In Dalmatia as well as in the Croatian hinterland, Glagolitic remained the preferred script until the 14th century for official documents written in Slavic. Afterward the Latin alphabet gradually came to prevail. Glagolitic survived only on the offshore islands of the Adriatic, which as Byzantine possessions were immune to papal pressure in favor of Latin. As a historical anachronism, Slavic liturgical books in the Glagolitic script continue to be used today in a few remote spots in Dalmatia.

Glagolitic lasted as an isolated phenomenon in a few other localities down to the end of the Middle Ages. In the 14th century King Charles I of Bohemia promoted its use. Wishing to emphasize the Slavic identity of the Czech people, he permitted a group of Croatian monks to occupy the Emmaus monastery near Prague. These monks celebrated Mass in Old Slavic and used Glagolitic in their writings. This monastery retained its Slavic character until the 17th century, but apparently had no imitators. In Poland likewise the Slavic liturgy found only limited application. In 1390 some monks from Emmaus settled in a cloister near Cracow; and in the town itself the Slavic rite was still celebrated in the Church of the Holy Cross as late as the 15th century. In 15th-century Croatia the homilies of the Czech religious reformer John Hus circulated in the Glagolitic script.

Old Slavic remained the language of the Orthodox Church long after the Slavs themselves had ceased to speak it. The original reason for Slavic translations of religious texts—namely, to enable ordinary worshippers to comprehend the meaning—had long since been forgotten. The Slavic liturgy had become traditional; and the Orthodox Church deeply venerated tradition. Even the Romanian Orthodox Church continued to use Old Slavic until the 18th century. Since this ecclesiastical language underwent few changes in the course of time, it became farther and farther removed from common speech. As a result, Old Slavic among the Slavs came to occupy a position similar to that of Latin among the speakers of Romance languages. Both had become incomprehensible to most believers, although late-classical Latin is an additional half-millennium farther removed from modern French, Spanish, or Italian than Old Slavic from the modern Slavic languages.

The earliest literature in Old Slavic consisted almost entirely of translations and reworkings of Greek texts. To some extent this was because the Balkan peoples had received their Christianity from Byzantium, which made their churches administratively subordinate to the patriarchate of Constantinople. Vastly more important was the overwhelming superiority of Byzantine civilization itself. Greek literature of the Byzantine period was erudite and sophisticated, even if no longer very original. It embodied the accumulated wisdom of many centuries, offering far greater riches than newly literate peoples could hope to assimilate for a long while. In any event, medieval people did not value originality, nor did they consider plagiarism improper. Quite the contrary: adherence to tradition and citations from ancient authorities rendered a writer's ideas more convincing. Imitation and borrowing without acknowledgment of sources were common practices. The Byzantines copied entire passages from the Bible, the Church Fathers, or earlier biographies of saints. Medieval writers treated the available fund of Christian literature as a common heritage upon which any Christian was free to draw, with or without (usually without) identifying his sources.

The earliest known apostles to the Slavs, Cyril and Methodius, initiated a massive project of translations from Greek into Slavic. Presumably they did not undertake this entire labor personally, but directed a group of bilingual translators. After some of Methodius's followers arrived as refugees in Bulgaria in 885, Tsar Boris and his successors supported a continuation of this work. In the late 9th and the 10th centuries the chief centers of Slavic translation in Europe were to be found at Preslav, the capital of Bulgaria, and at Ohrid in Macedonia, where the leading figures were Bishop Clement and his disciple Naum. Tsar Symeon (r. 893–927), himself a lover of Greek literature, was an enthusiastic patron of this literary activity. Indeed, several Byzantine literary works, or parts thereof, would have been lost forever had they not been preserved in Slavic recensions. The translations produced in Bulgaria were frequently recopied and spread abroad. After 1018, when Bulgaria was reabsorbed into the Byzantine Empire, the center of Slavic translation shifted to Serbia. Even so, the language of the early Old Slavic texts remained quite consistent, exhibiting only minor dialectical differences irrespective of the translator's country of origin.

Many translations of Greek texts into Old Slavic were religious in nature. They provided a liturgy for use in divine services, explained Christian doctrine, or commented upon Bible verses. Cyril and Methodius had set the example by rendering the Gospels, the Psalms, and the liturgical books from Greek into Slavic. Various of their disciples and successors translated the New Testament and most of the Old Testament, biographies of saints, and writings of the Fathers of the Church. Portions of the works of Greek Church Fathers like Saint John Chrysostom, Saint Basil, and Saint Gregory Nazianzen appeared in multiple versions. Also translated were fundamental Byzantine legal texts which were considered essential for the establishment of a Christian society.

The standard secular works of medieval European literature likewise found their way into Old Slavic. Among them were books of dreams, prophecies, and natural disasters; fables and wisdom literature; fantastic descriptions of birds, beasts, and reptiles; and pseudo histories like the tales of the Trojan War or the romance of Alexander the Great. A great favorite was George Hamartolos's historical chronicle, a naive account of major events since the beginning of the world which includes long theological discussions and laments concerning the alleged decline of Christian life since Jesus' time. Notably absent from the corpus of Old Slavic translations are the philosophical works or drama and poetry of classical Greece, except for religious poetry. Presumably a few educated Bulgarians of the 10th century, including Tsar Symeon himself, were capable of reading such works in the original. The translators, however, were usually not interested in high culture. Their objective was to produce works of edification and entertainment for the vast majority of Slavic speakers who were ignorant of Greek.

Some of these early translations into Old Slavic showed an astonishing literary sophistication. The earliest translators were generally learned monks thoroughly familiar with the Greek language and literature. In order to render properly the works of the Church Fathers, they were forced to develop an entirely new and complex philosophical terminology for Slavic. As a consequence many foreign words, usually of Greek origin, entered the Slavic language together with new Slavic terms specifically invented to express Greek concepts. The apostle Cyril even created Slavic equivalents for Greek stylistic devices. Frequently the Old Slavic translations became more elaborate than the original texts, either through the addition of epithets and proverbs not present in the originals or by the use of euphonic elements like alliteration. Inevitably the quality of the translations declined as the work was undertaken on a larger scale. The process became more mechanical; and quite frequently the translators misunderstood the original text.

Occasionally an original work was written in Old Slavic. Biographies of Slavic saints are the obvious examples, like the *Lives* of Saints Cyril and Methodius or the multiple accounts of the life and martyrdom of Saint Wenceslas of Bohemia. Cyril and Methodius may themselves have composed the Slavic poem with which they introduced their translation of the Gospels. However, most of the original

Old Slavic literature is of Bulgarian provenance. Clement of Ohrid produced many sermons for special occasions, either for instructional purposes or as praises to God. His compositions, largely derived from Byzantine originals, are written in a simple and easily comprehensible style. Another outstanding Old Slavic author was Bishop Constantine of Preslav, the first organizer of the Bulgarian Church. His *Didactic Gospel* includes an "Alphabet Prayer," the first known poem in Old Slavic which is not a translation. Each line begins with a different letter to form an acrostic of the alphabet as a whole. Even more directly concerned with the alphabet is another very early original work in Old Slavic, the short (85-line) poem entitled "On Letters" or "Apology," dating from the turn of the 9th–10th century. Its author, the Bulgarian monk Hrabr, argues in favor of the Slavic alphabet against certain unnamed critics (presumably Greek clerics serving in Bulgaria) who claimed that only the languages of the Bible and the Church Fathers (Hebrew, Greek, and Latin) were worthy to be used for religious purposes. Still another member of the Preslav literary school was John the Exarch, who produced an account of the creation of the world known as the *Šestodnev* ("Six Days"). This was a kind of encyclopedia of natural history, praising God for the perfection of His world and including polemics against pagan practices and heretical doctrines. Large portions of it contain word-for-word translations of Greek patristic treatises, although at certain points John also inserted his own comments. The oldest surviving original work of any length to be written in Slavic is a religious polemic—the tract attacking the Bogomils by the 10th-century Church elder Kozma. Consisting of a monologue interspersed with dramatic dialogues and prayers. Kozma's work is a major literary achievement.

Translations and original works in Old Slavic circulated also among the Vlachs. Geography had placed the Vlachs within the natural orbit of Slavic Christianity and given them Slavic speakers as their principal neighbors. Thus while the Vlachs' spoken vernacular was an offshoot of Latin, Old Slavic became their ecclesiastical and cultural language, employed for official documents and for the first original literary works by Vlach authors. The Orthodox Church in Walachia and Moldavia used an Old Slavic liturgy derived from Bulgarian sources. The dominance of this foreign tongue, both in religion and for all written communication, proved doubly disadvantageous to the Vlachs, since it offered neither the prestige of Greek and Latin nor the practical advantages of the vernacular. While Old Slavic remained comprehensible to all Slavic peoples for several centuries before it became archaic, the Vlachs from the beginning did not understand it. Until the 14th century no independent Romanian state existed which might have promoted the native tongue. By that time ecclesiastical practices had long since become ossified and hallowed by tradition. One fortunate, if unintended, consequence of this situation was that monasteries in Walachia and Moldavia preserved numerous Old Slavic writings which would otherwise have been lost. In the 15th century the Neamț monastery in Moldavia became famous for its production of exceptionally beautiful Slavic manuscripts.

Some early examples of literature in Old Slavic appeared also in the Catholic lands where Slavic was spoken, although the pressure of the Roman Church in favor of Latin caused them to have no successors. The oldest Old Slavic works from Bohemia, dating from the 10th and 11th centuries, are little more than copies which show very few local features. The only known center in Bohemia for the production of Old Slavic manuscripts was the Sázava monastery, founded in 1032. The liturgical text known as the *Prague Fragments*, written in Old Slavic though with pronounced Czech features, probably originated there. Sázava still used a Slavic liturgy as late as the 11th century—the only monastery in the Czech lands which is known to have done so. In Poland no Old Slavic manuscripts of any type have ever been discovered, although in some localities a Slavic liturgy apparently was in use until the 1030s. Pious legend attributed the famous old Polish hymn *Bogurodzica* ("Mother of God") to Saint Adalbert, who lived in the late 10th century. However, scholars assign it to the 13th or 14th century; and all surviving manuscripts of the poem are no older than the 15th.

The most important Old Slavic work originating in early Bohemia deals with the life of Wenceslas, the first Czech saint. In this case the miraculous elements usually found in medieval biographies of saints are absent, making it a valuable historical source. A Latin version of the Wenceslas legend, composed by Bishop Gumpold of Mantua about 975 but translated into Old Slavic, demonstrates that a Slavic literary tradition was alive in Bohemia at that time. The oldest known liturgical hymn in Old Slavic from Bohemia, *Hospodine, pomiluj ny* ("Lord, Have Mercy upon Us"), is essentially a translation from the Roman form of the church liturgy, although it includes original Slavic elements. This famous hymn, a mere seven lines in length, was sung on battlefields and in churches even as late as the 20th century. Whether it should be assigned to the 9th, 10th, or 11th century is uncertain, although the words are set to a very ancient tune and the text contains various archaic linguistic features. In any event, this is the last Old Slavic work known to have been produced in Bohemia. By 1100 the Slavic literary language had been pushed aside by Latin and German in that country.

In the Catholic lands of East Central Europe virtually all serious literature of the medieval period was written in Latin, although by the 15th century a few exceptions appear. One vernacular work is the *Chronicle of the Priest of Dioclea*, originally written in Slavic, although it survives only in a Latin translation made between 1149 and 1153. Whether the translator was also the author is not known. Dioclea (or Duklja) was a minor principality on the south coast of Dalmatia which included parts of Hercegovina, Montenegro, and Albania. This *Chronicle* is the oldest extant account of the history of its region, beginning with the Slavic invasions and ending with events of the author's own lifetime. Like many medieval works of its type, its historical reliability is open to serious question. The author accepts traditions and legends at face value and uses written sources without identifying them. However, the work has undoubted literary qualities. Its language is polemical and the style flowing, with many flights of fancy. An extended version, written in the Croatian Cyrillic script and known as the *Croatian Chronicle*, was produced shortly before the middle of the 14th century.

In Bohemia the first known Latin chronicle was probably written in the year 994 by a member of the reigning Přemyslid dynasty, the monk called Christian, who retold once again the popular and familiar story of the martyrdom of Saint Wenceslas, the country's patron saint (d. 929). However, the real founder of historical literature in Bohemia was Cosmas of Prague, whose *Chronica Bohemorum* (written about 1119–22) relates the entire history of Bohemia down to his own time. Cosmas is a generally reliable author who demonstrates a critical spirit unusual for his day. While beginning his chronicle in typical medieval fashion with the Tower of Babel, he concludes with material derived from actual documents, recollections of his contemporaries, and his own personal experiences. Employing an elegant Latin style which is greatly indebted to classical Roman models, he quotes extensively from Christian writers and makes frequent use of poetry and rhythmic sequences. Another major historical work of Bohemian provenance is the *Zbraslav Chronicle*, so named after the cloister where it originated, which covers events from 1253 to 1338. Its principal author, the German abbot Peter of Zittau, was likewise a master of Latin literary style. Bohemia's most eminent medieval monarch, Charles I (r. 1347–78), who as German emperor was Charles IV, never found a suitable chronicler for his reign, but compensated for this lack by writing his autobiography, the *Vita Caroli*. The collections of Latin *exempla*, or "examples," represent another type of literature from medieval Bohemia, very different from either the historical chronicles or the lives of saints. Quite secular in nature, these are didactic tales which often draw explicit morals, composed for the purpose of providing priests with suitable anecdotes for use in sermons. Collections of Bohemian *exempla* are extant from as early as the 14th century. Many of them have earlier parallels in other medieval European literatures.

Whether in Latin or in Old Slavic, the medieval historical chronicles and lives of saints share many of the same features. A single literary work might be written partly in poetry, partly in prose, containing elements of fantasy as well as reality. The chronicles deal only with significant figures, particularly ruling princes. Even the nobility remains in the background, while townsmen and peasants are usually ignored, unless mentioned in passing as members of an obviously inferior species. Medieval chronicles record only memorable events like great triumphs or defeats, battles and wars, works of piety, and deaths. The object was to glorify a sovereign and create loyalty to his dynasty. Almost identical phrases are applied to nearly all monarchs, who are praised for their military prowess, courage, righteousness, devotion to religion, and care for their land and people. Characteristics which might give them individuality, such as physical appearance or personality traits, are interpreted symbolically if mentioned at all. In contrast to the critical and skeptical tone of much modern historical writing, medieval chronicles admire monarchs and extol their deeds. The biographies of saints are in many respects similar. Like the chronicles, they were composed with a purpose, which in this case was religious edification. They too describe nothing trivial, but rather the saint's extraordinary feats of pious devotion, charity, and renunciation. A similar tone of admiration and awe for the subject marks both types of medieval literature. The fact that so many early saints belonged to ruling dynasties shows that no strict boundaries existed between the supposedly secular historical works and the lives of saints.

Although Bohemia was the first country in East Central Europe where a strong demand arose for the use of the vernacular in religion, even the most prominent advocates of the Czech language were slow to renounce Latin in their own writings. The famous 14th-century preacher John Milíč of Kroměříž, for example, delivered his sermons in both Czech and German, but composed them originally in Latin. Other Latinists among the Bohemian reformers were Matthew of Janov and John of Jesenic, who strongly encouraged religious education in Czech for the laity. A gradual transition to the vernacular for secular purposes occurred in the final two decades of the 14th century, when Czech began to be used in legal and administrative documents. Several surviving word-lists from the period show that a technical vocabulary in Czech was being developed. In the 15th century the Hussites' advocacy of Czech was one cause of their split with the Catholic establishment. Nonetheless, even good Hussites continued to use Latin, no doubt partly in hopes of reaching an international audience. Peter of Mladoňovic composed a vivid account in Latin of the trial and burning of John Hus at the Council of Constance in 1414. Lawrence of Březova, the principal chronicler of the Hussite movement, wrote a famous "learned poem" in Latin celebrating the Hussites' victory over a Catholic army at Domažlice in 1431. It consists of 1,760 verses in eight-syllable lines, including epic fragments, monologues, dialogues, and lyrics, all interspersed with numerous Bible quotations.

Medieval Poland produced several major historical chronicles in Latin. The earliest is that of Gallus Anonymous, a monk of presumably French extraction employed in the chancellery of Duke Boleslav III. Writing in about 1115, Gallus recounted the history of the Polish state up to his own time, giving particular attention to the epic deeds of the three early Polish dukes who were all named Boleslav. Gallus's chronicle is very valuable as a historical source and does not hesitate to make critical judgments. A literary as well as a historical work, it is written in a rhythmic prose which is often rhymed as well. The author clearly was a man of considerable erudition, familiar with both ancient and modern literature. From the century after him comes the much less valuable *Polish Chronicle* by Vincent Kadłubek, bishop of Cracow (d. 1223), which recounts the history of Poland from its beginnings until 1206. Kadłubek used historical material chiefly to draw moral lessons, which in his case meant obedience to the Church. His work is largely a recital of allegories and paradoxes, all recounted in rhetorical style with little effort to distinguish legend from fact. Unlike Gallus's more solid work, Kadłubek's *Chronicle* became very popular in Poland, and was even used in the universities as a textbook of ethics and rhetoric.

The outstanding Polish historical work of the 14th century is the chronicle attributed to Janko of Czarnków, a canon and archdeacon who ultimately became vice-chancellor of the realm under King Casimir the Great. It is an authentic diary covering events between 1333 and 1384, full of court rumors and personal comments, although marred by the author's prejudices and sympathies. More valuable still is the work of John Długosz (1415–80), the greatest of all Polish medieval chroniclers, whose *Annales* consist of twelve books covering the history of Poland up to the time of his death. A member of the court of the powerful Cardinal Oleśnicki, Długosz was a versatile diplomat often employed on missions abroad. Despite a strong theological bias in his explanations of events, he was nonetheless capable of critical evaluation of his sources; and his chronicle drew upon an unusual wealth of material. Another important 15th-century Polish author was Paul Włodkowic, rector of the university at Cracow, who composed two Latin treatises on political morality for the Council of Constance in 1415 and 1418. Włodkowic eloquently defended Poland's policy of military resistance to the Teutonic Knights, whom the Church protected. In particular, he condemned the Knights' use of force to convert the heathens of Prussia to Christianity.

In Hungary the first Latin authors were clerics of German or Italian extraction who arrived in the country shortly after its official acceptance of Christianity in the year 1000. Probably it was one of these who penned the famous *Injunctions* of King Stephen I to his son Emeric, enjoining the youth to wisdom and tolerance. Other Latin literature from 11th-century Hungary recounts the pious deeds of persons admired for advancing the cause of Christianity. The biographies of royal saints were obvious favorites. Various examples of this genre survive, dealing especially with King Stephen I, his son Emeric, and King Ladislas I, all 11th-century figures. The Mongol invasion and occupation of Hungary in 1241–42 inspired a noteworthy example of medieval Latin poetry, the "Lament" (*Planctus*) of an unknown cleric, who presented a devastating picture of these events. Hungary also produced a number of Latin historical chronicles which sought to enhance the fame of the ruling dynasty and its ancestors. Most of these were patched together from material taken from earlier works and recast to suit the interests of the reigning king or the faction currently in power.

The oldest extant Hungarian chronicle is the *Gesta Ungarorum* ("Deeds of the Hungarians"), written in the reign of King Béla III (r. 1172–96) by a Latin author known simply as Anonymous, or King Béla's Notary. However, it draws upon references suggesting that other similar texts had preceded it. The Notary writes more like a novelist than a historian, relating dramatic episodes which for the most part cannot be verified from other sources. Similarly noted for its considerable literary skill is the Latin chronicle of Simon Kézai, a work in rhythmic prose. Writing in about 1283, Kézai was the first author to assign a heroic past to the Hungarians by claiming that their ancestors were Attila's 5th-century Huns. This idea had earlier been floated by foreign writers seeking to denigrate the Magyars as barbarians; but by the 13th century the devastating raids of the Magyar horsemen in Western Europe several centuries before had been largely forgotten, and Attila could be presented as a great conqueror. Since Pannonia had been the center of the Hun realm, Kézai saw that a claim of Hun ancestry could serve as an argument to validate the Hungarians' right to their country by virtue of ancient possession. His work was perpetuated and brought up to date in a major chronicle of the 14th century known as the *Chronica Hungarorum*, which in 1473 became the first book to be printed in Hungary. Another version of the *Chronica* is the Hungarian *Illuminated Chronicle*, containing lavish decorations that make it a masterpiece of medieval miniature painting.

In the Catholic lands of East Central Europe the changeover from Latin to the vernacular began fairly late in the Middle Ages and took an amazingly long time to complete. Latin retained its status as an official language in Hungary, Croatia, and Poland even in the 19th century. It ceased to be spoken in the Hungarian Diet only in 1836, and in the Croatian Diet in 1847. Since Latin was by definition the vehicle of all serious discourse, the early compositions in the vernacular lacked scholarly prestige. Throughout Western Christendom Latin was the lingua franca of the universities, of all literature with any pretensions to seriousness, and of international communication. Vernacular literature was addressed chiefly to people of limited education, either as entertainment, as religious instruction, or for the expression of religious emotion. Furthermore, the early medieval vernaculars all lacked the sophistication necessary for expressing complex ideas. Finally, no acceptable standard of correctness for the many variants of a spoken language had yet been defined.

This dominance of Latin made it natural for the languages of common speech in Catholic Europe to adopt the Latin alphabet when they were put into writing, although some modifications were necessary. The Czechs in the 15th century developed a system of diacritical marks to distinguish between different sounds (or lengths of sounds) rendered by the same basic Latin letter, for example: ď, d, and đ; e and ě; n and ň; r and ř; u, ú and ů; y and ý. For Polish a standard alphabet was slower to develop. Since certain specifically Polish sounds had no exact counterparts in Latin, various authors invented their own systems of writing. A widely accepted Polish alphabet came into existence only in the 16th century, greatly aided by the printing press. The Hungarian alphabet developed from the method invented by early medieval scribes, who in composing their Latin texts wished to insert occasional Magyar words to indicate persons and places. The Poles, Hungarians, and Croatians, like the Czechs, solved the problem of adapting the Latin alphabet to their respective languages by using diacritical marks. On the other hand, when the Orthodox peoples of East Central Europe began to write in the vernacular, they retained the Cyrillic alphabet familiar from Old Slavic, again with some modifications. Even the essential unity of the Serbian and Croatian languages, whose differences are no more profound than those between British and American English, proved insufficient to breach this alphabetic line of demarcation. The distinction grew out of the language of religion, since the Serbs are Orthodox, the Croats Catholic. Modern Serbo-Croatian in its Serbian variant is written in Cyrillic letters, while Croatian uses Latin letters, although the two alphabets are entirely interchangeable. For the Romanian language the changeover to the Latin script was completed only in the 19th century, promoted by nationalists eager to emphasize links between modern Romanians and the ancient Roman Empire.

The dominance of Old Slavic as the literary language of the Balkan Slavs went unchallenged in the Middle Ages except in Croatia, where the Church continued to promote Latin. However, Croatian literature profited greatly from the decision of the Lateran Councils at Rome in the early 13th century to loosen the Church's ban on the Slavic liturgy. In 1248 and 1252 Pope Innocent IV specifically authorized the use of this liturgy, apparently in an effort to improve relations with the Eastern Church. However, he stipulated that all Old Slavic religious texts must conform to the wording of the Latin Vulgate, the Church's official Bible. (The Glagolitic liturgical books reproduced Saint Cyril's translation of the church service as used in Salonika in the 9th century, which included Greek elements and differed in certain respects from the Roman version.) The Roman Church's new willingness to tolerate a language other than Latin stimulated an outburst of literary activity among the Croats. The pope's decision generated a whole new series of translations into a contemporary form of Slavic, reflecting changes which the spoken language had undergone in the centuries since Old Slavic was originally put into writing. Secular Croatian literature now drew increasingly upon the vernacular as well. The *Vinodol Codex*, for example, written in 1288 in Glagolitic script in the contempary form of Croatian, is one of the oldest law codes in any Slavic language.

By contrast, the religious texts used in Serbia were modified only slightly prior to the 17th century. Old Slavic "in Serbian version" stayed very close to the language of the 9th- and 10th-century Slavic translations. It continued to employ the ancient vocabulary, although sometimes the spelling of words was altered to accord with current pronunciation. Beside this Serbian variant of Old Slavic a second type of written Serbian developed which stayed fairly close to the vernacular. This became the literary language of the Serbian Empire in the 13th and 14th centuries, although it was used mainly for letters, songs, and laws rather than for the more solemn works of religion. Serbia in those days was an important European state maintaining close contacts with the sophisticated milieu of neighboring Byzantium. Many Serbian monks received part of their education abroad, especially in the cloisters of Mount Athos in Greece, which was then the chief center of literary activity in the Orthodox world. By actively copying and translating Greek manuscripts, these monks created fine libraries for the monasteries of Serbia itself, containing both religious and secular works. Original literary compositions were produced as well.

The oldest known work of Serbian secular literature is the legend of Vladimir and Kosara, recorded in writing in the minor Serbian state of Duklja in the 11th century. Surviving only in excerpts and in translation, it is both a love story and a heroic song about the righteous Prince Vladimir, executed unjustly in 1016 in consequence of a struggle for the throne. Two major early Serbian works of history are the biographies of Stephen Nemanya, the founder of the Serbian royal dynasty, composed early in the 13th century by his two notable sons, Archbishop Sava I and King Stephen "the First-Crowned." Sava, who wrote before his father was canonized, describes his subject in secular terms as an admirable ruler and monk, while focusing in particular on Nemanya's two renunciations—his abdication of the throne and his death. This short biography of no more than one hundred pages ranks among the outstanding achievements in the Serbian language. The parallel account by King Stephen recounts primarily his subject's worldly activities. A sovereign himself, Stephen depicts his royal father chiefly in his role as a military leader and founder of a dynasty and state. Both these works were written in the Serbian form of Old Slavic. In the 14th century, Archbishop Danilo composed an extensive series of biographies of Serbian monarchs and archbishops, lauding his subjects for the religious zeal exemplified by their rich gifts to the monks and their support for monasteries and churches. Later in the 14th century appeared the brief genealogy of the Serbian sovereigns known as the *Rodoslov* as well as the very valuable *Serb Annals*, a composite product of various authors describing campaigns, earthquakes, and eclipses together with exact dates.

A literary revival occurred in Bulgaria in the late 14th century, the period known as the Silver Age of medieval Bulgarian literature. Its major patron was Tsar John Alexander (r. 1331–71), who encouraged original writing in Slavic as well as translations and the copying and illuminating of manuscripts. Compositions from this era are overwhelmingly religious and contemplative in nature, apparently affected by the ever-present Turkish danger. The literature of the Silver Age was strongly influenced also by the mystical religious movement known as Hesychasm, which encouraged silent contemplation as a means of attaining knowledge of God. However, it was the Hesychasts' views on language which made them a literary force. They regarded language not merely as a means of transmitting sacred truth, but as an actual component of that truth. Believing that the language of divine revelation was faultless, they held that humans had corrupted it by careless and inaccurate transmission. Therefore perfect language was a requirement of doctrinal orthodoxy.

The chief effect of Hesychasm upon literature came from its concern for the correctness of texts and the importance of using precise terminology. The central figure of this movement was the monk Evtimii (or Euthymius), who in 1375 became the last patriarch of the medieval Bulgarian Church. Evtimii was the author of several biographies of Bulgarian saints, including Saint John of Rila, as well as a treatise on the ascetic life. He also introduced a spelling reform which incorporated the changes that had occurred in spoken Bulgarian since the creation of the original Cyrillic alphabet. However, he was most important as the founder of the Tirnovo literary school, a group of dedicated monks whose principal activity was "correction of the books," referring to the Old Slavic liturgical books currently in use. Firmly believing that erroneous readings could lead to heresy, Evtimii and his associates compared the Old Slavic translations with their Greek originals in order to eliminate errors which had crept into them through frequent recopyings over the centuries. The Evtimiians sought to restore certain archaic features of Old Slavic and promoted a more ornate literary style.

Evtimii's work was cut short by the Ottoman conquest of Bulgaria, since after the fall of Tirnovo in 1393 he was deposed as patriarch and sent into exile. However, the basic unity of Old Slavic as the language of Eastern Orthodoxy made it possible for many Bulgarian monks to continue their activities abroad. The literary movement which Evtimii founded had a profound effect on other Orthodox lands. One of his disciples, the Bulgarian monk Cyprian, became archbishop of Kiev and subsequently Metropolitan of All Russia, using his position to acquire many Old Slavic manuscripts for the Russian monasteries. His zeal caused many old texts to be preserved which have survived nowhere else. Another influential member of this literary school was Cyprian's contemporary, Gregory Camblak, who served for a time as abbot of the important Dečani monastery in Serbia, later became active in Moldavia and Lithuania, and spent his last years as metropolitan of Kiev. An even more important Evtimiian was Constantine Kostenečki, also known as "the Philosopher," a major author who settled in Serbia after fleeing Bulgaria in 1410. Literary life in 15th-century Bulgaria was chiefly confined to monasteries in the western part of the country, the area farthest from the centers of Ottoman power. There the outstanding figure was Dimitri Kantakuzin, a monk devoted to Greek classical antiquity who collected many manuscripts. While residing in the famous Rila monastery in 1469 he wrote a biography of Saint John of Rila and a touching "Prayer to the Holy Virgin" imploring her aid in combating sins. The biography attempts to explain the reasons for the Christians' defeat by the Turks and includes speculations concerning the end of the world.

The influence of the Bulgarian refugees proved very significant for Serbian literary life. The similarity in spoken vernaculars as well as the monks' familiarity with Old Slavic allowed the Bulgarians freely to interact with their Serbian colleagues. While Bulgaria in the 15th century was an Ottoman province, Serbia retained a degree of internal autonomy until 1459 under the native rulers known as despots. This reprieve permitted a Slavic literature to flourish in Serbia until midcentury. One of its principal patrons was Despot Stephen Lazarević (r. 1389–1427), himself a Serbian poet as well as a loyal Ottoman vassal. Lazarević promoted literary studies and founded a school at the Resava monastery which continued the Evtimiian tradition. His successor as despot, George Branković (r. 1427–56), collected a large library of Slavic, Latin, and Greek manuscripts and made his capital of Smederevo on the Danube a center of Serbian culture.

The outstanding literary figures in Serbia in the early 15th century were the two immigrant monks from Bulgaria, Gregory Camblak and Constantine Kostenečki. Camblak produced religious homilies as well as a biography of the Serbian King Stephen Dečanski, so-called because he founded the Dečani monastery where Camblak served as abbot. A tragic figure in Serbian history, Stephen Dečanski was condemned by his own father, King Milutin, to be blinded. In his biography Camblak sought to explain why God permitted such evil, reaching the conclusion that He meant it as a test of faith. The tragedy itself he attributed to the gullibility of a woman, Milutin's wife, who turned father against son at the Devil's urging. (Camblak's fellow biographer, Archbishop Danilo, blamed the act on Dečanski's "disobedience" in plotting against his father.) Constantine Kostenečki wrote a biography of Despot Stephen Lazarević, the best surviving example of historical writing from medieval Serbia despite its ornate, artificial style and numerous Hellenisms. Kostenečki is also noted for his essay *On Letters*, a work in the Hesychast tradition which contended that Slavic literature should faithfully imitate Greek models and that incorrect language is dangerous because of its potential for producing misunderstandings and heresies. Since the true divine language is unchangeable, local linguistic variants are impermissible. According to Kostenečki, the task of literary scholars is to separate the "genuine" from the "corrupt" forms in each local tradition.

South Slavic literature suffered a permanent loss with the downfall of the Serbian Despotate in 1459, since even those monks who survived the debacle received no further support for literary endeavors. Elimination of the native Christian nobility after the Ottoman conquest meant impoverishment for the monasteries, even though the Turks usually did not destroy them physically. As Muslims, the Ottoman overlords naturally had no interest in sponsoring Christian literature. New works were not produced; old ones were neglected. The Slavic literary imagination could find expression only through unwritten folktales and folk songs preserved by oral transmission. The position of the Vlach monasteries was scarcely better. Unlike their immediate neighbors to the south and west, Walachia and Moldavia in the 15th century were not ruled directly as Ottoman provinces. Nonetheless both Romanian principalities were plagued by chronic political instability, as the Ottoman and Hungarian governments competed to maintain vassal princes on the two Romanian thrones. Needless to say, this situation was hardly propitious for the cause of a national literature.

In Walachia and Moldavia the Old Slavic literary tradition continued virtually intact until the 17th century, although Ottoman control of the Balkans had the effect of isolating the two principalities from European intellectual influences. Bulgaria had fallen to the Turks in 1396; Serbia followed suit in 1459, while the former Kievan state in Ukraine had long since come under the aegis of the Mongol Golden Horde. Old Slavic now ceased to be a vehicle for fruitful cultural interchange between the Vlachs and their Orthodox neighbors. On the other hand, the dominance of Slavic hindered the development of a Romanian literary language. The Vlachs possessed (as their descendants still do) a rich oral folk literature. Popular ballads, accompanied by music, were often recited at popular festivals in which even the nobility participated. However, documents and books in the Romanian language date back no farther than to about 1490, and even these show little originality. The oldest texts in Romanian are translations from Old Slavic works which themselves had been rendered from Greek. The four Gospels with commentary, the Book of Acts, and the Psalms all appeared in the Romanian language in the late 15th or early 16th century. The development of a small educated class in the principalities in the 16th century created a demand for material in the vernacular. In the towns Romanian gradually became the medium of written communication, using the Cyrillic letters already familiar from Old Slavic. The nobility and the Church hierarchy held on longer to Slavic, which they fostered as a culture language distinguishing them from the lower classes. Old Slavic continued to be used for literary and religious purposes in some areas of Walachia and Moldavia as late as the 18th century.

The oldest of the Slavic vernacular literatures is Czech, although the precise boundary which separates Old Slavic from medieval Czech is sometimes difficult to identify. The language of the famous *Hospodine, pomiluj ny*, often loosely described as the oldest Czech hymn, might equally well be classified as Old Slavic "in Czech recension," since it dates from the 10th or 11th century, well before Czech speech had become markedly different from the other forms of Slavic. A few isolated fragments of a 12th-century Slavic literature from Bohemia still survive, including some ancient songs and prayers in verse. Among them are the glosses in Czech written on the margins of Latin books to help the reader comprehend the contents. The outstanding work of this early period is the hymn to Saint Wenceslas, dating from the 12th or 13th century—a concise and solemn prayer of the Czech people to the patron saint of their country. The first verse runs: "Saint Wenceslas, duke of the Czech land, our prince, pray for us to God and the Holy Ghost. Kyrie eleison." Like the earlier *Hospodine, pomiluj ny*, it was sung in churches during solemn processions and by Czech soldiers in battle. No doubt as a concession to the popularity of these two hymns, the Prague synod permitted them and two other Czech songs to be sung during divine services, although everything else was required to be in Latin.

A continuous tradition of Czech vernacular literature begins in the early 14th century, using the dialect of the Prague region. This is the period of the oldest Czech poetry, epic in form, which developed a characteristic style using rhymed couplets of eight-syllable lines in an irregular rhythm. This early poetry took its subject matter from internationally known themes, such as the legendary exploits of Alexander the Great. An outstanding example of this Czech epic poetry from the mid-14th century is the *Legend of Saint Catherine*, containing over 3,500 verses by an unknown author. Since Saint Catherine was the patron of students and educated clergy, the poem is connected in part with the foundation of King Charles's university at Prague. It includes the typical medieval themes of devotion to Christ, miracles, martyrdom, and scholarly disputation. The oldest major Czech epic on a secular theme is the *Alexandreis*, dating from the late 13th or early 14th century and employing a rich and correct language with skillfully constructed, rhymed eight-syllable lines. Freely adapted from a Latin poem of the same name by a 12th-century French author, it is ostensibly an account of the deeds of Alexander the Great. The unknown Czech poet, apparently unaware of any anachronism, presents Alexander as a Christian king who fights the heathen, behaves gallantly to women, and surrounds himself with a feudal nobility, many of whom bear Czech names and use medieval Czech weapons. The poem also betrays a pronounced aristocratic bias, exalting the standard virtues of the knight while expressing open contempt for peasants. In typical medieval fashion, the *Alexandreis* emphasizes the transient nature of all human greatness, even for a world conqueror.

In sharp contrast to the feudal mentality of the *Alexandreis* is the early 14th-century poem attributed to "Dalimil" (the author's true name is unknown). A lively account of the history of Bohemia from ancient times until the writer's own day, this work is the earliest extant rhymed chronicle in Czech. Notable for its vivid expressions and gnomic sayings, it comes close to the spoken language of its time, using a simpler vocabulary and syntax than the *Alexandreis*. Dalimil voiced an intense nationalism unusual in the medieval age. Acutely conscious of his Czech identity, he rejected everything foreign and unfeignedly expressed his resentment of the German influence in Bohemia. Typically medieval in his uncritical acceptance of earlier sources, including some fairly improbable legends, he was reasonably accurate concerning events of a more recent period, from about 1230 to 1310. Recopied many times, the chronicle of Dalimil remains the prime achievement of late medieval Czech historiography.

Quite a few lyrical works of the genre known as "dawn songs"—poems set to music which evidently were intended to accompany tavern revels—have survived from 14th-century Bohemia. These ballads depict the pain of young lovers being forced to part as the sun rises. As usual in medieval literature, neither author nor lovers in these poems reveal any personal characteristics, while the emotions described are the standard ones of traditional romance. Many of these dawn songs stem from a new social milieu created in Prague during the second half of the century—that of teachers and students at the university. A few are entirely in Czech, although the majority use Latin, the common language of university students throughout Catholic Europe. Some of the songs employ an irregular mixture of Latin and Czech (the so-called macaronic style). These compositions were of many types: beggar songs, drinking songs, and love songs, as well as satires and parodies. Entirely secular in nature, they express pure joy in life and delight in the pleasures of love and drink. Most of them imitate foreign themes and styles, usually taking Latin or German poems as their models. A particularly original dawn song, regarded as the outstanding example of the genre, is the *Song of Záviś*, an artfully constructed ballad on the theme of love as suffering. Záviś, whose work demonstrates great erudition as well as musical talent, is the earliest Czech composer whose name has come down to us. He was active in the 1370s and 1380s, writing the music to both secular and spiritual texts.

Originating likewise in 14th-century Bohemia was satirical poetry of quite a sophisticated sort, full of aphorisms as well as decorative elements. The outstanding writer in this genre was Smil Flaška, a highly educated noble who apparently was a member of the opposition to King Wenceslas IV. Flaška collected both Czech and foreign proverbs, which he adapted for his poetic work entitled *A Father's Advice to His Son*. Folk wisdom appears also in his long allegorical piece entitled *The New Council of the Animals*, written in the 1390s. This represents a style then popular throughout Europe, perhaps inspired by the conciliar movement in the Church, in which animals conduct discussions in their own parliament. The young lion of Flaška's tale inherits a throne and summons an assembly of animals to ask for advice on how best to rule. The lion is meant to represent the king of Bohemia, and the poem develops the ideal of a Christian state.

Other prominent examples of this period and genre in Bohemia are three anonymous student works of the 14th century, filled with playful humor, self-mockery, and acute awareness of contemporary social conflicts and injustices. One is *The Quarrel Between Water and Wine*, which parodies the academic disputes and legalistic quibbling characteristic of the university milieu. The water brings forth superior arguments, but the dialogue concludes with the compromise that the world requires both water and wine. Another satirical Czech poem of the same period is *The Song of Merry Poverty*, which portrays both the carefree quality and the misery of student life. Most interesting of the three is *The Groom and the Student*, a vehement disputation between an aged servant from the countryside and an impoverished young student. Unlike medieval Latin poems, which usually deal with the upper classes, this Czech satire depicts members of the poorest social strata comparing the hardships of their respective occupations. Intended as entertainment rather than edification, it reflects the atmosphere of Czech taverns in a realistic way.

Czech was not the only vernacular to be used for literary purposes in medieval Bohemia. In the 13th century the preferred language of the Bohemian court and nobility was German. Among the ruling classes of East Central Europe generally, spoken German was widely cultivated in the 13th and 14th centuries. As a vernacular current in the more advanced West, it ranked as the vehicle of a higher culture. (At this same period, for analogous reasons of prestige, French became popular with the upper classes of Germany.) High German was often the language of the ballads that troubadours sang to entertain knights and ladies at the royal, ducal, or noble courts of Bohemia, Poland, or Hungary. Every self-respecting knight was expected to know it. Similarly, German architectural styles became fashionable among Bohemian and Polish noblemen in the 13th century, inspiring them to give their castles German names like "Rosenberg" or "Falkenstein." Many nobles as well as kings took German wives, which inevitably led to a further influx of Germans into high society. Like foreigners everywhere, those Germans who lived in an alien Slavic or Magyar environment became more acutely conscious of their cultural affinities than they had been at home. Although they spoke a variety of Germanic dialects and identified themselves chiefly by regional affiliation as Bavarians, Saxons, Swabians, and so forth, the distinctions that had seemed so crucial in the homeland faded into the background abroad. This tendency toward amalgamation of everything German fostered the beginnings of a standard literary form of the German language. Known as Middle High German, it flourished from the 14th century onward particularly in the mixed Germanic-Slavic borderlands of Bohemia and Meissen. This standardization also reflected the fact that Czechs, Poles, and Hungarians, who usually were incapable of distinguishing one German dialect from another, tended to lump all Germans together. In the Slavic vernaculars, as in Hungarian, the word for "German" means "mute" or "silent," since Germans often could not speak the local language.

Ottokar II of Bohemia, the so-called Golden King (r. 1253–78), welcomed German poets and singers to his court. One of them was Ulrich of Eschenbach, a native of Bohemia, who with the king's encouragement composed his great epic poem about Alexander the Great. Antedating the Czech *Alexandreis* which was written on the same theme, Ulrich's work includes generous praise for his royal patron, who enjoyed comparing himself with Alexander. Ottokar's son Wenceslas II (r. 1278–1305) himself wrote love poetry in German and maintained a splendid court at Prague which attracted many traveling poets and singers. Even in 14th-century Bohemia, when the rulers of the Luxemburg dynasty promoted French culture, the love lyrics of German troubadours continued to find an audience. The noted Czech preacher John Milíč of Kroměříž wrote prayers in German as well as Czech. The presence of the German imperial court at Prague while King Charles I was emperor clearly contributed to this cultivation of the German language in Bohemia. John of Neumarkt, Charles's imperial chancellor, produced letters and diplomatic correspondence in German which subsequently found their way into collections of formulas for the use of officials, serving as an important basis for the rise of a literary New High German. Similarly influential was Neumarkt's German version of a Latin text attributed to Saint Augustine, *The Book of Caresses*, consisting of the dialogue of a sinful soul with God. However, some Czechs obviously disliked this German influence, since satirical Czech polemics against Germans appeared in this period as well.

From the town milieu of Bohemia in the early 15th century, where the ethnic German element was strong, came the popular novel by John of Tepl, *Ackermann aus Böhmen* ("The Plowman from Bohemia"), which is considered the high point of medieval Bohemian German prose. It also served as model for the Czech allegorical novel *Tkadleček* ("The Little Weaver")—"weaver" having the double meaning of craftsman in the cloth trade and "weaver of words." Written sometime after 1407 by an unnamed courtier, *Tkadleček* is regarded as the outstanding achievement of medieval Czech prose. Closely resembling the *Ackermann* in its first chapters, it is approximately four times as long, and stands out for its brilliant rhetoric and imagery. The theme of both works is a quarrel between a plowman or weaver, on the one hand, and Death and Misfortune in personified form on the other, with the latter two characters assuming an attitude of class superiority. Analogous in concept to the popular medieval dialogues between soul and body, these novels were influenced by Renaissance humanism and exhibit a comparatively secular attitude. The protagonist in each case lays claim to earthly happiness, even though Misfortune (in the form of a lover who ignores all entreaties) is triumphant. The ultimate conclusion is that human beings must bear misfortune, while death is a law of nature and thus unavoidable.

The Czech language in the 14th century became the medium for a greatly enhanced level of popular religiosity, despite the Church's dislike of employing the language of common people for "higher" subjects. Portions of the Bible were rendered into Czech as early as the 1370s, even prior to the appearance of John Wyclif's English Bible. The first complete Bible in Czech, ascribed to the 1380s and certainly finished by the year 1400, was translated from the Latin Vulgate. Frequently recopied and several times corrected, it enabled literate Czechs who lacked a Latin education to read the Scriptures in their own tongue. This continuous polishing and revision of the Biblical language contributed in a major way to the development of the Czech literary language. Numerous Czech Bibles in manuscript form have survived from the 15th century—clear evidence of their wide dissemination. Czech was also the vehicle for a number of forceful preachers whose writings circulated extensively in the last two decades of the 14th century. John Milíč of Kroměříž, for example, employed an entire group of copyists to reproduce his sermons. However, the outstanding literary figure among the Czech religious reformers of that time was Thomas Štítný, a provincial scholar without academic degrees or clerical rank. Writing originally for the moral and spiritual education of his own children, he naturally used his native tongue. Subsequently he revised his works for a larger audience. Štítný was a master at rendering scholarly Latin into understandable Czech. With considerable literary skill he sought to justify church dogma and promote Christian morality. His religious and philosophical tracts found many readers and ultimately were collected into several books. By encouraging a wider public to discuss theological issues, Štítný helped set the stage for the Hussite reforms.

John Hus himself was a famous preacher and the author of several academic Latin works on theology (mainly paraphrases of earlier authors) before he began to write in Czech. Ultimately he played a major role in the development of the Czech language. Eschewing the more formal style of earlier Czech literature, he used instead the living tongue as spoken in his native region or in Prague.

Hus's literary style was vivid and picturesque, full of exclamations and questions. He sought to purge Czech of the Germanisms found in contemporary Prague speech, taking care as well to avoid the inconsistent spelling found in so many medieval works. Hus was probably also responsible for the present system of Czech spelling, which employs diacritical marks instead of double letters to render certain sounds. The earlier attempts at using purely Latin letters for Czech had clearly proved unsatisfactory, since Czech contains sounds which are not present in Latin. The standard form of modern Czech closely resembles the system in *De orthographia bohemica*, a treatise on spelling originating in the early 15th century and generally attributed to Hus, although irrefutable proof of his authorship is lacking.

Without doubt the Hussite movement contributed greatly to the use of written Czech. Hussites vigorously asserted the dignity of the Czech language and insisted upon preaching in the vernacular. Many authors of the period expressed the opinion that Czech was fully equal to Latin with respect to beauty and flexibility of expression. Nonetheless literary Czech adopted many elements of classical Latin sentence structure. In the 15th century, Czech came to be widely used for administrative and legal purposes, and to some extent even for scholarly and technical writings. The simplified spelling facilitated the copying of books and documents, which still had to be done by hand until printing came into wide use toward the end of the century.

Hus is often considered the greatest of all medieval Czech writers. The works on which his literary reputation rest all date from the period of his enforced exile in south Bohemia, when he began preaching to large crowds of peasants in the fields and meadows. His most popular book was a collection of sermons entitled *Postilla, or Explication of Holy Readings for Sundays*, which first appeared in 1413, two years before he was condemned by the Council of Constance to die at the stake. Similarly well known were his *Explication of the Faith* and the treatise *On Simony*, an impassioned moral critique of the selling of church offices. Hus was a master of the epistolary style. All of his works read like sermons, punctuated by frequent rhetorical questions to engage the reader's attention. The Hussite movement in general gave rise to a considerable literature, all of which was intended for a mass audience. Even the poetry is readily intelligible, consisting of simple songlike verses. One popular Hussite literary form was the biting satire and witty polemic, often presented in the style of a medieval academic disputation. The more sober educational texts explained the Bible with straightforward rationalism, aided by allegory and a passionate intensity of feeling. On the whole, the Hussite literature rejected the rich symbolism and metaphor characteristic of medieval writing and favored a more dogmatic and polemical approach.

All factions within the Hussite movement showed great fondness for religious hymns. This was true even of the radical Taborites, who disapproved of other forms of music or literature. The successive invasions of Bohemia by foreign armies in league with the Catholic Church solidified the Hussites' resistance and enhanced the mood of religious exaltation to which these songs bear witness. Hussite hymns were both pious and belligerent, asserting an unshakable determination to fulfill God's will on earth, eradicate sin, and hasten the second coming of Christ. They also encouraged righteous Christians to please God by punishing His enemies. The most famous of all Hussite hymns, "Ye Warriors of God," is reliably ascribed to the entourage of John Žižka, the Taborite leader and commander whose military genius was reinforced by the religious dedication of his troops. This hymn expresses fiery religious passion and moral righteousness together with eagerness for battle and a cruel indifference toward opponents. Declaring that the Taborite troops are under God's direct command, it promises eternal life for those who lay down their lives for Christ. Like other songs of its type, it served both as an incitement to religious war and a stimulant to the religious emotion already amply present in Hussite Bohemia.

Another religious leader and prominent author in the Czech language was Peter Chelčický, the founder of the sect of Bohemian Brethren. Unlike reformers like Hus who were fully competent in Latin but employed Czech by choice, Chelčický had never acquired a traditional theological education. Knowing little Latin, he wrote exclusively in Czech in a vigorous and direct style. As a young man in Prague he had been profoundly affected by the fervent religiosity of the Hussite preachers; but unlike them, he refused to countenance war in the name of religion. A thoroughgoing pacifist, Chelčický opposed violence in all its forms and advocated a simple life-style like that of Jesus' twelve apostles. Viewing riches and worldly power as incompatible with a genuinely Christian life, he held that true Christians ought to reject all power and privilege, law, government, every form of war, and even their own nation. These ideas he expressed in two key literary works of the early 1440s: *Postilla, or a Book of Interpretations of the Gospel for the Whole Year*, and the far more important *Net of the Faith*. The latter was a work of social criticism, contending that the net of true Christianity had been broken when (as was then widely believed) the Roman Emperor Constantine I donated the Papal States to the pope.* The emperor and the pope were the two whales who had turned the faith of poor and humble people into a state religion. In his native village Chelčický gathered a circle of peasants and craftsmen around himself who sought to live according to his precepts. Convinced that only poor and humble people could be true Christians, the group at first denied any need for formal education. Subsequently they altered their opinion, realizing the need to defend their doctrines against learned adversaries. Ultimately the settlements of the Bohemian Brethren became centers of Czech literature and education, combining sincere Christian piety with a genuine love of knowledge.

The inhabitants of Slovakia, which was then part of the kingdom of Hungary, had very little contact during the Middle Ages with their brethren in Bohemia.

---

* This alleged donation was exposed as a forgery by the Italian scholar Lorenzo Valla in 1439—a fact obviously unknown to Chelčický.

The differences between spoken Czech and Slovak were minimal; but a political frontier divided them. Probably if the Czechs and Slovaks had always lived together in one country, a single Czechoslovak nationality and a unified literary language would have evolved; but when the new state of Czechoslovakia was finally created in the 20th century it was too late. Toward the end of the 15th century a few Bohemian humanists remarked upon the many resemblances between Czech and Slovak; but their discovery was treated as a curiosity, producing no results in either language or literature. The Slovaks of medieval Hungary neither adopted the literary language of the Czechs nor developed one of their own. Unlike the Czechs in Bohemia, they were not a "people of state" (i.e., the leading nationality in the kingdom they inhabited). More to the point, the centers of whatever literacy existed in Slovakia were the towns, which were dominated by Germans. This situation not only inhibited the development of a Slovak literary language but even encouraged the town-dwelling Slovaks to abandon their native speech and adopt German or Hungarian instead. Nonetheless, in 15th-century Slovakia the Czech language was used occasionally for administrative and legal functions and for sermons, with some modifications to accommodate certain clearly Slovak linguistic features. In the 16th century the Lutheran Reformation in Slovakia accepted Czech as its church language.

Literary Polish was slower to develop than its Czech counterpart, even though a few fragments in Polish are extant from as early as the 13th century. Among these surviving remnants are the co-called *Holy Cross Sermons*, as well as some glosses written above the words and phrases of Latin texts. The oldest extant poem in Polish is the famous *Bogurodzica* ("Mother of God"), which served for several centuries as a kind of national anthem and perhaps preserves elements of the Old Slavic liturgy. Scholars have tried to discover the date of this ancient hymn, which contains puzzling linguistic forms not found elsewhere in Polish sources. It has been variously assigned to the 10th, 12th, or 13th century, on the assumption that its unusual words come from Old Slavic, perhaps by way of Czech. A more recent hypothesis treats its unique expressions as Russicisms and places the poem in the reign of King Vladislav Jagiełło (r. 1386–1434), a former grand duke of Lithuania. This latter explanation would account for the quasi-official nature of the *Bogurodzica*, which was sung at court ceremonies and by soldiers marching to battle.

The oldest complete book extant in Polish, dating from about 1400, is the beautifully illuminated parchment manuscript of the *Psalter of Queen Jadwiga*, also known as *Saint Florian's Psalter*. A gift of Saint Florian's abbey to Jagiełło's royal consort, it contains a complete translation of the Psalms in Latin, Polish, and German. The clumsiness of the text to modern Polish ears illustrates the translator's difficulties in rendering sophisticated Latin into a language lacking a literary tradition, which at that time possessed only a limited vocabulary and no standard grammatical forms. A somewhat later rendition of the entire Old and

New Testaments into Polish, known as *Queen Sophia's Bible*, was done from an unknown Czech text (undoubtedly of Hussite origin) in the first half of the 15th century. The Hussite influences which entered Poland from Bohemia certainly contributed to the development of a Polish written vernacular. However, the Church succeeded so completely in eradicating all traces of this alleged heresy that only a single Polish poem modeled on the Czech Hussite songs has survived. This is the "Song on Wyclif" by Jędrzej Galka, a teacher at the university in Cracow who subsequently fled to Bohemia to escape being burnt at the stake. The poem in question reviles the pope as Antichrist and argues that the claims of the papacy to temporal power were based on falsification.

Another interesting example of Polish medieval poetry is the "Conversation of a Master with Death," adapted from a Latin original at the end of the 15th century. The "master" is a learned man, curious at first to see Death in person, whom the poem depicts in typically medieval style as a female apparition with scythe in hand. The man seeks to flee from this horrifying specter or to bribe her; she in turn spurns the expensive fabrics or delicacies he offers. Death boasts of her power over all people alike, whether king or peasant, rich or poor, and comments wittily on the sins and weaknesses of human beings. Similar in theme is the "Lament of a Dying Man," probably adapted into Polish from Czech, in which the speaker on his deathbed expresses fear for the fate of his soul and regret at having neglected its welfare through his absorption in worldly affairs. Works of this sort are typically medieval in their intense concern with humankind's relation to the supernatural. Nonetheless, the "Conversation of a Master with Death" is somewhat more modern in directing the reader's attention rather to the humorous aspects of life on earth than to pious reflections upon the hereafter.

A purely secular Polish literature also arose in the 15th century. A prominent example is *The Killing of Andrew Tęczyński*, a ballad based on an actual event occurring in Cracow in 1461. Tęczyński was a local knight, who expressed his dissatisfaction with the repairs done to his armor by administering a severe beating to the armorer. This act caused great indignation among a group of the armorer's acquaintances. They sought out the knight, murdered him in a church where he had taken refuge, and dragged his corpse through the gutter. The poem recounts these events entirely from the standpoint of the nobility, praising the arrogant knight, expressing outrage at his murder, and indicating satisfaction that the town councillors were executed for failing to prevent the lynching. Another example of noble disdain for social inferiors is the poem entitled *Satire on the Peasants*, which presents an amusing if one-sided picture of the alleged laziness of peasants and the many shrewd tricks they employ to avoid working for their lords.

In Hungary a vernacular literature came into existence in the early 13th century, although it was not extensive and certainly did not threaten the dominance of Latin. The oldest surviving text in Hungarian is a short funeral oration dating from about the year 1200. The author's use of literary devices like alliteration and rhythmic prose indicates that it belonged to a genre of which other examples probably existed at that time. Translation of secular Latin literature into Hungarian apparently also began in the 13th century. A notable stimulus to writing in the Hungarian vernacular was the outpouring of religious enthusiasm among laypeople stimulated by the popular preaching of Dominican and Franciscan friars. In response to the new demand for inspirational literature, religious hymns, legends, and portions of the Gospels were translated for the benefit of simple folk who did not know Latin. These works appealed especially to women, who rarely if ever were given a formal Latin education. Women's cloisters affiliated with the Dominican and Franciscan orders became centers of devotional writing in the vernacular. The single work in Hungarian which still survives from this 13th-century milieu, the poem known as the "Lamentation of Mary," was modeled on an existing Latin hymn and utilized the techniques of medieval Latin verse.

Conditions for development of the Hungarian language into a vehicle for literary expression improved in the 14th century, when formal education for laymen became more common and Hungarian students began to attend foreign universities. Appearing at that time were Hungarian versions of some of the standard European secular tales, such as the Alexander romance and stories of the Trojan War. The oldest original works in Hungarian date from the 15th century. Prominent among them are the comical or heroic tales recounted by professional troubadours, a genre favored by King Matthias, who particularly liked heroic epics telling of his own warlike deeds and the victories of his armies. The most important Hungarian epic of this period is the "Song of Ladislas," glorifying that 11th-century royal saint as a holy knight and defender of his nation against the pagans. Similar in type is the "Battle of Szabács," written in 1476 not long after Matthias captured this important Turkish fortress. The oldest legal document in the Hungarian language records the oath sworn by John Hunyadi upon taking office as regent in 1446. The use of the vernacular was essential in this instance because most of Hunyadi's supporters among the county nobility knew no Latin.

An extensive literature in Hungarian as well as Czech took its impetus from the Hussite reform movement, which spread outward from Bohemia quite widely after about 1410. Since Hussitism everywhere favored the vernacular language and addressed itself particularly to people ignorant of Latin, the first translators of the Bible into Hungarian quite naturally were two Hussite preachers, Thomas and Bálint, working about 1430. What proportion of the entire Bible they translated is not known, since only their versions of the Prophets, the Psalms, and the Gospels have survived. In order to combat Hussitism the Roman Church now began to sponsor Hungarian translations of certain approved devotional works (although not the Bible). Franciscan and Dominican preachers in particular felt the need of inspirational works for popular consumption. However, very little of this literature was original. Most of it consisted of translations into

Hungarian from popular Latin texts, especially religious legends, prayers, parables, monastic rules, and hymns. In the process the Hungarian written language was greatly enriched, since new terminology had to be invented and a suitable literary style developed.

In Croatia the new translations of the Slavic liturgy stimulated the flowering of additional vernacular literature. The earliest poetry in Croatian dates from the 14th century and is chiefly religious in character. Secular trends asserted themselves in the 15th century, when a considerable quantity of Croatian lyric and didactic poetry was produced. Some poets used the vernacular exclusively; others employed Latin as well. This literature developed initially in the coastal towns of Dalmatia, where an upper class of merchants possessed the money and leisure necessary to cultivate literature and learning. Meanwhile the Orthodox Serbs remained faithful to Old Slavic and the Cyrillic alphabet, so that cultural differences between Serbs and Croats became magnified despite their almost identical spoken vernaculars. As for Albanian—a non-Slavic tongue—the few scattered references to it in the 14th century come exclusively from foreign sources. The earliest extant fragments in this language, written in the Latin alphabet, date from the second half of the 15th century. Albania in the Middle Ages was never a unified country; and its coastal towns maintained close links with the Byzantine, Latin, or Slavic world. Chancelleries in the Albanian towns used Greek, Latin, or Slavic according to circumstances.

Folk literature in the medieval Balkans was dominated by heroic ballads in oral form which are difficult to date, but clearly are based on historical memory. One Serbian song cycle recounts the pious works and good deeds of the monarchs of the Nemanya dynasty. Another gives an account of the battle of Kosovo, where in 1389 the Turks put an end to the independence of medieval Serbia. As genuine history the Kosovo song cycle is suspect, since it shows obvious partiality toward certain Serbian noble families and describes the betrayal and defeat of the Serbian Prince Lazar in terms reminiscent of the story of Judas and Christ. Actually the Kosovo ballads are not concerned with the battle itself, but concentrate instead on the deeds of individual warriors.

This predilection for personal heroism appears again in the ballads describing the deeds of King Marko (or "Prince," as he is called in the epics), the best-loved character in Serbian folk literature. This warrior was an actual historical figure, the son of the Serbian King Vukašin and ruler of a small principality in Macedonia. His father and uncle were killed in 1371 at the battle of Černomen on the Maritsa, which forced many of the Balkan princelings to accept Ottoman overlordship. The epics depict Marko as a valiant Christian opponent of the Turks, although in reality he spent most of his career as a loyal Ottoman vassal. As such, he participated in many of the sultan's campaigns and died in 1395 at the battle of Rovine, fighting in the Turkish ranks against the Christian Voivode Mircea of Walachia. The tales about Marko emphasize his physical prowess in duels against opponents of unusual strength, such as the Albanian hero Musa.

Repeating a motif common to many folk epics, which proclaim that a famous hero cannot really have died but is merely in hiding, the legend claims that Marko remains alive in a cave somewhere, awaiting a propitious moment to return. In contrast to the tragic Kosovo cycle, the ballads in which Marko appears are often gay and humorous. Repeated in innumerable Serbian, Bulgarian, Vlach, and Albanian versions, they spread to every part of the Balkans.

Likewise popular among the Balkan Slavs in the Ottoman period were the epic ballads relating the brave deeds of haiduks—outlaws who conducted guerrilla raids against the Turkish occupiers from the relative safety of the mountains. No equivalents of these songs in praise of Christian heroism appear in Albanian or Vlach literature (though they do in Greek), since the majority of Albanians eventually accepted Islam, while the Romanian principalities remained vassal states which were never actually incorporated into the Ottoman Empire. The Albanian counterparts to the haiduk ballads are "soldier songs" which reflect the experiences of many Albanians in Ottoman military service. The earliest documentary evidence of these Balkan heroic epics dates from the early 16th century, although their main elements are obviously older. This literature has remained popular even in modern times. The Kosovo songs in particular have influenced the patriotism of the Serbs by reminding them of the grandeur of their medieval kingdom.

Still another type of medieval folk literature is the horror tale, of which the best known examples concern the blood-sucking vampire Dracula. The model for Dracula was the Walachian ruler Vlad III (r. 1456–62), known as "the Impaler" because of his preference for this form of torture. While some of Vlad's cruelties were undoubtedly political in intent—like his extermination of boyars who threatened his power—other reports suggest that he enjoyed committing atrocities for their own sake. The majority of his victims were Turks, which may be why Romanian folk tradition remembers him primarily as a hero of the anti-Turkish wars. Vlad's image abroad was very different. Refugees fleeing from Walachia into Transylvania spread reports of his cruelties; and their stories soon were repeated in the medieval German pamphlet literature. Narratives in German, the Slavic languages, and Turkish expanded upon the theme of his horrors, adding fantastic and demonic elements corresponding to popular taste. The printing press gave these tales wide dissemination. Dracula in Western literature appears as a corpse that leaves its grave at night to suck the blood of living persons. Although the real Dracula committed his atrocities in Walachia, the legend erroneously locates his activities in Transylvania.

Despite the growing popularity of the vernacular literatures, Latin remained the language of most scholarly and documentary writing throughout all of Catholic Europe even long after the end of the Middle Ages. However, in the hands of its most gifted exponents, 15th-century Latin had become very different from its predecessor of several centuries previously. More subtle and sophisticated, it was also grammatically more complex and closer to the classical Roman style. This improvement was the fruit of Renaissance humanism, which first took root in Italy in the 14th century and spread north of the Alps in the 15th. Humanist scholars were passionately attached to the literature of ancient Rome (and later to that of classical Greece as well). They admired it both for its elegance and for its concern with the position of human beings on this earth, which greatly enlarged the theologically focused medieval view of the world. Students from Hungary, Bohemia, Croatia, and even distant Poland attended Italian universities in the 15th century, where they came under strong humanist influences and often returned home as strong advocates of the new Renaissance learning. As lovers of classical literature, they themselves sought to cultivate the type of Latin used during the best period of the Roman Empire. Some of them followed the example of Italian poets like Petrarch or Boccaccio by writing in their native tongues also.

Hungary became an important center of Renaissance culture in the 15th century, although occasional evidence of a humanist attitude can be found there even earlier. The historical chronicle written by János Küküllei during the reign of King Louis the Great in the 14th century strikes a humanist note in the prominence it assigns to the human personality and the importance of worldly fame. Humanist standards in literature became more widely adopted in Hungary in the 15th century, when several leading Italian scholars resided at the royal court and created a thoroughly Renaissance atmosphere in this somewhat artificial milieu. Early in the century a prominent Italian humanist, Pier Paolo Vergerio, accepted a position in the chancellery of King Sigismund at Buda, where he remained from 1417 until his death in 1444. Under his influence a group of Hungarian, Polish, and Italian humanist scholars came together for discussions, and maintained close contacts with the Neo-Platonist circles of Florence in Italy. Renaissance Latin began to influence the style of written Hungarian, while the still-medieval Hungarian literature gradually came to be penetrated by Renaissance taste.

The decisive figure in the development of Hungarian humanism was King Matthias Corvinus (r. 1458–90), a Renaissance prince in the grand style. Educated by humanists himself, he became a generous patron of the new literature and art, which he cultivated out of personal inclination as well as for the cultural prestige they brought him. Like many Italian Renaissance princes, Matthias lacked the legitimacy of royal ancestry. As the son of the renowned general John Hunyadi and himself highly educated, he embodied in his own person the new idea that talent should prevail over royal lineage. His court was famous for its brilliant pageants and its pomp and magnificence. Matthias employed many Italian scholars and artists, among them the architects who rebuilt his palace at Buda. Surrounding himself with both foreign and Hungarian humanists, he engaged them in conversation and encouraged their scholarly efforts. As an accomplished Latinist, he carried on an extensive correspondence with Italian princes and scholars. To satisfy his taste for fine vellum manuscripts adorned with painted miniatures, he sent agents far and wide to procure beautiful and expensive specimens. He also patronized the new art of printing by setting up a press at Buda, which in 1473 brought out a Latin chronicle of Hungarian history as its first publication. Matthias established a marvelous library, the Corvina, on which he spent enormous sums of money amounting in some years to 30,000 gold florins. The conspiracy of 1472 against him, in which the leading Hungarian humanists were implicated, turned him temporarily aside from these preoccupations. Then his marriage in 1476 to Beatrice of Naples revived the old interests. Beatrice was an intelligent princess, well read in Latin literature, who had profited from the Renaissance advocacy of education for women. She used her cultivated taste in art to good effect, helping Matthias make his capital at Buda a brilliant center of Renaissance culture.

The most celebrated poet of Hungarian humanism was John Česmički, or "Janus Pannonius," as he called himself in the accepted Latin style.* The son of a Croatian nobleman from Slavonia (then part of the Hungarian kingdom), he wrote entirely in Latin, and from his teen years onward lived either in Italy or at Buda. His uncle was the well-known humanist scholar and royal Hungarian Chancellor John Vitéz, who financed his studies in Italy. After returning to Hungary, Pannonius became bishop of Pécs and eventually vice-chancellor of the kingdom. His exceptional talent was recognized at an early date; and his skillful use of Renaissance Latin won him an audience throughout Europe. Early in his career he was noted for his satirical Latin epigrams, in which he poked fun at enemies and fellow students, praised his friends, and ridiculed clerical greed and hypocrisy. After returning to Hungary he came to prefer panegyrics and elegies. Like many humanists of the period, Pannonius had little feeling for religion; and despite his position as bishop, was highly critical of the papacy. Some of his most trenchant lines vilified the clergy. Much of his poetry dealt with the wars against the Turks, praising the military life in general and the Hungarians in particular as Europe's defenders against the Ottoman menace. A great lyric poet, Pannonius wrote in a very personal and individual style, taking as his main subjects human beings in their natural surroundings, his own many illnesses, and the imminence of death. One of his principal works is a long epic in classical style praising the achievements of his Venetian friend Marcello. His most frequently reprinted poem is a fond eulogy of his former teacher, the famous Italian humanist Guarino of Verona.

King Matthias was well aware of the uses of humanism in enhancing the prestige of the monarchy. To glorify himself and his ancestors he commissioned historical chronicles written in the humanist style. Then in 1486 he engaged the Italian humanist Antonio Bonfini to write an exhaustive history of Hungary. The result was the immense *Rerum Ungaricorum Decades*, a compilation of native and

* Both Hungarians and Croats claim him as one of the great figures of their literary history, though he wrote in the vernacular of neither.

foreign sources beginning with the Magyars' settlement in Central Europe and ending in the year 1496. This work is the principal source for Matthias's reign and exerted a decisive influence on subsequent Hungarian historiography. Bonfini was a typical Renaissance scholar in his search for causal links between events. Following the fashion of that time, he composed humanist speeches for his characters and invented a fantastic genealogy which presented the Hunyadi family as descendants of the Romans. Naturally enough, the most prominent personage in his account is King Matthias himself. Another remarkable Renaissance scholar at Matthias's court was Regiomontanus, the greatest astronomer of the 15th century and the inventor of modern trigonometry. Matthias placed him in charge of the famous Corvina library and astronomical observatory. Regiomontanus's work constitutes the beginning of genuine scientific astronomy and contributed to the discovery of America. His book *Ephemerides*, a nautical almanac enabling sailors to calculate their position by observation of the stars, was used by Christopher Columbus. Fittingly, it is dedicated to King Matthias.

In Bohemia at the same period, humanists were neither numerous nor particularly eminent. Renaissance scholarship reached Bohemia in a minor way in the mid-14th century when two famous Italians visited Prague: Petrarch the poet and Cola di Rienzi, the advocate of an Italian republic. They were welcomed with enthusiasm, but their influence was restricted to a handful of literary men and had no wider impact. In the 15th century, literature and art in Bohemia were overwhelmed by the religious controversies and military conflicts arising out of the Hussite movement. Neither the "Hussite king" George Poděbrady nor his immediate successors were patrons of learning and the arts, so that humanist scholars could scarcely expect favors from the royal court. Later in the century some Bohemian students returning from Italian universities did bring Renaissance influences with them. Among the early Czech humanists may be counted the Utraquist Simon of Slaný, who sought to unite theological knowledge with literary sophistication, and John of Rabštein, a humanistically inclined Catholic prelate and diplomat. Humanist ideas also found an echo among the Bohemian Brethren, whose advocacy of peaceful discussion and nonviolence stood in sharp contrast to the religious polemics of the time. Ultimately the humanists' attention to classical studies promoted sounder scholarship at the university in Prague, which had become more a center for religious disputes than for disinterested study during the Hussite period.

The early Czech humanists, like their counterparts elsewhere in Renaissance Europe, tended to imitate Latin literary models with little or no attempt at originality. Inevitably their ideas were accessible only to an educated elite, while their scholarly and literary pursuits appealed to the even smaller number who remained relatively aloof from the religious strife. While some Czech humanists wrote in Latin only, others sought to apply the standards of Latin composition to their native tongue. The Czech language benefited from this synthesis by developing a more complex syntax and a sense of high style. The 15th-century writers who used Czech were usually also sympathetic to Hussitism, which favored the use of the vernacular. However, their interest in classical Roman civilization often tended toward its practical aspects, such as law and public speaking. The most successful attempt at synthesizing Latin humanism with Czech custom was made by Victor Kornel, whose *Nine Books Treating the Laws . . . of the Czech Lands* trace the development of the Czech legal tradition from a humanist standpoint.

In Croatia it was naturally the towns of the Adriatic coast which lay most open to influences from Renaissance Italy. In the 15th century many young men from wealthy Dalmatian families studied in Padua or Bologna, where they were exposed to humanist ideas. However, humanism in Dalmatia received its original impetus from Venice. The sizable Croatian colony residing in that city served to transmit Renaissance ideas back home, especially to Dubrovnik and the offshore islands. The themes of the Croatian humanist poets were at first usually religious, although occasionally they drew upon popular ballads for their subject matter. Generally they favored the lyric over the epic style. Some of these writers used the Croatian form of Slavic exclusively, while others employed both Croatian and Latin. Many took the works of Petrarch or Boccaccio as models.

Toward the end of the 15th century two major schools of Croatian humanist poetry arose, one in Dubrovnik, the other in Split. The most prominent members of the Dubrovnik school were Šiško Menčetić and Džore Držić, whose poems dealt largely with erotic themes, making frequent use of acrostics, mythological allusions, and classical and Biblical references. However, the most eminent poet of the Croatian Renaissance was Marko Marulić of Split. Educated at Padua, he wrote poetry in Latin and Italian as well as Croatian and enjoyed a high reputation throughout Europe. While essentially humanist in orientation, Marulić's works retain some traces of traditional medieval piety in their effort to promote moral renewal. His masterpiece, the poem *Judita*, is essentially the Old Testament Book of Judith told in verse. Penned in 1501, it was the first major poetic work in the Croatian language and gained great popular success. Marulić gave the familiar Biblical story contemporary relevance by suggesting that divine justice would punish the Turks one day, just as it formerly punished the enemies of the Hebrews.

Poland was the last of the Catholic lands of East Central Europe to be touched by humanist influences. The transmitters were Polish university students, some of whom had spent many years in Italy. Humanist visitors in Poland also played a role, like Filippo Buonacorsi, the Italian refugee from the Papal States who called himself Callimachus. Residing in Cracow from 1470 to 1496, he became the center of a humanist circle and wrote a biography of his patron, Bishop Gregory of Sanok. Callimachus subsequently became a diplomat, ambassador, royal secretary, and tutor to the sons of King Casimir IV. One of his royal pupils subsequently ascended the throne as King John Albert (r. 1492–1501), the first Polish sovereign to act as a patron of Renaissance scholars and bring them to court. Another influential foreign humanist in Poland was the Austrian Conrad Celtes, who resided in Cracow from 1488 to 1490. As he had done earlier at Buda,

Celtes organized a circle of interested intellectuals to discuss the new humanist ideas. On the whole, however, Renaissance humanism in Poland belongs to the 16th century.

A few Polish authors of the late 15th century may be regarded as precursors of humanism, standing on the border between medieval and Renaissance thought. The principal examples of this tendency are Cardinal Zbigniew Oleśnicki, the historian John Długosz, and especially the political writer John Ostroróg. These men all loved the old Roman classics and made a serious effort to write correct Latin, while Ostroróg on occasion even voiced opinions contrary to standard medieval modes of thought. Oleśnicki was the powerful bishop of Cracow and at times the virtual ruler of Poland. He insisted on correct Latin in the letters sent from his chancellery, but in other respects remained a medieval prelate who supported the authority of the Roman Church against the king and rejected on principle any political alliance with Hussite Bohemia. John Długosz was an official at Oleśnicki's court and a diplomat who undertook various missions abroad. Contacts with the culture of Renaissance Italy inspired him to model his Latin on Cicero and to take Livy as his ideal of historical method. Długosz became the outstanding Polish historian of the Middle Ages. He used sources expertly and examined critically the material he discovered in old annals and chronicles. Perhaps unavoidably, he defended the Catholic orthodoxy of his employer, Cardinal Oleśnicki. But despite his medieval readiness to place the cause of religion above reasons of state, Długosz attempted to be objective in his historical judgments. Some of his opinions were sufficiently unflattering to persons in high places to prevent portions of his chronicle from being printed until the 18th century.

The third of these Polish precursors of humanism was John Ostroróg (d. 1501), the first really secular Polish author. Holder of a doctorate in law from Padua, he gained practical experience in government by serving as voivode of Poznań. His *Memorial on the Governance of the Republic*, written in Latin about 1474–77, takes a modern view of the state as a fully sovereign entity independent of all external authorities, including the pope. Ostroróg criticized the existence of separate legal systems within a single country—canon law for clerics and German law for townsmen—and called for a single Polish law, albeit one which would uphold the class character of society. He advocated royal appointment of bishops, a voluntary church tithe, and state taxation of the clergy. At the same time he opposed the practice of sending tax money to Rome or appealing legal decisions to the papal curia. While never breaking openly with the Church, Ostroróg sought to subject the Church to the state.

Ultimately the intellectual promise of the late Middle Ages failed to bear fruit for the future in large parts of East Central Europe. Bulgaria, Serbia, and Albania all fell to the Turks, who did not support, even when they did not hinder, the literary and artistic activities of their Christian subjects. Precisely those social classes which formerly had underwritten indigenous culture with gifts and patronage—namely the nobility and the ecclesiastical hierarchy—had either disappeared or become impoverished. Circumstances were thus unpropitious for the flowering of a native literature. Ottoman conquest reinforced the isolation of the Balkan Christians from Western Europe, thus eliminating a possible source of foreign stimulus. Even without this hindrance, the close links between Renaissance humanism and Latin Christianity would have constituted a formidable obstacle to the spread of humanism into the lands dominated by Eastern Orthodoxy. Concurrently, religious barriers prevented the Balkan Christians from taking part in the Islamic-oriented cultural life of the Ottoman upper classes, who developed a rich formal literature of their own based largely on Arabic and Persian models. As a consequence, Christian civilization in the European lands of the Ottoman Empire remained essentially an oral folk culture. Catholic Hungary was similarly impoverished after its defeat in 1526 at the battle of Mohács, when most of the kingdom fell under Ottoman suzerainty. In the entire Balkan Peninsula, only the semi-independent towns of the Adriatic coast remained free to respond to Renaissance influences. In the 16th century in East Central Europe, Bohemia and Poland would prove unique in experiencing a major cultural efflorescence.

CHAPTER 15

Education and Literacy

*I*n East Central Europe, as everywhere in Europe north of the Alps in the early Middle Ages, literacy was a rare accomplishment. Aside from clerics, most people had no need for book learning in an era so overwhelmingly rural and technologically primitive. Peasants learned by example and practice the skills needed for farm or household work, just as boys of the noble class learned the art of warfare. Commerce was chiefly local in character and small in scale, demanding no great sophistication in the keeping of accounts. The economy produced very little beyond the minimum required for subsistence. Under the circumstances, it is scarcely surprising that literacy and written records were considered superfluous for most purposes. In the greater part of East Central Europe outside of the Byzantine Empire until about the 12th century, only the Church kept written records for even so important a matter as landholding. Secular lords supported their claims of estate ownership with oral evidence only, relying on the memory of living witnesses to a grant of land or citing the fact of possession over several generations. Most of the landed aristocracy were unable to read and write.

This nearly total illiteracy of the early Middle Ages represents a sharp departure from the situation in the ancient Greek and Roman worlds. Although at the height of the Roman Empire the general rural population was unlettered, among town dwellers of the middle and upper classes the ability to read and write was common. Literate and even highly educated laymen were fairly numerous, serving the requirements of the imperial bureaucracy and a far-flung commerce. Nor was general education a function of the Church, since schools and academies were run by the state. This remained the pattern in the East Roman (Byzantine) territories, where urban life and culture continued to exist for an entire millennium after the fall of Rome in the West. The bureaucracy, the legal system, and higher education remained in secular hands. Schools and universities in the Byzantine Empire existed essentially to train the imperial civil service. They did not teach theology, and the Orthodox Church did not monopolize education. Ecclesiastical schools for prospective clergy remained separate from the usual public educational institutions. By contrast, the barbarian invasions which afflicted the Western Empire caused secular education to disappear in the West after the 5th or 6th centuries. Urban life gradually declined, since the barbarian states could not provide the security necessary for commerce to flourish. Ruralization advanced together with increasing illiteracy.

Outside of Byzantine territory most schools in medieval Christian Europe were connected with churches or monasteries. Their primary function was to train boys for a clerical or monastic vocation, although some also accepted children from the neighborhood who had no intention of entering the Church. These early schools communicated only the minimum knowledge required for an ecclesiastical career, namely the reading of the liturgy and the most important prayers. Monks of the Western Church were supposed to know enough Latin to understand the Bible (the Latin Vulgate), the worship services, and the "Rule" of the monastery. Secular parish clergy maintained a still lower standard: most were content merely to acquire some slight knowledge of reading, and never did learn to write. In countries newly converted to Christianity, the need for priests was too pressing to permit anything more than the most cursory education. The famous Slavic school established by Saint Clement near Ohrid in Macedonia, which allegedly trained 3,500 pupils in the short space of seven years (886–93), was undoubtedly intended to turn out priests as rapidly as possible. Saint Naum's school at Preslav, the Bulgarian capital, was doubtless of the same type.

Moreover, until almost the end of the Middle Ages book learning in East Central Europe was confined to the languages used in church services— Latin, Greek, or Old Slavic. Long after the vernacular tongues had been put into writing and given rise to a genuine literature, only the church languages were considered suitable for the discussion of serious subjects. This too was a departure from ancient practice, since Greek and Latin were themselves spoken tongues at the time the ecclesiastical liturgies were created. However, while the forms of everyday speech gradually evolved, the languages of the divine service became ossified. In Western Europe, Latin had ceased to be anyone's vernacular tongue by the 8th century, which meant that it had to be learned as a foreign language. Knowledge of Latin thereby became the mark of an educated person, and usually denoted clerical status. The Slavic liturgy was considerably younger than its Greek and Latin counterparts, having been translated (generally from Greek) only in the 9th century. However, even Old Slavic (i.e., Church Slavonic) had become barely intelligible to most of the Slavic peoples by the 12th and 13th centuries.

Primary schooling was haphazardly organized in medieval Europe, and poorly differentiated from the later stages of education. Often it took place in parish churches or monasteries in the towns, with the town councils providing financial support. These grammar schools remained the most important element of medieval education. Open to boys only, they taught reading, writing, basic arithmetic, and simple Latin or Greek in addition to prayers, psalms, and church singing. At the instigation of townsmen, lay subjects like arithmetic, letter writing, and document writing eventually were added to the curriculum. Rote memory played a large part in grammar-school education, particularly since usually only the teacher possessed any books. In overall charge of the school was the vicar of the local church. He appointed the schoolmaster, who was paid either by the parishioners or by the vicar and parishioners jointly. The teacher normally possessed at least a grammar-school education and might also have attended a cathedral or collegiate school, although usually not a university. Typically he was poorly paid, and supplemented his earnings by serving as town notary or organist.

Prior to the 12th century the schools maintaining the highest intellectual standards were those connected with a cathedral (i.e., a bishop's church) They offered more advanced instruction than the parish schools; and their chief purpose was to educate clergy for work in the parishes. Together with the bishops, the canons of the cathedral chapters formed an intellectual elite in the towns. By the 14th and 15th centuries they often had received some form of higher education. Boys from the age of seven onward were taken into a bishop's household as part of his extended "family," where the bishop or his deputy sought to prepare them for the priesthood. At the head of the school stood one of the cathedral canons. The principal subjects of study were naturally those needed for a clerical vocation. In regions subject to the Roman Church this meant Latin and arithmetic—Latin for reading the liturgy; arithmetic to comprehend the tables which established the dates of Easter and the movable feasts. In the Orthodox lands Greek replaced Latin. At first the cathedral schools were chiefly concerned with training boys to assist at the Mass, although later some of these schools became genuine intellectual centers for the education of monks. Prior to the 12th century, lay persons seldom learned to read and write. The sons and daughters of the nobility were taught individually, if at all, by the chaplain of the noble household.

From the 12th century onward many schools were established in large endowed churches and administered by "colleges" (i.e., societies or guilds) of nonmonastic clergy. Each of these so-called collegiate schools apparently had a grammar school attached to it. From the beginning both the cathedral and the collegiate schools admitted a few lay pupils who did not aim at a clerical career, although this type of student became far more numerous in the 12th century and after. Gradually some of the parish churches founded schools also, while the cathedral schools began to offer a more advanced course of study. In Poland, for example, many styluses of the kind used for writing on wax tablets have been found on the sites of some rather small 12th-century settlements, indicating that parish schools were functioning at that period. In the 15th century every urban parish in Poland supported a school, although many country districts still did not. Even prior to the age of printing, some towns of East Central Europe in the late medieval period maintained small public libraries, either connected with the cathedrals or supervised by the town councils. For example, in 1442 the prosperous merchant town of Sibiu in Transylvania possessed a parish library containing 139 volumes, both literary and practical works.

The more important medieval churches often supported song-schools, intended chiefly to train choirboys. Those who attended were usually poor folk who received free board and instruction in return for their services in the church choir. Here in addition to choral singing the children were taught the basic elements of the faith, the Lord's Prayer, the Apostles' Creed, and a few anthems and psalms. Not uncommonly they learned to read Latin words without comprehending the meaning. Many children from poor families (including girls) passed through these schools, which often provided the only education the young people received. Great noblemen often required the priests in their private chapels to provide instruction for children of the aristocracy and for boys intending a clerical career. Even humble merchants and tradesmen, if they became well-to-do, sometimes founded "free" grammar schools in which instruction was given without a fee. Craft guilds and town governments often did likewise, employing a priest to provide schooling for the members' children. Finally, the growth of commercial activity in the towns stimulated a need for schools using the vernacular language. These were purely secular in intent and practical in purpose. Intended for the sons of town citizens, not for the masses, they promoted literacy in the language of ordinary speech and taught arithmetic as a useful instrument in business, not as one of the liberal arts.

Still another type of education was furnished by the mendicant or preaching friars, especially of the Dominican and Franciscan orders, whose numbers increased rapidly in Bohemia, Hungary, and Poland in the 13th century. Belonging to a community with branches throughout Europe, many of the mendicants participated in what amounted to an international scholarly exchange. Friars from East Central Europe frequently studied in schools belonging to their order in Western Europe, while some of their Western colleagues came eastward. The Dominicans in particular regarded the spread of learning as their particular mission, since preaching was viewed as an extension of scholarly activity. Each monastery was supposed to have its own teacher of grammar and logic for the training of novices. Even adult friars were required to listen to lectures. Novices in Dominican monasteries were exempted from domestic chores in order to have time for study.

The Dominicans also established a network of "general" schools to train teachers and lecturers for their order throughout Europe. In Poland several dozen such schools functioned in the 15th century. Some of them were closely allied with universities and offered similar instruction. Indeed, learned Dominicans often taught on the theological faculties of universities. The great monastic houses in the major cities often became important centers of scholastic theology and maintained well-endowed libraries. In Hungary, for example, the best schools were run by Dominicans, who accepted novices from the age of fourteen onward. Dominican higher schools (*studia*) existed in Pécs, Sibiu, and Košice. The Franciscans likewise paid much more attention to education than the older orders had done. Much of the devotional literature produced in 15th-century Hungary was inspired or produced by Franciscans; and some of it was in the Hungarian language.

The cloisters for women, by contrast, encouraged only very modest levels of learning. Medieval documents in fact have little to say about the nunneries, which in any case were far less numerous than the cloisters for men. The Rule of a convent usually required the nuns to be able to read; and each nunnery was supposed to maintain a school for novices. However, this was frequently not done. No doubt some of the noblewomen who took the veil could already read and write, although many others could not. In any case, the primary emphasis in nunneries was upon moral and religious training and (except for women of the nobility) manual work like sewing and weaving. Some of the women's cloisters did maintain schools attended by noblemen's daughters or wealthy town girls who were not taught privately at home. Since many convents were poorly endowed, the nuns were often willing to enhance their incomes by teaching girls. Nonetheless, formal education for girls in the Middle Ages was even more exceptional than instruction for boys. One obvious reason was that women were ineligible for the sacrament of priestly ordination; a nun's vows did not carry equivalent status. Similarly, the schooling which prepared young townsmen for careers in commerce was considered irrelevant for women. Although occasionally small girls were permitted to attend song-schools, the grammar schools were rigidly closed to them on the assumption that the presence of females would corrupt both the boys and the masters.

The nobility on the whole considered literacy unnecessary except in the case of boys destined for careers in the Church. Customarily a young noble at about age seven was sent as a page to the castle of a neighboring lord, where he was expected to acquire the manners and customs of upper-class society. Concurrently he might gain some knowledge of reading, writing, religion, and etiquette from the ladies of the court or from a priest. When he reached age fourteen or thereabouts the men of the court began to instruct him in riding, shooting, and hawking. Above all, the upper-class boy was taught the art of warfare. Although an occasional knight might possess some command of Latin, this was unusual. The daughters in a family of nobles or wealthy townspeople might have occasion to learn reading and writing from a chaplain, or even some Latin and French. However, the only really important attainments for an upper-class girl were polished manners, proficiency in dress, personal charm, and the skills needed to supervise a household. The behavioral code of the medieval aristocracy placed little value on book learning.

As in Catholic Europe, so also in the lands of Eastern Orthodoxy, book learning was imparted primarily in the schools attached to monasteries and cathedrals. The latter were usually found in the larger towns. Orthodox clergy were ordinarily educated in monastery schools, of which those in the Bulgarian capital of Tirnovo were especially famous. Both the cathedral and monastery schools emphasized religious subjects, and the teachers were clerics. Books and even the letters of the alphabet supposedly were divine instruments for attaining a more complete knowledge of God. The basic textbook was the Psalter (a collection of Old Testament Psalms designed for use in religious services). One of the pupils' chief tasks was to learn the Psalter and Book of Hours by heart. However, the 15th-century Bulgarian educational reformer Constantine Kostenečki opposed this method on the ground that memorization of these books must be accompanied by explanations from the teacher. For primary education the system in medieval Bulgaria was comparable to that in the Byzantine lands. In the first year the pupils were expected to learn ordinary reading and writing and memorize prayers and church songs. The school inculcated moral principles as well: fear of God, obedience, humility, uprightness, respect for elders, and the avoidance of sin.

In all the Orthodox states of the Balkans, including the Romanian principalities as well as Bulgaria and Serbia, Old Slavic was the basic medium of school instruction. Many of the monastery schools taught Greek as well, which some of the monks had learned on their wanderings or in one of the Orthodox cloisters on Mount Athos. Latin was not ordinarily a school subject, although some Balkan merchants apparently knew it, probably as a necessity in foreign trade. Purely Greek-language (i.e., non-Slavic) schools functioned in Bulgar territory also, since a considerable population of Greeks resided along the Black Sea coast and in Thrace and Macedonia. In such schools Greek grammar constituted the first level of instruction. Spelling was an important subject, since in the course of centuries the pronunciation of Greek had come to differ greatly from its written form. The pupils in these schools proceeded from grammar and spelling to the reading of the Psalter and then to the classical Greek authors, first of all Homer and Hesiod. However, literary works were treated from the standpoint of form rather than content, emphasizing choice of words, sentence construction, and metaphors. After grammar came rhetoric and finally philosophy. Many young Bulgars also attended educational institutions in the Byzantine Empire, thus preparing themselves for careers in the Church or in government service. Bulgaria lacked higher schools of the type found in the great Byzantine cities, which taught Greek philosophy and the great literary works of Greek antiquity.

Medieval Bulgaria did possess a small class of educated laymen. Some of the earliest such people were trained in the schools founded in Macedonia in the late 9th century by saints Clement and Naum. Some Bulgarian rulers were highly educated, like Tsar Symeon (r. 893–927), who became a noted patron of learning. Originally educated for a career in the Church, Symeon had studied in one of the famous schools of Constantinople, where mathematics, astronomy, rhetoric, and grammar were taught in addition to theology. Tsar John Asen II (r. 1218–41) reportedly spoke Greek; and Tsar John Alexander (r. 1331–71) knew it well. In the 13th and 14th centuries a school apparently existed at the royal court in Tirnovo for upper-class children, while middle-class pupils attended schools in some of the larger towns. Some craftsmen and soldiers of this period could read and write, while merchants unquestionably could do so. Literacy was widespread in the towns and cities of medieval Bulgaria, perhaps as high as 30 percent in the capital. This figure, while not at all remarkable by the standards of Byzantine cities, greatly exceeded the levels attained in the towns of Western Europe at that period. Undoubtedly the geographical proximity of Byzantium was a major factor in this situation. Medieval Bulgaria always stood under strong Greek influence, first as an independent state and later even more so when it was incorporated into the Byzantine Empire. Bilingualism in Greek and Slavic was common among the upper Bulgarian aristocracy and clergy.

In Latin Europe the widespread movement for Church reform in the 13th century helped to improve the condition of education, especially for clerics. Pious Christians were appalled at the all-too-common ignorance shown by priests and monks. Moreover, the institutional Church needed literate clerks to manage its constantly growing properties. In an effort to improve clerical education, the Lateran Council which met at Rome in 1215 ordered every cathedral church to maintain a teacher within its jurisdiction. Parish churches were told to do the same if possible. These schools were supposed to be open without fee to lay students as well as future clerics. While indicative of good intentions, this decree was widely ignored, usually owing to the unwillingness of local church authorities to set aside sufficient income to support a teacher. Although the number of schools continually increased during the 13th century, the typical one was still just a small-scale affair. Most supplied only a single instructor, although in major urban centers he might have one or more assistants. The usual classroom procedure consisted of imitation and memorization of texts, while the conversational method was used to impart a speaking knowledge of Latin. Since East Central Europe lagged behind the Latin West in education, many of the first teachers in Poland, Bohemia, or Hungary came from Western Europe. One proof of this is the striking similarity in the styles of handwriting on documents produced in both parts of Europe in the 12th and 13th centuries.

The curriculum of secondary schools in medieval East Central Europe conformed to the general European pattern, which in turn had been adopted from the models of classical antiquity. The old Greek theorists had recommended a program of liberal arts consisting of grammar, rhetoric, dialectic, arithmetic, geometry, music, astronomy, drawing, and gymnastics. The Romans had added medicine, law, and architecture. By the late 3rd century A.D., a fixed system of seven liberal arts had become fairly standard in the Roman Empire. Medieval Christian education largely followed this formal pattern, although the spirit had been vastly altered since ancient times. The seven arts were divided into the trivium (grammar, rhetoric, and dialectic) and quadrivium (arithmetic, geometry, music, and astronomy). However, the seven received very unequal attention, since grammar (which meant reading and writing in either Latin, Greek, or Old Slavic, depending on the region in question) easily took pride of place. It comprised grammatical theory as well as the study of texts, and constituted the foundation for all further study. Instruction was based on a few classical writings, which were used as manuals of style rather than for purposes of literary appreciation or mastery of the contents.

The other six liberal arts were relatively neglected in medieval education. Rhetoric to the Romans had meant the art of elegant expression, especially the use of dialogues and figures of speech in oratory. However, the civic function of oratory in debates on public policy had become irrelevant in the monarchical states of the Middle Ages. Europeans now cultivated oratory chiefly in the form of preaching, so that rhetoric usually meant the writing of documents and letters. Dialectic, which the ancients had defined as pure philosophy in the manner of Plato's dialogues, now denoted either formal logic or the art of argument as used in theological disputations. The first member of the quadrivium, arithmetic, was a purely abstract study of the nature of number. Considered essential to an understanding of God's universe, it was designed to lead the soul away from this world toward contemplation of the divine. Medieval arithmetic dealt with such concepts as unity, equality, ratio, and proportion. In practical form (i.e., the art of calculating with Roman numerals, aided by an abacus) it was needed to fix the dates of church festivals. Geometry extended the arithmetical notions of proportion and harmony to two- and three-dimensional figures. However, geometrical studies remained very elementary in medieval Europe until the 12th century, when contact with Muslim scholarship in Spain and southern Italy caused some revival of interest in this subject. Music in the medieval curriculum signified harmony, which meant ratio and proportion expressed in musical terms. The Greeks had considered music essential to the formation of character, since it was believed to promote harmony of the soul. Even in medieval times its connection with ethics was never forgotten. In addition, music was studied for its use in church services. Astronomy, the final discipline in the medieval program of liberal arts, applied proportion, harmony, and geometry to the study of the stars and planets. Nonetheless, practical knowledge of astronomy remained rudimentary in Europe until the 12th century, when contacts with the Muslim world became more frequent.

As society became more complex, literacy became more necessary in secular as well as clerical life. A fully literate person needed the ability to read not only the comparatively simple church books, but also the cursive script which was used for economic, political, and legal records. A growing commerce demanded that merchants be capable of keeping written accounts. By the late 12th and the 13th centuries (although much earlier in the southern sector of East Central Europe), writing began to be used for private documents, such as transfers of property. Governments began to record their official acts, and courts their judicial decisions. Additional scribes were added as governmental and judicial functions became more extensive.

For example, in Hungary by the early 12th century a fair number of higher state officials either were literate themselves or used the services of a scribe. Lay clerks, who were often minor nobles by origin, served in municipal, county, or royal judicial offices, where they needed not only a knowledge of Latin and penmanship but also some acquaintance with customary law. Laymen occasionally even worked for ecclesiastical institutions. Nonetheless, this growing use of written records did not mean that literacy became commonplace in secular society, even for the upper classes. It is safe to say that the overwhelming majority of nobles in medieval Hungary were illiterate and resorted to writing only on rare occasions. The archives of the great noble families ordinarily contained only the records pertaining to their landed properties (i.e., documents concerning royal gifts, mortgage deeds, or lawsuits). Sometimes these charters were entrusted to ecclesiastical institutions for safekeeping. By the 15th century, it is true, letter writing did develop to some extent among the aristocracy. Among townspeople the level of literacy was higher. Many 15th-century citizens of Buda could read and write in Hungarian and German, sometimes also in Latin.

A very important function in medieval society was that of the public notaries who drew up legal documents or copied records and manuscripts for the benefit of people unable to read or write. Students at the cathedral schools often performed this function. In Hungary King Andrew II (r. 1205–35) authorized the cathedral chapters and larger monasteries to provide this service and to keep copies of relevant documents. In the 13th century a class of secular lawyers also made its appearance, drawn from the sons of petty nobles, townsmen, or occasionally even peasants. After mastering sufficient Latin in one of the nearby schools, an aspiring lawyer served a practical apprenticeship with a respected notary to learn how to draft documents and represent clients in court. "Peasant scribes" functioned as notaries in some of the several hundred market towns existing in medieval Hungary. Probably such scribes were at least as numerous as literate noblemen. By the 15th century, Hungarian county administration had become more complex and employed some of the better-educated nobles. Great estates also began keeping written accounts, recording tenants' rents and dues for the information of overseers. Lords who held land in various parts of the kingdom communicated in writing with their stewards, whom they rarely met personally.

Lay literacy in medieval Europe benefited greatly from the increasing availability of paper, which eventually came to replace parchment for most writing purposes. Prior to the 12th century, when papyrus from Egypt or paper from the Middle East became widely available in Europe, writing had to be done on parchment produced from animal skins. As a result, books remained rare and expensive. Paper was thinner than parchment and very much cheaper. Its surface was also smoother, which facilitated the process of making an ink impression from carvings on wood. Although paper produced from mulberry bark or rags had been known in China ever since the 2nd or 3rd century A.D., it spread westward to the Arab world only in the 8th century. The art of papermaking was introduced into Europe by the Moors in the mid-12th century, and thereafter spread gradually throughout the continent. Paper made possible a more frequent use of the pen and contributed to the spread of vernacular literature. Nonetheless, important documents continued to be written on parchment, which was more durable than paper. Parchment could also be washed and used again, although it was more difficult to work than paper. It had the added advantage that its raw material was obtainable almost anywhere, from sheep, calves, or goats.

A still greater stimulus to literacy in the 15th century was the invention and spread of printing presses, which made possible the cheap and rapid multiplication of reading material. Like printing itself, movable type had been invented in China well before its appearance in Europe, although the Chinese had made no practical use of the idea and continued to use the old wood-block system. The operative printing press with movable type is a European invention, dating from about 1450 and usually credited to Johann Gutenberg of Mainz. This new device spread into East Central Europe with a speed remarkable for that period. Among the Slavic nations the first printers were Czechs. As early as 1468 a press was established at Plzeň in western Bohemia, which produced the first books in the Czech vernacular. The first Bible in a Slavic language was published in Prague in 1488, followed by another at Kutná Hora in 1489—the latter a genuine work of art done in black and red type with over a hundred woodcuts. Hungary and Poland saw the appearance of their first printed books during the same year: 1473. In Royal Prussia a press was established at Malbork in 1492 and at Gdańsk in 1499. The first Croatian book in the Glagolitic script appeared in Venice in 1483, although Glagolitic presses were set up soon afterward in Croatia itself, at Senj and Rijeka. The first press to use the Cyrillic alphabet was established at Cracow in 1491, where many leading nobles at the royal court were Lithuanian in origin and Orthodox in faith. However, since Cyrillic was the script of the Old Slavic books used in Orthodox church services, the Catholic Inquisition forced the printer (a German immigrant) to discontinue his activities by arresting him for heresy. Cyrillic printing continued at Cetinje in Montenegro in 1494–96, sponsored by the local prince, and at Tîrgoviște in Walachia in 1508–1512. Although none of these early presses survived for long, they set the example for the much more extensive Cyrillic printing of the 16th century. Most of the literature which came off the European presses in the 15th century was typically medieval in content—works of piety, didactic tracts, chronicles, and legal writings, generally in Latin. By contrast, the Muslim ulema regarded printing (even for religious purposes) as dangerous to the faith, and they firmly opposed its introduction. The earliest presses in the Ottoman Empire were established by the Greeks, Armenians, and Jews of the Empire for their own communities, although they also issued some books in the Arabic alphabet. The first Ottoman press to be founded by a Muslim dates only from the 18th century, authorized by the enlightened Grand Vizier Ibrahim Pasha (1718–30). Even then the printer—a man of Transylvanian origin but a convert to Islam—was allowed to publish only dictionaries and scientific or historical works, nothing of a religious nature.

The late 12th and early 13th centuries saw the rise of medieval Europe's first universities, providing more advanced instruction than the courses offered in cathedral or collegiate schools. The university as it took form at that time became the direct ancestor of the modern Western establishments of higher learning. Impetus for this development came from the growth of towns and trade, the inadequacy of the older schools to meet the needs of a developing society, and the increasing contacts of Europeans with Greek and Muslim scholars. The state-supported university at Constantinople, initially organized in A.D. 425, taught both Greek and Latin grammar as well as rhetoric, philosophy, and jurisprudence. Experiencing various periods of both decline and recovery, it was revived in 1045 with a curriculum based on the traditional trivium, quadrivium, and finally philosophy. The patriarch's school, which taught theology, was an institution entirely separate from the imperial university, although students sometimes attended both, either successively or concurrently. The Byzantines never considered theology and classical learning as mutually exclusive. Nor did they ever study canon law apart from secular law. The Church was a part of the body politic; and the Emperor was regarded as the source and guarantor of Christian law.

In Western Europe the first universities originated as a type of trade guild or corporation (in Latin: *universitas*), organized by either teachers or students to protect their mutual interests. In time they attracted most of the scholars with international reputations, so that the cathedral schools began limiting themselves to the teaching grammar and rhetoric. The original universities were associations consisting largely of laymen and independent of outside control. The earliest ones, like Oxford and Paris, were not established by any official act of an emperor, pope, or king, but evolved gradually through the expansion of a cathedral school. Students and teachers enjoyed the privileged status typically granted to clergy in medieval society. This included: (1) protection from violence on their travels; (2) the right to trial in special university courts; (3) the right of the university to suspend its existence and move to another place; (4) the right of graduates to teach anywhere in Christendom; (5) freedom from taxes on personal property; and (6) exemption from military service.

Eventually both the Church and the secular rulers sought to exert authority over the universities by granting them charters of foundation and guaranteeing their rights. In Latin Europe the first universities to be established by the specific act of a monarch arose in 1212 and 1220 in Spain. Soon afterward such acts of foundation became common. Sovereigns issued charters to universities and provided them with land, buildings, and endowments. However, the notion soon took hold that only the approval of the pope could give an institution complete legitimacy. Papal authorization was regarded as a guarantee of academic quality and religious orthodoxy. In 1346, when Charles I of Bohemia sought to establish a university at Prague, thirty such institutions already existed in Europe, including thirteen in Italy, six in France, six in the Iberian Peninsula, and two in England. All but one (Emperor Frederick II's university at Naples) had been authorized by the pope.

The medieval university was an institution for males only. Since one of its primary purposes was to train clergy, preparation for holy orders had the effect of excluding women. Whether or not a student intended to follow a clerical career, he usually received the "minor order" of tonsure (shaving of the head), wore clerical dress, and resided in an all-male community in some hostel or "college" of the university. The majority of students were exceedingly young by modern standards, often no more than fourteen years old, although they might sit together on the benches with mature men who had come to education later in life. Many were desperately poor, although some held church benefices which provided a comfortable income. Town boys in particular were likely to aspire to higher education, since they held no inherited social position and expected to make their own way in the world. However, wealth was not the invariable prerequisite for attending a university. Sometimes the children of poor artisans, and even an occasional peasant, managed to acquire the necessary grammar-school preparation. Talented boys of all classes might find well-situated patrons to help them toward a career in the Church. However, students needed a reasonable command of Latin in order to follow the lectures. This requirement frequently caused difficulties, since many young men arrived with insufficient prior knowledge. On the other hand, the ubiquity of Latin as the language of the Roman Church permitted a student to attend a university anywhere in Western Christendom with no language barrier.

The curriculum of a university was essentially similar throughout Latin Europe, consisting of advanced instruction in the seven liberal arts. The content of instruction was heavily influenced by Aristotle, whose authority was considered final. Ancient classical literature was ignored. Since books were scarce, teachers used the methods of lecture, dictation, and logical disputation, while students memorized class notes. Examinations on subject matter were often perfunctory. Much more important were the public disputations or debates, based on the scholastic method of argument, which gave students and teachers the opportunity to gain a scholarly reputation. If a man had fulfilled the prescribed length of residence at a university, possessed no obvious faults of character, swore that he had read the prescribed authorities, and paid the proper fees, he received his degree as master of arts. This diploma was a prerequisite to the study of medicine or theology and sometimes also of law. These further studies led to an additional master's or doctor's degree (in the medieval period the two titles were often used interchangeably).

University instruction began in the faculty of arts. The course in liberal arts normally lasted from four to seven years; courses in law and medicine required from five to eight years; and a knowledge of Roman law was prerequisite to the study of canon law. A doctorate in theology took longest, usually about eight years. However, most students at medieval universities never went beyond the study of arts. The bachelor's degree was not offered at first, but developed later out of the practice of letting advanced students give lectures. Eventually a formal examination was devised to test students who qualified for lectureships, and those who passed received a bachelor's degree. A master or doctor had the right to teach at any university in Western Christendom, provided that he could find students. However, possession of a degree did not guarantee adequate teaching. Especially in the arts faculty, most instructors were young and inexperienced and had not satisfied any real test of their knowledge. Unless they held a church benefice, their support came from the small and precarious fees paid by their hearers.

The universities of Western Christendom drew students and teachers from all countries where Latin was the language of the Church. Since no institution of higher learning existed anywhere in East Central Europe or even in the German Empire until the mid-14th century, students from these regions were obliged to seek higher education farther afield, usually in Italy or France. Matriculation records show that natives of Hungary (including Croatia) occasionally studied at the universities of Paris, Padua, Bologna, or Oxford in the 12th and 13th centuries, while many more did so during the 14th century. Students from Poland and Bohemia also attended these schools. Then after universities were founded at Prague, Cracow, and Vienna in the middle and late 14th century, many young men chose to study at one of the locations closer to home. The favored foreign institution for Poles was Prague until the Hussite reformers became dominant there early in the 15th century. From primarily Orthodox Moldavia, students who perhaps belonged to the small Catholic minority in that country came to study at Prague, Vienna, or Cracow.

The oldest university in either Central or East Central Europe was founded in Prague by King Charles I (Emperor Charles IV) in 1348. However, this was not the first attempt to establish a university for Bohemia. A half-century earlier King Wenceslas II had failed in his efforts to found one, frustrated by the opposition of nobles who feared that an institution of higher learning would enhance the prestige of king and Church. Charles was in a stronger position than his predecessor, since he was German emperor as well as king. Moreover, Pope Clement VI was his former teacher, and willing to approve the project. Charles's ambition was to make Prague the focal point of the German Empire. His new university was intended to provide not only spiritual leadership but also competent secular officials for the empire as well as for Bohemia. In 1347, Pope Clement authorized the establishment at Prague of all the four faculties necessary for a full-fledged medieval university: (liberal) arts, theology, medicine, and law. This made Charles's new foundation from the outset more complete than most other institutions of higher learning in Europe, which usually lacked one or more of the faculties. Papal permission for a faculty of theology was particularly valued, since the papacy had previously acted to maintain a monopoly of theological instruction for the universities of Paris, Oxford, and a very few others.

In April 1348, the new university was born at Prague. By its original charter Charles granted it "all the privileges, immunities and liberties" enjoyed by the two most prestigious universities in Western Europe, Paris and Bologna. He made a point of inviting scholars and students from all over Christendom to teach and study at Prague. Initially the largest number of masters there were Germans, most of whom had been educated at Paris, although the number of Czech masters gradually increased. For seventeen years Prague remained the only university in Central Europe. Then in rapid succession various others came into existence: Vienna, Erfurt, Heidelberg, and Cologne (founded in 1365, 1379, 1385, and 1388 respectively). Prague lost some personnel to the newer institutions, but retained its international stature until the Hussite period. In 1385, a year for which figures happen to be available, the university granted 234 bachelor's degrees, while 200 students were enrolled in the faculty of law—a very high number for that time. In all three faculties together, Prague had 50 masters with the rank of professor in addition to 200 graduates serving as unpaid teaching assistants. Prague's influence on neighboring universities was considerable, since some of its early graduates went on to teach at Vienna, Heidelberg, or Cracow.

In typical medieval fashion, the masters and students of the arts faculty at Prague were organized into "nations." This term referred only to a geographical area, not to nationality in the modern sense of ethnicity. A person's native language was considered irrelevant in the Latin-dominated world of higher education. At Prague the four nations corresponded to the four points of the compass. The "Bohemian" nation (South) included everyone from Bohemia, whether Czech-speaking or German-speaking, together with Hungarians. The "Polish" nation (East) encompassed not only ethnic Poles but also Silesians and Lusatians, who were subjects of the King of Bohemia but largely German in speech. The "Bavarian" nation (West) was defined to take in everyone from Western Europe, which in practice meant mostly Germans, while other Germans belonged to the "Saxon" nation (North). This division had considerable practical significance, since according to ancient custom, students took most of their courses and examinations with masters of their own "nation." It was also important for purposes of institutional governance, since each "nation" held one vote in the rector's advisory council, to which all masters and doctors of the university were admitted.

As natives of Bohemia became proportionately more numerous among the masters at Prague's university, this arrangement aroused objections. The spread of higher education had not been accompanied by a corresponding increase in the number of positions available in the Church or university, so that posts occupied by foreigners constituted a real grievance. As the Czech masters became more conscious of national identity, they came to resent the rigid division into "nations" which permitted the three predominantly German groups to outvote the Czechs in their own country. Moreover, during the quarrels over Wyclif's theology which erupted at the university in the early 15th century, Czechs and Germans usually found themselves on opposite sides of the argument. At this point the Czech masters pressed King Wenceslas IV to reform the university's voting system, pointing out that their teaching (like Wyclif's) assigned to the secular power the foremost role in carrying out church reforms. Finally in 1409 by the decree of Kutná Hora, Wenceslas granted the Bohemian nation three votes in university governance, reserving just one vote for all three of the German nations combined. The Germans lodged a vehement protest, but the King stood by his decision. The result was a large-scale exodus of Germans from Prague to Leipzig in Saxony, where they proceeded to found a new university.

The decree of Kutná Hora effectively deprived the university at Prague of its international standing. In complete contradiction to Charles IV's original intentions, it now became a purely national institution, overwhelmingly Czech in character. After Kutná Hora the university even lost its position of intellectual leadership within Bohemia itself. The burning at the stake of John Hus and his fellow reformer Jerome at Constance in 1415 brought about a radicalization of the Hussite movement. Thereafter the university largely followed in the wake of theological developments, rather than leading the way. When the Czech masters in 1417 finally passed a resolution approving the chalice (i.e., communion in both kinds for the laity), this practice had already been adopted by the entire Hussite movement. By granting scholarly legitimacy to this moderate reform, the Prague masters had hoped to prevent the Hussite movement from becoming more radical; but meanwhile the Hussites had become the dominant political force in Bohemia. Furthermore, by identifying itself with Hussitism in any way at all, the university effectively closed its doors to all Christians remaining loyal to the pope. Even within Bohemia, Catholics who sought higher education now gravitated toward foreign universities. Vienna, Leipzig, and Cracow became places of exile for anti-Hussite professors, while students from abroad usually avoided Prague for fear of the taint of heresy.

The second-oldest institution of higher learning in East Central Europe was founded in 1364 at Cracow by King Casimir III. His model was the university at Bologna, famous throughout Europe for its law faculty. Casimir viewed his new establishment chiefly as a place to train lawyers for the royal court and diplomatic service. Nonetheless, he wanted it to include all four faculties, including theology. Unfortunately for his plans, Pope Urban V was committed to maintaining the theological monopoly of Paris and Oxford, for fear that if theology was taught in too many places, the content of instruction would be difficult to control and might then lead to heresy. At two other universities founded during his pontificate—Vienna (1365) and Pécs (1367)—Urban similarly refused to authorize a theological faculty. With respect to Cracow the issue soon became irrelevant, since King Casimir's university proved to be short-lived. The king paid its expenses out of his own resources during his lifetime, since the bishop of Cracow, with whom he was then at loggerheads, refused to assign any ecclesiastical benefices for its support. This lack of a permanent endowment proved fatal. When Casimir died in 1370, the university did not yet stand on a firm financial basis. Shortly afterward it closed its doors.

The university of Cracow was reestablished at the end of the 14th century by King Jagiełło and Queen Jadwiga. In 1397 they asked the pope for permission to establish a theological faculty; and after long and difficult negotiations this was granted. The ostensible justification for this new foundation was the need to educate priests for the conversion of Lithuania, the large pagan territory recently united with Poland; and its designated chancellor was the bishop of Cracow. When Queen Jadwiga died in 1399, her final testament authorized the sale of her personal jewels in order to place the university's finances on a solid basis. The revived institution, known thereafter as the Jagiellonian University, opened its doors in 1400 as a full-fledged institution of higher learning with all four faculties. The king himself endowed many of its professorial chairs, chiefly those for theology and canon law. Already in the first years of its existence the university had a faculty of forty—a very large figure for the time. Its organizational model was Paris, while many of the early masters came from Prague.

Thanks to Queen Jadwiga's bequest, the existence of the Cracow university was not again interrupted. Polish monarchs often sought the opinion of its scholars, especially in the field of Roman law; and the university's influence over Polish intellectual life was enormous. Canon law became the dominant subject of study at Cracow, contrary to the earlier wishes of Casimir III, who had favored Roman law. Nor did the university always keep up with modern trends in thought. As late as the closing years of the 15th century it continued to be dominated by medieval scholastic philosophy, despite the increasing attraction of Renaissance humanism for many of its students. The works of classical Roman authors, so beloved by humanists, were long forbidden in Cracow's lecture halls. The study of Greek was introduced there only in about 1500. However, in the physical sciences, especially mathematics and astronomy, the university enjoyed a high reputation. Its most famous alumnus was a native of Royal Prussia, Nicholas Copernicus, the modern originator of the heliocentric theory of planetary motion. Copernicus studied at Cracow from 1491 to 1495, afterward completing his education in Italy.

By contrast, Hungary remained without a permanent institution of higher learning throughout the Middle Ages, although three different monarchs attempted to found one. The first was King Louis I, who established a university at Pécs in 1367, probably to train officials for the royal court. In 1395 and 1410, King Sigismund made two more attempts at Buda. In both towns the institution failed to last, apparently owing to the lack of a solid endowment. Hungarians who desired a higher education therefore had to seek it abroad. In the 13th and 14th centuries Italy was their favored destination, thanks to the reputation of the Italian law faculties. Subsequently the new universities founded at Prague, Cracow, and Vienna attracted many Hungarian students. In the latter part of the 15th century Vienna was popular for its offerings in astronomy, the favorite scholarly pastime at King Matthias's court. In 1465, Matthias himself founded a university at Bratislava (Pozsony), directed by the court humanist John Vitéz. However, like the two previous institutions of its type in medieval Hungary, it failed to outlive its founder. Similarly short-lived was the law faculty founded at Malbork by the grand master of the Teutonic Knights, Winrich of Kniprode (r. 1351–82), whose plans for a university at Chełmno also failed to materialize. In any case, as long as a military order set the tone for Prussian society, education did not enjoy a high priority, although the Order necessarily included some learned clerics to carry out the tasks of government.

The Ottoman conquests in the Balkan Peninsula inevitably had an adverse effect upon education for Christians. Formerly the Orthodox monasteries had provided schools for the clergy and a place for monks to engage in literary pursuits. Little specific information is available about the state of these monasteries under Turkish rule, but it is unlikely that they were in flourishing condition. The outstanding literary figures of the medieval Balkans all date from pre-Ottoman times. Even in Walachia and Moldavia, which never fell under direct Turkish hegemony, the monasteries lost many of their international connections. Nonetheless, they were the only places where Old Slavic scholarship was cultivated at all. Greek-language schools on the old Byzantine pattern presumably existed in a few of the larger Balkan towns, primarily for the benefit of the Greek merchant class. Jewish rabbinical schools likewise functioned in some places. However, education in the Ottoman Empire was predominantly Muslim in character, geared to the needs of the state or the Islamic religious community.

Basic education for Muslim boys was provided in schools where the pupils were taught to recite portions of the Koran from memory and sometimes also to read and write. These primary schools were quite numerous in the towns of the Ottoman Empire, including its European provinces. Usually attached to a mosque, they provided the basic religious instruction for Muslims in all the Islamic lands. In addition, boys preparing for higher education were taught to recite portions of the Koran in Arabic. However, the teachers made little attempt to explain the meaning of the texts, since ability to repeat the sacred words correctly was the desired accomplishment. The more advanced Muslim education was provided by the schools known as medrese, which were run by ulema (i.e., men learned in Islamic law). Graduates of the medreses often went on to become kadis, or judges, since no secular form of justice existed in the Ottoman world. The school itself was usually part of a larger complex, which included a mosque and perhaps a hospice or other charitable institution. Financial support usually came from charitable endowments (vakifs).

The ulema who taught in the Muslim schools were not a priestly class per se, since Islam recognizes no intermediary between God and man. Nonetheless, until the days of Ottoman decline the ulema were accorded high respect for their learning. Muslims believed that the highest form of education was religious, directed toward an understanding of God's word as recorded in the Koran and the Traditions (*Hadith*) handed down from the Prophet Mohammed. The method of scholarship was compilation and annotation of sources, followed by commentary upon them. Proof for any argument was sought first in the Koran, then in the Traditions, then in precedent. Reason was no more than the servant of religion, to be used as a last resort. The Ottomans practiced a type of analysis similar to the Scholasticism of Catholic Europe, which sought to affirm the unassailable truths of the faith through rational argument. Ultimately this kind of scholarship became a heavy weight upon Islamic thought, rendering intellectual innovation almost impossible.

The most eminent educational institution in the Ottoman Empire was the palace school at Istanbul, where young boys (largely products of the devşirme, or child tribute) were trained for government service. Instruction was based on the Arabic, Persian, and Turkish classics of poetry, history, and fine arts, with the addition of military skills like horsemanship, archery, fencing, and wrestling. The objective was to produce warrior statesmen who would be both loyal to the sultan and capable of filling the highest offices of the empire. Artists and scholars as well as soldiers and administrators were educated in this school, which served as the principal fount of Ottoman culture. In the 15th century, Sultan Murad II endowed schools in all of his larger cities, a tradition continued by Mohammed the Conqueror. On the other hand, little is known about the education provided by the nonimperial households in the empire or in the cities outside of Istanbul, though it is safe to assume that the sons of high Ottoman officials acquired a gentlemanly breeding similar to that provided at court. Certainly the Turkish sources do not give evidence of any difference in cultural or intellectual status between the men trained in the imperial palace and those educated elsewhere.

Despite important advances by the end of the 15th century, the number of university-educated, or even minimally literate persons in East Central Europe remained small down to the end of the medieval period. Admittedly, the process of economic and social development was gradually creating a more complex society in which higher educational standards would be required. Poland in the 16th century would experience a notable cultural Renaissance. At the same time the Protestant Reformation was promoting education in the spoken languages to enable ordinary believers to read the Bible. For a while the Reformation would make serious inroads in Poland, Bohemia and Hungary. However, the Ottoman-ruled lands were destined to stand aside both from this religious ferment and from the commercial revolution occurring in Western Europe. They remained aloof from the classical scholarship of the Renaissance and the spiritual upheaval of the Reformation. To be sure, even in the northern sector of East Central Europe until quite recent times the general level of learning would remain abysmally low by modern (or even Byzantine) standards. Education and literacy—the foundation of all higher culture—would continue to be the privilege of just a small (albeit influential) social and religious elite.

APPENDIX 1

Chronology of Important Events

681	Byzantium recognizes the existence of independent Bulgaria
863	Cyril and Methodius begin their mission to the Slavs; Khan Boris of Bulgaria accepts Christianity
889–93	Pagan reaction engulfs Bulgaria
893	Bulgarian Sabor (assembly) establishes Tsar Symeon on the throne and proclaims Cyrillic the official alphabet in Bulgaria
895–96	Magyar invaders occupy the plain of Hungary;
913	Bulgar Tsar Symeon advances to the walls of Constantinople
917 or 919	Tsar Symeon creates the first Bulgarian archbishopric
925	Synod of Split attempts to discourage the Slavic liturgy in Croatia
933	German coalition led by King Henry I defeats the Magyars at Merseburg
938–50	German King Otto I campaigns against the Slavs east of the Elbe
955	Germans under Otto I decisively defeat the Magyars at Lechfeld
962	Otto I "the Great" is crowned emperor by the pope, reviving in theory the Roman Empire in the West
963	The name of a Polish tribe first appears in historical sources
965	Jewish merchant Ibn Jakub reports on his travels in Bohemia
966	Duke Mieszko I of Poland accepts Christianity
967–72	Prince Sviatoslav of Kiev invades Bulgaria at Byzantine invitation and captures various towns on the lower Danube
971	Regent John Tzimiskes restores Byzantine rule in eastern Bulgaria
990–91	Document "Dagome iudex" declares Poland a fief of the Holy See
991–1014	Emperor Basil II campaigns against Bulgaria
997	Saint Adalbert, revered by Poles and Czechs alike, is martyred in pagan Prussia
1000	German emperor Otto III visits Gniezno and crowns Duke Boleslav I; the first Polish archbishopric is founded at Gniezno; King Stephen I orders the conversion of Hungary to Christianity
1014	Emperor Basil II definitively defeats the Bulgar Tsar Samuel
1018	Bulgaria reverts to Byzantine rule after long wars (remaining under Byzantine control until 1186)

1022	Heathen revolt flares up in Poland
1032–57	Sázava monastery in Bohemia functions with a Slavic liturgy
1034–40	Renewed heathen uprising occurs in Poland
1039	Bohemian invaders steal the body of Saint Adalbert from Poland
1040	Nobles attempt to place a Serbian prince on the throne of Bulgaria
1046	Heathen uprising occurs in Hungary
1054	Final split occurs between the Eastern and Western churches
1059–60	Second synod of Split continues to oppose a Slavic liturgy
1060s and 1070s	Pechenegs, Iazygs, and Cumans attack along the lower Danube
1072–73	Nobles attempt to place a Serbian prince in the throne of Bulgaria
1072–94	League of towns governs independently in Dobrudja
1079	Archbishop (later Saint) Stanislas is murdered in Cracow cathedral
1091	Hungarian army occupies Slavonia after the death of the last Croatian king
1096	Crusaders' persecution of Jews in Germany promotes Jewish immigration into East Central Europe
1096–99	First Crusade is fought to recover the Holy Land for Christianity
1102	Pacta Conventa set the terms of Croatia's union with Hungary
1115–18	Gallus Anonymous writes his history of the Polish state
1119–22	Cosmas of Prague composes his *Chronica Bohemorum*
1123 and 1139	Lateran councils at Rome forbid laypersons to be proprietors of churches or make priestly appointments
1138–1310	The Polish state remains divided into semi-independent appanages
1147–49	Second Crusade to the Holy Land is conducted by Conrad III of Germany and Louis VII of France
1163	Byzantine Emperor Manuel I campaigns successfully in Dalmatia
1165	Hungarian Prince Béla is named heir to Byzantine throne; Emperor Manuel lays claim to Syrmia and Dalmatia as Béla's inheritance
1168	Crusader William of Tyre records his impressions of Serbia
1172	Prince Béla returns from Constantinople to Hungary as King Béla III
1180	Emperor Manuel I Comnenus's death inaugurates a period of Byzantine weakness
1185	Synod of Latin bishops at Split declares the Orthodox to be heretics
1185–86	Asen brothers in Bulgaria successfully revolt against Byzantium and reestablish an independent Bulgar state
1187–1393	Bulgaria remains an independent state (Second Bulgarian Empire)
1189–90	Teutonic Order of Knights is founded in Palestine
1189–92	Third Crusade is fought in the Holy Land
1197	Polish Church issues its first injunctions on the subject of celibacy; province (march) of Moravia becomes subordinate to Bohemia
1199	Venetians gain extraterritorial rights in the Byzantine Empire

1202	Fourth Crusade takes and then abandons Zadar in Dalmatia
1204	Fourth Crusade captures Constantinople, establishing the Latin Empire
1204–61	Latin Empire (Constantinople and surrounding territories) is ruled by Western Christians, while Byzantine emperors rule from Nicaea
1205	Bulgar Tsar Kaloyan defeats the Latins in battle at Adrianople, occupies western Macedonia and Thrace
1207	Canons of Cracow cathedral freely elect a bishop for the first time
1211	Bulgarian church synod at Tirnovo proclaims the Bogomil doctrine to be heretical; King Andrew II of Hungary permits Teutonic Order of Knights to settle in eastern Transylvania
1212	Emperor Frederick II issues his "Sicilian" Golden Bull, renouncing some imperial rights over Bohemia
1217	Serbian ruler Stephen II receives a royal crown from the pope; King Andrew II of Hungary joins the Fifth Crusade;
1219	Monk (later Saint) Sava becomes the first archbishop of Serbia
1220	Orthodox patriarch agrees to an autonomous Serbian Church
1221	Vienna establishes a staple to create a trade monopoly; Mongol commander Subutai leads long-range campaign from Mongolia through southern Russia into Georgia and Crimea; Serbian church council proclaims parts of the Byzantine *Nomocanon* as legal foundation of the Serbian Church;
1222	Hungarian lords force King Andrew II to issue the Golden Bull, a charter of rights for the nobility
1223	The first known grant of municipal liberties to a Bohemian town is issued; Polish historian Vincent Kadłubek dies; Mongols under Subutai smash a coalition of Russian and Cuman princes on the Kalka River
1224	King Andrew II of Hungary issues the "Andreanum," granting rights of self–government to the Saxons of Transylvania
1225	Andrew II establishes separate territories for the Saxons and Szeklers of Transylvania, but expels the Teutonic Knights from that province
1226	Duke Conrad of Mazovia invites Teutonic Knights to settle in Prussia
1230	Teutonic Knights begin settlement in Prussia; Theodore of Epirus attacks Bulgaria but is defeated at Klokotnica
1231	Second Hungarian Golden Bull confirms provisions of the earlier one
1233	Pope Gregory IX founds the Inquisition to combat heresy
1234–38	Hungarians conduct a Crusade against alleged Bosnian heretics
1235	A Bulgar patriarchate is reestablished at Tirnovo

1237–40	Mongols (Tatars) conquer southern and central Russia
1238	Volhynian princes annex Galicia
1241	Mongol armies invade and devastate Poland and Hungary
1242	Mongols withdraw from Europe upon hearing of the Great Khan's death
1244	Duke Frederick of Austria issues his charter of privileges for Jews, which becomes widely imitated in East Central Europe
1246	Bulgaria gets a child ruler, enabling the Nicaeans to begin occupying Bulgar territory
1248 and 1252	Pope Innocent IV authorizes the use of a Slavic liturgy where it already exists
1251	King Béla IV issues the first Hungarian charter of privileges for Jews
1254	King Ottokar II issues the first Bohemian charter of Jewish privileges
1259	Mongols assault Sandomierz, Lublin, and Cracow, but then retreat
1260–73	Pagan uprising occurs in Prussia
1261	Nicaeans recapture Constantinople, overthrowing the Latin Empire
1264	Duke Boleslav the Pious of Great Poland issues the first Polish charter of privileges for Jews
1266	Church council in Wrocław recommends discrimination against Jews; at the battle of Beneventum Charles of Anjou wins the crown of the Two Sicilies, a base for his attempt to restore the Latin Empire
1267	Hungarian law forbids the king to judge a nobleman except in the presence of an assembly of nobles
1270 and 1272	Croatian Sabor refuses to recognize a king elected in Hungary
1270s	Swineherd Ivailo leads Bulgarians against the Tatars, becomes tsar
1274	Council of Lyons proclaims union of the Eastern and Western churches
1278	King Ottokar II of Bohemia is defeated and killed at the battle of Marchfeld, ending his efforts to annex several Austrian provinces
1280	Tatar chief Nogai makes himself independent of the Golden Horde
1281	Byzantines defeat Charles of Anjou at the battle of Berat in Albania
1282	"Sicilian Vespers" uprising prevents Charles of Anjou from invading the Byzantine Empire
1283	Simon Kézai produces his Latin chronicle of Hungarian history
1285	Byzantine rule is partly restored in Albania; synod at Łęczyca seeks to make the Church in Poland more Polish; Bulgar Tsar George Terter accepts the supremacy of Khan Nogai (replacing that of the Golden Horde)

1288	*Vinodol Codex*, an ancient Croatian law code in Glagolitic script, is produced; the first recorded meeting of a separate Transylvanian Diet takes place
1290–1301	Bohemian King Wenceslas II overruns Poland
1297	Catholic Inquisition is introduced into Bohemia
1301	Árpád dynasty dies out in Hungary
1306	Přemyslid dynasty dies out in Bohemia
1307–78	The pope maintains his residence at Avignon
1309	Teutonic Order moves its headquarters from Venice to Malbork in Prussia
1310	"Dalimil" writes his Czech chronicle; Anjou (Angevin) dynasty is established in Hungary; Luxemburg dynasty is established in Bohemia; Vladislav Łokietek reunifies much of Poland and becomes king
1310–11	King John of Bohemia agrees to limit his nobles' military obligation
1318	Catholic Inquisition is introduced into Poland
1321	King John of Bohemia gives Nürnberg merchants freedom to trade in his kingdom
1323	Hungarian King Charles Robert establishes a reliable gold currency; Hungarian Diet meets for the last time during Charles Robert's reign
1327	Hungary and Bohemia attempt to establish a joint currency
1330	Serbian King Stephen Dečanski defeats the Bulgars at Velbužd
1335	At a conference in Visegrád, the kings of Bohemia, Hungary, and Poland agree to joint regulation of trade to avoid the Vienna staple
1340	Polish King Casimir III campaigns against the Golden Horde in Galicia
1341	King Charles Robert of Hungary orders all his non-Christian subjects either to be baptized or to leave the country
1343	Casimir III of Poland concludes a long-lasting peace with the Teutonic Knights
1344	Prague receives an archbishopric independent of the German Church
1345	Stephen Dušan of Serbia proclaims himself "emperor of the Serbs and Greeks"
1346	Church council at Skopje creates a Serbian patriarchate at Peć; King John of Bohemia dies fighting at Crécy in the Hundred Years' War
1347	King Casimir III issues separate law codes for Great and Little Poland; King Charles I of Bohemia introduces his law code, *Maiestas Carolina*
1347–50	Black Death (bubonic plague) devastates much of Europe

1348	Charles I (Emperor Charles IV) founds the first university in Central Europe at Prague
1349 and 1354	Serbian Tsar Stephen Dušan issues a law code
1349	King Casimir III of Poland annexes Volhynia, giving Poland a common boundary with Moldavia
1351	Hungarian Diet meets for the only time in the reign of Louis the Great; King Louis confirms the Hungarian Golden Bull of 1222, giving lesser nobles the same status as magnates; all Hungarian nobles (including servientes) receive hereditary rights to their landed properties, making the fief extinct; King Louis decrees a uniform land rent for all Hungary (the nona), amounting to one-ninth of all peasant produce
1351–52	Genoa defeats Venice in a trade war and excludes Venetian merchants from the Black Sea
1352	Casimir III of Poland incorporates most of Galicia, with Lvov, into his realm
1354	Serbian law provides that anyone receiving a fugitive serf is subject to confiscation of property
1355	Bulgarian church synod at Tirnovo pronounces a curse on Bogomils and Hesychasts and condemns Jews and heretics
1356	Bohemian Diet meets for the last time in the 14th century; Golden Bull of Emperor Charles IV (King Charles I) confirms Bohemia's independent status within the German Empire
1358	King Louis of Hungary ends his war with Venice; Hungary gains suzerainty over Dalmatia from Rijeka to Durrës
1364	King Casimir III founds the first Polish university at Cracow
1365–69	Hungarians rule in the Vidin region of western Bulgaria and force many Orthodox Christians to be baptized as Catholics
1366	Bosnian nobles revolt against King Tvrtko
1367	King Louis establishes the first Hungarian university at Pécs
1369	Ottoman Turks capture Adrianople (Edirne), their first major urban acquisition in Europe (probable date)
1370	Death of King Casimir III of Poland brings the Piast dynasty to an end
1370–82	Poland and Hungary are united under rule of the Hungarian Anjou dynasty
1371	Turks defeat a major Christian coalition at Černomen on the Maritsa
1374	At the Diet of Košice King Louis abolishes all previous tax obligations of the Polish nobility; the nobles then agree to accept one of Louis's daughters as heir to the Polish throne; margravate of Brandenburg is united with the crown of Bohemia

1375	Evtimii becomes the last patriarch of the medieval Bulgarian Church
1376	King Louis of Hungary expels the Jews from Buda
1378–1418	Schism in the Western Church produces two (and finally three) rival popes
1382	Ottoman Turks capture Sofia in Bulgaria
1384	Interregnum in Poland leads to founding of Confederation of Radom
1385	Turks win decisive victory over the Albanians on the plain of Savra; union of Krewo, sealed by the betrothal of Jadwiga and Jagiełło, creates the combined state of Poland-Lithuania
1386	Jagiełło, grand duke of Lithuania, is elected king of Poland and founds the Polish Jagiellon dynasty; Ottomans capture Niš in Serbia and enter Bosnia
1387	Moldavia temporarily accepts Polish hegemony
1389	Turks win decisive victory over the Serbs in legendary battle at Kosovo Polje (Blackbirds' Field)
1393	Turks capture Tirnovo, capital of Bulgaria, and incorporate eastern Bulgaria into their empire; Voivode Mircea of Walachia pays his first tribute to the Ottoman sultan
1394	Bethlehem Chapel for preaching in the Czech tongue is established in Prague
1394–1405	Bohemian nobility insists that only nobles may hold important provincial and national offices
1395	Turkish victory at Rovine in Walachia leads to Ottoman annexation of the south Serbian principalities
1396	Ottoman army decisively defeats a major Christian force at Nicopolis (Nikopol); Bulgaria becomes a province of the Ottoman Empire
1400	Dubrovnik begins issuing laws against the slave trade; defunct university at Cracow is refounded as the Jagiellonian University; Sigismund, king of Hungary, is elected German emperor
1401	Agreements of Vilnius and Radom strengthen Polish-Lithuanian union
1402	John Hus becomes chief preacher at the Bethlehem Chapel; Sultan Bayezid I is defeated and captured by Tamerlane at Ankara; Ottoman civil war begins
1402–13	Bayezid I's three sons contend for the Ottoman throne
1403	Pope Boniface IX and King Sigismund of Hungary clash over church appointments; the pope attempts to depose the king
1409	Decree of Kutná Hora gives the Bohemian nation three votes at the university in Prague; the other three nations taken together receive only one

1410	Polish and Lithuanian armies defeat Teutonic Knights at battle of Tannenberg in Prussia
1411	Poland, Lithuania, and the Teutonic Order sign the Peace of Toruń; Pope Gregory XII excommunicates John Hus
1413	Union of Horodło further strengthens the Polish-Lithuanian union, but grants full political rights to Catholic nobles only
1415 and 1418	Paul Włodkowic of Cracow writes his two treatises on political morality for the Council of Constance, opposing conversion of the heathens by force
1415	First Czech-language translations of the Latin liturgy appear in Bohemia; John Hus is burned at the stake by order of the Council of Constance
1419	An angry mob throws anti-Hussite town councillors to their deaths from the windows of Prague's town hall (first Prague defenestration); Sigismund (German emperor and king of Hungary) inherits Bohemian throne, but the Bohemian Diet refuses to accept him
1420	Four Articles of Prague are drawn up, expressing basic Hussite demands; radical Hussite camp is established on the hill of Tabor in south Bohemia; Venetian hegemony over Dalmatia begins; Pope Martin V proclaims a crusade against Bohemian Hussites
1420–31	Emperor Sigismund leads five unsuccessful campaigns into Bohemia
1420–34	A council of the Diet governs Bohemia in the absence of a monarch
1422, 1430, and 1433	Polish laws forbid the king to arrest or punish a noble or confiscate his property without a legal court judgment
1424	King Jagiełło authorizes church courts in Poland to prosecute "heretics" (i.e., Hussites)
1430	Polish towns agree to support the succession of one of Jagiełło's sons; the Bible is translated into Hungarian for the first time; Serbian despot George Branković completes his fortress at Smederevo on the Danube
1432	Hussite-led revolt occurs in Hungary proper as well as in Transylvania; King Sigismund mobilizes the Hungarian nobility for war for the last time
1434	Conservative Utraquists in Bohemia defeat Hussite radicals at battle of Lipany; Council of Basel orders Jews to live in ghettos; Lithuanian charter exempts boyars from taxes
1435	Bohemian Diet elects John Rokycana as (Utraquist) archbishop
1436	Basel Compacts (or Compactata) recognize both Catholicism and Utraquism as legal faiths in Bohemia; Emperor Sigismund finally enters Prague as king of Bohemia; Albanians rebel against the Turks

1436–39	Hungary and Bohemia are ruled by a single king
1437	Peasant insurrection breaks out at Bobîlna in Transylvania and is brutally suppressed; Transylvanian Diet adopts the Union of Three Nations granting political rights to Hungarians, Saxons, and Szeklers (but not Vlachs)
1439	Council of Florence proclaims union of the Catholic and Orthodox churches; Ottomans capture Smederevo and occupy most of the Serbian despotate
1440–44	Poland and Hungary are ruled by one king (Vladislav VI and I)
1440	Prussian League is founded to oppose the Teutonic Order
1442	Dubrovnik agrees to a Turkish tribute of 1,000 gold ducats annually
1443–68	Guerrilla chief Skanderbeg leads Albanians in a 25-year revolt against the Turks
1443	John Hunyadi conducts his "Long Campaign" into the Balkans
1444	Venice, Aragon, the pope, and the German emperor agree to recognize Dubrovnik's neutrality; Peace of Szeged restores Serbia to Despot George Branković; failure of Varna crusade ends hopes of expelling the Turks from Europe
1445	John Hunyadi is elected regent of Hungary
1447	Casimir IV is recognized as king of Poland after three-year interregnum
1448	Turks under sultan Murad II defeat Hunyadi at second battle of Kosovo
1450	First European printing press is established, probably by Johann Gutenberg of Mainz
1452–57	Young Ladislas "Posthumous" reigns in both Hungary and Bohemia
1453	Ottoman Turks under Sultan Mohammed II capture Constantinople, bringing the Byzantine Empire to an end
1454	Hunyadi defeats a major Ottoman campaign against Serbia; Prussian League revolts against the Teutonic Knights; King Casimir IV at Nieszawa grants important privileges to his nobles in exchange for their agreement to fight the Teutonic Order;
1454–66	Poland and Teutonic Knights fight the Thirteen Years' War
1456	Hungarians under Hunyadi repulse a major Turkish attack on Belgrade; Moldavia pays its first tribute to the Ottoman sultan
1458	Dubrovnik receives a favorable trade agreement from the Turks
1459	A Bosnian monarch for the first time persecutes the Bosnian Church; religious radicals found a new sect, the Unity of Brethren (Bohemian or Moravian Brethren); Turks capture Smederevo a second time, definitively occupying the Serbian despotate
1460	Czech religious philosopher and pacifist Peter Chelčický dies
1461	Armenian millet is formed to include all non–Muslims in the Ottoman Empire who are neither Christians nor Jews

1461–62	Vlad III the Impaler defeats Turkish invasion of Walachia
1462	Pope Pius II denies ány obligation to respect the Basel Compacts
1463	Bosnia and Hercegovina fall to the Ottomans
1466	Second Peace of Toruń ends the Thirteen Years' War and cedes West Prussia to Poland; Pope Paul II places the Hussite king George of Bohemia under the ban of the Church; King Casimir IV issues a lawbook for Lithuania granting equal rights to all nobles
1471	Polish (Jagiellon) prince Vladislav "All Right" is elected king of Bohemia as successor to the Hussite King George
1473	The first printing presses are established in Hungary and Poland; King Matthias of Hungary guarantees the Szeklers' status as free warriors
1475	Voivode Stephen the Great of Moldavia wins a decisive victory over the Turks at Vaslui
1478	Stephen the Great makes peace with the Turks and resumes paying the Turkish tribute
1480	Tsar Ivan III of Muscovy renounces allegiance to the Golden Horde; John Długosz, greatest Polish medieval historian, dies
1480s	Albania becomes an Ottoman province
1481	Dubrovnik's tribute to the sultan becomes stabilized at 12,500 gold ducats yearly
1483	The first Croatian printing press begins operation
1484	Ottomans capture Moldavia's Black Sea ports of Kilia and Cetatea Alba
1485	Bohemian Diet passes the Kutná Hora statutes, permitting Catholicism and Utraquism to exist side by side in Bohemia; King Matthias of Hungary captures Vienna
1486	The first Bohemian printing press is set up at Plzeň; King Matthias issues a lawbook for Hungary; Matthias creates the Corporation of the Saxon Nation as an autonomous organization for the Transylvanian Saxons
1486–94	Tsar Ivan III of Muscovy fights his first major war with Lithuania
1490–1516	The crowns of Hungary and Bohemia are united under monarchs of the Polish Jagiellon dynasty
1490s	The first printing press in Europe to use the Cyrillic alphabet is established in Zeta (Montenegro)
1492	Many Jews settle in Ottoman Bulgaria after being expelled from Spain; a printing press is established at Malbork in Prussia;
1496	By the statutes of Piotrków the Great Sejm of Poland decrees that only nobles (not townsmen) may hold landed property; that peasants may not change their place of residence (thus becoming serfs); and that nobles (but not townsmen) may import and export goods duty-free

1500–1501	Voivode Stephen the Great of Moldavia joins Hungary and Venice for his last campaign against the Turks
1501	Marko Marulić writes *Judita*, the first major poetic work in Croatian;
1505	Polish Sejm passes laws reserving most of the higher church positions for nobles, prohibiting marriages between nobles and commoners, and restricting noble status to persons with two noble parents; Polish statute known as "Nihil Novi" forbids the king to issue any "new" laws without the consent of the nobility in the Sejm
1509 and 1515	Papal bulls proclaim crusades against alleged "heretics" (i.e., the Eastern Orthodox) in Poland-Lithuania
1512	Bohemian Diet reaffirms the statutes of Kutná Hora (passed in 1485)
1514	Transylvanian peasant insurrection develops out of preparations for an anti-Turkish crusade; lawyer Stephen Verböczy completes his influential law code for Hungary, the Tripartitum, which declares that all nobles have equal rights
1521	Ottomans Turks capture Belgrade, opening the way to conquest of Hungary
1526	Turks destroy the Hungarian army at Mohács, ending Hungary's existence as an independent state
1529	Semi-independent Mazovia is definitively incorporated into Poland; Ottoman army unsuccessfully besieges Vienna and withdraws
1620	Victory of the Catholic-led army at battle of White Mountain ends religious toleration in Bohemia
1699	Habsburg armies expel the Turks from Hungary

APPENDIX 2

List of Monarchs*

Bohemia

920–29	Wenceslas [Václav] (duke)
929–67	Boleslav I
1034–55	Břetislav I
1061–92	Vratislav I (first Czech king; *Duke* Vratislav II until 1086)
1140–73	Vladislav II (entitled *duke* until 1158, then *King* Vladislav I)
1198†–1230	Ottokar I
1230–53	Wenceslas I [Václav]
1253–78	Ottokar II
1278–1305	Wenceslas II [Václav]
1305–06	Wenceslas III
1310–46	John I of Luxemburg [Jan]
1346–78	Charles I (=Emperor Charles IV) [Karl]
1378–1419	Wenceslas IV (=Emperor, 1378–1400)
1424–27	Sigismund Korybut (of Lithuania)
1436–37	Sigismund I (king of Hungary and emperor)
1437–39	Albert I of Habsburg [Albrecht] (king of Hungary and emperor)
1453–57	Ladislas I Posthumous [Ladislav] (=Ladislas V of Hungary)
1457–71	George I Poděbrady [Jiří]
1471–1516	Ladislas II Jagiellon [Ladislav] (=Vladislav II of Hungary)
1516–26	Louis I Jagiellon [Ludvík] (=Louis II of Hungary)

Bosnia

1353–91	Tvrtko I

* Includes only the monarchs mentioned in this volume.
† After this date all Bohemian rulers held the royal title.

Bulgaria

852–89	Boris I
889–93	Vladimir I
893–927	Symeon I
927–69	Peter I
976–1014	Samuel
1185–97	John (Ivan) and Peter Asen
1197–1207	Kaloyan
1207–18	Boril
1218–41	John (Ivan) Asen II
1279–92	George Terter
1331–71	John (Ivan) Alexander
1371–93	John Šišman III

Byzantine Empire

311–37	Constantine I the Great*
582–602	Maurice
867–86	Basil I
886–912	Leo VI the Wise
912–59	Constantine VII Porphyrogenetos
969–76	John I Tzimiskes
976–1025	Basil II the Bulgar–slayer
1081–1118	Alexius I Comnenus
1143–80	Manuel I Comnenus
1185–95	Isaac II Angelus
1195–1203	Alexius III Angelus
1203–04	Isaac II Angelus (restored) and Alexius IV Angelus (ruled jointly)
1204–22	Theodore I Lascaris (of Nicaea)
1222–54	John III Vatatzes (of Nicaea)
1259–82	Michael VIII Paleologus
1282–1328	Andronicus II Paleologus
1448–53	Constantine XI Paleologus

Croatia

910–28 (?)	Tomislav
969–95	Stephen Držislav

* Too early to be termed "Byzantine," though he ruled from Constantinople.

1030–58	Stephen I
1058–73	Peter Krešimir IV
d. 1089	Zvonimir

German Empire

919–36	Henry I the Fowler
936–73	Otto I the Great
983–1002	Otto III
1039–56	Henry III
1056–1106	Henry IV
1138–52	Conrad III
1152–90	Frederick I Barbarossa
1215–50	Frederick II
1273–92	Rudolf I Habsburg
1308–13	Henry VII Luxemburg
1347–78	Charles IV Luxemburg
1410–37	Sigismund Luxemburg
1438–39	Albert II Habsburg
1440–93	Frederick III Habsburg

Hungary

972–97	Géza (duke)
997–1038	Stephen I [István] (saint)
1077–95	Ladislas I [László] (saint)
1095–1116	Koloman I the Book Lover
1131–41	Béla II the Blind
1141–62	Géza II
1162	Ladislas II
1162–73	Stephen III
1173–96	Béla III
1196–1204	Emeric I
1205–35	Andrew II
1235–70	Béla IV
1270–72	Stephen V
1272–90	Ladislas IV the Cuman
1290–1301	Andrew III
1310–42	Charles Robert
1342–82	Louis I the Great (= Louis of Poland)
1387–1437	Sigismund I [Zsigmond] (= emperor)

1438–39   Albert I (= Emperor Albrecht II)
1440–44   Vladislav I [Úlászló I] (= Vladislav VI of Poland)
1452–57   Ladislas V [László V] Posthumous (= Ladislas I of Bohemia)
1458–90   Matthias I Corvinus
1490–1516   Vladislav II "All Right" [Úlászló II] (= Ladislas II of Bohemia)
1516–26   Louis II (= Louis I of Bohemia)

Latin Empire

1228–61   Baldwin II

Moldavia

1401–31   Alexander the Good
1457–1504   Stephen the Great

Mongol Empire

1229–41   Ogadei
1260–94   Kubilai

Naples

1268–85   Charles I (Charles of Anjou)
1285–1309   Charles II

Ottoman Empire

1290–1326   Osman (Othman)
1326–61   Orkhan
1361–89   Murad I
1389–1402   Bayezid I the Thunderbolt
1413–21   Mohammed I
1421–51   Murad II
1451–81   Mohammed II the Conqueror
1481–1512   Bayezid II
1512–20   Selim I the Grim
1520–66   Suleiman I the Magnificent

Papacy

858–67	Nicholas I
999–1003	Sylvester II
1073–85	Gregory VII
1088–99	Urban II
1198–1216	Innocent III
1227–41	Gregory IX
1243–54	Innocent IV
1265–68	Clement IV
1342–52	Clement VI
1389–1404	Boniface IX
1406–15	Gregory XII
1410–15	John XXIII (antipope)
1417–31	Martin V
1458–64	Pius II (Aeneas Sylvius)
1464–71	Paul II
1513–21	Leo X

Poland

960–92	Mieszko I
992–1025	Boleslav I the Brave
1025–34	Mieszko II
1038–58	Casimir I the Restorer
1058–79	Boleslav II the Bold
1102–38	Boleslav III Wrymouth
1177–94	Casimir II the Just
1243–79	Boleslav V the Shameful
1300–1305	Wenceslas I (= Wenceslas II of Bohemia)
1310–33	Vladislav IV Łokietek (crowned king in 1320)
1333–70	Casimir III the Great
1370–82	Louis I (= Louis the Great of Hungary)
1384–99	Jadwiga (queen)
1386–1434	Jagiełło [Władysław] (= Vladislav V)
1434–44	Vladislav VI [Władysław] (= Vladislav I of Hungary)
1447–92	Casimir IV Jagiellonczyk
1492–1501	John Albert I

Serbia

1168–96	Stephen Nemanya I (grand župan and saint)
1196–1227	Stephen the First–Crowned (grand župan; king, 1217–27;)
1243–76	Stephen Uroš I
1276–82	Stephen Dragutin
1282–1321	Stephen Milutin (= Stephen Uroš II)
1321–31	Stephen Dečanski (= Stephen Uroš III)
1331–55	Stephen Dušan (= Stephen Uroš IV; tsar, 1346–55)
1355–71	Stephen Uroš V (tsar)
1369–71	Vukašin (regional king)
1370–95	Marko (regional king and epic hero)
1371–89	Lazar (prince)
1389–1427	Stephen Lazarević (despot)
1427–56	George Branković (despot)

Walachia

1386–1418	Mircea the Old
1436–37, 1443–47	Vlad II Dracul
1448, 1456–62, 1475	Vlad III the Impaler

Rulers of Two or More Kingdoms

In This Volume Called	Bohemia	Hungary	Poland	Empire
d. 1378 Charles I and IV	Karl I	. . .	. . .	Karl IV
d. 1382 Louis I	. . .	Lajos I	Ludwik I	. . .
d. 1419 Wenceslas IV (son of Charles I and IV)	Václav IV	. . .	. . .	Wenzel IV
d. 1437 Sigismund I (son of Charles I and IV; son-in-law of Louis I)	Zygmunt I	Zsigmond I	. . .	Sigismund (or Sigmund) I
d. 1439 Albert I (son-in-law of Sigismund I)	Albert I	Albert I	. . .	Albert (or Albrecht) I
d. 1444 Vladislav I and VI (son of Jagiełło of Poland)	. . .	Úlászló I	Władysław VI	. . .
d. 1457 Ladislav I and V (son of Albert)	Ladislav I	László V	. . .	. . .
d. 1516 Vladislav II (son of Casimir IV of Poland)	Ladislav II	Úlászló II	. . .	. . .
d. 1526 Louis II (son of Vladislav II)	Ludvík I	Lajos II	. . .	. . .

APPENDIX 3

Place Name Equivalents for Towns and Cities

Used in This Book	Equivalents
Adrianople (E)	Edirne (T)
Alba Iulia (R)	Gyulafehérvár (H); Apulum (L)
Banská Bystrica (Sl)	Neusohl (G); Beszterczebánya (H)
Banská Štiavnica (Sl)	Schemnitz (G)
Bar (SC)	Antivari (I)
Belgrade (E)	Beograd (SC); Singidunum (L); Nándorfehérvár (H)
Bistriţa (R)	Besztercze (H)
Bitolj (SC)	Monastir (SC); Bitola (E)
Braşov (R)	Kronstadt (G); Brassó (H)
Bratislava (Sl)	Pressburg (G); Pozsony (H)
Brno (Cz)	Brünn (G)
Bucharest (E)	Bucureşti (R)
Buda (H)	Ofen (G); Aquincum (L)
Budva (SC)	Budua (I)
Celje (Slovenian)	Cilli (G)
Cetatea Albă (R)	Belgorod (Rus); Akkerman (T); Maurocastro (I)
Cheb (Cz)	Eger (G) [Not to be confused with Eger in Hungary]
Chełmno (P)	Kulm (G)
Chojnice (P)	Konitz (G)
Cluj (R)	Klausenburg (G); Kolozsvár (H)
Constantinople (E)	Istanbul (T)
Cracow (E)	Kraków (P)
Drishti (A)	Drivasto (I)
Dubrovnik (SC)	Ragusa (I)
Durrës (A)	Durazzo (I); Drač (SC)
Edirne (T)	Adrianople (E)
Elbląg (P)	Elbing (G)
Esztergom (H)	Gran (G)
Gdańsk (P)	Danzig (G)

Abbreviations: (A) = Albanian; (B) = Bulgarian; (Cz) = Czech; (E) = English; (G) = German; (Gk) = Greek; (H) = Hungarian; (I) = Italian; (L) = Latin; (Lith) = Lithuanian; (M) = Macedonian; (P) = Polish; (R) = Romanian; (Rus) = Russian; (SC) = Serbo-Croatian; (Sl) = Slovak; (T) = Turkish; (U) = Ukrainian.

Used in This Book	*Equivalents ·*
Gniezno (P)	Gnesen (G)
Győr (H)	Raab (G)
Hradec Kralové (Cz)	Königgrätz (G)
Iaşi (R)	Jassy (E)
Istanbul (T)	Constantinople (E)
Jihlava (Cz)	Iglau (G)
Kołobrzeg (P)	Kolberg (G)
Košice (Sl)	Kassa (H); Kaschau (G); Kożyce (P)
Kotor (SC)	Cattaro (I)
Kremnica (Sl)	Kremnitz (G)
Kroměříž (Cz)	Kremsier (G)
Krujë (A)	Croia (I)
Krupina (Sl)	Karpfen (G)
Kutná Hora (Cz)	Kuttenberg (G)
Legnica (P)	Liegnitz (G)
Lezhë (A)	Alessio (I); Lesh (E)
Lvov (E)	Lwów (P); Lemberg (G); Lviv (U)
Malbork (P)	Marienburg (G)
Nicaea (E)	Izník (T)
Nicopolis (E)	Nikopol (B)
Niš (SC)	Nish (E); Naissus (L)
Nitra (Sl)	Neutra (G); Nyitra (H)
Olomouc (Cz)	Olmütz (G)
Pannonhalma (H)	Martinsberg (G)
Peć (SC)	Ipek (T)
Pécs (H)	Fünfkirchen (G)
Piotrków (P)	Petrikau (G)
Plovdiv (B)	Philippopolis (Gr, E)
Plzeň (Cz)	Pilsen (G)
Poznań (P)	Posen (G)
Prague (E)	Praha (Cz); Prag (G)
Rijeka (SC)	Fiume (I)
Salonika (E)	Thessaloniki (Gr)
Sandomierz (P)	Sandomir (Rus)
Serrai (E)	Sérrai (Gk); also Serres (E)
Shkodër (A)	Scutari (I)
Šibenik (SC)	Sebenico (I)
Sibiu (R)	Hermannstadt (G); Nagyszeben (H)
Sisak (SC)	Sissek (G); Sziszek (H)
Skopje (M)	Skoplje (SC); Üsküp (T); Scupi (L)
Smederevo (SC)	Semendria (G)

Used in This Book	*Equivalents*
Sofia (E)	Sofiya (B); Serdica (L)
Sopron (H)	Ödenburg (G)
Split (SC)	Spalato (I)
Syrmia (E)	Srem (SC)
Szczecin (P)	Stettin (G)
Szeged (H)	Szegedin (G)
Székesfehérvár (H)	Stuhlweissenburg (G)
Těšín (Cz)	Cieszyn (P); Teschen (G)
Tirnovo (B)	Trnovo (B); Veliko Tŭrnovo (B)
Toruń (P)	Thorn (G)
Trogir (SC)	Tragurium (L); Trau (G)
Ulcinj (SC)	Dulcigno (I)
Velbužd (SC)	Kyustendil (B)
Vilnius (Lith)	Wilno (P); Vilna (Rus)
Vlorë (A)	Valona (I)
Warsaw (E)	Warszawa (P)
Wrocław (P)	Breslau (G)
Zadar (SC)	Zara (I)
Zagreb (SC)	Agram (G)

BIBLIOGRAPHICAL ESSAY

*T*he volumes listed here under "General Works" deal with many of the themes discussed in the various chapters, but with few exceptions their titles are not repeated under the various chapter headings. Important books and articles of a more specialized nature appear under the chapter headings, but rarely more than twice even when some part of their contents touches on other themes. Citations appearing for the second time may be somewhat abbreviated.

General Works

Aside from the present volume, no general studies are extant that cover the history of medieval East Central Europe as a whole in more than cursory fashion (i.e., as introduction to the discussion of a later period). The works that come closest are by Francis Dvornik: *The Slavs: Their Early History and Civilization* (Boston: American Academy of Arts and Sciences, 1956) and *The Making of Central and Eastern Europe* (London: Polish Research Center, 1949), which deal with early Russia as well as the Slavic peoples of East Central Europe but exclude the Hungarians and Romanians.

For the BALKAN PENINSULA there exist the two volumes by John V. A. Fine, Jr., *The Early Medieval Balkans* (Ann Arbor: University of Michigan Press, 1983) and *The Late Medieval Balkans* (Ann Arbor: University of Michigan Press, 1987), based on extensive use of Serbo-Croatian and Bulgarian sources, very detailed and comprehensive. *The Cambridge Medieval History*, 2d ed., vol. 4, part 1 (Cambridge: University Press, 1923), includes a short section by M. Dinić on the Balkans from 1018 to 1499. A collaborative work produced in Yugoslavia by Vladimir Dedijer et al., *History of Yugoslavia* (New York: McGraw-Hill, 1974), contains some medieval material. Ferdinand Schevill's *The History of the Balkan Peninsula from the Earliest Times to the Present Day* (New York: Harcourt Brace, 1922; 2d ed., 1933) is still worth reading for its literary quality alone; the medieval section is very much oriented toward Byzantium.

For the BYZANTINE EMPIRE, which included large portions of the Balkan Peninsula for much of the medieval period, solid and readable works are Dimitri Obolensky, *The Byzantine Commonwealth: Eastern Europe, 500–1453* (London: Weidenfeld and Nicolson, 1971); George Ostrogorsky, *History of the Byzantine*

State (New Brunswick: Rutgers University Press, 1957); and A. A. Vasiliev, *History of the Byzantine Empire* (Madison: University of Wisconsin Press, 1961). Useful articles by Franz Dölger are collected in his *Byzanz und die europäische Staatenwelt: ausgewählte Vorträge und Aufsätze* (Darmstadt: Wissenschaftliche Buchgesellschaft, 1964). For Byzantine influences in the Balkans, see Constantine Porphyrogenitus, *De administrando imperio* (Washington, D.C.: Dumbarton Oaks Center for Byzantine Studies, 1967), the single most important primary source (English text); and the collection of articles by Jadran Ferluga, *Byzantium on the Balkans* (Amsterdam: Hakkert, 1976).

For the OTTOMAN EMPIRE, the best modern text is Halil Inalcik, *The Ottoman Empire: The Classical Age, 1300–1600* (London: Weidenfeld and Nicolson, 1973). The survey by H. A. R. Gibb and Harold Bowen, *Islamic Society and the West* (London: Oxford University Press, 1950), reads easily and contains much useful material, although its theoretical framework (i.e., "The Ruling Institution" and "The Religious Institution") has been questioned. The first quarter of Stanford Shaw's *History of the Ottoman Empire and Modern Turkey*, vol. 1 (Cambridge: University Press, 1976), deals with the years before 1500 and includes much useful bibliography. Michael Cook, ed., *A History of the Ottoman Empire to 1730* (Cambridge: University Press, 1976), contains chapters by V. J. Parry, H. Inalcik, A. N. Kurat, and J. S. Bromley from *The Cambridge History of Islam* and *The New Cambridge Modern History*. The single large volume by Lord Patrick B. Kinross, *The Ottoman Centuries: The Rise and Fall of the Turkish Empire* (New York: Morrow, 1977), is very readable, but uncritical and somewhat superficial. For the serious student of the Ottoman Empire the work of two 19th-century German historians remains indispensable. The ten volumes by the great Austrian Orientalist Joseph von Hammer-Purgstall, *Geschichte des Osmanischen Reiches* (Pest: C. A. Hartleben, 1827–35; reprinted Graz, 1963) are invaluable for their extensive use of Turkish-language sources inaccessible to most other historians. Volumes 1 and 2 deal with the period before 1500. Johann Zinkeisen's *Geschichte des Osmanischen Reiches in Europa*, vols. 1 and 2 (Hamburg: F. Perthes, 1840 and 1854) exhaustively utilizes the Western-language sources concerning the Ottomans; Volume 1 and the beginning of volume 2 cover the medieval era.

For medieval ALBANIA, the works of Alain Ducellier stand virtually alone. They include one large book, *La façade maritime de l'Albanie au Moyen Âge: Durazzo et Valona du XIe au XVe siècle* (Thessaloniki: Institute for Balkan Studies, 1981), and a collection of articles entitled *L'Albanie entre Byzance et Venise: X^e–XVe siècles* (London: Variorum Reprints, 1987). The best overview of Albanian history, though with a fairly brief treatment of the Middle Ages, is Stefanaq Pollo and Arben Puto, *The History of Albania from Its Origins to the Present Day* (London: Routledge and Kegan Paul, 1981).

Medieval BOHEMIA receives fairly extensive treatment by Karl Richter and Ferdinand Seibt in Karl Bosl, ed., *Handbuch der Geschichte der böhmischen*

Länder (Stuttgart: A. Hiersemann, 1967); and by Kamil Krofta in three separate sections of the *Cambridge Medieval History*, vols. 6 (1929), 7 (1932), and 8 (1936). The pioneering 19th-century work by František Palacký, *Geschichte von Böhmen*, 5 vols. (Prague: F. Tempsky, 1844–67), in Czech: *Dějiny národu českého* (Prague: Odeon, 1968), concluding with the year 1526, remains useful for its exhaustive consultation of original sources. Somewhat more recent are the two standard older works on Bohemia by Sudeten Germans, Adolf Bachmann, *Geschichte Böhmens*, 2 vols. (Gotha: F. A. Perthes, 1899), and Bertold Bretholz, *Geschichte Böhmens und Mährens*, 4 vols. (Reichenberg: Paul Sollers' Nachf., 1921–25). R. W. Seton-Watson, *A History of the Czechs and Slovaks* (London: Hutchinson, 1943) is a standard work; the first quarter of the book is devoted to the medieval period.

On BULGARIA, the old work by Konstantin Jireček, *Geschichte der Bulgaren* (Prague: F. Tempsky, 1876; reprinted 1977) remains valuable. For the period prior to 1018 the standard treatment is Stephen Runciman, *A History of the First Bulgarian Empire* (London: G. Bell and Sons, 1930). Robert Browning, *Byzantium and Bulgaria: A Comparative Study across the Early Medieval Frontier* (Berkeley: University of California Press, 1975), discusses Bulgaria in the 9th and 10th centuries.

For medieval CROATIA see Stanko Guldescu, *History of Medieval Croatia* (The Hague: Mouton, 1964); Ferdinand Šišić, *Geschichte der Kroaten* (Zagreb: Matica Hrvatska, 1917); and the collection of articles in Francis H. Eterovich and Christopher Spalatin, *Croatia: Land, People, Culture*, 2 vols. (Toronto: University of Toronto Press, 1964–70).

On HUNGARY (INCLUDING TRANSYLVANIA) the indispensable work on the Middle Ages is Bálint Hóman, *Geschichte des ungarischen Mittelalters*, 2 vols. (Berlin: W. de Gruyter, 1940). The best general history of Hungary in English, containing essays by specialists in various fields of Hungarian history, is Peter F. Sugar, Péter Hanák, and Tibor Frank, eds., *A History of Hungary* (Bloomington: University of Indiana Press, 1990). In addition, several adequate general histories of Hungary in Western languages are available which include considerable medieval materal: Thomas von Bogyay, *Gründzüge der Geschichte Ungarns* (Darmstadt: Wissenschaftliche Buchgesellschaft, 1967); Ervin Pamlényi, ed., *A History of Hungary* (Budapest: Corvina Press, 1973); Ştefan Pascu, *A History of Transylvania* (Detroit: Wayne State University Press, 1982); and László Makkai, *Histoire de Transylvanie* (Paris: Presses universitaires de France, 1946). The Hungarian Institute of History in Budapest has published several extensive collections of articles, many on medieval topics: *Nouvelles études historiques* (1965); *Études historiques* (1980) and *Études historiques hongroises* (1990).

For POLAND, Norman Davies's *God's Playground: A History of Poland*, 2 vols. (New York: Columbia University Press, 1982), is an outstanding work, eloquently written; the first quarter of volume 1 deals with the Middle Ages. An older and more purely political treatment by various authors may be found in *The Cambridge History of Poland*, vol. 1 (Cambridge: University Press, 1950). Useful also are the surveys by Gotthold Rhode, *Geschichte Polens: ein Überblick* (Darmstadt, 1966), and his *Kleine Geschichte Polens* (2d ed.; Darmstadt: Wissenschaftliche Buchgesellschaft, 1965). Leading Polish historians have collaborated to produce a recent history of their country: Aleksander Gieysztor et al., *History of Poland* (Warsaw: Polish Scientific Publishers, 1979). For those who read Polish, an excellent cultural history is Marian Friedberg, *Kultura polska a niemiecka*, 2 vols. (Poznań: Wydawnictwo Instytutu Zachodniego, 1946), while an extensive treatment of Polish government and law appears in Juliusz Bardach et al., *Historia państwa i prawa polskiego* (5th ed.; Warsaw: Panstwowe Wydawnictwo Naukowe, 1987; originally published Łodz, 1955), continued by Zdisław Kaczmarczyk and Bogusław Leśnodorski in *Historia państwa i prawa Polski od połowy XV w. do r. 1795* (Warsaw, 1957).

For PRUSSIA under the government of the Teutonic Knights, the most serious and scholarly work is P. Marjan Tumler, *Der deutsche Orden im Werden, Wachsen und Wirken bis 1400* (Vienna: Panorama, 1955).

For medieval SERBIA the work of the Czech historian J. Konstantin Jireček is in a class by itself, indispensable for its extensive use of original sources in various languages. His *Geschichte der Serben* (Gotha: F. A. Perthes, 1911) is both a political and a cultural history, free from nationalist prejudices; his *La civilisation serbe au Moyen Âge* (Paris: Bossard, 1900) is the French translation of volume 2, chapters 1–4 of *Geschichte der Serben*.

Since medieval SLOVENIA belonged to the German (Holy Roman) Empire, and did not constitute a separate Slavic province or state, the history of this region in Western languages can best be found in works dealing with the German-ruled duchies of Carinthia, Carniola, and Styria. Examples are Claudia Fräss-Ehrfeld, *Geschichte Kärntens: Das Mittelalter* (Celovec, 1982), and S. Vilfan, *Die deutsche Kolonisation nördlich der oberen Adria* (Sigmaringen, 1974). Dragotin Lončar's *The Slovenes: A Social History* (Cleveland: American Jugoslav Printing and Publishing Co., 1939) is a brief and uncritical overview.

For WALACHIA and MOLDAVIA the extensive writings of Nicolae Iorga at once come to mind, especially his *Histoire des Roumains et de la romanité orientale*, vols. 2–4 (Bucharest, 1937). However, the author's enormous erudition is not accompanied by a corresponding clarity; his work is impressionistic, imprecise, and difficult to use. R. W. Seton-Watson's *A History of the Roumanians from Roman Times to the Completion of Unity* (Cambridge: University Press, 1934) is the standard work in English on the Romanians, but passes with great rapidity over the Middle Ages. Shorter but more recent are Vlad Georgescu, *The Romanians: A History* (Columbus: Ohio State University Press, 1991); and George Castellan, *A History of the Romanians,* trans. from French (Boulder: East European Monographs, 1989). Other treatments of Romanian history are: A. Oţetea, ed., *The History of the Romanian People* (Bucharest: Scientific Publishing House, 1970); Victor Spinei, *Moldavia from the 11th to the 14th Centuries*

(Bucharest: Editura Academiei Republicii Socialiste România, 1986); and Ioan Lupaş, *Zur Geschichte der Rumänen: Aufsätze und Vorträge* (Sibiu: Krafft and Drotleff, 1943). Thorough and scholarly is Hugo Weczerka's *Das mittelalterliche und frühneuzeitliche Deutschtum im Fürstentum Moldau* (Munich: Oldenbourg, 1960), dealing with the history of Moldavia in much broader fashion than the title by itself would indicate.

Journals

Study of the history of East Central Europe has been greatly facilitated since World War II by the fact that historical institutes in most countries of the region have been issuing periodicals containing important monographs by their own historians in German, French, or English translations. The following series have been particularly useful in the preparation of the present book: *Acta poloniae historica* (Wrocław); *Balcanica* (Belgrade); *Balkan Studies* (Thessaloniki); *Bulgarian Historical Review* (identical to *Revue bulgare d'histoire*) (Sofia); *Byzantino-Bulgarica* (Sofia); *Études balkaniques* (Sofia); *Études historiques* (Sofia); *Historica* (Prague); *Revue des études sud-est européenes* (Bucharest); *Revue roumaine d'histoire* (Bucharest); *Studia Albanica* (Tirana); *Studia Historica* (Budapest).

Journals from German-speaking lands are also indispensable for anyone with a serious interest in East Central Europe. Among them are: *Bohemia: Jahrbuch des Collegium Carolinum* (Munich); *Jahrbücher für Geschichte Osteuropas* (Munich); *Österreichische Osthefte* (Vienna); *Südost-Forschungen* (Munich); *Sudostdeutsches Archiv* (Munich); *Ungarn-Jahrbuch* (Munich); and *Zeitschrift für Östforschung* (Marburg/Lahn).

Primarily in English are: *East Central Europe* (Bakersfield); *East European Quarterly* (Boulder); *Slavonic and East European Review,* formerly *Slavonic Review* (London); *Slavic Review* (Austin); *Journal of Turkish Studies* (Duxbury); *Turcica* (Louvain).

Chapter 1. Early Migrations

ALBANIANS: Alain Ducellier, "Les Albanais du XIᵉ au XIIIᵉ siècle: nomades ou sedentaires?" in Ducellier, *L'Albanie entre Byzance et Venise: Xᵉ–XVᵉ siècles* (London: Variorum Reprints, 1987).

BULGARS: V. Beševliev, *Die protobulgarische Periode der bulgarischen Geschichte* (Amsterdam: Hakkert, 1981), and "Aus der Geschichte der Protobulgaren," *Études balkaniques*, 1970, no. 2, pp. 39–56.

CUMANS: Petre Diaconu, *Les Coumans au Bas Danube aux XIᵉ et XIIᵉ siècles* (Bucharest: Editura Academiei Republicii Socialiste România, 1978).

HUNGARIANS (MAGYARS): Antal Bartha, *Hungarian Society in the 9th and 10th Centuries*, vol. 85 of *Studia Historica* (Budapest, 1975); Imre Boba, *Nomads, Northmen and Slavs: Eastern Europe in the Ninth Century* (The Hague: Mouton, 1967), and "A Twofold Conquest of Hungary or 'Secundus Ingressus,'" *Ungarn-Jahrbuch* 12 (1982–83): 23–41; György Györffy, "Landnahme, Ansiedlung und Streifzüge der Ungarn," *Acta Historica* 31 (1985): 231–70; C. A. Macartney, *The Magyars in the Ninth Century* (Cambridge: University Press, 1930); László Makkai, "Siebenbürgens Siedlungsgeschichte bis zum Ende des Mittelalters," in *Études historiques hongroises* (Budapest, 1990), 2: 1–9; Jenő Szücs, "The Peoples of Medieval Hungary," *Études historiques hongroises*, 2: 11–20, and "Theoretical Elements in Master Simon of Kéza's *Gesta Hungarorum* (1282–1285 A.D.)," *Studia Historica* 96 (1975): 5–45.

SLAVS: Marija Gimbutas, *The Slavs* (New York: Praeger, 1971), and Konrad Jazdzewski, *Poland* (London: Thames and Hudson, 1956), deal chiefly with archaeological remains, but include some pages on the Slavic migrations. See also Gerhard Mildenberger, "Vor- und Frühgeschichte der böhmischen Länder" in Karl Bosl, *Handbuch der Geschichte der böhmischen Länder* (Stuttgart, 1967); Lubor Niederle, *Manuel de l'antiquité slave*, 2 vols. (Paris: Champion, 1923); Helmut Preidel, *Die Vor- und Frühgeschichtlichen Siedlungsraüme in Böhmen und Mähren* (Munich: Oldenbourg, 1953).

Chapter 2. State Formation

ALBANIA: Alain Ducellier, "L'Arbanon et les Albanais au XIe siècle," in Ducellier, *L'Albanie entre Byzance et Venise: Xe–XVe siècles* (London, 1987).

BULGARIA: Dimitar Angelow(v), "Aufstand der Asseniden und die Wiedererrichtung des bulgarischen Staates im Mittelalter," *Bulgarian Historical Review* 12, no. 4 (1984): 31–52; G. Cankova-Petkova, "La liberation de la Bulgarie de la domination byzantine," *Byzantino Bulgarica* 5 (1978): 95–121; V. N. Zlatarski, "The Making of the Bulgarian Nation," in 2 parts, *Slavonic Review* 4 (1925–26): 362–83 and 629–44.

BOHEMIA: Josef Dobiás, "Seit wann bilden die natürlichen Grenzen von Böhmen auch seine politische Landesgrenze?" *Historica* 6 (1963): 5–44; František Graus, "Die Entstehung der mittelalterlichen Staaten in Mitteleuropa," *Historica* 10 (1965).

HUNGARY: Gy. Györffy, "Autour de l'état des semi-nomades: le cas de la Hongrie," *Studia Historica* 95 (1975): 5–20.

POLAND: Aleksander Gieysztor, "Recherches sur les fondements de la Pologne médiévale: état actuel des problèmes," *Acta poloniae historica* 4 (1961): 7–33; Tadeusz Grudziński, "The Beginnings of Feudal Disintegration in Poland," *Acta poloniae historica* 30 (1974): 5–31; Witold Hensel, *The Beginnings of the Polish State* (Warsaw: Polonia Publishing House, 1960).

WALACHIA AND MOLDAVIA: Eugen Stănescu, "Les Vlaques à la fin du Xᵉ siècle–début du XIᵉ et la restauration de la domination byzantine dans la Péninsule Balkanique," *Revue des études sud-est européenes* 6 (1968): 407–38; Șt. Ștefănescu, "The Emergence of the Romanian States," in A. Oțetea, *The History of the Romanian People* (Bucharest, 1970); Șt. Ștefănescu, "Reconstitution de la vie d'état sur le territoire de la Roumanie au cours du Haut Moyen Âge," *Revue roumaine d'histoire* 9 (1970): 3–18.

Chapter 3. Monarchies

BOHEMIA AND THE HOLY ROMAN (GERMAN) EMPIRE: František Graus, "Kirchliche und heidnische (magische) Komponenten der Stellungen der Přemysliden," in František Graus and Herbert Ludat, eds., *Siedlung und Verfassung Böhmens in der Frühzeit* (Wiesbaden: Harrassowitz, 1967); Otakar Odložilík, "Problems of the Reign of George of Poděbrady," *Slavonic and East European Review* 20 (1941): 206–22, and "Good King Wenceslas: A Historical Sketch," *Slavonic Review* 8 (1929–30): 120–30.

BULGARIA: Georgi Bakalov, "Quelques particularités de la titulature des souverains balkaniques du Moyen Âge," *Études balkaniques*, 1977, no. 2, pp. 67–86; Veselin Beševliev, "Souveränitätsansprüche eines bulgarischen Herrschers im 9. Jahrhundert," in his *Bulgarisch-byzantinische Aufsätze* (London: Variorum Reprints, 1978); Franz Dölger, "Bulgarisches Zartum und byzantinisches Kaisertum," "Die mittelalterliche 'Familie der Fürsten und Völker' und der Bulgarenherrscher," and "Die mittelalterliche Kulture auf dem Balkan als byzantinisches Erbe," all reprinted in Franz Dölger, *Byzanz und die europäische Staatenwelt* (Darmstadt, 1964); I. Gošev, "Zur Frage der Krönungszeremonien und die zeremonielle Gewandung der byzantinischen und der bulgarischen Herrscher im Mittelalter," *Byzantino Bulgarica* 2 (1966): 145–68; Hristo Matanov, "Problems of the State Structures in the South-West Balkan Lands during the Second Half of the 14th Century," and "Contribution to the Political History of South-Eastern Macedonia after the Battle of Černomen," *Études balkaniques*, 1984, no. 1, pp. 116–25, and 1986, no. 2, pp. 31–43.

HUNGARY: Janos M. Bak, *Königtum und Stände in Ungarn im 14.–16. Jahrhundert* (Wiesbaden: F. Steiner, 1973); Josef Deér, *Die heilige Krone Ungarns* (Vienna: Böhlau, 1966); Michael de Ferdinandy, "Ludwig I von Ungarn (1342–1382)," *Südost-Forschungen* 31 (1972): 41–80, and "Ludwig I von Ungarn (1342–1382)," in Vardy ed., *Louis the Great*, pp. 3–48; Erik Fügedi, "Coronation in Medieval Hungary," *Studies in Medieval and Renaissance History*, n.s. 3 (Vancouver, B.C., 1980); József Gerics, "An der Grenze zwischen West und Ost: Der Staatsgründer und Gesetzgeber Stephan der Heilige," *Études historiques hongroises* (Budapest, 1990), 4:1–10; Josef Karpat, "Die Lehre von der heiligen Krone Ungarns im Lichte des Schrifttums," *Jahrbücher für Geschichte Osteuropas*

6 (1958): 1–54; Z. J. Kosztolnyik, *Five Eleventh Century Hungarian Kings* (Boulder: East European Quarterly, 1981), and *From Coloman the Learned to Bela III, 1095–1196* (Boulder: East European Monographs, 1987); Elemér Mályusz, *Kaiser Sigismund in Ungarn, 1387–1437* (Budapest: Akadémiai Kiadó, 1990); Karl Nehring, "Herrschaftstradition und Herrschaftslegitimität. Zur ungarischen Aussenpolitik in der zweiten Hälfte des 15. Jahrhunderts," *Revue roumaine d'histoire* 13 (1974): 463–71; Gerhard Seewann, "Die Sankt-Stephans Krone," *Südost-Forschungen* 37 (1978): 148–78. S. B. Vardy, Geza Grosschmid, and Leslie Domonkos, eds., *Louis the Great, King of Hungary and Poland* (Boulder: East European Monographs, 1986).

OTTOMAN EMPIRE: Franz Babinger, *Mehmed the Conqueror and His Time* (Princeton: University Press, 1978).

SERBIA: Ruža Ćuk, "Carica Mara," *Istorijski Časopis* 25–26 (1978–79): 53–97; see also articles by Bakalov and Matanov under "Bulgaria," this section.

WALACHIA AND MOLDAVIA: Ion Donat, "Le Domaine princier rural en Valachie (XIVᵉ–XVIᵉ siècles)," *Revue roumaine d'histoire* 6 (1967): 201–31; Radu Florescu and Raymond T. McNally, *Dracula: A Biography of Vlad the Impaler, 1421–1476* (New York: Hawthorn Books, 1976); Nicolae Stoicescu, *Vlad Tepeş, Prince of Walachia* (Bucharest: Editura Academiei Republicii Socialiste România, 1978); Kurt W. Treptow, ed., *Dracula: Essays on the Life and Times of Vlad Tepes* (Boulder: East European Monographs, 1991).

Chapter 4. Nobles and Landowners

BOHEMIA: John M. Klassen, *The Nobility and the Making of the Hussite Revolution* (Boulder: East European Quarterly, 1978); Miloslav Polívka, "The Bohemian Lesser Nobility at the Turn of the 14th and 15th Century," *Historica* (Prague) 25 (1985): 121–75; Dušan Třeštík and Barbara Krzemieńska, "Zur Problematik der Dienstleute im frühmittelalterlichen Böhmen," in F. Graus and H. Ludat, eds., *Siedlung und Verfassung Böhmens* (Wiesbaden, 1967), pp. 70–103.

BULGARIA: G. Cankova-Petkova, "Beitrag zu einigen Fragen des bulgarischen und des byzantinischen Feudalismus im 11.–13. Jahrhundert," *Études historiques* (Sofia) 2 (1965): 85–99; Bistra A. Cvetkova, "Typical Features of the Ottoman Social and Economic Structure in South-Eastern Europe during the 14th to the 16th Centuries," *Études historiques* (Sofia) 9 (1979): 129–49; Elena Kojčeva, "À Propos de la question de l'évolution de certain titres et institutions balkaniques du Moyen Âge," *Études balkaniques* 18 (1982): 84–101; Vera P. Mutafchieva, *Agrarian Relations in the Ottoman Empire in the 15th and 16th Centuries* (Boulder: East European Monographs, 1988); and "De l'exploitation féodale dans les terres de population bulgare sous la domination turque au XV et XVI s.," *Études historiques* (Sofia) 1 (1960): 145–70.

HUNGARY: (INCLUDING TRANSYLVANIA): Gabriel Adrianyi, "Zur Geschichte des Deutschen Ritterordens in Siebenbürgen," *Ungarn-Jahrbuch*, 3 (1971): 9–22; János M. Bak, "Louis I and the Lesser Nobility in Hungary," in Vardy, ed., *Louis the Great*, pp. 67–80; Pál Engel, "Der Adel Nordostungarns zur Zeit Sigismunds (1387–1437)," in *Études historique hongroises* (1990), 1:27–47; Erik Fügedi, "The Aristocracy in Medieval Hungary," in his *Kings, Bishops, Nobles and Burghers* (collection of articles) (London: Variorum Reprints, 1986), pp. 1–14, and *Castle and Society in Medieval Hungary (1000–1437)* (Budapest: Akadémiai Kiadó, 1986); Maria Holban, "Variations historiques sur le problème des cnèzes de Transylvanie," *Revue roumaine d'histoire* 4 (1965): 901–23; Anthony Komjáthy, "Hungarian *Jobbágyság* in the Fifteenth Century," *East European Quarterly* 10 (1976): 77–111; J. Lupaş, "Réalités historiques dans le voïvodat de Transylvanie du XIIe au XVIe siècle," in Académie Roumaine, *La Transylvanie* (Bucharest, 1938); F. Maksay, "Le Pays de la noblesse nombreuse," *Études historiques* (Budapest, 1980) 167–91; E. Malyusz, "Die Entstehung der ständischen Schichten im mittelalterlichen Ungarn," *Studia Historica* 137 (1980): 5–34; Ilona Tárnoky, "Ungarn vor Mohács," *Südost-Forschungen* 20 (1961): 90–129.

POLAND: Oswald P. Backus, "Die Rechtsstellung der litauischen Bojaren, 1387–1506," *Jahrbücher für Geschichte Osteuropas* 6 (1958):1–32; Janusz Bieniak, "Knight Clans in Medieval Poland," in A. Gąsiorowski, ed., *The Polish Nobility in the Middle Ages* (Wrocław: Zakład Narodowy im. Ossolinskich, 1984), pp. 123–76; Marian Biskup, "Der Kreuzritterorden in der Geschichte Polens," *Österreichische Osthefte* 5 (1963): 283–97; Karol Buczek, "The Knight Law and the Emergence of the Nobility Estate in Poland," in Gąsiorowski, ed., *The Polish Nobility*, pp. 87–122; Włodzimierz Dworzaczek, "Perméabilité des barrières sociales dans la Pologne du XVIe siècle," *Acta poloniae historica* 24 (1971): 22–50; A. Gąsiorowski, "Research into Medieval Polish Nobility," in Gąsiorowski, ed., *The Polish Nobility*, pp. 7–20; Stanisław Grodziski, "Les devoirs et les droits politiques de la noblesse polonaise," *Acta poloniae historica* 36 (1977): 163–76; Henryk Łowmianski, "The Rank Nobility in Medieval Poland," in Gąsiorowski, ed., *The Polish Nobility* 21–54; Stanisław Russocki, "Le Rôle de la 'fidelitas' et du 'beneficium' dans la formation des états slaves," *Acta poloniae historica* 26 (1972): 171–88; Michał Sczaniecki, "Les origines et la formation de la noblesse polonaise au Moyen Âge," *Acta poloniae historica* 36 (1977): 101–8; P. Skwarczyński, "The Problems of Feudalism in Poland up to the Beginning of the 16th Century," *Slavonic and East European Review* 34 (1955–56): 292–310.

WALACHIA AND MOLDAVIA: Neagu Djuvara, "Les Grands Boïars ont-ils constitué dans les principautés roumaines une véritable oligarchie institutionnelle et héréditaire?" *Südost-Forschungen* 46 (1987): 1–56; Ion Donat, "Le Domaine princier rural en Valachie (XIVe–XVIe siècles)," *Revue roumaine d'histoire* 6 (1967): 201–31; Dan Gr. Pleşia, "La noblesse roumaine de Transylvanie: structure et évolution," *Revue roumaine d'histoire* 26 (1987): 187–215; Şt. Ştefănescu,

"L'évolution de l'immunité féodale en Valachie aux XIVᵉ–XVIᵉ siècles," *Revue roumaine d'histoire* 7 (1968): 17–27.

Chapter 5. *Peasants, Herders, Serfs, and Slaves*

BOHEMIA: František Graus, "Die Problematik der deutschen Ostsiedlung aus tschechischer Sicht," in Walter Schlesinger, ed., *Die deutsche Ostsiedlung des Mittelalters* (Sigmaringen: J. Thorbecke, 1975), pp. 31–75; Josef Macek, "The Emergence of Serfdom in the Czech Lands," *East Central Europe* (Special Volume), 9 (1982).

BULGARIA: Bistra Cvetkova, "Typical Features of the Ottoman Social and Economic Structure," *Études historiques* (Sofia) 9 (1979): 129–49; Vera Mutafchieva, *Agrarian Relations in the Ottoman Empire* (Boulder, 1988), and "De l'exploitation féodale," *Études historiques* (Sofia) 1 (1960): 145–70; P. Tivcev and G. Cankova-Petkova, "Au sujet des relations féodales dans les territoires bulgares sous la domination byzantine à la fin du XIᵉ et pendant la première moitié du XXIIᵉ siècle," *Byzantino Bulgarica* 2 (1966): 107–25.

HUNGARY: (INCLUDING TRANSYLVANIA): Joseph Held, "The Peasant Revolt of Bábolna, 1437–1438," *Slavic Review* 36 (1977): 25–38; A. Komjáthy, "Hungarian *Jobbágyság* in the Fifteenth Century," *East European Quarterly* 10 (1976): 77–111; E. Lederer, "La structure de la société hongroise du début du Moyen-Âge," *Studia Historica* 45 (1960): 1–23; L. Makkai, "Agrarian Landscapes of Historical Hungary in Feudal Times," *Studia Historica* 140 (1980): 5–18; and "Die Hauptzüge der wirtschaftlich-sozialen Entwicklung Ungarns im 15–17. Jahrhundert," *Studia Historica* 53 (1963): 27–46; Zs. P. Pach, "Das Entwicklungsniveau der feudalen Agrarverhältnisse in Ungarn in der zweiten Hälfte des XV. Jahrhunderts," *Studia Historica* 46 (1960): 1–49; Ştefan Pascu, "Les caractéristiques principales des révoltes paysannes de Transylvanie au Moyen Âge," *Revue roumaine d'histoire* 3 (1964): 5–31.

OTTOMAN EMPIRE: Alan Fisher, "Studies in Ottoman Slavery and Slave Trade. II: Manumission," *Journal of Turkish Studies* 4 (1980): 49–56; Halil Inalcik, "Servile Labor in the Ottoman Empire," in A. Ascher, T. Halasi-Kun, and Bela Kiraly, *The Mutual Effects of the Islamic and Judeo-Christian Worlds: The East European Pattern* (Brooklyn: Brookyn College Press, 1979).

POLAND (INCLUDING PRUSSIA): Oskar Kossmann, "Altpolnisches Bauerntum in neuem Licht: zur Kritik von Karol Buczek," and "Bauernfreiheit im mittelalterlichen Böhmen und Polen," *Zeitschrift für Ostforschung* 25 (1976): 193–247, and 28 (1979): 193–238; Walter Kuhn, "Siedlungsgeschichte des Auschwitzer Beskidenvorlandes," *Zeitschrift für Ostforschung* 24 (1975): 1–78; and "Westslawische Landesherren als Organisatoren der mittelalterlichen Ostsiedlung," in Walter Schlesinger, ed., *Die deutsche Ostsiedlung* (Sigmaringen, 1975), pp. 225–61; Stanisław Trawkowski, "Die Rolle der deutschen Dorfkolonisation und des deutschen Rechtes in Polen im 13. Jahrhundert," in Schlesinger, *Die deutsche Ostsiedlung*, pp. 349–68; Reinhard Wenskus, "Der deutsche Orden und die nichtdeutsche Bevölkerung des Preussenlandes mit besonderer Berücksichtigung der Siedlung," in Schlesinger, ed., *Die deutsche Ostsiedlung*, pp. 417–38.

SERBIA: E. A. Hammel, "Some Mediaeval Evidence on the Serbian Zadruga: A Preliminary Analysis of the Chrysobulls of Dečani," *Revue des études sud-est européenes* 14 (1976): 449–63; Vuk Vinaver, "Crno roblje u starom Dubrovniku (1400–1600)," *Istoriski Časopis* 5 (1954–55): 437–42.

WALACHIA AND MOLDAVIA: Emil Cernea, "Quelques considérations sur le *Jus Valachicum* dans la Pologne féodale," *Revue roumaine d'histoire* 10 (1971): 845–52; Costin Feneşan, "Beziehungen der Wlachen aus dem Cetina-Tal zur Stadt Šibenik gegen Ende des 14. und zu Beginn des 15. Jahrhunderts," *Revue des études sud-est européenes* 17 (1979): 3–15; Damaschin Mioc, "Les vignobles au Moyen Âge en Valachie. I. Les formes de la propriété viticole," *Revue roumaine d'histoire* 6 (1967): 865–79; Şt. Ştefănescu, D. Mioc, and H. Chircă, "L'évolution de la rente féodale en travail en Valachie et en Moldavie aux XIVe–XVIIIe siècles," *Revue roumaine d'histoire* 1 (1962): 39–60.

Chapter 6. Towns and Townspeople

GENERAL: Gerda Baudisch, "Deutsche Bergbausiedlungen auf dem Balkan," *Süddeutsches Archiv* 12 (1969): 32–61; Dietrich Claude, *Die byzantinische Stadt im 6. Jahrhundert* (Byzantinisches Archiv, Heft 13) (Munich: Beck, 1969); Pierre Lavedan, *Histoire de l'urbanisme: Renaissance et temps modernes* (2d ed.; Paris: Henri Laurens, 1959); Danuta Molenda, "Mining Towns in Central-Eastern Europe in Feudal Times," *Acta poloniae historica* 34 (1976): 165–88; Roger Mols, *Introduction à la démographie historique des villes d'Europe du XIVe au XVIIIe siècle*, vol. 2: *Les résultats* (Louvain: J. Duculot, 1954); Zdravko Pljakov, "Le statut de la ville byzantine balkanique aux XIIIe–XIVe siècles," *Études balkaniques*, 1985, no. 3, pp. 73–96; Metodi Sokoloski, "Le développement de quelques villes dans le sud des Balkans au XVe et XVIe siècles," *Balcanica* 1 (1970): 81–106; Nikolai Todorov, *The Balkan City* (Seattle: University of Washington Press, 1983; originally published Sofia, 1972).

BOHEMIA: Jiři Kejř, "Organisation und Verwaltung des königlichen Städtewesens in Böhmen zur Zeit der Luxemburger," in Wilhelm Rausch, ed., *Stadt und Stadtherr im 14. Jahrhundert* (Linz: Österreichische Arbeitskreis für Stadtgeschichtsforschung, 1972), pp. 79–90; and "Zwei Studien über die Anfänge der Städteverfassung in den böhmischen Ländern," *Historica* (Prague) 16 (1969): 81–142; Maria Tischler, "Böhmische Judengemeinden, 1348–1519," in F. Seibt, ed., *Die Juden in den böhmischen Ländern* (Munich: Oldenbourg, 1983), pp. 37–56.

BOSNIA: Adem Handzić, "Die ältesten türkischen Quellenangaben über die

Bergwerke und Marktflecke in Bosnien," *Bulletin, Association internationale d'études du sud-est européen* 12 (1974), 131–39.

BULGARIA: Dimiter Angelov, "Die Stadt im mittelalterlichen Bulgarien," *Zeitschrift für Geschichtswissenschaft* (Berlin) 10 1962: 405–16; Ivan Dujčev, "Quelques traits spécifiques de la civilisation bulgare aux IXe–Xe siècles," *Revue des études sud-est européenes* 15 (1977): 63–73; R. F. Hoddinott, *Bulgaria in Antiquity: An Archaeological Introduction* (New York: St. Martin's Press, 1975); Alexandăr Kuzev, "Zur Lokalisierung der Stadt Vicina," *Études balkaniques*, 1977 no. 3, pp. 112–25; Strašimir Lišev (Lischev), "Zur Frage über die Lage der Stadtgemeinden in den Feudalstaaten der Balkanhalbinsel (X.–XV. Jh.)," *Études historiques* (Sofia) 3 (1966): 95–109; Nicolas Oikonomides, "Presthlavitza, the Little Preslav," *Südost-Forschungen*, 42 (1983): 1–9; Atanas Popov, "La ville médiévale bulgare d'après les recherches archéologiques," *Bulgarian Historical Review* 12, no. 2 (1984): 63–73.

DALMATIA: Dušanka Dinić-Knežević, "Položaj tekstilnih radnika u Dubrovniku u prvoj polovini XV veka," *Jugoslovenski istorijski časopis* 17 (1978): 126–42; Jadran Ferluga, "Les Îles dalmates dans l'empire byzantin," in his *Byzantium on the Balkans* (Amsterdam: Hakkert, 1976); Bariša Krekić, *Dubrovnik in the 14th and 15th Centuries: A City between East and West* (Norman: University of Oklahoma Press, 1972).

HUNGARY: Marianna D. Birnbaum, "Buda between Tatars and Turks," in Bariša Krekić, ed., *Urban Society of Eastern Europe in Premodern Times* (Berkeley: University of California Press, 1987), pp. 137–57; Erik Fügedi, "Die Ausbreitung der städtischen Lebensform–Ungarns Oppida im 14. Jahrhundert," in Rausch, ed., *Stadt und Stadtherr*, pp. 165–92, and "Die Entstehung des Städtwesens in Ungarn," in his *Kings, Bishops, Nobles and Burghers*, (London, 1986), pp. 101–18; László Gerevich, *Towns in Medieval Hungary* (Boulder: Social Science Monographs, 1990); András Kubinyi, "Zur Frage der deutschen Siedlungen im mittleren Teil des Königreiches Ungarn (1200–1541)," in Walter Schlesinger, ed., *Die deutsche Ostsiedlung* (Sigmaringen, 1975), pp. 527–66; and "Topographic Growth of Buda up to 1541," *Nouvelles études historiques* (Budapest; 1965), 133–57; and "Der ungarische König und seine Städte im 14. und am Beginn des 15. Jahrhunderts," in Rausch, ed., *Stadt und Stadtherr*, pp. 193–220; O. Paulinyi, "Der erste Anlauf zur Zentralisation der Berggerichtsbarkeit in Ungarn," *Études historiques* (Budapest, 1980), pp. 209–33; Günther Probszt, *Die niederungarischen Bergstädte; ihre Entwicklung und wirtschaftliche Bedeutung bis zum Übergang an das Haus Habsburg (1546)* (Munich: Oldenbourg, 1966); and "Die niederungarischen Bergstädte," *Zeitschrift für Ostforschung* 1 (1952): 220–52; Martyn C. Rady, *Medieval Buda; A Study of Municipal Government and Jurisdiction in the Kingdom of Hungary* (Boulder: East European Monographs, 1985); György Székely, "Elemente des regulierten und des organischen Wachstums in der ungarischen Städtentwicklung im feudalen Zeitalter," *Études historiques hongroises* (Budapest, 1990), 1:49–61; J. Szücs,

"Das Städtewesen in Ungarn im 15.–17. Jahrhundert," *Studia Historica* 53 (1963): 97–164.

POLAND: Wojciech M. Bartel, "Stadt und Staat in Polen im 14. Jahrhundert," in Rausch, ed., *Stadt und Stadtherr*, pp. 129–64; Marian Biskup, "Der Zusammenbruch des Ordenstaates in Preussen im Lichte der neuesten polnischen Forschungen," *Acta poloniae historica* 9 (1964): 59–76; Karol Buczek, *Targi i miasta na prawie polskim* (Kraków: Zakład Narodowy im. Ossolinskich, 1964); F. W. Carter, "Cracow's Early Development," *Slavonic and East European Review* 61 (1983): 197–225; Aleksander Gieysztor, "Recherches sur les fondements de la Pologne médiévale," *Acta poloniae historica* 4 (1961): 7–33; Paul W. Knoll, "The Urban Development of Medieval Poland, with Particular Reference to Krakow," in Krekić, ed., *Urban Society of Eastern Europe*, pp. 63–136; Walter Kuhn, "Die deutschen Stadtgründungen des 13. Jahrhunderts im westlichen Pommern," *Zeitschrift für Ostforschung* 23 (1974): 1–58; and "Die Stadtdörfer der mittelalterlichen Ostsiedlung," *Zeitschrift für Ostforschung* 20 (1971): 1–69; Tadeusz Lalik, "La genèse du réseau urbain en Pologne médievale," *Acta poloniae historica* 34 (1976): 97–120; Lech Leciejewicz, "Early-Medieval Sociotopographical Transformations in West Slavonic Urban Settlements in the Light of Archaeology," *Acta poloniae historica* 34 (1976): 29–56; Jan Ptaśnik, *Miasta i mieszczaństwo w dawnej Polsce* (Kraków: Nakl. Polskiej Akademiji Umicjetności, 1934).

SERBIA: Sima Ćirković, "Unfulfilled Autonomy: Urban Society in Serbia and Bosnia," in Krekić, ed., *Urban Society of Eastern Europe*, pp. 158–84.

WALACHIA AND MOLDAVIA: Nicoară Beldiceanu, "Un règlement minier ottoman du règne de Süleyman le Législateur," *Südost-Forschungen* 21 (1962): 144–67; Ştefan Pascu, "Le développement des métiers et du marché en Transylvanie au Moyen Âge jusqu'à la fin du XVIe siècle," *Revue roumaine d'histoire* 1 (1962): 19–38; Maja Philippi, "Cives civitatis Brassoviensis: Untersuchungen über die soziale Struktur des Bürgertums von Braşov im 14. und 15. Jahrhundert," *Revue roumaine d'histoire* 15 (1976): 11–28; Eugen Stănescu, "Beiträge zur Paristrion-Frage," *East European Quarterly* 4 (1970): 119–40.

Chapter 7. Religion and the Churches

ALBANIA: Stavro Skendi, *Balkan Cultural Studies* (Boulder: East European Monographs, 1980); Georg Stadtmüller, "Die Islamisierung bei den Albanern," *Jahrbücher für Geschichte Osteuropas* 3 (1955): 404–29.

BOGOMILS: G. Cankova-Petkova, "Apparition et diffusion du Bogomilisme et les rapports des Bulgares avec l'Europe occidentale au Moyen Âge," *Études historiques* (Sofia) 7 (1975): 69–87; Ivan Dujčev, "I Bogomili nei paesi e la loro storia," *Medioevo bizantino-slavo* (Rome: Edizione di Storia e Letteratura,

1965), 1: 251–82; John V. A. Fine, Jr., *The Bosnian Church: A New Interpretation* (Boulder: East European Quarterly, 1975); and "The Bulgarian Bogomil Movement," *East European Quarterly* 11 (1977): 385–412; Borislav Primov, "Medieval Bulgaria and the Dualistic Heresies in Western Europe," *Études historiques* (Sofia) 1 (1960): 79–106.

BOHEMIA: Imre Boba, *Moravia's History Reconsidered* (The Hague: Martinus Nijhoff, 1971); William R. Cook, "Negotiations between the Hussites, the Holy Roman Emperor, and the Roman Church, 1427–36," *East Central Europe* 5 (1978): 90–104; Zdenek Fiala, "Die Organisation der Kirche im Přemyslidenstaat des 10.–13. Jahrhunderts," in F. Graus and H. Ludat, *Siedlung und Verfassung Böhmens in der Frühzeit* (Wiesbaden, 1967), pp. 133–47; Frederick G. Heymann, *George of Bohemia, King of Heretics* (Princeton: University Press, 1965), and *John Žižka and the Hussite Revolution* (Princeton: University Press, 1955); Howard Kaminsky, *A History of the Hussite Revolution* (Berkeley: University of California Press, 1967); M. D. Lambert, "The Bohemian Reform Movement" and "Politics and Hussitism, 1409–1419," in *Medieval Heresy: Popular Movements from Bogomil to Hus* (London: Edward Arnold, 1977), pp. 272–87 and 228–313; Franz Machilek, "Böhmen, Polen und die hussitische Revolution," *Zeitschrift für Ostforschung* 22 (1974): 401–30; Alexander Patschovsky, *Die Anfänge einer ständigen Inquisition in Böhmen* (Berlin: W. de Gruyter, 1975); Johanna Schreiber, "Devotio moderna in Böhmen," *Bohemia: Jahrbuch des Collegium Carolinum* 6 (1965): 93–122; František Smahel, "Leben und Werk des Magisters Hieronymus von Prag," *Historica* 13 (1966): 81–111; Maria Tischler, "Die Juden in Böhmen und Mähren im Mittelalter und die ersten Privilegien," in Ferdinand Seibt, *Die Juden in den böhmischen Ländern* (Munich, 1983), pp. 37–56; Vladimir Vavřinek, "Die Christianisierung und Kirchenorganisation Grossmährens," *Historica* 7 (1963): 5–56.

BULGARIA: Dimiter Angelov, "Clement of Ochrida and Bulgarian Nationhood," *Études historiques* (Sofia) 3 (1966): 61–78; and "Hesychasm in Medieval Bulgaria," *Bulgarian Historical Review* 17, no. 3 (1989): 41–61; Vasil Gjuzelev, "Das Papsttum und Bulgarien im Mittelalter (9.–14.Jh.)," *Bulgarian Historical Review* 5 (1977): 34–58; Nikolaj Kočev, "De certains aspects des relations ecclésiastico-politiques dans la péninsule balkanique aux XIV–XVe s.," *Études balkaniques*, 1984, no. 4, pp. 51–61; D. Obolensky, "Clement of Ohrid," in *Six Byzantine Portraits* (Oxford: Clarendon Press, 1988); Borislav Primov, "Medieval Bulgaria and the Dualistic Heresies in Western Europe," *Études historiques* (Sofia) 1 (1960): 79–106; M. Sokoloski, "Islamizacija u Makedoniji u XV i XVI–veku," *Istorijski Časopis* 22 (1975): 75–89; A. E. N. Tachiaos, "Die Aufhebung des bulgarischen Patriarchats von Tirnovo," *Balkan Studies* 4 (1963): 67–82.

BYZANTINE INFLUENCES: Slobodan Ćurčić, "Byzantine Legacy in Ecclesiastical Architecture of the Balkans after 1453," in Lowell Clucas, ed., *The Byzantine Legacy in Eastern Europe* (Boulder: East European Monographs,

1988), pp. 59–81; Joan M. Hussey, *Church and Learning in the Byzantine Empire, 867–1185* (New York: Russell and Russell, 1963); Dušan Lj. Kašić, "Die griechisch-serbische Kirchensymbiose in Norddalmatien vom XV. bis zum XIX. Jahrhundert," *Balkan Studies* 15 (1974): 21–48; M. D. Lambert, "Early Western Heresy and Eastern Dualism," in *Medieval Heresy: Popular Movements from Bogomil to Hus* (London: Edward Arnold, 1977), pp. 7–23; Hristo Matanov, "Le Mont Athos et les rapports politiques dans les Balkans durant la deuxième moitié du XIVe siècle," *Études balkaniques*, 1981, no. 2, pp. 69–100; Dimitri Obolensky, *The Byzantine Commonwealth* (London: Weidenfeld and Nicolson, 1971); Steven Runciman, *The Great Church in Captivity: A Study of the Patriarchate of Constantinople from the Eve of the Turkish Conquest to the Greek War of Independence* (Cambridge: University Press, 1968); also *The Orthodox Churches and the Secular State* (Auckland: Auckland University Press, 1971).

GERMANS: Hans-Dietrich Kahl, "Zum Geist der deutschen Slawenmission des Hochmittelalters," *Zeitschrift für Ostforschung*, 2 (1953): 1–14; Ulrich Stutz, "The Proprietary Church as an Element of Mediaeval Germanic Ecclesiastical Law," in Geoffrey Barraclough, ed. and trans., *Mediaeval Germany, 911–1250* (Oxford: Blackwell, Barnes and Noble, 1938), 2:35–70; Fritz Valjavec, *Geschichte der deutschen Kulturbeziehungen zu Südosteuropa* (Munich: Oldenbourg, 1953); Franz Zagiba, "Die bairische Slawenmission und ihre Fortsetzung durch Kyrill und Method," *Jahrbücher für Geschichte Osteuropas* 9 (1961): 1–56.

HUNGARY: Gabriel Adrianyi, "Der Beitrag der Kirchen zur ungarischen Kultur zur Zeit der Staatsgründung und der Reformation," *Südostdeutsches Archiv* 14–15 (1981–82): 19–30, and "Der Eintritt Ungarns in die christlich-abendländische Völkergemeinschaft," *Ungarn-Jahrbuch* 6 (1974–75): 24–37; also "Die Kirchenpolitik des Matthias Corvinus (1458–1490)," *Ungarn-Jahrbuch* 10 (1979): 83–92; Smail Balić, "Der Islam im mittelalterlichen Ungarn," *Südost-Forschungen* 23 (1964): 19–35; Andor Csizmadia, "Die rechtliche Entwicklung des Zehnten (Decima) in Ungarn," *Zeitschrift der Savigny-Stiftung*, Kanonistische Abteilung, 92 (1975): 228–57; Erik Fügedi, "La formation des villes et les ordres mendiants en Hongrie," "Hungarian Bishops in the Fifteenth Century," and "Die Wirtschaft des Erzbistums von Gran," all in his *Kings, Bishops, Nobles and Burghers* (London, 1986); Z. J. Kosztolnyik, "The Church and the Hungarian Court under Coloman the Learned," *East European Quarterly* 18 (1984): 129–41; Elemér Mályusz, "Das Konstanzer Konzil und das königliche Patronatsrecht in Ungarn," *Studia Historica* 18 (1959): 1–120; Gyula Moravcsik, "Byzantine Christianity and the Magyars in the Period of Their Migration," *American Slavic and East European Review*, 5 (1946): 29–45; C. Mureşan and G.S. Ardeleanu, "La politique fiscale de la papauté en Transylvanie au cours de la première moitié du XIVe siècle," *Nouvelles études d'histoire* (Rome, 1955), pp. 225–40.

JEWS: Salo W. Baron, *A Social and Religious History of the Jews* (2d ed.; New York: Columbia University Press, 1957), vols. 3 and 9; S. M. Dubnow, *History of the Jews in Russia and Poland from the Earliest Times until the Present Day,* vol. I (Philadelphia: Jewish Publication Society of America, 1916); Heinrich H. Graetz, *History of the Jews*, vol. 3 (Philadelphia: Jewish Publication Society of America, 1894); Nikolaj Kočev, "The Question of Jews and the So-Called Judaizers in the Balkans from the 9th to the 14th Century," *Bulgarian Historical Review* 6 (1978): 60–79; James Parkes, *The Jew in the Medieval Community* (London: Soncino Press, 1938); Adam Vetulani, "The Jew in Medieval Poland," *Jewish Journal of Sociology* 4 (1962): 274–94.

MUSLIMS: Smail Balić, "Der Islam im mittelalterlichen Ungarn," *Südost-Forschungen* 23 (1964): 19–35, and "Der Islam in Bosnien," *Österreichische Osthefte* 7: (1964): 470–76; Gustave E. von Grunebaum, *Medieval Islam* (Chicago: University of Chicago Press, 1946); Nenad Moačanin, "Some Remarks on the Supposed Muslim Tolerance toward *dhimmis*," *Südost-Forschungen* 48 (1989): 209–15.

OTTOMAN EMPIRE: B. Braude and B. Lewis, "Foundation Myths of the Millet System," in their *Christians and Jews in the Ottoman Empire* (New York: Holmes and Maier, 1982), 1: 69–88; Charles A. Frazee, *Catholics and Sultans: The Church and the Ottoman Empire, 1453–1923* (London: Cambridge University Press, 1983); F. W. Hasluck, *Christianity and Islam under the Sultans*, 2 vols. (Oxford: Clarendon Press, 1973; originally published 1929); Nicolas Oikonomides, "Monastères et moines lors de la conquête ottomane," *Südost-Forschungen* 35 (1976): 1–10; N. J. Pantazopoulos, *Church and Law in the Balkan Peninsula during the Ottoman Rule* (Thessaloniki: Institute for Balkan Studies, 1967); Speros Vryonis, Jr., "The Byzantine Legacy and Ottoman Forms," and "Decisions of the Patriarchal Synod in Constantinople as a Source for Ottoman Religious Policy in the Balkans prior to 1402"; also "Religious Changes and Patterns in the Balkans, 14th–16th Centuries," all in his *Studies on Byzantium, Seljuks, and Ottomans* (Malibu: Undena Publications, 1981).

POLAND: Helmut Holzapfel, *Tausend Jahre Kirche Polens* (Würzburg: Echter Verlag, 1966); Jerzy Kłoczowski, "Dominicans of the Polish Province in the Middle Ages," in Kłoczowski, ed., *The Christian Community of Medieval Poland* (Wrocław: Zakład Narodowy im. Ossolinskich, 1981), pp. 73–118; and "Les ordres mendiants en Pologne à la fin du Moyen Âge," *Acta poloniae historica* 15 (1967): 5–38; Karolina Lanckorońska, *Studies on the Roman-Slavonic Rite in Poland* (Orientalia Christiana Analecta, no. 161) (Rome: Pont. Institutum Orientalium Studiorum, 1961); Erich Maschke, *Der Peterspfennig in Polen und dem deutschen Osten* (2d ed.; Sigmaringen: Thorbecke, 1979; originally published 1933); Karl Völker, *Kirchengeschichte Polens* (Berlin, 1930); Erich Weise, "Der Heidenkampf des deutschen Ordens," *Zeitschrift für Ostforschung* 12 (1963): 420–73 and 622–72, and 13 (1964): 401–20; Eugeniusz Wiśniowski, "Parish Clergy in Medieval Poland," in Kłoczowski, *The Christian Community*, pp. 119–48.

SERBIA: Ladislas Hadrovics, *Le peuple serbe et son église sous la domination turque* (Paris: Presses universitaires de France, 1947); D. Obolensky, "Sava of Serbia," in *Six Byzantine Portraits* (Oxford, 1988); George C. Soulis, *The Serbs and Byzantium during the Reign of Stephen Dušan (1331–1355) and His Successors* (Washington, D.C.: Dumbarton Oaks Library, 1984); Slavko P. Todorovich, *The Chilandarians: Serbian Monks on the Great Mountain* (Boulder: East European Monographs, 1989).

SLAVS (GENERAL): Z. R. Dittrich, "Zur religiösen Ur- und Frühgeschichte der Slaven," *Jahrbücher für Geschichte Osteuropas* 9 (1961): 481–510; Ivan Dujčev [Duichev], "Le mont Athos et les Slaves au Moyen Âge," *Medioevo bizantino-slavo*, 1: 487–510; Francis Dvornik, "The Significance of the Missions of Cyril and Methodius," *Slavic Review* 23 (1964): 195–211; František Graus, "Die Entwicklung der Legenden von Konstantin und Method," *Jahrbücher für Geschichte Osteuropas* 19 (1971): 161–211; Ihor Ševčenko, "Three Paradoxes of the Cyrillo-Methodian Mission," *Slavic Review* 23 (1964): 220–36; A.P. Vlasto, *The Entry of the Slavs into Christendom* (Cambridge: University Press, 1970).

Chapter 8. The Art and Practice of War

GENERAL: Philippe Contamine, *War in the Middle Ages* (London: Guild, 1985); Kelly DeVries, *Medieval Military Technology* (Peterborough, Ontario: Broadview Press, 1992); J. F. C. Fuller, *Armament and History: A Study of the Influence of Armament on History from the Dawn of Classical Warfare to the Second World War* (New York: Scribner's, 1945), and *A Military History of the Western World*, 2 vols. (New York, 1954); Konstantin Jireček, *Die Heerstrasse von Belgrad nach Constantinople und die Balkanpässe* (Prague: F. Tempsky, 1877); Archer Jones, *The Art of War in the Western World* (Urbana: University of Illinois Press, 1987); H. W. Koch, *Medieval Warfare* (Greenwich: Bison Books, 1978); Ferdinand Lot, *L'Art militaire et les armées au Moyen Âge*, 2 vols. (Paris: Payot, 1946); Lynn Montross, *War through the Ages* (3d rev. ed., New York: Harper, 1960); C. W. C. Oman, *The Art of War in the Middle Ages, A.D. 378–1515*, rev. and ed. John Beeler (Ithaca: Cornell University Press, 1953), and *A History of the Art of War in the Middle Ages* (2d ed., New York: Houghton Mifflin, 1924); Richard A. Preston and Sidney F. Wise, *Men in Arms: A History of Warfare and Its Interrelationships with Western Society* (4th ed.; New York: Holt, Rinehart and Winston, 1979); Steven Runciman, *A History of the Crusades*, 3 vols. (Cambridge: University Press, 1951).

BOHEMIA: Frederick G. Heymann, *John Žižka and the Hussite Revolution* (Princeton: Princeton University Press, 1955). A discussion of Hussite strategy and tactics appears in many general accounts of the history of warfare.

BULGARIA: D. Angelov, "Certain aspects de la conquête des peuples balkaniques par les Turcs," *Byzantinoslavica* 17 (1956): 220–75; Borislav Primov, "The Third and Fourth Crusades and Bulgaria," *Études historiques* (Sofia) 7 (1975): 43–67.

BYZANTINE EMPIRE: Mark C. Bartusis, *The Late Byzantine Army: Arms and Society 1204–1453* (Philadelphia: University of Pennsylvania Press, 1992); Djurdjica Petrović, "Fire-arms in the Balkans on the Eve of and After the Ottoman Conquest of the Fourteenth and Fifteenth Centuries," in V. J. Parry and M. E. Yapp, eds., *War, Technology and Society in the Middle East* (London: Oxford University Press, 1975), pp. 164–94; Steven Runciman, *The Fall of Constantinople* (Cambridge: University Press, 1965).

CROATIA: Ivan Babić, "Military History," in F. Eterovich and C. Spalatin, *Croatia*, (Toronto, 1964), 1: 131–66; Willy A. Bachich, "Maritime History of the Eastern Adriatic," in Eterovich and Spalatin, *Croatia*, 2: 119–56.

HUNGARY: Gabriel Adrianyi, "Zur Geschichte des Deutschen Ritterordens in Siebenbürgen," *Ungarn-Jahrbuch* 3 (1971): 9–22; Aziz Suryal Atiya, *The Crusade of Nicopolis* (London: Methuen, 1934); János Bak and Béla Király, eds., *From Hunyadi to Rákoczi: War and Society in Late Medieval and Early Modern Hungary* (New York: Brooklyn College Press, 1982); János Bak, "Politics, Society and Defense in Medieval and Early Modern Hungary," in *From Hunyadi to Rákoczi*, pp. 1–22; András Borosy, "The *Militia Portalis* in Hungary before 1526," in *From Hunyadi to Rákoczi*, pp. 63–80; Pál Engel, "János Hunyadi: The Decisive Years of His Career, 1440–1444," in *From Hunyadi to Rákoczi*, pp. 103–23; Erik Fügedi, "Medieval Hungarian Castles in Existence at the Start of the Ottoman Advance," in *From Hunyadi to Rákoczi*, pp. 59–62; Horst Glassl, "Der deutsche Orden im Burzenland und in Kumanien (1211–1225)," *Ungarn-Jahrbuch* 3 (1971): 22–49; Hansgerd Göckenjan, *Hilfsvölker und Grenzwächter im mittelalterlichen Ungarn* (Wiesbaden: F. Steiner, 1972); Gustav Gündisch, "Siebenbürgen in der Türkenabwehr, 1395–1526," *Revue roumaine d'histoire* 13 (1974): 415–43; and "Die Türkeneinfälle in Siebenbürgen bis zur Mitte des 15. Jahrhunderts," *Jahrbücher für Geschichte Osteuropas* 2 (1937): 393–412; Konrad G. Gündisch, "Siebenbürgen und der Aufruhr von 1403 gegen Sigismund von Luxemburg," *Revue roumaine d'histoire* 15 (1976): 399–420; Joseph Held, *Hunyadi, Legend and Reality* (Boulder: East European Monographs, 1985), and "Military Reform in Early Fifteenth Century Hungary," *East European Quarterly* 11, (1977): 129–39; also "Peasants in Arms, 1437–1438 and 1456," in *From Hunyadi to Rákoczi*, pp. 81–101; also "The Peasant Revolt of Bábolna, 1437–1438," *Slavic Review* 36 (1977): 25–38; Béla K. Király, "Society and War from Mounted Knights to the Standing Armies of Absolute Kings: Hungary and the West," in *From Hunyadi to Rákoczi*, pp. 23–55; Anthony Komjáthy, *A Thousand Years of the Hungarian Art of War* (Toronto: Rakoczi Foundation, 1982); András Kubinyi, "The Road to Defeat: Hungarian Politics and Defense in the Jagiellonian Period," in *From Hunyadi to Rákoczi*, pp. 159–78; Gabriel S. Pellathy, "The Dozsa Revolt: Prelude and Aftermath," *East European Quarterly* 21 (1987): 275–95; Gyula Rázsó, "The Mercenary Army of King Matthias Corvinus," in *From Hunyadi to Rákoczi*, pp. 125–40; Ferenc Szakály, "The Hungarian-Croatian Border Defense System and Its Collapse," in *From Hunyadi to Rákoczi*, pp. 141–58, and "Phases of Turco-Hungarian Warfare before the Battle of Mohács (1365–1526)," *Acta Orientàlia Academiae Scientiarum Hungaricae* 33 (I) (Budapest: 1979): 65–111.

MONGOLS: Harold T. Cheshire, "The Great Tartar Invasion of Europe," *Slavonic Review* 5 (1926–27): 89–105; David Morgan, *The Mongols* (Oxford: Basil Blackwell, 1986); Alfred von Pawlikowski-Cholewa, *Die Heere des Morgenlandes* (Berlin: W. de Gruyter, 1940); Michael Prawdin, *The Mongol Empire: Its Rise and Legacy* (2d ed.; New York: Macmillan, 1942); J. J. Saunders, *The History of the Mongol Conquests* (London: Barnes and Noble, 1971); Denis Sinor, "Horse and Pasture in Inner Asian History," *Oriens Extremis* 19 (1972): 171–83; John Masson Smith, Jr., "Mongol Campaign Rations: Milk, Marmots, and Blood?" *Journal of Turkish Studies* 8 (1984): 223–28; Bertold Spuler, *History of the Mongols: Based on Eastern and Western Accounts of the Thirteenth and Fourteenth Centuries* (London: Routledge and Kegan Paul, 1972).

OTTOMAN EMPIRE: D. Angelov, "Certain aspects de la conquête des peuples balkaniques par les Turcs," *Byzantinoslavica* 17 (1956), 220–75; H. Inalcik, "Ottoman Methods of Conquest," *Studia Islamica* 2: 103–29; Paul Wittek, "De la défaite d'Ankara à la prise de Constantinople (un demi-siècle d'histoire ottomane)" in his *La formation de l'empire ottoman* (London: Variorum Reprints, 1982); E.A. Zachariadou, "The Conquest of Adrianople by the Turks," in her *Romania and the Turks* (London: Variorum Reprints, 1985).

POLAND: Sven Ekdahl, "Der Krieg zwischen dem Deutschen Orden und Polen-Litauen im Jahre 1422," *Zeitschrift für Ostforschung* 13 (1964): 614–51; Stanisław M. Zajączkowski, "Udział ludności wiejskiej w polskiej wojskowości do połowy XV stulecia," *Studia i materiały do historii wojskowości* (Wrocław) 27 (1984): 3–80.

PRUSSIA: Friedrich Benninghoven, "Der Gotlandfeldzüge des deutschen Ordens, 1398–1408," *Zeitschrift für Ostforschung* 13 (1964): 421–77; William Urban, *The Prussian Crusade* (Lanham: University Press of America, 1980); Erich Weise, "Der Heidenkampf des deutschen Ordens," *Zeitschrift für Ostforschung* 12 (1963): 420–73.

SERBIA: Thomas Allen Emmert, *Serbian Golgotha: Kosovo, 1389* (Boulder: East European Monographs, 1990); Olga Zirojević, *Tursko vojno uredjenje u Srbiji (1459–1683)* (Belgrade: Istorijski Institut, 1974).

WALACHIA AND MOLDAVIA: Ştefan Andreescu, "L'action de Vlad Tepeş dans le sud-est de l'Europe en 1476," *Revue des études sud-est européenes* 15 (1977): 259–72; Nicoară Beldiceanu, "La campagne ottomane de 1484: ses préparatifs militaires et sa chronologie," *Revue des études roumaines* (Paris) 5–6 (1960): 67–77; and "La conquête des cités marchandes de Kilia et de Cetatea Alba par Bayezid II," *Südost-Forschungen* 23, (1964): 36–90; R. Rosetti, "Stephen the Great of Moldavia and the Turkish Invasion (1457–1504)," *Slavonic Review* 6 (1927–28): 86–103; Nicolae Stoicescu, "Contribution à l'histoire de l'armée roumaine au Moyen Âge," *Revue roumaine d'histoire* 6 (1967): 731–63; and "La victoire de Vlad l'Empaleur sur les Turcs (1462)," *Revue roumaine d'histoire* 15 (1976): 377–97.

Chapter 9. Governments

ALBANIA: Antonina L. Zeljazkova, "Ottoman-Turkic Colonization in Albania and Some Aspects of the Ensuing Demographic Changes," *Études balkaniques*, 1984, no. 2, pp. 67-84.

BOHEMIA: Krzysztof Baczkowski, "Die Städte in den Ständevertretungen Ostmitteleuropas gegen Ende des Mittelalters," *Bohemia* 30, no. 1 (1989): 1–17; Frederick Heymann, "The National Assembly of Časlav," *Medievalia et Humanistica* 8 (1954): 32–55; Ivan Hlavaček, "Die Geschichte der Kanzlei König Wenzels IV und ihre Beamten in den Jahren 1376–1419," *Historica* 5 (1963): 5–69.

BOSNIA: Nicoara Beldiceanu, "Les Valaques de Bosnie à la fin du XVᵉ siècle et leurs institutions," in *Turcica* 7 (1975): 122–34, reprinted in Beldiceanu, *Le monde ottoman des Balkans*, 1402–1566 (London: Variorum Reprints, 1976).

BULGARIA: Genoveva Cankova-Petkova, "Certains aspects du pouvoir royal et des institutions d'état sous le second royaume bulgare," *Études balkaniques*, 1978, no. 3, pp. 102–8; Dragoljub Dragojlović, "La župa chez les slaves balkaniques au Moyen Âge," *Balcanica* 2 (1971): 85–115; Elena Kojčeva, "À Propos de la question de l'évolution de certains titres et institutions balkaniques du Moyen Âge," *Études balkaniques*, 1982, no. 4, pp. 84–101; Petar Koledarov, "Administrative Structure and Frontier Set Up of the First Bulgarian Tsardom," *Études balkaniques*, 1978, no. 3, pp. 132–40.

CROATIA: Jadran Ferluga, "Tema Dalmacija," in *Byzantium on the Balkans* (Amsterdam, 1976), 151–72; Hrvoje Jurčić, "Die sogenannten 'Pacta conventa' in kroatischer Sicht," *Ungarn-Jahrbuch* 1 (1969): 11–22.

HUNGARY: János Bak, *Königtum und Stände in Ungarn* (Wiesbaden, 1973); Gábor Barta, "Siebenbürgen im Königreich Ungarn (997–1690)," in *Études historiques hongroises* (Budapest, 1990) 1:79–96; György Bonis, "The Hungarian Feudal Diet (13th–18th Centuries)," *Recueils de la Société Jean Bodin*, 25 (1965): 287–307, and "Ständisches Finanzwesen in Ungarn im frühen 16. Jahrhundert," *Nouvelles études historiques* (Budapest: 1965), pp. 83–103; L. Elekes, "Essai de centralisation de l'état hongrois dans la seconde moitié du XVᵉ siècle," *Studia historica* 22 (1960): 1–31; Erik Fügedi, "Castles and Castellans in Angevin Hungary" (with map), in S. B. Vardy et al., *Louis the Great* (Boulder, 1986), pp. 49–65; Hungarian "Golden Bull," quoted in Alfred J. Bannan and Achilles Edelenyi, *Documentary History of Eastern Europe* (New York: Twayne Publishers, 1970); Gyula Kristó, "Die Entstehung der Komitatsorganisation unter Stephan dem Heiligen," in *Études historiques hongroises* (Budapest, 1990), 1:13–25; E. Malyusz, "Les débuts du vôte de la taxe par les ordres dans la Hongrie féodale," *Nouvelles études historiques* (Budapest, 1965), pp. 55–82, and "Die Zentralisationsbestrebungen König Sigismunds in Ungarn," *Studia historica*, 50 (1960): 1–42; Heinrich Marczali, *Ungarische Verfassungs-Geschichte* (Tübingen: Mohr, 1910); O. Paulinyi, "Der erste Anlauf zur Zentralisation der Berggerichtsbarkeit in Ungarn," *Études historiques* (Budapest, 1980), pp. 209–33; Herbert Schönebaum, "Der politische und kirchliche Aufbau Siebenbürgens bis zum Tatareneinfall," *Leipziger Vierteljahrschrift für Südosteuropa* 1 (1937): 14–53; Ilona Tárnoky, "Ungarn vor Mohacs," *Südost-Forschungen* 20 (1961): 90–129.

OTTOMAN EMPIRE: Benjamin Braude, "Foundation Myths of the Millet System," in Braude and Lewis, *Christians and Jews in the Ottoman Empire*, pp. 69–88; Metin Kunt, *The Sultan's Servants: The Transformation of Ottoman Provincial Government, 1550–1650* (New York: Columbia University Press, 1983); Arno Mehlan, "Der Einfluss der Raja-Privilegierung auf die Balkanwirtschaft zur Türkenzeit," *Leipziger Vierteljahrschrift für Südosteuropa* 5 (1941): 205–22; Vera P. Mutafchieva, *Agrarian Relations in the Ottoman Empire in the 15th and 16th Centuries* (Boulder: East European Monographs, 1988); Michael Ursinus, "Zur Diskussion um '*millet*' im Osmanischen Reich," *Südost Forschungen* 48 (1989): 195–207; Speros Vryonis, Jr., "The Byzantine Legacy and Ottoman Forms," in his *Studies on Byzantium, Seljuks, and Ottomans* (Malibu: Undena Publications, 1981), 2: 253–308.

POLAND: Juliusz Bardach, "L'État polonais du Haut Moyen Âge," in *Acta poloniae historica* 5 (1962): 7–47; Karol Górski, "The Origins of the Polish Sejm," *Slavonic and East European Review* 44 (1966): 122–38; Stanisław Grodziski, "Les devoirs et les droits politiques de la noblesse polonaise," *Acta poloniae historica* 36 (1977): 163–76; Oskar Kossmann, "Aufsätze und Forschungsberichte," *Zeitschrift für Ostforschung* 32 (1983): 173–233; Walter Kuhn, "Kastellaneigrenzen und Zehntgrenzen in Schlesien," *Zeitschrift für Ostforschung* 21 (1972): 201–47; Henryk Łowmianski, "Economic Problems of the Early Feudal Polish State," *Acta poloniae historica* 3 (1960): 7–32; Stanisław Russocki, "'Consilium Baronum' en Pologne médiévale," *Acta poloniae historica* 35 (1977): 5–19; Michał Sczaniecki, "Les origines et la formation de la noblesse polonaise du Moyen Âge," *Acta poloniae historica* 36 (1977): 101–8.

PRUSSIA: Marian Biskup, "Royal Prussia in the Times of Copernicus," in Bogdan Suchodolski, ed., *Poland: The Land of Copernicus* (Wrocław: Ossolineum, 1973), pp. 43–53, and "Der Zusammenbruch des Ordensstaates in Preussen im Lichte der neuesten polnischen Forschungen," *Acta poloniae historica* 9 (1964): 59–76; Karol Górski, "The Teutonic Order in Prussia," *Medievalia et Humanistica* 17 (1966): 20–37; and "The Royal Prussia Estates in the Second Half of the XVth Century and Their Relation to the Crown of Poland," *Acta poloniae historica* 10 (1964): 49–64; Heinrich G. von Treitschke, *Das deutsche Ordensland Preussen* (Göttingen: Vandenhoeck and Ruprecht, 1958; originally published, 1862); P. Marjan Tumler, *Der deutsche Orden* (Vienna, 1955); Erich Weise,

"Entwicklungsstufen der Verfassungsgeschichte des Ordensstaates Preussen im 15. Jahrhundert," *Zeitschrift für Ostforschung*, 7 (1958): 1–17.

SERBIA: Miloš Blagojević, "L'exploitation fiscale et féodale en Serbie du XIIIᵉ au XVᵉ siècle," *Revue roumaine d'histoire*, 22 (1983): 137–46.

WALACHIA AND MOLDAVIA: Franz Babinger, "Beginn der Türkensteuer in den Donaufürstentümer (1394 bzw. 1455)," *Südost-Forschungen* 8 (1943): 1–35; Ion Donat, "Le Domaine princier rural en Valachie (XIVᵉ–XVIᵉ siècles)," *Revue roumaine d'histoire* 6 (1967): 201–31; Ion Matei, "Quelques problèmes concernant le régime de la domination ottomane dans les pays roumains," *Revue des études sud-est européenes* 10 (1972): 65–81 and 11 (1973): 81–95.

Chapter 10. Laws and Justice

BOHEMIA: Wilhelm Hanisch, "Die Luxemburger und die Juden," in F. Seibt, ed., *Die Juden in den böhmischen Ländern* (Munich: Oldenbourg, 1983), pp. 27–35; Peter Hilsch, "Die Juden in Böhmen und Mähren im Mittelalter und die ersten Privilegien," in Seibt, ed., *Die Juden*, pp. 13–26; Alexander Patschovsky, *Die Anfänge einer ständigen Inquisition in Böhmen* (Berlin, 1975).

BULGARIA: Emil Alexandrov, "The International Treaties of Medieval Bulgaria (Legal Aspects)," *Bulgarian Historical Review* 17, no. 4 (1989): 40–56; Mihail Andréev, "Sur l'origine du 'Zakon sudnyi Ljudem' (Loi pour juger les gens)," *Revue des études sud-est européenes* 1 (1963): 331–44; Dragoljub Dragojlović, "Dispositions légales concernant les néomanichéens dans les nomocanons byzantins et slaves," *Balcanica* 3 (1972): 133–55; Harold D. Hazeltine, "Roman and Canon Law in the Middle Ages," *Cambridge Medieval History*, vol. 5 (Cambridge: University Press, 1929), pp. 697–764; Fani Milkova, "Le droit byzantin et la première loi écrite bulgaro-slave," *Études balkaniques*, 1988, no. 2, pp. 81–86; Vicki Tamir, *Bulgaria and Her Jews: The History of a Dubious Symbiosis* (New York: Yeshiva University Press, 1979).

HUNGARY: János M. Bak, György Bónis, and James Ross Sweeney, *The Laws of the Medieval Kingdom of Hungary, 1100–1301* (Bakersfield: C. Schlacks, 1989); György Bonis, "Men Learned in the Law in Medieval Hungary," *East Central Europe* 4, part 2 (1977): 181–91; Erik Fügedi, "Das mittelalterliche Königreich Ungarn als Gastland," in Schlesinger, ed., *Die deutsche Ostsiedlung des Mittelalters*, pp. 471–507; András Kubinyi, "Zur Frage der deutschen Siedlungen im mittleren Teil des Königreiches Ungarn (1200–1541)," in Walter Schlesinger, ed., *Die deutsche Ostsiedlung* (Sigmaringen, 1975), pp. 527–66; J. Lupaş, "Réalités historiques dans le voïvodat de Transylvanie du XIIᵉ au XVIᵉ siècle," in Académie roumaine, *La Transylvanie* (Bucharest, 1938); László Revesz, "Staat und Recht in Ungarn im Zeitalter des Humanismus und der Renaissance," *Ungarn-Jahrbuch* 10 (1979): 93–107; Valeriu Şotropa, "Conditions sociales et politiques de la formation du droit transylvain," *Revue roumaine d'histoire* 14 (1975): 549–59; Reinhard Wenskus, "Der deutsche Orden und die nicht-deutsche Bevölkerung des Preussenlandes mit besonderer Berücksichtigung der Siedlung," in Schlesinger, ed., *Die deutsche Ostsiedlung*, pp. 417–38.

OTTOMAN EMPIRE: Ilber Ortayh, "Some Observations on the Institution of Qadi in the Ottoman Empire," *Bulgarian Historical Review* 10 (1982): 57–68; N. J. Pantazopoulos, *Church and Law in the Balkan Peninsula during the Ottoman Rule* (Thessaloniki: Institute for Balkan Studies, 1967); Speros Vryonis, Jr., "The Byzantine Legacy and Ottoman Forms," in Vryonis, *Studies on Byzantium, Seljuks, and Ottomans* (Malibu, 1981), 2: 253–308.

POLAND: Juliusz Bardach, Bogusław Leśnodorski, and Michał Pietrzak, *Historia państwa i prawa polskiego* (Warsaw, 1976); Zdisław Kaczmarczyk and Bogusław Leśnodorski, *Historia państwa i prawa Polski od połowy XV w. do r. 1795* (Warsaw, 1957).

SERBIA: Malcolm Burr, ed., "The Code of Stephen Dušan, Tsar and Autocrat of the Serbs and Greeks," *Slavonic Review* 28 (1949–50): 198–217 and 516–39.

WALACHIA AND MOLDAVIA: D. J. Deletant, "Some Aspects of the Byzantine Tradition in the Rumanian Principalities," *Slavonic and East European Review* 59 (1981): 1–14; Valentin Georgescu, "La place de la coutume dans le droit des états féodaux roumains de Valachie et de Moldavie jusqu'au milieu du XVIIe siècle," *Revue roumaine d'histoire* 6 (1967): 553–86; N. Smochina, "Le Procheiros Nomos de l'empereur Basile (867–879) et son application chez les Roumains au XIVe siècle," *Balkan Studies* 9 (1968): 167–208; Smochina, "L'application du droit romain-byzantin chez les roumains," *Balkan Studies* 12 (1971): 187–252.

Chapter 11. Commerce and Money

BALKAN PENINSULA: Willy A. Bachich, "Maritime History of the Eastern Adriatic, in Eterovich and Spalatin," *Croatia*, 2: 119–56; Michel Balard, "Les Genois et les regions bulgares au XIVe siècle," *Byzantino-Bulgarica* 7 (1981): 87–97; Matei Cazacu, "L'impact ottoman sur les pays roumains et ses incidences monétaires (1452–1504), *"Revue roumaine d'histoire* 12 (1973): 159–92; Paul Cernovodeanu, "Les échanges économiques dans l'évolution des relations roumano-turques (XVe–XVIIIe siècles)," *Revue des études sud-est européenes* 16 (1978): 81–90; S. Cirković and D. Kovačević-Kojić, "L'Économie naturelle et la production aux XIIIe–XVe siècles dans les regions actuelles de la Yougoslavie," *Balcanica* 13–14 (1982–83): 45–56; Dennis Deletant, "Genoese, Tatars and Rumanians at the Mouth of the Danube in the Fourteenth Century," *Slavonic and East European Review* 62 (1984): 511–30; Alain Ducellier, "Les Mutations de l'Albanie au XVe siècle (du monopole ragusain à la redecouverte des fonctions de transit)," *Études balkaniques*, 1978, no. 1, pp. 55–79; Jadran Ferluga, "Les Îles dalmates dans l'empire byzantin," in his *Byzantium on the Balkans* (Amsterdam,

1976); Vasil Gjuzelev, "Les relations bulgaro-venetiennes durant la première moitié du XIVe siècle," *Études historiques* (Sofia) 9 (1979): 39–76; Alexandru I. Gonta, "Urkundliche Aufschlüsse über die Münzen und Zahlungsmittel der Moldau im Handelsverkehr mit ihren Nachbarländern im 14. und 15. Jahrhundert," *Südost-Forschungen* 27 (1968): 51–82; Konstantin Jireček, *Die Heerstrasse von Belgrad nach Constantinopel und die Balkanpässe* (Prague: F. Tempsky, 1877); Bariša Krekić, *Dubrovnik in the 14th and 15th Centuries* (Norman, Okla., 1972); Luan Malltezi, "Le monopole de l'état de Venise sur les céreales en Albanie au XVe siècle," *Studia Albanica* 24, no. 1 (1987): 139–60; Arno Mehlan, "Die Handelsstrassen des Balkans während der Türkenzeit," *Südost Forschungen* 4 (1939): 243–96; D.M. Metcalf, *Coinage in South-Eastern Europe, 820–1396* (2d ed.; London: Royal Numismatic Society, 1979); Ilija Mitić, "O dubrovačkim konzulima na Balkanu," *Balcanica* 6 (1975): 63–76; Şerban Papacostea, "De Vicina à Kilia: Byzantins et Génois aux bouches du Danube au XIVe siècle," *Revue des études sud-est européenes* 16 (1978): 65–79; and "La Mer Noire: du monopole byzantin à la domination des Latins aux détroits," *Revue roumaine d'histoire* 27 (1988): 49–71; Ute Monika Schwob, *Kulturelle Beziehungen zwischen Nürnberg und den Deutschen im Südosten im 14. bis 16. Jahrhundert* (Munich: Oldenbourg, 1969); Ioanna D. Spisarevska, "Les relations commerciales entre Dubrovnik et les regions bulgares sous la domination ottomane (XVe–XVIe s.)," *Études historiques* (Sofia) 7 (1975): 101–32; Freddy Thiriet, "De l'importance des mers dans le système romaniote de Venise," *Byzantino-Bulgarica* 7 (1981): 73–86; Elisaveta Todorova, "River Trade in the Balkans during the Middle Ages," *Études balkaniques*, 1984, no. 4, pp. 38-50.

BOHEMIA: František Graus, "Die Handelsbeziehungen Böhmens zu Deutschland und Österreich im 14. und zu Beginn des 15. Jahrhunderts," *Historica* (Prague) 2 (1960): 77–110; Josef Janácek, "Der böhmische Aussenhandel in der ersten Hälfte des 15. Jahrhunderts," *Historica* 4 (1962): 39–58; Jaroslav Mezník, "Der ökonomische Charakter Prags im 14. Jahrhundert," *Historica* 17 (1969): 43–91; Helmut Preidel, "Handel und Verkehr in den Sudetenländern während der zweiten Hälfte des ersten Jahrtausends n. Chr.," *Südost-Forschungen* 5 (1940): 473–501.

HUNGARY: L. Makkai, "Die Hauptzüge der wirtschaftlich-sozialen Entwicklung Ungarns im 15.–17. Jahrhundert," *Studia Historica* 53 (1963): 27–46; Zs. P. Pach, "The Transylvanian Route of Levantine Trade at the Turn of the 15th and 16th Centuries," *Studia Historica* 138 (1980): 5–36; Artur Pohl, "Die Münzstätte Pressburg im Mittelalter," *Südost-Forschungen* 24 (1965): 81–102; Günther Probszt, "Absatzmärkte und Verkehrswege der niederungarischen Bergstädte," and "Deutsches Kapital in den niederungarischen Bergstädten," *Zeitschrift für Ostforschung* 3 (1954): 537–53, and 10 (1961): 1–25; also Probszt, *Die niederungarischen Bergstädte* (Munich, 1966); and "Die Rolle des ungarischen Goldguldens in der österreichischen Wirtschaft des Mittelalters," *Südost-Forschungen* 22 (1963): 234–58.

POLAND: M. Małowist, "Die Problematik der sozial-wirtschaftlichen Geschichte Polens vom 15. bis zum 17. Jahrhundert," *Studia Historica* 53 (1963): 11–26; Henryk Samsonowicz, "Recherches polonaises sur l'histoire de la Baltique au déclin du Moyen Âge (XIVᵉ–XVᵉ siècle)," *Acta poloniae historica* 23 (1971): 150–61; Charlotte Warnke, *Die Anfänge des Fernhandels in Polen* (Würzburg: Holzner, 1964); Hugo Weczerka, "Herkunft und Volkszugehörigkeit der Lemberger Neubürger im 15. Jahrhundert," *Zeitschrift für Ostforschung* 4 (1955): 506–30.

WALACHIA AND MOLDAVIA: Mihnea Berindei, "L'empire ottoman et la 'route moldave' avant la conquête de Chilia et de Cetatea Alba (1484)," *Journal of Turkish Studies* 10 (1986): 47–71.

Chapter 12. Foreign Affairs

ALBANIA: Stavri N. Naçi, "À propos de quelques truchements concernant les rapports de la papauté avec Skanderbeg durant la lutte albano-turque (1443–1468)," *Studia Albanica* 6, no. 1 (1968): 73–86; Francisc Pall, "Skanderbeg et Janco de Hunedoara (Jean Hunyadi)," *Studia Albanica* 6, no. 1 (1968): 103–17.

BALKAN PENINSULA: Franz Babinger, "Beginn der Türkensteuer in den Donaufürstentümer (1394 bzw. 1455)," *Südost-Forschungen* 8 (1943): 1–35; Mihnea Berindei et al., "Actes de Murad III sur la région de Vidin et remarques sur les qanun ottomans," *Südost-Forschungen* 35 (1976): 11–68; Boško Bojović, "Dubrovnik et les Ottomans (1430–1472): 20 Actes de Murad II et de Mehmed II en médio-serbe," *Turcica* 19 (1987): 119–73; Matei Cazacu, "L'impact ottoman sur les pays roumains et ses incidences monétaires (1452–1504)," *Revue roumaine d'histoire* 12 (1973): 159–92; Paul Coles, *The Ottoman Impact on Europe* (London: Thames and Hudson, 1968); Hans Joachim Kissling, "Die Türkenfrage als europäisches Problem," *Südostdeutsches Archiv* 7 (1964): 39–57; and "Türkenfurcht und Türkenhoffnung im 15./16. Jahrhundert: zur Geschichte eines Komplexes," *Südost-Forschungen* 23 (1964): 1–18; Momčilo Spremić, "Turci i Balkansko poluostrvo u XIV i XV veku," *Jugoslovenski istorijski časopis*, 1966, no. 1–2, pp. 37–49; Jorjo Tadić, "Venecija i Dalmacija u srednjem veku," *Jugoslovenski istorijski časopis*, 1968, no. 3–4, pp. 5–17.

BOHEMIA: Franz Machilek, "Böhmen, Polen und die hussitische Revolution," *Zeitschrift für Ostforschung* 23 (1974): 401–30; Otakar Odložilík, "Problems of the Reign of George of Podebrady," *Slavonic and East European Review* 20 (1941): 206–22; Wilhelm Wegener, *Böhmen, Mähren und das Reich im Hochmittelalter* (Cologne: Böhlau, 1959).

BULGARIA: Dimitar Angelov, "Das byzantinische Reich und der mittelalterliche bulgarische Staat," *Byzantino-Bulgarica* 8 (1986): 9–16; G. Cankova-Petkova, "Griechisch-bulgarische Bündnisse in den Jahren 1235 und 1246,"

Byzantino-Bulgarica 3 (1969): 49–79; Vasil Gjuzelev, "Bulgarien und das Kaiserreich von Nikaia (1204–1261)," *Jahrbuch der österreichischen Byzantinistik* 26 (1977): 143–54; Gjuzelev, "Das Papstum und Bulgarien im Mittelalter (9.–14. Jh.)," *Bulgarian Historical Review* 5 (1977): 34–58; Georgi Nešev, "Die bulgarische Kultur und die osmanische Eroberung," *Bulgarian Historical Review* 2 (1974): 46–61; Ilka Petkova, "Nordwestbulgarien in der ungarischen Politik der Balkanhalbinsel im 13. Jahrhundert," *Bulgarian Historical Review* 11, no. 1 (1983): 57–65; P. Petrov, "Le rôle de la Bulgarie dans la vie politique de l'Europe au Moyen Âge," *Études historiques* (Sofia) 2 (1965): 117–30; B. Primov, "La Bulgarie et l'Europe occidentale au début du XIIIe siècle," *Études historiques* (Sofia) 2 (1965): 101–16.

HUNGARY: Virgil Ciocîltan, "La campagne ottomane de Transylvanie (1438) dans le contexte politique international," *Revue roumaine d'histoire*, 15 (1976): 437–45; Gustav Gündisch, "Siebenbürgen in der Türkenabwehr, 1395–1526," *Revue roumaine d'histoire* 13 (1974): 415–43; and "Die Türkeneinfälle in Siebenbürgen bis zur Mitte des 15. Jahrhunderts," *Jahrbücher für Geschichte Osteuropa* 2 (1937): 393–412; Ferenc Makk, "Les relations hungaro-byzantines aux Xe siècles," *Études historiques hongroises* (Budapest, 1990), 4: 11–26; and "Relations hungaro-byzantines à l'époque de Bela III," *Acta Historica* 31 (1985): 1–32; Karl Nehring, "Herrschaftstradition und Herrschaftslegitimät: zur ungarischen Aussenpolitik in der zweiten Hälfte des 15. Jahrhunderts," *Revue roumaine d'histoire* 13 (1974): 463–71, and *Matthias Corvinus, Kaiser Friedrich III, und das Reich* (Munich: Oldenbourg, 1975); Géza Perjés, *The Fall of the Medieval Kingdom of Hungary: Mohács 1526–Buda 1541* (Boulder: Social Science Monographs, 1989).

POLAND: Wojciech Hejnosz, "Der Friedensvertrag von Thorn (Toruń) und seine Staatsrechtliche Bedeutung," *Acta poloniae historica* 17 (1968): 105–22; Stanislas Łukasik, *Pologne et Roumanie* (Paris: Librairie polonaise, 1938); Elinor von Puttkamer, "Die polnisch-ungarische Grenze im Mittelalter," *Jahrbücher für Geschichte Osteuropas* 4 (1956): 369–86; Gotthold Rhode, "Die Ostgrenze Polens im Mittelalter," *Zeitschrift für Ostforschung* 2 (1953): 15–65; Gerhard Sappok, "Polen, Reich und Pommern im 10. Jahrhundert," *Jahrbücher für Geschichte Osteuropas* 2 (1937): 201–23; Erich Weise, "Die staatsrechtlichen Grundlagen des Zweiten Thorner Friedens und die Grenzen seiner Rechtmässigkeit," *Zeitschrift für Ostforschung* 3 (1954): 1–25.

PRUSSIA: Marian Biskup, "Der Kreuzritterorden in der Geschichte Polens," *Österreichische Osthefte* 5 (1963): 283–97; Klaus Conrad, "Litauen, der Deutsche Orden und Karl IV, 1352–1360," *Zeitschrift für Ostforschung* 21 (1972): 20–41; Klemens Wieser, "Zur Geschichte des deutschen Ordens in Osteuropa in den ersten drei Jahrzehnten des 13. Jahrhunderts," *Österreichische Osthefte* 7 (1965): 12–21.

SERBIA: Mirco M. Mitrovich, "Serbian Participation in European History and Civilization from Early Times to 1389," *East European Quarterly* 9 (1975):

135–51; George C. Soulis, *The Serbs and Byzantium during the Reign of Tsar Stephen Dušan (1331–1355) and His Successors* (Washington, D. C. Dumbarton Oaks Library, 1984).

WALACHIA AND MOLDAVIA: Nicoară Beldiceanu, "La conquête des cités marchandes de Kilia et de Cetatea Alba par Bayezid IIe," *Südost-Forschungen* 23 (1964): 36–90; Matei Cazacu, "L'Impact ottoman sur les pays roumains et ses incidences monétaires (1452–1504)," *Revue roumaine d'histoire* 12 (1973): 159–92; Ştefan Gorovei, "Autour de la paix moldo-turque de 1489," *Revue roumaine d'histoire* 13 (1974): 535–44; Maria Lazarescu-Zobian, "Cumania as the Name of Thirteenth Century Moldavia and Eastern Wallachia: Some Aspects of Kipchak-Rumanian Relations," *Journal of Turkish Studies* 8 (1984): 265–72; Stanislas Łukasik, *Pologne et Roumanie* (Paris, 1938); Şerban Papacostea, "Un épisode de la rivalité polono-hongroise au XVe siècle: la campagne de Mathias Corvin en Moldavie (1467)," *Revue roumaine d'histoire* 8 (1969): 967–79, and "Kilia et la politique orientale de Sigismond de Luxembourg," *Revue roumaine d'histoire* 15 (1976): 421–36; Papacostea, "La Moldavie état tributaire de l'empire ottoman au XVe siècle," *Revue roumaine d'histoire* 13 (1974): 445–61; and "La politique exterieure de la Moldavie à l'epoque d'Étienne le Grand: points de repére," *Revue roumaine d'histoire* 14 (1975): 423–40; and "De Vicina à Kilia: Byzantins et Génois aux bouches du Danube au XIVe siècle," *Revue des études sud-est européenes* 16 (1978): 65–79; Eugen Stănescu, "Beiträge zur Paristrion-Frage," *East European Quarterly* 4 (1970): 119–40.

Chapter 13. Ethnicity and Nationalism

ALBANIANS: Aleks Buda, "Quelques questions de l'histoire de la formation du peuple albanais, de sa langue et de sa culture," *Studia Albanica* 17, no. 1 (1980): 43–61.

BULGARIANS: Dimiter Angelov, "Clement of Ochrida and Bulgarian Nationhood," *Études historiques* (Sofia) 3 (1966): 61–78; Ivan Dujčev, "Protobulgares et slaves," in Dujčev, *Medioevo bizantino-slavo*, 1 (1965): 67–82.

CZECHS: František Graus, "Die Bildung eines Nationalbewusstseins im mittelalterlichen Böhmen (die vorhussitische Zeit)," *Historica* 13 (1966): 1–49; Ernst Schwarz, "Die Volkstumverhältnisse in den Städten Böhmens und Mährens vor den Hussitenkriegen," *Bohemia* 2 (1961): 27–111; František Šmahel, "The Idea of the 'Nation' in Hussite Bohemia," *Historica* 16 (1969): 143–247 and 17 (1969): 93–197.

GERMANS: Janusz Małek, "Die Entstehung und Entwicklung eines Sonderbewusstseins in Preussen während des 15. und 16. Jahrhunderts," *Zeitschrift für Ostforschung* 31 (1982): 48–58; Wolfgang Zorn, "Deutsche und Undeutsche in der städtischen Rechtsordnung des Mittelalters in Ost-Mitteleuropa," *Zeitschrift für Ostforschung* 1 (1952): 182–94.

HUNGARIANS: Loránd Benkő and Ádám Szabó, "Die Szekler: zur Siedlungsgeschichte einer ungarischen Volksgruppe," *Ungarn-Jahrbuch* 14 (1986): 207–24; Thomas von Bogyay, "Über Herkunft, Gesellschaft und Recht der Székler," *Ungarn-Jahrbuch* 2 (1970): 20–33; Erik Fügedi, "Das mittelalterliche Königreich Ungarn als Gastland," in Walter Schlesinger, ed., *Die deutsche Ostsiedlung,* (Sigmaringen, 1975), pp. 471–507; Gy. Györffy, "Autour de l'état des seminomades: le cas de la Hongrie," *Studia Historica* 95 (1975): 5–20; and "Einwohnerzahl und Bevölkerungsdichte in Ungarn bis zum Anfang des XIV. Jahrhunderts," *Studia Historica* 42 (1960): 1–31; Jenő Szűcs, *Nation und Geschichte* (Cologne: Böhlau Verlag, 1981); Miklos Tomka, "Die Zigeuner in der ungarischen Gesellschaft," *East European Quarterly* 4 (1970): 2–24; Ernst Wagner, *Geschichte der siebenbürger Sachsen* (Innsbruck: Wort und Welt, 1981).

POLES: Kazimierz Ślaski, "Ethnic Changes in Western Pomerania," *Acta poloniae historica* 7 (1962): 7–27; Hugo Weczerka, "Herkunft und Volkszugehörigkeit der Lemberger Neubürger im 15. Jahrhundert," *Zeitschrift für Ostforschung* 4 (1955): 506–30; Reinhard Wenskus, "Der deutsche Orden und die nichtdeutsche Bevölkerung des Preussenlandes mit besonderer Berücksichtigung der Siedlung," in Schlesinger, ed., *Die deutsche Ostsiedlung,* pp. 417–38; Benedykt Zientara, "Foreigners in Poland in the 10th–15th Centuries: Their Role in the Opinion of Polish Medieval Community," *Acta poloniae historica* 29 (1974): 5–27.

SERBS: Alex N. Dragnich and Slavko Todorovich, *The Saga of Kosovo: Focus on Serbian-Albanian Relations* (Boulder: East European Monographs, 1984); Alois Schmaus, "Zur Frage der Kulturorientierung der Serben im Mittelalter," *Südost-Forschungen* 15 (1956): 179–201.

SLAVS (GENERAL): Aleksandar Stojanovski and Galaba Palikruševa, "Situation ethnique dans la Macédoine du nord-ouest au XVe siècle," *Jugoslovenski istorijski časopis* 1 (1970): 33–40; Benedykt Zientara, "Nationality Conflicts in the German-Slavic Borderland in the 13th–14th Centuries and Their Social Scope," *Acta poloniae historica* 22 (1970): 207–25.

VLACHS (ROMANIANS): Costin Feneşan, "Beziehungen der Wlachen aus dem Cetina-Tal zur Stadt Šibenik gegen Ende des 14. und zu Beginn des 15. Jahrhunderts," *Revue des études sud-est européenes* 17 (1979): 3–15; Eugen Stănescu, "Les Vlaques à la fin du Xe siècle–début du XIe et la restauration de la domination byzantine dans la Péninsule Balkanique," *Revue des études sud-est européenes* (1968): 407–38.

Chapter 14. Languages and Literatures

ALBANIAN: Aleks Buda, "Quelques questions de l'histoire de la formation du peuple albanais, de sa langue et de sa culture," *Studia Albanica* 17, no. 1 (1980): 43–61; Eqrem Çabej, "Le problème du territoire de la formation de la langue albanaise," *Studia Albanica* 9, no. 2 (1972): 125–51; Mahir Domi, "Problèmes de l'histoire de la formation de la langue albanaise, resultats et tâches," *Studia Albanica* 19, no. 2 (1982): 31–51; Kristo Frasheri, "Les territoires albanais dans le Haut Moyen Âge," *Studia Albanica* 19, no. 2 (1982): 93–107; Jorgji Gjinari, "De la continuation de l'Illyrien en Albanais," *Studia Albanica* 9, no. 1 (1972): 143–54; Stuart E. Mann, "Albanian as an Indo-European Language," *Studia Albanica* 2, no. 2 (1965): 45–47.

BULGARIAN: Veselin Beševliev, "Les inscriptions protobulgares et leur portée culturelle et historique," *Byzantinoslavica* 32 (1971): 35–51; V. Beševliev, *Die protobulgarische Periode der bulgarischen Geschichte* (Amsterdam: Hakkert, 1981); Ivan Duichev [Dujčev], ed., *Kiril and Methodius: Founders of Slavonic Writing* (primary sources from Old Bulgarian literature, with translations and commentary) (Boulder: East European Monographs, 1985); Ivan Dujčev "Demetrius Cantacuzène, écrivain byzantino-slave du XVᵉ siècle," in Dujčev, *Medioevo bizantino-slavo*, 3:311–21; and "Klassisches Altertum im mittelalterlichen Bulgarien," in Dujčev, *Medioevo bizantino-slavo*, 1: 467–85; Charles A. Moser, *A History of Bulgarian Literature, 865–1944* (The Hague: Mouton, 1972); Vivian Pinto, "Bulgarian," in Alexander M. Schenker and Edward Stankiewicz, *The Slavic Literary Languages: Formation and Development* (New Haven: Yale Concilium on International and Area Studies, 1980), pp. 37–52; Anton-Emil Tachiaos, "L'oeuvre littéraire de Cyrille et de Methode d'après Constantin Kostenecki," *Balkan Studies* 14 (1973): 293–302.

CZECH AND SLOVAK: Robert Auty, "Czech," in Schenker and Stankiewicz, *The Slavic Literary Languages*, pp. 163–82; Winfried Baumann, *Die Literatur des Mittelalters in Böhmen: deutsch-lateinisch-tschechische Literatur vom 10. bis zum 15. Jahrhundert* (Munich: Oldenbourg, 1978); F. Chudoba, *A Short Survey of Czech Literature* (London: Kegan Paul, Trench, Trubner and Company, 1924); Ľubomir Ďurovič, "Slovak," in Schenker and Stankiewicz," *The Slavic Literary Languages*, pp. 211–28; Alfred French, ed., *Anthology of Czech Poetry* (Ann Arbor: Czechoslovak Society of Arts and Sciences in America, 1973); William E. Harkins, *Czech Prose, an Anthology* (Ann Arbor: Michigan Slavic Publications, 1983); Andreas Mráz, *Die Literatur der Slowaken* (Berlin: Volk und Reich Verlag, 1943); Arne Novák, *Czech Literature* (Ann Arbor: Michigan Slavic Publications, 1976).

HUNGARIAN: Anonymous, "Aus der Geschichte der ungarischen Schriftsprache," *Österreichische Osthefte* 4 (1962): 190–95; Lórant Czigány, *The Oxford History of Hungarian Literature from Earliest Times to the Present* (Oxford: Clarendon Press, 1984); László Hadrovics, "Rapports de la Poésie hongroise ancienne avec celles de l'Europe centrale," in Hungarian Academy of Sciences, *Littérature hongroise, littérature européene* (Budapest, 1964), pp. 105–27; T. Kardos, "Zentralisierung und Humanismus im Ungarn des 15. und 16. Jahrhunderts," *Studia Historica* 53 (1963): 397–414; T. Klaniczay, "La littérature de la Renaissance et la noblesse hongroise," in *Studia Historica* 53 (1963): 243–52;

Tibor Klaniczay, József Szauder, and Miklos Szabolcsi, *A History of Hungarian Literature* (Budapest: Corvina, 1964). Peter Kulcsár, "Der Humanismus in Ungarn," in *Études historiques hongroises* (Budapest, 1990), 4; 27–37.

POLISH: Manfred Kridl, *A Survey of Polish Literature and Culture* (The Hague: Mouton, 1956); Julian Krzyżanowski, *A History of Polish Literature* (Warsaw: Polish Scientific Publishers, 1978); Stanisław Łempicki, *Renesans i humanizm w Polsce: materiały do studiów* (Kraków: Czytelnik, 1952); Michael J. Mikoś, *Medieval Literature of Poland: An Anthology* (New York: Garland Publishing, Inc., 1992); Czesław Miłosz, *The History of Polish Literature* (New York: Macmillan, 1969; 2d ed.; Berkeley: University of California Press, 1983); A. Wagner, "Johannes Heydeke, 1443–1512, Stadtschreiber, Archpresbyter und Humanist in Krakau," *Jahrbücher für Geschichte Osteuropas* 1 (1936): 48–62.

ROMANIAN: M. Berza, "Problèmes majeurs et orientations de la recherche dans l'étude de l'ancienne culture roumaine," *Revue roumaine d'histoire* 9 (1970): 485–506; Petre V. Haneş, *Histoire de la littérature roumaine* (Paris, 1934); Basil Munteanu, *Modern Rumanian Literature* (Bucharest: Curentul, 1939); P. P. Panaitescu, "Les premier textes écrits en langue roumaine," *Revue roumaine d'histoire* 1 (1962): 427–49; Émile Turdeanu, "L'activité littéraire en Moldavie à l'époque d'Étienne le Grand (1457–1504)," *Revue des études roumaines* 5–6 (1957–58): 21–66.

SERBO-CROATIAN: Antun Barac, *A History of Yugoslav Literature* (Belgrade: Committee for Foreign Cultural Relations of Yugoslavia, 1955); Thomas Butler, *Monumenta Serbocroatica: A Bilingual Anthology of Serbian and Croatian Texts from the 12th to the 19th Century* (Ann Arbor: Michigan Slavic Publications, 1980); Ante Kadić, "Croatian Humanists at the Hungarian Court," *East European Quarterly* 22 (1988): 129–46; Milan Kašanin, *Srpska kniževnost u srednjem veku* (Belgrade: Prosveta, 1975); Nada Klaić, "Historijska podloga hrvatskoga glagoljastva," *Jugoslovenski istoriski časopis* 4 (1965): 3–15; Albert B. Lord, "Tradition and Innovation in Balkan Epic, from Heracles and Theseus to Digenis Akritas and Marko," *Revue des études sud-est européenes* 18 (1980): 195–212; Kenneth Naylor, "Serbo-Croatian," in Schenker and Stankiewicz, *The Slavic Literary Languages*, pp. 65–84; D. Obolensky, "Cyprian of Kiev and Moscow," in *Six Byzantine Portraits* (Oxford: Clarendon Press, 1988); Franjo Trogrančić, "Literature, 1400–1835," in Eterovich and Spalatin, *Croatia*, 2: 175–250.

SLAVIC (GENERAL): Dmitrij Čiževskij, *Comparative History of Slavic Literatures* (Nashville: Vanderbilt University Press, 1971); Riccardo Picchio, "Church Slavonic," in Schenker and Stankiewicz, *The Slavic Literary Languages*, pp. 1–33.

Chapter 15. Education and Literacy

GENERAL: Margaret Deanesly, "Medieval Schools to c. 1300," *Cambridge*

Medieval History, vol. 5 (1929), pp. 765–79; James Mulhern, *A History of Education* (New York: Ronald Press 1946); G. R. Potter, "Education in the Fourteenth and Fifteenth Centuries," *Cambridge Medieval History*, vol. 8 (Cambridge: University Press, 1936), pp. 688–717; Hastings Rashdall, "The Medieval Universities," *Cambridge Medieval History*, vol. 6 (Cambridge: University Press, 1929), pp. 559–601; David Wagner, ed., introduction to *The Seven Liberal Arts in the Middle Ages* (Bloomington: Indiana University Press, 1983).

BOHEMIA: R. R. Betts, "The University of Prague: 1348," *Slavonic Review* 26–27 (1947–49): 57–66; František Kavka and Jan Havranek, "Der kulturelle und geistige Einfluss der Wiener Universität auf die Tschechen und Slowaken," *Österreichische Osthefte* 7 (1965), 195–212; František Šmahel, "Le mouvement des étudiants à Prague dans les années 1408–1412," *Historica* 14 (1967): 33–75.

BULGARIA: Vasil Gjuzelev, "Bildungsstand in Bulgarien während des Hochmittelalters (13.–14. Jh.)," *Bulgarian Historical Review* 12, no. 3 (1984): 72–96.

BYZANTIUM: Friedrich Fuchs, *Die höheren Schulen von Konstantinopel im Mittelalter*, Byzantinisches Archiv, Heft 8 (Leipzig, 1926), pp. 1–79; Joan M. Hussey, *Church and Learning in the Byzantine Empire, 867–1185* (New York: Russell and Russell, 1963.)

HUNGARY: György Bonis, "Men Learned in the Law in Medieval Hungary," *East Central Europe* 4, part 2 (1977): 181–91; Erik Fügedi, "Verba Volant . . . Oral Culture and Literacy among the Medieval Hungarian Nobility," in his *Kings, Bishops, Nobles and Burghers* (London, 1986), pp. 1–25; Astrik L. Gabriel, *The Mediaeval Universities of Pécs and Pozsony* (Notre Dame: Mediaeval Institute, 1969); S. Jakó, "Les débuts de l'écriture dans les couches laïques de la société féodale en Transylvanie," *Nouvelles études d'histoire, présentées au Xe Congrès des sciences historiques* (Rome, 1955), pp. 209–23; B. L. Kumorivitz, "Die erste Epoche der ungarischen privat-rechtlichen Schriftlichkeit im Mittelalter (XI.–XII. Jahrhundert)," *Studia Historica* 21 (1960): 3–38.

POLAND: J. Dąbrowski, "Les relations de Cracovie et son université avec la Hongrie à l'époque de l'humanisme," *Studia Historica* 53 (1963): 451–64; Jerzy Dowiat, "Le livre et l'école dans l'éducation des seigneurs laïcs en Pologne et dans les pays voisins du Xe au XIIe siècle," *Acta poloniae historica* 28 (1973): 7–22; Charlotte B. and Howard V. Evans, "Nicholas Copernicus: A Renaissance Man," *East European Quarterly* 7 (1973), 231–47; Jerzy Kłoczowski, "Dominicans of the Polish Province in the Middle Ages," in his *The Christian Community of Medieval Poland* (Wrocław, 1981); Adam Vetulani, "Les origines de l'université de Cracovie," *Acta poloniae historica* 13 (1966): 14–40; Eugeniusz Wiśniowski, "The Parochial School System in Poland towards the Close of the Middle Ages," *Acta poloniae historica* 27 (1973): 29–43; Szczepan K. Zimmer, *The Beginning of Cyrillic Printing in Cracow, 1491* (Boulder: East European Monographs, 1983).

WALACHIA AND MOLDAVIA: Radu Manolescu, "L'Écriture latine en Valachie et en Moldavie au Moyen Âge," *Revue roumaine d'histoire* 25 (1986): 59–68.

INDEX*

* Entries marked with an asterisk (*) may be found as subheads under the country and regional listings. Page numbers given immediately after the asterisk indicate subject matter of a general nature.

Boldface type denotes major headings.

* Entries marked with an asterisk (*) may be found as subheads under the country and regional listings. Page numbers given immediately after the asterisk indicate subject matter of a general nature.

    Boldface type denotes major headings.

* Entries marked with an asterisk (*) may be found as subheads under the country and regional listings. Page numbers given immediately after the asterisk indicate subject matter of a general nature.

Boldface type denotes major headings.

* Entries marked with an asterisk (*) may be found as subheads under the country and regional listings. Page numbers given immediately after the asterisk indicate subject matter of a general nature.

Boldface type denotes major headings.

* Entries marked with an asterisk (*) may be found as subheads under the country and regional listings. Page numbers given immediately after the asterisk indicate subject matter of a general nature.

Boldface type denotes major headings.

---

* Entries marked with an asterisk (*) may be found as subheads under the country and regional listings. Page numbers given immediately after the asterisk indicate subject matter of a general nature.
Boldface type denotes major headings.

* Entries marked with an asterisk (*) may be found as subheads under the country and regional listings. Page numbers given immediately after the asterisk indicate subject matter of a general nature.

Boldface type denotes major headings.

* Entries marked with an asterisk (*) may be found as subheads under the country and regional listings. Page numbers given immediately after the asterisk indicate subject matter of a general nature.

Boldface type denotes major headings.

* Entries marked with an asterisk (*) may be found as subheads under the country and regional listings. Page numbers given immediately after the asterisk indicate subject matter of a general nature.

Boldface type denotes major headings.

* Entries marked with an asterisk (*) may be found as subheads under the country and regional listings. Page numbers given immediately after the asterisk indicate subject matter of a general nature.

Boldface type denotes major headings.

* Entries marked with an asterisk (*) may be found as subheads under the country and regional listings. Page numbers given immediately after the asterisk indicate subject matter of a general nature.
    Boldface type denotes major headings.

* Entries marked with an asterisk (*) may be found as subheads under the country and regional listings. Page numbers given immediately after the asterisk indicate subject matter of a general nature.
Boldface type denotes major headings.

* Entries marked with an asterisk (*) may be found as subheads under the country and regional listings. Page numbers given immediately after the asterisk indicate subject matter of a general nature.

Boldface type denotes major headings.

---

* Entries marked with an asterisk (*) may be found as subheads under the country and regional listings. Page numbers given immediately after the asterisk indicate subject matter of a general nature.

Boldface type denotes major headings.

* Entries marked with an asterisk (*) may be found as subheads under the country and regional listings. Page numbers given immediately after the asterisk indicate subject matter of a general nature.

Boldface type denotes major headings.